A–Z OF VOLUNTARY AGENCIES

10:10

8 Delancey Passage, London NW1 7NN
T: 020 7388 6688
E: hello@1010uk.org
www.1010global.org
Executive Director: Heidi Proven
We're on the way to a cleaner, cleverer, low-carbon world and everyone deserves a chance to help build it. 10:10 creates these chances, and brings people together to make the most of them. 10:10ers work together to: celebrate the good stuff already happening, and help it spread; save energy at home, work and locally; light up our best-loved places with crowdfunded clean energy; and convince people in power to tackle the stuff we don't control.
Employees: 13
Regional offices: 1

25% ME Group - Support for Severe ME Sufferers

21 Church Street, Troon, Ayrshire KA10 6HT
T: 01292 318611
E: enquiry@25megroup.org
www.25megroup.org
The 25% ME Group is a unique nationwide charitable organisation managed entirely by volunteers (most of whom are severely affected by ME) and was set up to offer support services to those severely affected by ME (myalgic encephalomyelitis), and their carers.
Employees: 2
Volunteers: 12

3 Villages Youth Project

2, Elms Close Terrace, Newlyn, Penzance, Cornwall TR18 5AU
T: 01736 364707
E: julyan.drew@gmail.com
www.3villagesyouthproject.org.uk
Chair of Trustees: Julyan Drew
Working with and for children and young people in Newlyn, Mousehole and Paul in Cornwall.
Employees: 1
Volunteers: 11
Regional offices: 1

3H Fund (Helping hands for Holidays)

B2 Speldhurst Business Park, Langton Road, Speldhurst, Tunbridge Wells, Kent TN3 0AQ
T: 01892 860207
E: info@3hfund.org.uk
www.3hfund.org.uk
Charity Manager: Lynne Loving
3H Fund organises subsidised group holidays for physwlunteer helpers, so that family carers can have a separate and much-needed period of respite.
Employees: 5
Volunteers: 100

4Children

City Reach, 5 Greenwich View Place, London E14 9NN
T: 020 7512 2112
F: 020 7512 2010
E: info@4children.org.uk
www.4children.org.uk
Chief Executive: Anne Longfield
4Children is a national children's charity that aims to place children and young people at the centre of policy development and service delivery, creating and supporting opportunities that enable all children to fulfil their potential and all parents to access the support they need. The organisation has led the lobbying for, and development of, childcare and out-of-school activities over the last 20 years whilst supporting a major growth in childcare places.
Employees: 80
Regional offices: 1

A Rocha UK

13 Avenue Road, Southall, Middlesex UB1 3BL
T: 020 8574 5935 (also fax)
E: uk@arocha.org
www.arocha.org
The advancement of the Christian faith and understanding of its relevance to the environment.
Employees: 13
Volunteers: 30

Abbeyfield Society

Abbeyfield House, 53 Victoria Street, St Albans AL1 3UW
T: 01727 857536
F: 01727 846168
E: post@abbeyfield.com
www.abbeyfield.com
Abbeyfield is one of the largest voluntary sector providers of housing and care for older people in the UK. Abbeyfield believes older people should be able to obtain the support and care they need to remain independent and involved in life. Founded in 1956 by Richard Carr-Gomm, Abbeyfield has grown to include about 700 houses throughout the UK providing accommodation and support for around 7,500 older people, run by professional staff and more than 7,500 volunteers.

AbilityNet

PO Box 94, Birmingham Road, Warwick, Warwickshire CV34 5WS
T: 0870 240 4455
Helpline: 0800 269545
E: enquiries@abilitynet.org.uk
www.abilitynet.org.uk
A national charity helping disabled adults and children use computers and the internet by adapting and adjusting their technology.

AbleChildAfrica

Southbank House, Black Prince Road SE1 7SJ
T: 020 7793 4144
E: info@ablechildafrica.org.uk
www.ablechildafrica.org.uk
Executive Director: Jane Anthony
AbleChildAfrica specialises in advocating for and supporting disabled children and young people in Africa. In order to achieve this we support partner organisations to carry out life-changing work with disabled children and young people and work alongside them to use their experiences and learning to campaign for more widespread change in attitudes and practice.
Employees: 6
Volunteers: 2

Academy of Youth Limited

University of The First Age, The Toll House, 180-182 Fazeley Street, Digbeth, Birmingham B5 5SE
T: 0121 766 8077
E: info@ufa.org.uk
www.aoy.org.uk
Advances the education of children, young people and adults through an institution that is committed to: raising educational achievement; preparing children and young

people for the challenge of adult life; transforming educational opportunities.

Access Community Trust

28 Gordon Road, Lowestoft NR32 1NL
T: 01502 527200
F: 01502 527241
E: julie.gordon@accessct.org
www.accessct.org
Chief Executive: Emma Ratzer
To promote social inclusion, reducing vulnerability and homelessness by providing accommodation, education, training and practical support tailored to individual needs. We offer mental health and wellbeing services, have two recruitment mentors and a youth-led project addressing social issues faced by young people who are vulnerable, socially excluded and isolated. It is our mission to provide our clients and local community with unrivalled services.
Employees: 60
Volunteers: 20
Regional offices: 1

ACCURO (Care Services)

South Side Suite 5 (North), Level 11, Terminus House, Terminus Street, HARLOW CM20 1XA
T: 01279 433667 (also fax)
E: arthur@accuro.org.uk
www.accuro.org.uk
CEO: Arthur Steward
Accuro provides a range of services for children, young people and adults with a disability resident in West Essex. Services include youth groups, a Saturday Play Club, an Adult Friendship Scheme, etc.
Employees: 75
Volunteers: 80
Income: £530,000 (2014-15)

Achieve Lifestyle

Egham Leisure Centre, Vicarage Road, Egham, Surrey TW20 8NL
T: 01784 437695
E: admin@achievelifestyle.co.uk
www.achievelifestyle.co.uk
Central Services Manager: Debbie Wilmott

Action Against Allergy

PO Box 278, Twickenham TW1 4QQ
T: 020 8892 4949
Helpline: 020 8892 2711
E: aaa@actionagainstallergy.freeserve.co.uk
www.actionagainstallergy.co.uk
Executive Director: Patricia Schooling
Advances understanding, awareness, and recognition of allergic medical conditions and allergy-related illness and the actions needed for research, diagnosis and treatment.
Employees: 3
Volunteers: 3

Action Against Hunger UK

1st Floor, Rear Premises, 161-163 Greenwich High Road, London SE10 8JA
T: 020 8293 6190
E: m.eaton@actionagainsthunger.org.uk
www.actionagainsthunger.org.uk
Executive Director: Jean-Michel Grand
Action Against Hunger is an international humanitarian organisation committed to ending child hunger. Recognised as a leader in the fight against malnutrition, ACF works to save the lives of malnourished children while providing communities with sustainable access to safe water and long-term solutions to hunger.
Employees: 55
Volunteers: 25
Income: £12,523,575 (2014-15)

Action Against Medical Accidents

Christopher Wren Yard, 117 High Street, Croydon, Surrey CR0 1QG
T: 020 8688 9555
Helpline: 0845 123 2352
F: 020 8667 9065
E: support@avma.org.uk
www.avma.org.uk
Chief Executive: Peter Walsh
Action against Medical Accidents (AvMA) is an independent UK charity that works for better patient safety and justice for people who have been affected by a medical accident.
Employees: 22
Volunteers: 70

Action for Blind People

Action House, 53 Sandgate Street, London SE15 1LE
T: 020 7635 4800
Helpline: 0303 123 9999
E: info@actionforblindpeople.org.uk
www.actionforblindpeople.org.uk
Chief Executive: Miriam Martin
Action for Blind People provides practical and emotional advice and support across England to people who are blind or partially sighted and their friends and family.
Employees: 365
Volunteers: 573
Regional offices: 16
Income: £20,530,000 (2013-14)

Action for Children

3 The Boulevard, Ascot Road, Watford, Hertfordshire WD18 8AG
T: 01923 361500
Helpline: 0300 123 2112
E: ask.us@actionforchildren.org.uk
www.actionforchildren.org.uk
Chief Executive: Sir Tony Hawkhead
Action for Children exists to help the most vulnerable children and young people break through injustice, deprivation and inequality so they can achieve their full potential. We work across the UK, Northern Ireland and internationally. Action for Children works directly with more than 300,000 children, young people, parents and carers each year and runs more than 650 services.

Action for ME

42 Temple Street, Keynsham, Bristol BS31 1EH
T: 0117 927 9551
F: 0117 986 1152
E: admin@actionforme.org.uk
www.actionforme.org.uk
Chief Executive: Sonya Chowdhury
At Action for ME we provide information and support for people affected by Myalgic Encephalomyelitis (ME), and work collaboratively to raise awareness, campaign for better health and welfare services and fund and driver vital research. People affected by ME can access support and information through our publications, Welfare Rights Line and online Services Directory, available via our Online ME Centre at www.actionforme.org.uk
Employees: 14
Regional offices: 1

Action for Prisoners' Families

Action for Prisoners' and Offenders' Families, part of Family Lives, 15-17 The Broadway, Hatfield, Hertfordshire AL9 5HZ
T: 020 7553 3080
E: luke.evans@prisonersfamilies.org.uk
www.prisonersfamilies.org.uk
Director: Deborah Cowley
Membership organisation for prisoners' and offenders' families and those who work with them. Works for the benefit of prisoners' and offenders' families by: providing advice,

information and training; providing opportunities for members to share experiences, concerns and successes; listening to prisoners' families and promoting, developing and supporting services and resources that they need or would like; lobbying for improved structures, procedures, conditions and services to promote the wellbeing of prisoners' and offenders' families.
Employees: 7
Income: £708,640 (2011-12)

Action for Sick Children

32b Buxton Road, High Lane, Stockport SK6 8BH
T: 01663 763004
Helpline: 0800 074 4519
E: enquiries@actionforsickchildren.org
www.actionforsickchildren.org
CEO: Val Jackson
To join parents and professionals in promoting high-quality healthcare for children in hospital and at home.
Employees: 2
Volunteers: 100
Regional offices: 15

Action Medical Research

Vincent House, North Parade, Horsham, West Sussex RH12 2DP
T: 01403 210406
F: 01403 210541
E: info@action.org.uk
www.action.org.uk
Chief Executive: Julie Buckler
Action Medical Research is the leading UK-wide medical research charity saving and changing children's lives. Since we began in 1952, we've been funding medical breakthroughs that have helped save thousands of children's lives and changed many more. We want to make a difference in: tackling premature birth and treating sick and vulnerable babies; helping children affected by disability, disabling conditions and infections; targeting rare diseases that together severely affect many forgotten children.
Employees: 51
Volunteers: 1050
Regional offices: 1
Income: £7,500 (2013-14)

Action on Addiction

Head Office, East Knoyle, Salisbury, Wiltshire SP3 6BE
T: 0300 330 0659
F: 01747 832028
E: admin@actiononaddiction.org.uk
www.actiononaddiction.org.uk
Chief Executive: Graham Beech
The charity Action on Addiction takes action to disarm addiction in all its forms through a uniquely comprehensive approach that encompasses research, treatment (both residential and non-residential), rehabilitation, family support, education, training and campaigning. Our vision is to see people free from addiction and its effects.
Employees: 145
Regional offices: 5

Action on Disability and Development

ADD International, The Foundry, 17-19 Oval Way, London SE11 5RR
T: 0300 303 8835
F: 01373 452075
E: supportercare@add.org.uk
www.add.org.uk
Building strong associations of disabled people; self-advocacy and influence; access; economic empowerment; information and education; recreation, sport and drama.
Employees: 159
Volunteers: 25
Regional offices: 10

Action on Disability and Work UK

The Vassall Centre, Gill Avenue, Fishponds, Bristol BS16 2QQ
T: 0117 961 7900
E: andy.rickell@adwuk.org
www.adwuk.org
Chief Executive Officer: Andy Rickell
Action on Disability and Work UK (ADWUK) is a Disabled People's User-Led Organisation that supports disabled people to have successful working lives. Our national Advice Service provides advice on work-related issues to disabled people, employers and professionals. We run a local Work Club supporting disabled people looking for work, volunteering opportunities or self-employment. We provide consultancy and training for employers on any disability issue.
Employees: 10
Volunteers: 12
Regional offices: 1
Income: £260,000 (2012-13)

Action on Elder Abuse

PO Box 60001, London SW16 9BY
T: 020 8835 9280
Helpline: 0808 808 8141
F: 020 8696 9328
E: enquiries@elderabuse.org.uk
www.elderabuse.org.uk
Chief Executive: Gary FitzGerald
Aims to prevent abuse in old age through raising awareness, education, promoting research and the collection and dissemination of information.

Action on Hearing Loss (the new name for RNID)

19-23 Featherstone Street, London EC1Y 8SL
T: 020 7296 8000
F: 020 7296 8199
E: rebecca.griffin@hearingloss.org.uk
www.actiononhearingloss.org.uk
We aim to make daily life better for deaf and hard of hearing people. Our campaigns, information, services and support of scientific and technological research are some of the ways we're trying to help. We also support other organisations in their aim to provide better services to their deaf and hard of hearing employees and customers.
Employees: 1400
Volunteers: 200
Regional offices: 7

Action on Pre-Eclampsia

The Stables, 80 B High Street, Evesham, Worcestershire WR11 4EU
T: 01386 761848
Helpline: 020 8427 4217
E: info@apec.org.uk
www.apec.org.uk
Chief Executive Officer: Ann Marie Barnard
Aims to raise public and professional awareness of pre-eclampsia, improve care and ease or prevent physical and emotional suffering caused by the condition. To educate, inform and advise the public and health professionals about the prevalence, nature and risks of pre-eclampsia.
Employees: 2
Volunteers: 10

Action on Smoking and Health

Suites 59-63, 6th Floor, New House, 67-68 Hatton Garden, London EC1N 8JY
T: 020 7404 0242
F: 020 7404 0850
E: phil.rimmer@ash.org.uk
www.ash.org.uk
Chief Executive: Deborah Arnott
ASH is an organisation that provides information on all aspects of tobacco and works to advance policies and measures that will help to prevent the addiction, disease and unnecessary premature death caused by smoking. ASH was established in 1971 by the Royal College of Physicians.
Employees: 8

Action to Regenerate Community Trust

67 Market Place, Warminster, Wiltshire BA12 9AZ
T: 01225 290595
E: nicholas.gardham@regeneratetrust.org
www.rslm.org
Chief Executive Officer: Stephen Kearney
RE:generate is an enterprising social action charity and grant making trust. Our mission is to tackle poverty and the root causes of poverty and disadvantage. We work with people to encourage them to: develop local enterprising solutions to problems, participate in public life and wake up to their potential to make change in their lives and their community. We aim to transform the relationship between communities, agencies, organisations and the state.
Employees: 6
Volunteers: 103
Regional offices: 1

Action with Communities in Rural England

Suite 109, Unit 9, Cirencester Office Park, Tetbury Road, Cirencester, Gloucestershire GL7 6JJ
T: 01285 653477
F: 01285 654537
E: acre@acre.org.uk
www.acre.org.uk
Chief Executive: Sylvia Brown
Action with Communities in Rural England is the national umbrella body of the Rural Community Action Network (RCAN), which operates at national, regional and local level in support of rural communities across the country. We aim to promote a healthy, vibrant and sustainable rural community sector that is well connected to policy and decision-makers who play a part in delivering this aim.
Employees: 16

ActionAid

33-39 Bowling Green Lane, London EC1R 0BJ
T: 020 3122 0561
F: 020 7278 5667
E: rachel.leonard@actionaid.org
www.actionaid.org
Working in partnership with poor people to eradicate poverty by overcoming the injustice and inequity that cause it.
Employees: 244
Volunteers: 7500
Regional offices: 3

Active Training and Education Trust

8 St Ann's Road, Malvern, Worcestershire WR14 4RG
T: 01684 562400
Helpline: 0845 456 1205
F: 01684 562716
E: info@ate.org.uk
www.ate.org.uk
Director of Operations: Liz Macartney
The trust runs and promotes educational residential experiences for children and young people, through a programme of imaginative and creative summer camps, and through weekend and weekday sessions for schools, as well as FunDays in schools. It also runs training, INSET, conferences, etc., on the subject of fun and imagination in education.
Employees: 3
Volunteers: 200
Income: £200,000 (2012-13)

Actors Benevolent Fund

E: willie.bicket@abf.org.uk

ADD Information Services

5th Floor Premier House, 112 Station Road, Edgware, Middlesex HA8 7BJ
T: 020 8952 1515
E: info@addiss.co.uk
www.addiss.co.uk
The object of the charity is to relieve children and those persons suffering from attention deficit hyperactivity disorder (ADHD), and to advance the education of the public about the disorder.
Employees: 3

Addaction

67-69 Cowcross Street, London EC1M 6PU
T: 020 7251 5860
F: 020 7251 5890
E: info@addaction.org.uk
www.addaction.org.uk
Chief Executive: Simon Antrobus
Addaction reduces both the use of, and the harm caused by, drugs and alcohol.
Employees: 640
Volunteers: 100
Regional offices: 2

Addiction Recovery Agency

King's Court, King Street, Bristol BS1 4EE
T: 0117 930 0282
E: info@addictionrecovery.org.uk
www.addictionrecovery.org.uk
Aims to support those who are affected by addiction to drugs, alcohol and gambling. We provide accommodation to clients in Bristol engage in treatment to address their addiction. We also provide counselling to clients affected by Gambling addiction. A newly developed service Connect Psychology is part of the Increasing Access to Psychological Therapies services in Bristol.

Adfam

25 Corsham Street, 1st Floor, London N1 6DR
T: 020 7553 7640
F: 020 7253 7991
E: admin@adfam.org.uk
www.adfam.org.uk
Chief Executive: Vivienne Evans
Adfam is a registered charity working with families affected by drugs and alcohol. Adfam provides accessible, clear and accurate information via their website and publications for families affected by drug and alcohol, including good practice guides and training manuals for professionals working with family members. We challenge and influence policy makers, planners and the media to understand and represent more accurately the issues affecting families of drug and alcohol users.
Employees: 13
Regional offices: 2

Adhar Project

E: admin.box@adharproject.org

ADHD Solutions cic

St Gabriel's Community Centre, Kerrysdale Avenue, Leicester, Leicestershire LE4 7GH
T: 0116 261 0711
E: info@adhdsolutions.org
www.adhdsolutions.org
Director/CEO: Christine Jarvis
ADHD Solutions aims 'To improve the life chances of people with Attention Deficit Hyperactivity Disorder (ADHD) by delivering a quality service that supports and empowers children/young people, adults and

their families to develop strategies for use at home, school and the work place. Identifying critical times and triggers, preventing crises occurring. Reducing social isolation and the risk of adverse outcomes, including, antisocial behaviour, long term mental health problems, educational underachievement, worklessness, family breakdown and social exclusion'
Employees: 12
Volunteers: 35
Regional offices: 1
Income: £312,004 (2013-14)

Adoption UK

**Linden House, 55 The Green,
South Bar Street, Banbury,
Oxfordshire OX16 9AB
T: 01295 752240
F: 01295 752241
E: non@adoptionuk.org.uk
www.adoptionuk.org.uk**
Adoptions UK helps to make adoptions work, and promotes loving and supportive relationships between children and their adoptive families. It provides independent support and advice to all concerned with adoption, offering a wealth of relevant experience from generations of adoptive families to prospective and established adopters and those who work with them.
Employees: 28
Volunteers: 130
Regional offices: 50

Adullam Homes Housing Association

**Walter Moore House, 34 Dudley Street,
West Bromwich, West Midlands B70 9LS
T: 0121 500 2828
F: 01250 02824
E: info@adullam.org.uk
www.adullam.uk.net
Chief Executive: Trevor Palfreyman**
Adullam Homes is a specialist provider in quality housing and support services and was founded in 1972. Adullam Homes now houses and supports 1,200 people at any one time, throughout the North West and the Midlands. The Association is renowned for its expertise in supporting and developing vulnerable and excluded people in addition to integrating service users and residents into the world of work.
Employees: 220
Volunteers: 30
Regional offices: 2

Adults Affected by Adoption-NORCAP

**112 Church Road, Wheatley,
Oxfordshire OX33 1LU
T: 01865 875000
F: 01865 875686
E: jeanm@norcap.org
www.norcap.org.uk
CEO: Jean Milsted**
Support, advice and specialist services provided to adult adopted people, birth-relatives and other family members to assist with locating and reunion issues. AAA-NORCAP is a national registered voluntary adoption support agency and intermediary agency. We assist adopted adults to access birth and adoption records and provide birth relatives with an intermediary service to seek renewed contact with relatives who were adopted.
Employees: 8
Volunteers: 85

Adventist Special Needs Association (ASNA)

**ASNA, Howbery Park, Suite W-05,
Windrush Innovation Centre,
Wallingford, Oxon, Oxfordshire OX10 8BA
T: 01491 821104
Helpline: 01491 833395
E: info@asna.info
www.asna.info
Honorary Secretary/Development Director:
Sophia Nicholls**
Supporting people living with special needs and disabilities by providing respite care residential short breaks, family fun days, resources, volunteer carers, advice and information. We also support professionals and other people working with people living with disabilities and special needs by providing advice, information, resources, disability training and awareness programmes.
Employees: 1
Volunteers: 30

Adventure Service Challenge Scheme

**East Lynn, Lansdown Lane, Bath BA1 4NB
T: 01225 329838 (also fax)
E: asc@asc-scheme.org.uk
www.asc-scheme.org.uk
Chair: Roger Crocker**
ASC Scheme is a nationally available, structured, flexible scheme of activities for children aged eight to 14 and over. It is used by schools, youth clubs, uniformed organisations, special needs groups etc. It offers young people adventure, the chance to give service to their community and a challenge. It is a three-fold programme helping young people develop in today's world, achieve their potential and prepare for a fulfilling and responsible adult life.
Volunteers: 15
Regional offices: 7

Adventure Unlimited

**64 Edward Street, Brighton,
East Sussex BN2 0JR
T: 01273 681058
E: info@aultd.org
www.aultd.org
Director: Louise Stone**
Adventure Unlimited is a registered charity based in Brighton and Hove. Its aim is to enrich the lives of disadvantaged young people through outdoor education events run by formerly unemployed adults. We run adventure activity and climbing events for groups and individuals of all ages. For more information about its work, please go to the website.
Employees: 10
Volunteers: 30
Regional offices: 1

Adverse Psychiatric Reactions Information Link (APRIL)

**Room 311, Linen Hall, London W1B 5TD
T: 020 7998 1561
E: info@april.org.uk
www.april.org.uk
Chair: Millie Kieve**
The objective of APRIL is to promote greater awareness, recognition and safe treatment of adverse psychiatric reactions and withdrawal symptoms that may be caused by prescribed and over-the-counter medicines and anaesthetics.
Employees: 1
Volunteers: 5

Advice on Individual Rights in Europe

**3rd Floor, 17 Red Lion Square,
London WC1R 4QH
T: 020 7831 4276
F: 020 7404 7760
E: info@airecentre.org
www.airecentre.org**
Operates a law centre specialising in European Union law and international human rights law, in particular, the European Convention on Human Rights.

Advice Services Alliance

7th Floor, Tavis House, Tavistock Square, London WC1H 9NA
T: 07904 377460
E: info@asauk.org.uk
www.asauk.org.uk
Director: Lindsey Poole
ASA is the umbrella body for the independent not-for-profit advice sector. It aims to: promote collaboration between advice agencies; provide a voice for the sector; analyse advice needs and provision; support the development of high-quality independent advice services; encourage better information on and public awareness of the rights of the citizen
Employees: 1
Income: £80,000 (2013-14)

AdviceUK

WB1, PO BOX 70716, London EC1P 1GQ
T: 0300 777 0107
E: mail@adviceuk.org.uk
www.adviceuk.org.uk
Chief Executive: Steve Johnson
AdviceUK promotes the provision of independent advice services across the UK; supports centres delivering independent advice to the public; acts as a coordinating network and voice for centres; provides a discussion forum on issues of concern to centres and their clients and helps formulate and promote policies with regard to advice work.
Employees: 17
Regional offices: 2

Advisory Centre for Education (ACE) Ltd

ACE Education Advice & Training, 72 Durnsford Road, London N11 2EJ
T: 020 8888 3377
Helpline: 0300 011 5142
F: 020 7354 9069
E: enquiries@ace-ed.org.uk
www.ace-ed.org.uk
ACE provides a free advice service for parents of children in state-maintained schools. It advocates changes in state schools to help them to become more responsive to the needs of parents and children. It offers training in specialist areas of education and supports local organisations giving advice on education.
Employees: 18
Volunteers: 2
Regional offices: 1

Advisory Committee on the Protection of the Sea

Anne-Laure Riber, Trinity College (Julian Hunt), Saint Johns Street, Cambridge CB2 1TQ
T: 01223 746918
E: info@acops.org
www.acops.org.uk
The committee exists to promote the preservation of the seas of the world from pollution by human activities; promote and conduct research into the causes and effects of pollution of the seas; advance public education by the study of the impact of human activities upon the natural resources of the sea.

Advisory Council for the Education of Romany and Other Travellers

ACERT, 12 Leinster Road, London N10 3AN
T: 020 8374 1286
E: info@acert.org.uk
www.acert.org.uk
Chair: Rosemarie McCarthy
ACERT campaigns for: equal access and opportunities in education; safe and secure accommodation; equal access to health and other community services; good community relations; an end to discrimination for all Gypsy, Roma and Traveller families.
Volunteers: 15
Regional offices: 1
Income: £13,000 (2014-15)

Afasic

20 Bowling Green Lane, London EC1R 0BD
T: 020 7490 9410
Helpline: 0845 355 5577
F: 020 7251 2834
E: info@afasic.org.uk
www.afasic.org.uk
Chief Executive: Linda Lascelles
Afasic is a UK-wide charity that helps children and young people with speech, language and communication impairments and their families. Afasic operates a helpline for parents, a website, produces information and literature, is a membership organisation, and has local groups across the country. Afasic runs training events and conferences for parents and professionals and activities for children and young people.
Employees: 21
Volunteers: 150
Regional offices: 2

African Caribbean Leukaemia Trust (ACLT)

2A Garnet Road, (Off Gillett Road), Thornton Heath, Surrey CR7 8RD
T: 020 3757 7700
E: info@aclt.org
www.aclt.org
Chief Executive: Orin Lewis
ACLT is a UK charity established in 1996 with the aim of raising awareness and registering potential lifesaving donors onto the stem cell (bone marrow), blood & organ donor registers. We have a particular focus on Black, Asian and Mixed race communities due to the severe lack of representation on the registers from individuals in these communities. To date ACLT have signed up approx. 70,000 people of all ethnicities to the stem cell register.
Employees: 4
Volunteers: 110
Regional offices: 1
Income: £218,302 (2013-14)

African Community Development Foundation

Ilex House, 1 Barrhill Road, Streatham Hill, London SW2 4RJ
T: 020 8671 2666
E: info@acdf.org
www.acdf.org
The foundation has been established to alleviate poverty and deprivation, promote social inclusion, and to help build capacity for self-reliance within the African community in the UK, serving as the umbrella organisation for the community.

African Community Involvement Association

Justin Plaza 3, Viceroy Suite 1, 341 London Road, Croydon CR4 4BE
T: 020 8687 2400
F: 020 8646 4363
E: membership@acia.org.uk
www.acia-uk.org
Works towards the relief of sickness among persons with AIDS or HIV infection particularly by the provision of culturally appropriate care and support services for people from the African community.

African Community Partnership

Barnes Wallis Community Centre, 74 Wild Goose Drive, New Cross, London SE14 5LL
T: 020 7635 9000
F: 020 7635 9600
E: africap@btconnect.com
Employees: 2
Volunteers: 12

African Health Policy Network

107-109 The Grove, Stratford, London E15 1HP
T: 020 8555 5778
F: 020 7017 8919
E: info@ahpn.org.uk
www.ahpn.org
CEO: Francis Kaikumba
The principal object of the network is to alleviate the suffering of persons subject to or affected by HIV and to promote sexual health amongst African communities in the UK and elsewhere by providing training, support, research and information and increasing public awareness of effective policies and good practice.
Employees: 7
Volunteers: 14

African Pastors Fellowship

Station House, Station Approach, Adisham, Canterbury, Kent CT3 3JE
T: 01227 812021
E: admin@africanpastors.org
africanpastors.org
CEO: Revd. David Stedman
The mission of APF is to work in partnership with local agencies and denominations supporting their strategies for pastoral, leadership and community development by providing training, help and equipment.
Employees: 3
Income: £90,000 (2014-15)

AFTAID Aid for the Aged in Distress

Epworth House, 25 City Road, London EC1Y 1AA
T: 0870 803 1950
F: 0870 803 2128
E: info@aftaid.org.uk
www.aftaid.org.uk
Chair: Susan Elson
AFTAID makes grants for the purchase of essential items to enable older people in need of vital financial assistance maintain independent living in the familiar surroundings of their home. AFTAID provides a safety net when distressed elderly people cannot obtain the help they require from social services, caring agencies or their own family.

After Adoption

Unit 5 Citygate, 5 Blantyre Street, Manchester, Lancashire M15 4JJ
T: 0161 839 4932
Helpline: 0800 056 8578
F: 0161 832 2242
E: information@afteradoption.org.uk
www.afteradoption.org.uk
Chief Executive: Lynn Charlton
After Adoption is a Voluntary Adoption Agency and the leading provider of adoption support services within the UK. We specialise in finding families for children with complex needs and deliver a full range of adoption services from our 7 regional offices across England and Wales
Employees: 126
Volunteers: 99
Regional offices: 7
Income: £3,278,562 (2012-13)

Aftermath Support

c/o Merseyside Police, Bromborough Village Road, Bromborough, Wirral, Merseyside CH62 7JG
T: 0845 634 4273
F: 0151 777 2583
E: support@aftermathsupport.org.uk
www.aftermathsupport.org.uk
Manager: Jackie Briscoe
Aftermath Support provides emotional and practical help to all victims of road collisions, including families and witnesses. Help is available for those who have been bereaved as well as those sustaining injury. We offer a choice of face-to-face and/or telephone support in Merseyside, Cheshire and Lancashire (where we have support workers based) or telephone support in other areas.
Employees: 3
Volunteers: 36
Regional offices: 1

AGCAS

Millenium House, 30 Junction Road, Sheffield S11 8XB
T: 0114 251 5750
F: 0114 251 5751
E: sarah.nichols@agcas.org.uk
www.agcas.org.uk
AGCAS has established an enviable position within the UK and beyond as a strong, collaborative body for HE careers professionals. Our primary aim is to help our members improve the accessibility and quality of careers information, advice and guidance. We work in partnership with organisations not only across the UK and Ireland but also with careers practitioners throughout the world.
Employees: 5
Volunteers: 1000

Age Concern Central Lancashire

Arkwright House, Stoneygate, Preston, Lancashire PR1 3XT
T: 01772 552850
E: help@55plus.org.uk
www.55plus.org.uk
Chief Executive: Linda Chivers
Age Concern Central Lancashire is a well established charity delivering services and support to meet the needs of local people who are over 55 and their carers primarily in Preston and South Ribble. Our aim is to support individuals to maintain and re-establish daily living skills, promoting independence and encouraging physical and mental well being.
Employees: 120
Volunteers: 250+
Regional offices: 1
Income: £2,500,000 (2014-15)

Age Concern Eastbourne

William and Patricia Venton Centre, Junction Road, Eastbourne, East Sussex BN21 3QY
T: 01323 638474
E: john.trainor@ageconcerneastbourne.co.uk
www.ageconcerneastbourne.or.uk
Chief Executive: John Trainor
To enhance and improve the experience in later life of people in Eastbourne and the surrounding area through the delivery of first class activities, services, information and advice designed to promote wellbeing for all.
Employees: 31
Volunteers: 200
Regional offices: 1
Income: £600,000 (2012-13)

Age Concern Hassocks and District

Pauline Thaw Centre, Dale Avenue, Hassocks, West Sussex BN6 9BX
T: 01273 844461
E: enquiries@achassocks.co.uk
www.achassocks.co.uk
Chairman: John Rose
We operate a Social Day Centre offering a freshly cooked, three course meal every weekday (cost £5 at October 2015). Minibus transport available. Coffee shop and charity shop open weekdays and Saturday mornings. Chiropody and Hairdressing available on site. Regular outings, events and entertainment. Pre-lunch chair-based exercises.

Wheelchairs for hire. Monthly hearing aid maintenance. Membership is free but registration is required after first visit. New volunteers always welcome.
Employees: 9
Volunteers: 70+
Income: £180,000 (2013-14)

Age Concern Havering

E: r.krishnan@achavering.co.uk

Age UK

Tavis House, 1-6 Tavistock Square, London WC1H 9NA
T: 0800 169 6565
E: contactageuk@ageuk.org.uk
www.ageuk.org.uk

Age UK Portsmouth

The Bradbury Centre, 16-18 Kingston Road, Portsmouth PO1 5RZ
T: 023 9286 2121
F: 023 9288 3523
E: kathy.kay@ageukportsmouth.org.uk
www.ageukportsmouth.org.uk
Chief Executive Officer: Dianne Sherlock
Mission: To help adults in Portsmouth & South East Hampshire enjoy a better quality of life, with a specific focus on all aspects of getting older. We assist older people to live independently and exercise choice. We are dynamic and driven by results and constantly deliver for older people. We are passionate about what we do and care about each individual. We are experts, authoritative and quality orientated.
Employees: 80
Volunteers: 40

Age UK Runnymede and Spelthorne

The Orchard, Staines Lane, Chertsey, Surrey KT16 8PS
T: 01784 444200
E: tdocker@ageukrunnymedeandspelthorne.org.uk
www.ageukrunnymedeandspelthorne.org.uk
Chief Officer: Tony Docker
As the independent local charity for people aged 50+, we provide information and advice, products and services; assessing what is right for each individual to help with maintaining independence at home.
Employees: 35
Volunteers: 170
Regional offices: 2
Income: £461,401 (2014-15)

AgeCare

Head Office, High Broom, Stone Cross, Crowborough, East Sussex TN6 3SL
T: 01892 611542
E: enquiries@agecare.org.uk
www.agecare.org.uk
AgeCare establishes and supports residential care homes for older people and promotes education and training of staff employed to care for older people.

AIESEC (UK) Ltd

29-31 Cowper Street, London EC2A 4AT
T: 020 7549 1800
E: aimee@aiesec.co.uk
www.aiesec.co.uk
President: Lubka Mieresova
AIESEC is a 65-year-old global organisation that develops students into leaders by running and participating in an international exchange programme. We are present in 125 countries and send more than 600 students from the UK abroad every year.
Employees: 11
Volunteers: 987
Regional offices: 22

Air Cadets

Headquarters Air Cadets, Royal Air Force, Cranwell, Sleaford, Lincolnshire NG34 8HB
T: 01400 267632
E: acfo@atc.raf.mod.uk
www.raf.mod.uk/aircadets/
Promotes and encourages among young people a practical interest in aviation and in the Royal Air Force; provides training which will be useful both in the services and civil life; fosters the spirit of adventure and develops the qualities of leadership and good citizenship.

Airey Neave Trust

The Airey Neave Trust, PO Bo 111, Leominster HR6 6BP
T: 020 7833 4440
E: aireyneavetrust@gmail.com
www.aireyneavetrust.org.uk/
The advancement of education by the furtherance of research into personal freedom under the law of any nation in the world and the dissemination of the useful results of such research.

Al-Anon Family Groups UK and Eire

Family Groups Limited, 57B Great Suffolk Street, London SE1 0BB
T: 020 7593 2070
Helpline: 020 7403 0888
E: enquiries@al-anonuk.org.uk
www.al-anonuk.org.uk
Al-Anon Family Groups provide support to anyone whose life is, or has been, affected by someone else's drinking, regardless of whether that person is still drinking or not.

Albany Trust

239A Balham High Rd, London SW17 7BE
T: 020 8767 1827
E: practicemanager@albanytrust.org
www.albanytrust.org.uk
The Trust provides counselling and psychotherapy, which aim to create a better climate for more honest and open relationships. We work with couples and individuals experiencing difficulties in their relationship or with their sexuality.
Employees: 1

Albert Kennedy Trust

Unit 112, Cremer Business Centre, 37 Cremer Street, London E2 8HD
T: 020 7831 6562
F: 020 7405 6929
E: admin@akt.org.uk
www.akt.org.uk
Chief Executive: Tim Sigsworth
The Trust's aim is to ensure that all lesbian, gay and bisexual young people are able to live in accepting, supportive and caring homes by providing a range of services to meet the individual needs of those who would otherwise be homeless or in a hostile environment.
Employees: 22
Volunteers: 200
Regional offices: 3

Albrighton Trust Ltd

Albrighton Moat and Gardens, Blue House Lane, Albrighton, Wolverhampton WV3 3FL
T: 01902 372441
E: moat@albrightontrust.org.uk
www.albrightontrust.org.uk
Operations Manager: Sandie Jackson
The Trust is dedicated to providing sports, arts, training & recreational activities for people of all ages who have disabilities or are disadvantaged, it enables and empowers them, regardless of disabilities, to participate

in and enjoy activities that are otherwise denied them
Employees: 5
Volunteers: 20
Income: £120,000 (2013-14)

Alcohol Concern

25 Corsham Street, London N1 6DR
T: 020 7566 9800
Helpline: 0300 123 1110
F: 020 7488 9213
E: contact@alcoholconcern.org.uk
www.alcoholconcern.org.uk
Chief Executive: Don Shenker
Alcohol Concern is the national agency on alcohol misuse campaigning for effective alcohol policy and improved services for people whose lives are affected by alcohol-related problems.
Employees: 20
Volunteers: 1
Regional offices: 1

Alcohol Research UK

Room 178, Queen Anne Business Centre, 28 Broadway, London SW1H 9JX
T: 020 7340 9502
F: 020 7340 9505
E: andrea.tilouche@alcoholresearchuk.org
www.aerc.org.uk
The Council administers a charitable foundation, the Alcohol Education and Research Fund, which finances projects within the UK for education and research and for novel forms of help for people with drinking problems, including offenders.
Employees: 3
Volunteers: 15

Alcoholics Anonymous

PO Box 1, 10 Toft Green, York YO1 7NJ
T: 01904 644026
F: 01904 629091
E: aainformation@gsogb.org.uk
www.alcoholics-anonymous.org.uk
To stay sober and to help other alcoholics to achieve sobriety. A fellowship of men and women who share their experience, strength and hope with each other that they may solve their common problem and help others to recover from alcoholism. The only requirement for membership is a desire to stop drinking. AA has no dues or fees.
Employees: 10
Regional offices: 3

Alexandra Rose Day

5 Mead Lane, Farnham, Surrey GU9 7DY
T: 01252 726171
F: 01252 727559
E: dleclercq@alexandraroseday.org.uk
www.alexandraroseday.org.uk
Chief Executive: Diana le Clercq
Alexandra Rose Day is an umbrella organisation that helps small and local charities across England and Wales raise funds. Any charity that helps children, young people, disabled people and the elderly can apply to take part in a Rose Day collection or Rose Charities Raffle. Participating charities can also apply for a grant from our Special Appeal Fund.
Employees: 3
Volunteers: 2

Alington House Community Association

4 North Bailey, Durham, Durham DH1 3ET
T: 0191 386 4088
E: abpegasus553@gmail.com
www.alingtonhouse.org.uk
Co-ordinator: Alan Barnett
Alington House Community Centre is situated in historical Durham City close to the Cathedral. An ideal venue for conferences, seminars, meetings, parties. We have a number of different size rooms to hire and free wi fi available. Parts of the centre are from the 17th century and is a grade 2* listed building and with views of Durham City this makes a fantastic place to hire.
Employees: 2
Volunteers: 15
Income: £90,000 (2013-14)

Alkaptonuria Society

66 Devonshire Road, Cambridge CB1 2BL
T: 01223 322897
E: info@alkaptonuria.info
www.akusociety.org
Advances the education of the public into all matters relating to Alkaptonuria disease and its causes.

Allergy UK

Planwell House, LEFA business park, Edington Way, Sidcup, Kent DA14 5BH
T: 01322 619898
E: info@allergyuk.org
www.allergyuk.org
Allergy UK is the country's leading national patient information charity dealing with allergy. We provide up-to-date information on all aspects of allergy and food intolerance. Our fully trained helpline staff guide callers to the appropriate allergy specialist.
Employees: 11
Volunteers: 12

Alliance of Healing Associations

Secretary's Office, 21 Mitchell Road, St Austell, Cornwall PL25 3AX
T: 01726 74843
F: 01726 67148
E: frances.evans@tesco.net
www.britishalliancehealingassociations.com/
President: Ken Baker
The Alliance consists of over 43 different organisations to date. This covers nearly 4,000 accredited spiritual healers and in the region of 1,000 student healers. Our object is the promotion and advancement of spiritual healing. The Alliance was formed in 1976 acquiring charitable status in 1982.
Employees: 1
Volunteers: 3
Regional offices: 4

Almshouse Association

Billingbear Lodge, Maidenhead Road, Wokingham, Berkshire RG40 5RU
T: 01344 452922
F: 01344 862062
E: naa@almshouses.org
www.almshouses.org
The Association advises members on any matters concerning almshouses and the welfare of the elderly; promotes improvements in almshouses and studies and research into all matters concerning them; makes grants and loans to members; keeps under review existing and proposed legislation affecting almshouses and when necessary takes action; encourages the provision of almshouses.
Employees: 8

Alone in London

Unit 6, 48 Provost Street, London N1 7SU
T: 020 7278 4224
F: 020 7837 7943
E: enquiries@als.org.uk
www.als.org.uk
Aims to relieve the homelessness of young people aged under 26; enable young people to live as independently as possible; provide practical and emotional support for young people at risk of homelessness; and bring young people's homelessness to public attention.
Employees: 39
Volunteers: 40

Alopecia UK

39 Wykeham Drive, Basingstoke, Hampshire RG23 8HW
T: 07763 293687
E: info@alopeciaonline.org.uk
www.alopeciaonline.org.uk
Charity Manager: Jen Chambers
Alopecia UK works to improve the lives of those affected by alopecia. The work of the charity is focused around its three aims: Support - to provide impartial information, advice, and support to help people feel less isolated. Awareness - to raise awareness to the general public and healthcare professionals about alopecia and its psychological impact. Research - to support medical and psychological researchers who aim to find effective treatments.
Employees: 1
Volunteers: 30
Income: £30,280 (2012-13)

Alternatives to Violence Project, Britain

The Grayston Centre, 28 Charles Square, London N1 6HT
T: 020 7324 4755
E: info@avpbritain.org.uk
www.avpbritain.org.uk
Director: Richard Drake
The Alternatives to Violence Project (AVP) runs a network of trained volunteers, who provide workshops for anyone who wants to find ways of resolving conflict in their lives without resorting to physical or verbal violence. AVP also runs a distance learning course for prisoners anywhere in the UK.
Employees: 5
Volunteers: 147
Regional offices: 6

Alzheimer's Society

Devon House, 58 St Katharine's Way, London E1W 1JX
T: 020 7423 3500
F: 020 7423 3501
E: enquiries@alzheimers.org.uk
www.alzheimers.org.uk
The Society's principal objectives are the provision of practical support, information and advice to people with Alzheimer's disease and other dementias and those who care for them, and the promotion of research into the disease and other dementias.
Employees: 1200
Regional offices: 260

Amal Trust

15h Bourne House, Westbourne Grove W2 4UA
T: 020 7727 5882
F: 020 7727 5859
E: info@amaltrust.org
www.amaltrust.org
Chairman: Hashim Charif
The object of the charity is to propagate Islam to young Muslims and non-Muslims through classes, lectures and seminars; to guide the youth of today away from bad street culture through Light of the Youth social activities like summer camps, sporting competitions and other social activities.
Employees: 3
Volunteers: 12
Regional offices: 2
Income: £37,460 (2012-13)

Ambition

371 Kennington Lane, London SE11 5QY
T: 020 7793 0787
E: info@ambitionuk.org
www.ambitionuk.org
Chief Executive: Helen Marshall
Ambition is the UK's leading youth club charity. Our members work with over 3,500 youth clubs and youth community projects across the UK, supporting more than 350,000 young people. We develop the services our members need and use our influence to open up exciting opportunities for them.
Employees: 13

Amnesty International Secretariat

1 Easton Street, London WC1X 0DW
T: 020 7413 5500
F: 020 7956 1157
E: amnestyis@amnesty.org
www.amnesty.org
Amnesty International is a worldwide campaigning movement that works to promote all human rights enshrined in the Universal Declaration of Human Rights and other international standards.
Employees: 469
Volunteers: 86
Regional offices: 12

Amnesty International United Kingdom

The Human Rights Action Centre, London EC2A 3EA
T: 020 7033 1500
F: 020 7033 1503
E: sct@amnesty.org.uk
www.amnesty.org.uk
Campaigns within Britain about Amnesty International's (AI) worldwide concerns. AI is a worldwide human rights movement independent of any government, political faction, ideology, economic interest or religious creed. It works for the: release of people imprisoned for their ethnic origin, sex, colour or beliefs, provided they have neither used nor advocated violence; abolition of torture and the death penalty; fair and early trial of all political prisoners; end to extra-judicial executions and 'disappearances'; observance of the UN Universal Declaration of Human Rights.
Employees: 120
Volunteers: 80
Regional offices: 3

Amref Health Africa

15-18 Lower Ground Floor, White Lion Street, London N1 9PD
T: 020 7269 5520
E: info@amrefuk.org
www.amrefuk.org
CEO: Samara Hammond
Amref Health Africa -is an international African organisation. AMREF was founded in Kenya in 1957 as the Flying Doctors of East Africa, we are now Africa's largest health NGO with programmes in Ethiopia, Kenya, Senegal, South Sudan, South Africa, Tanzania and Uganda. Last year we brought better health to over 12 million people across Africa.
Employees: 18

AMSPAR

Tavistock House North, Tavistock Square, London WC1H 9LN
T: 020 7387 6005
F: 020 7388 2648
E: info@amspar.co.uk
www.amspar.com
CEO: Thomas Brownlie
AMSPAR promotes quality and coherence in the delivery of vocational qualifications aimed at medical secretaries, practice managers, administrators and receptionists, and encourages and supports standards of excellence in the pursuit of continuous professional development and lifelong learning.
Employees: 3

Anaphylaxis Campaign

PO Box 275, Farnborough, Hampshire GU14 6XS
T: 01252 546100
Helpline: 01252 542029
F: 01252 377140
E: info@anaphylaxis.org.uk
www.anaphylaxis.org.uk
Chief Executive: Lynne Regent

The campaign fights for people with life-threatening allergies by providing education, information and support, campaigning on their behalf and promoting research.
Employees: 13
Volunteers: 75

Anchor Trust

1st Floor, 408 Strand, London WC2R 0NE
T: 020 7759 9107
E: office.support-lon@anchor.org.uk
www.anchor.org.uk
The Anchor Trust offers relief to older people, together with those in need by reason of physical or mental frailty, illness or disability, through the provision of housing, amenities and services for their accommodation, care, support, relief and treatment.

Ancient Monuments Society

St Ann's Vestry Hall, 2 Church Entry, London EC4V 5HB
T: 020 7236 3934
E: office@ancientmonumentssociety.org.uk
www.ancientmonumentssociety.org.uk
Secretary: Matthew Saunders
Founded in 1924 to campaign for historic buildings of all ages and all types.
Employees: 2
Volunteers: 30

Andover Neighbourcare

14 Union St, Andover, Hampshire SP10 1PA
T: 01264 351579
E: neighbourcare3@andover.co.uk
www.andoverneighboucare.co.uk
General Manager: Pam Delderfield
Remit of Andover Neighbourcare: To relieve persons resident in area of benefit who are in need by reason of age, disability, sickness or poverty by the provision of such voluntary care work as may be charitable. Andover Neighbourcare offers many services to predominantly older people in Andover and surrounding villages. Services include: transport to doctors, hospitals and clubs; cleaning; gardening; shopping; lunch club; drop-in centre; health and general information; minibus hire; outings and computer lessons.
Employees: 6
Volunteers: 120
Regional offices: 1
Income: £150,000 (2012-13)

Angel Foundation

Angel House, Borough Road, Sunderland, Tyne and Wear SR1 1HW
T: 0191 568 0800
E: info.uk@god.tv
www.god.tv
Head of Network Development: Tevon Jordan
Employees: 72
Volunteers: 30

Anglo Jewish Association

The Anglo-Jewish Association, 28 Queen Street, London EC4R 1BB
T: 020 7449 0909
E: info@anglojewish.org.uk
www.anglojewish.org.uk
The Association promotes the education of Jews and other persons in Jewish matters. Membership of the Association is open to all British citizens who wish to retain their Jewishness, and comprises a representative cross-section of the Anglo-Jewish community.

Angolan Civic Communities Alliance (ACCA)

C/O Sangat Advice Centre, Sancroft Road, Harrow, Middlesex HA3 7NS
T: 020 8423 3003
Helpline: 07940 556897
F: 020 8864 8881
E: acca.enquiries@gmail.com
Executive Director: Alex da Costa
The Angolan Civic Communities Alliance (ACCA) is one of the main drop-in centres for Angolan refugees and migrants and for other refugees and migrants from the Portuguese-speaking communities in Britain.
Employees: 2
Volunteers: 25

Animal Rescue Charity

Foxdells Sanctuary, Foxdells Lane, Rye Street, Bishop's Stortford, Hertfordshire CM23 2JG
T: 01279 501547
E: cbmitchell@animalrescue.org.uk
www.animalrescuecharity.org.uk
The charity provides a safe and caring environment for neglected and unwanted domestic animals and helps and rehabilitates wildlife wherever possible.
Employees: 10
Volunteers: 50
Regional offices: 1

Animal Welfare Foundation

7 Mansfield Street, London W1G 9NQ
T: 020 7908 6375
E: florenceb@bva.co.uk
www.bva-awf.org.uk
Chairman: Tiffany Hemming
The Animal Welfare Foundation is committed to improving the welfare of animals through veterinary science, education and debate. We apply the knowledge, skill and compassion of veterinary surgeons in an effective way by funding a variety of projects and activities.
Employees: 2
Volunteers: 30
Income: £112,057 (2013-14)

Ann Craft Trust

University of Nottingham, University Park, Nottingham NG7 2RD
T: 0115 951 5400
F: 0115 951 5232
E: ann-craft-trust@nottingham.ac.uk
www.anncrafttrust.org
CEO: Deborah Kitson
The Trust responds nationally to the needs and concerns of staff working in the statutory, voluntary and independent sectors in the interests of adults and children with learning disabilities who may be at risk of abuse. It improves working practices through research, training, publications, information and advice.

Anna Freud Centre

12 Maresfield Gardens, London NW3 5SU
T: 020 7794 2313
F: 020 7794 6506
E: rose.palmer@annafreud.org
www.annafreud.org
Chief Executive: Professor Peter Fonagy
The Anna Freud Centre is committed to developing innovative methods of prevention and treatment for children and young people with emotional and behavioural difficulties. We provide a vital lifeline for families under pressure and are the UK's only children's mental health organisation to combine practice, training and world-class research, with a focus on family wellbeing. We provide specialist help, we train others and we carry out innovative research.
Employees: 170
Volunteers: 1

Anne Frank Trust UK

Star House, London NW5 4BA
T: 020 7284 5858
E: info@annefrank.org.uk
www.annefrank.org.uk

Drawing on the power of Anne Frank's diary, we aim to inspire and educate a new generation to build a world of mutual respect, compassion and social justice.

Anthony Nolan Trust

2 Heathgate Place, 75-87 Agincourt Road, London NW3 2NU
T: 0303 303 0303
E: info@anthonynolan.org
www.anthonynolan.org.uk
The Trust maintains a register of 350,000 volunteer bone marrow donors who are prepared to give some of their marrow to save the life of another person, irrespective of country, colour, race or creed. It carries out research into the causes of failure in bone marrow transplants when donor and recipient appear to be matched.

Anti-Slavery International

Thomas Clarkson House, Unit 4, The Stableyard, Broomgrove Road, London SW9 9TL
T: 020 7501 8920
F: 020 7738 4110
E: info@antislavery.org
www.antislavery.org
Director: Aidan McQuade
Anti-Slavery International, founded in 1839, is committed to eliminating all forms of slavery throughout the world. Slavery, servitude and forced labour deny basic dignity and fundamental human rights. Anti-Slavery International works to end these abuses by campaigning for slavery's eradication, exposing current cases, supporting the initiatives of local organisations to release people and pressing for more effective implementation of international laws against slavery.
Employees: 24
Volunteers: 10

Antiquarian Horological Society

New House, High Street, Ticehurst, East Sussex TN5 7AL
T: 01580 200155
E: secretary@ahsoc.org
www.ahsoc.org
Chairman: David Thompson
A learned Society founded to encourage the study and conservation of timepieces.
Employees: 2

Anxiety Care UK

8 Nicholas Court, 3 Wallwood Road, London E11 1DQ
T: 07552 877219
E: admin@anxietycare.org.uk
www.anxietycare.org.uk
Anxiety Care UK works with clients towards recovery from anxiety and provides cognitive behavioural therapy (CBT), together with support, information and encouragement while undergoing this therapy. It promotes the reality of anxiety disorders, and encourages those affected to use their strengths to work towards recovery and to maintain it.

Anxiety UK (formerly National Phobics Society)

c/o Zion Community Resource Centre, 339 Stretford Road, Hulme, Manchester M15 4ZY
T: 0844 477 5774
F: 0161 226 7727
E: info@anxietyuk.org.uk
www.anxietyuk.org.uk
Chief Executive: Nicky Lidbetter
Anxiety UK is a user-led charity for those suffering from anxiety disorders, including panic attacks, phobias, obsessive/compulsive disorders, social anxiety and other associated anxiety disorders. We provide a helpline service offering information, support and understanding, run by sufferers and ex-sufferers of anxiety disorders. We provide information on self-help groups in the UK and provide self-help resources, factsheets and a quarterly magazine. Therapy is available across the UK for members face-to-face and over the phone.
Employees: 6
Volunteers: 500
Regional offices: 1

Apex Charitable Trust Limited

Tontine House, 24 Church Street, St. Helens, Merseyside WA10 1BD
T: 01744 612898
E: sthelens@apextrust.com
www.apextrust.com
Chief Executive: Godfrey Allen
The Trust aims to help people with criminal records obtain appropriate jobs or achieve self-employment by providing them with the skills they need in the labour market, and by working with employers to break down barriers to their employment. Provision only available in the Merseyside area.
Employees: 4
Regional offices: 1

Apex-Works

E: srowe@apex-works.co.uk

Apostleship of the Sea

National Headquarters, Stella Maris, Herald House, Lamb's Passage, Bunhill Row, London EC1Y 8LE
T: 020 7588 8285
F: 020 7588 8280
E: salvina@apostleshipofthesea.org.uk
www.aos-usa.org
Promotes the spiritual and material welfare of seafarers and their families.
Employees: 15
Volunteers: 30

Aquaterra Leisure

Suite 1.40 Millbank Tower, 21-24 Millbank, London SW1P 4QP
T: 020 3474 0552
E: laura.gray@aquaterra.org
www.aquaterra.org

Arbours Association Limited

6 Church Lane, London N8 7BU
T: 020 8340 7646
E: info@arboursassociation.org
www.arboursassociation.org
Director: T.J.Ryan
The Arbours Association provides long-term residential accommodation and psychotherapeutic support for those in emotional distress. It also offers a low-to-high cost psychotherapy service for members of the public. It also runs the Arbours Association Training Programme for those wishing to qualify as psychoanalytic psychotherapists, with a postgraduate professional support organisation (AAP).
Employees: 20
Volunteers: 1

ARC

ARC House, Marsden Street, Chesterfield, Derbyshire S40 1JY
T: 01246 555043
F: 01246 555045
E: contact.us@arcuk.org.uk
www.arcuk.org.uk
ARC is a UK-wide umbrella body for providers of services to people with a learning disability. We promote best practice and support good-quality provision by training, projects and partnerships between providers. We represent providers' views at local, regional, national and European levels. We have a large training consortium and hold UK and national conferences to bring providers

together to promote best practice and share problems and solutions.
Employees: 55
Regional offices: 4

ARC (Antenatal Results and Choices)

345 City Road, London EC1V 1LR
T: 020 7713 7356
Helpline: 0845 077 2290
E: info@arc-uk.org
www.arc-uk.org
Director: Jane Fisher
ARC offers information and support to parents who are: making decisions before, during and after the antenatal testing process; told that their unborn baby has an abnormality; having to make difficult decisions about continuing the pregnancy; having to make difficult decisions about ending the pregnancy; dealing with the consequences of their decisions. ARC also works with health professionals, providing training, support and publications.
Volunteers: 43

Architects Benevolent Society

43 Portland Place, London W1B 1QH
T: 020 7580 2823
E: help@absnet.org.uk
www.absnet.org.uk
The Society relieves persons engaged or formerly engaged in the practice of architecture, and the wives, widows, children and other dependants of such persons being in necessitous circumstances.

Architectural Heritage Fund

The Architectural Heritage Fund, 3 Spital Yard, Spitalfields E1 6AQ
T: 020 7925 0199
F: 020 7930 0295
E: diane.kendal@ahfund.org.uk
www.ahfund.org.uk
Promotes the permanent preservation of historic buildings in the UK by providing advice, information and financial assistance in the form of grants and loans for projects undertaken by building preservation trusts and other charities.

Army Cadet Force Association

Holderness House, 51-61 Clifton Street, London EC2A 4DW
T: 020 7426 8370
E: exec-asst@armycadets.com
www.armycadets.com
The association develops among its members the qualities of good citizenship and the spirit of service to Queen, country and local community, and gives encouragement and training to those considering a career in the regular army or service in the reserve forces. The ACF is a voluntary youth movement, sponsored principally by the army, and takes part in both military and community activities.

Army Families Federation

IDL 414, Floor 1, Zone 6, Ramilies Building, Marlborough Lines, Monxton Road, Andover SP11 8HJ
T: 01264 382326
F: 01264 382327
E: us@aff.org.uk
www.aff.org.uk
The AFF is a unique two-way communications link between the British Army and its families. As a registered charity with branches in Northern Ireland, Germany and Cyprus, its objectives are to voice the views and concerns of army families about their way of life, helping to get things changed for the better.
Employees: 54
Regional offices: 3

ARNI Institute

PO Box 68, Lingfield, Surrey RH7 6QQ
Helpline: 07712 211378
E: tom@arni.uk.com
www.arni.uk.com
Secretary: Dr Tom Balchin
The Institute aims to encourage and advance the rehabilitation of those suffering from the effects of stroke and other brain injuries that have resulted in partial paralysis.
Volunteers: 43
Regional offices: 1

Arthritis Action

64 Victoria Street, 9th Floor, London SW1E 6QP
T: 020 3781 7120
Helpline: 01323 408617
E: info@arthritisaction.org.uk
www.arthritisaction.org.uk
Chief Executive: Shantel Irwin
Arthritis Action's vision is for people to live active lives, free from arthritis pain. Our aim is to empower people with arthritis to take control of their lives, manage their condition and reduce the need for medical intervention. Working in partnership with members, health professionals, other charities, researchers, arthritis experts and corporates is very important to us.
Employees: 13
Regional offices: 2
Income: £376,000 (2013-14)

 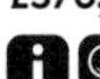 

Arthritis and Musculoskeletal Alliance

Bride House, 18-20 Bride Lane, London EC4Y 8EE
T: 020 7842 0910
F: 020 7842 0901
E: lynnlevi@arma.uk.net
www.arma.uk.net
The Arthritis and Musculoskeletal Alliance (ARMA) is the UK umbrella association bringing together support groups, professional bodies and research organisations in the field of arthritis and other musculoskeletal conditions.
Employees: 2
Volunteers: 45

Arthritis Care

Floor 4, Linen Court, 10 East Road, London N1 6AD
T: 020 7380 6540
Helpline: 0808 800 4050
F: 020 7380 6502
E: peter@arthritiscare.org.uk
www.arthritiscare.org.uk
Chief Executive: Neil Betteridge
Arthritis Care is a user-centred and user-led charity, with people with all types of arthritis at the heart of what we do. We are the voice of people with arthritis and their families, providing high-quality information and support to enable people living with arthritis to make positive and practical changes to their lives.
Employees: 120
Volunteers: 200
Regional offices: 5

Arthritis Research UK

Copeman House, St Mary's Court, St Mary's Gate, Chesterfield, Derbyshire S41 7TD
T: 0300 790 0400
F: 01246 558007
E: enquiries@arthritisresearchuk.org
www.arthritisresearchuk.org
Raises funds and finances research into the causes and cure of the rheumatic diseases; encourages the teaching of rheumatology to medical and paramedical under- and postgraduates; stimulates public authorities to provide better treatment facilities.
Employees: 150
Volunteers: 5000
Regional offices: 4

Arthur McDougall Fund

McDougall Trust Unit W219, Second Floor, West Building,

Westminster Business Square 1-45,
Durham Street, London SE11 5JH
T: 020 7620 1080
F: 020 7928 1258
E: admin@mcdougall.org.uk
www.mcdougall.org.uk
Aims to advance knowledge and encourage study and research in: political and economic science, the functions of government and the services provided to the community by public and voluntary organisations; methods of election of, and the selection and government of, representative organisations, whether national, civic, commercial, industrial or social.
Employees: 1
Volunteers: 10

Arthur Rank Centre

Stoneleigh Park, Kenilworth,
Warwickshire CV8 2LG
T: 024 7685 3060
F: 024 7641 4808
E: info@germinate.net
www.germinate.net
CEO: Jerry Marshall
The ARC is committed to helping create sustainable vibrant rural communities and has a particular concern for the 900,000 rural households living in poverty, those who feel isolated, and families experiencing difficulties. We offer support directly and work to equip the UK's 13,000 rural churches to bring physical, social and spiritual transformation to communities.
Employees: 7
Volunteers: 2

Article 19

Free Word Centre, 60 Farringdon Road,
London EC1R 3GA
T: 020 7324 2500
E: renato@article19.org
www.article19.org
Executive Director: Thomas Hughes
Article 19 is an international human rights organisation that works to promote, protect and develop freedom of expression, including access to information and the means of communication.

Arts and Business

137 Shepherdess Walk, London N1 7RQ
T: 020 7566 6650
E: jessica.stockford@bitc.org.uk
www.artsandbusiness.org.uk
Arts and Business strengthens communities by developing creative partnerships between business and the arts.
Employees: 114
Regional offices: 13

Arts Council England

14 Great Peter Street, London SW1P 3NQ
T: 0845 300 6200
F: 0161 934 4426
E: enquiries@artscouncil.org.uk
www.artscouncil.org.uk
Arts Council England is the national development agency for the arts in England, distributing public money from government and the National Lottery. We believe in the transforming power of the arts - power to change the lives of people throughout the country. Our ambition is to place the arts at the heart of national life, reflecting the country's rich and diverse cultural identity as only the arts can. We want people throughout England to experience arts activities of the highest quality. We believe that access to the arts goes hand in hand with excellence.

Artswork

Second Floor, Cadogan House,
37 Commercial Road, Southampton,
Hampshire SO15 1GG
T: 023 8033 2491
E: alice@artswork.org.uk
www.artswork.org.uk
Chief Executive: Jane Bryant
Artswork is the national, independent youth arts development agency, committed to making a difference to the lives of children and young people.
Employees: 26

Arun Co-ordinated Community Transport

Unit S3, Rudford Industrial Estate,
Ford Road, Arundel,
West Sussex BN18 0BD
T: 01903 723584
F: 01903 718631
E: manager@arun-cct.org
www.arun-cct.org
Chairman of Trustees: Graham Paull
Arun Co-Ordinated Community Transport is a registered not for profit, charity based in Littlehampton that offers a range of transport solutions for the residents of the local community within the Arun area who have difficulty using public transport due to a mobility or visual disability, illness, frailty, age or other impairment.
Employees: 5
Volunteers: 35
Regional offices: 1
Income: £153,678 (2014-15)

ARVAC Association for Research in the Voluntary and Community Sector

c/o School of Business and Social Sciences,
Roehampton University,
Southlands College, 80 Roehampton Lane,
London SW15 5SL
F: 020 7704 9995
E: arvac@arvac.org.uk
www.arvac.org.uk
ARVAC promotes effective community action through research.
Employees: 5
Volunteers: 1

ASDAN

Wainbrook House, Hudds vale Road,
St George, Bristol BS5 7HY
T: 0117 941 1126
F: 0117 935 1112
E: sallyfinn@asdan.org.uk
www.asdan.co.uk
ASDAN's aim is the advancement of education, by providing opportunities for all learners to develop their personal and social attributes and levels of achievement through the use and attainment of ASDAN resources and awards, and the relief of poverty, where poverty inhabits such opportunities for learners.
Employees: 40

Asha Projects

13 Shrubbery Road, London SW16 2AS
T: 07870 570861
Helpline: 020 8696 0023
F: 020 8677 9920
E: admin@asha.org.uk
www.ashaprojects.org.uk
Asha means 'hope'. Our mission is to empower Asian women to live independently and achieve the goals that they have set for themselves.
Employees: 9
Volunteers: 2

Ashoka (UK) Trust

15 Old Ford Road, Bethnal Green,
London E2 9PJ
T: 020 8980 9416
E: ppelimanni@ashoka.org
www.ashoka.org
UK Director: Mark Cheng
Ashoka contributes to the social progress of developing countries by encouraging and empowering outstanding individuals in those countries who have shown they have the capacity and character to achieve substantial change, in a wide variety of fields, through the organisations they lead.
Regional offices: 2

Asian Family Counselling Service

Suite 51, The Lodge, Windmill Place,
2-4 Windmill Lane, Southall UB2 4NJ
T: 020 8571 3933 (also fax)
E: afcs@btconnect.com
www.asianfamilycounselling.org
Director: Kulbir Randhawa

Asian Family Counselling Service provides family, marital and individual counselling for the Asian community resident in the UK. Counsellors offer caring, personal and confidential counselling in the client's language with an awareness of their cultural and ethnic backgrounds.

Employees: 6
Volunteers: 6
Regional offices: 2
Income: £139,790 (2013-14)

Asian Foundation for Help

BIA House, 116 Ealing Road, Wembley, Middlesex HA0 4TH
T: 020 8903 3019
E: ketan@asianfoundation.org.uk
www.asianfoundation.org.uk
Chairman: Hitesh Popat

A voluntary organisation raising funds to help the poor and needy.

Volunteers: 20
Regional offices: 3
Income: £125,000 (2014-15)

Asian People's Disability Alliance Ltd

Daycare And Development Centre,
Alric Avenue, off Bruce Road, Harlesden,
London NW10 8RA
T: 020 8830 4220
F: 020 8830 3890
E: apdmcha@aol.com
www.apda.org.uk
CEO Joint: Zeenat Jeewa

Aims to ensure that Asian people with disabilities are accorded full status, rights and facilities to enable them to participate fully and represent their own interests in all areas of society.

Employees: 15
Volunteers: 10
Regional offices: 1

ASPIRE

Aspire National Training Centre,
Wood Lane, Stanmore HA7 4AP
T: 020 8954 5759
E: info@aspire.org.uk
www.aspire.org.uk

Aspire is a national charity that provides practical help to people who have been paralysed by Spinal Cord Injury, helping them move from injury to independence. Every eight hours in the UK someone is paralysed by a spinal cord injury; it can happen to anyone at any time and no one is prepared for how it will change their life. Our services include: Aspire Grants, Aspire Housing, Independent Living, Assistive Technology, Campaigning and Research.

Employees: 80
Volunteers: 20

ASSERT

PO Box 4962, Nuneaton CV11 9FD
Helpline: 0300 999 0102
F: 01268 415940
E: assert@angelmanuk.org
www.angelmanuk.org

Aims to relieve the need of those with Angelman Syndrome and their families, to advance the education of the public in Angelman Syndrome and to promote research into Angelman Syndrome.

Volunteers: 10

Assist UK

Redbank House, 4 St Chad's Street,
Manchester M8 8QA
T: 0161 832 9757
E: general.info@assist-uk.org
www.assist-uk.org
CEO: Alan Norton

Assist UK is an umbrella organisation for a UK-wide network of locally situated disabled/independent living centres. Most centres include a permanent exhibition of products and equipment that provide people with opportunities to see and try products and equipment and get information and advice from professional staff about what might suit them best.

Employees: 5
Volunteers: 18
Regional offices: 41

Associated Board of the Royal Schools of Music

24 Portland Place, London W1B 1LU
T: 020 7636 5400
F: 020 7467 8223
E: abrsm@abrsm.ac.uk
www.abrsm.ac.uk

Aims to advance the arts, science and skills of music, speech and drama throughout the UK and overseas.

Employees: 95
Volunteers: 250

Associated Country Women of the World

Mary Sumner House, 24 Tufton Street,
London SW1P 3RB
T: 020 7799 3875
F: 020 7340 9950
E: info@acww.org.uk
www.acww.org.uk
Operations Manager: Tish Collins

An international membership organisation that aims to raise the standard of living of rural women and their families through education, training, support and community development programmes. It gives women a voice at international level through its links with United Nations agencies and liaises with other NGOs. It has an administrative office in London and organises a World conference every three years. ACWW connects and supports women and communities worldwide.

Employees: 8
Volunteers: 50

Association for Child and Adolescent Mental Health

St Saviour's House, 39-41 Union Street,
London SE1 1SD
T: 020 7403 7458
F: 020 7403 7081
E: martin.pratt@acamh.org
www.acamh.org

The Association undertakes the scientific study of all matters concerning the mental health and development of children, young people and their families.

Employees: 7

Association for Continence Advice

Fitwise Management Ltd, Blackburn House,
Redhouse Road, Bathgate EH47 7AQ
T: 01506 811077
E: aca@fitwise.co.uk
www.aca.uk.com

The Association acts as a multidisciplinary forum for healthcare professionals with a special interest in the promotion of continence and the management of incontinence and to educate professionals about the prevention and treatment of incontinence.

Association for Family Therapy

7 Executive Suite, St James Court,
Wilderspool Causeway,
Warrington WA4 6PS
T: 01925 444414
E: s.kennedy@aft.org.uk
www.aft.org.uk
Chair: Jeanette Neden

AFT's key aim is to benefit the public by working to continually improve standards of

professional family therapy and systemic practice. Members promote family therapy through practice, training, management and research. AFT provides the Journal and Context magazine for its members and a number of conferences.
Employees: 4
Volunteers: 30

Association for Glycogen Storage Disease (UK)

Old Hambledon Racecourse, Sheardley Lane, Droxford, Hampshire SO32 3QY
T: 0300 123 2790
E: allan.muir@agsd.org.uk
www.agsd.org.uk
Chairman: Andrew Wakelin
The Association is a contact and support group for all persons affected by some form of glycogen storage disease. It also creates public awareness of GSD and acts as a focus for educational, scientific and charitable activities related to this disorder.
Employees: 2
Regional offices: 1

Association for Humanistic Psychology

BM Box 3582, London WC1N 3XX
T: 0845 707 8506
E: admin@ahpb.org
www.ahpb.org
The Association educates the public about humanistic psychology, disseminates alternative ways of dealing with human problems, both personal and societal and encourages the development of the individual to his/her full potential.
Volunteers: 6

Association for Language Learning

University of Leicester, University Road, Leicestershire LE1 7RH
T: 0116 229 7600
F: 0116 223 1488
E: info@all-languages.org.uk
www.all-languages.org.uk
Director: Linda Parker
The aims of the association are to support members' professional work and development; to develop policies that reflect views and interests of members; to promote improved standards of language teaching and learning; and to encourage understanding of the importance of languages, communication and cultural issues.
Employees: 4
Volunteers: 50+

Association for Learning Technology

Gipsy Lane, Headington, Oxford OX3 0BP
T: 01865 484125
F: 01865 484165
E: thomas.palmer@alt.ac.uk
www.alt.ac.uk
Chief Executive: Maren Deepwell
ALT is a professional and scholarly Association that seeks to bring together all those with an interest in the use of learning technology. We represent and support our members and provide services for them; facilitate collaboration between practitioners, researchers, and policy makers; spread good practice in the use of learning technology; raise the profile of research in learning technology and support the professionalisation of learning technologists.
Employees: 6
Volunteers: 42
Regional offices: 1

Association for Multiple Endocrine Neoplasia Disorder

The Warehouse, Draper Street, Southborough, Tunbridge Wells TN4 0PG
T: 01892 516076
E: jo.grey@amend.org.uk
www.amend.org.uk
CEO and Chair of Trustees: Jo Grey
AMEND provides information and support services to families affected by multiple endocrine neoplasia (MEN) disorders and associated endocrine tumours and syndromes. We maintain a Research Registry, award research grants and produce patient information with the help of our expert medical advisory team. Membership is free and open to all via our HONCode certified website at www.amend.org.uk.
Volunteers: 20
Income: £178,000 (2014-15)

Association for Perioperative Practice

Daisy Ayris House, 42 Freemans Way, Harrogate, North Yorkshire HG3 1DH
T: 01423 881300
Helpline: 01423 880997
E: stephanie.oates@afpp.org.uk
www.afpp.org.uk
Chief Executive Officer: Dawn Stott
Improving patient care in perioperative practice.
Employees: 22

Association for Physical Education

Room 17, Bredon, University of Worcester, Henwick Grove, Worcester WR2 6AJ
T: 01905 855584
E: enquiries@afpe.org.uk
www.afpe.org.uk
The Association for Physical Education (afPE) is committed to being the UK representative organisation of choice for people and agencies delivering or supporting the delivery of physical education in schools and in the wider community.
Employees: 10

Association for Post-Natal Illness

145 Dawes Road, Fulham, London SW6 7EB
T: 020 7386 0868
E: info@apni.org
www.apni.org
The Association advises and supports women suffering from post-natal depression.
Employees: 7
Volunteers: 300+
Regional offices: 1

Association for Project Management

Ibis House, Regent Park, Summerleys Road, Princes Risborough, Buckinghamshire HP27 9LE
T: 0845 458 1944
F: 0845 458 8807
E: mike.robinson@apm.org.uk
www.apm.org.uk
Chief Executive: Andrew Bragg
Association for Project Management (APM) is the largest independent body of its kind in Europe, a professional membership association with the mission to develop and promote the professional disciplines of project and programme management for the public benefit. APM currently forms a community of around 19,500 individual and 500 corporate members in all sectors and industries, including public sector, civil engineering, financial services, retail, logistics, science and arts.
Employees: 60
Volunteers: 400

Association for Science Education

College Lane, Hatfield AL10 9AA
T: 01707 283000
F: 01707 266532
E: info@ase.org.uk
www.ase.org.uk
Chief Executive: Shaun Reason
ASE is the largest subject association in the UK. As the professional body for all those involved in science education from pre-school to higher education, the ASE provides a national network supported by a dedicated staff team. Members enjoy benefits such as journals, book sales service, publishing and Public Liability insurance.
Employees: 20
Volunteers: 50

Association for the Study of Obesity

PO Box 410, Deal, Kent CT14 4AL
T: 01304 367788
E: asooffice@aso.org.uk
www.aso.org.uk
Promotes medical research into the causes, prevention and treatment of obesity. It facilitates contact between individuals and organisations interested in any aspect of the problem of obesity and body weight regulation. An organisation for health professionals.

Association of Blind and Partially Sighted Teachers and Students

BM Box 6727, London WC1N 3XX
T: 0117 966 4839
E: e.standen@btinternet.com
www.abapstas.org.uk
Provides support to visually impaired teachers and students and those with an interest in education or training and to campaign on their behalf.

Association of Blind Piano Tuners

31 Wyre Crescent, Darwen, Lancashire BB3 0JG
T: 0844 736 1976
E: abpt@uk-piano.org
www.uk-piano.org
The aims of the association are to further the interests and raise the status of blind and partially sighted piano tuners, give them all possible assistance in their work, and to maintain or raise the standard of service given by blind piano tuners.

Association of Breastfeeding Mothers

PO Box 207, Bridgwater, Somerset TA6 7YT
T: 0844 412 2948
Helpline: 0300 330 5453
E: admin@abm.me.uk
www.abm.me.uk
We offer mother-to-mother breastfeeding support and up-to-date breastfeeding information.
Volunteers: 100

Association of British Credit Unions

T: 0161 832 3694
E: info@abcul.org
www.abcul.org/home

Association of Charitable Foundations

314-320 Acorn House, 14 Upper Woburn Place, Gray's Inn Road, London WC1X 8DP
T: 020 7255 4499
F: 020 7255 4496
E: charlotte@acf.org.uk
www.acf.org.uk
Chief Executive: David Emerson
The Association of Charitable Foundations (ACF) is the membership association for foundations and grant-making charities in the UK. For 25 years we have supported trusts and foundations; respecting and safeguarding their independence, and helping them to be effective in the many ways that they use their resources. www.acf.org.uk
Employees: 6

Association of Charitable Organisations

Acorn House, 314-320 Gray's Inn Road, London WC1X 8DP
T: 020 7255 4480
F: 020 7255 4496
E: info@aco.uk.net
www.aco.uk.net
Chief Executive: Dominic Fox
The Association of Charitable Organisations (ACO) is the national UK umbrella body for charities that give grants and welfare support to individuals in need. ACO provides support to its members through networking, raising standards, promoting good practice, lobbying and campaigning, information, advice and online services.
Employees: 2

Association of Charity Independent Examiners

The Gatehouse, White Cross, South Road, Lancaster, Lancashire LA1 4XQ
T: 01524 34892
E: info@acie.org.uk
www.acie.org.uk
ACIE Chair: Chris Smith
Promotes the greater effectiveness of charities in the UK in the achievement of their charitable objectives by: providing advice, support and training to any person acting or wishing to act as an independent examiner; promoting and maintaining high standards of practice and professional conduct; and providing charity trustees with information in connection with the selection and appointment of independent examiners.
Employees: 2
Volunteers: 500
Income: £62,719 (2014-15)

Association of Chief Executives of Voluntary Organisations

Regents Wharf, 8 All Saints Street, London N1 9RL
T: 020 7014 4600
E: marketing@acevo.org.uk
www.acevo.org.uk
Chief Executive: Stephen Bubb
ACEVO is the only professional association for voluntary sector CEOs in England and Wales. We connect, develop, support and represent over 2,000 members. Over the last 20 years, our aim has been to increase the professionalism of our members and raise standards across the voluntary sector.
Employees: 30
Regional offices: 2

Association of Community Based Business Advice

2nd Floor, 200A Pentonville Road, London N1 9JP
T: 020 7832 5842
E: info@acbba.org.uk
www.acbba.org.uk
Executive Director: Armando Pardo
We provide business training, advice and mentoring support to people interested in small business with a focus on self-employment. Our aim is to promote viable, income generating, enterprises that enable people to make a living out of their business activities.
Employees: 3

Association of Dance Therapists (International)

Flat 1, Penlee, Lindridge Road, Babbacombe, Torquay, Devon TQ1 3SD
T: 01803 314366
E: deniseputtock@yahoo.co.uk
www.schoolofdancetherapy.com
Director of Studies: Denise Puttock
Volunteers: 6

Association of Disabled Professionals

The Vassall Centre, Gill Avenue, Gill Avenue, Bristol BS16 2QQ
T: 0844 445 7123
E: advice@adwuk.org
www.adwuk.org
Chief executive: Andy Rickell
ADP exists to improve the educational/employment opportunities available to disabled people, allowing disabled people to retain employment commensurate with their abilities and to participate fully in the everyday life of society. It aims to improve public knowledge of the capabilities and needs of disabled people. ADP provides employment advice, information and peer support to disabled people. Also operates the Disabled Entrepreneurs' Network providing advice and support to self-employed disabled people www.disabled-entrepreneurs.net. It is part of ADWUK

Association of Governing Bodies of Independent Schools

3 Codicote Road, Welwyn, Hertfordshire AL6 9LY
T: 01438 840730
F: 05603 432632
E: comms@agbis.org.uk
www.agbis.org.uk
General Secretary: Stuart Westley
The Association of Governing Bodies of Independent Schools supports and advises governing bodies of schools in the independent sector under the umbrella of ISC. The objectives of the Association are the advancement of education in independent schools and the promotion of good governance in such schools.
Employees: 3

Association of Interchurch Families

6th Floor, 10 Aldersgate Street, London EC1A 4HJ
T: 020 3384 2947
E: info@interchurchfamilies.org.uk
www.interchurchfamilies.org.uk
Executive Development Officer: Doral Hayes
The association is a focus for all concerned with marriages between committed Christians of different church allegiances, and more widely with 'mixed marriages'. It promotes Christian unity and offers a support network for interchurch families (usually where one partner is Roman Catholic) and a voice for such families in the churches.
Employees: 1
Volunteers: 50
Income: £35,000 (2014-15)

Association of Jewish Ex-Servicemen and Women

Shield House, Harmony Way, Hendon, London NW4 2BZ
T: 020 8202 2323
E: headoffice@ajex.org.uk
www.ajex.org.uk
AJEX is the only UK Jewish Charity totally devoted to the care and welfare of Jewish ex-service personnel and their dependants in need. The Association provides practical support in assisting with mobility equipment, household emergency repairs, respite breaks and general wellbeing.

Association of Jewish Refugees in Great Britain

Jubilee House, Merrion Avenue, Stanmore, Middlesex HA7 4RL
T: 020 8385 3070
E: carolhart@ajr.org.uk
www.ajr.org.uk
The Association aims to assist Jewish refugees from Nazi oppression and their families, primarily from Central Europe, by providing a wide range of services.

Association of Medical Research Charities

Charles Darwin House, 12 Roger Street, London WC1N 2JU
T: 020 7685 2620
F: 020 7685 2621
E: ceoffice@amrc.org.uk
www.amrc.org.uk
Chief Executive: Aisling Burnand
The Association of Medical Research Charities (AMRC) is a membership organisation of the leading medical and health research charities in the UK. Working with our member charities and partners, we aim to support the sector's effectiveness and advance medical research by developing best practice, providing information and guidance, improving public dialogue about research and science, and influencing government.
Employees: 10
Volunteers: 1

Association of Natural Burial Grounds

Natural Death Centre, In The Hill House, Watley Lane, Twyford, Winchester SO21 1QX
T: 01962 712690
E: contact@naturaldeath.org.uk
www.naturaldeath.org.uk
Manager: Rosie Inman-Cook
Run by the Natural Death Centre charity.
Volunteers: 5

Association of Radical Midwives

Rothley Lake House, Longwitton, Morpeth, Northumberland NE61 4JY
T: 07810 665733
E: rothleylakehouse@gmail.com
www.midwifery.org.uk
Administration Secretary: Katherine Hales
The aims of the Association are to improve maternity services, especially within the NHS; to preserve and enhance choices in childbirth for all women; to re-establish the full role of the midwife; to encourage the evaluation of maternity care; to encourage research.
Employees: 3
Volunteers: 12

Association of Reflexologists

5 Fore Street, Taunton, Somerset TA1 1HX
T: 01823 351010
F: 01823 335246
E: info@aor.org.uk
www.aor.org.uk
Chief Executive: Carolyn Story
The Association was set up to create an independent, fully democratic network of professional reflexologists, providing them with support and ongoing education through seminars and workshops.
Employees: 10

Association of Research Ethics Committees

AREC Office 13, Cherry Drive, Durham DH6 2BG
T: 0845 604 5466
E: jackiemaull@arec.org.uk
www.arec.org.uk
Chief Executive: Jackie Maull
AREC is an independent, voluntary organisation established to set standards within the field of research ethics. AREC is the voice of research ethics within the UK.
Employees: 2
Volunteers: 16

Association of Therapeutic Communities

Waterfront, Kingsdown Road, Walmer, Kent CT14 7LL
T: 01242 620077
E: post@therapeuticcommunities.org
www.therapeuticcommunities.org
The Association acts as a focus for information, debate, training and support for people who work in therapeutic communities, or who are interested in this way of working. Members are drawn from all sectors of the healthcare and social-work professions, and share a belief in the importance of participation by both staff and patients in creating and maintaining a therapeutic environment.

Association of Volunteer Managers

Po box 1449, Bedford, Bedfordshire MK44 5AN
E: info@volunteermanagers.org.uk
www.volunteermanagers.org.uk
Chair: Heather Baumohl
The Association of Volunteer Managers is an independent body that aims to support, represent and champion people who manage volunteers in England regardless of field, discipline or sector. It has been set up by and for people who manage volunteers.
Volunteers: 15
Income: £12,000 (2013-14)

Association of Young People with ME

10 Vermont Palce, Tongwell, Milton Keynes MK12 8JA
T: 01908 379737
Helpline: 0845 123 2389
E: info@ayme.org.uk
www.ayme.org.uk
Chief Executive: Mary-Jane Willows
AYME is a national service for young people suffering from the condition known as ME/CFS. It works on behalf of those young people whose lives are affected, through media coverage, representations to government and other agencies, and through talks and presentations. Providing advice, guidance, information and support for young people and their families. Promote campaigns for the recognition, diagnosis, treatment and acceptance of ME/CFS.
Employees: 6
Volunteers: 45
Regional offices: 1
Income: £20,000 (2013-14)

Asthma UK

Summit House, 70 Wilson Street, London EC2A 2DB
T: 020 7786 4900
F: 020 7256 6075
E: reception@asthma.org.uk
www.asthma.org.uk
Asthma UK aims to help and advise people with asthma to understand and control their condition so that they may live healthier and more active lives. It promotes research into asthma, its causes, treatments and cure.
Employees: 90
Regional offices: 75

Asylum Aid

Asylum Aid, Club Union House, 253-254 Upper Street, London N1 1RY
T: 020 7354 9631
Helpline: 020 7354 9264
F: 020 7354 5620
E: jessicac@asylumaid.org.uk
www.asylumaid.org.uk
Chief Executive: Wayne Myslik
Provides advice and representation to refugees and asylum seekers in the UK.
Employees: 14
Volunteers: 5
Regional offices: 1

Ataxia UK

Lincoln House, Kennington Park, 13 Brixton Road, London SW9 6DE
T: 020 7582 1444
Helpline: 0845 644 0606
E: smillman@ataxia.org.uk
www.ataxia.org.uk
CEO: Sue Millman
Ataxia UK raises money for research into ataxia and provides information, advice and support to people affected by ataxia.

Ataxia-Telangiectasia Society (A-T Society)

Rothamsted, Harpenden, Hertfordshire AL5 2JQ
T: 01582 760733
F: 01582 760162
E: info@atsociety.org.uk
www.atsociety.org.uk
Chief Executive: William Davis
The A-T Society provides information and practical support to people with A-T and their families to enable them to live their lives to the full. It also funds bio-medical and clinical research to improve treatments and find a cure. The Society provides advocacy, counselling and financial grants. It provides opportunities for people living with A-T to meet and organises activity breaks. It has established two national specialist clinics and works to raise standards of care locally.
Employees: 3
Volunteers: 18

ATD Fourth World UK Ltd

48 Addington Square, London SE5 7LB
T: 020 7703 3231
F: 020 7252 4276
E: atd@atd-uk.org
www.atd-uk.org
ATD Fourth World is an anti-poverty organisation committed to ending extreme poverty by working in partnership with those living in and experiencing poverty. We regard the existence of poverty as a denial of human rights and work to enable people living in poverty to take on active roles within their communities. We believe that people in poverty are the real experts on poverty issues and should become the key partners in all anti-poverty projects.
Employees: 10
Volunteers: 30
Regional offices: 2

ATTEND

London W1G 0AN
T: 020 7307 2570 (also fax)
E: info@attend.org.uk
www.attend.org.uk
Chief Executive: David Wood
ATTEND aims to relieve patients and former patients of hospitals in the UK and other persons in the community who are sick, convalescent, disabled, handicapped, infirm, socially isolated or in need of financial assistance. It supports the work of health bodies and those who care for people using healthcare services or courts or the prison services.
Employees: 18
Volunteers: 31000
Regional offices: 1

Attlee Foundation

5 Thrawl Street, London E1 6RT
T: 020 7375 3212
Helpline: 020 7183 0093
E: tania.shaikh@attleeycc.org.uk
www.attlee.org.uk
The Foundation honours the memory of Clement Richard Attlee, Prime Minister 194551, by initiating projects for young people and for the alleviation of poverty and hardship.
Employees: 4
Volunteers: 10

Aurora Health Foundation

Head Office, 4 Ebor Cottages, Kingston Vale, London SW15 3RT
T: 020 8541 1951
E: info@aurorafoundation.org.uk
www.aurorahealthfoundation.org.uk
Chief Executive Officer: Susannah Faithfull
Aurora is a charity that provides specialist counselling, support and complementary therapies to people abused in childhood.
Employees: 12
Volunteers: 4
Regional offices: 1

Autism Independent UK

Kettering, Northamptonshire NN16 9AT
T: 01536 523274
E: autism@autismuk.com
www.autismuk.com
Director: Keith Lovett
The Autism Society exists to increase awareness of autism, together with well-established and newly developed approaches in the diagnosis, assessment, education and treatment. The main goal is to improve the quality of life for persons with autism.

Autism Plus

The Exchange Brewery, 2 Bridge Street, Sheffield, South Yorkshire S3 8NS
T: 0114 384 0284
F: 0114 384 0292
E: melanie.russell@autismplus.co.uk
www.autismplus.org
Managing Director : Glynis Davidson
The Charity aims to provide innovative and person-centred solutions for people with ASD and other disabilities, irrespective of where and how they live. To improve their quality of life and to extend and exercise their rights to access more control over their lives.
Employees: 346
Volunteers: 87
Regional offices: 2

Autism Research Ltd – The International Autistic Research Organisation

49 Orchard Avenue, Shirley, Croydon CR0 7NE
T: 020 8777 0095
E: iaro@autismresearch.wanadoo.co.uk
www.iaro.org.uk
Director/Secretary: Gerda McCarthy
Autism Research carries out and encourages research into the mental and emotional condition of autism and any other conditions that might be associated with autism. It disseminates the results of such research.
Volunteers: 4

AVERT

4 Brighton Road, Horsham, West Sussex RH13 5BA
T: 01403 210202
E: info@avert.org
www.avert.org
Chief Executive: Sarah Hand
AVERT is an international HIV and AIDS charity based in the UK. Through our HIV/AIDS information website community projects in sub-Saharan Africa and information and advocacy service, we provide education, treatment and care to avert the spread of AIDS.
Regional offices: 1

Aviation Environment Federation

Broken Wharf House, 2 Broken Wharf, London EC4V 3DT
T: 020 7248 2223
F: 020 7329 8160
E: info@aef.org.uk
www.aef.org.uk
Director: Tim Johnson
The AEF is the principal UK non-profit-making environmental association concerned with the environmental effects of aviation, ranging from aircraft noise issues associated with small airstrips or helipads, to the contribution of airline emissions to climate change. The AEF was established in 1975 and now has over 120 affiliated members comprising community and environmental groups, local authorities, parish councils, businesses and consultancies. Individual and student members are also welcomed.
Employees: 3
Volunteers: 3
Regional offices: 1

AVID (Association of Visitors to Immigration Detainees)

Archway Resource Centre, 1b Waterlow Road, London N19 5NJ
T: 020 7281 0533
E: enquiries@aviddetention.org.uk
www.aviddetention.org.uk
Director: Ali McGinley
National network of volunteer visitors to immigration detainees. We support those held under immigration acts in the UK with our network of 20 voluntary groups and over 400 visitors.

AVIF (Able Volunteers International Fund)

Flat 1, 13 Cheltenham Parade, Harrogate, North Yorkshire HG1 1DD
E: alowndes@avif.org.uk
www.avif.org.uk
Founder Trustee: Alison Lowndes
AVIF is an innovative online charity, assisting with sustainable development via online and onsite volunteering in rural Kenya, East Africa. AVIF does not charge fees.
Volunteers: 200
Regional offices: 2
Income: £1,000 (2012-13)

Avocet Trust

Clarence House, Hull, Humberside HU9 1DN
T: 01482 329226
E: info@avocettrust.co.uk
www.avocettrust.co.uk
Chief Executive: LC Howell
Avocet provides lifetime support to vulnerable people to enable them to live valued lives. Avocet provides a range of services including 24-hour support in clients' homes, as well as short stay care and through-the-door domiciliary services. Going forward the Trust plans to provide employment training services as well as employment placement services.
Employees: 300

Aylesham Neighbourhood Project

Ackholt Road, Aylesham, Canterbury, Kent CT3 3AJ
T: 01304 840134
E: office@aylesham-np.org.uk
www.aylesham-np.org.uk
Chief Executive: Kathryn Rogers
Aylesham Neighbourhood Project (the Project) is a charitable company that works in local communities to inspire children and families to recognise potential, make positive change and achieve bright futures. The

Project delivers community based services across Dover District that are person centred and give positive opportunities for children and families.
Employees: 22
Volunteers: 9

Back Up (transforming lives after spinal cord injury)

Jessica House, Red Lion Square,
191 Wandsworth High Street,
London SW18 4LS
T: 020 8875 1805
E: admin@backuptrust.org.uk
www.backuptrust.org.uk
Chief Executive: Louise Wright
Our vision is a world where people with a spinal cord injury can realise their full potential. Our mission is to: inspire people affected by spinal cord injury to transform their lives; challenge perceptions of disability; deliver services that build confidence and independence and offer a supportive network.
Employees: 30
Volunteers: 400

BackCare

16 Elmtree Road, Teddington,
Middlesex TW11 8ST
T: 020 8977 5474
F: 020 8943 5318
E: info@backcare.org.uk
www.backcare.org.uk
BackCare helps people manage and prevent back pain by providing advice, promoting self-help, encouraging debate and funding scientific research into back care.
Employees: 8
Volunteers: 180
Regional offices: 30

Bank Workers Charity

E: jenna.southgate@bwcharity.org.uk

Bar Pro Bono Unit

289-293 High Holborn,
London WC1V 7HZ
T: 020 7092 3960
E: enquiries@barprobono.org.uk
www.barprobono.org.uk
The unit provides free legal advice and representation for deserving cases where Legal Aid is not available and where the applicant is unable to afford legal assistance. Applicants are strongly encouraged to approach an advice agency or solicitor before applying to the unit.

Barnardo's

Tanners Lane, Barkingside, Ilford,
Essex IG6 1QG
T: 020 8550 8822
F: 020 8551 6870
E: supportercare@barnardos.org.uk
www.barnardos.org.uk
Chief Executive: Javed Khan
As one of the UK's leading children's charities, Barnardo's believes in children regardless of their circumstances, gender, race, disability or behaviour. We believe in the abused, the vulnerable, the forgotten and the neglected. We will support them, stand up for them and bring out the best in each and every child. We do this because we believe in children.
Employees: 6800
Volunteers: 12000
Regional offices: 9

Barnsley Hospice

Church Street, Gawber, Barnsley,
South Yorkshire S75 2RL
T: 01226 244244
E: enquiries@barnsley-hospice.org
www.barnsleyhospice.org
Chief Executive/Chair: Ian Carey
Barnsley Hospice is a charity dedicated to providing quality specialist palliative and end of life care to all adults in Barnsley, as well as their family and friends. The Hospice's vision is to: be the first choice for patients, referrers, customers and donors of all our services; provide more services to more people; strive to be one of the best hospices in England.
Employees: 120
Volunteers: 400

BASIC

The Brain And Spinal Injury Centre,
554 Eccles New Road, Salford M5 5AP
T: 0161 707 6441
Helpline: 0870 750 0000
E: enquiries@basiccharity.org.uk
www.basiccharity.org.uk
CEO: Wendy Edge
The Brain And Spinal Injury Centre - or BASIC, provides community rehabilitation and support services to help people re-build their lives following acquired brain injury and neurological illness.
Employees: 14
Volunteers: 35
Regional offices: 1
Income: £435,000 (2014-15)

BasicNeeds UK

158a Parade, Leamington Spa,
Warwickshire CV32 4AE
T: 01926 330101
E: jess.mcquail@basicneeds.org
www.basicneeds.org
Executive Director: Jess McQuail
BasicNeeds is an International Non-Governmental Organisation working to improve the lives of people living with mental illness and epilepsy. Predominantly focused on low and middle income countries, we work right across the system: with individuals and communities, local and national governments, and international organisations. To date, over 640,700 people have benefitted from our programmes in Africa and Asia.
Employees: 7

BBC Children in Need Appeal

PO Box 1000, London W12 7WJ
T: 020 8576 7788
F: 020 8576 8887
E: pudsey@bbc.co.uk
www.bbc.co.uk/pudsey
Chief Executive: David Ramsden
The Children in Need appeal provides grants to properly constituted organisations working with children and young people aged 18 and under, who may have experienced mental, physical or sensory disabilities; behavioural or psychological disorders; are living in poverty or situations of deprivation; or suffering through distress, abuse or neglect.
Employees: 43
Regional offices: 12

BCS – The Chartered Institute for IT

First Floor, Block D, North Star House,
North Star Avenue, Swindon,
Wiltshire SN2 1FA
T: 01793 417417
F: 01793 480270
E: customerservice@hq.bcs.org.uk
www.bcs.org
CEO: David Clarke
Professional membership association representing over 70,000 people worldwide working in IT and computing. We promote wider social and economic progress through

the advancement of information technology science and practice. We bring together industry, academics, practitioners and government to share knowledge, promote new thinking, influence the development of computing education, shape public policy and inform the public.
Employees: 220
Regional offices: 2

Be Your Best Foundation

Portsmouth Guildhall, Guildhall Square, Portsmouth, Hampshire PO1 2AB
T: 023 9298 5716
E: dan@rockchallenge.co.uk
www.rockchallenge.co.uk
Chairman of the Board of Directors: Juno Hollyhock
The Foundation aims to improve quality of life by encouraging young people to take an active role in building safe and healthy communities. The primary aim of the Foundation is to raise funds to stage Rock Challenge events across the UK, an anti-drug and crime initiative that takes the form of a friendly performing arts competition for 11 to 18 year olds. Rock Challenge encourages a natural high through live performance.
Employees: 3
Volunteers: 100
Regional offices: 1

Beacon Awards

12 Angel Gate, 320-326 City Road, London EC1V 2PT
T: 020 7713 9326
E: contact@beaconfellowship.org.uk
www.beaconawards.org.uk
The Beacon Awards were established in 2003 with the aim of promoting effective philanthropic giving through the creation of a nationally recognised awards scheme to highlight best practice and innovation in philanthropy. In addition to the biennial awards ceremony Beacon also runs a programme of roundtables that offer opportunities for philanthropists to connect with each other in order to share best practice and learn about the best philanthropic work in the UK today.
Employees: 1
Volunteers: 6

Beanstalk

6 Middle Street, London EC1A 7JA
T: 020 7729 4087
E: info@beanstalkcharity.org.uk
www.beanstalkcharity.org.uk
Chief Executive: Ginny Lunn
Beanstalk is a national literacy charity that recruits, vets, trains and supports volunteers to work in primary schools with children who have fallen behind with their reading. Our vision is that all children and young people will have the essential skills they need to grow up and lead successful lives.
Employees: 115
Volunteers: 3000
Regional offices: 17

Beat

2nd Floor, Wensum House, 103 Prince of Wales Road, Norwich, Norfolk NR1 1DW
T: 0300 123 3355
Helpline: 0345 634 1414
F: 01603 664915
E: info@b-eat.co.uk
www.b-eat.co.uk
Chief Executive: Andrew Radford
Beat is the leading UK-wide charity providing information, help and support for people affected by eating disorders anorexia, bulimia nervosa and binge eating disorder through helplines, online services and emails.
Employees: 30
Volunteers: 850

BECHAR

The Prebend Day Centre, 12 Prebend Street, Bedford, Bedfordshire MK40 1QW
T: 01234 365955
Helpline: 01234 376835
F: 01234 352717
E: pdc@bechar.org.uk
www.bechar.org.uk
Chief Executive: Ryan Flecknell
Bedford Concern for the Homeless and Rootless provides a Day Centre where our clients can get cheap hot food, clothing and washing facilities and somewhere to relax in comfort. We provide counselling services to help our clients get access to jobs, housing and generally re-enter normal society.
Employees: 10
Volunteers: 30
Regional offices: 1

Behcet's Syndrome Society

Kemp House, 152-160 City Road, London EC1V 2NX
T: 0845 130 7328
Helpline: 0845 130 7329
E: info@behcetsdisease.org.uk
www.behcets.org.uk
Chairman: Alan Booth
Behçet's (pronounced Betjets) is a rare, complex and life-long condition caused by disturbances in the body's immune system. Behçet's can affect people of any age, but it most commonly affects those between the ages of 20 and 40. The Behcets Syndrome Society (Charity Reg No 326679) runs a helpline, funds research, and offers financial support for patients in need.
Employees: 1
Volunteers: 20
Income: £75,000 (2012-13)

Beth Johnson Foundation

Parkfield House, 64 Princes Road, Hartshill, Stoke-on-Trent, Staffordshire ST4 7JL
T: 01782 844036
F: 01782 746940
E: debbie.everden@bjf.org.uk
www.bjf.org.uk
Chief Executive: Steve Robinson
The Foundation undertakes innovative work to develop evidence-based approaches to the social aspects of ageing. Currently we have UK programmes in intergenerational work, positive ageing and advocacy. Our work is approached from a life course perspective and we provide resources, training and consultancy in support of our aims.
Employees: 24
Volunteers: 40
Regional offices: 1

Bethany Children's Trust

Office 211, 22 Eden Street, Kingston Upon Thames, Surrey KT1 1DN
T: 020 8977 7571
E: admin@bethanychildrenstrust.org.uk
www.bethanychildrenstrust.org.uk
Director: Susie Howe
The Bethany Children's Trust's vision is to see every child in the world loved, safe, nurtured and free to reach their God-given potential. We are strengthening churches and Christian projects that care for vulnerable children throughout the world, with training workshops, prayer and financial support. BCT also works with other Christian organizations worldwide, to speak out with, and for, children at risk and challenge the Church, local communities and world leaders to address their needs.
Employees: 3
Volunteers: 2
Regional offices: 1
Income: £180,000 (2013-14)

Bexley Snap

Thames Innovation Centre, 2 Veridion Way, Erith, Kent DA18 4AL
T: 020 8320 1488
E: ceo@bexleysnap.org.uk
www.bexleysnap.org.uk
Chief Executive: Carol Penny

Our vision is that disabled children have choices and a right to a fulfilling life. We aim to increase choice of services and activities available to children and young people while reducing the isolation and frustration experienced by their families. We offer a range of weekend, evening and school holiday play and leisure activities for disabled children, a pre-school programme for disabled babies and toddlers, and a comprehensive support programme for parents/carers
Employees: 42
Volunteers: 23
Income: £379,095 (2012-13)

BHA

Democracy House, 609 Stretford Road, Old Trafford, Manchester M16 0QA
T: 0845 450 4247
F: 0845 450 3247
E: info@thebha.org.uk
www.thebha.org.uk
Chief Executive: Priscilla Nkwenti
BHA challenges health inequalities for disadvantaged and marginalised communities. We make a positive contribution in health provision and service delivery. Using expertise in the field of health, social care policy and service development, we provide efficient and appropriate advice and services to communities at grass-root level. We take a strategic and consultative role by working with policy makers and legislators to ensure effective service development and delivery to people from disadvantaged and marginalised communities.
Employees: 36
Volunteers: 33
Regional offices: 2
Income: £1,700,000 (2014-15)

BIBIC

Knowle Hall, Knowle, Bridgwater, Somerset TA7 8PJ
T: 01278 684060
F: 01278 685703
E: info@bibic.org.uk
www.bibic.org.uk
BIBIC exists to maximise the potential of children with sensory, social, communication, motor and learning difficulties. We work with parents and carers, offering a valuable support system that offers time to talk, expert advice and practical help.
Employees: 39
Volunteers: 8

Bible Society

Stonehill Green, Westlea, Swindon SN5 7DG
T: 01793 418100
E: contactus@biblesociety.org.uk
www.biblesociety.org.uk
Chief Executive: James Catford
Employees: 105
Volunteers: 700

Big Issue Foundation

1-5 Wandsworth Road, London SW8 2LN
T: 020 7526 3200
F: 020 7526 3401
E: foundation@bigissue.com
www.bigissue.org.uk
CEO: Stephen Robertson
The Big Issue Foundation is a national charity that connects vendors with the vital support and solutions that enable them to rebuild their lives and journey away from homelessness.
Employees: 23
Volunteers: 15
Regional offices: 7
Income: £922,040 (2012-13)

Big Society Capital

Chronicle House, 72-78 Fleet Street, London EC4Y 1HY
T: 020 7186 2500
E: enquiries@bigsocietycapital.com
www.bigsocietycapital.com/
Chief Executive: Cliff Prior
Big Society Capital is an organisation set up to help grow the social investment market, so that charities and social enterprises who want to borrow money can access the finance they need to maintain and increase their support for people in need in the UK. Since 2012, we have committed £140 million in investments to specialist organisations who lend to charities and social enterprises.

Bipolar UK

11 Belgrave Road, London SW1V 1RB
T: 020 7931 6480
F: 020 7931 6481
E: info@bipolaruk.org.uk
wwww.bipolaruk.org.uk
Bipolar UK is the national charity dedicated to supporting individuals with the much misunderstood and devastating condition of bipolar, their families and carers.
Regional offices: 3

BirdLife International

Wellbrook Court, Girton Road, Cambridge CB3 0NA
T: 01223 277318
F: 01223 277200
E: tracy.spraggon@birdlife.org
www.birdlife.org
BirdLife International is a partnership of people for birds and the environment. Over 10 million people worldwide support the BirdLife Partnership of national NGO conservation organisations and local networks. BirdLife's vision is of a world rich in biodiversity, with people and nature living in harmony, equitably and sustainably. BirdLife's aim is to conserve wild birds, their habitats and global biodiversity by working with people towards sustainability in the use of natural resources.
Employees: 65
Volunteers: 8
Regional offices: 6

Birth Companions

PO Box 64597, London SW17 1DR
T: 07855 725097
Helpline: 020 7117 0037
E: info@birthcompanions.org.uk
www.birthcompanions.org.uk
Director: Annabel Kennedy
Our overall aim is to improve the wellbeing of pregnant women and new mothers who are, have been or are at risk of being detained. We do this by improving their mental health, reducing isolation, enabling them to give their babies the best possible start in life and improving their conditions. We work in HMP Holloway as well as in the community supporting women antenatally, during birth and postnatally.
Employees: 5
Volunteers: 34

Black and Ethnic Minority Diabetes Association

c/o ONE WESTMINSTER, 37 CHAPEL STREET, London NW1 5DP
T: 07401 097733
Helpline: 07831 046824
E: info@bemda.org
www.bemda.org
Executive Director: Aderonke Kuti
BEMDA, founded in 1995, is a user-led, health-focused organisation that was established to promote the health of diabetics in the community and reduce the impact of diabetes-related health problems in black and ethnic minority communities in particular,

without excluding diabetics and their carers from other communities from our services.
Employees: 2
Volunteers: 8
Income: £25,007,000 (2013-14)

Black Environment Network

UK Office, 268 Bannerdale Road, Sheffield S11 9FE
E: ukoffice@ben-network.org.uk
www.ben-network.org.uk
Development Manager: Max Ghani
BEN works for full ethnic participation in the built and natural environment. BEN uses the word 'black' symbolically recognising that the black communities are the most visible of all ethnic communities. We work with black, white and other ethnic communities.
Volunteers: 2

Black Training and Enterprise Group

2nd Floor, 200A Pentonville Road, London N1 9JP
T: 020 7832 5800
F: 020 7832 5829
E: jeremy@bteg.co.uk
www.bteg.co.uk
The group aims to ensure fair access and outcomes for black communities in employment, training and enterprise and to help black organisations to play an active role in the economic regeneration of local communities through partnership with others.
Employees: 5
Volunteers: 2

Bladder and Bowel Foundation

SATRA Innovation Park, Rockingham Road, Kettering, Northamptonshire NN16 9JH
T: 01536 533255
Helpline: 0845 345 0165
F: 01536 533240
E: heather.ellison@bladderandbowelfoundation.org
www.bladderandbowelfoundation.org
Executive Director: Robert Dixon
B&BF is now the UK's largest advocacy charity providing information and support for all types of bladder and bowel-related problems, including incontinence, prostate problems, constipation and diverticular disease, for patients, their families, carers and healthcare professionals.
Employees: 3
Volunteers: 1
Regional offices: 1

Blesma, The Limbless Veterans

Frankland Moore House, 185-187 High Road, Chadwell Heath, Romford, Essex RM6 6NA
T: 020 8590 1124
F: 020 8599 2932
E: chadwellheath@blesma.org
www.blesma.org
Chief Executive: Barry Le Grys
Blesma, The Limbless Veterans is the national charity for all limbless serving and ex-service men and women, their widows and dependants. It is a membership organisation which helps wounded service men and women rebuild their lives by providing rehabilitation activities and welfare support. Their membership includes those who have lost the use of a limb, an eye or the sight of an eye.
Employees: 62
Volunteers: 28
Income: £4,000,000 (2013-14)

Blind Children UK

Hillfields, Reading Road, Burfield Common, Reading, Berkshire RG7 3YG
T: 0800 781 1444
E: enquiries@blindchildrenuk.org
www.blindchildrenuk.org
Chief Executive: Richard Leaman
Blind Children UK provides services for the families of children and young people with a visual impairment from birth to 25 years. Our services include family support, educational advocacy, IT advice, activities and CustomEyes large-print children's books and as part we are part of Guide Dogs we can also provide Habilitation and Mobility support. Subject to criteria grants may be given for computers for home use.

Blind Veterans UK

12-14 Harcourt Street, London W1H 4HD
T: 020 7723 5021
Helpline: 0800 389 7979
F: 020 7262 6199
E: info@blindveterans.org.uk
www.blindveterans.org.uk
Chief Executive: Nick Caplin CB
Blind Veterans UK, formerly St Dunstan's, believe that no one who's served our country should battle blindness alone. We're here to help with a lifetime's practical and emotional support, regardless of when people served or how they lost their sight. We get our members back on their feet, recovering their independence and discovering a life beyond sight loss.
Employees: 380
Volunteers: 349
Regional offices: 12

Blindaid Africa

Prospect Cottage, Wells Road, Radstock, Avon BA3 3RP
T: 01761 434385
E: peter@blindaid.org
www.blindaid.org
Director: Rosalie Lees
The provision of tools for learning and living for blind young people in Africa that is our motto and objective. We provide minimal cost (mostly pre-used) materials and equipment to enable blind students to participate and compete effectively in their national education systems and to integrate effectively in the school and community social environments.
Employees: 2
Volunteers: 10
Regional offices: 2

Bliss

2nd and 3rd Floors, 9 Holyrood Street, London SE1 2EL
T: 020 7378 1122
F: 020 7403 0673
E: reception@bliss.org.uk
www.bliss.org.uk
Bliss, the premature baby charity, is dedicated to making sure that more babies born prematurely or sick in the UK survive and that each one has the best quality of life.
Employees: 21
Volunteers: 250
Regional offices: 25

Blond McIndoe Research Foundation

E: debbie.mitchell@blondmcindoe.org

Blood Pressure Association

60 Cranmer Terrace, London SW17 0QS
T: 020 8772 4994
F: 020 8772 4999
E: info@bpassoc.org.uk
www.bpassoc.org.uk
The BPA aims to significantly improve the prevention, diagnosis and treatment of high blood pressure in order to prevent death and disability from stroke and heart disease.
Employees: 6
Volunteers: 2
Regional offices: 1

Bloodwise

**43 Great Ormond Street,
London WC1N 3JJ
T: 020 7405 0101
E: info@lrf.org.uk
www.bloodwise.org.uk**
Works to defeat the leukaemia and related blood diseases (lymphomas, myeloma, myelodysplasia, myeloproliferative disorders, aplastic anaemia).

Blue Cross

**Shilton Road, Burford,
Oxfordshire OX18 4PF
T: 0300 777 1897
E: kerry.lane@bluecross.org.uk
www.bluecross.org.uk
CEO : Sally de la Bedoyere**
Blue Cross has been dedicated to the health and happiness of pets since 1897. Abandoned or unwanted, ill or injured – we do what's needed to give every pet a healthy life in a happy home. We're a charity, so the more help you give us, the more help we can give pets.
**Employees: 650
Regional offices: 16**

BMS World Mission

**PO Box 49, 129 Broadway,
Didcot OX11 8XA
T: 01235 517700
F: 01235 517601
E: mail@bmsworldmission.org
www.bmsworldmission.org
General Director: David Kerrigan**
The purpose of the Society is to enable Baptist Churches to respond to the call of God throughout the world by pursuing the following objectives: to make known the Gospel of Jesus Christ; to prevent and relieve poverty; to relieve sickness and promote and protect health; to advance education; to alleviate human suffering caused by disaster overseas.
**Employees: 180
Volunteers: 186
Regional offices: 1**

Board of Deputies of British Jews

**6 Bloomsbury Square, London WC1A 2LP
T: 020 7543 5400
E: info@bod.org.uk
www.bod.org.uk**
The Board acts as the representative body of the UK Jewish community, composed of some 330 deputies elected by synagogues and by certain national communal bodies. It is the voice of the Jewish community and protects the rights and interests of Jews in the UK. It monitors legislation and any discriminatory measures, legal or social, affecting the Jewish community and watches over the interests of co-religionists in countries where they are oppressed and persecuted.

Boaz Trust

**First Floor, 110 Oldham Road,
MANCHESTER,
Greater Manchester M4 6AG
T: 0161 202 1056
F: 0161 228 7332
E: info@boaztrust.org.uk
www.boaztrust.org.uk
Chief Executive: Ros Holland**
Boaz provides accommodation and holistic support to destitute refused asylum seekers and refugees in Greater Manchester.
**Employees: 10
Volunteers: 250
Income: £310,000 (2012-13)**

Bobath Centre for Children with Cerebral Palsy

**Bradbury House, 250 East End Road,
London N2 8AU
T: 020 8444 3355
F: 020 8444 3399
E: kevin.gillespie@bobath.org.uk
www.bobath.org.uk
Director of Administrative Services: Jayne Pearce**
The Centre provides specialist Bobath therapy for children with cerebral palsy. It also provides training in the Bobath Concept to physiotherapists, occupational therapists and speech and language therapists from all over the UK and abroad.
**Employees: 26
Volunteers: 6
Income: £1,150,000 (2012-13)**

Body and Soul

**99-119 Rosebery Avenue,
London EC1R 4RE
T: 020 7923 6880
E: info@bodyandsoulcharity.org
www.bodyandsoulcharity.org
Director: Emma Colyer**
A charity supporting children, teenagers and adults who are living with and closely affected by HIV in the UK. Our strategy aims to impact five key areas of member wellbeing: physical health, mental health, psychosocial wellbeing, practical support and maximising productivity.
**Employees: 12
Volunteers: 200+
Regional offices: 1
Income: £1,264,735 (2012-13)**

Body Shop Foundation

**Watersmead, Littlehampton,
West Sussex BN17 6LS
T: 01903 844039
F: 01903 844202
E: bodyshopfoundation@thebodyshop.com
www.thebodyshopfoundation.org
CEO: Lisa Jackson**
The Body Shop Foundation funds projects across the globe. The groups we support address human and civil rights, animal and environmental protection issues.
**Employees: 8
Volunteers: 150**

Bond

**Regents Wharf, 8 All Saints Street,
London N1 9RL
T: 020 7837 8344
F: 020 7837 4220
E: mwright@bond.org.uk
www.bond.org.uk
Chief Executive: Ben Jackson**
Bond is the network of UK-based voluntary organisations working in international development and development education. Bond members aim to improve the extent and quality of the UK and Europe's contribution to international development, the eradication of global poverty and the upholding of human rights.
**Employees: 35
Income: £3,000,000 (2013-14)**

Book Aid International

**39-41 Coldharbour Lane, Camberwell,
London SE5 9NR
T: 020 7733 3577
F: 020 7978 8006
E: info@bookaid.org
www.bookaid.org
Director: Alison Hubert**
Book Aid International works in partnership with libraries in Africa, providing books, resources and training to support an environment in which reading for pleasure, study, and life-long learning can flourish.
**Employees: 20
Volunteers: 50**

Booktrust

Book House, 45 East Hill, London
T: 020 8875 4584
E: trudi.kent@booktrust.org.uk
www.booktrust.org.uk
PA To Chief Executive: Trudi Kent

Born Free Foundation

3 Grove House, Foundry Lane, Horsham, West Sussex RH13 5PL
T: 01403 240170
E: info@bornfree.org.uk
www.bornfree.org.uk
The foundation works to investigate, expose and alleviate animal suffering in zoos and to promote the protection of wildlife in its natural habitat.

Bowel Cancer UK

9 Rickett Street, London SW6 1RU
T: 020 7381 9711
F: 020 7381 5752
E: admin@bowelcanceruk.org.uk
www.bowelcanceruk.org.uk
The principal objectives of the Charity are to help all people concerned about colorectal cancer by: providing authoritative information, support and advice for those affected by the disease, their carers and their families; raising awareness of the disease to increase knowledge and understanding of the symptoms; educating the public and healthcare professionals about methods of prevention and treatments; campaigning for improved choice, equality of access to treatments and best care.
Employees: 13
Volunteers: 20

Boys' Brigade

Felden Lodge, Felden, Hemel Hempstead HP3 0BL
T: 01442 231681
F: 01442 235391
E: enquiries@boys-brigade.org.uk
www.boys-brigade.org.uk
Brigade Secretary: Steve Dickinson
Christian Youth Organisation for children and young people of all faiths and none, from 4-18 years. Through its activity programme and resources the Boys' Brigade partners churches and communities to care for and challenge young people for life by a programme of informal education underpinned by the Christian faith.
Employees: 40
Volunteers: 15000
Regional offices: 3

Bracknell Forest Voluntary Action

Amber House, Market Street, Bracknell, Berkshire RG12 1JB
T: 01344 304404
E: carole.allen@bfva.org
www.bfva.org
Chief Officer: Janet Dean
Bracknell Forest Voluntary Action is an independent organisation whose role is to enhance the quality of life of the people of Bracknell Forest by promoting and supporting the work of voluntary, community and faith organisations. We are a central support for voluntary and community action, a local development agency and provide back office support for our members
Employees: 7
Volunteers: 10
Regional offices: 1
Income: £368,448 (2012-13)

Brain and Spine Foundation

3.36 Canterbury Court, Kennington Park, 1-3 Brixton Road, London SW9 6DE
T: 020 7793 5900
Helpline: 0808 808 1000
F: 020 7793 5939
E: emma@brainandspine.org.uk
www.brainandspine.org.uk
CEO: Ken Walker
The Brain and Spine Foundation is a national charity that aims to improve the care, treatment and prevention of neurological disorders through patient and carer information programmes.
Employees: 8
Volunteers: 100
Income: £620,000 (2012-13)

Brain Research Trust

Dutch House, 307-308 High Holborn, London WC1V 7LL
T: 020 7404 9982
E: info@brt.org.uk
www.brt.org.uk
The Brain Research Trust was founded as an independent medical charity, not part of the NHS, with the aim of supporting research at the Institute of Neurology, London, into diseases of the brain and nervous system.

Braintree District Voluntary Support Agency

E: judy@bdvsa.org

Brainwave Centre Ltd

Marsh Lane, Huntworth Gate, Bridgwater, Somerset TA6 6LQ
T: 01278 429089
E: joannesmith@brainwave.org.uk
www.brainwave.org.uk
Chief Executive: Phil Edge
Brainwave is a Charity that exists to help children with disabilities and additional needs to achieve greater independence. Aiming to improve mobility, communication skills, and learning potential, through a range of educational and physical therapies. The children we work with have a range of conditions including autism, brain injuries such as cerebral palsy and genetic conditions such as Down's Syndrome.
Employees: 96
Volunteers: 200+
Regional offices: 3

Breaking Free – Primarily Supporting Women Survivors of Child Sexual Abuse

Marshall House, 124 Middleton Road, Morden, Surrey SM4 6RW
T: 0845 108 0055
F: 020 8687 4134
E: breakingfreecharity@hotmail.com
Breaking Free provides a confidential, safe, supportive and understanding environment in which women can deal with issues arising from their experiences of abuse. It offers support to women survivors regardless of race, colour, creed, religious beliefs or ability/disability and increases awareness of the issue of child sexual abuse.
Employees: 3
Volunteers: 44

Breakthrough UK Ltd

The Kevin Hyett Suite, Abraham Moss Centre, Crescent Road, Crumpsall, Manchester, Greater Manchester M8 5UF
T: 0161 234 3950
E: reception@breakthrough-uk.co.uk
www.breakthrough-uk.co.uk
Chief Executive: Michelle Scattergood
Our mission is to promote the rights, responsibilities and respect of disabled people. Our mission is broken into 4 main aims. These are: Influencing government, local, regional and national agencies about barriers to disabled people's participation; Enabling disabled people to pursue and develop their careers; Providing greater choice, control and independent living; Working towards being financially stable, politically aware with healthy growth.
Employees: 16
Regional offices: 1

Breast Cancer Care

5-13 Great Suffolk Street, London SE1 0NS
T: 0845 092 0800
Helpline: 0808 800 6000
E: joanne.stewart@breastcancer.org.uk
www.breastcancercare.org.uk
Breast Cancer Care is here for anyone affected by breast cancer. We bring people together, provide information and support, and campaign for improved standards of care. We use our understanding of people's experience of breast cancer and our clinical expertise in everything we do. All our services are free.
Employees: 119
Volunteers: 350
Regional offices: 4

Breast Cancer Now

Ibex House, 42-47 Minories, London EC3N 1DY
T: 0333 207 0300
E: community@breastcancernow.org
www.breastcancernow.org
Chief Executive: Delyth Morgan
We're Breast Cancer Now, the UK's largest breast cancer charity – and we're dedicated to funding research into this devastating disease. We believe that if we all act now, by 2050, everyone who develops breast cancer will live.
Employees: 180
Volunteers: 600
Regional offices: 2
Income: ££23.00 (2014-15)

Breast Cancer Research Trust

PO Box 861, Bognor Regis PO21 9HW
T: 01243 583143 (also fax)
E: bcrtrust@btinternet.com
www.breastcancerresearchtrust.org.uk
Executive Administrator: Rosemary Sutcliffe
The Trust promotes scientific research into the origins, causes and nature of breast cancer. It improves methods of prevention and techniques in the treatment, cure and control of breast cancer and develops aids to assess the clinical needs of patients and potential patients. It establishes clinics for the therapeutic treatment of breast cancer and encourages the public to take appropriate measures.
Income: £76,597 (2012-13)

Bridging the Gap

c/o SMCA, Cobham Court, Haslemere Avenue, Mitcham, Surrey CR4 3PR
T: 020 8090 1486
E: james@btguk.org
www.btguk.org
Chief Executive: Dr James Stevens-Turner
A registered charity helping prisoners and ex-prisoners adjust to life outside prison. It encourages local and global understanding of problems faced by people leaving prison and helps people leaving prison to restart their lives, stay crime free and become useful members of society.
Volunteers: 20
Regional offices: 1

Britain-Nepal Medical Trust

Export House, 130 Vale Road, Tonbridge, Kent TN9 1SP
T: 01732 360284
E: info@britainnepalmedicaltrust.org.uk
www.britainnepalmedicaltrust.org.uk
Co-Chairs: Dr G Holdsworth and Dr S. Subedi
BNMT aims to assist the people of Nepal to improve their health through realisation of their health rights. It does this by working in partnership with the Ministry of Health, international and local non-governmental organisations, local committees and communities.
Employees: 54
Volunteers: 11
Regional offices: 2

British Accreditation Council for Independent Further and Higher Education

Ground Floor, 14 Devonshire Square, London EC2M 4YT
T: 0300 330 1400
E: info@the-bac.org
www.the-bac.org
Chief Executive: Paul Fear
The British Accreditation Council has provided a comprehensive quality assurance scheme for independent further and higher education in the UK since 1984. Our accreditation is recognised the world over by students, agents and government officials as a clear mark of educational quality in the private sector.
Employees: 8
Regional offices: 1

British Acoustic Neuroma Association

Oak House B, Ransomwood Business Park, Southwell Road West, Mansfield, Nottinghamshire NG21 0HJ
T: 01623 632143
E: admin@bana-uk.com
www.bana-uk.com
Formed in 1992, BANA is organised and administrated by people affected by acoustic neuroma. It is a registered charity and exists for mutual support, information exchange and listening. We aim to support those affected (both patients and family members) by acoustic neuroma and other similar conditions.
Employees: 2
Volunteers: 50+
Regional offices: 1

British Acupuncture Council

63 Jeddo Road, London W12 9HQ
T: 020 8735 0400
F: 020 8735 0404
E: info@acupuncture.org.uk
www.acupuncture.org.uk
The Council works to establish the status, maintain a register, regulate the conduct and protect the interests of practitioners of acupuncture, so as to promote and maintain, in the public interest, proper standards for the practice of acupuncture. It promotes and encourages the study and knowledge of acupuncture, which is a branch of medicine founded upon the principle that health is dependent upon a proper balance of vital energy forces within the body.
Employees: 9
Volunteers: 15

British Albanian Kosovar Council

21 Winchester Road, London NW3 3NR
T: 020 7586 8731
F: 020 8674 0860
E: carolineffrenchblake@gmail.com
www.bakc.org.uk/
The charity's object and its principal activity is that of providing assistance to Albanian-speaking young people, children and families, as well as unaccompanied minors.
Employees: 7
Volunteers: 6

British and International Federation of Festivals

Festivals House, 198 Park Lane, Macclesfield, Cheshire SK11 6UD
T: 01625 428297
F: 01625 503229
E: info@federationoffestivals.org.uk
www.federationoffestivals.org.uk
Chief Executive Officer: Terry Luddington

The Federation is the largest UK organisation for the participatory arts of music, dance and speech. Our aim is to advance, promote and encourage generally, and by means of the amateur festival movement in particular, the study and practice of the arts of music, dance, speech, literature and acting.

Employees: 4
Volunteers: 16500
Income: £250,000 (2013-14)

British Archaeological Association

18 Stanley Road, Oxford OX4 1QZ
E: dacruz@liv.ac.uk
www.archeologyuk.org

The Association promotes the study of archaeology. It aims to preserve our national antiquities, encourages original research and publishes new work, covering art and antiquities from the Roman to the post-medieval periods.

British Association and College of Occupational Therapists

106-114 Borough High Street, Southwark, London SE1 1LB
T: 020 7357 6480
F: 020 7480 2299
E: vandita.chisholm@cot.co.uk
www.cot.org.uk

The British Association and College of Occupational Therapists champions the unique and vital work of occupational therapy staff. Occupational therapy promotes health, wellbeing and independence through participation in activities or occupation. It gives people the tools and skills to do the things they need or want to do, removing obstacles to disability, injury, illness or other conditions.

Employees: 60
Volunteers: 200
Regional offices: 20

British Association for Adoption and Fostering

Saffron House, 6-10 Kirby Street, London EC1N 8TS
T: 020 7421 2600
F: 020 7421 2601
E: mail@baaf.org.uk
www.baaf.org.uk

Membership organisation for local authorities, voluntary adoption agencies, fostering agencies, legal advisers, childcare practitioners and the general public with an interest in adoption and fostering. The organisation aims to promote high standards in adoption and fostering, to promote public and professional understanding of the issues and to be an independent voice in the field of childcare, informing and influencing policy makers.

Employees: 140
Volunteers: 5
Regional offices: 9

British Association for Cancer Research

c/o Leeds Institute of Cancer & Pathology, Clinical Sciences Building, St James University Hospital, Beckett Street LS9 7TF
T: 0113 206 5611 (also fax)
E: bacr@leeds.ac.uk
www.bacr.org.uk

The Association aims to advance research in all aspects of cancer by encouraging the exchange of information.

Employees: 1
Volunteers: 1200

British Association for Counselling and Psychotherapy

BACP House, 15 St John's Business Park, Lutterworth, Leicestershire LE17 4HB
T: 01455 883300
F: 01455 550243
E: bacp@bacp.co.uk
www.bacp.co.uk

The Association promotes education and training for those involved in counselling and psychotherapy, full or part time, in either professional or voluntary contexts, with a view to raising standards. It also promotes the understanding of counselling and psychotherapy.

Employees: 75
Volunteers: 180

British Association for Early Childhood Education

136 Cavell Street, London E1 2JA
T: 020 7539 5400
F: 020 7539 5409
E: office@early-education.org.uk
www.early-education.org.uk
Chief Executive: Beatrice Merrick

The British Association for Early Childhood Education (Early Education), founded in 1923, is the leading national voluntary organisation for early years practitioners and parents, with members and branches across the UK. Early Education promotes the right of every child to education of the highest quality. It provides support, training, advice and information on best practice for all those concerned with the education and care of young children from birth to eight years.

Employees: 7
Volunteers: 200

British Association for Immediate Care

Turret House, 2 Turret Lane, Ipswich, Suffolk IP4 1DL
T: 01473 218407
F: 01473 280585
E: cx@basics.org.uk
www.basics.org.uk
Chief Executive: Phill Browne

The aims of BASICS are to foster co-operation between immediate care schemes and to encourage the formation of new schemes; to strengthen and develop cooperation between all services in coping with emergencies that may result in injury or risk to life; to encourage and assist research into all aspects of immediate care; to raise standards of care and training of practitioners; to disseminate information and encourage and assist international exchange of information and co-operation.

Employees: 3
Volunteers: 1

British Association for Local History

PO Box 6549, Somersal Herbert, Ashbourne, Staffordshire DE6 5WH
T: 01283 585947
E: mail@balh.co.uk
www.balh.co.uk

The association works to advance understanding and knowledge of local history.

Employees: 4
Volunteers: 22

British Association for the Advancement of Science

Wellcome Wolfson Building, 165 Queen's Gate SW7 5HD
T: 020 7973 3503
F: 0870 770 7102
E: info@britishscienceassociation.org
www.britishscienceassociation.org
Chief Executive: Sir Roland Jackson

We are the UK's nationwide, open membership organisation, which provides opportunities for people of all ages to learn about, discuss and challenge the sciences and their implications.

Employees: 40
Volunteers: 5000
Regional offices: 14

British Association of Dermatologists

4 Fitzroy Square, London W1T 5HQ
T: 020 7383 0266
E: rachael@bad.org.uk
www.bad.org.uk
The Association publishes and promotes information, teaching and research in dermatology.

British Association of Friends of Museums

141A School Road, Brislington, Bristol, Avon BS4 4LZ
T: 0117 977 7435
E: jayneselwood@live.co.uk
www.bafm.org.uk
BAFM encourages support for museums of all kinds. Its aims are to publicise the achievements of museums, and their friends; to advise those wishing to set up new groups; and to assist and encourage existing groups. It liaises with all other bodies concerned with museums, art galleries and heritage centres, and voluntary support for them.
Employees: 1

British Association of Social Workers

16 Kent Street, Birmingham B5 6RD
T: 0121 622 3911
F: 0121 622 4860
E: info@basw.co.uk
www.basw.co.uk
Chief Executive: Hilton Dawson
BASW is the main professional association for social workers in the UK.
Employees: 48
Volunteers: 200
Regional offices: 3

British Blind Sport

Pure Offices, Plato Close, Tachbrook Park, Warwick, Warwickshire CV34 6WE
T: 01926 424247
E: info@britishblindsport.org.uk
www.britishblindsport.org.uk
Chief Executive: Alaina MacGregor
Provides sport and recreation for blind and visually impaired people.
Employees: 3

British Cardiac Patients Association

15 Abbey Road, Bingham, Nottingham NG13 8EE
T: 01949 837070
E: admin@bcpa.co.uk
www.bcpa.co.uk
Chairman: Keith Jackson
The Association provides support, reassurance and advice to cardiac patients, their families and carers. Whether it be heart attack, angina, cardiac investigations, arrhythmias, implantable cardiac devices, or surgery for bypass, valve replacement aneurysm or transplant, we are able to offer free advice and information.
Volunteers: 80

British Cardiovascular Society

9 Fitzroy Square, London W1T 5HW
T: 020 7383 3887
E: enquiries@bcs.com
www.bcs.com
The objective of the British Cardiac Society is to advance the knowledge of diseases of the heart and circulation for the benefit of the public.
Employees: 12

British Cave Research Association

Old Methodist Chapel, Great Hucklow, Buxton, Derbyshire SK17 8RG
T: 01298 873810
F: 01298 873801
E: publications@british-caving.org.uk
www.bcra.org.uk
Chairman: David Checkley
Promotes cave research and exploration, and related activities.
Employees: 1
Volunteers: 20+
Regional offices: 1

British Centre for Science Education

12 Millbeck Approach, Morley, West Yorkshire LS27 8WA
E: committee@bcseweb.org.uk
www.bcseweb.org.uk
The British Centre for Science Education is a single-issue pressure group dedicated solely to keeping creationism and intelligent design out of the science classroom in publicly funded schools in the UK.

British Colostomy Association

Enterprise Hose, 95 London Street, Reading, Berkshire RG1 4QA
T: 0118 939 1537
Helpline: 0800 328 4257
E: jo.mckenzie@colostomyassociation.org.uk
www.colostomyassociation.org.uk
Chairman: Monty Taylor
The Association offers help and reassurance to anyone who has had, or is about to have, a colostomy operation and runs a 24 hour helpline, provides a range of literature, publishes a quarterly magazine and promotes a network of support groups. Its team of UK wide volunteers provide one to one support on the phone or in person if needed.
Employees: 4
Volunteers: 100

British Council

10 Spring Gardens, London SW1A 2BN
E: general.enquiries@britishcouncil.org
www.britishcouncil.org
The UK's international organisation for educational opportunities and cultural relations.

British Deaf Association

18 Leather Lane, London EC1N 7SU
F: 020 7405 0090
E: bdn@bda.org.uk
www.bda.org.uk
Chairman: Terry Riley
Promoting the rights of deaf people who use British Sign Language.
Employees: 25
Volunteers: 120
Regional offices: 4

British Dental Health Foundation

Smile House, 2 East Union Street, Rugby, Warwickshire CV22 6AJ
T: 01788 546365
Helpline: 0845 063 1188
F: 01788 541982
E: sharon@dentalhealth.org
www.dentalhealth.org
Chief Executive: Dr Nigel Carter
The UK's leading oral health charity, with a 40-year track record of providing public information and influencing government policy. It maintains a Dental Helpline consumer free-advice service; runs a product accreditation scheme to provide consumer assurance; publishes and distributes a wide range of educational literature for the profession and consumers; and runs National Smile Month between May and June, and Mouth Cancer Action Month throughout November.
Employees: 15

British Dyslexia Association

**Unit 8, Bracknell Beeches,
Old Bracknell Lane, Bracknell,
Berkshire RG12 7BW
T: 0333 405 4555
Helpline: 0333 405 4567
F: 0333 405 4570
E: helpline@bdadyslexia.org.uk
www.bdadyslexia.org.uk
Chief Executive: Dr Kate Saunders**

The British Dyslexia Association is the voice for 10% of the population that experience dyslexia. We aim to influence government to promote a dyslexia friendly society that enables dyslexic people of all ages to reach their full potential. We provide the only national helpline supporting tens of thousands of people each year.

Employees: 25
Volunteers: 50

British Ecological Society

**Charles Darwin House, 12 Roger Street,
London WC1N 2JU
T: 020 7685 2500
F: 020 7685 2501
E: amelia@britishecologicalsociety.org
www.britishecologicalsociety.org**

The British Ecological Society aims to promote the science of ecology through research and to use the findings of such research to educate the public and influence policy decisions that involve ecological matters.

Employees: 20

British Endodontic Society

**PO Box 707, Gerrards Cross,
Buckinghamshire SL9 0XS
T: 01494 581542 (also fax)
E: enquiries@bes-administrator.org
www.britishendodonticsociety.org**

The object of the charity is to promote and advance the study of endodontology and to ensure that the dental health of the nation is both maintained and improved.

Employees: 1
Volunteers: 20

British False Memory Society (BFMS)

**The Old Brewery, Newtown,
Bradford-on-Avon, Wiltshire BA15 1NF
T: 01225 868682
F: 01225 862251
E: carolyn@bfms.org.uk
www.bfms.org.uk
Director: Madeline Greenhalgh**

Formed 1993 to raise awareness of dangers of recovered memory through flawed therapeutic trauma theories and investigative systems. Aims to promote accurate differentiation between true and false allegations of child sexual abuse through raising public, professional and policy maker awareness, organising conferences and seminars, through information provision, newsletters and encouraging academic research plus working with the media. BFMS incorporates a telephone helpline to support families and individuals affected by false memory and false accusations.

Employees: 3
Regional offices: 1

British Federation of Film Societies Cinema For All

**Unit 320, The Workstation,
15 Paternoster Row, Sheffield,
South Yorkshire S1 2BX
T: 0114 221 0314
E: jaq.bffs@gmail.com
www.bffs.org.uk**

BFFS is the national support and development agency for the film society and community cinema sector. BFFS has supported specialised (art-house) cinema exhibition in the voluntary sector since its inception over 60 years ago and today continues to provide advice, technical support and education opportunities to communities across the UK.

British Future

**Kean House, 6 Kean Street,
London WC2B 4AS
T: 020 7632 9069
E: elizabeth@britishfuture.org
www.britishfurture.org
Director: Sunder Katwala**

British Future is an independent, non-partisan thinktank seeking to involve people in an open conversation that addresses people's hopes and fears about identity and integration, migration and opportunity, so that we feel confident about Britain's future.

Employees: 5

British Geriatrics Society

**Marjory Warren House, 31 St John's Square,
London EC1M 4DN
T: 020 7608 1369
E: ionajaneharris@bgs.org.uk
www.bgs.org.uk**

The society promotes better care in old age and seeks to improve the quality and provision of healthcare services for older people.

British Heart Foundation

**Great London House, 180 Hampstead,
London NW1 7AW
T: 020 7554 0000
F: 020 7554 0100
E: internet@bhf.org.uk
www.bhf.org.uk**

Plays a leading role in the fight against heart disease.

Employees: 1584
Volunteers: 26000
Regional offices: 9

British HIV Association

**BHIVA Secretariat, Mediscript Ltd,
1 Mountview Court, 310 Friern Barnet Lane,
London N20 0LD
T: 020 8369 5380
F: 020 8446 9194
E: bhiva@bhiva.org
www.bhiva.org
Chair: Dr David Asboe**

The objectives of BHIVA are to relieve sickness and to protect and preserve health through the development and promotion of good practice in the treatment of HIV and HIV-related illnesses; to advance public education in the subjects of HIV and the symptoms, causes, treatment and prevention of HIV-related illnesses through the promotion of research.

British Holistic Medical Association

**PO Box 371, Bridgwater,
Somerset TA7 9AA
E: contactbhma@aol.co.uk
www.bhma.org
Chair: David Peters**

The BHMA is an open association of mainstream healthcare professionals, CAM practitioners and members of the public who want to adopt a more holistic approach in their own life and work. We do not endorse, accredit or recommend individual practitioners or organisations.

Employees: 4
Volunteers: 7
Regional offices: 1

British Home and Hospital for Incurables

**Crown Lane, London SW16 3JB
T: 020 8670 8261
E: home.stmvolunteercoord@thebritishhome.co.uk
www.britishhome.org.uk**

The British Home provides specialist nursing care and support to chronically sick and disabled people. Our residents are offered the highest standard of care and support to: maintain their independence; participate in the planning of their care; retain personal prospects; and have access to their health records.

British Homeopathic Association

Hahnemann House, 29 Park Street West, Luton LU1 3BE
T: 0870 444 3950
F: 0870 444 3960
E: info@trusthomeopathy.org
www.britishhomeopathic.org
Chief Executive: Cristal Sumner
The charity was founded in 1902 to promote homeopathy and raise money for research and the homeopathic training of healthcare professionals including doctors, dentists, nurses, podiatrists, pharmacists and vets. It is committed to making homeopathy more widely available on the NHS and provides information for the public and lobbies and campaigns for NHS homeopathy.
Employees: 9
Volunteers: 1

British Horse Society

Abbey Park, Stareton, Kenilworth, Warwickshire CV8 2XZ
T: 024 7684 0500
F: 024 7684 0501
E: enquiries@bhs.org.uk
www.bhs.org.uk
The Society aims to improve standards of care for horses and ponies, improve standards of riding and driving, encourage the use of horses and ponies and promote the interests of horse and pony breeding.
Employees: 71
Volunteers: 1000
Regional offices: 9

British Humanist Association

1 Gower Street, London WC1E 6HD
T: 020 7079 3580
F: 020 7079 3588
E: info@humanism.org.uk
www.humanism.org.uk
Chief Executive: Andrew Copson
The BHA promotes Humanism and supports and represents people who seek to live good lives without religious or superstitious beliefs. The BHA provides educational resources for schools and students; organises public lectures and other events; campaigns against religious privilege and for equality on grounds of religion or beliefs; and provides humanist funerals, weddings, civil partnership celebrations, namings and other ceremonies.
Employees: 12
Volunteers: 6

British Institute of Human Rights

School of Law, Queen Mary University of London, Mile End Road, London E1 4NS
T: 020 7882 5850
E: info@bihr.org.uk
www.bihr.org.uk
Director: Stephen Bowen
The Institute aims to further the education of the public and public authorities in the field of human rights in the UK and internationally.
Employees: 10
Volunteers: 3

British Institute of Learning Disabilities

Campion House, Green Street, Kidderminster DY10 1JL
T: 01562 723010
F: 01562 723029
E: enquiries@bild.org.uk
www.bild.org.uk
Chief Executive: Keith Smith
BILD aims to improve the quality of life for people with learning disabilities by involving them and their families in all aspects of our work. This includes working with Government and public bodies to achieve full citizenship and human rights for people with learning disabilities, turning research and policy into practice and supporting service providers to develop and share person-centred approaches.
Employees: 28
Volunteers: 1

British Institute of Radiology

Farringdon, London EC1M 4DT
E: admin@bir.org.uk
www.bir.org.uk
The Institute brings together all the professions in radiology, medical and scientific disciplines to share knowledge and educate the public, thereby improving the prevention and detection of disease and the management and treatment of patients.
Employees: 15

British Kidney Patient Association

3 The Windmills, St Mary's Close, Turk Street, Alton, Hampshire GU34 1EF
T: 01420 541424
F: 01420 89438
E: info@britishkidney-pa.co.uk
www.britishkidney-pa.co.uk
Chief Executive: Paddy Tabor
The British Kidney Patient Association exists to provide support for the benefit and welfare of kidney patients throughout the UK, offering information, advice, financial aid,direct patient support services as well as funding improvements in health and social care practice and campaigning on behalf of patients and their families.
Employees: 11
Volunteers: 20

British Liver Trust

2 Southampton Road, Ringwood, Hampshire BH24 1HY
T: 01425 481320
Helpline: 0800 652 7330
E: emma.bowering@britishlivertrust.org.uk
www.britishlivertrust.org.uk
Chief Executive: Andrew Langford
We aim to help everyone affected by liver disease, through information, support and research.
Employees: 15
Volunteers: 2

British Lung Foundation

73-75 Goswell Road, London EC1V 7ER
T: 020 7688 5555
Helpline: 0300 003 0555
F: 020 7688 5556
E: enquiries@blf.org.uk
www.blf.org.uk
Chief Executive: Penny Woods
The British Lung Foundation is here for everyone affected by a lung condition. It understands lung disease and fights to beat it through prevention, support and research.
Employees: 75
Volunteers: 500
Regional offices: 3

British Lymphology Society

Garth House, Rushey Lock, Tadpole Bridge, Buckland Marsh, Oxfordshire SN7 8RF
T: 01452 790178
E: info@thebls.com
www.thebls.com
Chair: Jane Rankin
The Society's objects are: to advance education and knowledge in the field of lymphology and related subjects; to foster interest in and co-ordinate a strategy for improving the management of chronic oedema, particularly lymphoedema; to produce and maintain a register of specialist centres in the United Kingdom and Ireland; to benefit patients by improving the knowledge,

expertise and skills of health care professionals treating them.
Employees: 2
Volunteers: 14
Regional offices: 1
Income: £137,184 (2012-13)

British Medical Acupuncture Society

Royal London Hospital for Integrated Medicine, 60 Great Ormond Street, London WC1N 3HR
T: 020 7713 9437
F: 020 7713 6286
E: bmaslondon@aol.com
www.medical-acupuncture.co.uk
Support Manager to Medical Director: Allyson Brown
A registered charity established to encourage the use and scientific understanding of acupuncture within medicine for the public benefit. BMAS seeks to enhance the education/training of suitably qualified practitioners, and to promote high standards of working practices in acupuncture.
Employees: 5

British National Temperance League

18 Warwick Avenue, Carlton in Lindrick, Worksop, Nottinghamshire S81 9BP
T: 01909 731435
E: bntl@btconnect.com
www.bntl.org
Chief Executive: Barbara Pike
BNTL is an organisation that responds to alcohol and other drug-related problems by seeking to promote healthy drug-free lifestyles and to inform on the effect of alcohol and drugs on individuals and communities. This is achieved through the production of teaching resources based around the national curriculum for teachers and others working with young people.
Employees: 2
Volunteers: 15

British Naturalists' Association

BNA, BM 8129, London WC1N 3XX
T: 0844 892 1817
E: mo.norrington@bna-naturalists.org
www.bna-naturalists.org
President: David Bellamy
One of the UK's oldest natural history societies, BNA was founded in 1905 for the sole purpose of promoting awareness and the study of all aspects of British natural history, an aim which it continues to pursue to the present day.
Volunteers: 300
Regional offices: 10

British Obesity Surgery Patient Association

PO Box 805, Taunton, Somerset TA1 9DU
T: 0845 602 0446
E: enquiries@bospa.org
www.bospa.org
BOSPA (British Obesity Surgery Patient Association) was launched in December 2003 to provide support and information to the thousands of patients in the UK for whom obesity surgery can provide an enormous benefit.
Employees: 1

British Ornithologists' Union

Department of Zoology, University of Oxford, South Parks Road, Oxford OX1 3PS
E: bou@bou.org.uk
www.bou.org.uk
The Union promotes the study of the science of ornithology, encourages links between amateur and professional ornithologists, and encourages and supports research and training.

British ORT

Ort House, 126 Albert Street, London NW1 7NE
T: 020 7446 8520
E: info@ortuk.org
www.ortuk.org
ORT's mission is to provide education and vocational training, helping the young and not so young to gain skills they need to become proud, independent, contributing members of their own culture and society.

British Pain Society

3rd Floor, Churchill House, 35 Red Lion Square, London WC1R 4SG
T: 020 7269 7840
F: 020 7831 0859
E: info@britishpainsociety.org
www.britishpainsociety.org
The Society promotes the advancement of health by raising the standard of management of pain by promotion of education, research and training.

British Polio Fellowship

Ground Floor Unit A, Eagle Office Centre, The Runway, South Ruislip, Middlesex HA4 6SE
T: 0800 018 0586
F: 020 8842 0555
E: info@britishpolio.org.uk
www.britishpolio.org.uk
Chief Executive: Ted Hill
The aims of the Fellowship are to enable polio survivors to lead full, independent and active lives and to ensure their needs are met. It ensures that post polio syndrome (late effects of polio) is recognised and managed effectively in every polio survivor and campaigns for the rights and equality of polio survivors.

British Pregnancy Advisory Service

20 Timothys Bridge Road, Stratford Enterprise Park, Stratford upon Avon CV37 9BF
T: 0845 365 5050
Helpline: 0845 730 4030
F: 0845 365 5051
E: info@bpas.org
www.bpas.org
Chief Executive: Ann Furedi
bpas was established in 1968 to provide a safe, legal abortion service and is a charitable, non-profit making organisation with sites nationwide. The organisation offers information and treatment in relation to unplanned pregnancy, vasectomy, abortion, contraception and online STI testing and treatment.
Employees: 60

British Psychological Society

St Andrew's House, 48 Princess Road East, Leicester LE1 7DR
T: 0116 254 9568
F: 0116 227 1314
E: enquiries@bps.org.uk
www.bps.org.uk
Chief Executive: Professor Ann Colley
The British Psychological Society is the representative body for psychology and psychologists in the UK. The Society and its members develop, promote and apply psychology for the public good. We enhance the efficiency and usefulness of psychologists by setting high standards of professional education and knowledge. We cover all areas of psychological research and practice.
Employees: 100
Regional offices: 4

British Red Cross

UK Office, 44 Moorfields EC2Y 9AL
T: 0844 871 1111
E: information@redcross.org.uk
www.redcross.org.uk
The British Red Cross provides caring and emergency service to those most in need in their local communities through some 30,000 volunteers and staff. It raises funds to support the international work of the British Red Cross. The British Red Cross is part of the International Red Cross Movement, the largest voluntary organisation in the world with 10 million volunteers worldwide and 181 partner organisations.
Employees: 3000
Volunteers: 30000
Regional offices: 4

British School of Osteopathy

Avon House, 275 Borough High Street, London SE1 1JE
T: 020 7089 5307
E: n.waters@bso.ac.uk
www.bso.ac.uk
The School undertakes osteopathic research, to deliver osteopathic education and healthcare for the benefit of the whole community.

British Sjögren's Syndrome Association

PO Box 15040, Birmingham B31 3DP
T: 0121 478 0222
Helpline: 0121 478 1133
E: office@bssa.uk.net
www.bssa.uk.net
The Association provides mutual support and information to individuals affected by Sjogren's syndrome. We aim to educate people about the condition, raise awareness surrounding its existence and symptoms, and support research into its cause and treatment.
Employees: 3

British Society For Immunology

Vintage House, 37 Albert Embankment, London SE1 7TL
T: 020 3031 9800
E: e.thomas@immunology.org
www.immunology.org
Office Co-ordinator/PA To CEO: Emilie Thomas
Employees: 9

British Society for Rheumatology

Bride House, 18-20 Bride Lane, London EC4Y 8EE
T: 020 7842 0900
F: 020 7842 0901
E: bsr@rheumatology.org.uk
www.rheumatology.org.uk
To promote excellence in the treatment of people with arthritis and musculoskeletal conditions and to support those delivering it.
Employees: 24

British Society of Disability and Oral Health

Dental Special Needs, Chorley and District Hospital, Preston Road, Chorley, Lancashire PR7 1PP
E: margaret.gregory2@nhs.net
www.bsdh.org.uk
The aims of the Society are to promote the oral health of disabled people of all ages. It promotes links with organisations representing disabled people, consults with disability groups to identify their needs and demands and studies the barriers relating to the provision of oral healthcare for disabled people.

British Society of Psychosomatic Obstetrics Gynaecology and Andrology

Porterbrook Clinic, 75 Osborne Road, Nether Edge, Sheffield, South Yorkshire S11 9BF
E: info@bspoga.org
www.bspoga.org
BSPOGA aims to advance the education of the general public and medical profession by encouraging the development of a better understanding and improved management of the psychological problems associated with reproductive and associated conditions in women and men.

British Sociological Association

Bailey Suite, Palatine House, Belmont Business Park, Belmont, Durham DH1 1TW
T: 0191 383 0839
F: 0191 383 0782
E: judith.mudd@britsoc.org.uk
www.britsoc.co.uk
Chief Executive: Judith Mudd
The BSA advances knowledge of sociology by lectures, publications, the promotion of research and encouragement of contact between workers in all relevant fields of enquiry.
Employees: 13
Volunteers: 500
Income: £1,246,366 (2012-13)

British Spiritualist Federation

T: 01475 700706
E: sandramcfadden@yahoo.co.uk
www.sagb.org.uk

British Stammering Association

15 Old Ford Road, London E2 9PJ
T: 020 8981 8818
E: mail@stammering.org
www.stammering.org
The Association aims to help stammerers live satisfactorily with their speech and encourage research into stammering.
Employees: 9
Volunteers: 10

British Thyroid Foundation

2nd Floor, 3 Devonshire Place, Harrogate, North Yorkshire HG1 4AA
T: 01423 709707
Helpline: 01423 709448
E: info@btf-thyroid.org
www.btf-thyroid.org
Director and Secretary to the Trustees: Janis Hickey
Provides reliable information and support to people with thyroid disorders.
Employees: 4
Volunteers: 44
Regional offices: 1
Income: £100,000 (2013-14)

British Tinnitus Association

Unit 5, Acorn Business Park, Woodseats Close, Sheffield, South Yorkshire S8 0TB
T: 0114 250 9933
Helpline: 0800 018 0527
F: 0114 258 2279
E: info@tinnitus.org.uk
www.tinnitus.org.uk
Chief Executive: David Stockdale
The British Tinnitus Association (BTA) provides help, support and advice to people with tinnitus, their families, friends and professionals caring for them. We provide accurate, reliable and authoritative information via: our helpline; over 20 information leaflets; Quiet, our quarterly journal; our website; attending awareness-

raising events. We also support clinical research and provide training.
Employees: 12
Volunteers: 80
Income: £674,331 (2013-14)

British Trust for Ornithology

The Nunnery, Thetford, Norfolk IP24 2PU
T: 01842 750050
F: 01842 750030
E: sophie.foulger@bto.org
www.bto.org
The BTO promotes and encourages the wider understanding, appreciation and conservation of birds through scientific studies, using the combined skills and enthusiasm of its members, other birdwatchers and staff.
Employees: 95
Volunteers: 30000
Regional offices: 130

British Voice Association

330 Gray's Inn Road, London WC1X 8EE
T: 0300 123 2773
F: 020 3456 5092
E: administrator@britishvoiceassociation.org.uk
www.britishvoiceassociation.org.uk
The BVA recognises the human voice as an essential element of our communication and wellbeing. It is devoted to people with voice problems, ranging from severe pathology and cancer to subtle difficulties of artistic performance, all of whom are entitled to the best care available.
Volunteers: 10

British Waterways

64 Clarendon Road
T: 01442 278738
E: robin.evans@britishwaterways.co.uk
www.britishwaterways.co.uk
Chief Executive: Robin Evans

British Wireless for the Blind Fund

10 Albion Place, Maidstone, Kent ME14 5DZ
T: 01622 754757
F: 01622 751725
E: dave@blind.org.uk
www.blind.org.uk
The Fund provides, on a permanent free-loan basis, radios, radio-cassette recorders, CD radio cassette recorders to UK registered blind and partially sighted persons, over the age of eight, who are in need.
Employees: 5
Volunteers: 300

British Youth Council

London N1 6AH
T: 0845 458 1489
E: mail@byc.org.uk
www.byc.org.uk
The Council works to advance the spiritual educational and physical welfare of young people in conjunction with similar bodies working in the same field in countries overseas.

Broken Rainbow LGBT Domestic Violence Service UK

J414, 83 Ducie Street, Greater Manchester M1 2JQ
T: 0845 260 5560
Helpline: 0300 999 5428
E: mail@brokenrainbow.org.uk
www.broken-rainbow.org.uk
Broken Rainbow UK runs the only National LGBT Domestic Violence Helpline providing confidential support to all members of the lesbian, gay, bisexual and transgender (LGBT) communities, their family and friends, and agencies supporting them.
Employees: 6
Volunteers: 15
Regional offices: 1

Bromley Y

E: valeriemichelet@gmail.com

Brook

50 Featherstone Street, London EC1Y 8RT
T: 020 7284 6040
Helpline: 0808 802 1234
F: 020 7284 6050
E: admin@brook.org.uk
www.brook.org.uk
National Director: Simon Blake
The country's largest young people's sexual health charity. For 50 years, we have been providing sexual health services, support and advice to young people under 25. Brook wants a society that values all children, young people and their developing sexuality. We want all children and young people to be supported to develop the self-confidence, skills and understanding they need to enjoy and take responsibility for their sexual lives, sexual health and wellbeing.
Employees: 27
Volunteers: 21
Regional offices: 23

Brothers of Charity Services

Lisieux Hall, Dawson Lane, Whittle-le-Woods, Chorley PR6 7DX
T: 01257 266311
F: 01257 265671
E: info@brothersofcharity.org.uk
www.brothersofcharity.org.uk
Aims to assist people who have learning difficulties to live an ordinary life in which they are respected and valued in their local community.

BSS

163 Eversholt Street, London NW1 1BU
T: 020 7419 3800
E: peter.calderbank@bss.org
www.bss.org
Chief Executive: Peter Calderbank
The purpose of BSS is to enable people to take action to improve the quality of their lives and society, through the provision and management of information and advice. This is done by providing comprehensive, high-quality, specialist contact centre and information services to our customers in the public, voluntary and commercial sectors.
Employees: 750
Regional offices: 6

BUAV

16A Crane Grove, London N7 8NN
T: 020 7700 4888
F: 020 7700 0252
E: meg.griffiths@buav.org
www.crueltyfreeinternational.org
Chief Executive: Michelle Thew
The BUAV's vision is to create a world where nobody wants or believes we need to experiment on animals.
Employees: 18
Volunteers: 2

Buglife - The Invertebrate Conservation Trust

Bug house, Ham Lane, Orton Waterville, Peterborough, Cambridgeshire PE2 5UU
T: 01733 201210
F: 01733 315410
E: info@buglife.org.uk
www.buglife.org.uk
Chief Executive: Matt Shardlow
The food we eat, the birds we see, the flowers we smell and the hum of life we hear, simply would not exist without bugs. Invertebrates truly underpin all life on earth. Sadly, many amazing and beautiful creatures are declining. Three species of bumblebees are now extinct in the UK and over 70% of butterfly species are in significant decline. Buglife is the only

organisation in Europe devoted to the conservation of all invertebrates.
Employees: 24
Volunteers: 50
Regional offices: 4
Income: £1,175,816 (2014-15)

Build Africa

Vale House, Clarence Road, Tunbridge Wells, Kent TN1 1HE
T: 01892 519619
E: hello@build-africa.org.uk
www.build-africa.org.uk
Build Africa combines education and livelihoods projects to help communities in Kenya and Uganda live happier, healthier and more fulfilled lives.

Building and Social Housing Foundation

Memorial Square, Coalville, Leicestershire LE67 3TU
T: 01530 510444
F: 01530 510332
E: bshf@bshf.org
www.bshf.org
Director: David Ireland
BSHF is an independent housing research organisation which identifies and promotes good practice in housing throughout the world.
Employees: 10

Business and Education London South

E: michaelmanningprior@bels.org.uk

Business in the Community

137 Shepherdess Walk, London N1 7RQ
T: 020 7566 8650
E: hq.reception@bitc.org.uk
www.bitc.org.uk
Chief Executive: Julia Cleverdon
Business in the Community is a unique movement of over 800 member companies, representing one in five of the UK private sector workforce. A further 3,000 companies are engaged through our programmes and campaigns, which we operate through a local network of more than 100 business-led partnerships and we lead a global partners network of 112 organisations operating in over 60 countries.
Employees: 343
Regional offices: 11

Butler Trust

Howard House, 32-34 High Street, Croydon, Surrey CR0 1YB
T: 020 8688 6062
F: 020 8688 6056
E: info@butlertrust.org.uk
www.butlertrust.org.uk
Director: Simon Shepherd
The Butler Trust is an independent charity that recognises excellence and innovation by people working with offenders in the UK. Through its Annual Award Scheme and Development Programme, the Trust helps to identify and promote excellence and innovation; develop and disseminate best practice in the care and resettlement of offenders throughout the UK; and provide professional and personal development opportunities for award-winning staff.
Employees: 6
Volunteers: 14

Buttle UK

Audley House, 13 Palace Street, London SW1E 5HX
T: 020 7828 7311
E: info@buttleuk.org
www.buttleuk.org
Chief Executive: Gerri McAndrew
Buttle UK helps children and young people living in poverty, in the UK. We make grants to meet the critical needs of individual children and young people whose safety, health or development are at risk, launching them into a brighter future. Objectives include providing grant aid, carrying out research, policy work and fundraising.
Employees: 20
Regional offices: 4

BYHP

2 Chandos Close, Banbury, Oxfordshire OX16 4TL
T: 01295 259442
E: linda.slide@byhp.org.uk
www.byhp.org.uk
Head Of Business: Tim Tarby Donald
BYHP is a registered charity that exists to support and assist vulnerable young people aged 13 – 25 in finding and maintaining a safe home. We provide free, confidential advice, information and support services and have developed a range of services to support young people in securing and maintaining housing.
Employees: 8
Volunteers: 8
Regional offices: 1

CAADA

3rd Floor, Maxet House, 28 Baldwin Street, Bristol BS1 1NG
T: 0117 317 8750
E: queries@caada.org.uk
www.caada.org.uk
CAADA's goal is to transform the UK's response to domestic abuse to make sure that victims are identified as early as possible and that they and their children are supported to live in safety.
Employees: 45

Cabrini Children's Society

E: himare.peterkin@cabrini.org.uk

Caldecott Foundation

Caldecott House, Hythe Road, Smeeth, Ashford, Kent TN25 6SP
T: 01303 815678
F: 01303 815677
E: info@caldecottfoundation.co.uk
www.caldecottfoundation.co.uk
The Caldecott Foundation provides high-quality childcare and education within a therapeutic setting, enabling children to attain life skills and self-esteem. We ensure children and young people achieve their educational potential via personal educational plans and delivery of the National Curriculum.
Employees: 178

CALIBRE Audio Library

New Road, Weston Turville, Aylesbury, Buckinghamshire HP22 5XQ
T: 01296 432339
F: 01296 392599
E: membershipservices@calibre.org.uk
www.calibre.org.ok
Director: Mike Lewington
The CALIBRE Audio Library is a free nationwide postal library of audio books for people with sight problems or physical disabilities. 7,000 fiction and non-fiction books recorded on cassette or MP3 disks (unabridged) and no special playback equipment is required. 1,200 titles are available in the Young Calibre library. A small

charge is made for print catalogues full catalogue available on the website. Contact the Membership Services Team for further details and an application form.
Employees: 52
Volunteers: 95

Camberwell After School Project

14 Badsworth Road, Camberwell, London SE5 0JY
T: 020 7708 2711
E: carmen.lindsay@caspuk.org
www.caspuk.org
Chief Executive Officer: Carmen Lindsay MBE
To advance the education of children by the provision of safe and satisfying group play and supplementary learning. For primary school children, this entails the provision of a safe and happy environment before and after school, safe travel to and from school, full day service during school holiday. The mission is also to enable children to develop both socially and academically both by the provision of appropriate group play and through structured learning.
Employees: 17
Volunteers: 5
Regional offices: 2
Income: £280,737 (2014-15)

Cambridge House

1 Addington Square, London SE5 0HF
T: 020 7358 7000
E: kwoodley@ch1889.org
www.ch1889.org
Chief Executive: Karin Woodley
Cambridge House is a people's social action centre that works innovatively to tackle poverty and social injustice. Occupying our own building in Southwark for more than 126 years, we deliver specialist frontline services to address the needs of people facing multiple disadvantage and complex interrelated needs. Working nationally and internationally, we remain firmly rooted in our local neighbourhood as a community asset and hub working one person, one family and one community at a time.
Employees: 51
Volunteers: 43
Income: £1,500,000 (2014-15)

Camfed International

St Giles Court, 24 Castle Street, Cambridge CB3 0AJ
T: 01223 362648
E: info@camfed.org
www.camfed.org
Camfed is an international non-profit organisation tackling poverty and inequality by supporting girls to go to school and succeed, and empowering young women to step up as leaders of change. Since 1993, Camfed's innovative education programmes in Zimbabwe, Zambia, Ghana, Tanzania and Malawi have directly supported over 1,202,000 students to attend primary and secondary school, and over 3 million children have benefited from an improved learning environment.

Campaign Against Drinking and Driving

1st Floor, 16 Market Street, Brighouse, West Yorkshire HD6 1AP
T: 01484 723649 (also fax)
Helpline: 0845 123 5542
E: info@cadd.org.uk
www.scard.org.uk
Chair: Carole Whittingham
Campaigns against drink and/or drug driving. Supports victims who have been bereaved or injured as a result of drink/drugs or any other bereavement related to road collisions or incidents.

Campaign for Better Transport Charitable Trust

44-48 Wharf Road, London N1 7UX
T: 020 7566 6480
E: info@bettertransport.org.uk
www.bettertransport.org.uk
We are the Campaign for Better Transport and since 1973 we have been helping to create transport policies and programmes that give people better lives. Working nationally and locally, collectively and as individuals, through high-level lobbying and strong public campaigning, we make good transport ideas a reality and stop bad ones from happening.
Employees: 11
Volunteers: 3

Campaign for Freedom of Information

Suite 102, 16 Baldwins Gardens, London EC1N 7RJ
T: 020 7831 7477
F: 020 7831 7461
E: admin@cfoi.demon.co.uk
www.cfoi.org.uk
The Campaign for Freedom of Information is a non-profit organisation working to improve public access to official information and ensure that the Freedom of Information Act is implemented effectively.
Employees: 2

Campaign for Learning

24 Greencoat Place, Westminster, London SW1P 1RD
T: 020 7798 6067
F: 020 7798 6001
E: jwright@cflearning.org.uk
www.campaignforlearning.org.uk
Chief Executive: Tricia Hartley
The Campaign for Learning is working for a society where learning is at the heart of social inclusion. Research shows that lifelong learners are more likely to be happier, healthier, have better jobs, contribute more to society and live longer and more fulfilled lives. We work to build motivation, create opportunities and provide support for learning in families and communities, workplaces and schools that leads to positive change.
Employees: 17
Volunteers: 2
Regional offices: 2

Campaign for Nuclear Disarmament (CND)

Mordechai Vanunu House, 162 Holloway Road, London N7 8DQ
T: 020 7700 2393
F: 020 7700 2357
E: enquiries@cnduk.org
www.cnduk.org
Chair: Dave Webb
CND campaigns non-violently to rid the world of nuclear weapons and other weapons of mass destruction and to create genuine security for future generations. CND is funded entirely by its members and supporters.
Employees: 11
Volunteers: 20
Regional offices: 6

Campaign to Protect Rural England

5-11 Lavington Street, London SE1 0NZ
T: 020 7981 2800
F: 020 7981 2899
E: vickis@cpre.org.uk
www.cpre.org.uk
Chief Executive: Shaun Spiers
CPRE campaigns for a sustainable future for the English countryside, a vital but undervalued environmental, economic and social asset to the nation. We highlight threats and promote positive solutions. Our in-depth research supports active campaigning, and through reasoned argument and lobbying we

seek to influence public opinion and decision-makers at every level.
Employees: 38
Volunteers: 1500
Regional offices: 43
Income: £4,000,000 (2013-14)

Camphill Village Trust Ltd

9 Saville Street, Malton, North Yorkshire YO17 7LL
T: 01653 228322
F: 0845 094 4639
E: trustoffice@cvt.org.uk
www.cvt.org.uk
CEO: Huw John
To provide support for adults with special needs by establishing and maintaining intentional communities of purpose where all may continue to develop as individuals through meaningful work of a productive nature alongside a range of chosen therapeutic activities and further education, as well as a healthy cultural, social and spiritual life.
Employees: 470
Regional offices: 10

CAN

Southwark, London SE1 0EE
T: 020 7922 7700
E: r.chadha@can-online.org.uk
www.can-online.org.uk
Chief Executive: Adele Blakebrough
Employees: 16

Cancer Care Society

48 Mountbatten Drive, Ferndown, Dorset BH22 9EL
T: 01202 894896
E: peter.j.hayes@btinternet.com
The Society aims to relieve, aid and support persons who are suffering or have suffered from cancer. Grants are given to associated charities and not to individuals.

Cancer Laryngectomee Trust

PO Box 618, Halifax HX3 8WX
T: 01422 205522 (also fax)
E: info@cancerlt.org
www.cancerlt.org
Trustee: Carole Stainton
The Trust exists to improve the quality of life for all neck breathers in the UK and to provide support for all cancer of the larynx patients after surgery.
Volunteers: 20
Income: £13,111 (2013-14)

Cancer Research UK

Angel Building, 407 St Johns Street, London EC1V 4AD
T: 020 7242 0200
F: 020 7269 3100
E: supporter.services@cancer.org.uk
www.cancerresearchuk.org
The aims of the Trust are to carry out world-class research into the biology and causes of cancer; develop effective treatments and improve the quality of life for cancer patients; reduce the number of people getting cancer and provide authoritative information on cancer.
Employees: 3380
Volunteers: 30000
Regional offices: 1000

Cancerkin

The Cancerkin Centre, Royal Free Hospital, Pond Street, London NW3 2QG
T: 020 7830 2323
F: 020 7830 2324
E: info@cancerkin.org.uk
www.cancerkin.org.uk
Cancerkin provides information, treatment, supportive care and rehabilitation for breast cancer patients and support for relatives. It also offers support for, and collaboration in, research; education and training for health professionals, students and volunteers; and evolves with the changing management of breast cancer.

CANS Legal Information

Camelford House, London SE1 7TP
T: 020 7820 3456
F: 020 7820 7890
E: canstrust@aol.com
www.cans.org.uk
Legal Editor: Robert Jack
We provide legal information that is comprehensive, accurate, affordable and always up to date. We work to promote a better understanding of the law by widening access to legal information.
Employees: 4
Regional offices: 1

Canterbury Diocesan Board of Finance

Diocesan House, Lady Wootton's Green
T: 01227 459401
E: cmccaulay@diocant.org
www.canterburydiocese.org
Reception and Hospitality Manager: Charlotte McCaulay

Canterbury Oast Trust

Highlands Farm, Woodchurch, Ashford, Kent TN26 3RJ
T: 01233 861493
F: 01233 860433
E: enquiries@c-o-t.org.uk
www.c-o-t.org.uk
Chief Executive: David Jackson
The Trust provides homes, training and supported employment for people with a learning disability.
Employees: 178
Volunteers: 130
Regional offices: 1

CapeUK

31 The Calls, Leeds LS2 7EY
T: 0845 450 3700
E: lisa.ibbetson@capeuk.org
www.capeuk.org
Chief Executive: Pat Cochrane
We are an independent not-for-profit organisation committed to improving the lives of children and young people, preparing them to face the future with creativity and self-belief. We work with schools, youth and community organisations, universities, the cultural and creative sector and other agencies that share our aims.
Employees: 21
Regional offices: 3
Income: £133,606 (2013-14)

Capital Project

Safe Haven, 32 Sudley Road, Bognor Regis, West Sussex PO21 1EL
T: 01243 869662
E: clare.ockwell@capitalproject.org
www.capitalproject.org
CEO: Clare Ockwell
CAPITAL is a peer run charity committed to helping people in West Sussex who experience mental distress to reach their full potential through training, involvement opportunities, a wide variety of peer led activities and mutual support.
Employees: 16
Volunteers: 31
Income: £20,500 (2013-14)

CARA (Centre for Action on Rape and Abuse)

PO Box 548, Colchester, Essex CO1 1YP
T: 01206 367881
Helpline: 01206 769795
E: info@caraessex.org.uk
www.caraessex.org.uk
Director: Helen Parr
CARA supports children, young people and adult women who have experienced any form of sexual violence, directly or indirectly, recently or in the past. We operate across the whole of mid, north and west Essex.
Employees: 12
Volunteers: 16
Regional offices: 1
Income: £208,000 (2013-14)

Cara Trust

240 Lancaster Road, London W11 4AH
T: 020 7243 6147
F: 020 7243 5821
E: mail@caralife.com
www.caralife.com
Director: Chris Woolls
The Cara Trust works to reduce the impact of HIV on people living with the virus through provision of a range of social welfare and spiritual support services. We also offer education services to faith communities. Our service guides can be downloaded from our website.
Employees: 4
Volunteers: 30

Cardiomyopathy UK

Unit 10 Chiltern Court, Asheridge Road, Chesham, Buckinghamshire HP5 2PX
T: 01494 791224
Helpline: 0800 018 1024
F: 01494 797199
E: fundraising@cardiomyopathy.org
www.cardiomyopathy.org
Chief Executive: Joel Rose
Our vision is for everyone affected by cardiomyopathy to lead long and fulfilling lives. We are at an important point in our 25 year history, with ambitious plans for growth, so that we can improve diagnosis and care and increase support for everyone affected by the heart muscle disease cardiomyopathy. Although it is the most common medical cause of sudden death under 35, most of those affected can lead a long and fulfilling life if diagnosed promptly and given correct treatment.
Employees: 10
Volunteers: 200
Income: £600,000 (2013-14)

Cards for Good Causes Ltd

1 Edison Gate, West Portway, Andover, Hampshire SP10 3SE
T: 01264 361555
F: 01264 362333
E: jill.grigg@cfgc.org.uk
www.cardsforcharity.co.uk
Cards for Good Causes assists charities through a forum where charities can exchange useful information and share ideas and solutions relating to their administration, promotion and fundraising. It encourages and promotes voluntary work for these charities by their members, supporters, local community groups and the general public.
Employees: 20
Volunteers: 6300

Care and Repair England

The Renewal Trust Business Centre, 3 Hawksworth Street, Nottingham, Nottinghamshire NG3 2EG
T: 0115 950 6500
E: info@careandrepair-england.org.uk
www.careandrepair-england.org.uk
Chief Executive: Sue Adams
Care and Repair England innovates, develops, promotes and supports housing-related policies and practical initiatives that enable older people to live independently in their own homes for as long as they wish.
Employees: 7
Volunteers: 11
Regional offices: 3

Care for the Wild International

72 Brighton Road, Horsham, West Sussex RH13 5BU
T: 01403 249832
E: info@careforthewild.com
www.careforthewild.org
Chief Executive Officer: Philip Mansbridge
Care for the Wild is dedicated to the protection of wildlife in the UK and around the world. Our vision is to live in a world where caring for wildlife is a global priority. Our mission is to rescue, protect and defend wildlife. Join us today www.careforthewild.org
Employees: 10
Volunteers: 48
Regional offices: 1

CARE International UK

9th Floor, 89 Albert Embankment, Vauxhall, London SE1 7TP
T: 020 7091 6000
F: 020 7582 0728
E: thomas@careinternational.org
www.careinternational.org.uk
Chief Executive: Geoffrey Dennis
CARE International is a leading development and humanitarian charity supporting the poorest communities in 84 countries around the world. Our aim is to bring sustainable and innovative solutions to complex poverty issues and last year we supported 1,015 poverty-fighting projects that reached more than 122 million people. Our mission is to create lasting change in poor communities and we put money where it is needed most.
Employees: 110
Volunteers: 4

Careers Research and Advisory Centre Ltd

Sheraton House, Castle Park, Cambridge CB3 0AX
T: 01223 460277
E: hayley.evans@vitae.ac.uk
www.crac.org.uk
CRAC works to advance the education of the public in lifelong career-related learning for all; to enable employers and the world of education to work successfully together and promote best practice and the highest standards of professionalism and execution amongst those offering careers advice and development. Vitae (CRAC's biggest programme) is the UK organisation championing the personal, professional and career development of doctoral researchers and research staff in higher education institutions and research institutes.
Employees: 16
Regional offices: 1

Carer Support Wiltshire

Independent Living Centre, St George's Road, Semington, Trowbridge, Wiltshire BA14 6JQ
T: 01380 871690
Helpline: 0800 181 4118
E: dianaf@carersinwiltshire.co.uk
www.carersinwiltshire.co.uk
Chief Executive: Catharine Hurford
Our aim is to ensure carers in Wiltshire are supported. We do this partly by delivering support services directly to carers, and partly by raising awareness of carers and the issues they face. As part of this work, we provide training on good practice with health and social care staff, and run a GP award scheme and employers' award scheme (Working For Carers).
Employees: 46
Volunteers: 75
Regional offices: 2
Income: £1,260,279 (2014-15)

Carers Association Southern Staffordshire

E: michele.mcdonald@carersinformation.org.uk

Carers Centre (Leicestershire & Rutland)

Unit 19 Matrix House, Constitution Hill, Leicester, Leicestershire LE1 1PL
T: 0116 251 0999
F: 0116 251 3514
E: enquiries@claspthecarerscentre.org.uk
www.org.uk
Centre Manager: Charles Huddleston
To promote any charitable purposes for the benefit of carers in the city and county of leicestershire (hereinafter called the area of benefit) and in particular the advancement of education and furtherance of health and the relief of poverty distress and sickness.
Employees: 9
Volunteers: 25
Income: £230,000 (2012-13)

Carers Network

E: bernadette.scott@carers-network.co.uk

Carers Trust

32-36 Loman Street, London SE1 0EH
T: 0844 800 4361
F: 0844 800 4362
E: info@carers.org
www.carers.org / www.babble.carers.org / www.matter.carers.org
Chief Executive: Gail Scott-Spicer
Carers Trust is a major new charity for, with and about carers. We work to improve support, services and recognition for anyone living with the challenges of caring, unpaid, for a family member or friend who is ill, frail, disabled or has mental health or addiction problems. To find your nearest Carers Trust Network Partner, call 0844 800 4361 or visit www.carers.org
Employees: 50+
Volunteers: 2
Regional offices: 6

Carers UK

20 Great Dover Street, London SE1 4LX
T: 020 7378 4999
Helpline: 0808 808 7777
F: 020 7490 8824
E: david.titmas@carersuk.org
www.carersuk.org
Chief Executive: Heléna Herklots
Carers UK makes life better for the millions of people who look after older, ill or disabled family and friends.
Employees: 65
Volunteers: 250
Regional offices: 4
Income: £4,292,034 (2012-13)

Carers' Support - Canterbury, Dover & Thanet

80 Middle Street, Deal, Kent CT14 6HL
T: 01304 364637
E: admin@carers-doverdistrict.org
www.carers-doverdistrict.org
CEO: Patricia Cole
Supporting those who care for a relative or friend.
Employees: 11

CARITAS – Social Action

39 Eccleston Square, London SW1V 1BX
T: 020 7901 4875
F: 020 7901 4874
E: caritas.admin@cbcew.org.uk
www.csan.org.uk
Promotes Catholic social action in England and Wales.
Employees: 7
Regional offices: 100

Carplus Trust

Round Foundry Media Centre, Foundry Street, Leeds, West Yorkshire LS11 5QP
T: 0113 394 4590
E: info@carplus.org.uk
www.carplus.org.uk
Chief Executive: Chas Ball
Carplus is the UK's pioneering transport NGO supporting the development of affordable, accessible and low-carbon car-sharing clubs and ride-sharing services. It is Carplus' mission to promote sustainable transport and, specifically, to stimulate and facilitate a rethink in the role of the private car as part of the urban mobility mix.
Employees: 7
Regional offices: 2

CASE Kent

Berwick House, 8 Elwick Road, Ashford, Kent TN23 1PF
T: 01233 610171
E: janperfect@casekent.org.uk
www.casekent.org.uk
CEO: Jan Perfect
CASE Kent provides specialist expertise, information and support to develop the skills local people need to run successful not-for-profit organisations and groups, primarily in the districts of Ashford, Dover, Shepway and Thanet.
Employees: 7
Volunteers: 4
Regional offices: 3
Income: £137,015 (2013-14)

Caspari Foundation for Educational Therapy and Therapeutic Teaching

Gregory House, Coram Campus, 48-49 Mecklenburgh Sq, London WC1N 3NY
T: 020 7923 6270
E: admin@caspari.org.uk
www.caspari.org.uk
The Foundation aims to develop the theory and practice of therapy as a mode of treatment for children and young people with emotional, behavioural and learning difficulties, to establish professional standards in its practice and to disseminate knowledge and understanding of the method.

Cass Centre for Charity Effectiveness

Cass Business School, 106 Bunhill Row, London EC1Y 8TZ
T: 020 7040 5562
E: casscce@city.ac.uk
www.cass.city.ac.uk/cce
Director: Professor Paul Palmer
The Centre for Charity Effectiveness at Cass (Cass CCE) is the leading nonprofit and philanthropy centre in the UK. Cass CCE focuses on driving positive change within the nonprofit sector, enabling organisations and individuals to extend their reach into wider society by increasing their operating effectiveness. The Centre achieves this through a mix of consulting assignments, professional development programmes and five specialist MScs.
Employees: 15
Volunteers: 20
Income: £1,200,000 (2014-15)

Castle Point Association of Voluntary Services (CAVS)

The Tyrells Centre, 39 Seamore Avenue, Thundersley, Essex SS7 4EX
T: 01268 638416
F: 01268 638415
E: office@castlepointavs.org.uk
www.castlepointavs.org.uk
CEO: Janis Gibson

CAVS provides support and guidance to voluntary sector organisations in the borough of Castle Point. Frontline projects include Children's Services, Volunteer Centre, Befriending Service and Be Safer Essex.
Employees: 30
Volunteers: 220
Regional offices: 1
Income: £939,435 (2013-14)

Catholic Agency for Overseas Development

Romero Close, Stockwell Road, London SW9 9TY
T: 020 7733 7900
F: 020 7274 9630
E: cafod@cafod.org.uk
www.cafod.org.uk
CAFOD funds relief and development projects overseas and raises awareness in England and Wales of the root causes of poverty.
Employees: 172
Volunteers: 80
Regional offices: 12

Catholic Association for Racial Justice

9 Henry Road, Manor House, London N4 2LH
T: 020 8802 8080
F: 020 8211 0808
E: rosie@carj.org.uk
www.carj.org.uk
National Coordinator: Rosie Bairwal
To overcome racial discrimination in the Church and in society through policy work and programmes. Each year we produce materials for Racial Justice Sunday (on the second Sunday in September each year) with CTBI. We work with parishes, dioceses, networks and others throughout the year to promote equality for all disadvantaged groups including black minority ethnic people, Muslim communities, migrants, sanctuary seekers and refugees, gypsies, Roma and travellers, disadvantaged white communities and Dalits.
Employees: 3
Volunteers: 2

Catholic Children's Society

E: paulw@cathchild.org.uk

Catholic Clothing Guild

5 Dark Lane, Shrewsbury, Shropshire SY2 5LP
T: 01743 243858
E: carmel.edwards@btinternet.com
www.catholicclothingguild.org.uk
The guild supplies new, useful and warm clothing for those who, through unfortunate circumstances, are unable to provide for themselves and their families.

Catholic Concern for Animals

15 Rosehip Way, Bishops Cleeve, Cheltenham, Gloucestershire GL52 8WP
T: 01242 677423
E: deborahjark@aol.com
www.catholic-animals.org
Chairman: Mgr John Chaloner
We aim to put animals on the agenda of the Church, and to promote authentic Christian teaching on animals. The wellbeing of all animals is our priority, and cultivating non-cruelty, to help make this a better, gentler and more compassionate world for all.
Employees: 1
Volunteers: 10

Catholic Truth Society

40-46 Harleyford Road, London SE11 5AY
T: 020 7640 0042
E: f.martin@ctsbooks.org
www.ctsbooks.org
The Society publishes and disseminates low-priced devotional and teaching works; assists all Catholics to a better knowledge of their religion; spreads information about the faith among non-Catholics and assists the circulation of Catholic books.

Catholic Women's League

PO Box 303, Malvern WR14 9DX
T: 01684 540414 (also fax)
E: natsec@cwlhq.org.uk
www.catholicwomensleague.org
The League aims to unite Catholic women in a bond of common fellowship; promotes religious, educational and social welfare interests on parish, diocesan, national and international levels; ensures Catholic representation of these interests on major public bodies and initiates and maintains charitable works.

Cats Protection

National Cat Centre, Chelwood Gate, Haywards Heath, West Sussex RH17 7TT
T: 01825 741211
F: 01825 741005
E: volunteering@cats.org.uk
www.cats.org.uk
From humble beginnings in 1927, Cats Protection has grown to become the UK's leading feline welfare charity. We now help around 235,000 cats and kittens every year through our network of over 260 volunteer-run branches, 29 adoption centres and our homing centre.
Employees: 350
Volunteers: 9000
Regional offices: 260

Cavell Nurses' Trust

Grosvenor House, Prospect Hill, Redditch, Worcestershire B97 4DL
T: 01527 595999
Helpline: 0808 123 4999
F: 01527 67245
E: vickyl@cavellnursestrust.org
www.cavellnursestrust.org
Chief Executive Officer: Stephen Charlton
Cavell Nurses' Trust nurses, midwives and healthcare assistants, whether student, working or retired, who are in need or suffering hardship or distress. Support is offered in the form of financial grants and advice as well as signposting to other agencies.
Employees: 11
Volunteers: 20
Income: £516,860 (2012-13)

Caxton Trust (working name Catch Up)

Catch Up, Keystone Innovation Centre, Croxton Road, Thetford, Norfolk IP24 1JD
T: 01842 752297
F: 01842 824490
E: info@catchup.org
www.catchup.org
Director: Julie Lawes
To address the problem of underachievement that has its roots in literacy and numeracy difficulties.
Employees: 11

CCS Adoption

162 Pennywell Road, Easton, Bristol, Avon BS5 0TX
T: 0117 935 0005
E: info@ccsadoption.org
www.ccsadoption.org
Chief Executive: Jadwiga Ball
CCS Adoption is a voluntary, independent and registered adoption agency that offers a comprehensive adoption service that includes recruiting, assessing and preparing adoptive families, supporting child and family throughout the adoption process and beyond, working with birth parents who may be considering adoption for their child in partnership with Local Authority Social Services Departments and providing a counselling service to adult adoptees and their relatives.
Employees: 20
Volunteers: 2
Regional offices: 1

CDH UK

The Denes, Lynn Road, Tilney All Saints, King's Lynn, Norfolk PE34 4RD
T: 01553 828382
Helpline: 0800 731 6991
E: committee@cdhuk.org.uk
www.cdhuk.org.uk
Chair: Brenda Lane
The charity supports families whose children are diagnosed with congenital diaphragmatic hernia; it supports both those who survive and those who are bereaved. It also aims to educate and raise awareness both to the general public and medical professionals and promotes research. The association supports families whose children are diagnosed with congenital diaphragmatic hernia; it supports both those who survive and those who are bereaved. It also aims to educate and raise awareness both to the general public and medical professionals and promotes research.
Volunteers: 10
Regional offices: 2

Centre 404

404 Camden Road, London N7 0SJ
T: 020 7607 8762
F: 020 7700 0085
E: amyc@centre404.org.uk
www.centre404.org.uk
Chief Executive: Amy Curtis
Centre 404 is working towards a world where people with a learning disability and their families have the support they need to enjoy the same rights, freedom, responsibilities, respect, choices and quality of life as people within the wider community. We aim to contribute to this by providing excellent quality services and by supporting people with a learning disability and their carers to get their voices and views heard.
Employees: 173
Volunteers: 90
Regional offices: 1
Income: £2,932,543 (2012-13)

Centre for Accessible Environments

Holyer House, 20-21 Red Lion Court, London EC4A 3EB
T: 020 7822 8232
E: info@cae.org.uk
www.cae.org.uk
Director: Jean Hewitt
The Centre for Accessible Environments is a leading authority on inclusive design and management. We provide training, guidance publications, research and consultancy on access and inclusion - offering pan disability access audits, design reviews and workplace assessments. We produce regular professional journals for our subscribing members.
Employees: 6
Volunteers: 1
Income: £250,000 (2014-15)

Centre for Crime and Justice Studies

2 Langley Lane, London SW8 1GB
T: 020 7840 6110
E: info@crimeandjustice.org.uk
www.crimeandjustice.org.uk
The Centre promotes the exchange of knowledge and experience of criminal justice matters among all interested people, both professional and lay; initiates and disseminates research into the causes, prevention and treatment of crime and delinquency.

Centre for Effective Dispute Resolution

International Dispute Resolution Centre, 70 Fleet Street, London EC4Y 1EU
T: 020 7536 6000
E: artims@cedr.com
www.cedr.co.uk
The Centre encourages and develops mediation and other dispute resolution and prevention techniques in commercial and public sectors.

Centre for Fun and Families Limited

177/179 Narborough Road, Leicester, Leicestershire LE3 0PE
T: 0116 223 4254
F: 0116 275 8558
E: robert@funandfamilies.org.uk
www.funandfamilies.co.uk
Chief Executive: Jayne Ballard
The Centre assists families where parents are experiencing behaviour difficulties with their children/young people; promotes good practice by providing parent training packs based on social learning theory; provides services direct to families and offers skills training to professional staff in both statutory and voluntary agencies.
Employees: 7
Volunteers: 22

Centre for Innovation In Voluntary Action

9-10 Mansfield Place, London NW3 1HS
T: 020 7431 1412
E: norton@civa.org.uk
www.civa.org.uk
The Centre promotes new ideas and approaches, encourages innovation in voluntary action in the UK and abroad; facilitates the dissemination of ideas, experiences and issues and promotes exchanges.

Centre for Policy on Ageing

28 Great Tower Street, London EC3R 5AT
T: 020 7553 6500
F: 020 7553 6501
E: cpa@cpa.org.uk
www.cpa.org.uk
The Centre encourages better services for older people by initiating informed debate, stimulating awareness of the needs of older people, formulating and promoting social policies and encouraging the spread of good practice.
Employees: 7

Centre for Studies on Inclusive Education

The Park Centre, Daventry Road, Knowle, Bristol BS4 1DQ
T: 0117 353 3150
F: 0117 353 3151
E: admin@csie.org.uk
www.csie.org.uk
CSIE Director: Dr Artemi Sakellariadis
The Centre for Studies on Inclusive Education (CSIE) is an independent centre, set up in 1982, actively supporting inclusive education as a basic human right of every child. The Centre is funded by charitable donations, with additional income from sale of publications and small grants for research or other projects. CSIE's work is driven by a

commitment to overcome barriers to learning and participation for all children and young people.
Employees: 3

Centre for Sustainable Energy

3 St Peters Court, Bedminster Parade, Bristol BS3 4AQ
T: 0117 934 1400
E: info@cse.org.uk
www.cse.org.uk
Chief Executive: Simon Roberts OBE
We are an independent national charity that shares our knowledge and experience to help people change the way they think and act about energy
Employees: 50

Centre for the Advancement of Interprofessional Education

PO Box 680, Fareham PO14 9NH
E: admin@caipe.org.uk
www.caipe.org.uk
Chair: Marilyn Hammick
CAIPE promotes and develops interprofessional education as a way of improving collaboration between practitioners and organisations, engaged in both statutory and non-statutory public services and improving the quality of care that is delivered to the public. CAIPE's some 200 members form a network of mutual support and interest that facilitates intellectual engagement with interprofessionalism.
Employees: 1

Centre for Volunteering and Community Leadership

University of Central Lancashire, School of Education and Social Science, Livesey House, Room 213, Preston, Lancashire PR1 2HE
T: 01772 893662
Helpline: 01772 893669
E: amelling@uclan.ac.uk
www.communityleadership.org.uk
Director of the Centre for Volunteering : Alethea Melling
The University of Central Lancashire's award-winning Centre for Volunteering and Community Leadership (CVCL) is a social enterprise that has delivered significant regional, national and international high-impact outcomes in the areas of youth development and community volunteering programmes alongside academic, vocational and bespoke Continuing Professional Development (CPD) courses at UCLan. We aim to engage, empower and enable everyone who comes into contact with our work in local, national and international settings.
Employees: 7
Volunteers: 2000+
Regional offices: 2

Centre for Youth and Community Development

94-106 Leagrave Road, Luton, Bedfordshire LU4 8HZ
T: 01582 519500
E: mir.juma@cycd.org.uk
www.cycd.org.uk
Director: Mir Juma
Through a dedicated and professional system of youth and community development work, the Bangladesh Youth League will seek to improve the quality of life of the community, alleviate poverty and promote good health through the provision of: education and training, including social education programmes; advocacy; advice; information; outreach and centre-based activities; and liaison with other similar service providers. BYL actively promotes equality of opportunity and diversity, is non-religious and non-political.

Centrepoint

Central House, 25 Camperdown Street, London E1 8DZ
T: 0845 466 3400
E: info@centrepoint.org.uk
www.centrepoint.org.uk
Centrepoint aims to give young people on a downward spiral a chance to turn things around and build a more fulfilling future.
Employees: 250
Volunteers: 70
Regional offices: 2

Centris

Crane House, 19 Apex Business Village, Annitsford, Northumberland NE23 7BF
T: 0191 250 1969
F: 0191 250 2563
E: centris@cranehouse.eu
www.centris.org.uk
The Centre exists to advance education, to promote the relief of sickness and the preservation and protection of health and to promote the relief of poverty in particular by promoting research into the role of individual self-awareness, self-development and personal responsibility in these fields and the dissemination of the useful results of that research.

CfBT Education Trust

60 Queens Road, Reading RG1 4BS
T: 0118 902 1000
F: 0118 902 1434
E: enquiries@cfbt.com
www.cfbt.com
Chief Executive: Steve Munby
CfBT Education Trust is a top 30 UK charity providing education services in the UK and internationally. Established more than 40 years ago, CfBT has an annual turnover exceeding £100 million and employs 2,000 staff worldwide. We teach in schools, academies and the secure estate, manage national programmes in the UK and special projects overseas, provide support for school improvement as well as consultancy services to education professionals. CfBT finances a substantial research and development programme.
Employees: 2000

Challenge Fund the Fight Against Cancer in the Emerging World

INCTR Challenge Fund, Prama House, 267 Banbury Road, Oxford OX2 7HT
T: 01865 339510
F: 01865 339300
E: mlodge@canet.org
www.challengefund.org
Executive Director: Mark Lodge
65% of cases of cancer and 70% of all cancer deaths occur in the Developing Countries. We are the UK charity that raises money to treat children and adults with cancer in these poorer countries. We support the work of the International Network for Cancer Treatment and Research (www.inctr.org) and help build capacity in cancer control in Africa, Asia and Latin America through professional training and carefully managed treatment programmes.

Chance UK

2nd Floor, London Fashion Centre, 89-93 Fonthill Road, London N4 3JH
T: 020 7281 5858
F: 020 7281 4402
E: admin@chanceuk.com
www.chanceuk.com
Chance UK provides a year-long, one-to-one mentoring programme for primary school children with behavioural difficulties who are at risk of developing anti-social or criminal behaviour.
Employees: 25
Volunteers: 160
Regional offices: 1

CHANGE

Unit 11, Shine, Harehills Road, Leeds, West Yorkshire LS8 5HS
T: 0113 388 0011
F: 0113 388 0012
E: info@changepeople.org
www.changepeople.org
Director: Philipa Bragman
CHANGE is a national rights organisation led by disabled people. We campaign for equal rights for all people with learning disabilities. We make information accessible and we give a strong voice to parents with a learning disability.
Employees: 12
Volunteers: 14
Regional offices: 1

Changing Faces

The Squire Centre, London WC1E 6JN
T: 0845 450 0275
F: 0845 450 0276
E: info@changingfaces.org.uk
www.changingfaces.org.uk
Chief Executive: James Partridge
Changing Faces supports and represents the interests of children, teenagers, adults and their families who have disfigurements from birth, accident or disease, helping them to build self-esteem, to gain access to the best health and social services and to enjoy full civil rights and equal opportunities in all aspects of life.
Employees: 24
Volunteers: 150
Regional offices: 3

Chapter 1

2 Exton Street, London SE1 8UE
T: 020 7593 0470
F: 020 7593 0478
E: mail@chapter1.org.uk
www.ch1.org.uk
Chief Executive: Geoff Hawkins
Changing lives one by one. Supported housing for vulnerable people and those at risk. Work with single parents and their children, women's refuge, family contact centres, single homeless persons, private sector leasing schemes, student accommodation, empty homes and social enterprise
Employees: 300
Volunteers: 20
Regional offices: 1

Charities Advisory Trust

Radius Works, Back Lane, London NW3 1HL
T: 020 7794 9835
E: pa@charitiesadvisorytrust.org.uk
www.charitiesadvisorytrust.org.uk
The Trust works to relieve poverty throughout the world; to advance education; to preserve buildings and monuments of architectural merit; and to assist charities to make better use of their assets and resources both generally and in relation to trading and/or fundraising activities on their behalf.

Charities Aid Foundation

25 Kings Hill Avenue, Kings Hill, West Malling, Kent ME19 4TA
T: 0300 012 3000
Helpline: 01732 520000
F: 01732 520001
E: enquiries@cafonline.org
www.cafonline.org
CEO: John Low
The Charities Aid Foundation is a registered charity that works to create greater value for charities and social enterprise. We do this by transforming the way donations are made and the way charitable funds are managed. We also help shape the charitable sector through our research and events.
Employees: 375
Regional offices: 3

Charities HR Network

43 Kingfisher Way, Marchwood, Southampton SO40 4XS
T: 023 8086 0984
E: charhrnet@aol.com
www.chrn.org.uk
Chair of Steering Group: Peter Reeve
A network of senior HR representatives who work together to advance the education in and promote improved standards of human resource management in national charities, with the aim of increasing their effectiveness and efficiency.
Income: £11,000 (2013-14)

Charity Administration, Resourcing and Accountability

5 St George's Avenue, Rugby, Warwickshire CV22 5PN
T: 01788 810146
F: 01788 522888
E: carargd@aol.com
Executive Director: Greyham Dawes
CARA (Regd. Charity No.1117929) provides free advice via its volunteer executive director on best practice in annual financial reporting and regulatory compliance issues for small charities generally (on request) and 'Special Trust' administration services for spiritually minded charitable projects/activities designed to awaken and nurture the mutually respectful, caring humanity revealed to us as the ideal we can and must now attain to here on earth in the New Knowledge from the Holy Grail.
Volunteers: 6
Regional offices: 1
Income: £24,000 (2013-14)

Charity Bank

194 High Street, Tonbridge, Kent TN9 1BE
T: 01732 774040
F: 01732 774069
E: mhowland@charitybank.org
www.charitybank.org
Charity Bank is a specialist lender to charities, voluntary organisations and social enterprises, providing affordable loans from 5,000 up to 1,000,000 on favourable terms. We offer loan finance where other banks won't or can't. We have stable interest rates, which are not linked to the Bank of England's base rate, no early repayment penalties, usually no trustee personal guarantees and no requirement to change banks.
Employees: 10
Volunteers: 30

Charity Finance Group

15-18 White Lion Street, London N1 9PG
T: 0845 345 3192
F: 0845 345 3193
E: info@cfg.org.uk
www.cfg.org.uk
Chief Executive: Caron Bradshaw
CFG (Charity Finance Group) is the charity that champions best practice in finance management in the voluntary sector. Our training and development programmes enable finance managers to give the essential leadership on finance strategy and management that their charities need. With more than 2,000 members, managing over 18 billion, we are uniquely placed to challenge regulation that threatens the effective use of charity funds.
Employees: 24

Charity IT Leaders (CITL)

Chester House, 68 Chestergate, Macclesfield, Cheshire SK11 6DY
T: 01625 664500
E: admin@charityitleaders.org.uk
www.charityitleaders.org.uk
Chair: Laura Dawson
As the premier membership group for IT Directors of major UK Charities, the object is the promotion for the public benefit of the efficiency and effectiveness of charities and not-for-profit organisations through the promotion of study, sharing of knowledge and advancement of the use of information technology. We do this by providing

opportunities of networking, sharing and giving advice.
Volunteers: 15
Income: £91,500 (2012-13)

Charity Retail Association

356 Holloway Road, London N7 6PA
T: 020 7697 4080
Helpline: 020 7697 4252
E: liam@charityretail.org.uk
www.charityretail.org.uk
Chief Executive : Warren Alexander
Aims to: monitor policy and legislative changes affecting charity retailing and lobby governments to achieve and maintain a supportive regulatory environment; promote charity retailing to public and policy makers including its reuse/recycling/sustainability contributions; respond to developments in charity retailing and the needs of members through provision of services and activities; be a major source of expertise and information on issues affecting the sector; promote good practice, efficiency and self-regulation through sharing of information; work closely with organisations to support the sector.
Employees: 8

Chartered Institute of Environmental Health

Chadwick Court, 15 Hatfields, London SE1 8DJ
T: 020 7928 6006
E: membership@cieh.org
www.cieh.org
The Institute maintains, enhances and promotes improvements in public and environmental health.

Chartered Institute of Housing

Octavia House, Westwood Way, Coventry CV4 8JP
T: 024 7685 1700
E: louise.fisher@cih.org
www.cih.org
Chief Executive: Grainia Long
The Chartered Institute of Housing is the independent voice for housing and the home of professional standards. Our goal is simple we want to provide everyone involved in housing with the advice, support and knowledge they need to be brilliant.

Chartered Institute of Library and Information Professionals

7 Ridgmount Street, London WC1E 7AE
T: 020 7255 0500
F: 020 7255 0501
E: memberservices@cilip.org.uk
www.cilip.org.uk
CILIP works to enable its members to achieve and maintain the highest professional standards and encourages and supports them in delivery and promotion of high-quality library and information services responsive to the needs of users.
Employees: 45
Regional offices: 2

Chartered Institute of Taxation

First Floor, Artillery House, 11-19 Artillery Row, London SW1P 1RT
T: 020 7340 0550
E: info@ciot.org.uk
www.tax.org.uk
Head of Finance: Stephen Hines
Employees: 56
Volunteers: 140

Chartered Institution of Highways and Transportation

119 Britannia Walk, London N1 7JE
T: 020 7336 1555
E: daniel.isichei@ciht.org.uk
www.ciht.org.uk
Chief Executive: Sue Percy
CIHT, founded in 1930, has over 12,000 members concerned with the design, construction, maintenance and operation of transport systems and infrastructure across all transport modes in both the public and private sectors. CIHT promotes excellence in transport systems and infrastructure.
Employees: 20
Volunteers: 250
Income: £2,000,000 (2013-14)

Chartered Quality Institute

2nd Floor North, Chancery Exchange, 10 Furnival Street, London EC4A 1AB
T: 020 7245 6722
E: sreeve@thecqi.org
www.thecqi.org
Chief Executive: Simon Feary
The Chartered Quality Institute is the chartered body for quality management professionals. Established in 1919, we gained a Royal Charter in 2006 and became the CQI shortly afterwards. The philosophy that came with the new name was simple through innovation and care we create quality'. This is something that we now base all our activity on and will continue to do so.
Employees: 50
Volunteers: 300

Chaseley Trust

South Cliff, Eastbourne, East Sussex BN20 7JH
T: 01323 744200
F: 01323 744208
E: info@chaseleytrust.org
www.chaseley.org.uk
Chief Executive: Sue Wyatt
The Chaseley Trust operates two nursing care homes in Eastbourne, providing residential, respite and day care for people with spinal injury, acquired brain injury, a wide range of neurological conditions and other severe physical disabilities. It also has a multidisciplinary therapy team experienced in assessments, treatment, rehabilitation and bespoke splinting.
Employees: 136
Volunteers: 45

Child Accident Prevention Trust

Canterbury Court (1.09), 13 Brixton Rod, London SW9 6DE
T: 020 7608 3828
F: 020 7608 3674
E: safe@capt.org.uk
www.capt.org.uk
Chief Executive: Katrina Phillips
The Trust encourages investigation and research into accidents in childhood, examining their pattern, causes, relationship to child development, social and environmental context and methods of prevention; promotes a better understanding of the importance of a child's need for a safe but stimulating environment; spreads information about the incidence and nature of childhood accidents and their prevention.
Employees: 9

Child Bereavement UK

Claire Charity Centre, Wycombe Road, Saunderton, Buckinghamshire HP14 4BF
T: 01494 568900
Helpline: 0800 028 8840
F: 01494 568920
E: support@childbereavementuk.org
www.childbereavementuk.org
Chief Executive: Ann Chalmers
Child Bereavement UK supports families and educates professionals both when a baby or child of any age dies or is dying, or when a child is facing bereavement. Every year we deliver training across a breadth of issues to

around 6,000 professionals at the frontline of bereavement support.
Employees: 38
Volunteers: 50+

Child Brain Injury Trust

Unit 1, The Great Barn,
Baynards Green Farm, Bicester,
Oxfordshire OX27 7SG
T: 01869 341075
Helpline: 0303 303 2248
E: info@cbituk.org
www.childbraininjurytrust.org.uk
Chief Executive: Lisa Turan
The Child Brain Injury Trust is a UK-wide charity offering support to anyone affected by childhood brain injury that has happened after birth. Acquired brain injury isn't something families prepare for. The Child Brain Injury Trust responds to the needs of these families by providing child and family support, training, information and awareness raising.
Employees: 19
Volunteers: 5
Regional offices: 6

Child Death Helpline

York House, 37 Queen Square,
London WC1N 3BH
T: 0800 282986
Helpline: 0808 800 6019
F: 020 7813 8516
E: rachel.cooke@gosh.nhs.uk.org
www.childdeathhelpline.org.uk
The Child Death Helpline aims to provide a quality freephone service to anyone affected by the death of a child of any age, from pre-birth to adult, under any circumstances, however recently or long ago. It is a listening service that offers emotional support to all those affected by the death of a child.
Volunteers: 50

Child Growth Foundation

2 Mayfield Avenue, London W4 1PW
T: 020 8912 0720
E: ros.chaplin@childgrowthfoundation.org
www.childgrowthfoundation.org
Honorary Chairman: Tam Fry
The Foundation offers support to anybody who is concerned about the growth of a child. It aims to promote a wider understanding of the importance of monitoring growth from birth by running training sessions and publishing booklets on growth disorders. It also funds research into treatments for conditions as yet untreatable. It is the umbrella organisation for growth hormone insufficiency, Turner syndrome, IUGR/Russell Silver, bone dysplasia, Sotos and premature sexual maturation patient/parent support groups.
Employees: 5

Child Migrants Trust

124 Musters Road, West Bridgford,
Nottingham, Nottinghamshire NG2 7PW
T: 0115 982 2811
F: 0115 981 7168
E: enquiries@childmigrantstrust.com
www.childmigrantstrust.com
CMT provides a professional social work, counselling, family research and advisory service for former child migrants and their families. The Trust is an international agency that enables former child migrants to reclaim their personal identity and reunite with members of their families.
Employees: 9
Regional offices: 1

Child Poverty Action Group

94 White Lion Street, London N1 9PF
T: 020 7837 7979
F: 020 7837 6414
E: info@cpag.org.uk
www.cpag.org.uk
Chief Executive: Alison Garnham
Promotes action for the relief, directly or indirectly, of poverty among children and families with children. We get a better life for low-income families through campaigning and lobbying, and ensure they get good advice with our welfare rights work, publications and training.
Employees: 35
Regional offices: 2
Income: £2,820,000 (2012-13)

Child Soldiers International

4th Floor, 9 Marshalsea Road, Borough,
London SE1 1EP
T: 020 7367 4110
F: 020 7367 4129
E: info@child-soldiers.org
www.child-soldiers.org
Child Soldiers International is an international human rights research and advocacy organisation. We seek to end the military recruitment and the use in hostilities, in any capacity, of any person under the age of 18 by state armed forces or non-state armed groups. We advocate for the release of unlawfully recruited children, promote their successful reintegration into civilian life, and call for accountability for those who unlawfully recruit or use them.
Employees: 8
Income: £675,000 (2013-14)

Childhood Eye Cancer Trust

The Royal London Hospital,
Whitechapel Road, London E1 1BB
T: 020 7377 5578
F: 020 7377 0740
E: info@chect.org.uk
www.chect.org.uk
Chief Executive: Patrick Tonks
The Childhood Eye Cancer Trust is a UK-wide charity for families and individuals affected by retinoblastoma. Our aims are to provide information and support to individuals and families affected by retinoblastoma; to raise awareness of retinoblastoma; to raise funds for research; to influence those bodies responsible for healthcare delivery in the UK; to ensure retinoblastoma patients get the best possible quality of care.
Employees: 9
Volunteers: 20

ChildLine

45 Folgate Street, London E1 6GL
T: 020 7650 3200
F: 020 7650 3201
E: help@nspcc.org.uk
www.childline.org.uk
ChildLine is the UK's free, 24-hour helpline for children and young people. Trained volunteer counsellors provide comfort, advice and protection to the children who call and refer children in danger to appropriate helping agencies. ChildLine also works to bring to the attention of the public and of government issues affecting children's welfare and rights.
Employees: 246
Volunteers: 1000
Regional offices: 11

Childlink

10 Lion Yard, Tremadoc Road,
London SW4 7NQ
T: 020 7501 1700
F: 020 7498 1791
E: enquiries@adoptchildlink.org.uk
www.adoptchildlink.org.uk
Chief Executive: Caroline Hesslegrave
Recruitment, preparation, assessment and approval of adopters.
Employees: 20

Childnet International

Studio 14, Brockley Cross Business Centre, 96 Endwell Road, London SE4 2PD
T: 020 7639 6967
F: 020 7639 7027
E: info@childnet.com
www.childnet.com
Chief Executive Officer: Will Gardner
Childnet International is a registered charity, established in 1995, with the aim of helping to help make the internet a great and safe place for children, both in the UK and on a global level. For the past 20 years, Childnet has sought to promote the positive use of technology, by highlighting the creative and beneficial things that children are doing with new technology, as well as responding to the potential risks.
Employees: 10

Children and Families Across Borders (Formerly ISS UK)

Unit 1.03 Canterbury Court, 1-3 Brixton Road, London SW9 6DE
T: 020 7735 8941
F: 020 7582 0696
E: laura.parker@cfab.org.uk
www.cfab.org.uk
CEO: Laura Parker
CFAB identifies and protects children who have been separated from family members due to conflict, trafficking, abduction, migration, divorce and asylum. It is the only charity specifically set up to help children, families and vulnerable people whose socio-welfare problems involve the UK and another country. We provide expert advice, guidance, skilled professional services, and emotional support and are guided by the UN Convention on the Rights of the Child.
Employees: 16

Children and Young People's Empowerment Project

11 Southey Hill, Southey, Sheffield, South Yorkshire S5 8BB
T: 0114 234 8846
E: lesley.pollard@chilypep.org.uk
www.chilypep.org.uk
Manager: Lesley Pollard
Chilypep works with children and young people to make the most of opportunities to influence and improve their lives and communities through empowerment and participation in a challenging, fun and action-packed way. We aim to increase children and young people's involvement in decision-making processes; increase their skills base through training and personal development; develop, deliver and promote models that remove barriers to participation and provide training to organisations and projects that promote good youth work practice.
Employees: 8
Volunteers: 50
Regional offices: 1
Income: £358,081 (2014-15)

Children England

Unit 30 Angel Gate, City Road, London EC1V 2PT
T: 020 7833 3319
E: nick.davies@childrenengland.org.uk
www.childrenengland.org.uk
Chief Executive: Kathy Evans
We are the leading membership organisation and collective voice for the CYPF voluntary sector. Our mission is to create a fairer world for children, young people and families by championing the voluntary organisations working on their behalf. We act as an independent, fearless voice for the values, contribution and expertise of the sector. We empower the sector through brokering strong relationships and active networks. We build the capacity of a thriving, sustainable sector.

Children of Africa

1 Beechwood, Cavendish Road, Bowdon, Altrincham, Cheshire WA14 2NH
T: 07974 161027
E: liezl.hesketh@btinternet.com
www.childrenofafrica.org/en
Trustee: Liezl Hesketh
We support orphaned children in South Africa suffering from or orphaned as a result of HIV/AIDS and advancement of education among children and young people attending schools, by the provision of financial support to meet the costs of progressing to higher education.

Children's Burns Trust

2 Grosvenor Gardens, London SW1W 0DH
T: 020 7881 0902
F: 020 7233 8200
E: info@cbtrust.org.uk
www.cbtrust.org.uk
The Trust offers support to specialist burns units and assistance with long-term rehabilitation of children suffering from burns. It provides education for children in burn prevention and activates public awareness of the severe problem of scalding.
Employees: 3
Volunteers: 25
Regional offices: 1

Children's Country Holidays Fund

Stafford House, 91 Keymer Road, Hassocks, West Sussex BN6 8QJ
T: 01273 847770
E: info@cchf-allaboutkids.org.uk
www.cchf-allaboutkids.org.uk
CCHF exists to provide holidays for children in need and their families from London.
Employees: 8
Volunteers: 600

Children's Family Trust

MKA House, 46 St Andrews Road, Droitwich, Worcestershire WR9 8DN
T: 01905 798299
F: 01905 798230
E: shelley.candlin@thecft.org.uk
www.thecft.org.uk
Chief Executive: Thomas Gormley
The charity's aims are the relief of children and young people in need, in particular those in the care of, or accommodated by, a local authority.
Employees: 19
Regional offices: 2

Children's Heart Federation

Level 1, 24 Great Eastern Street, London EC2A 3NW
T: 020 7422 0630
Helpline: 0808 808 5000
F: 020 7247 2087
E: info@chfed.org.uk
www.chfed.org.uk
Chief Executive: Anne Keatley-Clarke
The Federation works to relieve children suffering from heart conditions and supports their families. It advances public education about the problems experienced by children with heart conditions and their families.
Employees: 5
Volunteers: 30

Children's Hope Foundation

15 Palmer Place, London N7 8DH
T: 020 7700 6855
Helpline: 020 7700 6919
F: 020 7700 4432
E: tomdoran@childrenshopefoundation.org.uk
www.childrenshopefoundation.org.uk
Chief Executive: Tom Doran
Our aim is to improve the quality of life for children affected by illness, disability or indeed poverty, by responding to their needs in a practical way, based on the recommendation of their health and/or education professionals, to ensure they have

the opportunity to fulfil their dreams and achieve their full potential.
Employees: 5
Volunteers: 10
Regional offices: 2

Children's Links

Holland House, Horncastle College, Mareham Road, Horncastle, Lincolnshire LN9 6BW
T: 01507 528300
F: 01507 528301
E: info@childrenslinks.org.uk
www.childrenslinks.org.uk
Children's Links promotes the care and education of children and provides facilities for recreation and leisure time for children in the interests of social welfare.
Employees: 61
Volunteers: 8
Regional offices: 2

Children's Society

c/o The Children's Society, Edward Rudolf House, Margery Street, London WC1X 0JL
E: venisha.douse@childrenssociety.org.uk
www.childrenssociety.org.uk
One of the UK's leading children's charities, for more than 120 years the Church of England Children's Society has worked with and for children, helping them face life's toughest challenges. Whoever they are and whatever their issues, we believe that no child is beyond hope, love or understanding, and we work with those most in need to help them face the future with confidence.
Employees: 1050
Regional offices: 3

Children's Trust

Tadworth Court, Tadworth, Surrey KT20 5RU
T: 01737 365000
F: 01737 365001
E: enquiries@thechildrenstrust.org.uk
www.thechildrenstrust.org.uk
The Children's Trust was established for the care, treatment, rehabilitation and education of children with physical disabilities, learning disabilities and complex medical needs, including life-limiting or life-threatening conditions and neurological damage acquired through accident or other causes; for the support of families and other carers involved; and for the prevention of such disabilities and disorders.
Employees: 380
Volunteers: 330

Chinese in Britain Forum

239 Old Street, London EC1V 9EY
T: 020 7553 7180
F: 020 7251 3130
E: enquiries@cibf.co.uk
www.cibf.co.uk
Provides support and access to resources and services for the Chinese communities organisations in Britain.
Employees: 6
Volunteers: 18
Regional offices: 1

Chinese Information and Advice Centre

Lower Ground Floor, London Chinatown Market, 71-73 Charing Cross Road, London WC2H 0ND
T: 020 7437 0112
F: 020 7734 1039
E: info@ciac.co.uk
www.ciac.co.uk
Chair: Mr Edmond Yeo, JP
Since founded in 1982, the Chinese Information and Advice Centre (CIAC) has been a leading Chinese charity providing immigration legal services, women's support, refugee and asylum support, benefits advice and information development. We aim to help the disadvantaged Chinese individuals and groups with compassion, care and professionalism and have successfully assisted a great number of service users in getting immigration status and welfare benefits as well as supporting women domestic violence victims.
Employees: 3
Volunteers: 20
Regional offices: 1

Chinese Mental Health Association

2/F Zenith House, 155 Curtain Road, London EC2A 3QY
T: 020 7613 1008
F: 020 7739 6577
E: info@cmha.org.uk
www.cmha.org.uk
The charity exists to promote the preservation and the safeguarding of mental health and the relief of persons who are of Chinese origin suffering from mental illness or distress.
Employees: 8

Chiropractic Patients' Association

Twingley Centre, The Portway, Winterbourne Gunner, Salisbury, Wiltshire SP4 6JL
T: 01980 610218
F: 01980 611947
E: backs@chiropatients.org.uk
www.chiropatients.org.uk
Chairman: Maureen Atkinson
The association aims to raise public awareness and hasten acceptance of chiropractic by the health professions and health service. It promotes research and chiropractic treatment for the benefit of patients, encourages the adoption of chiropractic as a professional career and assists in the education of chiropractic students.
Volunteers: 7

Choices 4 All

The 21 Building, 21 Pinner Road, Harrow, Middlesex, Harrow HA1 4ES
T: 020 8424 0848
E: rachel@choices4all.co.uk
www.choices4all.co.uk
Choices 4 All: Rachel Chronnell
Choices 4 All is a specialist non-profit learning provider which encourages individuals with learning difficulties and disabilities to progress towards independence. We believe in people's abilities and in creating new and fresh ways of providing opportunities to help overcome barriers. Learners are given the tools in a person-centered environment to gain confidence for their future and make their own Choices.
Employees: 15
Volunteers: 2
Income: £350,000 (2012-13)

Christian Aid

35-41 Lower Marsh, Waterloo SE1 7RL
T: 020 7523 2000
E: mraffay@christian-aid.org
www.christian-aid.org.uk
Chief Executive : Loretta Minghella
Christian Aid is supported and sustained by the churches of the UK and Ireland. Our essential purpose is to expose the scandal of poverty, contribute to its eradication and challenge structures and systems that keep people poor and marginalised.

Christian Camping International

World Vision House, Opal Drive, Fox Milne, Milton Keynes, Buckinghamshire MK15 0DH
T: 01908 477951
E: office@cci.org.uk
www.cci.org.uk
Executive Director: Keith Hagon
CCI is an association of Christian residential providers across the UK. Members offer a wide range of conference and meeting facilities to meet all budgets. The automated online venue finding service is a great place to find your conference venue.
Employees: 4
Volunteers: 20
Income: £90,000 (2013-14)

Christian Education

1020 Bristol Road, Selly Oak, Birmingham B29 6LB
T: 0121 472 4242
E: diane.horton@christianeducation.org.uk
www.christianeducation.org.uk
Promotes human development within a context of faith, aspiring to an education system that offers full opportunities for spiritual and moral development.

Christian Family Concern

Wallis House, 42 South Park Hill Road, South Croydon CR2 7YB
T: 020 8688 0251
F: 020 8686 7114
E: info@christianfamilyconcern.org.uk
www.christianfamilyconcern.org.uk
Operations Manager: Mari Walters
The charity's main purpose is the care of children, parents and young mothers in need of support, through our nursery, out-of-school clubs and bed-sit scheme.
Employees: 35
Volunteers: 8

Chronic Granulomatous Disorder Society

199A Victoria Street, London SW1E 5NE
T: 0800 987 8988
E: hello@cgdsociety.org
www.cgdsociety.org
Chief Executive: Caroline Harding
The CGD Society is the leading source of support for individuals and families affected by chronic granulomatous disorder in the UK. The charity provides comprehensive information on CGD and associated issues; offers direct support to patients and affected families; funds nursing services and patient and family events; supports research to improve treatments and find a cure.
Volunteers: 10

CHS Alliance

Resource Centre, 356 Holloway Road, London N7 6PA
T: 020 3137 3590
E: info@chsalliance.org
www.chsalliance.org
The Alliance supports its organisational members to advance their performance, credibility and reputation, both operationally and among the international community and donors, through strengthening quality, accountability and people management in their activities and management practices.
Employees: 20

Church Action on Poverty

Dale House, 35 Dale Street, Manchester M1 2HF
T: 0161 236 9321
E: info@church-poverty.org.uk
www.church-poverty.org.uk
Director: Niall Cooper
CAP works to achieve lasting solutions to problems of poverty, debt and exclusion amongst communities across the UK. We advocate for local and national policies that enable people in poverty to achieve more sustainable livelihoods; enable people with first-hand experience of poverty to speak out and campaign for lasting changes in their own communities and nationally; and equip churches to work with others to achieve real and long-term change.
Employees: 10
Volunteers: 2
Regional offices: 1

Church Army

Wilson Carlile Centre, 50 Cavendish Street, Sheffield, South Yorkshire S3 7RZ
T: 0300 123 2113
E: info@churcharmy.org.uk
www.churcharmy.org.uk
Chief Executive: Mark Russell
Church Army is a charity affiliated with the Church of England which is committed to sharing the Christian faith through words and action with those in need across the United Kingdom and Ireland. To find out more about its work visit www.churcharmy.org.uk

Church Housing Trust

PO Box 50296, London, County Londonderry EC1P 1WF
T: 020 7269 1630
E: info@churchhousingtrust.org.uk
www.churchhousingtrust.org.uk
The Trust raises funds to support projects to benefit homeless people.

Church of England: Archbishops' Council

Archbishops' Council, Church House, 27 Great Smith Street SW1P 3AZ
T: 020 7898 1000
E: william.nye@churchofengland.org
www.churchofengland.org
Secretary-General: William Nye
The Archbishops' Council is a body charged with the responsibility at national level to coordinate, promote, aid and further the work and mission of the Church of England.
Employees: 252

Church Pastoral Aid Society

Sovereign Court One (Unit 3), Sir William Lyons Road, University of Warwick Science Park, Coventry CV4 7EZ
T: 0300 123 0780
E: info@cpas.org.uk
www.cpas.org.uk
General Director: John Dunnett
The Church Pastoral Aid Society exists to inspire and enable churches to reach everyone in their communities with the good news of Jesus Christ.
Employees: 22
Regional offices: 1

Church Urban Fund

Church House, Great Smith Street, London SW1P 3NZ
T: 020 7898 1647
F: 020 7898 1601
E: esther.edmund-allen@gov.org.uk
www.cuf.org.uk
Promotes any charitable purpose in urban areas within the provinces of Canterbury and York that are in need of spiritual and material assistance by reason of social and economic changes with a view to reinforcing the work of the Church of England among the people of those areas.
Employees: 16
Regional offices: 43

Churches Child Protection Advisory Service

PO Box 133, Swanley, Kent BR8 7UQ
T: 0845 120 4550
F: 0845 120 4552
E: info@ccpas.co.uk
www.ccpas.co.uk
Chief Executive Officer: Simon Bass
CCPAS is a professional Christian-based safeguarding charity offering resources, training, advice and support in all areas of safeguarding children and vulnerable adults to churches, faith groups and organisations, and those with no religious affiliation. CCPAS offers a 24-hour helpline and is an umbrella body for the Criminal Records Bureau.
Employees: 24
Volunteers: 1
Regional offices: 1

Churches Community Work Alliance

St Chad's College, North Bailey, Durham DH1 3RH
T: 0191 334 3346
F: 0191 334 3371
E: uk@ccwa.org.uk
www.ccwa.org.uk
We initiate, support and encourage community development work in the life of the churches; we help the churches to reflect theologically on their response to social and economic change; we promote good community development work practice; and we provide help and guidance for community development work projects and we support practitioners.
Employees: 2
Volunteers: 20
Regional offices: 4

Churches Together in Britain and Ireland

39 Eccleston Square, London SW1V 1BX
E: info@ctbi.org.uk
www.ctbi.org.uk
General Secretary: Revd Bob Fyffe
To assist the many different Christian churches of Britain and Ireland to work together for the good of all people, deepening their fellowship with each other and, without losing their distinctive differences, to work towards a greater visible unity.
Employees: 7

Cicely Northcote Trust

Camelford House, 15th Floor, 87-89 Albert Embankment, London SE1 7TP
T: 020 7582 9996
E: cntrust@btconnect.com
www.cicelynorthcotetrust.org.uk
Chairman: Gary Loke
The Trust sets up projects that address gaps in the health and social services provided by statutory and voluntary organisations and, where possible, identifies ways of filling these gaps.
Employees: 1

Circles Network

Potford's Dam Farm, Coventry Road, Cawston, Rugby CV23 9JP
T: 01788 816671
F: 01788 816672
E: info@circlesnetwork.org.uk
www.circlesnetwork.org.uk
The ultimate aim of Circles Network is to build inclusive communities where everyone belongs and to demonstrate that people of all ages can be supported to live self-determined lives, regardless of their ability or difference.
Employees: 45
Volunteers: 30

Circles UK

E: stephen.hanvey@circles-uk.org.uk

Circulation Foundation

Leeds Vascular Institute, Leeds General Infirmary, Great George Street, Leeds LS1 3EX
T: 0113 392 3190
E: bvf@care4free.net
www.bvf.org.uk
The Foundation encourages, promotes and assists research into the treatment of vascular disease and its related problems.

Citizen's Income Trust

286 Ivydale Road, London SE15 3DF
T: 020 7635 7916
E: info@citizensincome.org
www.citizensincome.org
Director: Malcolm Torry
The Citizen's Income Trust promotes debate on the feasibility and desirability of a citizen's income: an automatic, unconditional and non-withdrawable income for every citizen.
Volunteers: 15
Income: £4,303 (2014-15)

Citizens Advice

Myddelton House, London N1 9LZ
T: 020 7833 7118
F: 020 7837 0279
E: alistair.gibbons@citizensadvice.org.uk
www.citizensadvice.org.uk
Citizens Advice helps people resolve their money, legal and other problems by providing information and advice, and by influencing policy makers.
Employees: 5000
Volunteers: 20000
Regional offices: 2000

Citizens Online

1 Town Square, West Swindon Centre, Tewkesbury Way, Swindon, Wiltshire SN5 7DL
T: 01793 882800
F: 01793 882801
E: info@citizensonline.org.uk
www.citizensonline.org.uk
Citizens Online's initial remit was to explore the impact of the internet and IT on today's society. From these findings we campaign and work with other not-for-profit organisations to ensure all citizens are given the opportunity to experience the internet and IT, especially those citizens which could be judged as socially excluded.
Employees: 17
Volunteers: 5
Regional offices: 7

Citizens UK

112 Cavell Street, London E1 2JA
T: 020 7375 1658
F: 020 7375 2034
E: colin.weatherup@cof.org.uk
www.citizensuk.org
The Citizen Organising Foundation (COF) has built a large, broad-based and diverse alliance of organisations, such as faith congregations, trade unions, schools and local community associations. Our experience, as community organisers, has demonstrated that the connectivity between individuals, family, community and society is extremely fragile and that these alliances are vital for a healthy democracy and vibrant civil society.
Employees: 7
Regional offices: 2

Citizenship Foundation

50 Featherstone Street, London EC1Y 8RT
T: 020 7566 4141
F: 020 7566 4131
E: info@citizenshipfoundation.org.uk
www.citizenshipfoundation.org.uk
CEO: Andy Thornton
The Citizenship Foundation inspires young people to take part in society as equal members. We help them to understand the

law, politics and democratic life. We promote participation, we help teachers to teach citizenship and we work with young people on issues that concern them. Our work involves:
Shaping schools - Helping teachers to help young people take responsible action in their lives and communities and shape the world around them;
Inspiring action - Motivating young people to shape the world for everyone's benefit;
Influencing policy - Helping school leaders, policy-makers and community leaders to understand the importance of citizenship education.
We want society to be fairer, more inclusive and more cohesive. We want a democracy in which everyone has the knowledge, skills, and confidence to take part and drive change as effective citizens, both as individuals and as communities.
Employees: 25
Volunteers: numerous
Regional offices: 1

City Bridge Trust

City of London, PO Box 270, Guildhall, London EC2P 2EJ
T: 020 7332 3710
F: 020 7332 3127
E: citybridgetrust@cityoflondon.gov.uk
www.citybridgetrust.org.uk
Chief Grants Officer: David Farnsworth
City Bridge Trust, the City of London Corporation's charity, is the grant-making arm of Bridge House Estates. We aim to address disadvantage by supporting charitable activity across Greater London through quality grant-making and related activities within clearly defined priorities.
Employees: 16

City South Manchester

Turing House, Archway 5, Hulme, Manchester, Lancashire M15 5RL
T: 0161 227 1360
E: sarah.roberts@citysouthmanchester.co.uk
www.citysouthmanchester.co.uk
Placement and Volunteer Coordinator: Sarah Roberts
Our vision: By 2014 City South will be a strong, viable business focused on our customers, providing cost-effective services City South will grow in terms of the number of homes we own and manage, the range of products we offer, and the areas in which we work. We will be more than a landlord; providing supportive services and products to our customers that will help build and sustain neighbourhoods, households and our business.
Employees: 140
Volunteers: 20
Regional offices: 1

City Year UK

58-62 White Lion Street, London N1 9PP
T: 020 7014 2680
E: shaque@cityyear.org.uk
www.cityyear.org.uk
Chief Executive: Sophie Livingstone
City Year UK is a leading youth and education charity and a beacon for a volunteer service year. Its mission is to galvanise the talent, energy and idealism of young role models to help vulnerable children succeed in school.
Employees: 25
Volunteers: 150
Regional offices: 2
Income: £2,200,000 (2012-13)

Civic Trust

Essex Hall, London WC2R 3HU
T: 020 7539 7900
F: 020 7539 7901
E: info@civictrust.org.uk
www.civictrust.org.uk
Managing Director: Peter Bembridge
An independent and national organisation. It is the umbrella body for over 750 civic societies, representing over 250,000 individuals committed to improving and caring for places where people live and work. It is the leading UK charity dedicated to bringing vitality, sustainability and high-quality design to the built environment. The Trust works with people to promote thriving towns and villages, developing dynamic partnerships between communities, government and business to deliver regeneration and local improvement.
Employees: 35
Volunteers: 5
Regional offices: 1

Civil Service Retirement Fellowship

Suite 2, 80a Blackheath Road SE10 8DA
T: 020 8691 7411
E: enquiries@csrf.org.uk
www.csrf.org.uk
Chief Executive: Jean Cooper
The CSRF provides social welfare assistance to retired civil servants, their widows/widowers and dependants to ensure they do not become isolated in retirement. We have a UK-wide network of social groups, national befriending schemes and provide advice, signposting and information to any beneficiary needing help.
Employees: 6
Volunteers: 1000

CIWEM

15 John Street, London WC1N 2EB
T: 020 7831 3110
F: 020 7405 4967
E: reception@ciwem.org
www.ciwem.org.uk
The Chartered Institution of Water and Environmental Management (CIWEM) is the leading professional and examining body for scientists, engineers, other environmental professionals, students and those committed to the sustainable management and development of water and the environment.
Employees: 17
Volunteers: 180
Regional offices: 17

Claire House Hospice For Children

Clatterbridge Road, Bebington, Wirral, Merseyside CH63 4JD
T: 0151 343 0883
F: 0151 334 5493
E: keelan.early@claire-house.org.uk
www.claire-house.org.uk
CEO: David Pastor
The principal aim of Claire House is to provide specialist palliative and end-of-life care for children and young people across the North West (Merseyside, Cheshire, North Wales and the Isle of Man) who are living with a life-threatening or life-limiting illness, and to provide support for their families.

CLCGB - Church Lads' and Church Girls' Brigade

2 Barnsley Road, Wath-upon-Dearne, Rotherham, South Yorkshire S63 6PY
T: 01709 876535
F: 01709 878089
E: audreysimm@clcgb.org.uk
www.clcgb.org.uk
Chief Executive: Audrey Simm
The Church Lads' and Church Girls' Brigade (CLCGB) is the Anglican Churches own uniformed youth organisation and was established in 1891. The CLCGB traditionally works in inner-city areas where there is little or no positive youth provision but more recently within highly diverse communities, with significant ethnic, cultural and faith diversity. We provide a safe environment, for

youth to engage in positive, structured activities and self development programmes.
Employees: 9
Volunteers: 3500

Clean Break

2 Patshull Road, London NW5 2LB
T: 020 7482 8600
F: 020 7482 8611
E: general@cleanbreak.org.uk
www.cleanbreak.org.uk
Clean Break uses theatre for personal and political change, working with women whose lives have been affected by the criminal justice system.
Employees: 15
Volunteers: 4

Climb

Climb Building, 176 Nantwich Road, Crewe, Cheshire CW2 6BG
T: 0845 241 2173
Helpline: 0800 652 3181
F: 0845 241 2174
E: pam@climb.org.uk
www.climb.org.uk
Interim Executive Director: Pam Davies
The only charity to provide information on over 700 inherited metabolic diseases. CLIMB is also the National Information Centre for Metabolic Disease. Supporting everyone linked with a metabolic disease.
Employees: 5
Volunteers: 40

Clinks

Tavis House, 1-6 Tavistock Square, London WC1H 9NA
T: 020 7383 0966
E: info@clinks.org
www.clinks.org
Director: Clive Martin
Clinks supports the voluntary and community sector working with offenders in England and Wales. Our aim is to ensure the sector and all those with whom it works, are informed and engaged in order to transform the lives of offenders and their communities.
Employees: 20
Regional offices: 1

Clothing Solutions for Disabled People

Unit 13, Inspire Bradford Business Park, Newlands Way, Bradford, West Yorkshire BD10 0JE
T: 01274 292291
E: enquiries@clothingsolutions.org.uk
www.clothingsolutions.org.uk
Manager: Sandra Hunt
Clothing Solutions for Disabled People is a registered charity providing a unique clothing service for learning and physically disabled children, adults and elderly people. The service offers solutions to dressing and undressing difficulties by offering a made-to-measure garment alteration/adaptation and dressmaking facility. We also provide an outreach service where we visit the person for consultation, as well as an information service about specialist clothing. We make beanbags with unique breathable and waterproof lining.
Employees: 4
Volunteers: 2
Regional offices: 1
Income: £79,436 (2013-14)

CMT United Kingdom

PO Box 5089, Christchurch, Dorset BH23 7ZX
T: 01202 432048
Helpline: 0800 652 6316
E: secretary@cmt.org.uk
www.cmt.org.uk
Chair: Lisa Welsh
We are the national support group for people affected by Charcot-Marie-Tooth disease, the most common inherited neurological condition in the UK, affecting approximately 25,000 individuals. We provide a service of support, advice and information, with publications, a magazine and an annual conference.
Employees: 1
Volunteers: 20
Regional offices: 8

Co-operatives UK

Holyoake House, Hanover Street, Manchester M60 0AS
T: 0161 246 2900
F: 0161 831 7684
E: linda.barlow@uk.coop
www.uk.coop
Secretary General: Ed Mayo
Represents and promotes the interests of the co-operative sector, and develops and extends the co-operative sector through provision of a range of targeted services to members.
Employees: 28
Regional offices: 1

Coeliac UK

Suites AD, Octagon Court, High Wycombe, Buckinghamshire HP11 2HS
T: 01494 437278
Helpline: 0870 444 8804
F: 01494 474349
E: generalenquiries@coeliac.org.uk
www.coeliac.org.uk
Chief Executive: Sarah Sleet
Coeliac UK is a national charity, providing support and advice to those living with coeliac disease and dermatitis herpetiformis. The charity also campaigns for awareness of the disease and promotes the need for early diagnosis. Advice is given by a team of dietetic professionals and ranges from the gluten-free diet to symptoms of the disease and related health issues.
Employees: 20
Volunteers: 1000
Regional offices: 1

Collage Arts

Chocolate Factory 2, 4 Coburg Road, Wood Green, London N22 6UJ
T: 020 8365 7500
F: 020 8365 8686
E: info@collage-arts.org
www.collage-arts.org
Executive Director: Manoj Ambasna
A leading arts development, training and creative regeneration organisation based in Haringey's Cultural Quarter and established in 1985. For over 20 years the organisation has created opportunities for greater access and participation in the arts and creative industries for the whole community.
Employees: 15
Volunteers: 10

College of Sexual and Relationship Therapists (COSRT)

PO Box 13686, London SW20 9ZH
T: 020 8543 2707 (also fax)
E: info@cosrt.org.uk
www.cosrt.org.uk
National specialist charity for sexual and relationship therapy.
Employees: 2

College of St Barnabas

Blackberry Lane, Lingfield,
Surrey RH7 6NJ
T: 01342 870260
F: 01342 871672
E: bursar@collegeofstbarnabas.com
www.st-barnabas.org.uk
Bursar: Paul Wilkin
A retirement home providing sheltered flats and nursing rooms for those who are Clergy or who have worked with a Bishop's license for the Church of England or recognised Anglican missionary bodies overseas. The spouses, widows and widowers of the above along with those in communion with the Church of England.
Employees: 80
Volunteers: 5
Income: £1,970,640 (2013-14)

Comic Relief

5th Floor, Camelford House,
87-89 Albert Embankment,
London SE1 7TP
T: 020 7820 5555
F: 020 7820 5500
E: info@comicrelief.com
www.comicrelief.com
Comic Relief tackles poverty and social injustice by helping disadvantaged people in the UK and Africa.
Employees: 90
Volunteers: 20

Common Ground

Gold Hill House, 21 High Street,
Shaftesbury, Dorset SP7 8JE
T: 01747 850820
E: adrian@commonground.org.uk
www.commonground.org.uk
Common Ground helps people explore, celebrate and take action for their place by emphasising the value of our everyday surroundings and the positive investment people can make in their own localities. It forges links between the arts and the conservation of nature and our cultural landscapes.

Common Purpose

Discovery House, London EC1Y 8QE
T: 020 7608 8134
E: enquiries@commonpurpose.org.uk
www.commonpurpose.org.uk
For a democracy to be strong, it needs an active civil society in which citizens are both informed and connected. Common Purpose's vision is that we can improve the way society works by increasing the number of informed and engaged individuals who are actively involved in the future of the areas in which they live and work.

Commonwealth Education Trust

New Zealand House, 80 Haymarket,
London SW1Y 4TE
T: 020 7024 9822
F: 020 7024 9833
E: jcurry@cet1886.org
www.cet1886.org
Chief Executive: Judy Curry
The Trust invests in primary and secondary education and the training and professional development of teachers in the Commonwealth, thereby enhancing the opportunities for children in the Commonwealth to develop the skills necessary to contribute to the economic and social development of their communities. CET works in partnership with educationalists to use financial and business skills to structure sustainable, scalable and transferrable projects based on applied research.

Commonwork Land Trust

Bore Place, Chiddingstone, Edenbridge,
Kent TN8 7AR
T: 01732 463255
F: 01732 740264
E: info@commonwork.org
www.commonwork.org
Director: Jacqueline Leach
Commonwork's vision is of a fairer world in which people work together and with nature, recognising that all are interconnected. We work towards this vision in practical ways, through our study centre and education programmes on an organic farm in Kent. We offer: hands-on activities in food, farming, sustainable development, global citizenship, climate change, renewable energy; CPD for teachers and school leaders; and share the lessons from our practical work locally, regionally and nationally.
Employees: 26
Volunteers: 26
Regional offices: 1

Community Accountancy Self-Help

E: tom@cash-online.org.uk

Community Action Network

E: c.mott@can-online.org.uk
Head of CAN Mezzanine Operations: Peter Murray

Community Action Project

The CAP Centre, Windmill Lane,
Smethwick, West Midlands B66 3LX
T: 0121 565 3273
F: 0121 565 0471
E: cap.smeth@talk21.com
The project fosters and supports the needs and aspirations of the African Caribbean community primarily but not exclusively, as CAP adopts an open-door policy whereby anyone is welcome to utilise our services.
Employees: 9
Volunteers: 10

Community Action Wyre Forest

Suite B, 3rd floor, 26 Church Street,
Kidderminster, Worcs DY10 2AR
T: 01562 67008
Helpline: 01384 671060
E: cvs@communityactionwf.org.uk
www.communityactionwf.org.uk
Chief Officer: Irene Walker
Supporting the community and voluntary sector across Worcestershire. Delivering front line services supporting long term unemployed, people with mental ill health and other barriers to well being. Developing micro business and social enterprise
Employees: 6
Volunteers: 12
Regional offices: 2
Income: £110,000 (2012-13)

Community Development Finance Association (cdfa)

Hatton Square Business Centre,
16 Baldwin Gardens, London EC1N 7RJ
T: 020 7430 0222
F: 020 7430 2112
E: info@cdfa.org.uk
www.responsiblefinance.org.uk
Chief Executive: Bernie Morgan
The Community Development Finance Association (cdfa) is the trade association for UK Community Development Finance Institutions (CDFIs). CDFIs are independent organisations that provide finance and support to people who have had trouble getting such services from the usual sources, such as banks and building societies. CDFIs typically work to benefit businesses and individuals in disadvantaged communities.
Employees: 12
Regional offices: 3

Community Development Foundation

Unit 5, Angel Gate, 320-326 City Road,
London EC1V 2PT
T: 020 7833 1772
E: diane.williams@cdf.org.uk
www.cdf.org.uk
Chief Executive: Alison Seabrooke
CDF is the leading national organisation in community development and engagement. We are passionate about empowering communities where local people are at the centre of change. We have unique expertise in working alongside local communities to strengthen local voices, improve people's lives

and create better places to live. Our purpose is to bring together resources, insight and people so that communities can thrive.
Employees: 22
Income: £567,904 (2012-13)

Community First

Wyndhams, St Josephs Place, Devizes, Wiltshire SN10 1DD
T: 01380 722475
F: 01380 728476
E: reception@communityfirst.org.uk
www.communityfirst.org.uk
Chief Executive: Philippa Read
Community First is Wiltshire's Rural Community Council, a charity that works at the forefront of community development to help improve the quality of life and economic well being of people and local communities throughout Wiltshire and Swindon. We have been a dependable source of support to communities in Wiltshire and Swindon since 1965. Our extensive networks involve parish and town councils, village and community hall committees, youth clubs, community transport and community leaders across the county.
Employees: 65
Volunteers: 2
Regional offices: 1
Income: £2,600,000 (2012-13)

Community Foundation for Lancashire & Merseyside

Third Floor, Stanley Building, 43 Hanover Street, Merseyside L1 3DN
T: 0151 232 2444
E: james.mcmahon@cflm.email
www.cfmerseyside.org.uk
Community Foundations for Lancashire & M: Cathy Elliott
As an independent registered charity, we are part of a national movement of community foundations that undertakes strategic grant making, facilitates philanthropy and contributes to achieving positive social change in our local communities.

Community Housing and Therapy

24/5-6 Coda Studios, 189 Munster Road, London SW6 6AW
T: 020 7381 5888
F: 020 7610 0608
E: co@cht.org.uk
www.cht.org.uk
Chief Executive: John Gale
Community Housing and Therapy is a charity that runs residential and non-residential services for those with severe and enduring mental ill health, and ex-service personnel who are homeless and have psychological difficulties. The charity's objectives are to help people experiencing mental ill-health and emotional distress by providing residential accommodation with psychotherapy, care and support. Its therapeutic and rehabilitative programme is designed to create a structure that will lead to recovery, employment and eventual independence.
Employees: 43
Volunteers: 8
Regional offices: 6

Community Hygiene Concern

22 Darin Court, Crownhill, Milton Keynes, Bucks MK8 0AD
T: 01908 561928
F: 01908 261501
E: bugbusters2k@yahoo.co.uk
www.chc.org
Manager: Frances Fry
Community Hygiene Concern offers advise on head lice.
Employees: 3
Regional offices: 1

Community Integrated Care

2 Old Market Court, Miners Way, Widnes, Cheshire WA8 7SP
T: 0151 422 5326
F: 0151 424 0299
E: information@c-i-c.co.uk
www.c-i-c.co.uk
CIC was founded to assist vulnerable people to have a life rather than an existence.
Employees: 3500

Community Links

105 Barking Road, London E16 4HQ
T: 020 7473 2270
E: athena.lamnisos@community-links.org
www.community-links.org
CEO: Athena Lamnisos
Leading social action charity based in east London working with the whole community to find new solutions to old problems. We focus on early action programmes that prevent problems. Our focus is on helping young people gain skills, getting adults into work, providing spaces for families to thrive and supporting entrepreneurs to develop. We have a national policy and campaigning programme which is driven by the learning and insights from our service delivery.
Employees: 300
Volunteers: 600
Income: £8,000,000 (2012-13)

Community Links Bromley

E: alisonn@communitylinksbromley.org.uk

Community Matters

London N1 9LL
T: 020 7837 7887
Helpline: 0845 847 4253
F: 020 7278 9253
E: liz.cleverly@communitymatters.org.uk
www.communitymatters.org.uk
Chief Executive: David Tyler
Community Matters supports organisations across the UK whose aim is to build stronger communities in which everyone is valued and can play their part. We are a membership body delivering services to organisations and representing their interests at a national level.
Employees: 20
Volunteers: 12

Community Media Association

The Workstation, 15 Paternoster Row, Sheffield S1 2BX
T: 0114 279 5219
Helpline: 0844 357 0442
E: info@commedia.org.uk
www.commedia.org.uk
Chair: Dom Chambers
The Community Media Association is the UK representative body for the community broadcasting sector and is committed to promoting access to the media for people and communities. We enable people to establish and develop community-based communications media promoting: social cohesion and inclusion; cultural and creative expression; social and economic regeneration; empowerment through giving communities a voice; media literacy; tackling the digital divide; inter-cultural and inter-generational dialogue; training and employment opportunities; and provide information and entertainment.
Regional offices: 1

Community Network

1B Waterlow Road, London N19 5NJ
T: 020 7923 5250
E: angela@community-network.org
www.communitynetworkprojects.org
Chief Executive: Angela Cairns
Community Network is a national charity combating loneliness and isolation by bringing people together in groups on the telephone and online, helping them to remain active & connected to others via peer support. We provide training to other organisations in facilitating groups on the phone. NB. Our teleconferencing service is now operated by The Phone Co-op. You can contact them on

020 3559 9000. Please tell them you have been referred by Community Network.
Employees: 5
Volunteers: 25
Income: £214,864 (2013-14)

Community of Congolese Refugees in Great Britain (CORECOG)

Stephen Laurence House,
90 Greengate Street, Plaistow,
London E13 0AS
T: 020 8548 4073
F: 020 8552 0473
E: wgpambu@aol.co.uk
www.corecog.org.uk
The Community of Congolese Refugees in Great Britain (CORECOG) is a charity registered in England and Wales since 1993. Created as a national charity for all groups in the UK, its headquarters is based in the London Borough of Newham, which has the largest population of Congolese in England.
Employees: 4
Volunteers: 3
Regional offices: 25

Community of Reconciliation and Fellowship

Prideaux House,
10 Church Crescent E9 7DL
T: 020 8986 6000
E: prideaux.house@btconnect.com
Director: Rev Gualter De Mello
The main aim of the fellowship is the improvement of conditions of life in the community, including the relief of poverty, distress and sickness, and the provision of facilities in the interest of social welfare.
Employees: 7
Volunteers: 38

Community Resilience

16th Floor Portland House,
Bressenden Place, London SW1E 5RS
T: 0300 999 2004
F: 0300 999 2005
E: contact-us@emergencyaid.org.uk
www.communityresilience.cc
CEO: David Cloake
A not-for-profit social enterprise dedicated to helping communities respond to, and recover from major emergencies.

Community Security Trust (CST)

Shield House, Harmony Way, Hendon,
London NW4 2BZ
T: 020 8457 9999
E: enquiries@cst.org.uk
www.cst.org.uk
Chief Executive: David Delew
CST advises on and provides security for the UK Jewish community, monitors levels of antisemitism, and represents the Jewish community on antisemitism, terrorism and security to Police, Government and the media. The Trust promotes good race relations between the Jewish community and other members of society by working towards the elimination of racism in the form of antisemitism.
Employees: 58
Volunteers: 1000

Community Transport

National Office, Office Suite E107,
Dean Clough, Halifax,
West Yorkshire HX3 5AX
T: 01422 364964
F: 01422 322720
E: murray.seccombe@communitytransport.org
www.communitytransport.org
Chief Executive: Murray Seccombe
We provide services in three themed areas: passenger transport for individuals with mobility needs, VCS groups and statutory agencies; furniture re-use/recycling; training, volunteering and work experience. We operate in Tyne and Wear, Greater Manchester, West Midlands and Staffordshire.
Employees: 130
Volunteers: 100
Regional offices: 15

Community Transport Association

Highbank, Halton Street, Hyde,
Cheshire SK14 2NY
T: 0161 351 1475
Helpline: 0845 130 6195
F: 0161 351 7221
E: info@ctauk.org
www.ctauk.org
Chief Executive: Keith Halstead
The Community Transport Association is a not-for-profit organisation that provides advice and training for operators of community and voluntary transport. We also administer the prestigious MiDAS and Pats range of training courses for minibus drivers and passenger assistants.
Employees: 30
Regional offices: 6

Compassion in World Farming

River Court, Mill Lane, Godalming,
Surrey GU7 1EZ
T: 01483 521950
F: 01483 861639
E: compassion@ciwf.org.uk
www.ciwf.org.uk
Chief Executive: Philip Lymbery
Compassion in World Farming is the leading charity campaigning exclusively for the welfare of farm animals throughout the world. Our vision is a world where farm animals are treated with compassion and respect and where cruel factory farming practices end. Our mission is to advance the wellbeing of farm animals worldwide. We have pioneered engagement with the food industry, rewarding good practice and highlighting welfare failures.
Employees: 40
Volunteers: 6

Computers for Charities

Cemetery Lodge, Ersham Road, Hailsham,
East Sussex BN27 3LJ
T: 01323 840641
E: info@computersforcharities.org
www.computersforcharities.org
Chair: Simon Rooksby
Computers for Charities as a registered charity. It provides IT advice and services to UK and overseas charities and voluntary organisations including low-cost refurbished PC and Mac computer systems. CfC also undertakes social, educational, vocational and humanitarian projects.
Employees: 1
Volunteers: 40
Regional offices: 1

Concern Universal

21 King Street, Hereford HR4 9BX
T: 01432 355111
F: 01432 355086
E: cu.uk@concern-universal.org
www.concern-universal.org
Chief Executive Officer: Kathryn Llewellyn
Concern Universal is an international development organisation tackling poverty from the grassroots. We create opportunities for people around the world to improve their lives and shape their own futures. By building skills and connecting people at all levels in society, we help communities deliver practical solutions with long term impact.
Employees: 30
Volunteers: 20
Income: £14,000,000 (2012-13)

Concern Worldwide UK

13/14 Calico House, Clove Hitch Quay
T: 020 7801 1850
E: rose.caldwell@concern.net
www.concern.org.uk
Executive Director: Rose Caldwell

Concordia International Volunteers

19 North Street, Portslade BN41 1DH
T: 01273 422218
F: 01273 421182
E: info@concordiavolunteers.org.uk
www.concordiavolunteers.org.uk
Concordia is a charity committed to international volunteering as a means to promoting intercultural understanding and peace. Our International Volunteer Programme offers the opportunity to join international teams of volunteers working on short-term projects in over 60 countries worldwide. Types of international volunteer projects include conservation, restoration, archaeology, construction, arts, children's play-schemes and teaching. Projects last from two to four weeks up to one year.
Employees: 4
Volunteers: 1

Confederation of Indian Organisations (UK)

25 Buller Road, Leicester, Leicestershire LE4 5GB
T: 0116 266 8068
F: 0116 266 8072
E: info@conf-indian.org.uk
www.ciostrokeproject.co.uk
Project Coordinator: Vinod Kotecha
The South Asian Stroke Prevention Project aims to set up an outreach, advocacy and support services in the East Midlands for people from South Asian communities who have suffered from a Stroke or are at a high risk. The project is a partnership between the Confederation of Indian Organisations (UK) and The Big Lottery Fund.
Employees: 4
Volunteers: 113
Regional offices: 1

CONNECT the Communication Disability Network

St Alphege Hall, King's Bench Street, London SE1 0HX
T: 020 7367 0840
E: info@ukconnect.org
www.ukconnect.org
Chief Executive: Sally McVicker
Connect exists to improve the lives of people with the communication disability 'aphasia', caused most commonly by stroke. Aphasia can affect a person's ability to speak, read, write and manage numbers. We aim to empower people with aphasia by helping them re-connect with life. We do this through a range of activities including drop-ins, special interest groups and befriending schemes around the country.
Employees: 12
Volunteers: 20

Conquest Art - Enriching the Lives of People with Disabilities

Conquest Art Centre, Cox Lane Centre, Cox Lane, West Ewell, Surrey KT19 9PL
T: 020 8397 6157 (also fax)
E: conquestart@hotmail.com
www.conquestart.org
Conquest Art promotes the relief and rehabilitation of people with disabilities, in particular by encouraging them to lead fuller and more active lives, and wherever possible, assisting them to cope with their disability through active participation in the visual arts.
Employees: 1
Volunteers: 80

Conscience: taxes for peace not war

Archway Resource Centre, 1b Waterlow Road, London N19 5NJ
T: 020 3515 9132
E: info@conscienceonline.org.uk
www.conscienceonline.org.uk
Conscience: taxes for peace not war, works for a world where taxes are used to nurture peace, not pay for war. We campaign for an increase in the amount of UK tax spent on peace-building and a decrease in the amount spent on war and preparation for war. We campaign for the legal right of those with a conscientious objection to war to have the entire military part of their taxes spent on peace-building.
Employees: 3
Volunteers: 1

Conservation Foundation

1 Kensington Gore, London SW7 2AR
T: 020 7591 3111
E: info@conservationfoundation.co.uk
www.conservationfoundation.co.uk
Executive Director: David Shreeve
The Conservation Foundation was launched by David Bellamy and David Shreeve in 1982 to provide a means for people in public, private and not-for-profit sectors to collaborate on environmental causes.

Consortium of Bengali Associations

100 Gatesden (Basement Offices), Argyle Street, London WC1H 8EB
T: 020 7713 8610
F: 020 7289 8115
E: enquiries@cba-uk.org.uk
www.cba.dsl.pipex.com
Since being established CBA has played an important part in the development of many Bengali-led voluntary organisations that serve the Bengali community. It provides a range of services to encourage and support voluntary action and to promote the increasingly important role of the Bengali voluntary and community sector in the UK.
Employees: 1

Consortium of Lesbian, Gay, Bisexual and Transgendered Voluntary and Community Organisations

Unit 204, 34 Buckingham Palace Road, London SW1W 0RH
T: 020 7064 6500
E: information@lgbconsortium.org.uk
www.lgbconsortium.org.uk
CEO: Paul Roberts
We are a national membership organisation focusing on the development and support of LGBT groups, projects and organisations, so they can deliver direct services and campaign for individual rights.
Employees: 5
Volunteers: 10

Consortium of Voluntary Adoption Agencies

Caritas Care, 218 Tulketh Road, Ashton on Ribble, Preston, Lancashire PR2 1ES
Helpline: 07775 910009
E: info@cvaa.org.uk
www.cvaa.org.uk
Chief Executive Officer: Annie Crombie
The CVAA work to ensure CVAA member agencies of voluntary adoption are enabled to deliver services of excellence to children, adoptive families, and all those considering adoption, or who have been affected by it.
Employees: 6

Construction Industry Trust for Youth

The Building Centre, 26 Store Street, London WC1E 7BT
T: 020 7467 9540
E: cyt@cytrust.org.uk
www.constructionyouth.org.uk
Executive Director: Christine Townley

Consumers' Association

2 Marylebone Road, London NW1 4DF
T: 020 7770 7810
E: which@which.co.uk
www.which.net
The Association aims to improve the standards of goods and services available to the public as consumers.

Contact a Family

209-211 City Road, London EC1V 1JN
T: 020 7608 8700
F: 020 7608 8701
E: debbie.gordon@cafamily.org.uk
www.cafamily.org.uk
Contact a Family is the only UK-wide charity providing advice, information and support to parents of all disabled children no matter what their health condition.
Employees: 65
Volunteers: 100
Regional offices: 13

Contact the Elderly

2 Grosvenor Gardens, London SW1W 0DH
T: 020 7240 0630
Helpline: 0800 716543
F: 020 7379 5781
E: info@contact-the-elderly.org.uk
www.contact-the-elderly.org.uk
CEO: Mary Rance
Contact the Elderly aims to relieve the loneliness of frail, isolated elderly people, who live alone with little or no support from family or friends. Our volunteer network offers a simple yet effective act of friendship. Every month our volunteer drivers take otherwise-housebound elderly guests to the home of volunteer hosts, enjoying the warmth of friendship for a few hours. The effect becomes cumulative as new friendships blossom.
Employees: 32
Volunteers: 7199

Conway Hall Ethical Society

Conway Hall, 25 Red Lion Square, London WC1R 4RL
T: 020 7405 1818
E: jim@ethicalsoc.org.uk
www.conwayhall.org.uk
CEO: Dr Jim Walsh
The landmark of London's independent intellectual, political and cultural life.
Employees: 11
Volunteers: 12
Regional offices: 1
Income: £800,000 (2014-15)

Coram Children's Legal Centre

University of Essex, Wivenhoe Park, Colchester, Essex CO4 3SQ
T: 01206 877910
F: 01206 877963
E: clc@essex.ac.uk
www.childrenslegalcentre.com / www.lawstuff.org.uk
Managing Director: Kawaldip Sehmi
Coram Children's Legal Centre, part of the Coram group of charities, specialises in law and policy affecting children and young people. CCLC provides free legal information, advice and representation to children, young people, their families, carers and professionals, as well as international consultancy on child law and children's rights.
Employees: 41
Regional offices: 2

Coram Family

49 Mecklenburgh Square, London WC1N 2QA
T: 020 7520 0300
F: 020 7520 0301
E: matt@coram.org.uk
www.coram.org.uk
Coram Family works with vulnerable children and young people to enable them to take responsibility for their lives and achieve their full potential.
Employees: 144
Volunteers: 100

Coram Voice

320 City Road, London EC1V 2NZ
T: 020 7833 5792
Helpline: 0808 800 5792
F: 020 7713 1950
E: info@voiceyp.org
www.voiceyp.org
Managing Director: Andrew Radford
Coram Voice exists to enable children and young people to actively participate in shaping their own lives and to hold to account the services that are responsible for their care. We serve children and young people who are vulnerable to harm or exclusion from society, and who rely on the state or its agencies for their rights and wellbeing.
Employees: 60
Volunteers: 25
Regional offices: 3

Cord

1 New Street, Leamington Spa, Warwickshire CV31 1HP
T: 01926 315301
E: info@cord.org.uk
www.cord.org.uk
Chief Executive: Brian Wakley
Cord is an international organisation working to build lasting peace in partnership with people living and working in conflict, or post-conflict situations. We believe these people hold the keys to peace and we work alongside them to make lasting peace a reality.
Employees: 800
Volunteers: 20
Regional offices: 1

CORDA preventing heart disease and stroke

Chelsea Square, London SW3 6NP
T: 020 7349 8686
E: corda@rbht.nhs.uk
www.corda.org.uk
The charity raises funds to support high-quality clinical research into the early diagnosis and prevention of heart disease and stroke through non-invasive methods (magnetic resonance and ultrasound).

CORE

3 St Andrews Place, London NW1 4LB
T: 020 7486 0341
F: 020 7224 2012
E: info@corecharity.org.uk
www.corecharity.org.uk
Chief Executive: Warren Alexander
CORE works for the advancement of science and the practice of medicine and surgery for the benefit of the public in the field of gastroenterology. It promotes the study of and research into medicine and surgery with reference to the physiology and pathology of the digestive system and disseminates the results.
Employees: 4

Cornelia de Lange Syndrome Foundation

The Tower, Guardian Ave, North Stifford, Grays, Essex RM16 5US
T: 01375 376439
E: info@cdls.org.uk
www.cdls.org.uk
Chairman: James May
The CdLS Foundation exists to ensure early and accurate diagnosis of CdLS; promotes research into the causes and manifestations of the syndrome and helps people with a

diagnosis of CdLS to make informed decisions throughout their lifetime.
Employees: 1
Volunteers: 16
Regional offices: 1

Corona Worldwide

Southbank House, Black Prince Road, London SE1 7SJ
T: 020 7793 4020
E: corona@coronaworldwide.org
www.coronaworldwide.org
Corona Worldwide helps and educates people going to live and work overseas, and helps returners and foreigners adjust to life in the UK.

Coronary Prevention Group

Buckinghamshire Chilterns University, Newland Park, Gorelands Lane, Chalfont St Giles, Buckinghamshire HP8 4AD
T: 020 7927 2125
E: cpg@bcuc.ac.uk
www.healthnet.org.uk
The Group contributes to the prevention of coronary heart disease, the UK's major cause of death.

Council for Awards in Care, Health and Education

CACHE Head Office, Apex House, 81 Camp Road, St Albans, Hertfordshire AL1 5HL
T: 01727 818616
F: 01727 818618
E: info@cache.org.uk
www.cache.org.uk
Chief Executive: Richard Dorrance
Employees: 124

Council for British Archaeology

Beatrice de Cardi House, 66 Bootham, York YO30 7BZ
T: 01904 671417
F: 01904 671384
E: mikeheyworth@archaeologyuk.org
www.archaeologyuk.org
Director: Dr Mike Heyworth MBE
The Council aims to advance the study and care of Britain's historic environment, and to improve public awareness and enjoyment of Britain's past.
Employees: 15
Volunteers: 600
Income: £1,125,000 (2014-15)

Council for Dance Education and Training

Old Brewers Yard, Covent Garden, London WC2H 9UY
T: 020 7240 5703
F: 020 7240 2547
E: info@cdet.org.uk
www.cdet.org.uk
Director: Sean Williams
The Council aims to advance the education of all people in the art, practice and appreciation of the cultural significance of dance.
Employees: 3

Council for Music in Hospitals

74 Queens Road, Surrey KT12 5LW
T: 01932 252809
E: info@music-in-hospitals.org.uk
www.music-in-hospitals.org.uk
The Council uses high-quality live music to improve the quality of life of patients and residents in hospitals, nursing homes, hospices etc.

Council of British Pakistanis

415 Bordesley Green, Birmingham B9 5RE
T: 0845 658 1057
F: 0845 658 1067
E: info@thedoliproject.net
The prime objective of the Council is the welfare of British Pakistanis, to promote better understanding between the British and Pakistani community, and to promote social, cultural and educational activities of British Pakistanis.
Employees: 7
Volunteers: 25
Regional offices: 15

Council of Christians and Jews

1st Floor, 89 Albert Embankment, London SE1 7TP
T: 020 7820 0090
F: 020 7820 0504
E: cjrelations@ccj.org.uk
www.ccj.org.uk
The Council exists to combat all forms of religious and racial intolerance; to promote mutual understanding and goodwill between Christians and Jews, and to foster cooperation in educational activities and in social and community service.

Council of Voluntary Welfare Work

Room 118/119, Block 16, Chelsea Barracks, Chelsea Bridge Road, London SW1H 8RF
T: 020 7259 9392
E: gensec@cvww.org.uk
The Council advances charitable work carried out by member organisations among the armed forces.

Counsel and Care

6 Avonmore Road, West Kensington, London W14 8RL
T: 020 7605 4200
Helpline: 0845 300 7585
F: 020 7605 4201
E: sara.campbell@counselandcare.org.uk
www.independentage.org
Chief Executive: Janet Morrison
Counsel and Care merged with Independent Age in 2011. Independent Age is a unique and growing charity, providing information, advice and support for thousands of older people across the UK and the Republic of Ireland. Not only did it merge with Counsel and Care but also with UBS and so together the whole organisation is able to provide a broader range of services than any of the charities could provide separately.
Volunteers: 6

Counselling

62 Douglas Towers, Radwell Drive, Bradford, West Yorkshire BD5 0QR
T: 01924 377119
E: info@counselling.ltd.uk
www.counselling.ltd.uk
Aims to relieve poverty by the provision of counselling. We do this by compiling and displaying a web-based database of trained and experienced counsellors and providing free counselling to those on low incomes.

Counselling and Support For Young People

16 London Road, Newark, Nottinghamshire NG24 1TW
T: 01636 704620
E: n.hunter@casy.org.uk
www.casy.org.uk
CEO: Neil Hunter
We promote the preservation of good mental and emotional health among young people 6-25 within Nottinghamshire and Lincolnshire. We do this through the provision of a confidential counselling service and by working in the community delivering training courses, workshops and conferences. We focus on the individual needs of the young person, building our service around them, to help them reach their full potential.
Employees: 6
Volunteers: 40
Regional offices: 1
Income: £260,000 (2014-15)

Countryside Restoration Trust

Bird's Farm, Haslingfield Road, Barton, Cambridgeshire CB23 7AG
T: 01223 262999
E: martin@countrysiderestorationtrust.com
www.countrysiderestorationtrust.com
Director: Martin Carter
The Countryside Restoration Trust is a farming and conservation charity that aims to protect and restore Britain's countryside through wildlife-friendly and commercially viable land management. Through education, demonstration and community involvement, the Trust is committed to promoting the importance of a living and working countryside.
Employees: 9
Volunteers: 75
Income: £3,128,849 (2013-14)

Countrywide Holidays Association

16 Stoneleigh Gardens, Grappenhall, Warrington, Lancashire WA4 3LE
T: 01925 263664
F: 01925 263464
E: info@cha-walking.org.uk
www.cha-walking.org.uk
The Association organises holidays at reasonable prices at home and abroad for people of all ages, creeds and backgrounds, with a special emphasis on walking and the enjoyment of the countryside.
Employees: 4
Volunteers: 130

Cranfield Trust

Court Room Chambers, 1 Bell Street, Romsey, Hampshire SO51 8GY
T: 01794 830338
F: 01794 830340
E: admin@cranfieldtrust.org
www.cranfieldtrust.org.uk
The Trust helps charities improve their effectiveness through the provision of free management consultancy and online HR support.
Employees: 7
Volunteers: 850

Cranstoun

1st Floor St Andrew's House, St Andrew's Road, Surbiton, Surrey KT6 4DT
T: 020 8335 1830
F: 020 8399 4153
E: info@cranstoun.org.uk
www.cranstoun.org
Chief Executive Officer: Steve Rossell
Since 1969 Cranstoun has been making life better for those affected by alcohol and drugs. Our skilled and compassionate people work closely with services users and their families to change and save lives. We combine proven expertise in treatment and recovery with innovative approaches and actively involve those we help in improving the design of the services we provide.
Employees: 156
Volunteers: 93
Regional offices: 15
Income: £11,103,000 (2013-14)

CRASH

10 Barley Mow Passage, London W4 4PH
T: 020 8742 0717
F: 020 8747 3154
E: info@crash.org.uk
www.crash.org.uk
CRASH is the construction and property industry charity for the homeless. It harnesses the skills, products, talents and goodwill of the industry to improve buildings and premises for voluntary agencies working with homeless people, throughout the UK.
Employees: 3

Creative and Supportive Trust

37-39 King's Terrace, Camden Town, London NW1 0JR
T: 020 7383 5228
F: 020 7388 7252
E: info@castwomen.org.uk
www.castwomen.org.uk
The Trust provides free education and training to women ex-offenders or those at risk of offending due to drug, alcohol or mental health issues. It aims to realise the potential of each woman for their development (personal, education, employment) and make effective changes.

Creative Youth Network

Kingswood Estate, 20 Old School House, Britannia Road, Bristol, Avon BS15 8DB
T: 0117 947 7948
E: info@creativeyouthnetwork.org.uk
www.creativeyouthnetwork.org.uk
CEO: Sandy Hore Ruthven
Inspiration through the arts. We provide creative opportunities and challenges to unlock young people's talent and personality. Our aim is for young people to excel. We help them grow and succeed through the inspiration of the arts. Our work takes place across sites in Bristol and beyond, with the aim of reaching as many young people as we can.
Employees: 45
Volunteers: 5
Regional offices: 2

CreativePeop!e

PO Box 2677, Caterham, Surrey CR3 6WJ
T: 01883 371112
F: 01883 381155
E: info@creativepeople.org.uk
www.creativepeople.org.uk
Director: Barbara Brunsdon
CreativePeople is a UK network of organisations offering information, advice and guidance on professional development in the arts, crafts and creative industries. The network currently has 200 member organisations from across the UK. There is a shared website www.creativepeople.org.uk designed to help visitors find the organisation or resources most appropriate to their needs. The website is a signposting site channelling visitors through to the sites of member organisations.
Employees: 1

CRI

3rd Floor, North West Suite, Tower Point, 44 North Road, Brighton, West Sussex BN1 1YR
T: 01273 677019
F: 01273 693183
E: queries@cri.org.uk
www.cri.org.uk
Chief Executive: David Biddle
CRI is a social care and health charity working with individuals, families and communities across England and Wales that are affected by drugs, alcohol, crime, homelessness, domestic abuse and antisocial behaviour. Our projects, delivered in communities and prisons, encourage and empower people to regain control of their lives and motivate them to tackle their problems.
Employees: 2128
Volunteers: 1100
Regional offices: 4

Crimestoppers Trust

Apollo House, 66A London Road, Morden, Surrey SM4 5BE
T: 020 8254 3200
F: 020 8254 3201
E: cst@crimestoppers-uk.org
www.crimestoppers-uk.org
Crimestoppers is an independent UK-wide charity working to stop crime. Crimestoppers works for you, your family and your community.
Employees: 30
Volunteers: 500

Crisis

66 Commercial Street, London E1 6LT
T: 0300 636 1967
F: 0300 636 2012
E: enquiries@crisis.org.uk
www.crisis.org.uk
Chief Executive: John Sparkes
Crisis is the national charity for single homeless people. Our purpose is to end homelessness. Crisis helps people rebuild their lives through housing, health, education and employment services. We are also determined campaigners, working to prevent people from becoming homeless and to change the way society and government think and act towards homeless people.
Employees: 200
Volunteers: 10,000

Crisis Counselling for Alleged Shoplifters

Box 147, Stanmore, Middlesex HA7 2QT
T: 020 8954 8987
E: crisiscounselling@gmail.com
Chairman: Harry Kauffer
Provides counselling and advice to people wrongfully accused of shoplifting offences and refers such cases to a solicitor, doctor or social worker where appropriate. It has a particular concern for the problems of children accused of shoplifting offences and liaises with MPs, local authorities and other organisations to discuss aspects of social or legal policy and practice. We do not condone premeditated shoplifting, which is theft. Office hours: 9:30am to 18:30pm Monday to Friday.

Crohn's and Colitis Uk

4 Beaumont House, Sutton Road, St Albans, Hertfordshire AL1 5HH
T: 01727 830038
Helpline: 0845 130 2223
F: 01727 862550
E: gill.lamb@crohnsandcolitis.org.uk
www.crohnsandcolitis.org.uk
Chief Executive: David Barker
Crohn's and Colitis UK offers support and information for patients. It has over 30,000 members and 70 area groups throughout the UK. Since 1984 Crohn's and Colitis UK members have raised over 2.5 million for research into the causes inflammatory bowel disease. Membership is open to patients, relatives, health professionals and to anyone interested in the activities of the association.
Employees: 40
Volunteers: 100
Regional offices: 66

Crohn's in Childhood Research Association

Parkgate House, 356 West Barnes Lane, Motspur Park, Surrey KT3 6NB
T: 020 8949 6209
E: support@cicra.org
www.cicra.org
Chair - Board of Trustees: Margaret Lee
The association funds research into the causes and treatment of inflammatory bowel disease. It aims to increase overall public understanding of Crohn's disease and ulcerative colitis, particularly as it affects children and young people. It supports sufferers, their families and carers and the medical professionals who care for them.
Employees: 2
Volunteers: 6
Income: £339,771 (2012-13)

Crowthorne Old Age To Teen Society (COATS)

The COATS Centre, Pinewood Avenue, Crowthorne, Berkshire RG45 6RQ
T: 01344 773464
E: secretary@coatscrowthorne.org.uk
www.coatscrowthorne.org.uk
Chairman of Trustees: John Barnes
The welfare of older people living in and around Crowthorne, Berkshire. At present we run a day centre, providing companionship, freshly cooked meals, activities and entertainment. We own a minibus to transport older people to the centre from their own homes.
Employees: 7
Volunteers: 100
Income: £232,726 (2014-15)

Cruse Bereavement Care

PO Box 800, Richmond, Surrey TW9 1RG
T: 020 8939 9530
Helpline: 0844 477 9400
F: 020 8940 1761
E: jill.sanders@cruse.org.uk
www.cruse.org.uk
Chief Executive: Debbie Kerslake
Cruse Bereavement Care exists to promote the wellbeing of bereaved people and to enable anyone bereaved by death to understand their grief and cope with their loss. We offer information, advice and support with helplines, publications and face to face sessions through a network of branches; also external education and training with bespoke courses. Cruse welcomes and trains new volunteers. There's a special interactive website for bereaved young people: www.rd4u.org.uk.
Employees: 129
Volunteers: 5500
Regional offices: 12

CSV

237 Pentonville Road, London N1 9NJ
T: 020 7278 6601
E: information@csv.org.uk
www.volunteeringmatters.org.uk
Chief Executive: Lucy de Groot
CSV creates opportunities for people to play an active part in the life of their community through volunteering and learning.

CSV Cathedral Camps

CSV Social Action and Volunteering, 237 Pentonville Road, London N1 9NJ
T: 020 7278 6601
E: cathedralcamps@csv.org.uk
www.cathedralcamps.org.uk
Helps conserve, restore and maintain Cathedrals, Churches and Historical buildings through community engagement and volunteering.

CTBI Christians Abroad

22 Ebenezer Close, Witham, Essex CM8 2HX
Helpline: 0300 012 1201
E: support@cabroad.org.uk
www.cabroad.org.uk
Lead Consultant: Colin South
Christians Abroad provides opportunities for those who wish to work overseas for short periods within the Christian community in Africa, Asia the Caribbean and South America. It provides travel insurance with accident and emergency and other specialist insurances for those working overseas in mission and development.
Employees: 2
Volunteers: 3
Income: £10,000 (2013-14)

CTC – UK's National Cycling Organisation

Parklands, Railton Road, Guildford, Surrey GU2 9JX
T: 0870 873 0060
F: 0870 873 0064
E: carol.mckinley@ctc.org.uk
www.ctc.org.uk
CEO: Kevin Mayne

Promotes and encourages the use of cycles and provides services to cyclists.
Employees: 60
Volunteers: 400
Regional offices: 200

Cued Speech Association UK

9 Jawbone Hill, Dartmouth,
Devon TQ6 9RW
Helpline: 01803 832784
E: info@cuedspeech.co.uk
www.cuedspeech.co.uk
Executive Director: Anne Worsfold
We provide information about and training in Cued Speech throughout the UK with the aim of improving the communication and literacy skills of deaf and hearing-impaired children and adults by giving them full access to spoken language through vision.

Cult Information Centre

BCM Cults, London WC1N 3XX
T: 01689 833800
E: info@cultinformation.org.uk
www.cultinformation.org.uk
The centre researches and supplies information on cults. It offers advice and an international network of contacts for further information and counselling.

Cumberland Lodge

The Great Park, Windsor,
Berkshire SL4 2HP
T: 01784 432316
Helpline: 01784 497780
F: 01784 497799
E: martinnewlan@cumberlandlodge.ac.uk
www.cumberlandlodge.ac.uk
Principal: Canon Dr Edmund Newell
Cumberland Lodge is an educational charity in a 17th century royal house, established in 1947 to provide a place where university students could consider wider moral, ethical and social issues than their courses permit. The objective remains the same, but Cumberland Lodge is now a comfortable and inspiring residential conference centre in the stunning and peaceful surroundings of Windsor Great Park,only forty minutes from London Waterloo and twenty minutes from Heathrow.
Employees: 70
Volunteers: 18
Income: £2,750,000 (2014-15)

Cumbria CVS

6 Hobson Court, Gillan Way, Penrith,
Cumbria CA10 2NH
T: 01768 800350
E: info@cumbriacvs.org.uk
www.cumbriacvs.org.uk
Chief Officer: Karen Bowen
Cumbria CVS is a membership organisation, a registered charity and a company limited by guarantee. It is the only provider of generalist infrastructure support to third sector organisations in Cumbria. The third sector comprises community and voluntary groups and organisations, as well as faith groups, sports groups and social enterprises.
Employees: 25
Volunteers: 3
Income: £1,321,351 (2012-13)

CXK Limited

The Old Court House, Tufton Street,
Ashford, Kent TN23 1QS
T: 01233 645852
E: info@cxk.org
www.cxk.org
CEO: Sean Kearns
CXK Limited is a charity with a 12 year track record supporting young people and adults to raise their aspirations and maximise their potential, in particular by helping them to build their resilience & resourcefulness to make successful transitions into adult life including progression into education, employment and training. Services include impartial and independent careers advice and guidance, emotional health and wellbeing services, youth services, vocational training and reintegration programmes
Employees: 248
Volunteers: 10
Regional offices: 3
Income: £10,412,699 (2012-13)

Cyclical Vomiting Syndrome Association UK

77 Wilbury Hills Road,
Letchworth Garden City,
Hertfordshire SG6 4LD
Helpline: 0151 342 1660
E: info@cvsa.org.uk
www.cvsa.org.uk
Chair: Dr Robin Dover
The Association offers relief to people suffering from cyclical vomiting syndrome by providing and assisting in the provision of treatment, advice, information and counselling for sufferers and their families.
Volunteers: 10

Cystic Fibrosis Trust

11 London Road, Bromley, Kent BR1 1BY
T: 020 8464 7211
Helpline: 0845 859 1000
E: enquiries@cftrust.org.uk
www.cftrust.org.uk
Chief Executive: Ed Owen
The trust funds medical research, provides advice, information and support to all those affected by Cystic Fibrosis.
Employees: 90
Volunteers: 200
Income: £10,000,000 (2013-14)

Daisy Network

PO Box 183, Rossendale BB4 6WZ
E: daisy@daisynetwork.org.uk
www.daisynetwork.org.uk
The Daisy Network Premature Menopause Support Group is a registered charity for women who have experienced a premature menopause.
Volunteers: 20

Dance UK

Unit A402A, The Biscuit Factory,
100 Clements Road,
Bermondsey SE16 4DG
T: 020 7713 0730
F: 020 7223 0074
E: info@danceuk.org
www.danceuk.org
Dance UK works to create a diverse, dynamic and healthy future for dance and to build a stronger sense of a UK-wide dance community.
Employees: 7
Volunteers: 25
Regional offices: 1

Dartington Social Research Unit

Lower Hood Barn, Totnes, Dartington, Devon TQ9 6AB
T: 01803 762400
E: jaddy@dartington.org.uk
www.dartington.org.uk
The Dartington Social Research Unit (DSRU) is an independent charity that brings science and evidence to bear on policy and practice in children's services to improve the health and development of children and young people.
Employees: 25

darts (Doncaster Community Arts)

The Point, 16 South Parade, Doncaster, South Yorkshire DN1 2DR
T: 01302 341662
F: 01302 341668
E: ssylvester@thepoint.org.uk
www.thepoint.org.uk
Co-Directors: Elaine Hirst / Duncan Robertshaw
darts is a participatory arts organisation, firmly rooted in and focused on Doncaster communities. At the heart of our work is a passionate belief that the arts can fuel change for individuals and communities and that creativity enhances the abilities and opportunities of every person who participates in it. Our mission is to engage those who are described as hard to reach and/or who have little or no access to the arts.
Employees: 43
Volunteers: 50
Regional offices: 1
Income: £1,408,143 (2014-15)

David Lewis

Mill Lane, Warford, Near Alderley Edge, Cheshire SK9 7UD
T: 01565 640000
F: 01565 640100
E: enquiries@davidlewis.org.uk
www.davidlewis.org.uk
CEO: Anthony Waters
David Lewis is the UK's largest provider of care, education, assessment, treatment and life skill development for people aged 16 upwards with complex epilepsy, physical and learning disabilities and other neurological conditions.
Employees: 1000

Deaf Education through Listening and Talking (DELTA)

DELTA, 83 Sherwin Road, Nottingham, Nottinghamshire NG7 2FB
T: 0300 365 7200
E: enquiries@deafeducation.org.uk
www.deafeducation.org.uk
Chair: Andy Stubbs
DELTA is a national charity that supports deaf children, their families and practitioners following the Natural Aural Approach. This approach helps the deaf child learn to listen and talk using their residual hearing and natural spoken language, even those with a severe or profound loss. DELTA provides a range of information, advice and practical help at summer schools, weekend and information days for parents, teachers and other professionals.
Employees: 1
Volunteers: 250
Regional offices: 1

Deaf Ex-Mainstreamers Group

Unit 9, Milner Way, Ossett, Wakefield, West Yorkshire WF5 9JN
F: 01226 700326
E: info@dex.org.uk
www.dex.org.uk
Chair: Brian Daltrey
The Deaf Ex-Mainstreamers' Group (DEX) is a deaf-led organisation concerned about the limited lack of access deaf children have to the National Curriculum and to the school environment. DEX has conducted a Best Value Review of deaf children in the UK, Sweden, Norway and Canada, a literature review, and a study of the needs of parents of deaf children and deaf young people. DEX now markets its services to local government and health.
Employees: 1

Deaf PLUS

1st Floor, Trinity Centre, Key Close, Whitechapel, London E1 4HG
T: 020 7790 6147
E: clare.kennedy@deafplus.org
www.deafplus.org
Chief Executive: Clare Kennedy
Deaf and hearing people working together to achieve equality.
Employees: 26
Volunteers: 15
Regional offices: 6

Deafax

Clare Charity Centre, Wycombe Road, Saunderton, Buckinghamshire HP14 4BF
T: 01494 568885
E: info@deafax.org
www.deafax.org
Chief Executive: Helen Lansdown
Deafax works with deaf people providing innovative and high-quality deaf-friendly resources and training courses (online and face to face) which cover areas such as life skills, personal health, drug and alcohol awareness, sexual health, identity issues etc.

Deafblind UK

National Centre For Deafblindness, John and Lucille Van Geest Place, Cygnet Road, Hampton, Peterborough, Cambridgeshire PE7 8FD
T: 01733 358100
Helpline: 0800 132320
F: 01733 358356
E: info@deafblind.org.uk
www.deafblind.org.uk
Chief Executive: Jeff Skipp
Deafblind UK is a national charity offering specialist services and human support to deafblind people and those who have progressive sight and hearing loss acquired throughout their lives. Our aim is to enable people living with this unique disability to maintain their independence, quality of life and to reduce the isolation that Deafblindness creates. Further information about Deafblind UK is available on our website.
Employees: 200
Volunteers: 200
Regional offices: 1

Deafconnect

Spencer Dallington Community Centre, Tintern Avenue, Northampton NN5 7BZ
T: 01604 589011
F: 01604 754529
E: joanna.steer@deafconnect.org.uk
www.deafconnect.org.uk
CEO: Joanna Steer
Deafconnect supports and empowers Deaf and Hearing Impaired people to be independent. We offer support, advice, information and Advocacy to Deaf and hearing impaired people of all ages, their families, carers and professionals working with them. We provide an interpreting service for Hearing Impaired communication to support our aims. We work closely with other organisations to improve access to other services and information. We also offer

competitively priced sign language courses and Deaf awareness training.
Employees: 7
Volunteers: 30
Regional offices: 1
Income: £200,000 (2012-13)

Deafness Support Network

144 London Road, Northwich, Cheshire CW9 5HH
T: 0808 208 2440
F: 01606 49456
E: dsn@dsnonline.co.uk
www.dsnonline.co.uk
Chief Executive Officer: Bob Birchall
Providing support services to Deaf, deafened & Hard of Hearing people of all ages, across Cheshire.
Employees: 70
Volunteers: 150
Regional offices: 3

Deafway

Brockholes Brow, Preston, Lancashire PR2 5AL
T: 01772 796461
F: 01772 693416
E: info@deafway.org.uk
www.deafway.org.uk
Chief Executive: David Hynes
Deafway works towards providing equality of opportunity and access in all areas of life for deaf, sign language users in the UK and abroad.
Employees: 64
Volunteers: 6
Regional offices: 1

DEBRA

Unit 13, Wellington Business Park, Dukes Ride, Crowthorne, Berkshire RG45 6LS
T: 01344 771961
E: debra@debra.org.uk
www.debra.org.uk
DEBRA is the national charity that supports individuals and families affected by Epidermolysis Bullosa (EB) – a genetic condition which causes the skin to blister and shear at the slightest touch. DEBRA provides an enhanced specialist EB Nursing Service, in partnership with the NHS and community support staff to work directly with families. The charity also commissions world-leading research into the condition with the aim of finding effective treatments and, ultimately, a cure for EB.

Depression Alliance

212 Spitfire Studios, London N1 9BE
T: 0845 123 2320
F: 020 7633 0559
E: information@depressionalliance.org
www.depressionalliance.org
Depression Alliance provides information and support to anyone affected by depression.
Employees: 10
Volunteers: 200
Regional offices: 3

Develop Enhancing Community Support

3-4 New Road, Chippenham, Wiltshire SN15 1EJ
T: 0845 034 5250
F: 01249 655696
E: enquiries@developecs.org.uk
www.developecs.org.uk
Chief Executive Officer: Janice Fortune
DEVELOP Enhancing Community Support is an independent organisation which operates across Wiltshire and the surrounding areas. We are a registered Charity set up, owned and run by local groups to support, develop and enhance local voluntary and community action.
Employees: 17
Volunteers: 5
Regional offices: 1

Development Trusts Association

33 Corsham Street, London N1 6DR
T: 0845 458 8336
E: info@dta.org.uk
www.dta.org.uk
The Association supports the development of new development trusts, helps existing trusts operate well and persuades other to support development trusts.

Diabetes Foundation

1 Constable's Gate, Winchester SO23 8GE
T: 01962 842070
E: judith.rich@btinternet.com
www.diabetesfoundation.org.uk
Chair: Judith Rich
Volunteers: 10

Diabetes UK

Macleod House, 10 Parkway, London NW1 7AA
T: 020 7424 1106
F: 020 7424 1080
E: info@diabetes.org.uk
www.diabetes.org.uk
Chief Executive: Chris Askew
Our aim is to improve the lives of people with diabetes and to work towards a future without diabetes and to set people free from the restrictions of diabetes. We work towards the highest quality care and information for all, an end to discrimination and ignorance, universal understanding of diabetes and Diabetes UK and a world without diabetes.
Employees: 180
Volunteers: 10000
Regional offices: 10

DIAL Basildon and South Essex

75 Southernhay, Basildon, Essex SS14 1EU
T: 01268 285676
E: jan@dialbasildon.co.uk
www.dialbasildon.co.uk
Manager: Jan Stevens
DIAL provides a free, confidential information and advice service on all issues affecting disabled people's everyday lives, to enable and empower individuals to improve their quality of life. We currently offer advice, support, advocacy and guidance service to local disabled people, assisting them with a number of topics related to disability. Our own unique experience of living with disability allows us to assist others with understanding and expertise.
Employees: 6
Volunteers: 19
Regional offices: 2
Income: £180,000 (2013-14)

DIAL UK

6 Market Road, London N7 9PW
F: 020 7619 7100
E: dialnetwork@scope.org.uk
www.dialuk.org.uk
Dial UK is the national organisation for the DIAL network 140 disability advice centres run by and for people with disabilities.
Employees: 8
Volunteers: 8

DIAL West Cheshire

DIAL House, Hamilton Place, Chester, Cheshire CH1 2BH
T: 01244 345655
E: k.roper@dialwestcheshire.org.uk
www.dialhousechester.org.uk
Chief Officer: Keith Roper
DIAL West Cheshire (DIAL House) aims to enable disabled people and older people to live sustained, independent lives. We provide a range of disability-related services including: Advice & Information, Community Cafe, Shopmobility, Volunteering & training.
Employees: 12
Volunteers: 80+
Income: £320,000 (2014-15)

Different Strokes

9 Canon Harnett Court, Wolverton Mill, Milton Keynes, Buckinghamshire MK12 5NF
T: 01908 317618
Helpline: 0845 130 7172
F: 01908 313501
E: info@differentstrokes.co.uk
www.differentstrokes.co.uk
Chief Executive: Debbie Wilson

Different Strokes provides a free service to younger stroke survivors throughout the UK. Run by stroke survivors for stroke survivors, for active self-help and mutual support. We help stroke survivors of working age to optimise their recovery and regain as much independence as possible by offering rehabilitative services, information and advice. Our services include the Strokeline, access to exercise sessions, practical information packs, an interactive website, regular newsletters and assistance finding counselling services.

Employees: 6
Volunteers: 150
Regional offices: 50

Dignity in Dying

13 Prince of Wales Terrace, London W8 5PG
T: 020 7937 7770
F: 020 7376 2648
E: info@dignityindying.org.uk
www.dignityindying.org.uk

Dignity in Dying is the leading campaigning organisation promoting patient choice at the end of life. We are also a major information source on end-of-life issues. Dignity in Dying is independent of any political, religious or other organisation. We are supported entirely by voluntary contributions from members of the public.

Employees: 6
Volunteers: 12

Dimbleby Cancer Care

4th Floor Management Offices, Bermondsey Wing, Guy's Hospital, Great Maze Pond, London SE1 9RT
T: 020 7188 7889
Helpline: 020 7188 5918
E: admin@dimblebycancercare.org
www.dimblebycancercare.org
Chairman of Trustees: Jonathan Dimbleby

Provides psychological and social support, complementary therapies and benefits advice to patients with cancer at Guy's and St Thomas' Hospitals, London. Provides research funding for national projects looking into the psycho-social and practical support needs of people with cancer and their families.

Employees: 2

DIPEx Charity

Oxford, Oxfordshire OX2 7LX
T: 01865 201330
E: info@healthtalkonline.org
www.healthtalkonline.org

In partnership with Oxford University we provide information about people's experiences of illnesses and health conditions via video interviews, shared on our websites Healthtalkonline and Youthhealthtalk. The award-winning websites are aimed at patients, their carers, family and friends, and health professionals. We aim to help them understand the impact of issues such as cancer, being a carer, bereavement, infertility and chronic pain on people's everyday lives.

Employees: 5
Volunteers: 20

Direct Help & Advice (DHA)

Phoenix Street, Derby, Derbyshire DE1 2ER
T: 01332 287850
Helpline: 0845 345 4345
F: 01332 287863
E: annette.barrett@dhadvice.org
www.dhadvice.org
Interim Chief Executive: Ian Grostate

DHA provides direct help via specialist advice, advocacy and representation for families and individuals facing crisis, to prevent and alleviate homelessness, debt and housing difficulty. Our free, independent and confidential services offer support to the most vulnerable people in our communities, often requiring immediate intervention, support and advice. We also offer accessible training and skills development to a wide range of people to help reduce unemployment and promote social and financial inclusion.

Employees: 36
Volunteers: 5
Regional offices: 2

Directory of Social Change – London

24 Stephenson Way, London NW1 2DP
T: 0845 077 7707
F: 020 7391 4804
E: dsc@dsc.org.uk
www.dsc.org.uk

The Directory of Social Change, set up in 1975, aims to be an internationally recognised independent source of information and support to voluntary and community sectors worldwide. We enable the community and voluntary sectors to achieve their aims through being an independent voice, providing training and information.

Employees: 45
Regional offices: 1

Disabilities Trust

32 Market Place, Burgess Hill, West Sussex RH15 9NP
T: 01444 239123
F: 01444 244978
E: info@thedtgroup.org
www.disabilities-trust.org.uk

The Trust provides purpose-built accommodation and a full range of support facilities for people with physical disabilities, acquired brain injuries and autism; provides the most modern facilities in a homely, caring atmosphere; offers residents a stage between institutionalised care and total independence, and encourages them to lead as independent a lifestyle as possible while receiving individual attention and the security offered by residential staff.

Employees: 1160

Disability Alliance

Universal House, 88-94 Wentworth Street, London E1 7SA
T: 020 7247 8776
F: 020 7247 8765
E: office@disabilityalliance.org
www.disabilityrightsuk.org
Chief Executive: Vanessa Stanislas

Disability Alliance is committed to breaking the link between poverty and disability by providing information to disabled people about their entitlements, and campaigning for improvements to the social security system and for increases in disability benefits so that they better reflect the real costs of disability.

Employees: 8

Disability Awareness in Action

46 The Parklands, Hullavington, Wiltshire SN14 6DL
T: 01666 837671
E: info@daa.org.uk
www.daa.org.uk

The Alliance provides information to disabled people, their organisations and allies worldwide; supports their self-help activities and ensures their equality of opportunity. It raises awareness that disability is a human rights issue.

Disability Foundation

RNOH, Brockley Hill, Stanmore, Middlesex HA7 4LP
T: 020 8954 7373
F: 020 8954 7414
E: info@tdf.org.uk
www.tdf.org.uk
TDF welcomes any person with a disability by offering help, support and guidance to them, their families and care/support associates, creating hope and inspiration for the future. TDF has a holistic approach offering complementary therapies at heavily reduced rates and provides information, promoting best practice at all times.
Employees: 6
Volunteers: 10
Regional offices: 1

Disability Law Service

London E1 2BP
T: 020 7791 9800
F: 020 7791 9802
E: advice@dls.org.uk
www.dls.org.uk
Director: Aydin Djemal
For over 30 years the Disability Law Service (DLS) has continued to provide high-quality information and advice to disabled and deaf people. As a national registered charity DLS is independent, run by and for disabled people.
Employees: 8

Disability Partnership and MOVE

Wooden Spoon House, 5 Dugard Way, London SE11 4TH
T: 020 7414 1495
E: office@disabilitypartnership.co.uk
www.disabilitypartnership.co.uk
The Disability Partnership is a small but influential charity that exists primarily as a launch-pad for initiatives that ultimately change the daily lives of many disabled people for the better. We change lives through working to overcome the attitudinal and physical barriers that most affect disabled people in the UK and worldwide.

Disability Pregnancy and Parenthood

N10 1HU
E: info@dppi.org.uk
www.disabledparent.org.uk
Disability, Pregnancy and Parenthood (DPPI) is Disability, Pregnancy & Parenthood is the national information charity on disability and parenthood. We promotes better awareness and support for disabled people considering, during and after pregnancy and as parents.

Disability Rights UK

12 City Forum, 250 City Road, London EC1V 8AF
Helpline: 0800 328 5050
E: skill4disabledstudents@disabilityalliance.org
www.disabilityalliance.org/skill.htm
Chief Executive: Liz Sayce
Disability Rights UK is a national registered charity, formed following the unification of Disability Alliance, Radar and National Centre for Independent Living. Disability Rights UK focuses on promoting meaningful independent living for disabled people, promoting disabled people's leadership and control and breaking the link between disability and poverty through our advice work and publications. We are a campaigning organisation for disability equality and human rights.
Employees: 33
Volunteers: 30
Regional offices: 1

Disability Snowsport UK (Bromley)

20 Foxearth Close, Biggin Hill, Kent TN16 3HQ
T: 01959 574108
E: m.martineau@btinternet.com
www.disabilitysnowsport.org.uk / www.uphill-skiing.org.uk
Chair of Bromley Group: Barbara Crow
Skiers and snowboarders with a disability should be able to ski alongside the able bodied as equals at all ski facilities and resorts. A disabled person chooses both freedom and independence when they snap into bindings or transfer from a wheelchair to sit ski. They also make a choice to actively access adventure, a choice that may be made in spite of chronic health problems or a physical or learning disability. Snowsport provides people with a method to conquer the barriers that confront them in daily life, and add to their potential.
Volunteers: 40
Income: £1,000 (2013-14)

Disabled Living Foundation

London W9 2HU
T: 020 7289 6111
Helpline: 0845 130 9177
F: 020 7266 2922
E: info@dlf.org.uk
www.dlf.org.uk
Chief Executive: Nicole Penn-Symons
Employees: 30
Volunteers: 4

Disabled Motoring UK

National Office, Ashwellthorpe, Norwich NR16 1EX
T: 01508 489449
E: info@disabledmotoring.org
www.disabledmotoring.org
CEO: Graham Footer
Disabled Motoring UK is the campaigning charity for Blue Badge holders, disabled motorists, wheelchair and scooter users. We run the Baywatch campaign against parking abuse and represent disabled people's needs at a national level. Membership includes a monthly magazine, one-to-one advice and member benefits and concessions. Membership is 24 a year 36 for joint members).
Employees: 10
Volunteers: 1

Disabled Motorists' Federation

145 Knoulberry Road, Washington, Tyne and Wear NE37 1JN
T: 0191 416 3172
E: jkillick2214@yahoo.co.uk
www.dmfed.org.uk
Chairman: Noel Muncey
The Federation helps disabled people overcome their handicaps and become as independent as possible so that they may lead fuller and more active lives. It gives free advice on motoring, travel etc. to all disabled people and their carers.
Volunteers: 8
Income: £6,000 (2012-13)

Disabled Parents Network

Poynters House, Poynters Road, Dunstable, Bedfordshire LU5 4TP
T: 0300 330 0639
E: information@disabledparentsnetwork.org.uk
www.disabledparentsnetwork.org.uk
Chair: Terri Balon
Disabled Parents Network (DPN) national user-led organisation providing information, advice & support to parents & parents to be, who are disabled or a have long term health condition, their families etc. Helping disabled

parent families access appropriate support, grow in knowledge and self-confidence. Support Service – confidential, providing information, support and advice on Peer Support Register. Contact with other parents with similar disability, or locality (DPN members only). Facebook & On-line Forum. Information. DPN resources.
Volunteers: 20

Disabled Photographers' Society

43 Burge Court, Cirencester, Gloucestershire GL7 1JY
T: 01285 654984
E: enquiries@disabledphotographers.co.uk
www.dps-uk.org.uk
The Society encourages disabled people to undertake photography as a therapeutic and creative activity.

Disaster Action

PO Box 849, Woking, Surrey GU21 8WB
T: 01483 799066
E: pameladix@disasteraction.org.uk
www.disasteraction.org.uk
Disaster Action provides support and guidance to individuals and groups affected by disasters.

Disasters Emergency Committee

1st Floor, 43 Chalton Street, London NW1 1DU
T: 020 7387 0200
F: 020 7387 2050
E: info@dec.org.uk
www.dec.org.uk
At times of overseas emergency, the DEC brings together a unique alliance of the UK's aid, corporate, public and broadcasting sectors to rally the nation's compassion, and ensure that funds raised go to DEC agencies best placed to deliver effective and timely relief to people most in need.
Employees: 9
Volunteers: 1

Disaway Trust

55 Tolworth Park Road, Surbiton, Surrey KT6 7RJ
T: 020 8390 2576
E: lynnesimpkins@hotmail.com
www.disaway.co.uk
Treasurer: Lynne Simpkins
We organise group holidays with physically disabled people. Each disabled person has their own helper, either a friend or family member or a helper supplied by the Trust. The helper pays approximately 50% of the cost.
Volunteers: Varies

Diversity Hub

The Learning Exchange, Wygston's House, Applegate, Leicester, Leicestershire LE1 5LD
T: 0116 222 9977
F: 0116 222 9970
E: info@diversityhub.org.uk
www.diversityhub.org.uk
Director: Val Carpenter
Diversity Hub is a leadership-training organisation dedicated to ending prejudice and discrimination, whether because of nationality, race, gender, religion, class, sexual orientation, age, physical ability, occupation or life circumstance.
Employees: 4
Volunteers: 30
Regional offices: 1

Diversity Role Models

5th Floor, 8/9 Harbour Exchange Square, London, Central E14 9JY
T: 020 7964 7009
E: office@diversityrolemodels.org
www.diversityrolemodels.org
Chief Executive: Suran Dickson
Our vision is a world where all children and young people can live, learn, grow and play safely, regardless of issues relating to gender and sexuality. Our mission is to eliminate homophobic and transphobic bullying. We achieve this by providing high quality, pioneering educational workshops involving role models and through collaborating with individuals and organisations. We value diversity and equality, creativity and innovation, communication and role modelling, and inter-generational learning.
Employees: 6
Volunteers: 136
Regional offices: 1
Income: £168,000 (2012-13)

Diving Diseases Research Centre

8 Research Way, Plymouth Science Park, Derriford, Plymouth, Devon PL6 8BU
T: 01752 209999
F: 01752 209115
E: info@ddrc.org
www.ddrc.org
Chief Executive Officer: Gary Smerdon
A medical research, training and service charity working with hyperbaric oxygen, its uses and effects in humans. Providing services to the NHS and private sector for difficult to heal wounds, soft tissue infections and carbon monoxide poisoning in particular as well as treatment for divers with decompression illness (the bends).
Employees: 28
Regional offices: 2

DoBe.org

NW1 1EU
E: info@alberyfoundation.org
www.alberyfoundation.org

Dog AID (Assistance In Disability)

CVS Building, Arthur Street, Chadsmoor, Cannock, Staffordshire WS11 5HD
T: 01543 899463
E: general_admin@dogaid.org.uk
www.dogaid.org.uk
Chairperson: Sandra Fraser
Dog AID provides access to dog training for people with physical disabilities, enabling them to train their own dog in basic control and specialised tasks, which will assist them manage their disability in everyday life.

Dogs for Good

The Frances Hay Centre, Blacklocks Hill, Banbury, Oxfordshire OX17 2BS
T: 01295 252600
F: 01295 252668
E: info@dogsforgood.org
https://www.dogsforgood.org
Chief Executive: Peter Gorbing
Dogs for the Disabled provides specially trained assistance dogs for adults and children with physical disabilities, and families with a child with autism, to help them lead fuller and more independent lives.
Employees: 50
Volunteers: 140

Dogs Trust

London EC1V 7RQ
T: 020 7837 0006
F: 020 7833 2701
E: info@dogstrust.org.uk
www.dogstrust.org.uk
Dogs Trust is working towards the day when all dogs can enjoy a happy life, free from the threat of unnecessary destruction. We care for stray and abandoned dogs through our network of 15 rehoming centres nationwide. No healthy dog is ever destroyed. Our subsidised neutering campaigns aim to prevent the birth of unwanted litters. Additionally, our schools education programme promotes responsible dog ownership to young people.
Employees: 400
Volunteers: 200
Regional offices: 15

Don'tDumpThat Ltd

PE20 3LH
E: contact@dontdumpthat.com
www.dontdumpthat.com
The majority of what is thrown away every day is probably reusable and only goes to landfill because most people don't know what else to do with it. Don'tDumpThat is 100% web

based and is all about helping people preserve the environment by keeping perfectly useful but otherwise unwanted items out of landfill sites.

Donkey Sanctuary

Slade Farm House, Sidmouth, Devon EX10 0NU
T: 01395 578222
F: 01395 579266
E: amanda.gordon@thedonkeysanctuary.com
www.thedonkeysanctuary.org.uk
Chief Executive: David Cook
The Donkey Sanctuary has taken over 13,000 donkeys into its care since 1969. Some of these donkeys may have been neglected, mistreated, retired from working on beaches or their owners could no longer care for them. The Donkey Sanctuary also brings urgent veterinary assistance to working donkeys in Egypt, Ethiopia, India, Kenya and Mexico. Further projects exist in Europe where more donkeys are in need of help. Admission is free at its headquarters in Sidmouth.
Employees: 526

Dorset and Somerset Air Ambulance

Landacre House, Castle Road, Chelston Business Park, Wellington, Somerset TA21 9JQ
T: 01823 669604
E: bill.sivewright@dsairambulance.org.uk
www.dsairambulance.org.uk
Chief Executive Officer: Bill Sivewright
To save and enhance lives through the funding and provision of a helicopter emergency medical service.
Employees: 17
Volunteers: 80
Regional offices: 2
Income: £4,834,506 (2012-13)

Dorset Youth Association

County Headquarters, Lubbecke Way, Dorchester, Dorset DT1 1QL
T: 01305 262440
E: info@dorsetyouth.com
www.dorsetyouth.com
Director: Dave Thompson
Improve the quality of life for children and young people in Dorset by: Delivering positive activities and support to affiliated clubs and groups; Providing information, advice and guidance for young people; Helping young people gain the skills and confidence to 'move on'; Supporting programmes which enable young people to make a positive contribution to their communities; Providing targeted support for young people who are disadvantaged; Administer and provide support to VCS 0-19 Forum and Sector.
Employees: 14
Volunteers: 300
Income: £638,000 (2014-15)

Douglas Haig Memorial Homes (Haig Homes)

Alban Dobson House, Green Lane, Morden, Surrey SM4 5NS
T: 020 8685 5777
E: haig@haighomes.org.uk
www.haighomes.org.uk
Provides housing for the ex-service community.

Down's Heart Group

PO Box 4260, Dunstable, Bedfordshire LU6 2ZT
T: 0300 102 1644
F: 0300 102 1645
E: info@dhg.org.uk
www.dhg.org.uk
Director: Penny Green
Provides support and information relating to heart problems associated with Down's syndrome.
Employees: 2
Volunteers: 10
Income: £15,000 (2014-15)

Down's Syndrome Association

2a Langdon Park, Langdon Centre, Teddington TW11 9PS
F: 0333 121 2300
E: info@downs-syndrome.org.uk
www.downs-syndrome.org.uk
We are the only organisation in this country focusing solely on all aspects of living successfully with Down's syndrome. We are a national charity with over 20,000 members, a national office in Teddington Middlesex, regional offices in Northern Ireland and Wales and over 130 affiliated local groups. We provide support, training, information and advice for people with Down's syndrome, their families and professionals.
Employees: 36
Regional offices: 130

Down's Syndrome Educational Trust

The Sarah Duffen Centre, Belmont Street, Southsea, Hampshire PO5 1NA
T: 023 9289 3889
F: 023 9289 3895
E: info@dseinternational.org
www.downsed.org
Promotes the development and education of individuals with Down's syndrome.
Employees: 20
Volunteers: 10
Regional offices: 3

Dr Hadwen Trust

Suite 8, Portmill House, Portmill Lane, Hitchin, Hertfordshire SG5 2DJ
T: 01462 436819
F: 01462 436844
E: info@drhadwentrust.org.uk
www.drhadwentrust.org.uk
Group Head of Operations: Kay Miller
The Dr Hadwen Trust funds and promotes non-animal medical research. We champion medical research that is humane and human-relevant.
Employees: 9
Volunteers: 10
Regional offices: 1
Income: £700,000 (2012-13)

Drake Music

60-61 Old Nichol Street, London E2 7HP
T: 020 7739 5444
E: info@drakemusic.org
www.drakemusic.org
CEO: Carien Meijer
Drake Music is the leading national charity working in music, disability and technology. We specialise in the use of assistive technology to break down both physical and societal barriers to music-making. We offer a wide range of high quality, lifelong-learning opportunities for people of all ages, working in partnership with schools, music hubs, universities, healthcare professionals, artists, technologists and more to improve access to music. Our team has an excellent track record in delivering outreach, training and education initiatives, as well as developing new technologies and commissioning disabled practitioners to produce new artistic works.
Employees: 8
Regional offices: 3

Dreamflight

7C Hill Avenue, Amersham, Buckinghamshire HP6 5BD
T: 01494 722733
F: 01494 722977
E: office@dreamflight.org
www.dreamflight.org
Dreamflight is a UK charity that takes seriously ill and disabled children on their 'holiday of a lifetime' to the theme parks of Central Florida. Other charities do some wonderful things like funding research or

purchasing medical equipment, but Dreamflight believes that fun and joy are just as important, especially for children who perhaps can't wait long enough for the breakthrough they need or whose illnesses and treatments have brought pain, distress and disruption.
Employees: 2

Dreams Come True Charity

Exchange House, 33 Station Road, Liphook, Hampshire GU30 7DW
T: 01428 726330
F: 01428 724953
E: info@dctc.org.uk
www.dctc.org.uk
Employees: 12
Volunteers: 3
Regional offices: 1

Drug and Alcohol Action Programme

KAS House, Unit K,
Middlesex Business Centre, Bridge Road, Southall, Middlesex UB2 4AB
T: 020 8843 0945
F: 020 8843 1068
E: info@daap.org.uk
www.daap.org.uk
The Programme advances the education of the public about all aspects of substance misuse and related issues particularly by working towards eradicating addiction by and through education; by developing and managing appropriate programmes and treatment services; by conducting research on addictive behaviour.
Employees: 4

Duchenne Family Support Group

78 York Street, London W1H 1DP
T: 0870 241 1857
Helpline: 0800 121 4518
E: info@dfsg.org.uk
www.dfsg.org.uk
Development Officer: Phillippa Farrant
We provide support to families affected by Duchenne muscular dystrophy by a national helpline,our website and a quarterly newsletter. We organise subsidised holidays and social events so that parents and siblings can share experiences. We also organise conferences and workshops on topics of interest to our families. We work with other related charities on a variety of topics including research and improving services.
Employees: 1
Volunteers: 55
Regional offices: 1

Dudley Caribbean and Friends Association

3rd Floor, Trident House,
14 Wolverhampton Street, Dudley, West Midlands DY1 1DB
T: 01384 868085
E: levene.bruce@btconnect.com
Manager: Levene Bruce
The Charity's objects are to impact the educational and socio-economic needs of ethnic communities, in particular the African Caribbean community within the metropolitan borough of Dudley and other likeminded community association in the wider West Midlands. To achieve this the Charity has established several projects to address the educational, training, employment and social welfare needs of the community.
Employees: 9
Volunteers: 6
Income: £134,931 (2013-14)

Durrell Wildlife Conservation Trust

Les Augres Manor, La Profonde Rue, Trinity, Jersey JE3 5BP
T: 01534 860000
F: 01534 860001
E: info@durrell.org
www.durrell.org
Employees: 88
Volunteers: 200

Dyslexia Action

Park House, Wick Road, Egham, Surrey TW20 0HH
T: 01784 222300
E: info@dyslexiaaction.org.uk
www.dyslexiaaction.org.uk
Chief Executive: Kevin Geeson
Dyslexia Action is a national charity and the UK's leading provider of services and support for people with dyslexia and literacy difficulties. We specialise in assessment, teaching and training. We also develop and distribute teaching materials and undertake research. Our services are available through our 26 centres and 160 teaching locations around the UK. Over half a million people benefit from our work each year.
Employees: 300
Regional offices: 26

Dyspraxia Foundation

8 West Alley, Hitchin, Hertfordshire SG5 1EG
T: 01462 455016
F: 01462 455052
E: admin@dyspraxiafoundation.org.uk
www.dyspraxiafoundation.org.uk
General Manager/Company Secretary: Eleanor Howes
The Foundation puts parents and children in contact with other sufferers, locally and nationally. It provides a regular newsletter, promotes better diagnostic and treatment facilities for dyspraxic children, and encourages a wider understanding of dyspraxia from childhood into adulthood by health and education professionals and by the general public.
Employees: 5
Volunteers: 100
Regional offices: 1

Dystonia Society

2nd Floor, 89 Albert Embankment, London SE1 7TP
T: 020 7793 3651
Helpline: 0845 458 6322
F: 0845 458 6311
E: info@dystonia.org.uk
www.dystonia.org.uk
Chief Executive: Guy Parckar
The Dystonia Society is a UK-wide charity providing practical and emotional support for the 70,000 people with dystonia and their families. Dystonia is a neurological movement disorder characterised by involuntary and sustained muscle spasms, which can be very painful and debilitating.
Employees: 15
Volunteers: 300
Income: £784,399 (2013-14)

Each one. Teach one

E: sarahmac77@gmail.com

Ealing Centre for Independent Living

E: ellen.collins@ecil.org

Ealing Community Transport

Greenford Depot, Greenford Road, Greenford, Middlesex UB6 9AP
T: 020 8813 3210
F: 020 8813 3211
E: ealing@ectcharity.co.uk
www.ectcharity.co.uk
Chief Executive: Anna Whitty
ECT is a national charity with a local focus on the specialist provision of high-quality, safe, accessible and affordable transport for the many communities we serve. We are committed to charity, partnership and social business excellence. Under the banner "ECT Charity", we operate in Ealing, Cheshire, Dorset, Bournemouth and Cornwall.
Employees: 180
Volunteers: 300
Regional offices: 3

Earl Mountbatten Hospice

Halberry Lane, Newport, Isle of Wight PO30 2ER
T: 01983 529511
E: richard.dent@iwhospice.org
www.iwhospice.org
Chief Executive: Nigel Hartley
Earl Mountbatten Hospice is an independent charity providing comprehensive end-of-life healthcare for the Isle of Wight community. We support and care for people living with and dying from a life-limiting illness.
Employees: 150
Volunteers: 550

Earthwatch (Europe)

267 Banbury Road, Summertown, Oxford, Oxfordshire OX13 5ET
T: 01865 318838
F: 01865 311383
E: info@earthwatch.org.uk
www.earthwatch.org/europe
Executive Director: Nigel Winser
Aims to advance the education and awareness of the public in the sciences and humanities and in all matters relating to the existence and development of life, human and non-human.
Employees: 55
Volunteers: 650

East Anglian Air Ambulance

Hangar E, Gambling Close, Norwich Airport, Norwich, Norfolk NR6 6EG
T: 01603 269320
E: info@eaaa.org.uk
www.eaaa.org.uk
Chief Executive: Tim Page
The East Anglian Air Ambulance is a 365-day helicopter emergency medical service covering Bedfordshire, Cambridgeshire, Norfolk and Suffolk. We fly with a doctor and critical care paramedic, bringing A&E to the patient. We are 100% charity and receive no government of lottery funding.
Employees: 48
Volunteers: 250
Regional offices: 6

East London Advanced Technology Training

E: orla@elatt.org.uk

Eaves Housing for Women Limited

Lincoln House, 13 Brixton Road, London SW9 6DE
T: 020 7735 2062
F: 020 7820 8907
E: post@eaveshousing.co.uk
www.eavesforwomen.org.uk
Provides housing for homeless women in need of supported housing; provides information about the causes of women's homelessness; campaigns for increased housing provision for single homeless women; encourages appropriate housing provision for single women.

ECPAT UK

4 A Chillingworth Road, Holloway, London N7 8QJ
T: 020 7607 2136
F: 020 7700 5435
E: info@ecpat.org.uk
www.ecpat.org.uk
Chief Executive Officer: Bharti Patel
ECPAT UK (End Child Prostitution, Pornography and Trafficking) is a leading children's rights organisation campaigning to protect children from commercial sexual exploitation in the UK. In particular, we focus on the protection of trafficked children and children exploited in tourism.
Employees: 7
Volunteers: 1
Income: £463,421 (2012-13)

Ecumenical Council for Corporate Responsibility

PO Box 500, Oxford, Oxfordshire OX1 1ZL
T: 01865 245349
E: info@eccr.org.uk
www.eccr.org.uk
ECCR works for economic justice, human rights and environmental sustainability. It acts as a forum where issues of corporate and investor responsibility are researched and studied, information and ideas are exchanged, and strategies are planned and implemented.
Employees: 4

EDP Drug and Alcohol Service

Suite 2:11, 2nd Floor, Renslade House, Bonhay Road, Exeter, Devon EX4 3AY
T: 01392 666710
E: info@edp.org.uk
www.edp.org.uk
Chief Executive: Lucie Hartley
When people have problems with drugs and alcohol they may feel they have less control over their lives, and they may struggle to engage with their families and communities. We provide accessible services in Devon and Dorset, which support people to move towards a place of wellbeing where they feel empowered and re-connected to their family and/or community.
Employees: 200
Regional offices: 17

Education and Services for People with Autism Ltd

2A Hylton Park Road, Wessington Way, Sunderland, Sunderland, Tyne and Wear SR5 3HD
T: 0191 516 5080
F: 0191 549 8620
E: lesley.lane@espa.org.uk
www.espa.org.uk
Chief Executive: Lesley Lane
Provides specialist further education, residential, day and domiciliary services for people with an autism spectrum disorder.
Employees: 425
Regional offices: 1

Education for Choice

The Resource Centre, 356 Holloway Road, London N7 6PA
T: 020 7700 8190 (also fax)
E: efc@efc.org.uk
www.efc.org.uk
Director: Lisa Hallgarten
Education For Choice is the only UK organisation dedicated to enabling young people to make and act on informed choices

about pregnancy and abortion. EFC works with young people, delivers training and consultancy for professionals and produces a range of information resources.
Employees: 4
Volunteers: 2

Educational Centres Association

21 Ebbisham Drive, Norwich NR4 6HQ
T: 0870 161 0302
E: info@e-c-a.ac.uk
www.e-c-a.ac.uk
The Educational Centres Association is a practice-based organisation concerned with adult education and lifelong learning. Its work in the arts and cultural sectors complements the role of its constituent institutions and organisations. These extend across the range of adult community learning, FE colleges and HE. In England, much of this work is funded by the Learning and Skills Council, LSC, with which we have effective relationships at national and local levels.

Edward's Trust

43A Calthorpe Road, Edgbaston, Birmingham, West Midlands B15 1TS
T: 0121 456 4838
E: christine.bodkin@edwardstrust.org.uk
www.edwardstrust.org.uk
The aims of Edward's Trust are to provide support to children with a serious illness and requiring hospital treatment, and their families; to provide support to families suffering a bereavement; to provide training to those involved in bereavement services following the death of a child; to raise awareness of complementary approaches to childhood concerns; and to promote and support research into complementary approaches to childhood illnesses.
Employees: 22

Ehlers-Danlos Support Group

PO Box 337, Aldershot GU12 6WZ
T: 01252 690940
E: director@ehlers-danlos.org
www.ehlers-danlos.org
Trustee: Frances Gawthrop
The aims of the Group are to support those with Ehlers-Danlos syndrome and provide education, information and research for medical and caring professionals. It produces books, information sheets and a newsletter. A national conference is held biennially. The group endeavours to heighten awareness of EDS among the medical professionals and support EDS research.
Volunteers: 24
Regional offices: 1

EIRIS Foundation

London SW8 1SF
T: 020 7840 5707
E: ethics@eiris.org
www.eiris.org
The foundation provides information on a wide range of issues to help concerned investors apply positive or negative ethical and social criteria. It identifies forms of investment that meet certain non-financial requirements on the part of the investor and promotes wider understanding of, and debate on, corporate responsibility.

Elderly Accommodation Counsel

3rd Floor, 89 Albert Embankment, London SE1 7TP
T: 020 7820 3755
Helpline: 020 7820 1343
F: 020 7820 3970
E: ros.lucas@eac.org.uk
www.housingcare.org
EAC provides information, advice and support to older people and their families on their housing and care options. It does this via its Advice Line service and its website.
Employees: 12
Volunteers: 10

Elfrida Society

34 Islington Park Street, London N1 1PX
T: 020 7359 7443
F: 020 7704 1358
E: elfrida@elfrida.com
www.elfrida.com
The Elfrida Society promotes and advances the welfare, education, training and advancement in life of people with learning difficulties.
Employees: 60
Volunteers: 7

Elimination of Leukaemia Fund

Regent House, Suite 131, 291 Kirkdale, London SE26 4QD
T: 020 8778 5353
E: admin@elf-fund.org.uk
www.elf-fund.org.uk
ELF is a major funder of leukaemia research at King's College Hospital, London, and is also funding work at a number of other major centres including the Institute of Child Health, Great Ormond Street Hospital and Belfast City Hospital. ELF favours patient-centred work so that there is an immediate or near future benefit to sufferers of leukaemia and the related blood disorders.

Elizabeth Finn Care

1 Derry Street, London W8 5HY
T: 020 7396 6700
F: 020 7396 6739
E: info@elizabethfinn.org.uk
www.elizabethfinncare.org.uk
Chief Executive: Jonathan Welfare
Employees: 750
Volunteers: 700
Regional offices: 8

Elizabeth Foundation

Southwick Hill Road, Cosham, Portsmouth PO6 3LL
T: 023 9237 2735
F: 023 9232 6155
E: sally.moger@elizabeth-foundation.org
www.elizabeth-foundation.org
Chief Executive: Sue Campbell
The Elizabeth Foundation facilitates early diagnosis for babies and preschool children with hearing loss, and provides comprehensive educational and support services to them and their families. By doing so we enable these children to develop their listening skills and natural speech and give parents the confidence and knowledge to make informed decisions on behalf of their child.
Employees: 20
Volunteers: 8
Regional offices: 1
Income: £857,938 (2013-14)

ella Forums CIC

17 Peters Lodge, 2 Stonegrove, Edgware, Middlesex HA8 7TY
T: 020 7164 6206
Helpline: 07703 291737
E: brian@ella-forums.org
www.ella-forums.org
CEO: Brian Chernett
ella Forums is a leadership development programme specifically designed to inspire and develop the leaders of Charities and Social Enterprises to grow their organisations.
Employees: 5
Volunteers: 12
Regional offices: 2
Income: £140,000 (2014-15)

Elmham Charitable Trust

224 Hills Road, Cambridge, Cambridgeshire CB2 2QE
T: 01223 247661
E: elmham@gn.apc.org
Very small family charity with no capital. It channels the income that trustees donate to charities the trustees agree upon. They do not

spend any money on running the charity and do not accept any applications for funding

Emily Jordan Foundation

Unit 9 Finepoint, Finepoint Way, Kidderminster, Worcestershire DY11 7FB
T: 01562 861484
E: chris.jordan@theemilyjordanfoundation.org.uk
www.theemilyjordanfoundation.org.uk
Chair of Trustees: Chris Jordan
The Aim: To help individuals with moderate learning and physical disabilities to lead fulfilled lives. This is done via developing and supplying good quality day opportunities alongside work development projects for those who may be able to enter the workplace
Employees: 5
Volunteers: 10

Emmaus UK

48 Kingston Street, Cambridge, Cambridgeshire CB1 2NU
T: 01223 576103
F: 01223 576203
E: contact@emmaus.org.uk
www.emmaus.org.uk
Director: Tim Page
Emmaus Communities enable people to move on from homelessness by providing home and work in a supportive, family environment. Residents work together, collecting donated furniture and selling it in community shops to support themselves and reduce waste going to landfill. Any surplus made by the Communities is used to benefit other people in need. Emmaus UK is the central support office for the Federation of Emmaus Communities in the UK.
Employees: 26
Volunteers: 5
Regional offices: 26

Empowering West Berkshire

Broadway House, 4-8 The Broadway, Northbrook Street, Newbury, Berkshire RG14 1BA
T: 01635 760501
E: shelly@empoweringwb.org.uk
www.empoweringwb.org.uk
Manager: Shelly Hambrecht
Providing support, information and training for the Voluntary Community Sector of West Berkshire. Working in partnership with West Berkshire's, statutory and community sector to ensure quality service provision for West Berkshire's communities.
Employees: 2
Regional offices: 1
Income: £70,000 (2014-15)

Empty Homes Agency

Downstream Building, 1 London Bridge, London SE1 9BG
T: 020 7828 6288
F: 020 7681 3214
E: info@emptyhomes.com
www.emptyhomes.com
Chief Executive: David Ireland
The Agency is an independent campaigning charity that aims to raise awareness of the potential of empty homes in England to meet housing need and to devise and promote, with others, sustainable solutions that will bring empty homes back into use.
Employees: 6
Volunteers: 5

End Child Poverty

94 White Lion Street, London N1 9PF
T: 020 7843 1913
F: 020 7843 1918
E: info@ecpc.org.uk
www.ecpc.org.uk
Employees: 5

Endeavour Training Ltd

Sheepbridge Lane, Chesterfield, Derbyshire S41 9RX
T: 0870 770 3250
F: 0870 770 3254
E: info@endeavour.org.uk
www.endeavour.org.uk
Employees: 26
Volunteers: 250
Regional offices: 3

Endometriosis SHE Trust (UK)

Unit 14, Moorland Way, Lincoln LN6 7JW
T: 01522 682300 (also fax)
E: shetrust@shetrust.org.uk
www.shetrust.org.uk
Chair: Diane Carlton
Aims include the relief of persons suffering from endometriosis by the provision of advice and guidance including that of holistic methods of treatment; the advancement of the education of the public, including the medical professions, by raising awareness in all matters relating to endometriosis and its treatment.
Volunteers: 12

Endometriosis UK

Suites 1 and 2, 46 Manchester Street, London W1U 7LS
T: 020 7222 2781
Helpline: 0808 808 2227
F: 020 7222 2786
E: admin@endometriosis-uk.org
www.endometriosis-uk.org
Chief Executive Officer: Helen North
1.5 million UK women live with endometriosis, a chronic gynaecological condition that has a huge impact on quality of life. Despite being so common, awareness and understanding is staggeringly low. Endometriosis UK is the lead charity offering vital support and information for those living with endometriosis, working hard to reduce the inherent isolation of this condition.
Employees: 5
Volunteers: 50
Regional offices: 30 (local support groups)

Energy Conservation and Solar Centre

Unit 327, 30 Great Guildford Street, London SE1 0HS
T: 020 7922 1660
E: enquiries@ecsc.org.uk
www.ecsc.org.uk
Advances public education in energy conservation and use, and all related subjects.

Enfield Carers Centre

Britannia House, 137-143 Baker Street, Enfield, Middx EN1 3JL
T: 020 8366 3677
E: info@enfieldcarers.org
www.enfieldcarers.org
Chief Executive: Pamela Burke
Enfield Carers Centre is a local charity offering support and advice for all unpaid carers living in Enfield. A Carer is someone of any age who provides unpaid support to a partner, relative or friend with a short or long-term illness, a disability, a substance-misuse problem, a life-limiting illness or terminal diagnosis. We support the following carers: Older carers; Working carers; Former carers; Parent carers; Bereaved Carers; Young Adult Carers (16-25 years); BME carers.
Employees: 14
Volunteers: 10
Income: £641,406 (2014-15)

Enfield Voluntary Action (EVA)

Community House, 311 Fore Street, London N9 0PZ
T: 020 8373 6268
F: 020 8373 6267
E: evanews@enfieldva.org.uk
www.enfieldva.org.uk
Chief Executive: Paula Jeffery
EVA provides services to local voluntary and community organisations in the London Borough of Enfield, including Community Accountancy, Development and Funding

Advice, News and Information Services and Volunteer Centre Enfield.
Employees: 8
Volunteers: 4
Income: £397,000 (2012-13)

Engineers Against Poverty

2nd Floor, Weston House,
246 High Holborn, London WC1V 7EX
T: 020 3206 0488
F: 020 3206 0401
E: p.matthews@engineersagainstpoverty.org
www.engineersagainstpoverty.org
Executive Director: Petter Matthews
Engineers Against Poverty works with industry, government and civil society to fight poverty and promote sustainable development.
Employees: 4
Volunteers: 2

English Federation of Disability Sport

SportPark, Loughborough University,
3 Oakwood Drive, Loughborough,
Leicestershire LE11 3QF
T: 01509 227750
F: 01509 227777
E: federation@efds.co.uk
www.efds.co.uk
Chief Executive: Barry Horne
The English Federation of Disability Sport (EFDS) was established in September 1998 as the national body and charity dedicated to disabled people in sport throughout England. We work closely with a number of key partners to improve and increase the opportunities offered, ensuring disabled people have a memorable experience of sport and physical activity. Our partners include the National Disability Sports Organisations (NDSOs) recognised by Sport England, who form part of our membership.
Employees: 19
Volunteers: 200
Regional offices: 1

Enham Trust

Enham Place, Enham Alamein, Andover,
Hampshire SP11 6JS
T: 01264 345850
E: info@enham.org.uk
www.enhamtrust.org.uk
Chief Executive: Peta Wilkinson
Enham delivers a wide range of essential services, from housing and employment to personal development and care, that provide choices and empower people to make their own decisions about their lives. Enham also operates a number of commercial enterprises that provide direct employment opportunities for disabled people, improve access to essential products and services and generate income to support Enham's charitable objectives.
Employees: 280
Volunteers: 90
Regional offices: 8

Enterprising Futures

Kingsley, The Brampton,
Newcastle under Lyme ST5 0QW
T: 01782 854803
E: wnixon@enterprisingfutures.org.uk
www.pmtraining.org.uk
CEO: Will Nixon
Employees: 7

Environment Africa Trust

110 Colleys Lane, Nantwich,
Cheshire CW5 6NT
T: 01270 662692 (also fax)
E: mike.chandler@environmentafricatrust.org.uk
www.environmentafricatrust.org.uk
Executive Director: Mike Chandler
Environment Africa Trust supports organisations and projects within Sub-Saharan Africa that encourage sound environmental management and biodiversity conservation through a strong community development focus to achieve sustainable livelihoods. Our partner Mpingo Conservation and Development Initiative in Tanzania is developing a fair trade in African Blackwood that is being promoted by Sound and Fair. EAT welcomes approaches from projects that have the above vision and focus in Sub-Saharan Africa that are seeking a UK partner.
Volunteers: 6

Environmental Investigation Agency Trust

62-63 Upper Street, London N1 0NY
T: 020 7354 7960
E: ukinfo@eia-international.org
www.eia-international.org
Executive Director: Mary Rice
The Environmental Investigation Agency (EIA) is an independent campaigning organisation committed to bringing about change that protects the natural world from environmental crime and abuse. Our vision is a future where humanity respects, protects and celebrates the natural world for the benefit of all
Employees: 26
Volunteers: 5

Environmental Law Foundation

Suite 309, 16-16a Baldwins Gardens,
London EC1N 7RJ
T: 020 7404 1030
E: info@elflaw.org
www.elflaw.org
ELF helps community groups and individuals gain access to the law in order to protect their environment.

Envision

3rd Floor, 63 Gee Street,
London EC1V 3RS
T: 020 7253 1677
E: vision@envision.org.uk
www.envsion.org.uk
CEO: Jennie Butterworth
Envision's programme supports 16-19 year olds from over 130 schools and colleges in Birmingham, Bristol and London. Envision programmes help young people to design their own local community projects tackling issues of their own choice. We seek to provide individuals with a powerful and rewarding experience of making a positive difference so they will be both willing and able to continue acting as effective role models for their communities building powerful legacies of their own.
Employees: 28
Volunteers: 180

Epic Arts

Bradbury Studios, 138 Kingsland Road,
London E2 8DY
T: 020 7613 6440 (also fax)
E: info@epicarts.org.uk
www.epicarts.org.uk
CEO: Rachel Duncombe-Anderson
The aim is to create arts opportunities for people who previously lacked access, especially those who are disadvantaged because of disability, poverty or age.
Employees: 6
Volunteers: 4
Regional offices: 1

Epilepsy Action

New Anstey House, Gate Way Drive,
Yeadon, Leeds LS19 7XY
T: 0113 210 8800
Helpline: 0808 800 5050
F: 0113 391 0300
E: epilepsy@epilepsy.org.uk
www.epilepsy.org.uk
Chief Executive: Philip Lee

Aims to increase public awareness and understanding of epilepsy; to provide information and advice; to promote research into the condition; to raise funds for epilepsy; to campaign for change.

Epilepsy Research UK

PO Box 3004, London W4 4XT
T: 020 8995 4781 (also fax)
E: info@eruk.org.uk
www.epilepsyresearch.org.uk
Epilepsy Research UK was formed by the merger of the Epilepsy Research Foundation and the Fund for Epilepsy in April 2007. It is the only national charity exclusively dedicated to research into epilepsy.
Employees: 4

Epilepsy Society

Chalfont Centre, Chalfont St Peter, Gerrards Cross, Buckinghamshire SL9 0RJ
T: 01494 601300
Helpline: 01494 601400
E: judy.consden@epilepsysociety.org.uk
www.epilepsysociety.org.uk
Chief Executive: Angela Geer
Epilepsy Society's mission is to enhance the quality of life of people affected by epilepsy by promoting research, education and public awareness, and by delivering specialist medical care and support services.

Equality and Diversity Forum

Tavis House, 1-6 Tavistock Square, London WC1H 9NA
T: 020 3033 1454
E: info@edf.org.uk
www.edf.org.uk/
CEO: Ali Harris
The Equality and Diversity Forum (EDF) is the network of national NGOs working on equality and human rights. Our vision is of a society: in which everyone can fulfil their potential and make a distinctive contribution; where diversity is celebrated, people can express their identities free from the threat of violence and everyone is treated with dignity and respect; where your chance to flourish is not limited by who you are or where you come from. EDF uses its strength as a network of committed and influential organisations to work for a society in which everyone can fulfil their potential, everyone is treated with respect regardless of background or circumstances, and diversity is celebrated. Our charitable aims are to promote: equality and in particular the elimination of discrimination on the grounds of age, disability, gender, gender identity, race, religion or belief, and sexual orientation or any combination of these grounds; understanding of and support for human rights; the efficiency and effectiveness of voluntary sector organisations working in the areas of equality and human rights.
Employees: 5
Volunteers: 1
Income: £279,285 (2014-15)

Equity Trust Fund

222 Africa House, 64 Kingsway, London WC2B 6BD
T: 020 7404 6041
E: kaethe@equitycharitabletrust.org.uk
www.equitytrustfund.org.uk
Aims to assist professional performers in need, in particular past and present members of British Actors Equity.

ERIC (Education and Resources for Improving Childhood Continence)

36 Old School House, Britannia Road, Kingswood, Bristol BS15 8DB
T: 0117 960 3060
Helpline: 0845 370 8008
F: 0117 960 0401
E: info@eric.org.uk
www.eric.org.uk
Interim CEO: David Derbyshire
ERIC provides information and support on bedwetting, daytime wetting, soiling and constipation, and potty training. Our telephone helpline is available Mondays and Wednesdays from 09:30 to 4:30. Leaflets and further information to download and a moderated message board are available on the ERIC website. Useful and practical resources are available to purchase from www.ericshop.org.uk.
Employees: 12
Volunteers: 2
Regional offices: 1
Income: £650,000 (2013-14)

Eritrean Relief Association (UK)

Robin House, 2a Iverson Road, London NW6 2HE
T: 020 7328 7888
Helpline: 07957 113307
E: seble@era-uk.org
www.era-uk.org
Chairman: Seble Ephrem
The Eritrean Relief Association (UK) is set up to provide relief, rehabilitation and development support and assistance to humans and their livestock affected by drought, war and displacement in Eritrea. ERA-UK also provides capacity building advice, information and guidance to people from Eritrea living in the UK.
Volunteers: 10
Regional offices: 1

Ernest Foundation

45 Cardiff House, Peckham Park Road, London SE15 6TT
T: 020 7635 9607
E: theernestfoundation@hotmail.com
www.theernestfoundation.org
Coordinator: Ernest Nkrumah
Carries out activities and projects that will bring support and relief to people living with HIV/AIDS and related diseases among the Ghanaian and other West African communities in England and Wales. Working with children and young people.

Esmee Fairbairn Foundation

Kings Place, 90 York Way, London N1 9AG
T: 020 7812 3700
F: 020 7812 3701
E: info@esmeefairbairn.org.uk
www.esmeefairbairn.org.uk
The Esmee Fairbairn Foundation aims to improve the quality of life throughout the UK by funding the charitable activities of organisations that have the ideas and ability to achieve change for the better. We take pride in supporting work that might otherwise be considered difficult to fund. Our primary interests are in the arts, children and young people, environment, social change and food.
Employees: 28

Ethical Property Foundation

Development House, London EC2A 4LT
T: 020 7065 0760
F: 020 7065 0768
E: victoriahowse@ethicalproperty.org.uk
www.ethicalproperty.org.uk
The Ethical Property Foundation is a charity committed to empowering charities and community groups to make the most of their property. The Foundation is also committed to improving the environmental and social performance of the commercial property sector.
Employees: 5
Regional offices: 1

Ethical Trading Initiative

8 Coldbath Square, London EC1R 5HL
Helpline: 020 7841 5180
F: 020 7831 7852
E: eti@eti.org.uk
www.ethicaltrade.org
Director: Dan Rees

We are an alliance of global brands and retailers, trade unions, campaigning organisations and charities that work together to improve the lives of workers in global supply chains. We provide practical tools and guidance for companies to help them implement codes of labour practice in their supply chains, and are widely recognised as a global leader in this area.
Employees: 15

Ethiopian Community Centre in the UK

Selby Centre, Selby Road, London N17 8JL
T: 020 8801 9224
F: 020 8801 0244
E: post@eccuk.org
www.embraceuk.org
Executive Director: Alem Gebrehiwot
Provides information, advice and guidance for migrants, refugees and asylum seekers (particularly but not exclusively of Ethiopian origin), on education and training, welfare benefits, housing, immigration, money and debt, health-related issues with a particular focus on HIV/AIDS and mental health, and also conducts research as necessary.
Employees: 12
Volunteers: 45

Ethiopian Community In Britain

2a Lithos Road, London NW3 6EF
T: 020 7794 4265
F: 020 7794 4116
E: postmaster@ethiopiancommunity.co.uk
www.ethiopiancommunity.co.uk
Coordinator: Eyoel F.Mengesha
Provides information, advice, advocacy and referral services and training for Ethiopians and members of other communities, as well as outreach, sports and leisure activities. It also runs ESOL and IT training courses for unemployed refugees and asylum seekers, irrespective of their country of origin.
Volunteers: 1

Europe Trust

PO Box MAR005, Markfield, Leicestershire LE67 9RY
T: 01530 245919
E: info@europetrust.eu.com
www.europetrust.eu.com
Provides support to community-based organisations.
Employees: 3

European Atlantic Movement

Start Farm, Harlow Road, Ongar, Essex CM5 0DT
T: 01277 890282
E: info@european-atlantic.org.uk
www.european-atlantic.org.uk
President: Lord Watson of Richmond
TEAM is an independent educational foundation that aims to promote understanding and discussion of European and world affairs.
Volunteers: 40

European Extension College

23 Castalia Square, Docklands, London E14 3NG
T: 0870 385 1213
Helpline: 0870 385 1218
F: 0870 385 1217
E: info@extensioncollege.org
www.extensioncollege.org
The European Extension College is a non-profit educational association established in London. The mission of the College is to provide opportunities for learning throughout life by enabling access to individualised and flexible quality education and training, and to support the advancement and improvement of education at all levels for the benefit of the public.
Volunteers: 10
Regional offices: 2

European League of Stuttering Associations

31 Grosvenor Road, Jesmond, Newcastle upon Tyne NE2 2RL
T: 0191 281 8003
E: elsa.europe@ymail.com
www.elsa.info
Chair: Edwin Farr
Coordinates, links together and furthers the cooperation of Europe's national stuttering associations.
Volunteers: 10
Regional offices: 2

Eva Women's Aid

E: julie@eva.org.uk

Evacuees Reunion Association

The Mill Business Centre, Mill Hill, Gringley-on-the-Hill, Nottinghamshire DN10 4RA
T: 01777 816166
E: era@evacuees.org.uk
www.evacuees.org.uk
Chief Executive: James Roffey
The Association has 2,200 members worldwide, mails out a monthly newsletter The Evacuee and organises events to raise the profile of the story of the evacuation of thousands of children both within the UK and abroad at the outbreak of war and the following years. We visit schools and give talks on the evacuation to numerous groups and have published Send Them to Safety, the story of the Great British evacuation.
Employees: 2
Volunteers: 100

Evangelical Alliance

176 Copenhagen Street, London N1 0ST
T: 020 7520 3830
E: info@eauk.org
www.eauk.org
General Director: Steve Clifford
A Christian charity founded in 1846 to promote unity and truth, and represent evangelical concerns to the wider world of the church, state and society.

Evelyn 190 Centre

190 Evelyn Street, Deptford, London SE8 5DB
T: 020 8691 7180
F: 020 8692 9305
E: admin@evelyn190centre.org.uk
Centre Manager : Elona Elliott
To provide Advice services (Housing, Welfare Rights, Employment and Debt) to the residents of the Borough of Lewisham
Employees: 6
Volunteers: 2
Income: £230,000 (2013-14)

EveryChild

4 Bath Place, Rivington Street, London EC2A 3DR
T: 020 7749 2468
F: 020 7729 8339
E: gen@everychild.org.uk
www.everychild.org.uk
EveryChild works with some of the world's most vulnerable and marginalised children to enable them to grow up free from disease, poverty and exploitation. We work with children, communities and governments across 18 countries to ensure that every child has the right to an education, healthcare and to grow up in a loving family environment.
Employees: 50
Volunteers: 15
Regional offices: 1

Evidence For Development

E: celiapetty@gmail.com

Ex-Services Mental Welfare Society (Combat Stress)

Tyrwhitt House, Oaklawn Road,
Leatherhead, Surrey KT22 0BX
T: 01372 587100
Helpline: 01372 587080
F: 01372 587081
E: contactus@combatstress.org.uk
www.combatstress.org.uk
Chief Executive: Commodore Andrew Cameron

Combat Stress seeks to help those of all ranks from the armed forces and the Merchant Navy suffering from psychological disability as a result of their service. To this end, the charity provides visiting welfare officers and treatment centres to aid former servicemen and women.

Employees: 171
Regional offices: 4

Examination Officers' Association

E: andrew.harland@examofficers.org.uk

Explore

The EWR Centre, Cloudesley Street,
London N1 0HU
T: 020 7278 0699
F: 020 7278 0589
E: enquiries@theexploreexperience.co.uk
www.theexploreexperience.co.uk

Explore is a registered educational charity that enables young people in schools, colleges and prisons to explore the experience of couples and, through this study, to appreciate lasting relationship skills, emotional literacy, family life and marriage.

EXTEND Exercise Training Ltd

2 Place Farm, Wheathampstead,
Hertfordshire AL4 8SB
T: 01582 832760 (also fax)
E: admin@extend.org.uk
www.extend.org.uk
CEO: Cynthia Robinson

EXTEND Exercise delivers accredited training courses and CPD to fitness teachers and provides Exercise to Music and Chair Based Exercise classes to 25,000 older adults and disabled people nationwide. EXTEND classes are delivered by qualified, insured and experienced instructors, working in the community or in care facilities. EXTEND Exercise ensures that all classes are tailored to meet the needs of every participant, delivering increased mobility, improved strength, coordination and balance and countering loneliness and isolation.

Employees: 6
Volunteers: 5

Eye on the Wild

Unit 10, The Glasshouse,
49a Goldhawk Road, London W12 8QP
T: 020 8204 8466
E: trustee4eow@hotmail.com
www.eyeonthewild.org
Chair: Lord Brian Hamilton

A small environmental charity that focuses on damage or influences caused by tourism. Identifies causes and concerns in flora, fauna, environment and communities globally directly or indirectly influenced by tourism and travel. Extensive operations and projects globally.

Volunteers: 4

Fable Charity

Lower Ground Floor, 305 Glossop Road,
Sheffield, South Yorkshire S10 2HL
T: 0114 275 5335
Helpline: 0800 521629
F: 0114 275 6444
E: sarah-fable@btconnect.com
www.fable.org.uk
Founder: Sandra Howard

For A Better Life with Epilepsy or FABLE is a national charity that helps people with epilepsy, or issues or associated with epilepsy, to increase their quality of life. It operates a free phone advice line and drop-in advice and information centre in Sheffield, along with a national patient support network.

Employees: 7
Volunteers: 10
Regional offices: 1

Fair Play for Children Association/ Charitable Trust

32 Longford Road, Bognor Regis,
West Sussex PO21 1AG
T: 0845 330 7635
E: fairplay@arunet.co.uk
www.fairplayforchildren.org
National Secretary: Jan Cosgrove

Campaigns for children's right to play, including more, better and safer facilities and services for all children. Provision of information, news and services such as CRB Enhanced Disclosures.

Employees: 3
Volunteers: 12

Fair Trials International

Temple Chambers, 3/7 Temple Avenue,
London EC4Y 0HP
T: 020 7822 2370
F: 020 7822 2371
E: office@fairtrials.net
www.fairtrials.net
Chief Executive Officer: Jago Russell

Works for fair trials according to international standards of justice and defends the rights of those facing charges in a country other than their own.

Employees: 9
Volunteers: 5
Regional offices: 1

Fairtrade Foundation

3rd Floor, Ibex House, 42-47 Minories,
London EC3N 1DY
T: 020 7405 5942
F: 020 7977 0101
E: mail@fairtrade.org.uk
www.fairtrade.org.uk
Chief Executive: Mike Gidney

Fairtrade is about better prices, decent working conditions and fair terms of trade for farmers and workers. We support over 1.5 million farmers and workers in 1,210 producer organisations across the Fairtrade system. But there are many more still urgently in need of a fair deal. As a certification scheme, our Fairtrade Standards provide one of our primary and also most visible tools for empowering small farmer and worker organisations. But beyond the standards and certification, the Fairtrade system also provides direct and indirect support to producers and their organisations to deepen social and environmental sustainability.

Employees: 125
Volunteers: 20
Income: £11,617,000 (2014-15)

Faith Based Regeneration Network UK

London N1 9LL
T: 020 7713 8193
E: doreenf@fbrn.org.uk
www.fbrn.org.uk
Executive Director: Doreen Finneron

FbRN UK is the leading national multi-faith network for community development, regeneration and social action. It encourages the active engagement of faith groups in civil society by linking practitioners across the different faith traditions for mutual learning, and provides an interface between policy makers and communities. It is managed by a trustee body drawn from nine faith traditions:

Baha'i, Buddhist, Christian, Hindu, Jain, Jewish, Muslim, Sikh and Zoroastrian.
Employees: 5

Faith in Families

7 Colwick Road, West Bridgford, Nottingham NG2 5AF
T: 0115 955 8811
F: 0115 955 8822
E: enquiries@faithinfamilies.org
www.faithinfamilies.org
Chief Executive Officer: Sumerjit Ram
Faith in Families is a registered charity and voluntary adoption agency. The charity is based in Nottingham and works throughout the East Midlands. Faith in Families vision is to provide nurturing, innovative, high quality services for children and families. We believe that the services we provide will enable all children to develop into confident, secure, caring individuals, with the capacity to reach their full potential in life.
Employees: 42
Volunteers: 150
Regional offices: 2

Families for Children

Southgate Court, Buckfast, Devon TQ11 0EE
T: 01364 645480
F: 01364 645499
E: marketing@familiesforchildren.org.uk
www.familiesforchildren.org.uk
CEO: Caroline Davis OBE
Families for Children is a vibrant adoption agency based in the south west. We place vulnerable children from all over country with adoptive families in Devon, Dorset and Cornwall. We are a specialist adoption agency providing advice and support for those who are considering adoption and also offer our 'forever' policy of support. This means that we can offer adoption support to the child and new family for as long as they need us.
Employees: 40
Regional offices: 2
Income: £1,300,000 (2012-13)

Families Need Fathers

Studio 206, 134 Curtain Road, London EC2A 3AR
T: 0300 030 0110
Helpline: 0300 030 0363
F: 020 7739 3410
E: admin@fnf.org.uk
www.fnf.org.uk
Chairman of Trustees: Jerry Karlin
Families Need Fathers is a registered UK charity that provides information and support to parents of either sex, grandparents and wider family members following divorce and separation. FNF is chiefly concerned with the problems of maintaining a child's relationship with both parents during and after family breakdown.
Employees: 4
Volunteers: 60-100

Family Action

London E8 4AU
T: 020 7254 6251
F: 020 7249 5443
E: info@family-action.org.uk
www.family-action.org.uk
Chief Executive: Helen Dent
Assists families and individuals to overcome the effects of poverty and disadvantage in tangible ways, by providing services offering practical, emotional and financial support.
Employees: 750
Volunteers: 500
Regional offices: 8

Family and Childcare Trust

2nd Floor, The Bridge, 81 Southwark Bridge Road, London SE1 0NQ
T: 020 7940 7510
E: info@familyandchildcaretrust.org
www.familyandchildcaretrust.org
Chief Executive: Julia Margo
The Family and Childcare Trust works to make the UK a better place for families. Our vision is of a society where government, business and communities do all they can to support every family to thrive. Through our research, campaigning and practical support we are creating a more family friendly UK.
Employees: 25

Family Education Trust (Family and Youth Concern)

The Atrium, 31 Church Road, Ashford, Middlesex TW15 2UD
T: 01784 242340
F: 01784 252343
E: info@familyeducationtrust.org.uk
www.familyeducationtrust.org.uk
Director: Norman Wells
An independent educational charity conducting and promoting research into the causes and consequences of family breakdown. Through its publications, media profile and responses to government consultations and inquiries, the Trust seeks to promote the welfare of children and families in line with the research evidence.

Family Holiday Association

16 Mortimer Street, London W1T 3JL
T: 020 7436 3304
E: info@fhaonline.org.uk
www.fhaonline.org.uk
Director: John McDonald
Aims to increase access to holidays for families on a low income.
Employees: 10
Volunteers: 100

Family Links

Units 2 & 3 Fenchurch Court, Bobby Fryer Close, Cowley, Oxford, Oxfordshire OX4 6ZN
T: 01865 401800
F: 01865 401820
E: info@familylinks.org.uk
www.familylinks.org.uk
Chief Executive: Annette Mountford
Family Links is a national charity that believes every child and parent deserves the best chance in life. We enable parents and teachers to become more effective, caring and confident in raising emotionally resilient and socially competent children. Our dynamic approach tackles the root causes of social problems with the Nurturing Programme, which challenges intergenerational dysfunction. Since 1997, we have helped 100,000 families achieve profound changes by training family support workers.
Employees: 28
Volunteers: 9
Regional offices: 1

Family Lives

CAN Mezzanine, 49-51 East Road, London N1 6AH
Helpline: 0808 800 2222
E: rachelt@familylives.org.uk
www.familylives.org.uk
Chief Executive: Jeremy Todd
Family Lives is a charity that supports parents, young people and families in England with all aspects of family life. They can be contacted via the helpline, as well as through email, Skype and live chat.

Family Matters Institute

Moggerhanger Park, Park Road, Moggerhanger, Bedfordshire MK44 3RW
T: 01767 641002 (also fax)
E: family@familymatters.org.uk
www.familymatters.org.uk
Family Matters Institute is an educational charity motivated by the Christian faith to provide affordable training in order to mobilise church and community groups to

support the family in marriage and couple relationships, parenting and money issues. We also carry out research in these areas.
Employees: 10
Volunteers: 4
Regional offices: 1

Family Rights Group

The Print House, 18 Ashwin Street, London E8 3DL
T: 020 7923 2628
F: 020 7923 2683
E: office@frg.org.uk
www.frg.org.uk
Supports and advises families involved with social services; promotes the involvement of children, parents and families in the decision-making process, so that the best decisions are made; develops and promotes policies and practices that help secure the best possible futures for children and families.
Employees: 16

Farm Africa

9th Floor, Bastion House, 140 London Wall, London EC2Y 5DN
T: 020 7430 0440
F: 020 7430 0460
E: farmafrica@farmafrica.org.uk
www.farmafrica.org
Chief Executive: Nigel Harris
Farm Africa reduces poverty permanently by unleashing African farmers' abilities to grow their incomes and manage their natural resources sustainably. We work with different types of farmers (pastoralists, agro-pastoralists, smallholders and forest dwellers) in a range of regions in eastern Africa. Their specific situations vary but most are facing increasing economic, health and environmental vulnerability.
Employees: 265
Volunteers: 2
Regional offices: 24

Farm Animal Welfare Network

Northfield Farmhouse, Wytham, Oxford OX2 8QJ
T: 01865 244315
E: fawcsecretariat@defra.gsi.gov.uk
www.farmanimalwelfaretrust.org.uk
Campaigns for the worldwide abolition of the battery cage system for laying hens, and opposes other intensive and cruel systems for all farmed animals.

Farms for City Children

Bridge House, 25 Fore Street, Okehampton, Devon EX20 1DL
T: 01837 55876
E: admin@farmsforcitychildren.org
www.farmsforcitychildren.org
Aims to enrich the lives and develop the potential of children from disadvantaged urban areas by providing a residential week on a working farm, where children participate purposefully in the life of the farm.

FAS Aware UK

c/o 4 Wakefield Crescent, Standish, Wigan, Lancashire WN6 0AU
T: 01257 432423
E: fasawareuk@blueyonder.co.uk
www.fasaware.co.uk
Full-time Volunteer Coordinator: Gloria Armistead MBE
To provide information, training and accredited courses. Support to improve the health and social wellbeing of all those affected by foetal alcohol spectrum disorders. To develop and support autonomous support groups.
Volunteers: 20

FATIMA Women's Network

Innovation Centre, Oxford Street, Leicester, Leicestershire LE1 5XY
T: 0845 331 2373
F: 0870 005 2608
E: parvin@fatima-network.com
www.fatima-network.com
Chief Executive: Parvin Ali
FATIMA (Forum for Advocacy, Training and Information in a Multicultural Arena) Women's Network is a BME-led socially responsible enterprise supporting the social and economic empowerment of women and their families, particularly those from diverse and disadvantaged communities, through personal development, advocacy, research, training, business support and cross-community networking. As a national infrastructure organisation we seek to build the resilience and connectivity of women's groups.
Employees: 6
Volunteers: 15

Fawcett Society

Unit 204, Linton House, 168-180 Union Street, London SE1 0LH
T: 020 3598 6154
E: info@fawcettsociety.org.uk
www.fawcettsociety.org.uk
Chief Executive: Sam Smethers
Fawcett is the UK's leading campaigning organisation for women's equality and rights – at home, at work and in public life. We are the UK's largest independent membership organisation with a dedicated focus on advancing women's equality and rights in modern Britain. We effect change by combining direct lobbying within the political system with campaigns that increase and demonstrate public support for action.
Employees: 9
Volunteers: 3

Federal Trust for Education and Research

31 Jewry Street, London EC3N 2EY
T: 020 7320 3045
E: info@fedtrust.co.uk
www.fedtrust.co.uk
Director: Brendan Donnelly
Promotes research and education about federal solutions to national, European and global problems.
Employees: 4

Federation for Community Development Learning

3rd Floor, The Circle, 33 Rockinghan Lane, Sheffield, South Yorkshire S1 4FW
T: 0114 253 6770
F: 0114 253 6771
E: info@fcdl.org.uk
www.fcdl.org.uk
Head of Agency: Janice Marks
FCDL welcomes the membership of everyone who is interested in or who practises community development, whether community activists or voluntary or paid workers. This includes generic CD practitioners or practitioners from other occupations (e.g. health, housing, environment) who are interested in using a CD approach to engage with and work effectively with communities. We support a network of individuals, groups and organisations who share information and good training practice and provide opportunities for CD learning.
Employees: 8

Federation of British Artists

17 Carlton House Terrace, London SW1Y 5BD
T: 020 7930 6844
E: info@mallgalleries.com
www.mallgalleries.org.uk
Director: Lewis McNaught
Provides exhibition space and other services to artists and administers the nine constituent societies of the Federation.
Regional offices: 1

Federation of City Farms and Community Gardens

The Greenhouse, Hereford Street, Bedminster, Bristol, Avon BS3 4NA
T: 0117 923 1800
E: admin@farmgarden.org.uk
www.farmgarden.org.uk
Director: Jeremy Iles
Supports, represents and promotes community-managed farms and gardens in the UK.
Employees: 32
Regional offices: 6

Federation Of English Karate Organisations (international)

234 West Park Drive West, Roundhay, Leeds, West Yorkshire LS8 2BD
T: 0113 269 0383
E: jimreece@tradka.org.uk
www.feko.co.uk
Chair: Noel Mantock
FEKO is a Federation of Karate Associations offering its members support, guidance and a range of services to enable them to manage their own organisations.

Federation of Merchant Mariners

16 Glebe Road, Brampton, Huntingdon, Cambridgeshire PE28 4PH
T: 01480 412958
E: info@merchant-mariners.co.uk
www.merchant-mariners.co.uk
FMM brings together many associations/organisations connected to the Merchant Navy, filling a gap that had existed in the maritime scene for over 60 years. Its aim is to gain recognition for the role that merchant seafarers have played in the defence and development of our nation.

Federation of Private Residents Associations Ltd

PO Box 10271, Epping, Essex CM16 9DB
T: 0871 200 3324
E: info@fpra.org.uk
www.fpra.org.uk
Chairman: Bob Smytherman
Volunteers: 20

Feline Advisory Bureau

Taeselbury, High Street, Tilsbury, Wiltshire SP3 6LD
T: 01747 871872
E: information@fabcats.org
www.icatcare.org
Promotes the wellbeing of cats in sickness and health; the increased understanding of feline diseases; the improvement of standards of boarding; humane behaviour towards, and increased understanding of, the cat.

Fellowship of Depressives Anonymous

Self Help Nottingham, Ormiston House, Nottingham NG1 2EG
T: 0870 774 4319
E: fdainfo@hotmail.com
www.depressionanon.co.uk
Supports and encourages people suffering from, or who have suffered from, depression and those who care about them, on a self-help/mutual support basis.

Fellowship of Postgraduate Medicine

12 Chandos Street, Cavendish Square, London W1G 9DR
T: 020 7636 6334
F: 020 7436 2535
E: admin@fpm-uk.org
www.fpm-uk.org
President: Donald Singer
The Fellowship achieves its objectives of development of postgraduate educational programmes in all branches of medicine through the publication of its international journal, the Postgraduate Medical Journal, and by hosting a range of seminars and conferences.
Employees: 1

Fellowship of Reconciliation

E: emma@for.org.uk

Fellowship of the School of Economic Science

11 Mandeville Place, London W1U 3AJ
T: 020 7034 4000
F: 020 7034 4001
E: secretary@fses.org
www.schooleconomicscience.org
Promotes the study of natural laws governing the relations between men in society and the study of the laws, customs and practices by which communities are governed.
Employees: 15

Female Prisoners Welfare Project and Hibiscus

18 Borough High Street, London SE1 9QG
T: 020 7357 6543
E: fpwphibiscus@aol.com
Provides welfare advice and support for women in prison, especially those disadvantaged by the criminal justice system such as foreign nationals and those from ethnic minorities.

FIA Foundation for the Automobile and Society

60 Trafalgar Square, London WC2N 5DS
T: 020 7930 3882
F: 020 7930 3883
E: j.pearce@fiafoundation.org
www.fiafoundation.org
Director General: David Ward
The Foundation was established in the UK by the Federation Internationale de l'Automobile (FIA), the non-profit federation of motoring organisations and the governing body of world motor sport. The foundation manages and supports an international programme of activities promoting road safety, environmental protection and sustainable mobility, as well as funding specialist motor sport safety research.
Employees: 13

Field Lane Foundation

16 Vine Hill, London EC1R 5EA
T: 020 7837 0412
E: info@fieldlane.org.uk
www.fieldlane.org.uk
Field Lane is a Christian charity that is committed to providing innovative accommodation and day-centre support services for families who are homeless, older people and people with disabilities.

Fieldfare Trust Ltd

Volunteer House, 69 Crossgate, Cupar KY15 5AS
T: 01334 657708
F: 0844 443 1139
E: info@fieldfare.org.uk
www.fieldfare.org.uk
Chief Executive: Ian Newman
The Fieldfare Trust works with, not for, people with disabilities to promote disabled access and provide environmental education opportunities for all.
Employees: 5
Regional offices: 3

Fields In Trust

2nd Floor, 15 Crinan Street, London N1 9SQ
T: 020 7427 2110
E: helen.griffiths@fieldsintrust.org
www.fieldsintrust.org
Chief Executive: Helen Griffiths
Fields in Trust (FIT) is the only independent UK-wide organisation dedicated to protecting and improving outdoor sports and play spaces and facilities. We want to make sure that everyone young and old alike, and wherever they live has somewhere nearby to go for healthy outdoor activities. Through our

work we improve the wellbeing of millions of people nationwide.
Employees: 18
Regional offices: 3

Filipino International Emergency Services Training

12 Montgomery Crescent, Bolbeck Park, Milton Keynes MK15 8PR
T: 01908 233120
E: dalejohno@aol.com
www.fiestauk.homestead.com/homepage.html
Chair: John Dale
Provides support for the emergency services of the Philippines in the form of equipment, training and other assistance. The website also lists all the countries of the world and their emergency telephone numbers.

Find a Future

157-197 Buckingham Palace Rd, London SW1W 9SZ
T: 0800 612 0742
F: 020 7543 7489
E: enquiries@worldskillsuk.org
www.findafuture.org.uk/
UK Skills is a charity that promotes excellence in vocational skills and training through competitions and major awards. UK Skills recognises that investing in high-quality training and vocational education lead to a well-equipped workforce that is the key to the success of the UK economy.
Employees: 10

Finn-Guild

1a Mornington Court, Mornington Crescent, London NW1 7RD
T: 020 7387 3508
F: 020 7529 8750
E: mail@finn-guild.org
www.finn-guild.org
Works for the advancement of Finnish culture and language in the UK, educating about Finland, supporting the work of the Finnish Church in London. Supports the wellbeing and relief of poverty among the Finnish-British community.
Employees: 8
Volunteers: 150

Fire Fighters Charity

Level 6, Belvedere, Basing View, Basingstoke RG21 4HG
T: 01256 366568
F: 01256 366599
E: sabbott@firefighterscharity.org.uk
www.firefighterscharity.org.uk
Employees: 136

First Step Trust

32-34 Hare Street, Woolwich, London SE18 6LZ
T: 020 8855 7386 (also fax)
E: comms@firststeptrust.org.uk
www.fst.org.uk
FST offers people with enduring mental health problems, learning disabilities and other disadvantages the chance to work; experiencing the challenges of working in a small business, trading with the local community. This enables them to overcome their problems, become less dependent on health and social care services. Many go on to make the transition to paid employment.

fit4funding

Lightwaves, Lower York Street, Wakefield, West Yorkshire WF1 3LJ
T: 01924 239063
E: info@fit4funding.org.uk
www.fit4funding.org.uk
fit4funding is nationally recognised as a quality provider of training (face to face and online) on all aspects of fundraising and commissioning for voluntary and community organisations, funders and funding advisers. Much of our training is OCN accredited. We can offer bespoke training for groups, infrastructure organisations or consortia. We provide extensive information through our website, the fit4funding e-newsletter and offer consultancy support on strategic planning and fundraising.
Employees: 5
Regional offices: 1
Income: £172,309 (2013-14)

FitzRoy

FitzRoy House, 8 Hylton Road, Petersfield, Hampshire GU32 3JY
T: 01730 711111
Helpline: 0808 168 4662
F: 01730 710566
E: info@fitzroy.org
www.fitzroy.org
Chief Executive: Anna Galliford
FitzRoy transforms the lives of people with disabilities and autism, helping them live more independently at home and in the community. We are a national charity that provides a mix of residential and community services and support including supported volunteering.
Employees: 800
Volunteers: 200
Regional offices: 3

FLACK Cambridge

City Life House, Sturton Street, Cambridge CB1 2QF
T: 01223 366532
E: info@flackcambridge.org.uk
www.flackcambridge.org.uk
Chairman of the Board of Trustees: Quentin Millington
FLACK supports adults in the Cambridge area who, through homelessness, have experienced social and economic exclusion. We assist individuals to explore their personal development needs, learn relevant skills and undertake meaningful activities. In a nurturing environment, we encourage creativity, foster a sense of belonging and help people to regain confidence and self-esteem. In providing this bridge back into the wider community, we also challenge unhelpful perceptions about individuals who have experienced exclusion.
Employees: 7
Volunteers: 5
Regional offices: 1
Income: £151,230 (2012-13)

Fledglings Family Services

Wenden Court, Station Approach, Wendens Ambo, Saffron Walden, Essex CB11 4LB
T: 0845 458 1124
F: 0845 280 1539
E: enquiries@fledglings.org.uk
www.fledglings.org.uk
Founder, Trustee & Director: Ruth Lingard
Fledglings helps parents and carers of disabled children and those with additional needs to find solutions to the practical problems of everyday living. We do this by searching for, testing and supplying a range of helpful products (at affordable prices) to address specific needs. We also share information via our monthly e-News, our product brochure and an informative website.
Employees: 9
Volunteers: 12
Income: £211,884 (2014-15)

FOCUS

73 Church Gate, Leicester LE1 3AN
T: 0116 251 0369
F: 0116 262 0187
E: admin@focus-charity.co.uk
www.focus-charity.co.uk
Director: Matt Lilley
FOCUS is a charity that aims to inspire and empower young people to become more actively involved in their local community and in so doing raise their aspirations, develop

their skills and self-confidence and improve their life chances.
Employees: 5
Volunteers: 50
Regional offices: 1
Income: £126,000 (2013-14)

Foley House Trust

115 High Garrett, Braintree, Essex CM7 5NU
T: 01376 326652
F: 01376 553350
E: enquiries@foleyhouse.org.uk
www.foleyhouse.co.uk
Director: Brenda Weavers
FHT is a registered charity established in 1851 providing long or short-term care, respite and short-break accommodation to profoundly deaf and deafblind men and women at its residential home. We also provide care to hearing elderly at the residential home.
Employees: 30
Volunteers: 6
Regional offices: 1

Food Chain (UK) Ltd

Acorn House, 314-320 Gray's Inn Road, London WC1X 8DP
T: 020 7843 1800
F: 020 7843 1818
E: katie.smith@foodchain.org.uk
www.foodchain.org.uk
Chief Executive: Siobhán Lanigan
The Food Chain provides nutrition services including home-delivered meals, essential groceries and nutrition advice to men, women and children who are chronically sick as a result of HIV-related illness. We aim to ensure that no one living with the virus has their ability to get well and stay well adversely affected by lack of access to appropriate food.
Employees: 11
Volunteers: 600
Income: £800,000 (2013-14)

Foresight the Association for the Promotion of Preconceptual Care

3 Lower Queens Road, Clevedon, Somerset BS21 6LX
T: 01275 878953
E: info@foresight-preconception.org.uk
www.foresight-preconception.org.uk
Promotes natural approaches to optimal health in both parents prior to the conception of a child, with a view to minimising the risks of miscarriage, foetal damage or compromised health in the infant. Promotes research on environmental hazards to foetal life.
Employees: 4
Regional offices: 2

Fostering Network

87 Blackfriars Road, London SE1 8HA
T: 020 7620 6410
F: 020 7620 6401
E: info@fostering.net
www.fostering.net
The network is the UK's leading charity for everyone involved in fostering. We are uniquely placed to bring people and organisations together to improve the lives of children in foster care. Our work is focused on improving foster care and making a positive difference for children and young people in and leaving foster care. We do this by working with foster carers, children and young people and fostering services.
Employees: 62
Volunteers: 2

Foundation for Community Dance

LCB Depot, 31 Rutland Street, Leicester, Leicestershire LE1 1RE
T: 0116 253 3453
F: 0116 261 6801
E: emma@communitydance.org.uk
www.communitydance.org.uk
Executive Director: Chris Stenton
The Foundation for Community Dance is the UK development agency for access, participation and progression in dance for all.
Employees: 14

Foundation for Conductive Education

Cannon Hill House, Russell Road, Moseley, Birmingham B13 8LD
T: 0121 449 1569
E: foundation@conductive-education.org.uk
www.conductive-education.org.uk
Aims to develop and advance the science and skill of conductive education and especially its teaching.

Foundation for Public Service Interpreting

12 Tudor Rose Court, Fann Street, London EC2Y 8DY
T: 020 7623 9191
E: director@fpsi.org
www.fpsi.org
Chief Executive: Mark Kiddle
The Foundation aims to promote a national minimum standard in public service interpreting, together with an affordable telephone interpreting service.
Employees: 3
Volunteers: 5

Foundation for the Study of Infant Deaths

Artillery House, London SW1P 1RT
T: 020 7222 8001
Helpline: 020 7233 2090
F: 020 7222 8002
E: joyce.epstein@sids.org.uk
www.fsid.org.uk
Director: Joyce Epstein
FSID aims to prevent unexpected infant death and promote infant health. We do this by funding research, supporting families, disseminating information on safe infant care and working with professionals to improve investigations of infant deaths.
Employees: 27
Volunteers: 200
Regional offices: 8

Foundation for Women's Health Research and Development

Unit 4, London NW10 5NY
T: 020 8960 4000
F: 020 8960 4014
E: yasmin@forwarduk.org.uk
www.forwarduk.org.uk
The Foundation aims to improve women's and children's health, with special emphasis on the eradication of female genital mutilation.
Employees: 3

Foundation of Nursing Studies (FoNS)

11-13 Cavendish Square, London W1G 0AN
T: 020 7307 2857
E: theresa.shaw@fons.org
www.fons.org
Chief Executive: Dr Theresa Shaw
Our Vision: To inspire and enable a culture across health and social care that values people, where patients experience care that is the best it can be and staff feel appreciated and supported. Our Mission: To work in partnership with health and social care organisations to a foster a commitment to person-centredness by valuing staff and enabling them to develop of the knowledge, skills and expertise to deliver care that is safe, effective and compassionate.
Employees: 4
Income: £365,941 (2013-14)

Foundation66

7 Holyrood Street, London SE1 2EL
T: 020 7234 9940
F: 020 7357 6712
E: info@foundation66.org.uk
www.foundation66.org.uk
CEO: Sally Scriminger
Foundation is a London-based charity and a registered social landlord. We exist to reduce the harm caused by problem alcohol and drug use. We provide client-focused community and accommodation-based services, supporting people to achieve positive change and freedom from the harmful effects of alcohol and other drugs.
Employees: 150
Volunteers: 6

Foundations UK

2 Augustine Road, London W14 0HZ
T: 020 7602 0862 (also fax)
E: deirdre@foundationsuk.org
www.foundationsuk.org
Aims to relieve those suffering with eating disorders or disordered eating and those affected by such suffering.
Employees: 1
Volunteers: 4

Fountain Society

Weathertop, Tower Hill, Dorking, Surrey RH4 2AP
T: 01306 883874
E: info@fountainsol.org.uk
www.fountainsol.org.uk
The society works to secure the conservation and restoration of fountains, cascades and waterfalls of aesthetic merit for public and domestic enjoyment. It also promotes the provision of fountains etc. in new developments to which the public have access.

Foyer Federation

3rd Floor, London EC1N 8HX
T: 020 7430 2212
F: 020 7430 2213
E: joel@foyer.net
www.foyer.net
Employees: 17

FPA

45 Park Mount, Harpenden, Hertfordshire AL5 3AS
T: 020 7923 5211
E: johng@fpa.org.uk
www.fpa.org.uk
The FPA promotes sexual health and the reproductive rights and choice of all people throughout the UK.

Fragile X Society

Rood End House, 6 Stortford Road, Great Dunmow, Essex CM6 1DA
T: 01371 875100
E: info@fragilex.org.uk
www.fragilex.org.uk
Managing Director: Tim Potter
The Society provides mutual support and information to families, encourages research and increases public and professional awareness of fragile X syndrome.
Employees: 6
Volunteers: 27
Income: £179,900 (2012-13)

Fraud Advisory Panel

Chartered Accountants' Hall, PO Box 433, Moorgate Place, London EC2P 2BJ
T: 020 7920 8721
F: 020 7920 8545
E: info@fraudadvisorypanel.org
www.fraudadvisorypanel.org
The Panel aims to raise awareness of fraud and financial crime in all its guises, and to develop effective remedies.
Employees: 2
Volunteers: 500

Free Word

60 Farringdon Road, London EC1R 3GA
T: 020 7324 2571
E: eleanor@freewordonline.com
Executive Director: Eleanor Lang

Freeplay Foundation

London W1S 2YZ
T: 020 7851 2616
E: jfairbairn@freeplayfoundation.org
www.freeplayfoundation.org
Chief Executive: Kristine Pearson
The Freeplay Foundation is unlike any other non-profit humanitarian organisation in the world. Our mission is to enable access to information and education for the most vulnerable populations through appropriate and sustainable technologies, particularly self-powered radios. The Freeplay Foundation collaborates with in-country non-governmental organisations (NGOs), government ministries, international organisations and broadcasters to ensure radio information and education reaches the widest possible rural populations.
Employees: 10

Freshwinds

Prospect Hall, 12 College Walk, Selly Oak, Birmingham, West Midlands B29 6LE
T: 0121 415 6670
F: 0121 415 6699
E: office@freshwinds.org.uk www.freshwinds.org.uk
Freshwinds offers care and support, without charge, to adults and children living with life-limiting illnesses, as well as to individuals from socially excluded backgrounds. The charity manages a wide range of projects, including the provision of integrated complementary therapy, advocacy, employment, debt counselling and community-based initiatives in HIV, substance misuse and crime.
Employees: 37
Volunteers: 200
Regional offices: 2

Friends of Cathedral Music

21 Bradford Road, Trowbridge, Wiltshire BA14 9AL
T: 01225 768607
E: info@fcm.org.uk
www.fcm.org.uk
The Friends publicise cathedral music, assist cathedrals in maintaining their musical activities and encourage as many people as possible to discover and enjoy cathedral music.

Friends of Friendless Churches

St Ann's Vestry Hall, 2 Church Entry, London EC4V 5HB
T: 020 7236 3934
E: office@friendsoffriendlesschurches.org.uk
www.friendsoffriendlesschurches.org.uk
Director: Matthew Saunders
Founded in 1957 to save redundant churches from demolition, decay and unsympathetic conversion. We now own 47 such buildings, half in England half in Wales (where our work is almost wholly funded by CADW and the Church in Wales). Joint membership with the Ancient Monuments Society.
Employees: 3
Volunteers: 100

Friends of the Earth

26-28 Underwood Street, London N1 7JQ
T: 020 7490 1555
F: 020 7490 0881
E: info@foe.co.uk
www.foe.co.uk
Executive Director: Andy Atkins
We campaign on issues of environmental and social justice, making life better for people by

inspiring solutions to environmental problems.
Employees: 170
Volunteers: 30
Regional offices: 12

Friends of the Elderly

London SW1W 0LZ
T: 020 7730 8263
E: enquiries@fote.org.uk
www.fote.org.uk
Supports older people, often frail, confused or with dementia, to maintain a level of independence and choice by providing a complete range of services for them in any one locality.

Friends of the Western Buddhist Order

51 Roman Road, Bethnal Green, London E2 0HU
T: 0845 458 4716
E: info@lbc.org.uk
www.lbc.org.uk
Aims to advance the Buddhist religion by encouraging members and others to live in accordance with the Buddha's teachings; to support ordained members of the Western Buddhist Order wherever possible; to maintain close contact with other groups with similar objectives.

Friendship Works

Studio 442, Highgate Studios, London NW5 1TL
T: 020 7485 0900
E: susan@friendshipworks.org.uk
www.friendshipworks.org.uk
Administrator: Richj
Employees: 12
Volunteers: 150

Fulham Football Club Foundation

Fulham FC Training Ground, Motspur Park
T: 020 8336 7432
E: enquiries@fulhamfc.com
Operations Manager: Jamie Morgan

Full Body and the Voice

The Lawrence Batley Theatre, Queen Street, Huddersfield, West Yorkshire HD1 2SP
T: 01484 484441
F: 01484 484443
E: fullbody@lbt-uk.org
www.darkhorsetheatre.co.uk
Promotes the education and training of the public in music, theatre and the performing arts, in particular enabling adults with learning disabilities to become independent and take control of their own lives, opening opportunities for employment.
Employees: 5

Fund for the Replacement of Animals in Medical Experiments

Nottingham NG1 4EE
T: 0115 958 4740
E: frame@frame.org.uk
www.frame.org.uk
Director: Robert Combes
FRAME was founded in 1969 to promote the concept of alternatives to the use of live animals in medical research and toxicity testing. FRAME believes in reducing the number of animals used, refining procedures so that the suffering of animals necessarily used is minimised and ultimately eliminating the need for live animal experiments altogether.
Employees: 8

Furniture Re-use Network

48-54 West Street, St Philips, Bristol, Avon BS2 0BL
T: 0117 954 3578
Helpline: 0845 602 8003
E: info@frn.org.uk
www.frn.org.uk
Chief Executive: Craig Anderson
The FRN promotes and supports the re-use of household and office items such as furniture, domestic appliances, TVs and computers to support low-income households and community-based organisations. We are a representative body with over 300 members working across the UK.
Employees: 10
Volunteers: 1
Regional offices: 1

Furzedown Family Centre

Graveny School Site, Welham Road, London SW17 8DN
T: 020 8672 6924
E: info@furzedownfamilycentre.org.uk
www.furzedownfamilycentre.org.uk
Centre Manager: Barbara Vine
We are a charitable organisation dedicated to providing a safe and nurturing environment for pre-school children to thrive and learn through play. The FFC is committed to providing parents/carents in the community with a warm and welcoming place to bring their children to learn by engaging with stimulating activities It is a place for both parents/carers and children to build friendships and provides an invaluable sense of belonging in the community
Employees: 7
Volunteers: 2-4

Fylde Coast YMCA

St Annes YMCA, St Albans Road, Lytham St Annes, Lancashire FY8 1XD
T: 01253 893928
E: enquiries@fyldecoastymca.org
fyldecoastymca.org
Chief Executive : John Cronin
Fylde Coast YMCA strives to transform people's lives by providing an inspirational journey which supports and develops individuals, with a focus on young people. We believe that by fulfilling this vision we can change and enhance lives.
Employees: 559
Volunteers: 50
Regional offices: 18
Income: £8,835,842 (2014-15)

Gaia House

West Ogwell, Newton Abbot, Devon TQ12 6EN
T: 01626 335256
F: 01626 352650
E: info@gaiahouse.co.uk
www.gaiahouse.co.uk
Preserves, protects and enhances physical mental emotional and spiritual health by the provision of a centre for the instruction and practice of meditation.
Employees: 6
Volunteers: 10

Galapagos Conservation Trust

28 Portland Place, London W1B 1LY
T: 020 7399 7440
E: gct@gct.org
www.galapagosconservation.org
Chief Executive: Sharon Johnson
The Galapagos Conservation Trust (GCT) was founded in 1995 with two aims: to raise awareness of the issues facing the Galapagos Islands; and to raise much needed funds to support the expanding conservation work.
Employees: 7
Volunteers: 15
Regional offices: 1

GamCare

2nd Floor, Clapham Junction,
London SW11 1TR
T: 020 7801 7000
F: 020 7378 5233
E: info@gamcare.org.uk
www.gamcare.org.uk
Works in a gambling-neutral manner with all sections of society, and delivers services that address the social impact of gambling; improves the understanding of gambling issues; promotes the concept of responsible gambling; and addresses the needs of those adversely affected by a gambling dependency.
Employees: 15
Volunteers: 15

Game & Wildlife Conservation Trust

Burgate Manor, Fordingbridge,
Hampshire SP6 1EF
T: 01425 652381
F: 01425 655848
E: info@gwct.org.uk
www.gwct.org.uk
Promotes for the public benefit the conservation and study of game species, their habitats and the other species associated with those habitats.
Employees: 120
Volunteers: 10
Regional offices: 6

Garden History Society, The

70 Cowcross Street, London EC1M 6EJ
T: 020 7608 2409
E: enquiries@gardenhistorysociety.org
www.gardenhistorysociety.org
Aims to promote the study of history of gardening, landscape gardening and horticulture; to promote protection and conservation of historic designed landscapes; to encourage creation of new parks and designed landscapes. GHS is a statutory consultee on all planning applications relating to or affecting sites entered on the English Heritage Register of Parks and Gardens of Historic Interest.

Garden Organic

Ryton Organic Gardens,
Coventry CV8 3LG
T: 024 7630 3517
F: 024 7663 9229
E: jgoold@gardenorganic.org.uk
www.hdra.org.uk
Garden Organic is the working name of the Henry Doubleday Research Association (HDRA). We are a registered charity, and Europe's largest organic membership organisation. We are dedicated to researching and promoting organic gardening, farming and food.
Employees: 120
Volunteers: 50
Regional offices: 3

Gardening for Disabled Trust

Appleton Oast, Frittenden, Kent TN17 2EG
T: 01580 852372
F: 01580 852218
E: sally@thetukes.com
www.gardeningfordisabledtrust.org.uk
Provides assistance, both practical and financial, to help disabled people wishing to take an active part in gardening. Grants may be made to help with the design of special gardens, both to individuals and to institutions, schools, hospitals etc.

Gateshead Voluntary Organisations Council

E: jennymcateer@gvoc.org.uk

Gateway Community Action

c/o Lee Omar, Refugee Action,
64 Mount Pleasant, Liverpool,
Merseyside L3 5SD
T: 07817 152444
E: festog@yahoo.com
www.gcscap.org

Gauchers Association Ltd

3 Bull Pitch, Dursley,
Gloucestershire GL11 4NG
T: 01753 646737
E: ga@gaucher.org.uk
www.gaucher.org.uk

General Assembly of Unitarian and Free Christian Churches

Essex Hall, London WC2R 3HY
T: 020 7240 2384
F: 020 7240 3089
E: amason@unitarian.org.uk
www.unitarian.org.uk
Chief Executive: Rev Steve Dick
Promotes a free and inquiring religion through the worship of God, the celebration of life, the service of humanity and respect for all creation; and the upholding of the liberal Christian tradition.
Employees: 9
Volunteers: 100
Regional offices: 177

General Council and Register of Naturopaths

1 Green Lane Avenue, Street,
Somerset BA16 0QS
T: 01458 840072
E: admin@naturopathy.org.uk
www.naturopathy.org.uk
President: Chris Burley
The Council is the largest naturopathic register in the UK. It sets and monitors educational standards in naturopathic training, sets and enforces a code of ethics, and publishes annually a listing of suitably qualified naturopathic practitioners, for the benefit and protection of the public. The GCRN operates, in association with the British Naturopathic Association, a HealthLine service for the public.
Employees: 1
Volunteers: 12

Generation for Change and Development

PO Box 2108, Ilford, Essex IG1 9LE
T: 020 8911 8767
E: abdirashid@gencad.org
www.gencad.org
GENCAD's vision is to be an exemplary organisation that contributes to the socio-economic development of pastoralist communities in the Horn of Africa. Pastoralist communities experience extreme poverty, lack of education, political and economic marginalisation in the Horn of Africa. GENCAD's mission is to increase their access to educational opportunities and health services, and to empower these communities to actively participate in and take ownership of their socio-economic development.

Genetic Alliance UK

Unit 4D, Leroy House, 436 Essex Road,
London N1 3QP
T: 020 7704 3141
E: contactus@geneticalliance.org.uk
www.geneticalliance.org.uk
Director: Alastair Kent
Genetic Alliance UK is the national alliance of patient organisations with a membership of over 150 charities supporting all those affected by genetic disorders. Our aim is to improve the lives of people affected by genetic conditions by ensuring that high-quality services and information are available to all who need them.
Employees: 15

Genetic Disorders UK

199A Victoria Street, London SW1E 5NE
T: 020 7199 3300
Helpline: 0800 987 8987
E: hello@geneticdisordersuk.org
www.geneticdisordersuk.org
Chief Executive: Caroline Harding
The mission of Genetic Disorders UK is to improve the lives of children and adults who are affected by genetic disorders. The charity aims to offer support and information to affected individuals and families as well as providing resources and grants for disorder-specific UK-based support groups and charities. Genetic Disorders UK organises the annual Jeans for Genes Day event in schools and workplaces to raise funds and awareness for its cause.
Employees: 9
Volunteers: 5

Get Connected Helpline

PO Box 7777, London W1A 5PD
T: 020 7009 2500
Helpline: 0808 808 4994
E: admin@getconnected.org.uk
www.getconnected.org.uk
Chief Executive: Fiona Clark
Get Connected is the UK's free, confidential helpline for young people under 25 who need help and don't know where to turn. Our service is available 365 days a year and young people can contact us by phone, webchat, email, text message or use our online directory, WebHelp 24/7. Our mission is to be the home of help and support for young people, enabling them to find free confidential help, whenever they need it, however they want it, no matter what the issue.
Employees: 15
Volunteers: 100

Get Hooked on Fishing

Old Billingham Business Centre,
Chapel Road, Billingham,
Stockton-On-Tees, Durham TE23 1EN
E: hello@ghof.org.uk
www.ghof.org.uk
Chief Executive Officer: Sarah Collins
We work with children and young people at risk of social exclusion across the UK. We use the vehicle of angling to help them access the personal, social, educational, community, health and well-being benefits.
Employees: 9
Volunteers: 100
Regional offices: 16

Get Well UK

9 Delancey Street, Camden Town NW1 7NL
T: 0870 438 9355
F: 0870 438 9356
E: boo@getwelluk.com
www.getwelluk.com
Managing Director: Boo Armstrong
Get Well UK makes it possible for GPs to confidently refer their patients to complementary therapists, by providing information, support and a team of highly skilled and qualified practitioners. With NHS funding, this service is free to patients. We believe that complementary medicine can play an important role in improving health and wellbeing and want to ensure that many more people have access to effective healthcare, not just people who can afford to pay for it privately.
Employees: 3

GFS Platform for Young Women

Unit 2, Angel Gate, 326 City Road,
London EC1V 2PT
T: 020 7837 9669
F: 020 7837 4107
E: info@gfsplatform.org.uk
www.gfsplatform.org.uk
Director: Joy Lauezzari
The Girls Friendly Society is a movement for young women that aims to widen horizons and celebrate individuality and talents, with love and understanding. Our vision is to inspire young women and challenge them to break down barriers, building on their achievements to become independent women.
Employees: 30
Volunteers: 175
Income: £748,881 (2013-14)

Gharweg Advice Training and Careers Centre

5 Westminster Bridge Road,
London SE1 7XW
T: 020 7620 1430
F: 020 7620 1431
E: gharweg@aol.com
Provision of welfare advice on benefits, immigration, health, housing, employment training and career guidance and counselling for black and minority communities.

Gideons International in the British Isles

24 George Street, Lutterworth,
Leicestershire LE17 4EE
T: 01455 554241
E: hq@gideons.org.uk
www.gideons.org.uk
Executive Director: Iain Mair
An interdenominational association of Christian business and professional men and their wives, which freely provides copies of the Bible or New Testament and psalms to public institutions such as hotels, hospitals, schools, homes for the elderly and prisons.
Employees: 15
Volunteers: 3600
Regional offices: 1

Gingerbread

530 Highgate Studios,
53-79 Highgate Road, London NW5 1TL
T: 020 7428 5400
F: 020 7482 4851
E: membership@gingerbread.org.uk
www.gingerbread.org.uk
Chief Executive: Fiona Weir
We provide expert advice, practical support and campaign for single parents.
Employees: 76
Regional offices: 2

Girlguiding UK

London SW1W 0PT
T: 020 7834 6242
F: 020 7828 8317
E: executive.assistant@girlguiding.org.uk
www.girlguiding.org.uk
Girlguiding UK, as part of a worldwide movement, enables girls and young women to fulfil their potential and to take an active and responsible role in society through a distinctive, stimulating and enjoyable programme of activities delivered by trained volunteer leaders. Our vision is to be recognised as the leading organisation for girls and young women and to widen and increase our membership.
Employees: 150
Volunteers: 80000
Regional offices: 9

Girls' Brigade England & Wales

Cliff College, Calver, Hope Valley,
Derbyshire S32 3XG
T: 01246 582322
E: gbco@girlsbrigadeew.org.uk
www.girlsb.org
National Director: Ruth Gilson
A membership organisation that specialises in working with churches to provide fun and inspiring local groups where girls and young women can belong, achieve and discover Jesus. GB companies are primarily for girls and young women, aged four to 18, and meet most weeks of the year in safe and friendly environments.

Girls' Venture Corps Air Cadets

1 Bawtry Gate, Sheffield S9 1UD
T: 0114 244 8405
E: gvcac@toucansurf.com
www.gvcac.org.uk
Corps Director: Brenda Layne
An organisation for girls aged between 11 and 20 years of age who are interested in aviation, Duke of Edinburgh award, leadership training, camps and courses, outdoor activities and community service.
Employees: 1
Volunteers: 300
Regional offices: 6

Glebe House

Church Road, Shudy Camps, Cambridge, Cambridgeshire CB21 4QH
T: 01799 584359
F: 01799 584098
E: jeanette.hurworth@glebehouse.org.uk
www.glebehouse.org.uk
Director: Peter Clarke
Glebe House (The Friends Therapeutic Community Trust) is a Quaker charity that provides holistic support for young men with challenging behaviour.
Employees: 55

Global Action Plan

9 Kean Street, London WC2B 4AY
T: 020 7420 4444
F: 020 7836 7345
E: all@globalactionplan.org.uk
www.globalactionplan.org.uk
CEO: Trewin Restorick
Global Action Plan is the UK's leading environmental behaviour change charity and, since 1993, has helped businesses, schools and communities reduce their impact on the environment. We achieve environmental and financial savings in the UK by empowering people to take action on energy, waste, water and travel. We are the only UK charity whose programmes are endorsed by the United Nations Environment Programme.
Employees: 27
Volunteers: 500
Regional offices: 1

Global Care

2 Dugdale Road, Coventry CV6 1PB
T: 024 7660 1800
F: 024 7660 1444
E: info@globalcare.org.uk
www.globalcare.org.uk
Employees: 21
Volunteers: 50

Global Connections

Caswell Road, Leamington Spa, Warwickshire CV31 1QD
T: 01926 487755
E: dwright@globalconnections.co.uk
www.globalconnections.org.uk
Executive Director: Martin Lee
Promotes and encourages the spread of the Christian Gospel by putting mission at the heart of the church and the church at the heart of mission.
Employees: 10

Global Witness Limited

PO Box 6042, London N19 5WP
T: 020 7561 6375
E: mail@globalwitness.org
www.globalwitness.org
Focuses on areas where environmental exploitation causes human rights abuses and funds conflict.

Golden Buddha Centre

The Grove, Totnes, Devon TQ9 5EP
T: 01803 897550
E: guidestar@goldenbuddha.org
www.goldenbuddha.org
The twin objectives of the Golden Buddha Centre project are to have an active Buddhist centre together with related residential accommodation for retired Buddhists.
Volunteers: 20

Good Gardeners' Association

Pinetum Lodge, Churcham, Gloucester GL2 8AD
T: 07901 815647
E: david@igeek.co.uk
www.goodgardeners.org.uk
The purpose of the Good Gardeners' Association is the improvement and encouragement of horticulture along compost or organic lines, and the daily study of organic methods of gardening.
Volunteers: 8

Gordon Moody Association

47 Maughan Street, Dudley, West Midlands DY1 2BA
T: 01384 241292
F: 01384 217649
E: elaine.smethurst@gordonmoody.org.uk
www.gordonmoody.org.uk
Managing Director: Elaine Smethurst
We provide advice, education and high quality and innovative therapeutic support to problem gamblers and those affected by problem gambling, through residential, online and outreach services. Gordon Moody Association offers a unique and intensive residential treatment programme in the UK for those gamblers most severely addicted as well as online support and advice to problem gamblers overseas through our Gambling Therapy website.
Employees: 18
Volunteers: 12
Regional offices: 2
Income: £909,308 (2014-15)

Gorlin Syndrome Group

11 Blackberry Way, Penwortham, Preston, Lancashire PR1 9LQ
Helpline: 01772 496849
E: info@gorlingroup.org
www.gorlingroup.porg
The Gorlin Syndrome Group was formed in the UK in 1992. It supports those affected by Gorlin syndrome and their families and carers; the advancement of the education of the medical profession and the general public regarding Gorlin syndrome and its implications; and the promotion and dissemination of research into the causes, effects, treatment and management of Gorlin syndrome.
Volunteers: 6

Gosport Voluntary Action

Martin Snape House, 96 Pavilion Way, St George's Barracks, Gosport, Hampshire PO12 1FG
T: 023 9258 3836
E: gosportvb@gva.org.uk
www.gosport-voluntary-action.org.uk
Chief Officer: GVA - Nicky Stavely - Gosport Voluntary Action
At the heart of the Gosport Community - providing support to voluntary sector organisations and running in-house projects to benefit under represented groups, as well as offering a Volunteer Centre service.
Employees: 20
Volunteers: 30
Regional offices: 1

Grail

125 Waxwell Lane, Pinner, Middlesex HA5 3ER
T: 020 8866 0505
E: m.grasar@grailsociety.org.uk
www.grailsociety.org.uk
President: Presidential Team
A Roman Catholic organisation involved in the education and formation of adults and young people, which encourages young people and adults to work out their Christian commitment in modern society and take

their full share in meeting the needs of the community.
Employees: 8

Grandparents Plus

18 Victoria Park Square, Bethnal Green, London E2 9PF
T: 020 8981 8001
Helpline: 0300 123 7015
E: info@grandparentsplus.org.uk
www.grandparentsplus.org.uk
Chief Executive: Lucy Peake
Grandparents Plus is the national charity (England and Wales) which champions the vital role of grandparents and the wider family in children's lives - especially when they take on the caring role in difficult family circumstances. Grandparents Plus provides: Evidence policy solutions and campaigns so that the contribution which the wider family make to children's well-being is better recognised, valued and supported; A free Support Network for the wider family raising children to reduce isolation and promote peer-to-peer support; An advice and information service for relatives and friends who are raising a child because their parents cannot; Training and guidance to professionals working with kinship carers.
Employees: 11

GrantScape

Office E, Whitsundoles, Broughton Road, Salford, Milton Keynes MK17 8BU
T: 01908 247630
E: steven.hargreaves@grantscape.org.uk
www.grantscape.org.uk
Chief Executive: Steven Hargreaves
The charity's aim is to improve the life of communities and the environment by managing and administering grant programmes for deserving and quality projects.
Employees: 7
Volunteers: 35

Great Ormond Street Hospital Children's Charity

Great Ormond Street Hospital, Great Ormond Street, London WC1N 3JH
T: 020 7405 9200
E: karen.atkinson@gosh.org
www.gosh.org

Greater London Volunteering

27 Old Gloucester Street, London WC1N 3AX
T: 020 7125 0151
E: info@glv.org.uk
www.glv.org.uk
Chief Executive Officer: James Banks
Greater London Volunteering is an umbrella body representing, consulting and co-ordinating Volunteer Centres and volunteer development agencies across Greater London. Activities include consultation, event organisation, training, marketing and promotion.
Employees: 2
Regional offices: 1
Income: £168,440 (2013-14)

Greater Manchester Centre for Voluntary Organisation

St Thomas Centre, Ardwick Green North, Manchester, Greater Manchester M12 6FZ
T: 0161 277 1000
F: 0161 273 8296
E: gmcvo@gmcvo.org.uk
www.gmcvo.org.uk
Chief Executive: Alex Whinnom
GMCVO supports local voluntary action by local people by providing specialist support, knowledge, voice, infrastructure and innovation, working in partnership with other support organisations and with the public and private sectors. We aspire to be a channel for information for and about our sector, and to provide co-ordination and leadership. A large element of our work involves representing the views and needs of people involved in local voluntary groups, sharing ideas and brokering relationships.
Employees: 28
Income: £1,500,000 (2012-13)

Greater World Christian Spiritualist Association

The Greater World Spiritual Centre, 3-5 Conway Street, Fitzrovia, London W1T 6BJ
T: 020 7436 7555
E: greaterworld@btconnect.com
www.greaterworld.co.uk
National President: Megan Long
To spread inall directions the truth of survival after death, of spirit communion, of healing by the power of Holy Spirit and to disseminate the teachings of Jesus the Christ and additional teachings received from highly evolved spirit messengers.
Employees: 3
Volunteers: many
Regional offices: 51
Income: £77,606 (2013-14)

Green Alliance

36 Buckingham Palace Road, London SW1W 0RE
T: 020 7630 4518
F: 020 7233 9033
E: ga@green-alliance.org.uk
www.green-alliance.org.uk
Green Alliance's mission is to promote sustainable development by ensuring that the environment is at the heart of decision-making.
Employees: 11
Volunteers: 3

Green Life UK

39 Marlborough Road, 39 Marlborough Road, London E7 8HA
T: 020 8472 6862
E: admin@greenlifeuk.org
www.greenlifeuk.org
Chairman: Jamal Uddin
Green Life UK is a non-governmental, non-profit-making, non-partisan charity striving to meet the basic human needs of the underprivileged and people of limited resources. The organisation was founded by a native Bangladeshi philanthropist, Jamal Uddin who is based in the UK.
Volunteers: 4
Regional offices: 1

GreenNet Educational Trust

Development House, London EC2A 4LT
T: 0845 055 4011
E: info@greenneteducationaltrust.org.uk
www.greenneteducationaltrust.org.uk
Promotes the strategic use of electronic networking for the benefit of social movements internationally and at home in the UK.

Greenpeace UK

Canonbury Villas, Islington, London N1 2PN
T: 020 7865 8100
Helpline: 0800 269065
E: info.uk@greenpeace.org
www.greenpeace.org.uk
Executive Director: John Sauven

Aims to protect the environment through peaceful direct action, scientific research and finding solutions to environmental problems.
Employees: 100
Volunteers: 40

Greenwich & Bexley Community Hospice

185 Bostall Hill, Abbey Wood, London SE2 0GB
T: 020 8312 2244
F: 020 8320 5780
E: info@gbch.org.uk
www.communityhospice.org.uk
Chief Executive: Kate Heaps
To provide specialist palliative care and support, free of charge, to patients and their families living within the boroughs of Greenwich and Bexley in our inpatient unit, day hospice, community, or outpatient clinic. Counselling and bereavement support are also offered.
Employees: 150
Volunteers: 600
Regional offices: 1
Income: £7,000,000 (2013-14)

Greyhound Rescue West of England (GRWE)

PO Box 4243, Radstock BA3 3ZL
Helpline: 07000 785092
E: enquiries@grwe.com
www.grwe.com
Chief Executive: Rachel Grocott
Our vision is that one day every greyhound will be free from risk or need. In the meanwhile we rescue, rehabilitate and find loving homes for abused and abandoned greyhounds and lurchers. The charity receives no financial help from the greyhound racing industry and is completely reliant on donations, legacies and public support. GRWE operates nationally and homes around 500 of these special dogs every year.
Employees: 4
Volunteers: 120
Income: £679,823 (2013-14)

Groundwork North East

Grosvenor House, 29 Market Place
T: 0191 567 2550 ext 32
E: stephen.armstrong@groundwork.org.uk
www.groundwork.org.uk/sites/northeast

Groundwork UK

Lockside, 5 Scotland Street, Birmingham B1 2RR
T: 0121 236 8565
F: 0121 236 7356
E: info@groundwork.org.uk
www.groundwork.org.uk
Chief Executive: Graham Duxbury
Groundwork supports communities in need, working with partners to help improve the quality of people's lives, their prospects and potential and the places where they live, work and play. Our vision is of a society of sustainable communities that are vibrant, healthy and safe, that respect the local and global environment and where individuals and enterprise prosper.
Employees: 31
Regional offices: 1
Income: £19,402,466 (2013-14)

Group B Strep Support

PO Box 203, Haywards Heath, West Sussex RH16 1GF
T: 01444 416176
F: 0870 803 0024
E: info@gbss.org.uk
www.gbss.org.uk
Chief Executive: Jane Plumb MBE
Group B Strep Support (GBSS) is the only UK charity dedicated to preventing group B Strep (GBS) infections in newborn babies and supporting affected families. GBS is the most common cause of life-threatening infection in newborn babies, infections which are usually preventable. GBSS regularly sends information materials to maternity units and GPs nationwide. We receive no Government funding – families affected by GBS raise most of the charity's funds.
Employees: 4
Income: £176,575 (2013-14)

Grubb Institute

Cloudesley Street, London N1 0HU
E: info@grubb.org.uk
www.grubbinstitute.org.uk
Executive Director: Bruce Irvine
The Institute is an applied research foundation working globally to mobilise values, faiths and beliefs as a resource for the transformation, healing and repair of organisations, people and society. The institutes work is informed by a Christian theology that recognises the heritage, culture and traditions of the many diverse faiths and spiritualities present in our society.

Guernsey Arts Commission

Guernsey Information Centre, North Esplanade, St Peter Port, Guernsey GY1 2LQ
T: 01481 709748
E: joanna.littlejohns@cultureleisure.gov.gg
www.arts.gg
Head of Arts Development: Littlejohns, Joanna
The Guernsey Arts Commission's aim is to help the arts in Guernsey to grow and develop and to involve more people in the arts; for the arts to be recognised and valued as a vital part of island life.
Employees: 4
Volunteers: 35

Guideposts Trust Ltd

Willow Tree House, Two Rivers, Station Lane, Witney, Oxfordshire OX28 4BH
T: 01993 893560
E: gpt@guidepoststrust.org.uk
www.guidepoststrust.org.uk
Guideposts aims to provide services to help all individuals lead independent lives, fulfil their aspirations and maximise their potential. We work with people who have mental health issues, dementia, learning disabilities, physical impairments, and their carers and families, to help them make the best possible choices for quality care. We seek to achieve excellence in our work and lead the way in researching, delivering and disseminating good practice.
Employees: 100
Volunteers: 100
Regional offices: 7

Guild of Health Ltd

9 St Georges Road, Folkestone, Kent CT19 4BE
T: 01303 277399
E: glan.izzard@ukgateway.net
www.gohealth.org.uk
Helps people to experience within the fellowship of God's family the freedom of life promised by Jesus Christ.

Guild of Pastoral Psychology

82 Boston Gardens, Brentford, Middlesex TW8 9LP
T: 020 8568 2195
E: administration@guildofpastoralpsychology.org.uk
www.guildofpastoralpsychology.org.uk
Acts as a meeting ground for all those interested in the relationship between religion and depth psychology, particularly the work of CG Jung and his followers and communicates the results of recent practice

and research to everyone interested professionally or personally.

Guild of St Raphael

St John's Church, 2 Green Lane, Stoneycroft, Liverpool L13 7EA
T: 0151 228 2023
E: straphael@enterprise.net
www.guild-of-st-raphael.org.uk
Teaches and practises the ministry of Christ's healing in the Church of England through the sacraments and prayer in full co-operation with the medical profession.

GuildHE Limited

Woburn House, 20 Tavistock Square, London WC1H 9HB
T: 020 3393 6132
E: info@guildhe.ac.uk
www.guildhe.ac.uk
CEO: Andrew Westwood
GuildHE is one of the two recognised representative bodies for Higher Education in the UK.
Employees: 7

Guillain Barre & Associated Inflammatory Neuropathies

Woodholme House, Heckington Business Park, Station Road, Heckington, Sleaford, Lincolnshire NG34 9JH
T: 01529 469910
Helpline: 0800 374803
F: 01529 469915
E: director@gaincharity.org.uk
www.gaincharity.org.uk
Director: Caroline Morrice
To provide support, information and other assistance to sufferers and their families; to promote research into causes, prevention and treatments; and to advance the education of the public and of the medical professionals.
Employees: 3
Volunteers: 150
Income: £232,674 (2014-15)

Habitat for Humanity Great Britain

10 The Grove, Slough, Berkshire SL1 1QP
T: 01295 264240
F: 01295 264230
E: supporterservices@habitatforhumanity.org.uk
www.habitatforhumanity.org.uk
Chief Executive: Rebecca Martin
Habitat for Humanity Great Britain is an international development charity. Our vision is for a world where everyone has a safe and decent place to live through the elimination of housing poverty and homelessness.
Employees: 18
Volunteers: 250
Regional offices: 2

Haemochromatosis Society

PO Box 6356, Rugby, Warwickshire CV21 9PA
T: 0303 040 1101
Helpline: 0303 040 1102
E: office@haemochromatosis.org.uk
www.haemochromatosis.org.uk
Chief Executive: David Head
Advice and support for people affected by genetic haemochromatosis (GH) and their families. A patient representative organisation.

Haemophilia Society

Petersham House, 57a Hatton Garden, London EC1N 8JG
T: 020 7380 0600
Helpline: 0800 018 6068
F: 020 7387 8220
E: sue@haemophilia.org.uk
www.haemophilia.org.uk
The Haemophilia Society works to secure the best possible care, treatment and support for people with haemophilia and related or associated bleeding disorders, and their families.
Employees: 9
Volunteers: 350
Regional offices: 18

Hambleton and Richmondshire Carers Centre

32 High Street, Northallerton, Northallerton, North Yorkshire DL7 8EE
T: 01609 780872
F: 01609 788489
E: info@hrcarers.org.uk
www.hrcarers.org.uk
Chief Executive: Andrea Hobbs
Our principal aim is to support carers of all ages in a way that is centred on individual needs and supports their general health and well-being. Provide advice and information to carers and their families; Provide emotional support; Work in partnership to raise awareness of issues; Provide social groups and activities to reduce isolation; Signpost and refer to other support agencies; Undertake Carers Assessments; Work in partnership and collaborate where appropriate to strengthen local and sub-regional services for carers.
Employees: 8
Volunteers: 10
Income: £200,000 (2013-14)

Hamlet Trust

c/o Mental Health Foundation, 9th Floor, Sea Containers House, 20 Upper Ground, London SE1 9QB
T: 020 7803 1160
E: office@hamlet-trust.org.uk
www.hamlet-trust.org.uk
Pursues development, education and research initiatives in mental health in central and Eastern Europe, with special emphasis on the social integration of people with long-term mental health problems in the community.

Hammersmith Management College

E: s.khan@hmclondon.com

Handicap International UK

CAN Mezzanine, London SE1 0EH
T: 0870 774 3737
F: 0870 774 3738
E: hi-uk@hi-uk.org
www.handicap-international.org.uk
We support people in situations of vulnerability who, due to a physical, mental or psychological condition, have difficulty in playing their role in society, thus finding themselves in a situation of disability.
Employees: 6

Volunteers: 155 Hannahs

Woodland Road, Ivybridge,
Devon PL21 9HQ
T: 01752 898100
F: 01752 898116
E: charlotte.simonds@discoverhannahs.org
www.discoverhannahs.org
Chief Executive Officer: Bronwen Hewitt
Hannahs offers education, care and life opportunities for children and adults with a range of disabilities. The Trust offers a school, respite centre, children's home, adult transition project and an innovative service for adults. We have two centres Hannahs at Ivybridge and Hannahs at Seale-Hayne.
Employees: 300
Volunteers: 150
Regional offices: 2

Hansard Society

London WC2A 1JA
T: 020 7438 1222
F: 020 7438 1229
E: pressoffice@lse.ac.uk
www.hansardsociety.org.uk
Chief Executive: Fiona Booth
The Hansard Society is the UK's leading non-partisan political research and education charity, which exists to strengthen parliamentary democracy and encourage greater public involvement in politics.
Employees: 22
Volunteers: 2

Happy Days Children's Charity

Clody House, 90-100 Collingdon Street, Luton, Bedfordshire LU1 1RX
T: 01582 755999
F: 01582 755900
E: happydayscharity@yahoo.co.uk
www.happydayscharity.org
Chief Executive: Ryan Sinclair
We fund and organise holidays, days out and theatre trips throughout the UK for disadvantaged young people with special needs. We help young people in special needs schools, in hospitals and in hospices, and we help individual families.
Employees: 10
Volunteers: 1
Income: £919,000 (2012-13)

Harvest Fields Commissioning International

PO Box 740, Hemel Hempstead, Hertfordshire HP1 3RH
T: 07941 502613
E: info@hfci.net
www.hfci.net
Offers leadership training and materials as well as TV, film and media production and media training in over 50 countries worldwide. We also provide humanitarian assistance in developing countries.

Havering Mind

Harrow Lodge House, Hornchurch Road, Hornchurch RM11 1JU
T: 01708 457040
F: 01708 457141
E: reach.us@haveringmind.org.uk
www.haveringmind.org.uk
CEO: Vanessa Bennett
We are a local mental health charity based in Hornchurch Havering. We provide advice and support to people who are experiencing mental health problems and also their carers. We campaign to improve local mental health services, raise awareness and promote understanding. We provide a range of services to support older people, younger adults and adolescents, children and those most at risk of social isolation.
Employees: 26
Volunteers: 73
Income: £385,940 (2013-14)

HCPT (Hosanna House and Children's Pilgrimage Trust)

Oakfield Park, 32 Bilton Road, Rugby, Warwickshire CV22 7HQ
T: 01788 564646
E: hq@hcpt.org.uk
www.hcpt.org.uk
Chief Executive: Phil Sparke
Disabled and disadvantaged children and adults enjoy life-changing pilgrimage holidays to Lourdes in the south of France, supported by volunteers, thanks to HCPT.
Employees: 15
Volunteers: 5000

Headliners (formerly known as Children's Express)

Rich Mix, London E1 6LA
T: 020 7749 9360
E: fiona.wyton@headliners.org
www.headliners.org
Director: Fiona Wyton
Employees: 25
Volunteers: 8
Regional offices: 4

Headlines, the Craniofacial Support Group

8 Footes Lane, Frampton Cotterell, Bristol BS36 2JQ
T: 01454 850557
E: info@headlines.org.uk
www.headlines.org.uk
Group Administrator: Gil Ruff
Provides help, advice and contact to anyone (including their families) having or dealing with craniosynostosis or craniostenosis and all of the associated conditions and syndromes. Merged with Apert Syndrome Support Group.
Employees: 1
Volunteers: 10

Headway – the Brain Injury Association

190 Bagnall Road, Old Basford, Nottingham NG6 8SF
T: 0115 924 0800
F: 0115 958 4446
E: services.director@headway.org.uk
www.headway.org.uk
Our aim is to promote understanding of all aspects of brain injuries and to provide information, support and services to people with brain injuries, their families and carers.
Employees: 35
Volunteers: 7
Regional offices: 112

Headway Devon

The XCentre, Commercial Road, Exeter, Devon EX2 4AD
T: 01392 211822
E: info@headwaydevon.org.uk
www.headwaydevon.org.uk
Chief Executive: Anne Mattock
Headway Devon is an independent registered charity working to provide information, support and advice for people with brain injuries and their families and carers. Centre-based social rehabilitation and respite care; Community outreach programme providing one-to-one support and enabling in the community; Carer support; Information and advice including signposting & advocacy; Training – internal and external; Campaigning and awareness raising – raising public awareness of brain injury ("the hidden disability").
Employees: 60
Regional offices: 1
Income: ££914.00 (2014-15)

Healing Foundation

The Royal College of Surgeons, London WC2A 3PE
T: 020 7869 6920
F: 020 7869 6929
E: info@thehealingfoundation.org
www.thehealingfoundation.org
Chief Executive: Brendan Eley
Employees: 5
Volunteers: 30

Health Foundation

90 Long Acre, London WC2E 9RA
T: 020 7257 8000
F: 020 7257 8001
E: jacquelyn.bell@health.org.uk
www.health.org.uk
Chief Executive: Stephen Thornton
Employees: 25

Health Poverty Action

Ground Floor, London SW8 1SJ
T: 020 7840 3777
F: 020 7840 3770
E: general@healthpovertyaction.org
www.healthpovertyaction.org
Director: Martin Drewry
Health Poverty Action works to strengthen poor and marginalised people in their struggle for health through development initiatives in 13 countries and campaigning for change.
Employees: 500
Volunteers: 10
Regional offices: 14

HealthProm

Star House, London NW5 4BA
T: 020 7284 1620
F: 020 7284 1881
E: general@healthprom.org
www.healthprom.org
Working in partnership to promote health and social care for women and children in Eastern Europe and Asia.
Employees: 4
Volunteers: 9

Hearing Dogs for Deaf People

The Grange, Wycombe Road, Saunderton, Princes Risborough, Buckinghamshire HP27 9NS
T: 01844 348100
F: 01844 348101
E: info@hearing-dogs.co.uk
www.hearingdogs.org.uk
Supplies trained dogs to assist the profoundly deaf by alerting them to specific household sounds by touch and provide companionship and independence.
Employees: 99
Volunteers: 500
Regional offices: 60

Hearing Link

27-28 The Waterfront, Eastbourne, East Sussex BN23 5UZ
T: 0300 111 1113
E: helpdesk@hearinglink.org
www.hearinglink.org
Chief Executive: Dr Lorraine Gailey
Hearing Link is a UK charity active in England, Scotland, Wales and Northern Ireland for people living with hearing loss, their family and friends. We offer a Helpdesk, support programmes, useful website and membership scheme. Find out more at www.hearinglink.org.
Employees: 18
Volunteers: 130
Regional offices: 3

Heart UK, the Cholesterol Charity

7 North Road, Maidenhead, Berkshire SL6 1PE
T: 01628 777046
Helpline: 0345 450 5988
E: jp@heartuk.org.uk
www.heartuk.org.uk
Chief Executive: Jules Payne
Over half of the adults in the UK have raised cholesterol. 1 in 500 people are born with an inherited high cholesterol condition, meaning they have a high risk of a heart attack, stroke or sudden death in their 20s, 30s and 40s. We provide expert support, guidance and education to people to have high cholesterol, their families and Health Care Professionals.
Employees: 10
Volunteers: 6

Helen & Douglas House

E: lcrowley@helenanddouglas.org.uk

Helen Arkell Dyslexia Centre

Frensham, Farnham, Surrey GU10 3BW
T: 01252 792400
E: enquiries@arkellcentre.org.uk
www.arkellcentre.org.uk
The Centre helps people of all ages with dyslexia and other specific learning difficulties to fulfil their potential by optimising their educational opportunities and quality of life; trains teachers in the special skills needed; helps schools manage dyslexics in the classroom; raises public awareness of how dyslexia can be helped.

Help A Poor Child

Devonshire House, Manor Way, Borehamwood, Hertfordshire WD6 1QQ
T: 020 8236 2953
F: 020 8731 4322
E: info@hapc.co.uk
www.hapc.co.uk
A non-profit, voluntary organisation, founded in 1980, to provide assistance to children and families struggling in terrible poverty.

Help Age International

PO Box 32832, London N1 9ZN
T: 020 7278 7778
E: info@helpage.org
www.helpage.org
Operates a global network of not-for-profit organisations with a mission to work with and for disadvantaged older people worldwide to achieve a lasting improvement in the quality of their lives.

Helplines Partnership

Business Design Centre, 52 Upper Street, London N1 0HQ
T: 0300 330 7777
E: mirelle.frost@helplines.org
www.helplines.org
Chief Executive: Theodore Spyrou
Helplines Partnership is the membership body for organisations that provide helpline services in the UK and internationally. We facilitate high quality service delivery to callers by providing a range of services, including training (accredited qualifications), innovative contact solutions, quality standards, individually tailored support and information resources through web portals. We raise the profile of the sector through representation of our members' interests and influencing the social policy agenda, giving providers of helpline services a voice to build sustainability and promote excellence, choice and accessibility for everyone.
Employees: 25
Volunteers: 10
Regional offices: 3

HemiHelp

6 Market Road, London N7 9PW
T: 0845 120 3713
E: info@hemihelp.org.uk
www.hemihelp.org.uk
Provides information and support for children and young people with hemiplegia and increases public awareness of the condition. Facilitates research into hemiplegia and its associated conditions.
Employees: 8

Henry George Foundation of Great Britain Ltd

212 Piccadilly, London W1J 9HG
T: 020 7377 8885
F: 020 8393 3526
E: office@henrygeorgefoundation.org
www.henrygeorgefoundation.org
Raises awareness of social injustice stemming from unjust property ownership and capitalisation of land rent and other resource rents.

Henry Smith Charity

65 Leadenhall Street, London EC3A 2AD
T: 020 7264 4970
E: dc@henrysmithcharity.org.uk
www.henrysmithcharity.org.uk
Director: Nick Acland

Heritage Care

Connaught House, 112-120 High Road, Loughton, Essex IG10 4HJ
T: 020 8502 3933
F: 020 8502 3543
E: dave.chopra@heritagecare.co.uk
www.heritagecare.co.uk
Chief Executive: Kim Foo
Heritage Care is a registered charity that provides a range of flexible individualised services that support independence and choice for people with learning disabilities, mental health support needs and older people. Our care and support services include supported living, domiciliary services, packages for self-directed support, extra-care schemes, registered care homes, day services and respite/short-break services. We support 1,000 service users each day and employ over 1,800 staff employed across 130 locations.
Employees: 1850
Volunteers: 50
Regional offices: 7

Herpes Viruses Association (also called HVA or SPHERE)

41 North Road, London N7 9DP
T: 020 7607 9661
Helpline: 0845 123 2305
E: info@herpes.org.uk
www.herpes.org.uk
Director: Marian Nicholson
Helps and advises people with herpes simplex (cold sores and genital herpes) and herpes zoster. The HVA answers phone calls, emails and letters; supports an informative and calming website; offers one-to-one counselling; promotes public awareness of the virus and reduces anxiety; disseminates information to the public and the medical profession; acts as a pressure group for research; undertakes research wherever possible; encourages and promotes self-help groups. Certified by the Information Standard.
Employees: 2
Volunteers: 15
Income: £105,000 (2014-15)

Herpetological Conservation Trust

655A Christchurch Road, Boscombe, Bournemouth, Dorset BH1 4AP
T: 01202 391319
E: enquiries@herpconstrust.org.uk
www.herpconstrust.org.uk
Co-ordinates and implements conservation efforts for threatened amphibians and reptiles, particularly in the UK and Europe and promotes research.

Hextol Foundation

E: chris.milner@hextol.org.uk

HFT the Home Farm Trust

Peter Needham, Merchants House North, Wapping Road, Bristol BS1 4RW
T: 0117 930 2600
E: info@hft.org.uk
www.hft.org.uk
Provides, for people with learning disabilities, residential and other services that develop their potential and sustain their rights.

Hi8us Projects Ltd

Ground Floor, Toepath House, Limehouse Court, London E14 7EQ
T: 020 7538 8070
F: 020 7987 4522
E: jerry@hi8us.co.uk
www.hi8us.co.uk
Hi8us Projects Limited was established in 1994 to produce innovative media with young people in their communities.
Employees: 5
Regional offices: 1

High/Scope UK

Anerley Business Centre, Anerley Road, Anerley, London SE20 8BD
T: 0870 777 7680
F: 0870 777 7682
E: susan.noble@southtyneside.gov.uk
www.high-scope.org.uk
Aims to improve the life chances of children through high-quality care and education using the high/scope approach. Disseminates information on the effectiveness of using the high/scope approach to care and education for young children. Aims to increase the use of the approach within social service, education, voluntary and independent settings.
Employees: 7

Highbury Vale Blackstock Trust

Elizabeth House, 2 Hurlock Street, London N5 1ED
T: 020 7690 1300
E: director@ehlc.co.uk
www.elizabeth-house.org.uk
Centre Director: Centre Director
Community Centre serving the local community by offering Play Services (After School's Club and Playscheme), Youth Work Programmes and meeting facilities to local groups and individuals.
Employees: 9
Volunteers: 2
Income: £243,224 (2012-13)

Hillingdon Autistic Care and Support

E: louise@hacs.org.uk

Historic Churches Preservation Trust

31 Newbury Street, London EC1A 7HU
T: 020 7600 6090
F: 020 7796 2442
E: info@historicchurches.org.uk
www.nationalchurchestrust.org
Provides for the preservation, repair, maintenance, improvement, upkeep, beautification and reconstruction of churches in the UK and of monuments, fittings, fixtures, stained glass, furniture, ornaments etc.
Employees: 5
Volunteers: 3

Historical Association

59a Kennington Park Road, London SE11 4JH
T: 0300 100 0223
F: 020 7582 4989
E: enquiries@history.org.uk
www.history.org.uk
The Historical Association is the national charity for history. It exists to bring together people of all communities who have an interest in the past. It promotes and supports the study and teaching of history at all levels: teacher, student, amateur and professional.
Employees: 9
Volunteers: 229
Regional offices: 50

Hollybank Trust

Roe Head, Far Common Road, Mirfield, West Yorkshire WF14 0DQ
T: 01924 490833
F: 01924 483902
E: s.hughes@hollybanktrust.com
www.hollybanktrust.com
Chief Executive and Principal: Steven Hughes

A charity trust working with children, young people and adults who have profound physical disabilities. We have a commitment for life for those in our care. We have a specialist school with an attached children's home, independence homes and homes for life in the neighbouring communities. We are open 52 weeks a year. Our multidisciplinary staff number 450. Internationally renowned for our work in IT, access technology and social care.

Employees: 450
Volunteers: 45
Regional offices: 1

Home from Hospital Care after Treatment

Prospect Hall, College Walk, Selly Oak, Birmingham, West Midlands B29 6LE
T: 0121 472 4499
E: enquiries@home-from-hospital-care.org.uk
www.home-from-hospital-care.org.uk
Director: Geraldine Amos

Volunteers from our Welcome Home Service offer practical, common-sense support for up to six weeks after discharge from hospital. We will shop, call in for a friendly chat, go to the bank, help with completing benefit forms etc. Our volunteers call in at least once a week. We can also supply lists of cleaners, gardeners, hairdressers, chiropodists etc.

Employees: 7
Volunteers: 60
Regional offices: 1

Home-Start Canterbury and Coastal

E: sari@homestartcanterbury.org

Home-Start Haringey

E: fatmata@home-start-haringey.org

Home-Start South Hams, Plymouth and Tavistock

Age Concern Building, Ilbert Road, Kingsbridge, Ilbert Road, Kingsbridge, Devon TQ7 1DZ
T: 01548 854513
E: andreachandler.homestart@gmail.com
www.homestart-southhams.org.uk
Scheme Manager: Andrea Chandler

We believe every child deserves the best start in life and parents are best placed to provide it but that sometimes, for some families this can be difficult. We offer one-to-one befriending and mentoring support to families with a child under 5, who are experiencing difficulties. We also offer gentle group support to parents at risk of exclusion.

Employees: 5
Volunteers: 100
Regional offices: 1
Income: £160,000 (2012-13)

Home-Start Stoke-on-Trent

E: chris.pointon@homestartstoke.org.uk

Home-Start UK

2 Salisbury Road, Leicester LE1 7QR
T: 0116 233 9955
Helpline: 0800 068 6368
F: 0116 233 0232
E: info@home-start.org.uk
www.home-start.org.uk
Chief Executive: Kay Bews

Home-Start offers support, friendship and practical help to parents with young children, in local communities throughout the UK and with British Forces in Germany and Cyprus. 337 independent schemes managed by and offering support from 20,226 volunteers, supported 34,952 families and 69,672 children during 2007/8.

Employees: 117
Volunteers: 20226
Regional offices: 12

Home-Start Worthing and Adur

E: lisa.green@wahomestart.org.uk

Homeless Action in Barnet

36B Woodhouse Road, London N12 0RG
T: 020 8446 8400
F: 020 8446 8480
E: joe@habcentre.org
www.habcentre.org
Chief Executive: Joe Lee

Our mission is to work with vulnerable people so that they gain access to housing, health and other services in order to achieve dignity; to make their own effective choices; and to express themselves as fully independent members of society. HAB should be a 'Place of Change' – enabling and facilitating practical change for individuals and promoting the needs of Homeless people within our society.

Employees: 16
Volunteers: 30
Income: £340,589 (2014-15)

Homeless International

Queen's House, 16 Queens Road, Coventry, West Midlands CV1 3EG
T: 024 7663 2802
F: 024 7663 2911
E: info@homeless-international.org
www.homeless-international.org
Chief Executive: Larry English

Aims to relieve poverty, in particular that caused by homelessness, internationally. We work through lasting relationships with local partners in Asia and Africa, within which there is confidence to create solutions to the challenge of urban poverty. Typically we provide resources, technical assistance and financial services for community-led processes.

Employees: 16

Homeless Link

1st Floor, London SE1 0RB
T: 020 7960 3010
F: 020 7960 3011
E: irmani.darlington@homelesslink.org.uk
www.homeless.org.uk
Employees: 30
Volunteers: 15

Homeopathy Action Trust

PO Box 9022, Melton Mowbray, Leicestershire LE13 9BZ
T: 0844 800 2840 (also fax)
E: info@homeopathyactiontrust.org
www.homeopathyactiontrust.org
Executive Director: Simon Wilkinson-Blake

The principal activity of the company is the promotion of homeopathy through funding of education and research and the raising of funds to support homeopathic activities.

Employees: 2
Volunteers: 8

HOPE

17 Queen Street, Worksop S80 2AN
T: 01909 531294
Helpline: 01909 489990
E: director@hopeservices.org.uk
www.hopeservices.org.uk
CEO: Alan Diggles

Aims to help those in crisis or without somewhere to live, through the provision of help, advice and practical support.
Employees: 25
Volunteers: 35
Income: £900,000 (2013-14)

Hope and Homes for Children

East Clyffe, Salisbury, Wiltshire SP3 4LZ
T: 01722 790111
F: 01722 790024
E: sue.rooke@hopeandhomes.org
www.hopeandhomes.org
Chief Executive: Rick Foulsham
Provides family-based care for orphaned and vulnerable children in Central and Eastern Europe and Africa.
Employees: 45
Volunteers: 7

Hope for Children

Hope House, 14a Queensway, Hemel Hempstead, Hertfordshire HP1 1LR
T: 0870 751 9861
E: hope@hope4c.org
www.hope4c.org
Aims to assist children, in particular those living in developing countries and the UK, who suffer through being handicapped, orphaned, poor and exploited.

Hope UK

25(F) Copperfield Street, London SE1 0EN
T: 020 7928 0848
F: 020 7401 3477
E: m.watson@hopeuk.org
www.hopeuk.org
Chief Executive Officer: Sarah Brighton
Hope UK enables children and young people to make drug-free choices. A network of 116 volunteer Drug Educators, trained to Open College Network accreditation standards, provide interactive drug awareness sessions for children and young people and any group with an interest in them. Hope UK also provides accredited two-day courses for family and youth workers.
Employees: 12
Volunteers: 116
Regional offices: 3
Income: £645,943 (2014-15)

HOPE worldwide

360 City Road, London EC1V 2PY
T: 020 7713 7655
F: 020 7812 1236
E: wil.horwood@hopeworldwide.org.uk
www.hopeworldwide.org.uk
Chief Executive: Wil Horwood
Bringing hope to, and changing the lives of, disadvantaged and vulnerable people. In the UK we work in the areas of homelessness and addiction recovery. Overseas, we support a wide range of poverty reduction initiatives through grants and management support. We have a strong volunteerism ethos and develop initiatives that connect volunteers with poverty issues.
Employees: 10
Volunteers: 890
Regional offices: 2

Horder Centre for Arthritis

St John's Road, Crowborough, East Sussex TN6 1XP
T: 01892 665577
E: info@hordercentre.co.uk
www.hordercentre.co.uk
Provides professional help by all available methods for people suffering the pain and disabling effects of all forms of arthritis in order to restore maximum independence and alleviate pain wherever possible.

Horse Rangers Association (Hampton Court) Ltd

E: director@horserangers.com

Horsham and Mid Sussex Voluntary Action

38 Church Road, Burgess Hill, West Sussex RH15 9AE
T: 01444 258102
E: adminfinance@hamsva.org.uk
www.hamsva.org.uk
Chief Executive Officer: Christine Hardisty
Practical support services to voluntary and community groups who work with people of all ages, faiths and abilities including community development, volunteer services, training opportunities, voluntary and statutory sector networking events, co-ordination and facilitation of open meetings, seminars and forums together with representation and liaison with local voluntary organisations and community groups encouraging them to put forward their views on local and national policies and events.
Employees: 8
Regional offices: 3

Hospice Information Service

Sydenham, London SE26 6DZ
T: 020 8768 4500
E: info@stchristophers.org.uk
www.stchristophers.org.uk
An information exchange and communication network for the hospice movement; phone and written enquiries welcomed from healthcare professionals and members of the public.

Hospice UK

Hospice House, 34-44 Britannia Street, London WC1X 9JG
T: 020 7520 8200
F: 020 7278 1021
E: info@hospiceuk.org
www.hospiceuk.org
Chief Executive: David Praill
Hospice UK is the national membership organisation for hospice care. It champions and supports the work of more than 200 services providing hospice care across the UK, so that they can deliver the highest quality care for people with terminal or life limiting conditions and support their families.
Employees: 60
Volunteers: 5

Hospitality Action

62 Britton Street, London EC1M 5UY
T: 020 3004 5500
F: 020 7253 2094
E: help@hospitalityaction.org.uk
www.hospitalityaction.org.uk
Chief Executive: Penny Moore
Hospitality Action helps those who work/have worked within the UK hospitality industry. We check all applicants are receiving their full state entitlement when unable to work and can assist where the state is unable to. In addition to signposting and support we offer one-off grants for essential needs, short-term ongoing support for periods of crisis and a befriending scheme for socially isolated individuals. We also provide educational seminars on drug and alcohol misuse.
Employees: 12
Volunteers: 40

HOST UK

Unit K106, Tower Bridge Business Complex, 100 Clements Road, London SE16 4DG
T: 020 7739 6292
E: info@hostuk.org
www.hostuk.org
Chief Executive: Susie Alemayehu
HOST's mission is to offer international students the chance to visit a British home and thereby promote international understanding and friendship.
Employees: 5
Volunteers: 1700

House of Saint Barnabas in Soho

1 Greek Street, Soho Square, Soho, London W1V 6NQ
T: 020 7434 1894
F: 020 7434 1746
E: finance@hosb.org.uk
hosb.org.uk
Provides temporary housing and care to homeless women (1855 years of age).

Housing Associations' Charitable Trust (HACT)

Octavia House, 50 Banner Street, London EC1Y 8ST
T: 020 7247 7800
F: 020 7247 2212
E: hact@hact.org.uk
www.hact.org.uk
Director: Heather Petch
HACT pioneers housing solutions for people on the margins. We identify emerging need, and then develop, test and promote practical solutions for social inclusion. We work through partnerships and networks, acting as a bridge between housing associations and the wider third sector.
Employees: 9
Volunteers: 1

Housing Justice

256 Bermondsey Street, London SE1 3UJ
T: 020 3544 8094
E: info@housingjustice.org.uk
www.housingjustice.org.uk
Chief Executive: Alison Gelder
The national voice for churches and Christians on housing and homelessness. We help churches help homeless people through practical support, training, resources, consultancy and events. We raise awareness about housing and homelessness and campaign for positive change, particularly through the annual Homeless Sunday campaign.
Employees: 10
Volunteers: 25
Regional offices: 2
Income: £414,340 (2012-13)

Howard League for Penal Reform

1 Ardleigh Road, London N1 4HS
T: 020 7249 7373
F: 020 7249 7788
E: info@howardleague.org
www.howardleague.org
The Howard League for Penal Reform works for a safe society where fewer people are victims of crime. The Howard League for Penal Reform believes that offenders must make amends for what they have done and change their lives. The Howard League for Penal Reform believes that community sentences make a person take responsibility and live a law-abiding life in the community.
Employees: 13
Volunteers: 300

Hubventures

E: eleri.smith@hubventures.org

Hull Churches Home from Hospital Service

E: administrator@hchfh.org.uk

Human Givens Foundation

Chalvington, East Sussex BN27 3TD
T: 01323 811662
E: info@hgfoundation.com
www.hgfoundation.com
Aims to promote research and public education into the 'givens' of human nature and their application in the treatment and care of those suffering from mental illness.
Employees: 1

Human Relief Foundation

PO Box 194, Bradford, Yorkshire BD7 1YW
T: 01274 392727
E: mohammed@hrf.co.uk
www.hrf.org.uk

Human Scale Education

Unit 8, Fairseat Farm, Chew Stoke, Bristol BS40 8XF
T: 01275 332516
E: info@hse.org.uk
www.hse.org.uk
The charity aims to promote education in small groups, in which effective learning can be encouraged and undertaken with mutual respect. The charity also supports and campaigns for state funding for small alternative schools and it supports the restructuring of state secondary schools.

Humane Research Trust

Brook House, 29 Bramhall Lane South, Bramhall, Stockport, Cheshire SK7 2DN
T: 0161 439 8041
E: info@humaneresearch.org.uk
www.humaneresearch.org.uk
The Humane Research Trust encourages and supports new medical research that does not include the use of animals, with the objectives of advancing the diagnosis and treatment of disease in humans. The Trust encourages scientists to develop innovative alternatives to the use of animals and so eliminate the suffering of animals that occurs in medical research and testing. The Trust fulfils an important role in educating the next generation of researchers.
Employees: 3
Volunteers: 50
Regional offices: 1

Humane Slaughter Association

The Old School, Brewhouse Hill, Wheathampstead, St Albans, Hertfordshire AL4 8AN
T: 01582 831919
E: info@hsa.org.uk
www.hsa.org.uk
Promotes humane methods of slaughter.

Humanity at Heart

Hassocks, West Sussex BN6 8AN
T: 01273 846135
E: humanity@humanityatheart.org.uk
www.humanityatheart.org.uk
Aims to relieve the suffering and poverty of children in Romania and elsewhere and to effect this by giving aid, support and training where appropriate, either directly or through the agency of other charities.

Huntington's Disease Association

Suite 24, Liverpool Science Park, Innovation Centre 1, 131 Mount Pleasant, Liverpool L3 5TF
T: 0151 331 5444
F: 0151 331 5441
E: info@hda.org.uk
www.hda.org.uk
Chief Executive: Cath Stanley
Provides care, advice, support and education to both families and professionals affected by Huntington's disease.
Employees: 30
Volunteers: 200+
Regional offices: 20

Hyperactive Children's Support Group

71 Whyke Lane, Chichester, West Sussex PO19 7PD
T: 01243 539966
E: hyperactive@hacsg.org.uk
www.hacsg.org.uk
Founder/Director: Sally Bunday MBE
Provides support, ideas and information to parents, carers and professionals concerned for ADHD/hyperactive children. Non-medication therapies a priority.
Employees: 2
Volunteers: 8

Hypothalamic Hamartoma Uncontrolled Gelastic Seizures UK

ABS House, 35 Chiltern Avenue, Amersham, Buckinghamshire HP6 5AE
T: 0800 999 4847
E: hhugsuk@hotmail.com
www.hhugs-uk.com
Trustee: Vivianne Gattoc
To provide support to individuals and families who are affected with Hypothalamic Hamartoma.
Income: ££500.00 (2013-14)

Hysterectomy Association

2 Princes Street, Puddletown, Dorchester, Dorset DT2 8UE
T: 0843 289 2142
E: info@hysterectomy-association.org.uk
www.hysterectomy-association.org.uk
CEO: Linda Parkinson-Hardman
The Hysterectomy Association provides impartial, timely and appropriate information, products, books and support to women facing a hysterectomy.
Volunteers: 2
Income: £20,000 (2012-13)

I CAN

8 Wakley Street, London EC1V 7QE
T: 020 7843 2552
Helpline: 020 7843 2544
F: 0845 225 4072
E: info@ican.org.uk
www.ican.org.uk
Chief Executive: Bob Reitemeier
Employees: 235

IA (The Ileostomy and Internal Pouch Support Group)

Peverill House, 15 Mill Road, Ballyclare BT39 9DR
T: 028 9334 4043
Helpline: 0800 018 4724
F: 028 9332 4606
E: info@iasupport.org
www.iasupport.org
National Secretary: Anne Demick
IA is a national support group run by and for people with ileostomies and internal pouches, their families and carers. The core objectives are to help those facing these operations to return to a normal active lifestyle as soon as possible after surgery. IA is totally funded by donations and subscriptions and most of the 10,000 members have either an ileostomy or an internal pouch.
Volunteers: 800
Regional offices: 50 member organisations

ICA:UK

41 Old Birley Street, Unit 14, Manchester M15 5RF
T: 0161 232 8444
E: martin@ica-uk.org.uk
www.ica-uk.org.uk
Chief Executive: Martin Gilbraith
Employees: 5
Volunteers: 30
Regional offices: 1

iDE UK

8a Accommodation Road, London NW11 8ED
T: 020 8905 5597
E: info@ide-uk.org
www.ide-uk.org
Chief Executive: Lewis Temple
International Development Enterprises UK (iDE UK) helps poor farming families in Africa and Asia to escape from poverty by doubling their income. IDE's mission is to create income and livelihood opportunities for the rural poor.
Employees: 3
Volunteers: 15

IGD

Grange Lane, Letchmore Heath, Watford WD25 8GD
T: 01923 851950
F: 01923 852531
E: itmanager@igd.com
www.igd.com
IGD is a charity that actively helps people to grow by bringing together intelligence, opinion and experience from the food and grocery chain. IGD's principal objectives are: to promote education and training, particularly industrial and technical education and training required for persons working in the food industry.
Employees: 78
Volunteers: 11

Imkaan

Tindlemanor, London EC1Y 8RT
T: 020 7250 3933
E: policy@imkaan.org.uk
www.imkaan.org.uk
Chair: Amrit Wilson
Our mission is to act as a collective voice for the South Asian women's and other refuges, by promoting their needs and views to relevant policy makers and agencies and by providing targeted organisational support.

Immigrant Counselling and Psychotherapy

96 Moray Road, Finsbury Park, London N4 3LA
T: 020 7272 7906
F: 020 7272 6920
E: info@icap.org.uk
www.icap.org.uk
The charity's objective and its principal activity is to provide culturally sensitive counselling for people of Irish origin.
Employees: 4
Volunteers: 15

Immigration Advisory Service

County House, 190 Great Dover Street, London SE1 4YB
T: 020 7967 1221
E: info@iasservices.org.uk
www.iasuk.org
Provides the best possible free legal advice and representation to immigrants and asylum seekers, without prejudice or discrimination, in which the interests and welfare of the client are paramount.

Impact Foundation

151 Western Road, Haywards Heath, West Sussex RH16 3LH
T: 01444 457080
F: 01444 457877
E: impact@impact.org.uk
www.impact.org.uk
Promotes activities for the prevention of disablement, and for the cure, mitigation and relief of disabling conditions.
Employees: 6
Volunteers: 8

Impetus – The Private Equity Foundation (Impetus-PEF)

183 Eversholt Street, London NW1 1BU
T: 020 3474 1000
E: lisa.dorstek@impetus-pef.org.uk
www.impetus-pef.org.uk
Chief executive officer: Daniela Barone Soares
Impetus-PEF is committed to transforming the lives of 11-24 year olds from disadvantaged backgrounds by ensuring they get the support they need to succeed in education, find and keep jobs, and achieve their potential. It finds the most promising charities and social enterprises working with these children and young people. It helps them become highly effective organisations that transform lives; then helps them expand significantly to dramatically increase the number of young people they serve.
Employees: 35
Income: £15,539,456 (2012-13)

In Kind Direct

62 Cornhill, London EC3V 3NH
T: 020 7398 5510
F: 020 7398 5544
E: robin@inkinddirect.org
www.inkinddirect.org
Chief Executive: Robin Boles
In Kind Direct, one of The Prince's Charities redistributes new goods donated by 930 of Britain's best-known manufacturers and retailers to UK voluntary and community organisations. Since 1997, we've distributed £130 million in value of goods to 6,700 organisations assisting millions of people in need. We created In Kind Direct International to spread product philanthropy to other countries. Start-up charity Innatura in Germany and Dons Solidaires in France are now members of the IKDI network.
Employees: 18
Income: £15,615,403 (2012-13)

Inclusion London

336 Brixton Road, London SW9 7AA
T: 020 7237 3181
E: info@inclusionlondon.org.uk
www.inclusionlondon.org.uk
CEO: Tracey Lazard
Inclusion London is a pan-London disability equality organisation. We provide policy, campaigning and capacity-building support for Deaf and Disabled people's organisations (DDPOs) in London. Inclusion London's mission is to promote Deaf and Disabled people's equality and inclusion by supporting Deaf and Disabled People's Organisations (DDPOs) and campaigning for rights for Deaf and Disabled people across the UK. Our work is rooted in the Social Model of Disability and the Cultural Model of Deafness.
Employees: 9
Income: £353,053 (2014-15)

Independence Initiative

Bootle, Liverpool L20 7EJ
T: 0151 284 1100
F: 0151 286 0015
E: joewelsh@independenceinitiative.co.uk
www.independenceinitiative.co.uk
The Independence Initiative works with individuals, agencies and the community to facilitate the long-term rehabilitation of people with a history of drug misuse and also provides support for their families. It provides a personal programme, addressing individual needs, overcoming barriers to social inclusion and assisting integration into the community.

Independent Custody Visiting Association

PO Box 1053, Colne, Lancashire BB9 4BL
T: 01282 870325
F: 020 7278 9027
E: info@icva.org.uk

Independent Home Solutions CIC

The Old Crumpet Factory, 16 Brockham Lane, Brockham, Surrey RH3 7EL
T: 01737 845630
F: 01737 841650
E: info@ihscic.org.uk
www.independenthomesolutions.org.uk
Managing director: Alison Goodall
Our experienced team specialises in providing quality and bespoke home adaptations for our disabled or elder clients. Popular alterations are: level access shower rooms, ground floor extensions, garage conversions, ramps, improved access, through floor or stair lifts. We help our clients to retain their independence, safety and dignity. The IHS team oversees every project from conception to completion so that we ensure a successful outcome and peace of mind for our clients.
Employees: 14
Volunteers: 2
Regional offices: 1
Income: £450,000 (2012-13)

Independent Living Alternatives

Trafalgar House, Grenville Place, Mill Hill, London NW7 3SA
T: 020 8906 9265
F: 020 8959 1910
E: paservices@ilanet.co.uk
www.ilanet.co.uk
Director: Tracey Jannaway
Independent Living Alternatives is a user-controlled disability organisation established in 1989 promoting the right of disabled people to live independently. ILA provides innovative and flexible alternatives to institutional and domiciliary care and has a comprehensive range of personal assistance services.
Employees: 4
Volunteers: 15
Regional offices: 1

Independent Theatre Council

The Albany, Douglas Way, London SE8 4AG
T: 020 7403 1727
E: admin@itc-arts.org
www.itc-arts.org
Chief Executive: Charlotte Jones
The Independent Theatre Council represents, supports and develops those producing professional performing arts in the UK. We are over 400 companies and producers, united in the knowledge that together we are stronger. ITC's commitment to represent your interests includes advice on management, financial and legal matters, peer learning, training opportunities and a professional network. ITC is a strong voice
Employees: 5

India Welfare Society

177 Kensal Road, London W10 5BJ
T: 020 8969 9493
F: 020 8960 2637
E: iwslondon@hotmail.com
www.nriwelfaresociety.com
Attends to the welfare of people in the UK, particularly members of the Indian community who are in need, hardship or distress.
Volunteers: 30

Industrial Careers Foundation

8 Nightingale Place, Buckingham, Buckinghamshire MK18 1UF
T: 01280 823363
E: geoff@icf.org.uk
www.icf.org.uk

Industry and Parliament Trust

Suite 101, 3 Whitehall Court,
London SW1A 2EL
T: 020 7839 9400
F: 020 7839 9401
E: admin@ipt.org.uk
www.ipt.org.uk
Chief Executive: Sally Muggeridge
Established in 1977, the Trust is dedicated to fostering mutual understanding between business and parliament for the public benefit. The IPT is independent, non-partisan and non-lobbying. IPT facilitates educational exchange Fellowships for MPs, MEPs, peers and officers of both Houses with a range of companies from different sectors of commerce and industry.
Employees: 10

Infertility Network UK

Charter House, 43 St Leonards Road,
Bexhill on Sea, East Sussex TN40 1JA
T: 0800 008 7464
F: 01424 731858
E: clarelewisjones@infertilitynetworkuk.com
www.infertilitynetworkuk.com
Chief Executive: Clare Lewis-Jones
At I N UK we aim to ease the feelings of isolation on both an emotional and practical level. Members of I N UK tell us frequently that by accessing our services, they are helped in the management of their illness.
Employees: 12
Volunteers: 80
Regional offices: 3
Income: £316,383 (2012-13)

Information Point for Centronuclear and Myotubular Myopathy

12 Bluebell Close, Huntington, Chester,
Cheshire CH3 6RR
T: 01244 316531
E: centronuclear.org@btinternet.com
www.centronuclear.org.uk
Founder: Toni Abram
The Information Point is a website for anyone affected by centronuclear/myotubular myopathy, the aim of which is to reach out to more families globally, to give them information about managing the condition. It is currently the only organisation in Europe/UK that provides comprehensive information and resources for the condition.
Volunteers: 1

Inland Waterways Association

Island House, Moor Road, Chesham,
Buckinghamshire HP5 1WA
T: 01494 783453
E: iwa@waterways.org.uk
www.waterways.org.uk
Chief Executive: Neil Edwards
The goals of the association are the preservation, conservation, restoration and development of the inland waterways of Great Britain.
Employees: 14
Volunteers: 17000

Innovative Vision Organisation (IVO)

123 High Cross Road, Tottenham,
London N17 9NR
T: 020 8365 0349
Helpline: 07943 317905
F: 020 8365 1477
E: info@ivo.org.uk
www.ivo.org.uk / www.ivouk.org [bc neither web address works]
Executive Director: Daisy Byaruhanga
Employees: 2
Volunteers: 25
Regional offices: 1

INQUEST

London N4 3JH
T: 020 7263 1111
F: 020 7561 0799
E: inquest@inquest.org.uk
www.inquest.org.uk
Co-Directors: Deborah Coles and Helen Shaw
INQUEST is the only registered charity in England and Wales that provides a free advice service to bereaved people and their advisors on contentious deaths and their investigation, with a particular focus on deaths in custody. INQUEST gives advice and a free handbook to any bereaved family about inquest procedure. Informed by casework, INQUEST undertakes research and develops policy proposals to campaign for changes to the inquest and investigation process.
Employees: 9
Volunteers: 3

Inspire!

E: david.blagbrough@inspire-ebp.org.uk

Institute for Community and Development Studies

Day Lewis House, 324 Bensham Lane,
Thornton Heath, London CR7 7EQ
T: 020 8664 2600
F: 020 8664 2656
E: icdsabcd@aol.com
www.partnershipventure.com
The charity exists primarily to advance education in accordance with Christian beliefs, values and identity, and biblical teachings in particular, by training students wishing to become community development leaders and facilitators working in inner-city areas.
Employees: 15
Volunteers: 80

Institute for Complementary Medicine

Unit 25, Tavern Quay Business Centre,
Sweden Gate, London SE16 7TX
T: 020 7231 5855
F: 020 7237 5175
E: info@i-c-m.org.uk
www.icnm.org.uk
Director: Frances Fewell
The ICM believes in promoting the standard of best practice and safe practice for all practitioners and therapists who work within complementary medicine. ICM facilitates the British Register of Complementary Practitioners and can supply names of highly qualified practitioners of various kinds of complementary medicine. It also has contact with other support groups.
Employees: 5
Volunteers: 1
Regional offices: 1

Institute for Conservation

3rd Floor, Downstream Building,
1 London Bridge, London SE1 9BG
T: 020 7785 3805
F: 020 7785 3806
E: admin@icon.org.uk
www.ukic.org.uk
Acts as a professional body for conservators of objects, for example, works of art, stonework, metalwork, etc. The Institute educates its members and the public about conservation techniques and developments in the profession.
Employees: 4
Volunteers: 80

Institute for European Environmental Policy London

28 Queen Annes Gate, London SW1H 9AB
T: 020 7799 2244
E: aglynn@ieep.eu
www.ieep.org.uk

Aims to analyse environmental policies in Europe, to increase the awareness of the European dimension of environmental policy and advance European environmental policy making.

Institute for Jewish Policy Research

4th Floor, 78 Market Place,
London W1W 8AG
T: 020 7436 1553
E: jpr@jpr.org.uk
www.jpr.org.uk
Executive Director: Dr Jonathan Boyd
The Institute for Jewish Policy Research is an independent think-tank that informs and influences policy, opinion and decision-making on social, political and cultural issues affecting Jewish life.
Employees: 6

Institute for Outdoor Learning

Plumpton Old Hall, Plumpton, Penrith,
Cumbria CA11 9NP
T: 01768 885800
E: institute@outdoor-learning.org
www.outdoor-learning.org
The aim of the Institute is to advance the education of the public in and through outdoor education.
Employees: 3

Institute for Philanthropy

2 Temple Place, London WC2R 3BD
T: 020 7240 0262
F: 020 7240 8022
E: contact@instituteforphilanthropy.org.uk
www.tpw.org
The Institute for Philanthropy works to increase effective philanthropy in the UK and internationally. We do this by: providing donor education and building donor networks; serving as a forum for new ideas; developing promising models for promoting philanthropy.
Employees: 15

Institute for War and Peace Reporting

48 Gray's Inn Road, London WC1X 8LT
T: 020 7831 1030
F: 020 7831 1050
E: gerryb@iwpr.net
www.iwpr.net
Aims to advance education and training in public-interest journalism and in the causes, conduct, effects and resolution of international, ethnic and group conflict and civil war for the public benefit. IWPR links local writers for story development, research, writing and training; organises public seminars and workshops; provides communications, networking, collaboration and financial support for local media; and undertakes consultancy and research.
Employees: 19
Volunteers: 5

Institute of Alcohol Studies

Elmgren House, 1 The Quay, St Ives,
Cambridgeshire PE27 5AR
T: 01480 466766
E: info@ias.org.uk
www.ias.org.uk
Chairman: Derek Rutherford
Aims to increase knowledge of alcohol and of the social health consequences of its use and abuse and to encourage and support the adoption of effective measures for the management and prevention of alcohol-related problems.

Institute of Business Ethics

24 Greencoat Place, London SW1P 1BE
T: 020 7798 6040
F: 020 7798 6044
E: info@ibe.org.uk
www.ibe.org.uk
Director: Philippa Foster Back
The Institute aims to advance public education and good practice in business ethics.
Employees: 9

Institute of Cancer Research

123 Old Brompton Road, London SW7 3RP
T: 020 7352 8133
F: 020 7370 5261
E: stewart.northcott@icl.ac.uk
www.icr.ac.uk
Chief Executive: Peter Rigby
The Institute is one of the world's leading cancer research organisations and is internationally renowned for the quality of its science. Together with the Royal Marsden NHS Foundation Trust it also forms the leading and largest comprehensive cancer centre in Europe. Our integrated work in genetics, molecular biology and drug development is unrivalled in the world and provides the opportunity for Institute scientists to transform the prospects for cancer patients.
Employees: 943

Institute of Fundraising

Park Place, 12 Lawn Lane,
London SW8 1UD
T: 020 7840 1000
F: 020 7840 1001
E: info@institute-of-fundraising.org.uk
www.institute-of-fundraising.org.uk
Chief Executive: Lindsay Boswell
The professional body for UK fundraising. We support fundraisers, through leadership, representation, setting standards and training, and we champion fundraising as a career choice.
Employees: 42
Volunteers: 300
Regional offices: 13

Institute of Group Analysis

1 Daleham Gardens, London NW3 5BY
T: 020 7431 2693
F: 020 7431 7246
E: sue@igalondon.org.uk
www.groupanalysis.org
The IGA was founded in 1971 by Dr SH Foulkes and a group of colleagues to provide clinical training in group analytic psychotherapy. Since then, group analysis has developed a strong presence in many regions of the UK, making the IGA a truly national organisation. Members come from different social and ethnic backgrounds, reflecting the social environment in which we live.
Employees: 6
Volunteers: 100

Institute of Money Advisers

T: 0113 242 0048
E: office@i-m-a.org.uk
www.i-m-a.org.uk

Institute of Psychoanalysis

Byron House, 112a Shirland Road,
London W9 2BT
T: 020 7563 5000
F: 020 7563 5001
E: nick.childs@iopa.org.uk
www.psychoanalysis.org.uk
CEO: Dr J Levett
Founded in 1924, the Institute of Psychoanalysis has trained psychoanalysts, many of whom have become leaders in the mental health field. The Institute welcomes applicants from all types of professional and academic backgrounds, from all over the world. Many students are psychiatrists or medically qualified, some are child or adult psychotherapists, psychologists, social workers or academics, and some come from other backgrounds altogether. The Institute

training leads to the title 'psychoanalyst', as recognised by the IPA.
Employees: 18
Regional offices: 1

Institute of Transactional Analysis

Broadway House, 149-151 St Neots Road, Hardwick, Cambridge CB23 7QJ
T: 0845 009 9101
E: admin@ita.org.uk
www.uktransactionalanalysis.co.uk
Promotes the study and application of transactional analysis in the UK; maintains a register of approved practitioners and monitors standards of application; provides information and support for any individual or organisation that wishes to know more about transactional analysis.

Insulin Dependent Diabetes Trust

PO Box 294, Northampton NN1 4XS
T: 01604 622837
F: 01604 622838
E: enquiries@iddtinternational.org
www.iddtinternational.org
Offers care and support to people with diabetes and their families and ensures that people with diabetes have an informed choice treatment; informs and disseminates information to the general public and health professionals to create a better understanding of life with diabetes.
Employees: 5
Volunteers: 50

Integrated Spinal Rehabilitation Foundation

Spinal Treatment Centre, Salisbury District Hospital, Odstock Road, Salisbury SP2 8BJ
T: 01722 336262
E: info@inspire-foundation.org.uk
www.inspire-foundation.org.uk
Promotes research into, and the development of, electronic, mechanical and medical aids to assist the mobility and enablement of people suffering spinal cord paralysis and its associated effects.

Inter Faith Network for the United Kingdom

Ground Floor, 2 Grosvenor Gardens, London SW1W 0DH
T: 020 7730 0410
F: 020 7730 0414
E: ifnet@interfaith.org.uk
www.interfaith.org.uk
Director: Harriet Crabtree
The Inter Faith Network for the UK works, with its member bodies, to advance public knowledge and mutual understanding of the teachings, traditions and practices of the different faith communities in Britain and to promote good relations between people of different faiths in this country. It links in membership national faith community representative bodies; national, regional and local inter faith organisations; and educational and academic bodies.

Inter-Action Associated Charitable Trusts and Companies

HMS President (1918), Near Blackfriars Bridge, Victoria Embankment, London EC4Y 0HJ
T: 020 7583 2652
F: 020 7515 4450
E: edbiaction@aol.com
Inter-Action applies entrepreneurial skills to obtain social and community benefits. It sets up model projects, especially in the areas of digital media, social enterprise training and education, which incorporate these aims, and offers training and consultancy to other groups locally and internationally, helping them to adapt model projects to their own communities' needs.
Employees: 3
Volunteers: 5

Interact Worldwide

325 Highgate Studios, London NW5 1TL
T: 020 7241 8500
F: 020 7267 6788
E: programmes@interactworldwide.org
www.interactworldwide.org
Interact Worldwide is an international charity with over 30 years' experience and relies on donations to fund its overseas projects and programmes. Interact Worldwide works on issues of sexual and reproductive health and HIV/AIDS in solidarity with indigenous partner organisations in Africa, Asia and Latin America. We take a rights-based approach, which is a framework that allows poor and marginalised people to demand as a 'right' the basic conditions that allow them to live in dignity.
Employees: 26
Volunteers: 5
Regional offices: 2

Interaction

3 Hoath Farm Cottages, Bekesbourne Lane, Canterbury, Kent CT3 4AB
T: 01227 455313
E: enquiries@pamhid.com
www.pamhid.com
Senior Trustee: Robert Hayward
InterAction has a vision of a world in which better mental health policy processes are created in developing countries and those in transition, which better involve people with mental health problems and grass-roots organisations, with better outcomes for individuals, households and communities.

Intercontinental Church Society

Unit 11 Ensign Business Centre, Westwood Way, Westwood Business Park, Coventry, West Midlands CV4 8JA
T: 024 7646 3940
F: 024 7767 5868
E: enquiries@ics-uk.org
www.ics-uk.org
Mission Director: Rev Richard Bromley
Aims to advance the Christian gospel by evangelical mission and ministry to English-speaking people throughout the world.
Employees: 5
Regional offices: 1

Intercountry Adoption Centre

22 Union Street, Barnet, Hertforshire EN5 4HZ
T: 020 8449 2562
Helpline: 020 8447 4753
E: pa@icacentre.org.uk
www.icacentre.org.uk
Chief Executive: Gill Haworth
Intercountry Adoption Centre (IAC) is a registered Voluntary Adoption Agency which specialises in intercountry adoptions but also offers a domestic service, including for adopters who have previously adopted overseas through IAC and who wish subsequently to adopt children from the UK. We provide intercountry adoption assessments and subscription services nationally to local authorities and other voluntary adoption agencies IAC is unique in being internationally accredited by some States of origin as their partner agency.
Regional offices: 1

InterHealth Worldwide

Partnership House, 157 Waterloo Road, London SE1 8US
T: 020 7902 9000
F: 020 7928 0927
E: info@interhealth.org.uk
www.interhealth.org.uk
InterHealth provides whole-person healthcare to individuals and organisations involved in service throughout the world. InterHealth is motivated by Christian beliefs and values and by humanitarian ideals to

provide compassionate and professional care without discrimination.
Employees: 22
Volunteers: 4

Interights

Lancaster House, 33 Islington High Street, London N1 9LH
T: 020 7278 3230
E: sharrington@interights.org
www.interights.org
Interights works to ensure that human rights are defended effectively in domestic courts and before regional and international bodies. We contribute to the development of a cumulative and progressive interpretation of universal human rights and to their effective use in both international and regional arenas as well as national courts.
Employees: 25

Interlink Foundation

Fourth Floor Offices, 97 Stamford Hill, London N16 5DN
T: 020 8802 2469
F: 020 8800 5153
E: admin@interlink-foundation.org.uk
www.interlink-foundation.org.uk
Chief Executive: Chaya Spitz
The Interlink Foundation strengthens and improves community services by supporting the work of Orthodox Jewish charities and community organisations. We provide specialist advice to community groups, advocate on their behalf and build bridges between the Orthodox Jewish community and public bodies.
Employees: 10
Regional offices: 2

International Action Network on Small Arms

London EC2V 4JX
T: 020 7065 0870
F: 020 7065 0871
E: contact@iansa.org
www.iansa.org
Employees: 4
Volunteers: 4

International Alert

346 Clapham Road, London SW9 9AP
T: 020 7627 6800
F: 020 7627 6900
E: general@international-alert.org
www.international-alert.org
Secretary General: Dan Smith
International Alert is one of the world's leading peace-building organisations. We help people find non-violent solutions to conflict and have nearly 30 years of experience working in 25 countries around the world to build lasting peace. We also seek to influence the policies and ways of working of governments, international organisations like the UN and multinational companies, to reduce conflict risk and increase the prospects of peace.
Employees: 200
Regional offices: 15

International Alliance of Patients' Organisations

49-51 East Road, London N1 6AH
T: 020 7250 8280
F: 020 7250 8285
E: info@patientsorganizations.org
www.patientsorganizations.org
CEO: Joanna Groves
IAPO is a unique global alliance representing patients of all nationalities across all disease areas and promoting patient-centred healthcare around the world. Our members are patients' organisations working at the international, regional, national and local levels to represent and support patients, their families and carers. A patient is a person with any chronic disease, illness, syndrome, impairment or disability.
Employees: 7
Volunteers: 3
Income: £572,248 (2013-14)

International Children's Trust

67A Lincoln Road, Peterborough, Cambridgeshire PE1 2SD
T: 01733 319777
E: admin@theict.org
www.theict.org
Executive Director: Dave Christie
The International Children's Trust funds, develops and supports partners who are working with severely disadvantaged and 'at risk' children, their families and their communities in low- and middle-income countries. It develops an effective network between its partners whose similarities and differences combine to form a collective experience in the field of international child development for the purpose of learning and giving strength through mutual support.
Employees: 3
Volunteers: 2
Income: £500,000 (2014-15)

International Community Assist

Churchview, 13 Woodland Road, Patney, Devizes, Wiltshire SN10 3RD
T: 01380 840990
E: icauk@btopenworld.com
www.ica-uk.co.uk
Aims to alleviate poverty through provision of general assistance in the developing world.

International Development Partnerships

5 Cleveland Mansions, Widley Road, London W9 2LA
T: 020 7286 9756
E: office@idp-uk.org
www.idp-uk.org
Chief Executive: Andrew Chadwick
We provide broad-based humanitarian assistance to rural communities in Ethiopia, particularly: improving access to healthcare; providing clean water and sanitation facilities; rehabilitating schools; improving agricultural production; protecting the environment and preserving Ethiopia's heritage.
Volunteers: 8
Income: £72,000 (2013-14)

International Fund for Animal Welfare

8th Floor, Camelford House, London SE1 7UD
T: 020 7587 6700
F: 020 7587 6720
E: info@ifaw.org
www.ifaw.org
Promotes the compassionate treatment of animals as sentient beings; to protect them from cruelty; to preserve their natural habitat; to preserve them from extinction.

International Glaucoma Association

Woodcote House, 15 Highpoint Business Village, Henwood, Ashford, Kent TN24 8DN
T: 01233 648164
Helpline: 01233 648170
F: 01233 648179
E: info@iga.org.uk
www.glaucoma-association.com
Chief Executive: David Wright
Provides a fellowship for those suffering from the eye disease glaucoma and those concerned in its diagnosis and treatment; presses for increased resources for what is frequently a neglected condition so that there is an improved awareness and better long-term monitoring of the disease. This is necessary because the loss of sight from glaucoma is largely preventable yet it accounts for 13% of the registered blind.
Employees: 14

International Guide Dog Federation

Hillfields, Burghfield Common, Reading RG7 3YG
T: 0118 983 8356
E: enquiries@igdf.org.uk
www.igdf.org.uk
First and foremost, membership of the IGDF enables guide dog organisations around the world to join a community dedicated to serving the visually impaired. That community needs and wants to share its knowledge and the IGDF facilitates that.
Employees: 1

International Institute for Environment and Development

3 Endsleigh Street, London WC1H 0DD
T: 020 7388 2117
F: 020 7388 2826
E: morris.kagkwo@iied.org
www.iied.org
Director: Camilla Toulmin
IIED seeks to make the world a fairer and more sustainable place, in alliance with like-minded partners. Acting as a catalyst, broker and facilitator, we seek to add voice to poorer and more vulnerable groups to ensure their interests are heard in decision-making and can bring about progressive change.
Employees: 70

International Institute of Communications

The Glasshouse, 177-187 Arthur Road, Wimbledon, London SW19 8AE
T: 020 8947 3535
F: 020 8944 6083
E: info@iicom.org
www.iicom.org
The Institute's principal activity is the organisation of overseas meetings and conferences, carrying out research and publishing material in the field of worldwide communications.
Employees: 5
Volunteers: 20

International League for the Protection of Horses

Anne Colvin House, Snetterton, Norfolk NR16 2LR
T: 0870 870 1927
F: 0870 904 1927
E: nagtrader08@gmail.com
www.ilph.org
Our aim is a world where horses are used but never abused. Our mission is to protect horses from abuse and alleviate their suffering by rehabilitation, campaigning and educating worldwide.
Employees: 131
Volunteers: 8
Regional offices: 5

International Longevity Centre-UK

Vauxhall, London SE1 7TJ
T: 020 7735 7565
E: louisetasker@ilcuk.org.uk
www.ilcuk.org.uk
Chief Executive: Baroness Sally Greengross
The International Longevity Centre-UK is an independent, non-partisan think-tank dedicated to addressing issues of longevity, ageing and population change. We develop ideas, undertake research and create a forum for debate.
Employees: 8
Regional offices: 1

International Network for the Availability of Scientific Publications

60 St Aldates, Oxford OX1 1ST
T: 01865 249909
F: 01865 251060
E: inasp@inasp.info
www.inasp.info/en/
The charity exists for the benefit of people in resource-poor countries, to promote education, knowledge and learning by enhancing local capabilities to manage and use information and knowledge.
Employees: 16

International Seafarers Welfare & Assistance Network

3rd Floor, Suffolk House, George Street, Croydon, Surrey CR0 1PE
T: 0300 012 4279
Helpline: 020 7323 2737
F: 0300 012 4280
E: iswan@iswan.org.uk
www.seafarerswelfare.org
Executive Director: Roger Harris
The objectives of ISWAN are to promote the relief of need, hardship or distress amongst seafarers of all nationalities, races, colours and creeds.
Employees: 16
Regional offices: 1

International Seafarers' Assistance Network

8th Floor, Cygnet House, Croydon, Surrey CR0 2EE
T: 020 8680 2232
F: 020 3251 0221
E: info@seafarerhelp.org
www.seafarerhelp.org
Provides support, information and advice to seafarers around the world, through a network of maritime agencies.
Employees: 3

International Service

2nd Floor, Rougier House, 5 Rougier Street, York YO1 6HZ
T: 01904 647799
F: 01904 652353
E: contact@internationalservice.org.uk
www.internationalservice.org.uk
Chief Executive: Jo Baker
An international development agency that has been changing lives for more than 60 years by empowering some of the world's poorest and most marginalised people. International Service works in Latin America, West Africa and the Middle East, supporting in-country partners to develop and deliver sustainable solutions to inequality and poverty. Partners range from a local, grassroots level to government departments. Promoting social and economic inclusion is at the core of our work.
Employees: 18
Volunteers: 250
Regional offices: 6

International Stress Management Association UK

PO Box 108, PO Box 108, Caldicot, Avon NP26 9AP
T: 0117 969 7284
E: stress@isma.org.uk
www.isma.org.uk
Chair: Jenny Edwards
ISMA is a registered charity with a multidisciplinary professional membership. It exists to promote sound knowledge and best practice in the prevention and reduction of human stress. It sets professional standards for the benefit of individuals and organisations using the services of its members.
Employees: 1

International Students House

229 Great Portland Street, London W1W 5PN
T: 020 7631 8300
F: 020 7631 8307
E: marketing@ish.org.uk
www.ish.org.uk
Helps students achieve the academic and personal aims that have brought them to the

UK; provides the best opportunities for international students to experience the many facets of life in the UK and give them a deeper understanding of British society; gives British students the opportunity for friendship with people from widely differing backgrounds and cultures and by these means makes an effective contribution to better international relations.
Employees: 130

International Tree Foundation

Mayfield House, 256 Banbury Road, Oxford, Oxfordshire OX2 7DE
T: 01865 318838
E: info@internationaltreefoundation.org
www.internationaltreefoundation.org
Chief Executive: Andy Egan
Since 1924 ITF has worked with communities in UK and internationally to protect the environment through safeguarding forests, re-forestation and improving livelihoods through agroforestry. Our programmes: Tree Power schools programme combining global and outdoor learning to encourage environmental awareness; Africa Drylands programme tackles desertification in the Sahel region; Sustainable Community Forestry Programme supports community-led forestry, bio-diversity and livelihoods projects across sub-Saharan Africa; UK Community Tree Planting provides grants for community and schools forestry projects.
Employees: 5
Volunteers: 2
Income: £267,490 (2013-14)

International Voluntary Service

Thorn House, 5 Rose Street, Edinburgh, Lothian EH2 2PR
T: 0131 243 2745
F: 0131 243 2747
E: info@ivsgb.org
www.ivsgb.org
Development Director: Helen Wass O'Donnell
IVS GB is a peace organisation that promotes intercultural cooperation and intercultural understanding through voluntary work. Volunteer projects work for sustainable development of local and global communities throughout the world. IVS is open to everyone from 18 to 70 years. We offer short-term projects of two to four weeks, long-term opportunities and we are a sending organisation for EVS (European Voluntary Service).
Employees: 4
Volunteers: 3
Regional offices: 1

International Youth Hostel Federation

2nd Floor, Gate House, Fretherne Road, Welwyn Garden City, Hertfordshire AL8 6RD
T: 01707 324170
F: 01707 323980
E: jpowell@hihostels.com
www.hihostels.com
Chief Executive: Mikael Hansson
Promotes the education of all young people by encouraging in them a greater knowledge, love and care of the countryside, towns and cities in all parts of the world; provides hostel accommodation with no distinction of race, nationality, colour, religion, sex, class or political opinions; and develops a better understanding of other people, both at home and abroad.
Employees: 20

Internet Watch Foundation

Suite 7310, First Floor Building 7300, Cambridge Research Park, Waterbeach CB25 9TN
T: 01223 203030
E: bill@iwf.org.uk
www.iwf.org.uk
Chief Executive: Susie Hargreaves
The IWF is the UK reporting hotline for images of child sexual abuse online, extreme adult pornography and non-photographic images of child sexual abuse. Our vision is to eliminate online child sexual abuse.
Employees: 20
Regional offices: 1

INTRAC

PO Box 563, Oxford OX2 6RZ
T: 01865 201851
F: 01865 201852
E: info@intrac.org
www.intrac.org
Provides specially designed management training, consultancy and research services to organisations involved in international relief and development; improves the organisational effectiveness and programme performance of northern NGOs and southern partners.
Employees: 28
Volunteers: 3
Regional offices: 3

Involvement and Participation Association (IPA)

42 Colebrook Row, London N1 8AF
T: 0171 354 8040
F: 020 7354 8041
E: involve@ipa-involve.com
www.ipa-involve.com
Promotes employee information and consultation processes, and partnership in the workplace.
Employees: 6

Iranian Association

Palingswick House, 241 King Street, London W6 9LP
T: 020 8748 6682
F: 020 8563 7549
E: info@iranian-association.org.uk
www.iranianassociation.org.uk
Aims to assist the development of the Iranian ethnic community in Britain in terms of settlement, social welfare, training and education.
Employees: 13
Volunteers: 35

Irish in Britain

356 Holloway Road, London N7 6PA
T: 020 7697 4081
F: 020 7697 4271
E: shutton@irishsocieties.org
www.irishinbritain.org
CEO: Jennie McShannon
Irish in Britain is the national representative body for the Irish in Britain. Working together with over 100 Irish cultural and community members we endeavour to raise the profile and contribution of the Irish community in Britain through research, policy and parliamentary work, campaigns and community development support. Our mission is to achieve a confident, healthy and empowered Irish community participating fully in Britain. Follow us on Twitter: @irishinbritain or Facebook: Irish in Britain
Employees: 11
Volunteers: 10
Regional offices: 3
Income: £529,437 (2012-13)

Irish Traveller Movement in Britain

The Resource Centre, 356 Holloway Road, London N7 6PA
T: 020 7607 2002
F: 020 7607 2005
E: info@irishtraveller.org.uk
ITM aims to develop the capacity and skills of members of the socially and economically disadvantaged community of Irish travellers in such a way that they are better able to identify, and help meet, their needs and to

participate more fully in society; and to promote equality and diversity and racial harmony for the benefit of the public by encouraging others to understand the culture and needs of Irish travellers.
Employees: 1
Volunteers: 11

Isbourne Foundation

Wolseley House, Oriel Road, Cheltenham GL50 1TH
T: 01242 254321
E: info@isbourne.org
www.isbourne.org
The Foundation helps individuals to develop their self-awareness in harmony with natural and spiritual laws.
Employees: 3
Volunteers: 10

Islamic Relief

19 Rea Street South, Digbeth, Birmingham, West Midlands B5 6LB
T: 0121 605 5555
F: 0121 622 5003
E: saleh.saeed@irworldwide.org
www.islamic-relief.com
Chief Executive Officer: Saleh Saeed
Dedicated to the service of the world's poorest people through emergency intervention at the time of disasters and through long-term development in the fields of education, health, income generation and water and sanitation.
Employees: 240
Volunteers: 100
Regional offices: 25

IVAR

26 Russell Square, Bloomsbury, London WC1B 5DQ
T: 020 7631 6608
F: 020 7631 6688
E: kulwinder@ivar.org.uk
www.ivar.org.uk
Director: Ben Cairns
IVAR's mission is to support the development and sustainability of charities and other voluntary, community and not-for-profit organisations through research, education and training.
Employees: 3

Iyengar Yoga Institute

223A Randolph Avenue, London W9 1NL
T: 020 7624 3080
F: 020 7372 2726
E: office@iyi.org.uk
www.iyi.org.uk
Aims to advance public education in the classical teachings of the science of yoga; promotes and advances the study and practice of yoga; supports research into the therapeutic effects of yoga as a means of improving the mental and physical health of the community and publishes the results of such research.

JAT

Berkeley House, 1st Floor, Edgware HA8 7RP
T: 020 8952 5253
F: 020 8952 8893
E: admin@jat-uk.org
www.jat-uk.org
Director: Janine Clements
JAT provides sexual health and HIV education for Jewish youth in schools, youth groups and summer camps. We also run a programme for parents on how to talk to their children about sex. We offer financial, practical and emotional support for Jewish people with HIV.
Employees: 4
Volunteers: 20

Jewish Association for the Mentally Ill

Olympia House, Armitage Road, London NW11 8RQ
T: 020 8458 2223
F: 020 8731 7395
E: info@jamiuk.org
www.jamiuk.org
Provides services and support to people with severe and enduring mental health problems.
Employees: 8
Volunteers: 37

Jewish Bereavement Counselling Service

Bet Meir, 44A Albert Road, Hendon, London NW4 2SJ
T: 020 8385 1874
E: enquiries@jbcs.org.uk
www.jvisit.org.uk
Offers emotional help and support to members of the Jewish community who have been bereaved, and serves as a resource and information centre to both the Jewish and the non-Jewish community within London and around the UK.

Jewish Council for Racial Equality (JCORE)

PO Box 47864, London NW11 1AB
T: 020 8455 0896
E: admin@jcore.org.uk
www.jcore.org.uk
Executive Director: Dr Edie Friedman
Since 1976, The Jewish Council for Racial Equality (JCORE) has been working to promote race equality in the UK through education, campaigning and dialogue. We have a particular interest in achieving justice for refugees and asylum seekers, safeguarding their human rights and giving them practical support. We also work closely with other ethnic minority groups in order to understand our common experiences and develop a collective voice on race and asylum issues.
Employees: 3
Volunteers: 30

Jewish Lads and Girls Brigade including Outreach/Kiruv and Hand-in-Hand Young Volunteers

3 Beechcroft Road, South Woodford, London E18 1LA
T: 020 8989 8990
F: 020 8530 3327
E: getinvolved@jlgb.org
www.jlgb.org
Aims to train its members in loyalty, honour, discipline and self-respect so that they may become a credit to their country and their community. We are committed to enhancing the lives of Jewish young people through a diverse range of experiences and activities within a friendly and safe environment, encouraging development within the Jewish and wider community.
Employees: 10
Volunteers: 250
Regional offices: 1

Jewish Marriage Council

23 Ravenshurst Avenue, Hendon, London NW4 4EE
T: 020 8572 2691
E: info@jmc-uk.org
www.jmc-uk.org
Chair: Martyn Zeidman
Provides confidential support for all Jewish people.
Employees: 2
Volunteers: 20
Regional offices: 1

Jewish Women's Aid

PO Box 2670, London N12 9ZE
T: 020 8445 8060
Helpline: 0808 801 0500
F: 020 8445 0305
E: info@jwa.org.uk
www.jwa.org.uk
Executive Director: Naomi Dickson
Aims to raise awareness of the issues of domestic abuse against women, within the Jewish community, and to campaign on their behalf; provides a refuge for Jewish women and their children fleeing domestic abuse; fosters links with organisations in both the Jewish and the wider community; provides professional advice services; and researches, develops and produces resources and publicity material.
Employees: 15
Volunteers: 160
Regional offices: 1

Jigsaw4U Ltd

40 Mill Green Road, Mitcham, Surrey CR4 4HY
T: 020 8687 1384
F: 020 8687 9730
E: info@jigsaw4u.org.uk
www.jigsaw4u.org.uk
Director of Operations: Pam Byfield
Jigsaw4u is a child-centred charity supporting children and young people through grief, loss and trauma whilst also empowering them to have a voice in decision-making about their own lives. The organisation delivers a wide range of projects including those that work with sexual exploitation, home school links, domestic abuse, participation for disabled young people, pre and post bereavement, advocacy and going missing.
Employees: 21
Volunteers: 60
Income: £655,021 (2013-14)

John Ellerman Foundation

Aria House, 23 Craven Street, London WC2N 5NS
T: 020 7930 8566
E: enquiries@ellerman.org.uk
www.ellerman.org.uk
Director: Nicola Pollock
The Foundation is a generalist grant-making trust, which mainly funds charities working in the arts, environment and welfare in the UK.
Employees: 5
Income: £3,692,000 (2014-15)

John Huntingdon's Charity

John Huntingdon House, Tannery Road, Sawston, Cambridge CB22 3UW
T: 01223 830599 (also fax)
E: jill@johnhuntingdon.org.uk
www.johnhuntingdon.org.uk
charity manager: Jill Hayden
To bring relief either generally or to individual persons who are in conditions of need, hardship or distress in particular, but not exclusively, for the benefit of those who live, work and study in the Parish of Sawston and elsewhere locally. We achieve these objectives by, supporting individuals and families with free advice through the JHC Support Service , giving grants to individuals and organisations and housing those most in need in our almshouses.
Employees: 5
Volunteers: 14
Income: £350,000 (2014-15)

Joint Committee of the Order of St John and British Red Cross Society

5th Floor, London SE1 7TJ
E: balwinder@jointcommittee.freeserve.co.uk
Provides financial assistance in the form of grants to ex-service war disabled men and women disabled in the First and Second World Wars. Help is also available for widows of war disability pensioners and for sick and elderly ex-members of the nursing services of HM Forces and to officers and members of the Voluntary Aid Detachment of the Red Cross and St John Ambulance who gave service to the wounded in the second World War or earlier.

Joint Council for the Welfare of Immigrants

115 Old Street, London EC1V 9RT
T: 020 7251 8708
F: 020 7251 8707
E: info@jcwi.org.uk
www.jcwi.org.uk
Chief Executive: Habib Rahman
JCWI was established in 1967 to provide immediate and direct support to immigrants and to respond to the injustice and unfairness of UK immigration control. JCWI exists to campaign for justice in immigration, nationality and refugee laws and policy.
Employees: 10
Volunteers: 2

Joint Epilepsy Council

PO Box 186, Leeds, West Yorkshire LS20 8WY
T: 01943 87182
E: sharon.jec@btconnect.com
www.jointepilepsycouncil.org.uk
Chief Executive: Sharon Wood
The Joint Epilepsy Council of the UK and Ireland (JEC) is an umbrella charity providing the representative voice working for the benefit of people affected by epilepsy.
Employees: 1
Volunteers: Varies

Joseph Levy Foundation

1 Bell Street, London NW1 5JY
T: 020 7616 1200
F: 020 7616 1206
E: info@jlf.org.uk
www.jlf.org.uk
Director: Sue Nyfield
The Foundation supports general charitable purposes, giving grants to registered charities. The trustees believe in an inclusive society and recognise the needs of all its citizens. The Foundation works with charities that enable people to build a better future in their communities and to improve their quality of life. The Foundation is currently closed to unsolicited applications.
Employees: 2

Joseph Rowntree Foundation

The Homestead, 40 Water End, York, North Yorkshire YO30 6WP
T: 01904 629241
F: 01904 620072
E: sarah.carrette@jrf.org.uk
www.rowntreesociety.org.uk
Chief Executive: Julia Unwin
The Joseph Rowntree Foundation's aim is to search, demonstrate and influence, providing research, evidence, solutions and ideas that will help to overcome the causes of poverty and inequality. Our three main research themes are Poverty, Place and An Ageing Society.
Employees: 700

Josephine Butler Educational Trust

4 The Hedges, Penenden Heath, Maidstone, Kent ME14 2JW
T: 01622 679630
E: jbt@liverpool.anglican.org
www.josephinebutler.org.uk
The Trust disseminates knowledge and educates the public about the law as it affects prostitution of women and children,

international sexual slavery and all forms of exploitation of prostitution by third parties.

Journalists Charity

Dickens House, 35 Wathen Road, Dorking, Surrey RH4 1JY
T: 01306 887511
F: 01306 888212
E: enquiries@pressfund.org.uk
www.journalistscharity.org.uk
Director: David Ilott
Helps journalists and their dependants in times of need. Also provides sheltered housing and a nursing home.
Employees: 20
Volunteers: 30

Jubilee Sailing Trust

Merlin Quay, Hazel Road, Southampton, Hampshire SO19 7GB
T: 023 8044 9108
F: 023 8044 9145
E: rebecca.withers@jst.org.uk
www.jst.org.uk
Chief Executive: Amanda Butcher
The JST was founded in 1977 to give disabled people the opportunity to discover the thrill and adventure of offshore tall ship sailing as a member of a mixed-ability crew. The JST operates two beautiful purpose designed and built tall ships, Lord Nelson and Tenacious and is the only organisation in the world that can integrate mixed-ability crews on year-round voyages to northern Europe, the Canaries and the Caribbean.
Employees: 58
Volunteers: 500

Judith Trust

5 Carriage House, 90 Randolph Avenue, London W9 1BG
T: 020 7266 1073
F: 020 7289 5804
E: judith.trust@lineone.net
www.judithtrust.org.uk
Chair: Annette Lawson
The Judith Trust's vision is a world without struggle: a better life for people with both learning disabilities and mental illness needs and their carers. The Trust funds commissioned research and, on the basis of outcomes, advocates for policy change and implementation.
Employees: 1

Julia Margaret Cameron Trust

Dimbola Museum and Galleries, Terrace Lane, Freshwater Bay, Isle of Wight PO40 9QE
T: 01983 756814
E: elissa.blizzard@dimbola.co.uk
www.dimbola.co.uk
Administrator: John Holsburt
Former home and work place of pioneering Victorian photographer Julia Margaret Cameron, now a museum and gallery. The charity aims to educate the public about the work of Cameron, the history of photography and the Freshwater Circle and to encourage an appreciation of modern photography as an art.
Employees: 3
Volunteers: 20
Income: £99,698 (2012-13)

Just a Drop

Gateway House, 28 The Quadrant, Richmond, Surrey TW9 1DN
T: 020 8910 7981
F: 020 8334 0555
E: nikki.davis@reedexpo.co.uk
www.justadrop.org
Polluted water is the world's biggest killer of children under five. Just a Drop raises money to build wells, install hand pumps and carry out health and sanitation programmes to give them and their families clean, accessible water.
Employees: 1
Volunteers: 10

JustGiving

1st Floor, 30 Eastbourne Terrace, London W2 6LA
E: press@justgiving.com
www.justgiving.com
CEO: Zarine Kharas

JUSTICE

59 Carter Lane, London EC4V 5AQ
T: 020 7329 5100
F: 020 7329 5055
E: lpepler@justice.org.uk
www.justice.org.uk
Director: Roger Smith
JUSTICE is an independent law reform and human rights organisation. Since its formation in 1957, JUSTICE has been at the cutting edge of the debate on legal reform. It is widely respected for the breadth, depth and quality of its analysis. Today, more than ever, JUSTICE is involved in the issues that will shape the future legal landscape.
Employees: 8
Volunteers: 6

Kairos Community Trust

110 Brixton Road, London SW9 6BE
F: 020 7582 4211
E: kairosoffice@kairoscommunity.org.uk
www.kairoscommunity.org.uk
Helps homeless people to recover from situations causing their marginalisation, providing detox and treatment for substance misuse and suitable accommodation. It fosters their recovery in a community residential setting and alleviates poverty.
Employees: 21
Volunteers: 20

Karuna Trust

72 Holloway Road, London N7 8JG
T: 020 7700 3434
F: 020 7700 3535
E: info@karuna.org
www.karuna.org
Works for the relief of poverty, the advancement of education, cultural conservation and advancement of the Buddhist religion. Continues to expand the funding work begun by Aid for India, both in India and elsewhere and promotes, amongst the poorest people of the world, dignity, initiative and self-reliance.
Employees: 9
Volunteers: 5

Keep Britain Tidy

Elizabeth House, The Pier, Wigan, Greater Manchester WN3 4EX
T: 01942 612621
F: 01942 824778
E: press@keepbritaintidy.org
www.keepbritaintidy.org
Chief Executive: Phil Barton
Keep Britain Tidy is a campaigning environmental charity that encourages everyone to be litter free, to waste less and to live more. It runs a variety of programmes including WasteWatch, Eco-Schools in England, the Blue Flag Award for beaches and the Keep Britain Tidy Network for local authorities and land managers as well as a number of volunteering programmes.
Employees: 100
Volunteers: 75000

Keep Fit Association

Suite 105, Astra House, Arklow Road, London SE14 6EB
T: 01403 266000
F: 020 8692 8383
E: office@emdp.org
www.keepfit.org.uk
Provides the opportunity for people of all ages and aptitudes to develop their individual potential through the medium of movement, dance and exercise by making full use of their physical and intellectual capabilities and social involvement.
Employees: 2
Volunteers: 20
Regional offices: 82

Kent Volunteers

E: caroline.reade@kent.gov.uk

Kenward Trust

Kenward Road, Yalding ME18 6AH
T: 01622 814187
F: 01622 815805
E: audrey.pie@kenwardtrust.org.uk
www.kenwardtrust.org.uk
Chief Executive: Angela Painter
Employees: 52
Volunteers: 29

Keratec

Keratec Eyebank, Department of Anatomy, St Georges, University of London, Cranmer Terrace, London SW17 0RE
T: 020 8672 2325
F: 020 8682 3026
E: rostron@sgul.ac.uk
www.kerateceyebank.co.uk
Medical Director: Chad Rostron
The charity is committed to developing the treatment of corneal disease. Corneal opacity is a major cause of blindness worldwide, and we are researching new methods of treatment to restore sight in those suffering from conditions such as keratoconus, trachoma and corneal scarring.
Employees: 1
Volunteers: 1

Keratoconus Self-Help and Support Association

PO Box 26251, London W3 9WQ
Helpline: 020 8993 4759
E: anneklepacz@aol.com
www.keratoconus-group.org.uk
The association provides information and support to those with this eye condition. It organises conferences, members meetings, and produces a regular newsletter and other information.
Volunteers: 12
Income: £10,802 (2012-13)

KeyChange Charity

5 St Georges Mews, 43 Westminster Bridge Road, London SE1 7JB
T: 020 7633 0533
E: info@keychange.org.uk
www.keychange.org.uk
Provides residential and nursing care for older people, provision for homeless women, and street outreach to women in the sex industry.

KeyRing

65, Dalston Lane E8 2NG
T: 020 3119 0960
E: enquiries@keyring.org
www.keyring.org
Chief Executive: Karyn Kirkpatrick
KeyRing supports vulnerable adults to live independently at the heart of their community. KeyRing has been supporting people for over 20 years and over 800 people across England and Wales are unlocking their potential through KeyRing.
Employees: 150
Volunteers: 100
Regional offices: 3

KIDS

49 Mecklenburgh Square, London WC1N 2NY
T: 020 7520 0420
F: 020 7520 0406
E: kevin.williams@kids.org.uk
www.kids.org.uk
Chief Executive: Kevin Williams
Provides services to disabled children and young people and their families.
Employees: 600
Volunteers: 200
Regional offices: 5

Kids Can Achieve

E: pat.lee@kidscanachieve.co.uk

Kidsaid

4 St Giles Terrace, Northampton NN1 2BN
T: 01604 630332
E: info@kidsaid.org.uk
www.kidsaid.org.uk
Chair of Trustees: Patrick Conrad
A Northamptonshire based charity that provides therapy and support to children who have suffered bereavement, abuse, domestic violence, family breakdown, bullying or any form of trauma.
Employees: 3
Volunteers: 10
Regional offices: 1
Income: £120,000 (2014-15)

Kidscape Campaign for Children's Safety

2 Grosvenor Gardens, London SW1W 0DH
T: 020 7730 3300
F: 020 7730 7081
E: contact@kidscape.org.uk
www.kidscape.org.uk
CEO: Claude Knights
Kidscape is committed to keeping children safe. Launched in 1985, it is the only nationwide charity dedicated exclusively to preventing child sexual abuse and bullying before it happens.
Employees: 22
Volunteers: 1
Regional offices: 1

Kidsout UK

14 Church Square, Leighton Buzzard, Bedfordshire LU7 1AE
T: 01525 385252
F: 01525 385533
E: kidsout@kidsout.org.uk
www.kidsout.org.uk
CEO: Gordon Moulds CBE
Our mission is to help transform the lives of disadvantaged children and young people in the UK by providing fun opportunities and positive experiences to significantly enhance their wellbeing and outlook for a happier future. Our projects currently support children who have experienced domestic violence, children with disabilities, children with English as an additional language, children struggling academically and those not in education, employment or training.
Employees: 7
Volunteers: 50
Regional offices: 1

King's Fund

London W1G 0AN
T: 020 7307 2400
F: 020 7307 2801
E: library@kingsfund.org.uk
www.kingsfund.org.uk
The King's Fund is an independent health charity that does work based on evidence of need and a commitment to the values of social justice and public service. It supports the health of the people of London by influencing health policy and stimulating good practice in service provisions. Works across

the UK to tackle problems, promote mutual learning and disseminate new ideas.
Employees: 113

King's Medical Research Trust

Weston Education Centre,
10 Cutcombe Road, London SE5 9RJ
T: 020 7848 5866
E: marc.masey@nhs.net
The Trust aims to relieve suffering and cure illness and disease by continuous research into causes, prevention, diagnosis and treatment, and by publishing the results for public good.

Kingham Hill Trust

Oak Hill College, Chase Side, Southgate
T: 020 8449 0467
E: tonys@oakhill.ac.uk
www.oakhill.ac.uk
Bursar: Tony Sims

Kingston Centre for Independent Living

River Reach, 31-35 High Street, Kingston, Surrey KT1 1LF
T: 020 8546 9603
E: robert.reilly@kcil.org.uk
www.kcil.org.uk
CEO: Lisa Ehlers
Enable disabled people in and around the Royal Borough of Kingston (RBK) to lead independent and empowering lives; Lobby for full equality of status, opportunity and inclusion for all; Promote the recognition and acceptance of the Social Model of Disability; Represent the interests of disabled people in and around RBK, using appropriate forms of user consultation and engagement;
Employees: 10
Volunteers: 10
Income: £365,000 (2014-15)

Kingsway International Christian Centre

KICC Prayer City, Buckmore Park, Maidstone Road, Chatham, Kent ME5 9QG
T: 020 8525 0000
E: ade_d'almeida@kicc.org.uk
www.kicc.org.uk
CEO: Oladipo Oluyomi
KICC is an independent, interdenominational and international church. KICC actively supports the community via a range of counselling services, skills training and a supplementary school for GCSE pupils. KICC also works in partnership with statutory and voluntary organisations to improve social conditions.
Employees: 51
Volunteers: 1200

Kingwood Trust

2 Chalfont Court, Chalfont Close, Lower Earley, Reading RG6 5SY
T: 0118 931 0143
F: 0118 931 1937
E: info@kingwood.org.uk
www.kingwood.org.uk
Chief Executive: Sue Osborn
Employees: 130

Kith and Kids

c/o Haringey Irish Centre, Pretoria Road, London N17 8DX
T: 020 8801 7432
F: 020 8885 3035
E: projects@kithandkids.org.uk
www.kithandkids.org.uk
Aims to achieve empowerment and social inclusion with families living with disability.

Koestler Trust

168A Du Cane Road, London W12 0TX
T: 020 8740 0333
E: bcrosland@koestlertrust.org.uk
www.koestlertrust.org.uk
The charity promotes the creative enterprise of inmates and former inmates of prisons, young offender institutions and secure units.
Employees: 6

Krishnamurti Foundation Trust

Brockwood Park, Bramdean, Hampshire SO24 0CQ
T: 01962 771525
F: 01962 771159
E: kft@brockwood.org.uk
www.kfoundation.org
The Trust works to advance the education of the public in philosophy, sociology, psychology and comparative religion and, in particular, to promote the study of the teachings in those fields of Jiddu Krishnamurti.
Employees: 48
Volunteers: 20

Kurdish Cultural Centre

14-16 Stannary Street, London SE11 4AA
T: 020 7735 0918
E: admin@kcclondon.org.uk
www.kcclondon.org.uk/english
Aims to assist and advise the Kurdish community in matters relating to education, health, immigration, integration, legal issues, housing, social activities and welfare; supports cultural events, meetings and seminars; encourages a positive relationship and wider co-operation between the Kurdish community and other communities.

Kurdish Human Rights Project

11 Guilford Street, London WC1N 1DH
T: 020 7405 3835
F: 020 7404 9088
E: khrp@khrp.org
www.khrp.org
KHRP is an independent, non-political human rights organisation and registered charity dedicated to the promotion and protection of the human rights of all persons in the Kurdish regions of Turkey, Iraq, Iran, Syria and elsewhere.
Employees: 9
Volunteers: 10

L'Arche

10 Briggate, Silsden, Keighley, West Yorkshire BD20 9JT
T: 01535 656186
F: 01535 656426
E: info@larche.org.uk
www.larche.org.uk
National Leader: John Sargent
We are people with and without learning disabilities sharing life in communities, belonging to an international federation. Our mission is to: nurture communities of faith in which mutually transforming relationships can flourish; promote the gifts of people with learning disabilities enabling them to take a full part in L'Arche and society; be open and outward looking and actively engaged with those around us responding to changing needs and circumstances.
Employees: 370
Volunteers: 178
Regional offices: 11

La Leche League Great Britain

PO Box 29, West Bridgford, Nottingham, Nottinghamshire NG2 7NP
T: 0845 456 1855
Helpline: 0845 120 2918
E: hfbutler.lllgb@btinternet.com
www.laleche.org.uk
Chair of Council of Directors: Helen Russ
Provides information and support for breastfeeding mothers through a national telephone helpline, email help and a network of local groups, all run by trained volunteers. Publishes books and leaflets on breastfeeding. Promotes the benefits of breastfeeding and works with health professionals nationally and locally; trains mothers with the help of health professionals through the national peer counsellor programme.
Employees: 4
Volunteers: 250
Regional offices: 77

Landlife

National Wildflower Centre, Court Hey Park, Liverpool L16 3NA
T: 0151 737 1819
E: info@landlife.org.uk
www.wildflower.co.uk
Aims to protect and promote wildlife, working with people for nature working with nature for people and creating new habitats for people to enjoy.

Landmine Action

1st Floor, 89 Albert Embankment, London SE1 7TP
T: 020 7820 0222
F: 020 7820 0057
E: info@landmineaction.org
www.aoav.org.uk
Landmine Action is a not-for-profit organisation committed to good governance and the development of civil society through the promotion of international humanitarian law, the relief of poverty and the empowerment of communities marginalised by conflict.
Employees: 7
Volunteers: 2

Landscape Design Trust

Bank Chambers, 1 London Road, Redhill, Surrey RH1 1LY
T: 01737 779257
E: lorraine@landscape.co.uk
www.landscapedesigntrust.org
Our object is the advancement of awareness and understanding of the landscape for the benefit of the environment and the community.
Employees: 8

Landscape Institute

33 Great Portland Street, London W1W 8QG
T: 020 7299 4508
E: mail@landscapeinstitute.org
www.landscapeinstitute.org
Employees: 20

Langley House Trust

PO Box 181, Witney, Oxfordshire OX28 6WD
T: 01993 774075
F: 01993 772425
E: info@langleyhousetrust.org
www.langleyhousetrust.org
The Langley House Trust is a national Christian charity that provides resettlement support for ex-offenders (and those at risk of offending) working towards crime-free independence and reintegration into society. The Trust's residential projects along with move-on accommodation provide a range of supported accommodation. The Trust works with those who are hard to place and accepts both men and women of any or no faith.
Employees: 205
Volunteers: 20
Regional offices: 3

LASA

E: cashcroft@lasa.org.uk

Lattitude Global Volunteering

Lattitude, 44 Queens Road, Reading RG1 4BB
T: 0118 959 4914
F: 0118 957 6634
E: nadie@lattitude.org.uk
www.lattitude.org.uk
Chief Executive: Belinda Coote
Lattitude Global Volunteering has 35 years' experience of working with young people. Every year we place 2,000 UK and overseas volunteers in 23 different countries. Our aims: to provide placements that allow young people to develop their skills and broaden their education; to promote access to volunteering opportunities for all young people, regardless of background; to help overseas communities by providing volunteer support whilst empowering our young people to make a real difference.
Employees: 28
Volunteers: 150

Law Centres Network

Floor 1 Tavis House, 1-6 Tavistock Square, London WC1H 9NA
T: 020 3637 1331
F: 020 3637 1342
E: info@lawcentres.org.uk
www.lawcentres.org.uk
Director: Julie Bishop
Established in 1978, the Law Centres Network (a business name of the Law Centres Federation) is a charity and a company limited by guarantee. LCN supports and promotes Law Centres in England, Wales and Northern Ireland. Law Centres provide free legal advice on social welfare law to disadvantaged people in their communities, helping them alleviate their poverty and disadvantage.
Employees: 10
Regional offices: 50

LawWorks

London EC3R 8DN
T: 020 7929 5601
F: 020 7929 5722
E: rg@lawworks.org.uk
www.lawworks.org.uk
Chief Executive: Robert Gill
Brokers and develops pro bono legal services linking those who need free legal help with lawyers willing to provide it.
Employees: 14
Volunteers: 2000
Regional offices: 1

LDN Research Trust

PO Box 1083, Buxton, Norwich, Norfolk NR10 5WY
T: 01603 279014
E: contact@ldnresearchtrust.org
www.ldnresearchtrust.org
Trustee: Linda Elsegood
We aim to raise awareness of LDN for autoimmune conditions, cancers and addictions, while helping initiate clinical trials for conditions where LDN could be of benefit.
Volunteers: 30
Income: £65,852 (2013-14)

Leadership Trust Foundation

Weston under Penyard, Ross on Wye, Herefordshire HR9 7YH
T: 01989 767667
F: 01989 768133
E: enquiries@leadership.co.uk
www.leadership.org.uk
Aims to enhance and develop leadership in all aspects of society.
Employees: 80
Volunteers: 200

League Against Cruel Sports

New Sparling House, Holloway Hill, Godalming, Surrey GU7 1QZ
F: 020 7378 7745
E: info@league.uk.com
www.league.org.uk

Campaigns for the abolition of cruel sports where animals are hurt, at risk of trauma, injury or death for sport. Seeks change where abolition is not politically achievable and provides protection for animals endangered by cruel sports.
Employees: 25
Volunteers: 50
Regional offices: 30

League of British Muslims

Ilford Muslim Community Centre, Eton Road, Ilford, Essex IG1 2UE
T: 020 8514 0706
F: 020 8599 7052
E: leagueofbm@btconnect.com
www.leagueofbritishmuslims.co.uk
The principal objectives of the charity are to advance the religion of Islam and to advance Islamic education amongst Muslims resident in England and Wales.
Employees: 1
Volunteers: 12

League of Jewish Women

6 Bloomsbury Square, London WC1A 2LP
T: 020 7242 8300
E: office@theljw.org
www.theljw.org
President: Marilyn Brummer
The League of Jewish Women (LJW) is one of the leading voluntary Jewish women's service organisations in the UK. Affiliated to more than 30 other national and international organisations, membership is open to all Jewish men and women. LJW is the UK affiliate of the International Council of Jewish Women. LJW is a voluntary service organisation that provides help wherever it is needed, within both the Jewish and the wider community.
Employees: 2
Volunteers: 2500
Regional offices: 1

League of Mercy

PO Box 68, Lingfield, Surrey RH7 6QQ
T: 020 8660 4496 (also fax)
E: admin@leagueofmercy.co.uk
www.leagueofmercy.co.uk
Works for the advancement of the Christian Faith; the relief of persons who are in need, hardship or distress and the advancement of education on the basis of Christian principles.

League of Remembrance

55 Great Ormond Street, London WC1N 3HZ
T: 020 7829 7818 (also fax)
E: hayley.dodman@gosh.nhs.uk
www.leagueofremembrance.org.uk
Provides companionship, financial assistance and support to dependants and retired members of the armed forces and retired nurses.
Employees: 1
Volunteers: 38

Learning for Life

2 Rickett Street, London SW6 1RU
T: 020 7385 8765
F: 020 7385 9154
E: info@learningforlifeuk.org
www.learningforlifeuk.org
Director: Ujwala Samant
Learning for Life assists and relieves needy persons and their dependants who are employed or have been employed in the motor, agricultural engineering and cycle and allied trades and industries.
Employees: 3
Volunteers: 30

Learning from Experience Trust

Goldsmiths College, Deptford Town Hall, New Cross Road, London SE14 6AF
T: 020 7919 7739
F: 020 7919 7762
E: su@gold.ac.uk
www.learningexperience.org.uk
Aims to advance education by promoting research into, and developing the concept of, experiential learning and its assessment, and encouraging its recognition and use in education, training, industry, commerce and the public service.
Employees: 5

Learning Plus Uk

1st Floor, Kings Lodge, 194 Kings Road, Reading, Berkshire RG1 4NH
T: 0118 956 8408
E: donna.roberts@learningplusuk.org
www.learningplusuk.org
Office Manager: Donna Roberts
Employees: 6

Learning South West

Bishops Hull House, Bishops Hull, Taunton, Somerset TA1 5EP
T: 01823 335491
F: 01823 323388
E: phil_barker@learning-southwest.org.uk
www.learning-southwest.org.uk
Chief Executive and Company Secretary: Paula Jones
The charity's objectives are to advance education of young persons and adults by: promoting excellence in the delivery of learning and skills; providing advice, training and the provision of resources to providers of learning and skills; and researching and disseminating good practice.
Employees: 31

Learning Through Landscapes

The Studio, Castle Hill, c/o The Castle, Winchester, Hampshire SO23 8UL
T: 01962 846258
E: enquiries@ltl.org.uk
www.ltl.org.uk
Executive Director: Juno Hollyhock
Learning through Landscapes is the UK charity dedicated to enhancing outdoor learning and play for children. Our vision is that every child benefits from stimulating outdoor learning and play in their education. We aim to enable children to connect with nature, be more active, be more engaged with their learning, develop their social skills and have fun!
Employees: 20
Volunteers: 8
Regional offices: 4

Leeds Church Institute

E: haydn@leedschurchinstitute.org

Legal Action Group

3rd Floor, Universal House, 88-94 Wentworth Street, London E1 7SA
T: 020 7833 2931
F: 020 7837 6094
E: lag@lag.org.uk
www.lag.org.uk
Director: Steve Hynes
LAG is a national, independent charity that aims to promote equal access to justice for all members of society who are socially, economically or otherwise disadvantaged. To this end, it seeks to improve law and practice, the administration of justice and legal services through campaigning as well as publishing legal books, its magazine Legal Action and providing training for solicitors, barristers and legal advisers.
Employees: 9
Volunteers: 2

Legislation Monitoring Service for Charities, Voluntary Organisations and their Advisers

Church House, Great Smith Street, London SW1P 3AZ
T: 020 7222 1265
E: info@lmsconline.org
www.charitylaw.info

LMSC's principal objective is monitoring and disseminating information about legislative and policy developments in the UK and Europe likely to have an impact on charities.

Leicestershire Centre for Integrated Living

West End Centre, Andrewes Street, Leicester, Leicestershire LE3 5PA
T: 0116 222 5005
F: 0116 222 5008
E: admin@lcil.org.uk
www.lcil.org.uk
CEO: Stephen Cooper
LCiL is an organisation of disabled people, supporting disabled people. Based upon our own experiences, and skills we work closely with Leicester City, the voluntary sector and areas of the private sector. To deliver support advice and guidance to anyone directly or indirectly affected by matters arising because of a disability. working to the social model of disability we offer support what ever age or condition.
Employees: 12
Volunteers: 4
Income: £373,000,000 (2013-14)

Leo Baeck College

The Sternberg Centre for Judaism, 80 East End Road, London N3 2SY
T: 020 8349 5600
E: info@lbc.ac.uk
www.lbc.ac.uk
Principal: Rabbi Dr Deborah Kahn-Harris
Established in 1956, Leo Baeck College trains rabbis and educators for Progressive Jewish congregations, communities and schools in the UK, Europe and worldwide with over 250 graduates; promotes the study of Judaism in a spirit of reverence for Jewish tradition; instils the love of learning in the Jewish community by raising the level of knowledge. Resources include Judaica and research library
Employees: 13
Volunteers: 2

Leo Trust

Boldshaves Oast, Woodchurch, Ashford, Kent TN26 3RA
T: 01233 860039
F: 01233 860060
E: leotrust@btconnect.com
www.leotrust.com
Chief Executive: Joe Graham
The Leo Trust is a residential care home for adults with learning difficulties, which seeks to promote the relief, welfare and preservation of health of the residents and to provide opportunities to develop them into productive members of the community.
Employees: 32
Volunteers: 1

Leonard Cheshire Disability

66 South Lambeth Road SW8 1RL
T: 020 3242 0200
F: 020 7802 8250
E: info@leonardcheshire.org
www.leonardcheshire.org
Chief Executive: Clare Pelham
We are the UK's leading charity supporting disabled people. We work for a society in which every person is equally valued. We believe that disabled people should have the freedom to live their lives the way they choose - to live independently, contribute economically, and participate fully in society.
Employees: 7100
Volunteers: 4000
Regional offices: 10
Income: £162,200,000 (2014-15)

Lepra

28 Middleborough, Colchester CO1 1TG
T: 01206 216700
E: lepra@lepra.org.uk
www.lepra.org.uk
Chief Executive: Sarah Nancollas
We are a UK-registered international charity fighting disease, poverty and prejudice. We work on the ground in Bangladesh, India and Mozambique with people affected by neglected diseases such as leprosy and lymphatic filariasis and also malaria and TB.
Employees: 50
Volunteers: 3
Regional offices: 1
Income: £4,970,000 (2014-15)

Lesbian and Gay Christian Movement

Oxford House, Derbyshire Street, London E2 6HG
T: 020 7739 1249 (also fax)
E: lgcm@lgcm.org.uk
www.lgcm.org.uk
Chief Executive: Rev Sharon Ferguson
We aim to encourage fellowship, friendship and support among individual lesbian and gay Christians and to help the whole church re-examine its understanding of human sexuality and to challenge homophobia.
Employees: 2
Volunteers: 10

Let's Face It Support Network for the Facially Disfigured

72 Victoria Avenue, Westgate-on-Sea, Kent CT8 8BH
T: 01843 833724
E: chrisletsfaceit@aol.com
www.lets-face-it.org.uk
Founder/Chief Executive: Christine Piff
Aims to provide counselling, advice and support to patients with facial disfigurement, however caused, and their families, by meetings, letter writing, telephone contact and hospital visits. This includes head and neck cancer patients.
Employees: 1
Volunteers: 40
Regional offices: 8
Income: £30,000 (2012-13)

Leukaemia Care

1 Birch Court, Blackpole East, Worcestershire WR3 8SG
T: 01905 755977
F: 01905 755166
E: care@leukaemia.org.uk
www.leukaemiacare.org.uk
Provides support, information and assistance to people affected by leukaemia or allied blood disorders.
Employees: 8
Volunteers: 125

Lewy Body Society

Hudson House, 8 Albany Street, Edinburgh EH1 3QB
T: 0131 473 2385
E: info@lewybody.org
www.lewybody.org
CEO: Jacqueline Cannon
Founded in 2006 & run entirely by volunteers, the LBSis the only charity in Europe dedicated exclusively to Lewy body disease, . The Society's mission is to support research into and raise awareness of this terrible neurogenerative disease. The Society is committed to not having paid employees nor ever soliciting donations.
Volunteers: 10

Liberal Judaism

The Montagu Centre, 21 Maple Street
E: shelley@liberaljudaism.org
Operations Director: Shelley Shocolinsky-Dwyer

Liberty

21 Tabard Street, London SE1 4LA
T: 020 7403 3888
Helpline: 0845 123 2307
E: webmaster@liberty-human-rights.org.uk
www.liberty-human-rights.org.uk

Liberty is also known as the National Council for Civil Liberties. Founded in 1934, we are a cross-party, non-party membership organisation at the heart of the movement for fundamental rights and freedoms in England and Wales. We promote the values of individual human dignity, equal treatment and fairness as the foundations of a democratic society.

Library Campaign

13 Shrublands Close, Chelmsford CM2 6LR
T: 01273 887321
E: www.librarycampaign.com
Supports friends and user groups of publicly funded libraries to advocate and lobby for library provision support.

LIFE

LIFE House, 1 Mill Street, Leamington Spa, Warwickshire CV31 1ES
T: 01926 312272
F: 01926 336497
E: vickyobrien@lifecharity.org.uk
www.lifecharity.org.uk
Chief Executive: Stephen Sharpe
LIFE is a charity that offers an innovative approach to supporting women and families throughout pregnancy and beyond, including the provision of supported housing for pregnant women and mothers of young children.
Employees: 190
Volunteers: 380
Regional offices: 60

Life Academy

9 Chesham Road, Guildford, Surrey GU1 3LS
T: 01483 301170
F: 01483 300981
E: info@life-academy.co.uk
www.life-academy.co.uk
Chief Executive: Stuart Royston
Life Academy is a charity that enables people to learn about managing the changes in their lives through life and retirement planning and financial education. We achieve this through: life and retirement planning courses; financial literacy education; qualifications in life and retirement planning; developing partnerships to reach individuals and creating innovative approaches for learning.
Employees: 5

Life Education Centres

County House, 14 Hatton Garden, London EC1N 8AT
T: 020 7831 9311
F: 020 7831 9939
E: jeani@lifeeducation.org.uk
www.lifeeducation.org.uk
National Director: Stephen Burgess
Helping children make healthy choices. Life Educations main work is with primary schools and with parents, delivered through local Trusts, to ensure that children develop the vital knowledge, skills and attitudes need to make informed choices about health that will enhance and enrich their lives.
Employees: 7
Volunteers: 400
Regional offices: 40

Life For The World

Micklefield Christian Centre, Buckingham Drive, High Wycombe, Buckinghamshire HP13 7YB
T: 01494 462008
Helpline: 0845 241 0973
E: wycombe@lftw.org
www.living-recovery.org
Chief Executive: John Lowton
Provides training, education, advice and consultancy for service providers (drug and alcohol misuse).
Employees: 5
Volunteers: 10
Regional offices: 2
Income: £47,760 (2012-13)

Life Opportunities Trust

Hempstead House, 1 Hempstead Road, Kings Langley, Hertfordshire WD4 8BJ
T: 01923 299770
F: 01923 299771
E: atierney@lot-uk.org.uk
www.lot-uk.org.uk
Chief Executive: Ralph Verlander
Provides domiciliary and residential services for adults with learning disabilities.
Employees: 165
Volunteers: 14

Lifeline Community Projects

LifeLine House, Neville Road, Dagenham, Essex RM8 3QS
T: 020 8597 2900
F: 020 8597 1990
E: andriasoteriou@lifelineprojects.co.uk
www.lifelineprojects.co.uk
PA to Chief Executive: Andria Soteriou
LifeLine is a social enterprise which impacts individuals and influences systems. Characterised by renewed hope, developed confidence and improved skills, our programmes release people to be agents of change in their communities.
Employees: 81
Volunteers: 5
Regional offices: 2

Lifeline International

25 Jellicoe Road N17 7BL
T: 020 8365 9815
F: 020 8805 9411
E: dupsy25@hotmail.com
www.lli.org.uk
Chair: Grace Labaran
Works to relieve the poverty and hardship of teenage mothers and their babies in Africa, whether through deprivation of family, skills, education, or otherwise, so that they may participate in a learning environment and/or life skills programme, enabling them to integrate into their communities and gain employment.
Employees: 10
Volunteers: 3
Regional offices: 5

Lifeline Project Ltd

Manchester M4 1NA
E: fazackerley2@btinternet.com
www.lifeline.org.uk
The charity aims to relieve poverty, sickness and distress among those persons affected by addiction to drugs of any kind, and to educate the public on matters relating to drug misuse.
Employees: 460

Lifeworks

Blacklers, Park Road, Dartington Hall Estate, Totnes, Devon TQ9 6EQ
T: 01803 840744
E: laurabambrey@lifeworks-uk.org
www.lifeworks-uk.org
CEO: Richard Hanlon
A charity that supports learning disabled children and young adults. Our services include respite care (short-breaks), residential care, a specialist FE college, youth clubs, life skills training and sports & leisure events.

Lifeworks Charity Ltd

E: joparsons@lifeworks-uk.org

Lightforce International

Christian Centre, Strudwick Drive, Oldbrook, Milton Keynes, Buckinghamshire MK6 2TG
T: 01908 553070
F: 01908 553077
E: grr@lightforce.org.uk
www.lightforce.org.uk
International Director: George Ridley
Aims to advance the Christian religion and to relieve people in any part of the world who are in condition of need, hardship and distress, in particular by deploying human and material resources.
Employees: 235
Volunteers: 15
Regional offices: 4

Lin Berwick Trust

Eastgate House, Upper East Street, Sudbury, Suffolk CO10 1UB
T: 01787 372343
E: info@thelinberwicktrust.org.uk
www.thelinberwicktrust.org.uk
Provides relief for physically disabled people, their families and carers, through the provision of holiday accommodation.
Employees: 3
Volunteers: 15

Linacre Centre for Healthcare Ethics

38 Circus Road, London NW8 9SE
T: 020 7806 4088
E: admin@linacre.org
www.linacre.org
Promotes understanding of the Catholic viewpoint on bioethical issues. The Centre's perspective is informed by Catholic moral teaching, but in defending such teaching it seeks also to appeal to non-religious, philosophical reasoning to enable dialogue with those of no religious faith.

Linkage Community Trust

Scremby Grange, Spilsby PE23 5RW
T: 01754 890339
F: 01754 890538
E: info@linkage.org.uk
www.linkage.org.uk
Works to advance the general education and social development of people with disabilities, to develop such skills as are necessary to enable such people to qualify for useful occupation and, where this is not possible, to provide long-term care facilities.

LionHeart

Surveyor Court, Westwood Way, Coventry, West Midlands CV4 8BF
T: 0845 603 9057
F: 024 7647 4701
E: mcarter@lionheart.org.uk
www.lionheart.org.uk
Chief Executive: Mike Carter
LionHeart provides advice, information, counselling, befriending, financial help by grant or loan, and help in kind to members of the Royal Institution of Chartered Surveyors (RICS) and their dependants who experience difficulties in their lives, including bereavement, unemployment, ill-health, accident or disability, separation of families or difficulties in retirement.
Employees: 11
Volunteers: 225

Lions Clubs International and British Isles and Ireland

257 Alcester Road South, Kings Heath, Birmingham B14 6DT
T: 0121 441 4544
F: 0121 441 4510
E: secretary@lions.org.uk
www.lionsmd105.org
Council Chairman: Martin Morgan
Lions Clubs International is the world's largest service club organisation. With 1.4 million members in 206 countries who work together through selfless, effective community service to answer the needs that challenge communities around the world.
Employees: 4
Volunteers: 17000
Regional offices: 13

Listening Books

12 Lant Street, London SE1 1QH
T: 020 7407 9417
E: info@listening-books.org.uk
www.listening-books.org.uk
Director: Bill Dee
Listening Books supplies an online and postal audiobook library service to anyone across the UK who struggles to read due to an illness, disability or learning difficulty. Members can choose from thousands of titles across a range of formats (MP3 CDs, internet streaming or downloads).
Employees: 9
Volunteers: 10+
Regional offices: 1

Little Hearts Matter

11 Greenfield Crescent, Edgbaston, Birmingham B15 3AU
T: 0121 455 8982
F: 0121 455 8983
E: info@lhm.org.uk
www.lhm.org.uk
The charity promotes the relief and welfare of persons affected by single ventricle cardiac disease and advances the education of the medical profession and the general public on the subject of single ventricle cardiac disease and its implications for the family.
Employees: 3
Volunteers: 12

Little Sisters of the Poor

St Peter's Residence, 2A Meadow Road, South Lambeth, London SW8 1QH
T: 020 7735 0788
E: lsplondonstpeter@aol.com
www.littlesistersofthepoor.co.uk
Cares for elderly people of modest means of all denominations or those of none.

Livability

50 Scrutton Street, London EC2A 4XQ
T: 020 7452 2000
F: 020 7452 2001
E: info@livability.org.uk
www.livability.org.uk
Chief Executive: Dave Webber
Livability offers a wide range of innovative services that support and enable disabled people throughout their lives and provides community organisations with the resources, advice and confidence to bring life to local neighbourhoods. Livability was formed in 2007 by the merger of John Grooms and the Shaftesbury Society.
Employees: 2000

Live Music Now!

Mill House, Newsham Bridge, Malton, North Yorkshire YO17 6TZ
T: 01653 668551
E: keisha@macfarlane.org.uk
www.livemusicnow.org.uk
Provides performance opportunities for talented young professional musicians under the age of 27 years and brings the experience of live music back into everyday life.

Living Paintings

Unit 8, Kingsclere Park, Kingsclere, Newbury, Berkshire RG20 4SW
T: 01635 299771 (also fax)
E: camilla@livingpaintings.org
www.livingpaintings.org
Charity Director: Camilla Oldland
Living Paintings helps blind and partially sighted people feel visual images. We make special versions of pictures with raised

surfaces that come to life when fingers feel them. Sound recordings direct the fingers, telling the stories of the pictures and describing their features. For children and adults the senses of touch and hearing combine to make up for the missing sense of sight.
Employees: 7
Volunteers: 120

Living Streets

London SW8 1SJ
T: 020 7820 1010
F: 020 7820 8208
E: info@livingstreets.org.uk
www.livingstreets.org.uk
Aims to improve conditions for walking journeys and for safe, convenient and environment friendly ways for people on foot. Represents the interests of walkers (particularly in urban areas) to central and local government and the media.
Employees: 12
Volunteers: 150
Regional offices: 76

Local Investment Fund

Seventh Floor, Ibex House,
London EC3N 1DY
T: 020 7680 1028
E: information@lif.org.uk
www.lif.org.uk
LIF is dedicated to providing loan finance to economically viable, community-based voluntary organisations that are run as not-for-profit enterprises. It bridges the gap between grant dependency and mainstream banking finance.

Local Trust

Unit 5, Angel Gate, 320-326 City Road,
London EC1V 2PT
T: 020 3588 0571
E: info@localtrust.org.uk
www.localtrust.org.uk
Funding Administrator: Michael Williams
Employees: 11

Localgiving

6th Floor, 233 High Holborn,
London WC1V 7DN
T: 0300 111 2340
E: help@localgiving.com
www.localgiving.com
Founder & CEO: Marcelle Speller
Localgiving is dedicated to providing funding opportunities and advocacy for local charities and community groups in the UK. Our mission is to safeguard the sustainability of the local voluntary sector by empowering charitable organisations to connect with supporters, fundraise online and take control of their future.
Employees: 14
Regional offices: 1

Locality

33 Corsham Street, London N1 6DL
T: 0845 458 8336
E: info@locality.org.uk
www.locality.org.uk
Locality is the leading nationwide network of settlements, development trusts, social action centres and community enterprises.

London Funders

314-320 Grays Inn Road,
London WC1X 8DP
T: 020 7255 4488
E: info@londonfunders.org.uk
www.londonfunders.org.uk
Director: David Warner
London Funders fulfils its mission by providing a unique space where funders can discuss issues affecting London and the work that they do, learn from each other, share experience and knowledge, be briefed on changes in public policy and the implications for London, and – increasingly – look at how they can work better together to improve the lives of Londoners.
Employees: 2

London Gypsy and Traveller Unit

6 Westgate Street, London E8 3RN
T: 020 8533 2002
F: 020 8533 7110
E: srowles@lgtu.org.uk
www.lgtu.org.uk
Joint Chief Executive: Debby Kennett and Lorraine Sweeney
We support Travellers and Gypsies living in London to: Influence decisions affecting their lives; Improve their quality of life and the opportunities available to them; Challenge the discrimination they routinely experience. By providing the following services: Community development; Youth work programme for young Irish Travellers in North and East London; Advocacy and advice service on accommodation, benefits and access to services; Learning support in literacy, IT and life skills; Strategic and policy work.
Employees: 12
Volunteers: 7
Income: £317,751 (2013-14)

Long-Term Conditions Alliance

202 Hatton Square, 16 Baldwins Gardens,
London EC1N 7RJ
T: 020 7813 3637
F: 020 7813 3640
E: thelongtrail@ltca.org.uk
www.ltca.org.uk
Chief Executive: David Pink
Umbrella body of over 100 patient groups and professional organisations working to improve the lives of people with long-term conditions.
Employees: 5

Look National Office

Queen Alexandra College,
49 Court Oak Road, Harborne,
Birmingham B17 9TG
T: 0121 428 5038
E: information@look-uk.org
www.look-uk.org
CEO: Aliona Laker
Provides practical help, support and information to families with visually impaired children. Promotes improved services nationally.
Employees: 4
Volunteers: 2

Lubavitch Youth

London N16 5RP
T: 020 8800 0022
F: 020 8809 7324
E: info@lubavitchuk.com
www.lubavitchuk.com
Works to further the needs of the Jewish ethnic minority, in the widest possible context.
Volunteers: 200
Regional offices: 18

LUpus Patients Understanding and Support (LUPUS)

8 Shakespeare Drive, Borehamwood,
Hertfordshire WD6 2FD
E: roz@lupus-support.org.uk
www.lupus-support.org.uk
Director: Rosalind Share
A non-profit organisation providing free information and free online psychological support for individuals affected by SLE, lupus variant conditions and the antiphospholipid antibody (Hughes) syndrome. The Lupus Counselling Service is maintained by qualified psychotherapists/counsellors. We offer online psychological support services and research into the unmet needs of individuals affected by lupus. We also offer information and support to carers, families as well as

doctors, nurses and other health professionals.
Volunteers: 3

LUPUS UK

St James House, Eastern Road, Romford, Essex RM1 3NH
T: 01708 731251
E: headoffice@lupusuk.org.uk
www.lupusuk.org.uk
Director: Chris Maker
Provides communication between patients; educates patients, the general public and the medical profession about the symptoms and problems of systemic lupus erythematosus; raises funds and provides practical help and lupus research.
Employees: 7
Volunteers: 250

Lutheran Council of Great Britain

30 Thanet Street, London WC1H 9QH
T: 020 7388 4044
E: enquiries@lutheran.org.uk
www.lutheran.org.uk
General Secretary: James Laing
Established in 1948, the Lutheran Council is a communion of churches that have come together to express their shared Lutheran heritage and identity through common work in Britain, enriched by their cultural and linguistic diversity.
Employees: 20
Income: £868,000 (2014-15)

Lyme Disease Action

Sand, Sidbury, Sidmouth, Devon EX10 0QN
E: lda@lymediseaseaction.org.uk
www.lymediseaseaction.org.uk
Chairman: Stella Huyshe-Shires
Lyme Disease Action was established for the relief of persons suffering from Lyme disease, other borrelioses and associated diseases by raising awareness of the public at large and scientific and medical education and research in topics related to Lyme disease, other borrelioses and associated diseases.
Volunteers: 8
Income: £17,300 (2012-13)

Lyme Trust

39 London Road, Newcastle, Staffordshire ST5 1LN
T: 01782 634725
F: 01782 634510
E: thelymetrust@tiscali.co.uk
www.thelymetrust.co.uk

The charity provides accommodation for people with mild to moderate mental health difficulties and assists them into a successful return to life in the community.
Employees: 18
Volunteers: 1

Lymphoedema Support Network

St Luke's Crypt, Sydney Street, London SW3 6NH
T: 020 7351 0990
Helpline: 020 7351 4480
F: 020 7349 9809
E: adminlsn@lymphoedema.freeserve.co.uk
www.lymphoedema.org/lsn
Chair: Anita Wallace
Provides information and support to people with lymphoedema and promotes better awareness of lymphoedema as a major health condition to local health authorities, healthcare professionals and politicians.
Employees: 2
Volunteers: 15

Lymphoma Association

PO Box 386, Aylesbury, Buckinghamshire HP20 2GA
T: 01296 619400
Helpline: 0808 808 5555
F: 01296 619415
E: j.coldwell@lymphomas.org.uk
www.lymphomas.org.uk
Chief Executive: Sally Penrose
The Lymphoma Association is the only specialist UK charity that provides accurate medical information and support to lymphatic cancer patients, their families, friends and carers. Support services include a freephone helpline, a buddy scheme that puts people in touch with others who have been through a similar experience of lymphoma, a network of support groups throughout the UK, free literature and an interactive website with a chatroom and forum.
Employees: 23

Macfarlane Trust

Alliance House, 12 Caxton Street, London SW1H 0QS
T: 020 7233 0057
F: 020 7233 0839
E: macfarlane@macfarlane.org.uk
www.macfarlane.org.uk
Works to meet the needs of those people with haemophilia who became infected with HIV through treatment with contaminated blood products in the UK, and their dependants; and dependants of those who have died.
Employees: 5
Volunteers: 10

MacIntyre Care

602 South Seventh Street, Milton Keynes MK9 2JA
T: 01908 230100
F: 01908 694452
E: bill.mumford@macintyrecharity.org
www.macintyrecharity.org
MacIntyre is a national charity that provides learning, support and care for more than 700 children and adults with learning disabilities, at more than 120 MacIntyre services across the UK.
Employees: 1320
Volunteers: 50

Macmillan Cancer Support

89 Albert Embankment, London SE1 7UQ
T: 020 7840 4648
F: 020 7840 7841
E: info@macmillan.org.uk
www.macmillan.org.uk
Volunteers: 70000

Macular Disease Society

PO Box 1870, Andover, Hampshire SP10 9AD
T: 01264 350551
Helpline: 0845 241 2041
F: 01264 350558
E: info@maculardisease.org
www.maculardisease.org
Chief Executive: Helen Jackman
Macular disease is the UK's most common cause of sight loss. The Macular Disease Society is the only UK charity supporting

people with macular disease and seeking a cure. We provide information and support to anyone affected by macular disease and professionals working with people with the condition. We have over 15,000 members and support many more through our national network of local support groups and our telephone helpline, counselling, advocacy and low vision services.
Employees: 23
Volunteers: 1000

Magdi Yacoub Institute

Heart Science Centre, Harefield, Middlesex UB9 6JH
T: 01895 828952
F: 01895 828954
E: preay@myi.ac
The Institute aims to improve the understanding of important clinical cardiac problems by combining a broad basis of research at both clinical and fundamental levels.
Employees: 3

Magistrates' Association

28 Fitzroy Square, London W1T 6DD
T: 020 7383 2672
F: 020 7383 4020
E: sandra.whitear@magistrates-association.org.uk
www.magistrates-association.org.uk
CEO: Chris Brace
We are a membership organisation that provides our members with information and training by publishing our magazine, email news bulletin and training materials. We promote public awareness of the magistracy and support our 60 local branches to work locally and regionally to promote the voice of the magistracy. We represent the magistracy at the highest levels of government and provide robust evidence for our policy positions using our own in-house research.
Employees: 13
Volunteers: 20000

Maharishi Foundation

The Golden Dome, Woodley Park Road, Skelmersdale, Lancashire WN8 6UQ
T: 01695 557403
E: info@t-m.org.uk
www.maharishifoundation.org.uk
Promotes the full development of the individual, using scientifically verified programmes that have been shown to unfold the full potential of the mind, create better health, improve social behaviour and relationships and establish a more peaceful world.

Maidstone Community Support Centre

E: matt@mcsc.org.uk

Make-A-Wish Foundation UK

Camberley, Surrey GU15 3HQ
T: 01276 24127
F: 01276 683727
E: info@make-a-wish.org.uk
www.make-a-wish.org.uk
Works to grant the wishes of children living with life-threatening illnesses.
Employees: 48
Volunteers: 750
Regional offices: 16

Making Space

46 Allen Street, Warrington, Cheshire WA2 7JB
T: 01925 571680
E: business.support@makingspace.co.uk
www.makingspace.co.uk
Senior Administrator: Sarah Thomas
Employees: 512
Volunteers: 116

Mammal Society

2b Inworth Street, London SW11 3EP
T: 020 7350 2200
F: 020 7350 2211
E: enquiries@mammal.org.uk
www.mammal.org.uk
The Society works to protect British mammals, halt the decline of threatened species, and advise on all issues affecting British mammals. We study mammals, identify the problems they face and promote conservation and other policies based on sound science.
Employees: 4
Volunteers: 20
Regional offices: 1

Management Strategies for Africa

Orion House, 104/106 Cranbrook Road, Ilford, Essex IG1 4LZ
T: 020 8636 9975
F: 020 8636 9994
E: info@msforafrica.org
www.msforafrica.org
Chairman/Chief Executive Officer: Marc A. Okunnu, Sr.
Management Strategies for Africa (MSA) is a charitable private company limited by guarantee, with country offices in Ghana and Nigeria. MSA advocates and supports organizational capacity development to strengthen the institutional effectiveness of public and civil society organizations engaged in social and health development. MSA is concerned with organisational effectiveness and performance improvement in relation to social development especially meeting sexual and reproductive health (SRH) goals, within the context of health systems strengthening.
Employees: 1
Volunteers: 3
Income: £19,807 (2013-14)

Mankind

PO Box 124, Newhaven, East Sussex BN9 9TQ
T: 01273 510447
E: admin@mankindcounselling.org.uk
www.mankindcounselling.org.uk
CEO: Martyn Sullivan
Mankind offers counselling services to men over the age of 18 who are suffering the continuing effects of childhood sexual abuse and/or adult sexual assault at any time in their lives. Counselling services are also offered to partners, family and those affected by sexual violence towards males.
Employees: 5
Volunteers: 15
Regional offices: 1

Marfan Association UK

Rochester House, 5 Aldershot Road, Fleet, Hampshire GU51 3NG
T: 01252 810472
F: 01252 810473
E: contactus@marfan-association.org.uk
www.marfan-association.org.uk
Chairman/Support Coordinator: Diane Rust
Provides updated Marfan information to patients, their families and the medical profession; provides means for patients and relatives to share their experience, to support one another, and to improve medical care; supports and fosters research.
Employees: 2
Volunteers: 3
Regional offices: 1

Marie Stopes International

London W1T 6QW
T: 020 7574 7400
E: services@mariestopes.org.uk
www.mariestopes.org.uk
Provides reproductive healthcare/family planning services and information, to enable individuals all over the world to have children by choice, not chance. MSI's goal is the prevention of unwanted births.

Marine Conservation Society

Unit 3, Wolf Business Park, Alton Road, Ross-on-Wye, Herefordshire HR9 5NB
T: 01989 566017
E: info@mcsuk.org
www.mcsuk.org
Chief Executive: Sam Fanshawe
UK charity is dedicated to the protection of the marine environment and its wildlife.
Employees: 50
Regional offices: 1

Marine Stewardship Council

3rd Floor, Mountbarrow House, London SW1W 9RB
T: 020 7811 3300
F: 020 7811 3301
E: info@msc.org
www.msc.org
Conserves marine fish populations and the ocean environment on which they depend, and promotes to the public the benefit of effective management of marine fisheries.
Employees: 12
Volunteers: 1

Mark Hall and Netteswell Community Association

Moot House, The Stow, Harlow, Essex CM20 3AG
T: 01279 424074
F: 01279 453200
E: moothouseca@moothouse.plus.com
www.moothouse.org.uk
President: Derek Fenny
Employees: 6
Regional offices: 1

Maroa Christian Counselling International

37 Clothworkers Road, Plumstead, London SE18 2PD
T: 020 8316 7074 (also fax)
Helpline: 07719 229897
E: maroacounselint@aol.com
www.maroa.org.uk
Director: Rebecca Adeosun
Our aim is to enable those we serve to live their lives to the fullest through counselling.
Volunteers: 2
Regional offices: 1

Marriage Care

Bishops Park House, 25-29 Fulham High Street, London SW6 3JH
T: 0800 389 3801
Helpline: 0845 660 6000
E: info@marriagecare.org.uk
www.marriagecare.org.uk
Chief Executive: Mark Molden
Marriage Care is an organisation committed to the lifelong support of marriage, relationships and family life through the provision of reliable, relevant and accessible services. We do this by offering two services: Marriage preparation via a group course for 10-12 couples presented by our trained practitioners or one-to-one facilitation following completion of an online inventory of the relationship (© FOCCUS) with one of our trained facilitator. Relationship counselling with one of our professionally trained counsellors.
Employees: 21
Volunteers: 750
Regional offices: 52

Mary Frances Trust

E: patrickwolter@maryfrancestrust.org.uk

Mary Ward Centre

42 Queen Square, London WC1N 3AQ
T: 020 7269 6061
E: mwenquiries@marywardcentre.ac.uk
www.marywardcentre.ac.uk
Aims to work for the advancement of public education and the promotion of social service for the benefit of the community.

Maternity Action

52-54 Featherstone Street, London EC1Y 8RT
T: 020 7253 2288
Helpline: 0845 600 8533
E: info@maternityaction.org.uk
www.maternityaction.org.uk
Director: Ros Bragg
To improve the health and well being of pregnant women, new parents and their babies. Maternity Action offers free advice on maternity and parental rights and benefits.
Employees: 5
Volunteers: 5

Mathematics in Education and Industry

Monckton House, Epsom Centre, White Horse Business Park, Trowbridge, Wiltshire SN12 6EL
T: 01225 776776
F: 01225 775755
E: office@mei.org.uk
www.mei.org.uk
Chief Executive: Charlie Stripp
MEI is an independent charity committed to improving mathematics education, and also an independent UK curriculum development body. Income generated through our work is used to support the teaching and learning of mathematics. MEI provides professional development for teachers and specialist tuition for students. We work with industry to enhance mathematical skills in the workplace. We also develop innovative teaching and learning resources, including extensive online materials. MEI manages the government-funded Further Mathematics Support Programme.
Employees: 50

Matthew Trust

PO Box 604, London SW6 3AG
T: 020 7736 5976
E: amt@matthewtrust.org
www.matthewtrust.org
The Matthew Trust is a small registered charity providing last-stop support and care for people aged eight years old and upwards, living in all communities of our society throughout the UK, who have a mental health problem of any kind.

ME Association

7 Apollo Office Court, Radclive Road, Gawcott, Buckinghamshire MK18 4DF
T: 01280 818968
Helpline: 0844 576 5326
E: meconnect@meassociation.org.uk
www.meassociation.org.uk
Chairman: Neil Riley
We are a campaigning national charity that provides information and support to an estimated 250,000 people in the UK who have ME/chronic fatigue syndrome, their families and carers. This is provided through a quarterly magazine, literature, education and training. We also run ME Connect, the UK's premier helpline for people with ME/CFS, and fund biomedical research.
Employees: 5
Volunteers: 30
Income: £778,647 (2012-13)

Medact

The Grayston Centre, 28 Charles Square, London N1 6HT
T: 020 7324 4739
E: office@medact.org
www.medact.org
Director: David McCoy
Medact educates, analyses and campaigns for global health on issues related to conflict, poverty and the environment.
Employees: 2
Volunteers: 10
Income: £130,000 (2013-14)

MEDFASH (Medical Foundation for HIV & Sexual Health)

BMA House, Tavistock Square, London WC1H 9JP
T: 020 7383 6345
E: enquiries@medfash.bma.org.uk
www.medfash.org.uk
Chief Executive: Ruth Lowbury
Promotes excellence in the prevention and management of HIV and other sexually transmitted infections.
Employees: 2

Media Trust

4th Floor, Block A, Centre House, Wood Lane, London W12 7SB
T: 020 7871 5600
F: 020 7871 5601
E: jades@mediatrust.org
www.mediatrust.org
CEO: Caroline Diehl
Media Trust works in partnership with the media industry to build effective voluntary and community sector communications. Its vision is of a society in which the voluntary and community sector is widely visible and celebrated for what it achieves; the public can easily access the voluntary and community sector; and voluntary organisations can access the resources, skills and contacts they need to communicate effectively with target audiences via a wide range of media and communication.
Employees: 70
Volunteers: 20
Regional offices: 1

Mediation Works Milton Keynes

Acorn House, 379 Midsummer Boulevard, Central Milton Keynes, Buckinghamshire MK9 3HP
T: 01908 200828
F: 01908 200842
E: mkcms@mkcommediation.org.uk
www.mediationworksmk.org.uk
The Chairman: Milton Keynes Community Mediation Service Ltd.
We operate in and around Milton Keynes, our main aim is to resolve conflict amicably and to open communication between all disputants. Our second aim is to recruit and train volunteers to CROCNAC and Community Legal Service QM standards in Community Mediation and provide support and ongoing training to our mediators.
Employees: 6
Volunteers: 35
Regional offices: 1
Income: £80,000 (2012-13)

MediaWise Trust

University of the West of England, Canon Kitson, Oldbury Court Road, Bristol, Avon BS16 2JP
T: 0117 939 9333
F: 0117 902 9916
E: info@mediawise.org.uk
www.mediawise.org.uk
Director: Mike Jempson
Provides information, advice, research and training on media ethics issues.
Employees: 2

Medical Council on Alcohol

5 St Andrews Place, London NW1 4LB
T: 020 7487 4445
F: 020 7935 4479
E: info@medicouncilalcol.demon.co.uk
www.m-c-a.org.uk
Aims to improve medical understanding of alcohol-related problems.
Employees: 5
Volunteers: 55
Regional offices: 33

Medical Engineering Resource Unit

Unit 2 Eclipse Estate, 30 West Hill, Epsom, Surrey KT19 8JD
T: 01372 725203
F: 01372 743159
E: info@meru.org.uk
www.meru.org.uk
Chief Executive: Jonathan Powell
Provides individual aids and services for disabled children and young adults that are not available commercially. Carries out research and development of devices and equipment that may have a more widespread use for the same disabled group.
Employees: 11
Volunteers: 20

Medical Foundation for the Care of Victims of Torture

111 Isledon Road, Finsbury Park, London N7 7JW
T: 020 7697 7777
F: 020 7697 7799
E: scarruth@torturecare.org.uk
www.freedomfromtorture.org
Chief Executive: Simon Carruth
Provides adult and child survivors of torture and organised violence living in the UK with medical, psychotherapeutic and social care and practical assistance; documents evidence of torture; provides training for health and social care professionals and others who work with torture survivors; educates the public and decision-makers about torture and its consequences; campaigns to improve the law and practice in the UK regarding the treatment of survivors in the asylum system.
Employees: 171
Volunteers: 250
Regional offices: 4

Medical Women's Federation

Entrance B, Tavistock House North, Tavistock Square, London WC1H 9HX
T: 020 7387 7765
E: admin.mwf@btconnect.com
www.medicalwomensfederation.co.uk
The MWF promotes the personal and professional development of women in medicine and women's health issues.

Medway Youth Trust

Connexions, 205-217 New Road, Chatham, Kent ME4 4QA
T: 01634 334343
F: 01634 335555
E: graham.clewes@themtrust.org
www.medwayyouthtrust.org
Chief Executive: Graham Clewes
We deliver the Connexions service in Medway to provide information and guidance to young people. Whilst our focus is careers we look to provide a much wider service to include delivery of the Prince's Trust programme, National Citizenship Service amongst others.
Employees: 49
Volunteers: 9
Regional offices: 1

Men's Health Forum

32-36 Loman Street, London SE1 0EH
T: 020 7922 7908
E: office@menshealthforum.org.uk
www.menshealthforum.org.uk
Chief Executive: Martin Tod
The Men's Health Forum works to improve the health of men and men's health services.
Employees: 8

Mencap

123 Golden Lane, London EC1Y 0RT
T: 020 7454 0454
Helpline: 0808 808 1111
F: 020 7696 5548
E: help@mencap.org.uk
www.mencap.org.uk
Mencap is the leading charity working with people with a learning disability in England, Wales and Northern Ireland. We campaign to ensure that people with a learning disability have the best possible opportunities to live as full citizens and aim to influence new legislation. We can support people with a learning disability to get a job, take a college course or find a place of their own to live in.
Employees: 5500
Volunteers: 20000
Regional offices: 15

Meniere's Society

The Rookery, Surrey Hills Business Park, Wotton, Dorking, Surrey RH5 6QT
T: 01306 876883
Helpline: 0845 120 2975
E: info@menieres.org.uk
www.menieres.org.uk
Director: Natasha Harrington-Benton
The Meniere's Society is the only registered charity in the UK dedicated solely to supporting people with vestibular (inner ear) disorders causing dizziness and imbalance. The Meniere's Society is a national organisation offering information and support to those affected by vestibular conditions and those who care for them; as well as health professionals and the general public. Research also funded.
Employees: 2
Volunteers: 15

Meningitis Now

Fern House, Bath Road, Stroud, Gloucestershire GL5 3TJ
T: 01453 768000
Helpline: 0808 801 0388
F: 01453 768001
E: lindseyb@meningitisnow.org
www.meningitisnow.org
Chief Executive: Sue Davie
Meningitis Now is a charity with almost 30 years' experience. Formed in 2013 by bringing together Meningitis UK and Meningitis Trust, founders of the meningitis movement in the UK. We exist to save lives and rebuild futures by funding research, raising awareness and providing support. Our vision is a future where no one in the UK loses their life to meningitis and everyone affected gets the support they need to rebuild their lives.
Employees: 66
Volunteers: 750

Meningitis Research Foundation

Midland Way, Thornbury, Bristol BS35 2BS
T: 01454 281811
Helpline: 0808 800 3344
E: info@meningitis.org
www.meningitis.org
Chief Executive: Christopher Head
Meningitis Research Foundation is a national registered charity whose vision is a world free from meningitis and septicaemia. The charity funds research to prevent meningitis and septicaemia, and to improve survival rates and outcomes. The Foundation promotes education and awareness to reduce death and disability, and gives support to people affected.
Employees: 50
Volunteers: 30
Regional offices: 4

Meningitis UK

25 Cleeve Wood Road, Downend, Bristol BS16 2SF
T: 0117 373 7373
F: 0117 373 7374
E: information@meningitisuk.org
www.meningitisuk.org
Chief Executive: Steve Dayman
Meningitis UK's sole focus is to eradicate meningitis. Meningitis is a terrifying disease, which can kill in less than four hours and tragically is most prevalent in children. We feel that focusing on prevention, as opposed to treatment, is the only way to successfully eradicate the disease and prevent its devastating consequences. We are confident that with enough support we will be able to put a stop to the heartache and devastation it causes.
Employees: 12
Volunteers: 5

Mental Health Foundation

1st Floor, Colechurch House, 1 London Bridge Walk, London SE1 2SX
T: 020 7803 1100
F: 020 7803 1111
E: info@mhf.org.uk
www.mentalhealth.org.uk
CEO: Jenny Edwards CBE
The Foundation provides information, carries out research, campaigns and works to improve services for anyone affected by mental health problems. We aim to help people survive, recover from and prevent mental health problems by learning what makes and keeps people mentally well; communicating our findings widely; turning our research into practical solutions that make a difference to peoples lives.
Employees: 50
Volunteers: 10
Regional offices: 4

Mental Health Matters

Avalon House, St Catherine's Court, Sunderland Enterprise Park, Sunderland, Tyne and Wear SR5 3XJ
T: 0191 510 3399
F: 0191 487 7945
E: ghiscox@mentalhealthmatters.co.uk
www.mentalhealthmatters.com
The principal aim of the charity is to act as a national organisation for all matters concerning mental health and mental illness, and to assist sufferers and carers of sufferers of mental health problems.
Employees: 200

Mental Health Providers Forum

c/o Mental Health Foundation, 9th Floor, Sea Containers House, 20 Upper Ground, London SE1 9QB
T: 020 7803 1107
F: 020 7803 1111
E: i.petit@mhpf.org.uk
www.mhpf.org.uk
Chief Executive: Judy Weleminsky
The Mental Health Providers Forum is a not-for-profit umbrella organisation that brings together voluntary sector service providers to improve services for people with mental health needs. We work to influence national and regional mental health strategies; improve the quality and accessibility of services in the community; and to increase opportunities for voluntary and community sector providers to delivery quality services.
Employees: 6

Mentor Foundation (International)

Unit 1, Elms Lodge Farm, Melton Road, Barrow upon Soar, Loughborough, Leicestershire LE12 8HX
T: 01509 221622
F: 01509 808111
E: mandy@mentorfoundation.org
www.mentorfoundation.org
Executive Director: Jeff Lee
The Mentor Foundation is an international non-government not-for-profit organisation with a focus on the prevention of drug misuse and the promotion of health and wellbeing of young people. Mentor seeks to identify, support and share information on effective practice that will protect young people from the harm that drugs can cause.
Employees: 5
Volunteers: 1
Regional offices: 1

Mentoring and Befriending Foundation

T: 0161 272 6042
E: infomandbf@ncvo.org.uk
www.mandbf.org
The Mentoring and Befriending Foundation (MBF) aims to increase the effectiveness and quality of mentoring and befriending as methods of enabling individuals to transform their lives and/or reach their full potential. MBF does this by providing training and resources, quality assurance, network membership, consultancy services and contract/project management for organisations and people interested in mentoring and befriending. Part of NCVO.

Merchant Navy Welfare Board

30 Palmerston Road, Southampton, Hampshire SO14 1LL
T: 023 8033 7799
F: 023 8063 4444
E: enquiries@mnwb.org.uk
www.mnwb.org
Chief Executive: David Parsons
The Board is the umbrella for those charities involved in the welfare of merchant seafarers, fishermen and their dependants visiting, or residing in, UK and Gibraltar. It manages 17 Port Welfare Committees and provides grants, training and support services for its constituent charities. It also advises and acts as a clearing house for seafarers and their families seeking assistance.
Employees: 6

Merlin

12th Floor, 207 Old Street, London EC1V 9NR
T: 020 7014 1600
F: 020 7014 1601
E: carolyn.miller@merlin.org.uk
www.merlin.org.uk
Chief Executive: Carolyn Miller
Merlin is the UK's leading international health charity. Undaunted and determined, Merlin saves lives. We deliver medical expertise to the toughest places and stay to help build lasting healthcare. Our mission is to end the needless loss of life in the poorest countries caused by a lack of effective healthcare. We help communities set up medical services for the long term including hospitals, clinics, surgeries and training nurses and other health workers.
Employees: 96 UK, 168 internationally
Regional offices: 16 international

Merseyside Jewish Community Care

Shifrin House, 433 Smithdown Road, Liverpool, Merseyside L15 3JL
T: 0151 733 2292
F: 0151 734 0212
E: info@mjccshifrin.co.uk
www.merseysidejewishcommunitycare.co.uk
Chief Executive: Lisa Dolan
MJCC offers caring welfare services to Jewish people facing a crisis or needing longer term support. We provide practical assistance to Jewish parents and children, older people, disabled people, the visually impaired, people coping with mental health problems, families on low income and people who have become isolated from the community. We offer daytime activities, kosher meals services, small crisis grants and links and referrals to other caring agencies.
Employees: 11
Volunteers: 263

Metamorphic Association

26 York Street, London W1U 6PZ
T: 0845 154 7222
E: office@metamorphicassociation.net
www.metamorphicassociation.org
Promotes good health and wellbeing through awareness, understanding and use of the metamorphic technique in the UK and internationally, and to uphold standards in practising and teaching the technique.

Metanoia Institute

13 North Common Road, Ealing, London W5 2QB
T: 020 8579 2505
F: 020 8832 3070
E: kate.fromant@metanoia.ac.uk
www.metanoia.ac.uk
Chief Executive: Sheila Owen-Jones
Metanoia Institute is a higher education institute and professional training establishment, specialising in the training of counsellors, psychotherapists, counselling psychologists, supervisors, coaches and organisational development consultants. We also have a clinic, staffed by students in fully supervised supervision, offering lower cost counselling and psychotherapy services to the general public.
Employees: 100
Volunteers: 100
Income: £3,000,000 (2013-14)

MHA Care Group

Epworth House, 3 Stuart Street, Derby DE1 2EQ
T: 01332 296200
E: enquiries@mha.org.uk
www.mha.org.uk
Provides a range of accommodation and care services, based on Christian principles, which are open to all older people in need, whatever their beliefs.

Middlesbrough Voluntary Development Agency

St Mary's Centre, 82-90 Corporation Road, Middlesbrough TS1 2RW
T: 01642 249300
F: 01642 249600
E: general@mvdauk.org.uk
www.mvda.info
CEO: Dinah Lane
MVDA exists to support an effective and enterprising voluntary and community sector (VCS) that makes a difference to the lives of Middlesbrough people. It supports, promotes and develops local voluntary and community action by: providing information, training and one-to-one support for VCOs; promoting and developing volunteering, through a brokerage service and support for good practice in volunteer management; representing the interests of the VCS and organising meetings and events to enable networking and collaboration.
Employees: 13
Volunteers: 3
Income: £933,527 (2012-13)

Migraine Action

Floor 4, 27 East Street, Leicester, Leicestershire LE1 6NB
T: 0845 601 1033
E: info@migraine.org.uk
www.migraine.org.uk
Chief Executive: Simon Evans
We are a National Charity supporting all those affected by migraine and their families. We provide information, advice, and reassurance helping people with migraine take control of their migraine and reduce its impact, both in their home life and in the workplace.
Employees: 6
Volunteers: 3
Regional offices: 1

Migrant Helpline

The Rendezvous Building, Freight Service Approach Road, Eastern Docks, Dover, Kent CT16 1JA
T: 01304 203977
F: 01304 203995
E: dover@migranthelpline.org
www.migranthelpuk.org
Provides relief for asylum seekers, refugees and migrants who are in distress.
Employees: 205
Volunteers: 28
Regional offices: 8

Migrants Resource Centre

24 Churton Street, London SW1V 2LP
T: 020 7834 2505
F: 020 7931 8187
E: info@migrants.org.uk
www.migrantsresourcecentre.org.uk
The Migrants Resource Centre works with migrants and refugees and in partnership with other agencies to effect social justice and change, enabling migrants and refugees to fully participate in this society.
Employees: 14
Volunteers: 12

Mind

Granta House, London E15 4BQ
T: 020 8519 2122
F: 020 8522 1725
E: contact@mind.org.uk
www.mind.org.uk
Aims to raise awareness of mental health and to campaign for the rights of everyone experiencing mental distress.
Employees: 116
Volunteers: 20

Mind in Camden

Barnes House, 9-15 Camden Road, London NW1 9LQ
T: 020 7911 0822
F: 020 7485 0842
E: rdean@mindincamden.org.uk
www.mindincamden.org.uk
Chief Executive: Brian Dawn
Mind in Camden provides services for people whose mental health and difficult life experiences are proving challenging including: hearing voices, extremes of mood, anxiety, unusual beliefs and post-traumatic reactions. We have a wellbeing and recovery service; a service to support people who are dependent on benzodiazepines; and projects for young voice hearers; for voice hearers in London prisons and a London-wide Paranoia project.
Employees: 14
Volunteers: 60
Income: £877,432 (2012-13)

Mind in Tower Hamlets and Newham

Open House, 13 Whitethorn Street
T: 020 7510 1081
E: cecilia.morkeh-yamson@mithn.org.uk
www.mithn.org.uk
Finance Manager: Cecilia Morkeh-Yamson Pelligrin

Mind the Gap

Silk Warehouse, Patent Street, Bradford, West Yorkshire BD9 4SA
T: 01274 487390
F: 01274 493973
E: arts@mind-the-gap.org.uk
www.mind-the-gap.org.uk
Mind the Gap believes in quality, equality and inclusion. Our mission is to dismantle the barriers to artistic excellence so that learning disabled and non-disabled artists can perform alongside each other as equals.

Minorities of Europe

Legacy House, 29 Walsgrave Road, Coventry CV2 4HE
T: 024 7622 5764 (also fax)
E: admin@moe-online.com
www.moe-online.com
Aims to develop a range of programmes and projects that meet the needs of young people and disadvantaged groups/communities in Europe.
Employees: 6
Volunteers: 36

Minority Rights Group International

54 Commercial Street, London E1 6LT
T: 020 7422 4200
E: minority.rights@mrgmail.org
www.minorityrights.org
MRG works to secure the rights of ethnic, religious and linguistic minorities, and indigenous peoples, and acts as an advocate of the rights of minorities. MRG works across groups to build units and raise awareness of minority rights within a clear framework of international standards in a non-partisan way.

Miscarriage Association

17 Wentworth Terrace, Wakefield, West Yorkshire WF1 3QW
T: 01924 200795
Helpline: 01924 200799
F: 01924 298834
E: info@miscarriageassociation.org.uk
www.miscarriageassociation.org.uk
National Director: Ruth Bender Atik
Miscarriage can be a very unhappy, frightening and lonely experience. The Miscarriage Association strives to make a positive difference to those it affects. We offer support, provide information, promote good practice amongst health professionals and work to raise public awareness about the facts and feelings of pregnancy loss.
Employees: 5
Volunteers: 100

Missing People

Roebuck House, 284 Upper Richmond Road West, London SW14 7JE
T: 020 8392 4590
Helpline: 116000
F: 020 8878 7752
E: info@missingpeople.org.uk
www.missingpeople.org.uk
Executive Director: Jo Youle
We are a lifeline when someone disappears. We are caring and highly trained staff and volunteers working in collaboration with partners across the UK. For those left behind, we provide specialised support to end the heartache and confusion and search for their missing loved one.
Employees: 67
Volunteers: 400
Regional offices: 1

Mission Aviation Fellowship UK

Castle House, Castle Hill Avenue, Folkestone, Kent CT20 2TQ
T: 01303 850950
F: 01302 852800
E: alex.finlow@maf-uk.org
www.maf-uk.org
Chief Executive: Ruth Whitaker
Mission Aviation Fellowship is a Christian organisation with the mission to fly light aircraft in developing countries so that people in remote areas can receive the help they need.
Employees: 79
Volunteers: 700
Regional offices: 2
Income: £12,000,000 (2012-13)

Mission Care

Graham House, 2 Pembroke Road, Bromley, Kent BR1 2RU
T: 020 8289 7925
E: admin@missioncare.org.uk
www.missioncare.org.uk
Works for the relief of sickness and poverty, the relief of the aged, handicapped or infirm and the advancement of the Christian religion.

Mobility Information Service

20 Burton Close, Dawley, Telford, Shropshire TF4 2BX
T: 01743 340269
E: info@starthere.org
www.mis.org
Provides an information service by letter, email and phone, with a 24-hour answering service. Leaflets are available covering various aspects of disability.
Volunteers: 10

Mobility Trust

17B Reading Road, Pangbourne, Reading, Berkshire RG8 7LR
T: 0845 450 0359
F: 0118 984 2544
E: mobility@mobilitytrust.org.uk
www.mobilitytrust.org.uk
Provides powered wheelchairs and scooters for severely disabled children and adults who cannot obtain them through statutory sources or purchase such equipment themselves. We do not give grants.
Employees: 4

MOC Foundation

341 Lauderdale Tower, Barbican, London EC2Y 8NA
T: 020 7256 6066
E: info@mocfoundation.org
www.mocfoundation.org
Chair: Jose Carlos Martines
Provides humanitarian aid for the relief of poverty in less developed regions of the world.
Volunteers: 9
Income: £35,000 (2014-15)

Money Advice Trust

21 Garlick Hill, London EC4V 2AU
T: 020 7489 7796
Helpline: 0808 808 4000
F: 020 7489 7704
E: info@moneyadvicetrust.org
www.moneyadvicetrust.org
Chief Executive: Joanna Elson
The Money Advice Trust (MAT) is a charity formed in 1991 to increase the quality and availability of free, independent money advice in the UK. MAT's vision: to help people across the UK to tackle their debts and manage their money wisely. MAT does this through direct service provision (National Debtline, Business Debtline and My Money Steps) as well as supporting the advice sector through training (wiseradviser).
Employees: 173

More Music

13-17 Devonshire Road, Morecambe, Lancashire LA3 1QT
T: 01524 831997
E: sandra.wood@moremusic.org.uk
www.moremusic.org.uk
Artistic Director: Peter Moser
More Music is a community music and education charity based in the West End of Morecambe, working throughout Lancashire, the North West and internationally. We provide a year round programme that covers a breadth of music making activity involving people of all ages and all backgrounds. We are one of the longest running and most highly regarded community music and education organisations in the UK.

MOSAIC Black and Mixed Parentage Family Group

Community Base, 113 Queens Road, Brighton BN1 3XG
T: 01273 234017
F: 01273 234018
E: info@mosaicbrighton.org.uk
www.mosaicequalities.org.uk
Director: Naima Nouidjem
MOSAIC exists to empower black, Asian and mixed-parentage families to combat racism and to support the development of positive cultural and racial identity.
Employees: 4
Volunteers: 30
Regional offices: 1

Mosaic Clubhouse

65 Effra Road, Brixton, London SW2 1BZ
T: 020 7924 9657
E: m.ness@mosaic-clubhouse.org
www.mosaic-clubhouse.org
Chief Executive: Maresa Ness
The aim of Mosaic Clubhouse is to provide opportunities for individuals, who have been socially and vocationally disadvantaged by mental ill health, to regain the confidence and skills necessary to lead productive and satisfying lives. The services we deliver assist our members with increased social networks; better mental health; improved skills; increased take up of education and employment opportunities; and the self-confidence to make informed choices about their future.
Employees: 16
Volunteers: 4
Regional offices: 1
Income: £900,174 (2014-15)

Mothers Apart from their Children

BM Box 6334, London WC1N 3XX
E: enquiries@matchmothers.org
www.matchmothers.org
MATCH offers non-judgemental emotional support to mothers apart because of their own short- or long-term mental or physical ill-health when children are fostered or adopted, to mothers whose children have been abducted abroad by their fathers, to mothers apart as a result of alienation following high-conflict family breakdown when children profess not to want to see their mothers, and to mothers of adult children apart as a result of family rows.
Volunteers: 10
Income: £5,000 (2013-14)

Mothers Union

Mary Sumner House, 24 Tufton Street, London SW1P 3RB
T: 020 7222 5533
F: 020 7222 1591
E: mu@themothersunion.org
www.themothersunion.org
The Mothers' Union is an Anglican organisation that promotes the wellbeing of families worldwide.
Employees: 47
Volunteers: 36000000
Regional offices: 70

Motivation

Brockley Academy, Brockley Lane, Backwell, Bristol BS48 4AQ
T: 01275 464012
F: 01275 464019
E: info@motivation.org.uk
www.motivation.org.uk
President : David Constantine
Motivation is an international charity transforming the lives of disabled people. Our wheelchairs and training give people independence, confidence and hope for the future.
Employees: 38
Volunteers: 4
Regional offices: 1

MS Trust Spirella Building, Bridge Road, Letchworth, Hertfordshire SG6 4ET
T: 01462 476700
Helpline: 0800 032 3839
E: info@mstrust.org.uk
www.mstrust.org.uk
Chief Executive: Pam Macfarlane
The MS Trust is dedicated to supporting people living with MS now. We provide the information you trust and support the health professionals you need.
Employees: 30
Volunteers: 2
Regional offices: 1

Multiple Births Foundation

Hammersmith House, Level 4, Queen Charlotte's Hospital, Du Cane Road, London W12 0HS
T: 020 3313 3519
E: mbf@imperial.nhs.uk
www.multiplebirths.org.uk
Director: Jane Denton
The Multiple Births Foundation offers professional advice, education and support to parents and carers of twins, triplets and more, and to the health professionals who care for them.

Multiple Sclerosis International Federation

3rd Floor, Skyline House, 200 Union Street, London SE1 0LX
T: 020 7620 1911
E: info@msif.org
www.msif.org
Works in worldwide partnership with member MS societies and the international research community to eliminate multiple sclerosis and its consequences, and speaks out globally on behalf of those affected by multiple sclerosis.

Multiple Sclerosis National Therapy Centres

Bradbury House, 155 Barkers Lane, Bedford MK41 9RX
T: 01234 325781
E: info@msntc.org.uk
www.ms-selfhelp.org
Supports multiple sclerosis therapy centres with training, education, information, etc.

Multiple Sclerosis Society of Great Britain and Northern Ireland

MS National Centre, 372 Edgware Road, London NW2 6ND
T: 020 8438 0739
F: 020 8438 0701
E: info@mssociety.org.uk
www.mssociety.org.uk
Supports people affected by MS; encourages people affected by MS to attain their full potential and promotes research into MS.
Employees: 529
Volunteers: 8000
Regional offices: 400

Muntham House School Ltd

Muntham Drive, Barns Green, Near Horsham, West Sussex RH20 2QZ
T: 01403 730302
F: 01403 730510
E: triciajeffs@muntham.org.uk
www.muntham.org.uk
Principal: Tricia Jeffs
Boarding & Day School for boys (8-18) with a range of social & emotional difficulties including ADHD, Asperger's Syndrome and conduct disorders. Muntham has a local, regional, national and international reputation for innovative practise, successful outcomes for young people and trains professionals in managing challenging behaviour.
Employees: 84

Muscular Dystrophy Campaign

61A Great Suffolk Street, London SE1 0BU
T: 020 7803 4800
Helpline: 0800 652 6352
F: 020 7401 3495
E: info@muscular-dystrophy.org
www.muscular-dystrophy.org
Chief Executive: Robert Meadowcroft
The Muscular Dystrophy Campaign is the leading UK charity fighting muscle-wasting conditions. We are dedicated to beating muscular dystrophy and related neuromuscular conditions by finding treatments and cures and to improving the lives of everyone affected by them.
Employees: 60
Volunteers: 30000
Regional offices: 11

Museums Association

24 Calvin Street, London E1 6NW
T: 020 7426 6910
F: 020 7426 6961
E: info@museumsassociation.org
www.museumsassociation.org
Director: Mark Taylor
Represents museums and art galleries and their staff; protects and develops professional standards in museums.
Employees: 26

Music Education Council

54 Elm Road, Hale, Altrincham, Cheshire WA15 9QP
T: 0161 928 3065
E: ahassan@easynet.co.uk
www.mec.org.uk
Promotes and advances music education and training in the UK.

Muslim Aid

PO Box 3, London E1 1WP
T: 020 7377 4200
F: 020 7377 4201
E: hr@muslimaid.org
www.muslimaid.org
Muslim Aid was established to provide humanitarian relief aid to the poorest, more deprived and most vulnerable in society worldwide. Emergency relief for victims of disasters like floods, earthquakes, famines as well as war is an important part of the aid we provide.
Employees: 10
Volunteers: 10
Regional offices: 5

Myaware

The College Business Centre, Uttoxeter New Road, Derby, Derbyshire DE22 3WZ
T: 01332 290219
Helpline: 0800 919912
E: mg@myaware.org
www.myaware.org
CEO: Ruth Bury
Funds research into the cause of myasthenia gravis in order to find a cure; provides a support network for myasthenics and their families, increases public and medical awareness of the problems of myasthenia gravis. (re branded from Myasthenia Gravis Association)
Employees: 15
Volunteers: 100+
Regional offices: 57

Myositis Support Group

146 Newtown Road, Woolston, Southampton SO19 9HR
T: 023 8044 9708
E: irene@myositis.org.uk
www.myositis.org.uk
Promotes the relief of persons suffering from dermatomyositis, polymyositis and inclusion body myositis; promotes research for a cure and better treatment. We also help to relieve the isolation felt when diagnosed with a rare condition and give support and up-to-date information to sufferers and their families.
Employees: 1
Volunteers: 8

Myotonic Dystrophy Support Group

19/21 Main Road, Gedling, Nottingham, Nottinghamshire NG4 3HQ
T: 0115 987 5869
Helpline: 0115 987 0080
E: mdsg@tesco.net
www.myotonicdystrophysupportgroup.org
National Coordinator: Margaret Bowler
We support families who have myotonic dystrophy, both congenital and adults. We supply information to the medical practitioners. There is a website and helpline, annual conference and area informal meetings.
Employees: 2
Volunteers: 25
Regional offices: 1

Nacro

First Floor, 46 Loman Street, London SE1 0EH
T: 0300 123 1889
E: contactus@nacro.org.uk
www.nacro.org.uk
CEO: Jacob Tas
As a champion of social justice, Nacro's mission is to positively change lives, strengthen communities, enhance social inclusion, reduce crime, and prevent offending behaviour. We deliver high quality, evidence based and outcome focused interventions throughout England and Wales, helping the most vulnerable in the community to change their lives and reach their full potential.
Employees: 725
Volunteers: 150
Income: £47,000 (2013-14)

NAGALRO

PO Box 264, Esher, Surrey KT10 0WA
T: 01372 818504
E: nagalro@globalnet.co.uk
www.nagalro.com
NAGALRO is the professional association for children's guardians, children and family reporters and independent social workers. NAGALRO promotes good practice; provides support and advice to individual members; contributes to developments in the Guardian and Family Court service; supports communication between individual guardians and Cafcass; encourages quality standards in independent social work with children and families; makes links with childcare solicitors and other professionals; provides professional insurance cover; produces a quarterly journal; and organises interdisciplinary conferences and training.
Volunteers: 15

Nakuru Environmental and Conservation Trust

5 Kingsend Court, Kingsend, Ruislip HA4 7DB
T: 01895 633650
E: nectecology@yahoo.co.uk
www.nectuk.org
Chair: Nim Njuguna
Promoting global citizenship and sustainable development through undertaking environmental service projects with communities in Kenya's Rift Valley Province. Encouraging young people from Kenya and the UK Diaspora to work and learn from each other by discovering, celebrating and exploring similarities and differences between their cultures through "Kenya's Story in a 100 Objects" programme.
Volunteers: 6
Income: ££800.00 (2012-13)

NAPAC

Weston House, 42 Curtain Road, London EC2A 3NH
T: 020 8313 9460 (also fax)
E: peter@napac.fsnet.co.uk
www.napac.org.uk
Provides relief and support to people who have experienced abuse in childhood and those affected by abuse and advances the education of the public and relevant professional bodies with regard to child abuse.
Employees: 7
Volunteers: 4

Narcolepsy Association UK (UKAN)

PO Box 13842, Penicuik EH26 8WX
T: 0845 450 0394
E: jennie@emms26.fsnet.co.uk
www.narcolepsy.org.uk
An association of people with narcolepsy, their relatives and others interested in improving their lot. Objectives are the benefit, relief and aid of persons suffering from narcolepsy; to promote awareness and provide authoritative information to narcoleptics, to the medical profession and to the public; and to encourage research into the causes and treatment of narcolepsy.
Employees: 1
Volunteers: 12

National AIDS Trust

New City Cloisters, 196 Old Street, London EC1V 9FR
T: 020 7814 6767
F: 020 7216 0111
E: info@nat.org.uk
www.nat.org.uk
Chief Executive: Deborah Gold
The National AIDS Trust is the UK's leading independent policy and campaigning charity on HIV. We develop policies and campaign to halt the spread of HIV and improve the quality of life of people affected by HIV, both in the UK and internationally.
Employees: 16
Volunteers: 15

National Alliance of Women's Organisations

Suite 405, Davina House, London EC1V 7ET
T: 020 7490 4100
E: info@nawo.org.uk
www.nawo.org.uk
Aims to bring together all women's organisations in the country working to eliminate all forms of discrimination against women.

National Animal Welfare Trust

Tyler's Way, Watford, Hertfordshire WD25 8WT
T: 020 8950 0177
F: 020 8420 4454
E: d.warner@nawt.org.uk
www.nawt.org.uk
Chief Executive: David Warner

The National Animal Welfare Trust's primary purpose is to rescue and re-home domestic animals and provide a place of sanctuary or retirement for animals of all types.
Employees: 110
Volunteers: 350

National Ankylosing Spondylitis Society (NASS)

4 Albion Court, Galena Road, Hammersmith, London W6 0QT
T: 020 8741 1515
E: admin@nass.co.uk
www.nass.co.uk
Director: Debbie Cook
NASS provides advice, support and information for patients with AS. We support research in this field, have over 100 branches in the UK and also campaign for access to treatments and better services for all AS patients.
Employees: 7
Volunteers: 200
Income: £350,000 (2013-14)

National Association for Able Children in Education

PO Box 242, Arnold's Way, Oxford OX2 9FR
T: 01865 861879
F: 01865 861880
E: info@nace.co.uk
www.nace.co.uk
NACE is a network of educators passionate about enabling able pupils to fulfil their potential within inclusive school communities. We develop and exchange strategies for effective practice and further the professional development of our members; provide responses on issues affecting the education of able children and advice to government agencies; undertake development projects; provide professional expertise, advice, training and consultancy services, conferences, events, publications and resources.

National Association for Children of Alcoholics

PO Box 64, Bristol, Avon BS16 2UH
T: 0117 924 8005
Helpline: 0800 358 3456
E: admin@nacoa.org.uk
www.nacoa.org.uk
CEO: Hilary Henriques MBE
Nacoa provides information, advice and support for children, young people and adults struggling with parental alcohol problems and people concerned with their welfare through our free, confidential telephone and email helpline and website. We raise awareness of the problems they face and services available to them. We also initiate and take part in research studies into the scope and scale of the problem and the prevention of alcoholism developing in this vulnerable group.
Employees: 3
Volunteers: 341
Regional offices: 1
Income: £86,000 (2013-14)

National Association for Environmental Education (UK)

University of Wolverhampton, Walsall Campus, Gorway, Walsall, West Midlands WS1 3BD
T: 07479 27183
E: info@naee.org.uk
www.naee.org.uk
Supporting those who deliver Environmental Education to young people. sharing good practice through social media and the production of our journal 'Enviroonmental Education'
Employees: 1
Volunteers: 10

National Association for Pastoral Care in Education

University of Warwick, Gibbet Hill Road, Coventry CV4 7AL
T: 024 7652 3810
E: base@napce.org.uk
www.napce.org.uk
NAPCE establishes links between all those who have an interest in pastoral care and personal-social education. It has a membership of 600 individuals and organisations. NAPCE supports all who have a professional concern for pastoral care; promotes the theoretical study of pastoral care; disseminates good practice; promotes the education, training and development of those engaged in pastoral care; and liaises with other organisations with similar aims.

National Association for Patient Participation

10 Rosegarth Avenue, Aston, Sheffield S26 2DD
T: 0870 774 3666 (also fax)
E: danny.daniels@napp.org.uk
www.napp.org.uk
NAPP is the umbrella group for patient participation groups (PPGs) in primary care. NAPP offers guidance on starting and maintaining PPGs, and advice to primary care organisations on PPGs as well as identifying and disseminating good practice.
Volunteers: 15

National Association for Premenstrual Syndrome

41 Old Road, East Peckham, Tonbridge, Kent TN12 5AP
T: 0870 777 2178
E: contact@pms.org.uk
www.pms.org.uk
Provides clinically authoritative, independent advice, information and support to all those experiencing, and treating, PMS and menstrual ill health.

National Association for Small Schools

Quarrenden, Upper Red Cross Road, Goring, Oxfordshire RG8 9BD
T: 01491 873548
E: quarrenden.tay@btinternet.com
www.smallschools.org.uk
Chairman: Bill Goodhand
Provides a voice and a link for those who believe that small schools, in rural and urban areas, have educational and social roles too precious to lose.

National Association for Special Educational Needs

NASEN House, Amber Close, Amington, Tamworth, Staffordshire B77 4RP
T: 01827 311500
F: 01827 313005
E: welcome@nasen.org.uk
www.nasen.org.uk
NASEN is the leading organisation in the UK that aims to promote the education, training, advancement and development of all those with special and additional support needs. NASEN reaches a huge readership through its journals: British Journal of Special Education, Support for Learning, the new online publication Journal of Research in Special Educational Needs and the magazine Special.
Employees: 14

National Association for the Relief of Paget's Disease (AKA The Paget's Association)

Suite 5, Moorfield House, Moorside Road, Swinton, Manchester M27 0EW
T: 0161 799 4646
E: diana.wilkinson@paget.org.uk
www.paget.org.uk
Chair: Prof Roger Francis
Our aims are to raise awareness of Paget's disease of bone among the public and the medical profession; to offer information and support to those with the condition; and to

support and sponsor research into the causes and treatment of the disease.
Employees: 2
Volunteers: 1
Regional offices: 1

National Association for the Teaching of English

50 Broadfield Road, Sheffield, South Yorkshire S8 0XJ
T: 0114 255 5419
F: 0114 255 5296
E: info@nate.org.uk
www.nate.org.uk
NATE currently has over 3,000 members, affiliated to a network of regional branches. The association has a range of committees and working parties that address current concerns, disseminate knowledge and ideas, promote the work of the association and seek to represent the views of the association to national bodies, local authorities, the DfES, OFSTED, QCA, examination boards, etc.
Employees: 8
Volunteers: 70

National Association for Voluntary and Community Associations

The Tower, 2 Furnival Square, Sheffield S1 4QL
T: 0114 278 6636
F: 0114 278 7004
E: navca@navca.org.uk
www.navca.org.uk
Chief Executive: Kevin Curley
NAVCA is the national voice of local voluntary and community sector infrastructure in England. Our 360 members work with 170,000 local community groups and voluntary organisations, which provide services, regenerate neighbourhoods, increase volunteering and tackle discrimination, in partnership with local public bodies.
Employees: 40
Volunteers: 8
Regional offices: 398

National Association of Child Contact Centres

Minerva House, Spaniel Row, Nottingham NG1 6EP
T: 0845 450 0280
E: contact@naccc.org.uk
www.naccc.org.uk
Chief Executive: Yvonne Kee
Promotes safe child contact within a national framework of around 350 child contact centres. These are safe, neutral places where children of separated families can spend time with one or both parents and sometimes other family members. NACCC offers a range of support services to its membership and also provides a voice for child contact centres, promoting their role with national and regional decision-makers.
Employees: 7
Volunteers: 12

National Association of Deafened People

NADP, Dalton House, 60 Windsor Avenue, London SW19 2RR
T: 0845 055 9663
E: enquiries@nadp.org.uk
www.nadp.org.uk
Chair: Lidia Best
NADP supports all those who have suffered hearing loss during their lifetime. We provide our newsletter Network and monthly EBulletins to provide information and updates on any developments affecting our members. We campaign and also provide information and advice on employment, telecommunications, equipment and other subjects. NADP has some local groups and other contacts in various parts of the country, which arrange social events and provide support at grassroots level.
Volunteers: 12
Income: £10,270 (2013-14)

National Association of Decorative and Fine Arts Societies

NADFAS House, 8 Guilford Street, London WC1N 1DA
T: 020 7430 0730
F: 020 7242 0686
E: enquiries@nadfas.org.uk
www.nadfas.org.uk
Aims to increase the enjoyment, knowledge and care of the arts, and to stimulate interest in the preservation of our cultural heritage.
Employees: 14
Volunteers: 10000

National Association of Independent Schools and Non Maintained Special Schools

PO Box 705, York YO30 6WW
T: 01904 621243 (also fax)
E: cdorer@nasschools.org.uk
www.nasschools.org.uk
Chief Executive: Claire Dorer
The umbrella organisation for non-maintained special schools and independent schools catering for pupils with special educational needs. Works as the voice of the sector to ensure high-quality education and care for children with special educational needs.
Employees: 2

National Association of Laryngectomee Clubs

Lower Ground Floor, 152 Buckingham Palace Road, London SW1W 9TR
T: 020 7381 9993
E: website@nalc.gov.uk
www.laryngectomy.org.uk
Promotes the welfare and rehabilitation, in any way possible, of laryngectomy patients and their families within the British Isles.

National Association of Local Councils

109 Great Russell Street, London WC1B 3LD
T: 020 7637 1865
F: 020 7436 7451
E: nalc@nalc.gov.uk
www.nalc.gov.uk
NALC represents the interests of around 8,500 town and parish councils in England. These councils serve electorates ranging from small rural communities to major cities, and are independently elected. Working with our member councils, NALC lobbies national government to advance and protect the interests of these councils and their communities. NALC provides support and advice to our members through a network of county associations and is committed to developing the role of town and parish councils.

National Association of Round Tables of Great Britain and Ireland

Marchesi House, 4 Embassy Drive, Edgbaston, Birmingham B15 1TP
T: 0121 456 4402
F: 0121 456 4185
E: john@roundtable.org.uk
www.roundtable.org.uk
General Secretary: John Handley
A young men's fellowship organisation.
Employees: 6
Regional offices: 670

National Association of Swimming Clubs for the Handicapped

The Willows, Mayles Lane, Wickham, Fareham, Hampshire PO17 5ND
T: 01329 833689
E: r.a.oleary@btinternet.com
www.nasch.org.uk
Chairman: Tracey Kitching

Encourages, promotes and develops swimming among handicapped people, in recognition of the immense value of swimming for both physical and psychological rehabilitation.

National Association of Women's Clubs

5 Vernon Rise, London WC1X 9EP
T: 020 7837 1434
E: nawc@btconnect.com
www.nawc.org.uk
National Chairman: Maureen Harwood
Provides facilities for social life and opportunities for informal education within the means of all women.
Employees: 3
Regional offices: 120

National Association of Youth Theatres

c/o York Theatre Royal, St. Leonard's Place, York YO24 3LD
T: 07515 651481
E: info@nayt.org.uk
www.nayt.org.uk
Chief Executive: Jill Adamson
NAYT works with over 1,000 groups and individuals to support the development of youth theatre activity through information and support services, advocacy, training, participation and partnerships.
Employees: 1

National Benevolent Fund for the Aged

32 Buckingham Palace Road, London SW1W 0RE
T: 020 7828 0200
F: 020 7828 0400
E: info@nbfa.org.uk
www.nbfa.org.uk
Interim Executive Director: Andrew Ross
NBFA was founded to improve the quality of life for older people who live on a low income. NBFA does this by providing direct, practical assistance through the provision of emergency alarms, TENS pain relief machines and free break-aways.
Employees: 4
Volunteers: 10

National Benevolent Institution

Peter Herve House, Eccles Court, Tetbury, Gloucestershire GL8 8EH
T: 01666 505500
Helpline: 01666 505200
F: 01666 503111
E: welfare@nbi.org.uk
www.thenbc.org.uk
The NBI was founded in 1812 by Peter Herve to provide a regular payment and one-off grants to people who have reached pension age or are over 50 years of age with a disability.
Employees: 5
Regional offices: 1

National Campaign for the Arts

1 Kingly Street, London W1B 5PA
T: 020 7287 3777
E: nca@artscampaign.org.uk
www.artscampaign.org.uk
Aims to inform the public, brief the media and alert politicians to the need for greater public funding of the arts and campaigns for improvements in arts funding, arts education and access to the arts.

National Centre for Social Research

35 Northampton Square, London EC1V 0AX
T: 020 7250 1866
E: info@natcen.ac.uk
www.natcen.ac.uk
Chief Executive: Norman Glass
Our aim is a society better informed through high-quality social research.

National Childbirth Trust

Alexandra House, Oldham Terrace, London W3 6NH
T: 0870 770 3236
Helpline: 0870 444 8707
F: 0870 770 3237
E: enquiries@national-childbirth-trust.co.uk
www.nct.org.uk
Chief Executive: Belinda Phipps
The NCT wants all parents to have an experience of pregnancy, birth and early parenthood that enriches their lives and gives them confidence in being a parent. It provides local support and puts parents in touch for social networking. The NCT also runs antenatal classes and provides information on maternity issues, breastfeeding and postnatal support, including specialist groups for caesareans and miscarriage. It has approximately 300 branches throughout the UK.
Employees: 80
Volunteers: 7000
Regional offices: 300

National Children's Bureau

8 Wakley Street, London EC1V 7QE
T: 020 7843 6000
E: pbell@ncb.org.uk
www.ncb.org.uk
Chief Executive: Anna Feuchtwang
The National Children's Bureau is a leading charity that for 50 years has been improving the lives of children and young people, especially the most vulnerable. We work with children and for children, to influence government policy, be a strong voice for young people and practitioners, and provide creative solutions on a range of social issues.
Income: £11,520,000 (2012-13)

National Children's Centre

Brian Jackson House, New North Parade, Huddersfield, West Yorkshire HD1 5JP
T: 01484 519988
F: 01484 435150
E: info@nccuk.org.uk
www.yorkshirechildrenscentre.org.uk
Aims to advance public awareness in subjects connected with the care and upbringing of children in order to promote a better quality of life for the child.
Employees: 30
Volunteers: 10

National Coastwatch Institution (NCI)

1 Walk Terrace, West Street, Polruan by Fowey, Cornwall PL23 1PN
T: 01726 870659 (also fax)
Helpline: 0300 111 1202
E: public.relations@nci.org.uk
www.nci.org.uk
Chairman: Alan Richards
NCI was set up in 1994 to restore a visual watch along the coast after many coastguard stations were closed. Today 50 stations are operational and manned by over 2,000 volunteers at no cost to the public purse. Our mission is to assist in saving lives at sea and along the UK coastline. NCI is part of the national Search and Rescue organisation and is dependent on public support to cover running costs.
Volunteers: 2000

National Communities Resource Centre

Trafford Hall, Ince Lane, Wimbolds Trafford, Chester CH2 4JP
T: 01244 300246
E: s.wyatt@traffordhall.com
www.traffordhall.com

Offering training and support to all those living and working in low-income communities around the UK. The centre develops skills, confidence and capacity to tackle problems and reverse poor conditions.

National Community Safety Network

1 Hunters Walk, Canal Street, Chester, Cheshire CH1 4EB
T: 01244 322314
E: enquiries@community-safety.net
www.communitysafetyinstitute.net
NCSN is the leading practitioner-led organisation supporting those involved in promoting community safety/crime reduction throughout the UK. It has just under 400 organisational members and individual members in the public, private and voluntary sectors, all with a common interest in promoting safer communities. NCSN gives a national voice to practitioners; influences national policy and practice; supports the professional development of practitioners; and promotes joint working in the UK and Europe.
Employees: 3
Volunteers: 1

National Confederation of Parent Teacher Associations

39 Shipbourne Road, Tonbridge, Kent TN10 3DS
T: 01732 375460
F: 01732 375461
E: dwb@ncpta.org.uk
www.pta.org.uk
NCPTA is the only membership organisation for PTAs and other home/school groups in England, Wales and Northern Ireland. Members enjoy high levels of support and advice on a variety of subjects such as fundraising ideas, running a PTA, registering as a charity and holding successful events.
Employees: 20
Volunteers: 130000
Regional offices: 11

National Confidential Enquiry Into Patient Outcome and Death

Ground Floor, Abbey House, 74-76 St John Street, London EC1M 4DZ
T: 020 7251 9060
F: 020 7250 0020
E: info@ncepod.org.uk
www.ncepod.org.uk
NCEPOD aims to review medical clinical practice and to make recommendations to improve the quality of the delivery of care. We do this by undertaking confidential surveys covering many different aspects of medical care and making recommendations for clinicians and management to implement.
Employees: 12

National Consumer Federation

24 Hurst House, Penton Rise, London WC1X 9ED
T: 020 7837 8545
E: secretary@ncf.info
www.ncf.info
Chair: Arnold Pindar
Aims to educate and inform consumers, with reference to the key guiding principles of choice, information, representation, access to goods and services, quality, fairness, safety and redress.
Employees: 1
Volunteers: 25

National Council for Palliative Care

The Fitzpatrick Building, London N7 9AS
T: 020 7697 1520
F: 020 7697 1530
E: enquiries@ncpc.org.uk
www.ncpc.org.uk
Chief Executive: Eve Richardson
NCPC is the umbrella organisation for all those providing, commissioning and using palliative care and hospice services in England, Wales and Northern Ireland. NCPC promotes the extension and improvement of palliative care services for all people with life-threatening and life-limiting conditions. NCPC promotes palliative care in health and social care settings across all sectors to government, national and local policy makers.
Employees: 17

National Council for Voluntary Organisations

Society Building, 8 All Saints Street, London N1 9RL
T: 020 7713 6161
F: 020 7713 6300
E: ncvo@ncvo.org.uk
www.ncvo.org.uk
Chief Executive: Sir Stuart Etherington
NCVO's vision is of a society in which people are inspired to make a positive difference to their communities. NCVO believes that a vibrant voluntary and community sector deserves a strong voice and the best support. NCVO aims to be that support and voice.
Employees: 130
Regional offices: 1
Income: £9,588,000 (2013-14)

National Council for Voluntary Youth Services (NCVYS)

28 Brunswick Place, London N1 6DZ
T: 020 7278 1041
E: mail@ncvys.org.uk
www.ncvys.org.uk
Chief Executive: Susanne Rauprich
NCVYS is the leading representative body for voluntary and community youth organisations working with or on behalf of young people in England. NCVYS supports a diverse network of 270 members, including regional and local networks. NCVYS has been working since 1936 to raise the profile of youth work, share good practice and influence policy that has an impact on young people and organisations that support them.
Employees: 12
Income: £800,000 (2013-14)

National Council of Women of Great Britain

72 Victoria Road, Darlington DL1 5JG
T: 01325 367375
E: info@ncwgb.org
www.ncwgb.org
President: Gwenda Nicholas
Works for the removal of discrimination against women; encourages the effective participation of women in public life and acts as a coordinating body to which societies with similar aims may affiliate.
Employees: 1

National Day Nurseries Association

National Early Years Enterprise Centre, Longbow Close, Huddersfield, West Yorkshire HD2 1GQ
T: 0870 774 4244
F: 0870 774 4243
E: info@ndna.org.uk
www.ndna.org.uk
NDNA is a national charity dedicated to the support and promotion of high-quality care and education for all children in the early years. It provides a code of practice for provider members and encourages all providers to follow the accreditation scheme, Quality Counts.
Employees: 50
Volunteers: 250
Regional offices: 5

National Deaf Children's Society (NDCS)

Ground Floor South, Castle House, 37-45 Paul Street, London EC2A 4LS
T: 020 7490 8656
Helpline: 0808 800 8880
F: 020 7251 5020
E: helpline@ndcs.org.uk
www.ndcs.org.uk
Chief Executive: Susan Daniels
In all our work we aim to: empower deaf children, young people and their families to determine what happens in their lives and shape the services they receive; increase awareness of the support deaf children and young people need to achieve and challenge social attitudes which prevent them achieving; influence and challenge key decision-makers to make deaf children and young people a political priority.
Employees: 140
Volunteers: 240
Regional offices: 5

National Development Team for Inclusion

First Floor, 30-32 Westgate Buildings, Bath BA1 1EF
T: 01225 789135
F: 01225 338017
E: mark.collings@ndti.org.uk
www.ndti.org.uk
Chief Executive: Rob Greig
The National Development Team for Inclusion is a not-for-profit organisation concerned with promoting inclusion and equality for people who risk exclusion and who need support to lead a full life. We have a particular interest in issues around age, disability, mental health and children and young people.
Employees: 20
Volunteers: 10

National Eczema Society

Hill House, Highgate Hill, London N19 5NA
T: 020 7281 3553
Helpline: 0800 089 1122
E: helpline@eczema.org
www.eczema.org
Chief Executive: M Cox
Provides information and support to people with eczema and their carers, including health professionals.
Employees: 8
Volunteers: 20

National Energy Action (NEA)

West One, Level 6 (Elswick), Forth Banks, Newcastle upon Tyne NE1 3PA
T: 0191 261 5677
F: 0191 261 6496
E: info@nea.org.uk
www.nea.org.uk
Chief Executive: Jenny Saunders OBE
The national energy efficiency charity which campaigns to end fuel poverty by influencing decision-makers and working with stakeholders to develop policies and practices to tackle the heating and insulation problems of low-income households through improvements in energy efficiency.
Employees: 68
Volunteers: 2
Regional offices: 9

National Energy Foundation

Davy Avenue, Knowlhill, Milton Keynes MK5 8NG
T: 01908 665555
F: 01908 665577
E: enquiries@nef.org.uk
www.nef.org.uk
CEO: Kerry Mashford
NEF aims to give people, organisations and government the knowledge, support and inspiration they need to understand and improve the use of energy in buildings.
Employees: 25
Volunteers: 3

National Extension College Trust Ltd

Joydon, 33 Adelaide Close, Stanmore, Middlesex HA7 3EN
T: 020 8420 6055
E: info@nec.ac.uk
www.nec.ac.uk
Provides the learning resources and opportunities to enable individuals to meet their vocational and personal goals.

National Eye Research Centre

Bristol Eye Hospital, Lower Maudlin Street, Bristol BS1 2LX
E: nerc-charity@bris.ac.uk
www.nerc.co.uk
The NERC funds and publishes research into the causes and treatment of eye diseases and disabilities and the prevention of blindness. The major part of the research it supports is carried out by the Unit of Ophthalmology at the University of Bristol, but research is also supported in Yorkshire, where it has a branch known as Yorkshire Eye Research, and in other eye research establishments throughout the UK.

National Family Mediation

4 Barnfield Hill, Exeter, Devon EX1 1SR
T: 0300 400 0636
F: 01392 271945
E: general@nfm.org.uk
www.nfm.org.uk
CEO: Jane Robey
Employees: 12
Volunteers: 1
Regional offices: 47

National Federation of Shopmobility UK

163 West Street, Fareham PO16 0EF
T: 0844 414 1850
E: info@shopmobilityuk.org
www.shopmobilityuk.org
Executive Director: Richard Ashdown
Provides advice, guidance and support to organisations and individuals considering developing Shopmobility in their locality. Influences policy on mobility and access issues and supports the organisations and individuals campaigning for improvements.
Employees: 2
Volunteers: 5
Regional offices: 1

National Federation of the Blind of the UK

Sir John Wilson House, 215 Kirkgate, Wakefield, West Yorkshire WF1 1JG
T: 020 8452 8336
Helpline: 01924 291313
F: 01924 200244
E: nfbuk@nfbuk.org
www.nfbuk.org
President: Norma Town
The Federation, through its blind and partially sighted membership, seeks to promote a better quality of life for all visually impaired people through local activities at branch level and nationally through campaigning.
Employees: 2
Volunteers: 1
Regional offices: 19

National Federation of Women's Institutes

104 New Kings Road, London SW6 4LY
T: 020 7371 9300
F: 020 7736 4333
E: pr@nfwi.org.uk
www.thewi.org.uk
General Secretary: Jana Osborne
The largest women's voluntary organisation in the UK, with over 212,000 members in over 6,600 WIs in England, Wales and the Islands. We offer women the best opportunity to

make an impact in their communities; to influence local, national and world issues affecting the social, economic and environmental life of families and communities; and to learn new and traditional skills.
Regional offices: 70

National Federation of Young Farmers' Clubs

YFC Centre, 10th Street, Stoneleigh Park, Kenilworth, Warwickshire CV8 2LG
T: 024 7685 7200
F: 024 7685 7229
E: james.eckley@nfyfc.org.uk
www.nfyfc.org.uk
Chief Executive: James Eckley
Employees: 70
Volunteers: 5000
Regional offices: 49

National Flood Forum

Old Snuff Mill Warehouse, Park Lane, Bewdley, Worcestershire DY12 2EL
T: 01299 403055
E: amanda.davies@floodforum.org.uk
www.nationalfloodforum.org.uk
Chief Executive: Paul Cobbing
The National Flood Forum is a charity dedicated to supporting and representing flood risk communities. It helps people to recognise, understand and reduce their flood risks and also helps people to recover if they have been flooded. The National Flood Forum also works to ensure that the needs of communities are fully recognised by Government, Environment Agency, local government and the insurance industry.
Employees: 14
Regional offices: 10
Income: £426,777 (2013-14)

National Gardens Scheme

Hatchlands, East Clandon, Guildford, Surrey GU4 7RT
T: 01483 211535
E: ngs@ngs.org.uk
www.ngs.org.uk
Opens gardens of quality, character and interest to the public for charity.

National Group on Homeworking

Office 26, 30-38 Dock Street, Leeds, Yorkshire LS10 1JF
T: 0113 245 4273
F: 0113 246 5616
E: admin@ngh.org.uk
www.ngh.org.uk/
Aims to educate the public and policy makers on issues concerning homeworking; to alleviate poverty among homeworkers by working, campaigning and lobbying to improve their working terms and conditions.
Employees: 8
Volunteers: 9

National Gulf Veterans and Families Association

Building E Office 8, Chamberlain Business Centre, Chamberlain Road, Hull, Humberside HU8 8HL
T: 0845 257 4853
F: 01482 808731
E: info@ngvfa.org.uk
www.ngvfa.org.uk
Chair: Nigel Graveston
Aims to relieve persons who served in the Gulf conflict and their families, and those involved in future desert conflicts who are in conditions of need, hardship, sickness or distress.
Employees: 6
Volunteers: 30
Income: £154,162 (2012-13)

National Housing Federation

Lion Court, 25 Procter Street WC1V 6NY
T: 020 7067 1010
F: 020 7067 1011
E: info@housing.org.uk
www.housing.org.uk
Chief Executive: David Orr
The National Housing Federation is the voice of affordable housing in England. We believe that everyone should have the home they need at a price they can afford. That's why we represent the work of housing associations and campaign for better housing. Our members provide two and a half million homes for more than five million people. Each year they invest in a diverse range of projects that help create strong, vibrant communities.
Employees: 135
Regional offices: 3

National Institute of Adult Continuing Education

Renaissance House, 20 Princess Road West, Leicester LE1 6TP
T: 0116 204 4200
F: 0116 285 4514
E: juliana.hancock@niace.org.uk
www.niace.org.uk
Director: Alan Tuckett
NIACE exists to encourage more and different adults to engage in learning of all kinds. We campaign for and celebrate the achievements of adult learners, young and old, in all their diversity. NIACE is the largest organisation working to promote the interests of learners and potential learners in England and Wales.
Employees: 275

National Institute of Medical Herbalists

Clover House, James Court, South Street, Exeter, Devon EX1 1EE
T: 01392 426022
F: 01392 498963
E: info@nimh.org.uk
www.nimh.org.uk
President: Desiree Shelley
Promotes the importance of herbal medicine. Makes people more aware of herbal medicine and its benefits. Assists with training to those who wish to pursue as a career.
Employees: 2

National Justice and Peace Network

NJPN, 39 Eccleston Square, London SW1V 1BX
T: 020 7901 4864
E: admin@justice-and-peace.org.uk
www.justice-and-peace.org.uk
Chair: Anne Peacey
We are a grassroots body working with groups and individuals of all faiths and none who share our aims and values based in the Christian Gospels. We engage with all who seek to challenge unjust structures which perpetuate poverty, violence and environmental degradation, including individuals, diocesan and local groups, national agencies and religious communities, offering opportunities for action, information sharing, friendship and mutual support.
Employees: 1
Volunteers: 9
Income: £70,000 (2014-15)

National Kidney Federation

The Point, Coach Road, Shireoaks, Worksop, Nottinghamshire S81 8BW
T: 01909 544999
Helpline: 0845 601 0209
F: 01909 481723
E: nkf@kidney.org.uk
www.kidney.org.uk
Chief Executive Officer: Timothy Statham
The National Kidney Federation (NKF) is the patient's voice and is fighting to achieve high-quality renal treatment across the UK. It is the only national kidney charity run by patients, for patients. It is funded entirely by donations and sponsorships. The Federation

is able to monitor and compare renal services across the country because of its unique structure. It is run by representatives of the 78 separate Kidney Patient Associations geographically spread across the UK.
Employees: 18

National Literacy Association

87 Grange Road, Ramsgate, Kent CT11 9QB
T: 01843 239952 (also fax)
Helpline: 07989 715732
E: wendy@nla.org.uk
www.nlaguide.co.uk
The NLA works in partnership with a range of organisations to promote awareness of and support children's literacy needs. As well as campaigning for the needs of the 20% of children who continue to underachieve, we do practical work in schools, with children in public care, with parent groups and in the wider community. We also produce a range of resources that are distributed free of charge to schools, parent groups and others.
Employees: 1
Volunteers: 15

National Literacy Trust

68 South Lambeth Road, London SW8 1RL
T: 020 7587 1842
F: 020 7587 1411
E: contact@literacytrust.org.uk
www.literacytrust.org.uk
Director: Jonathan Douglas
The National Literacy Trust is a national charity dedicated to raising literacy levels in the UK. Our research and analysis make us the leading authority on literacy. We run projects in the poorest communities, campaign to make literacy a priority for politicians and parents, and support schools.
Employees: 55
Volunteers: 5
Income: £3,144,000 (2014-15)

National Music for the Blind

2 High Park Road, Southport, Merseyside PR9 7QL
T: 01704 228010
E: music4blind@gmail.com
www.music4blind.webs.com
Director: Chris Mills
Provides a free fortnightly USB service to all visually handicapped persons in the UK. The USB memory stick contains nostalgic music programmes, plays, documentaries, comedy shows, old radio and much more from the vast library of the charity. 14 days to listen then return using freepost wallets.
Volunteers: 2

National Operatic and Dramatic Association

Peterborough PE1 2RZ
T: 0870 770 2480
F: 0870 770 2490
E: everyone@noda.org.uk
www.noda.org.uk
Promotes and improves the art of amateur theatre, to cultivate the improvement of public taste in the art.
Employees: 8
Volunteers: 180
Regional offices: 11

National Organisation for the Treatment of Abusers

PO Box 356, Hull HU12 8WR
T: 01482 896990 (also fax)
E: notaoffice@nota.co.uk
www.nota.co.uk
NOTA has a growing multidisciplinary membership comprising practitioners, managers and policy makers from the public, private and voluntary sectors. NOTA brings a wide variety of perspectives to interventions with sexual aggressors. It is the only professional multidisciplinary organisation in the UK and Ireland dedicated to work with sexual abusers. It is consequently in a unique position to promote and develop work in this area of public protection.
Regional offices: 13

National Osteoporosis Society

Camerton, Bath BA2 0PJ
T: 01761 471771
F: 01761 471104
E: h.kingman@nos.org.uk
www.nos.org.uk
The National Osteoporosis Society (NOS) campaigns to ensure that all people with or at risk of osteoporosis receive appropriate advice and treatment to enable them to avoid fractures and to enjoy a better quality of life. The NOS provides information and support for people with osteoporosis and their carers by promoting education for the public and health professionals, by lobbying government and health organisations and by encouraging fundraising for support services.
Employees: 60
Volunteers: 500

National Patients Support Trust

First Floor, 162 Shepherds Bush Road, Hammersmith, London W6 7PB
T: 020 7603 9770
E: npstcharity@btconnect.com
www.npst.co.uk
Trustee: Cornelius Oconnor
Provides relief and assistance for patients and former patients of NHS hospital trusts suffering from disease and from other physical and or mental disability or disabilities.
Employees: 6

National Pensioners Convention

Walkden House, 10 Melton Street, London NW1 2EJ
T: 020 7383 0388
E: admin@npcuk.org
www.npcuk.org
The NPC is Britain's biggest campaigning organisation for older people, representing over 1,000 local, regional and national pensioner groups with a total of 1.5 million members. The NPC promotes the welfare and interests of all pensioners. It lobbies MPs and government on policies affecting older people and stages an annual three-day Pensioners Parliament in Blackpool, where over 1,000 representatives discuss issues of concern.
Employees: 4
Regional offices: 18

National Playbus Association

Brunswick Court, Brunswick Square, Bristol BS2 8PE
T: 01458 850804
E: playbus@playbus.org.uk
www.workingonwheels.org
Promotes the use of playbuses and converted vehicles as mobile community resources, and acts as an umbrella organisation that promotes good practice in mobile community work.

National Portage Association

Kings Court, 17 School Road, Hall Green, Birmingham, West Midlands B28 8JG
T: 0121 244 1807
F: 0121 244 1801
E: info@portage.org.uk
www.portage.org.uk
Portage is a home-visiting educational service for pre-school children with additional support needs and their families.
Employees: 5

National Reye's Syndrome Foundation of the UK

15 Nicholas Gardens, Woking, Surrey GU22 8SD
T: 01932 346843
E: gordon.denney@ukgateway.net
www.reyessyndrome.co.uk
Promotes research into the cause, treatment, cure and prevention of Reye's syndrome and Reye-like illnesses; provides support for

parents whose children have suffered from these diseases and creates awareness and professional knowledge.

National Rheumatoid Arthritis Society

Unit B4, Westacott Business Centre, Westacott Way, Littlewick Green, Maidenhead, Berkshire SL6 3RT
T: 0845 458 3969
Helpline: 0800 298 7650
F: 0845 458 3971
E: enquiries@nras.org.uk
www.nras.org.uk
Chief Executive: Ailsa Bosworth
NRAS provides support, information and advocacy for people with rheumatoid arthritis and juvenile idiopathic arthritis, their families, friends and carers. We are also a resource for health professionals with an interest in rheumatology and work closely with rheumatology teams across the UK.
Employees: 20

National Society for Clean Air and Environmental Protection

44 Grand Parade, Brighton BN2 9QA
T: 01273 878777
E: pmitchell@nsca.org.uk
www.nsca.org.uk
Aims to secure environmental improvement by promoting clean air through the reduction of air pollution, noise and other contaminants, while having regard for other aspects of the environment.

National Society for Phenylketonuria (UK) Ltd

PO Box 3143, Purley CR8 9DD
T: 020 3397 7320
Helpline: 0303 040 1090
E: info@nspku.org
www.nspku.org
Chair: Eric Lange
The NSPKU exists to help and support people with PKU, their families and carers. The NSPKU actively promotes the care and treatment of people with PKU and works closely with medical professionals in the UK. It organises conferences and study days throughout the UK, produces a wide range of publications (including food lists) for parents, adults with PKU and medical professionals. The NSPKU also sponsors medical research into the condition.
Employees: 3
Volunteers: 15

National Society of Allotments and Leisure Gardeners

O'Dell House, Hunters Road, Corby, Northamptonshire NN17 5JE
T: 01536 266576
F: 01536 264509
E: geoff@nsalg.demon.co.uk
www.nsalg.org.uk
National Secretary: Geoff Stokes
National representative body for the allotment movement.
Employees: 5

National Trust

Heelis, Kemble Drive, Swindon, Wiltshire SN2 2NA
T: 01793 817400
F: 01793 817401
E: enquiries@thenationaltrust.org.uk
www.nationaltrust.org.uk
We protect and open to the public over 300 historic houses and gardens, and 49 industrial monuments and mills. We also look after forests, woods, fens, beaches, farmland, downs, moorland, islands, archaeological remains, castles, nature reserves and villages.
Employees: 4000
Volunteers: 40000
Regional offices: 11

National Voices

1st Floor, Bride House, 18-20 Bride Lane, London EC4Y 8EE
T: 020 3176 0738
E: info@nationalvoices.org.uk
www.nationalvoices.org.uk
Chief Executive: Jeremy Taylor
National Voices is the coalition of health and social care charities working to strengthen the voice of patients, service users and those who represent them
Employees: 9
Income: £506,474 (2013-14)

National Women's Register

23 Vulcan House, Vulcan Road North, Norwich, Norfolk NR6 6AQ
T: 01603 406767
F: 01603 407003
E: office@nwr.org.uk
www.nwr.org.uk
Chair of Trustees: Pamela McKee
Employees: 5
Volunteers: 24

National Youth Agency

Eastgate House, 19-23 Humberstone Road, Leicester, Leicestershire LE5 3GJ
T: 0116 242 7350
F: 0116 285 3777
E: nya@nya.org.uk
www.nya.org.uk
chief executive: Fiona Blacke
We are the national charity for youth work in England. Founded in 1964, we believe investing in young people's personal and social development helps them overcome challenges and reach their potential. We want to ensure young people get access to the youth workers they need, so we seek to secure youth work through policy and advocacy; supporting youth workers to do their jobs better and; securing new resources.
Employees: 48
Regional offices: 1

National Youth Orchestra of Great Britain

32 Old School House, Britannia Road, Kingswood, Bristol BS15 8DB
T: 0117 960 0477
E: info@nyo.org.uk
www.nyo.org.uk
Works to discover and foster exceptional musical talent in young people and to help provide them with tuition and experience in orchestral musical skills; to give concerts of the highest standard; and to inspire young people to take an interest in music.

National Youthbike

PO Box 27, Horncastle, Lincolnshire LN9 6XB
T: 01507 524432
E: nationalyouthbike@yahoo.co.uk
www.youthbike.com
Chair: Tony Nightingale
Promotes the education and social development of young people in the UK in life skills, engineering, design and information technology by assisting them in their preparation for and participation in the annual National Youthbike weekend event.
Volunteers: 17

Natural Death Centre

In The Hill House, Watley Lane, Twyford, Winchester SO21 1QX
T: 01962 712690
E: contact@naturaldeath.org.uk
www.naturaldeath.org.uk
Manager: Rosie Inman-Cook
Aim to improve the quality of dying and funerals. Information for families caring for the dying at home. Also how to get your affairs in order. Empowers people organising inexpensive and or environmentally friendly funerals, sometimes without funeral

directors. Advice on rights and laws concerning burials on private land or at natural burial grounds. List suppliers, who deal direct with the public. Advice on keeping costs down. Telephone helpline on all related topics.
Volunteers: 5

Nautilus International

12 The Shrubberies, George Lane,
South Woodford, London E18 1BD
T: 020 8989 6677
F: 020 8530 1015
E: mjess@nautilusint.org
www.nautilusint.org
General Secretary: Mark Dickinson
The Nautilus Welfare Fund, a charity administered by Nautilus International, provides support and assistance for retired seafarers and their dependants.
Employees: 65
Regional offices: 2

Naz Foundation International

2nd Floor, 5 Harbour Exchange,
London E14 9GE
T: 020 7570 6092
F: 020 7691 7062
E: kim@nfi.net
www.nfi.net
Chief Executive: Shivananda Khan
With a primary focus on males who have sex with males (MSM), NFI's mission is to empower socially excluded and disadvantaged males to secure for themselves social justice, equity, health and wellbeing through technical, institutional and financial support.
Regional offices: 1

NCVO Charities Evaluation Services (CES)

Society Building, 8 All Saints Street,
London N1 9RL
T: 020 7520 2535
E: consultancy@ncvo.org.uk
www.ncvo.org.uk/consultancy

Nell Bank

Denton Road, Ilkley,
West Yorkshire LS29 0DE
T: 01943 602032
F: 01943 601690
E: nell.bank@bradford.gov.uk
www.nellbank.com
Centre Manager: Bruce Fowler
Educates young people in the principles of responsible citizenship by providing them with training and recreation and community service opportunities. Provides affordable day and residential outdoor education experience in stunning and contrasting environments to 20,000 children and young people each year. Enables hard-to-reach groups to access outdoor experience via nationally significant activities, adapted accommodation and equipment.
Employees: 9
Volunteers: 100

Network 81

Stansted, Essex CM24 8AJ
T: 0845 077 4056
Helpline: 0845 077 4055
F: 0845 077 4057
E: network81@btconnect.com
www.network81.org
Chair: Eirwen Grenfell-Essam
Network 81 offers help and support to parents throughout all stages of assessment and statementing as outlined in the Education Act 1996 and Code of Practice 2001. Our national helpline offers an individual service linked to a national network of local contacts. Network 81 produces a range of literature aimed at familiarising parents with the assessment and statementing procedures. We also run extensive training programmes for parents and those working with parents.
Employees: 4
Volunteers: 80

Network for Peace

5 Caledonian Road, London N1 9DY
T: 07794 036602
E: mail@networkforpeace.org.uk
www.networkforpeace.org.uk
Coordinator: Claire Poyner
After the demise of the National Peace Council, one of the oldest peace organisations in the UK, Network for Peace was set up with the aim of continuing with the networking role of the NPC. NfP provides a regularly updated website, which includes links to websites of members, news and an extensive diary of events. This information is also available as a bi-monthly newsletter.
Employees: 1

Neuroblastoma UK

54 Forest Road, Richmond TW9 3BZ
T: 020 8940 4353
E: secretary@neuroblastoma.org.uk
www.neuroblastoma.org.uk
Chair: Susan Hay
Funding vital research to find new treatments and improve existing treatments for neuroblastoma, an aggressive childhood cancer.
Volunteers: 10
Income: £400,000 (2013-14)

Neurological Alliance

Stroke House, 240 City Road,
London EC1V 2PR
T: 020 7566 1540
F: 020 7735 1555
E: admin@neural.org.uk
www.neural.org.uk
The Neurological Alliance is a collaborative forum of a wide range of neurological charities. The Alliance campaigns for the highest standards of service and care for the 10 million people in the UK with a neurological condition.
Employees: 2
Regional offices: 13

New Bridge Foundation

1a Elm Park, London, 1a Elm Park SW2 2TX
T: 020 8671 3856
E: info@newbridgefoundation.org.uk
www.newbridgefoundation.org.uk
New Bridge was founded in 1956 to create links between the offender and the community. The keynote service remains the friendship and support given by volunteers to longer-term prisoners, especially those no longer in contact with family and friends.
Employees: 3
Volunteers: 200

New Choices for Youth

E: marcias@ncytrust.org

New Economics Foundation

3 Jonathan Street, Vauxhall,
London SE11 5NH
T: 020 7820 6300
F: 020 7820 6301
E: info@neweconomics.org
www.neweconomics.org
Executive Director: Stewart Wallis
Aims to put people and the environment at the centre of economic thinking. We aim to improve quality of life by promoting innovative solutions that challenge mainstream thinking on economic, environment and social issues. We work in partnership and put people and the planet first.
Employees: 45
Volunteers: 2
Regional offices: 1

New Horizon Youth Centre

68 Chalton Street, London NW1 1JR
T: 020 7388 5560
F: 020 7388 5848
E: info@nhyouthcentre.org.uk
www.nhyouthcentre.org.uk
Director: Shelagh O'Connor
New Horizon Youth Centre is a day centre working with young people age 16 to 21 who are vulnerable, homeless or at risk. New Horizon Youth Centre aims to enable young people to gain skills and knowledge to improve their life chances and to help them move from adolescence into adulthood.
Employees: 28
Volunteers: 45
Regional offices: 1

New Kadampa Tradition – International Kadampa Buddhist Union

Conishead Priory, Ulverston
T: 01229 588533
E: info@kadampa.org
www.kadampa.org
General Secretary: Stephen Cowing

New Philanthropy Capital

3rd Floor, Downstream Building, 1 London Bridge, London SE1 9BG
T: 020 7785 6300
F: 020 7785 6301
E: jjames@philanthropycapital.org
www.philanthropycapital.org
Chief Executive: Nigel Harris
NPC advises donors on how to make their giving to charities more effective. Our aim is to increase the quantity and quality of resources available to the charitable sector. We do this through a combination of independent research and tailored advice. Our research identifies charities that are achieving excellent results and where funds and resources can be targeted most effectively. Our advice for donors guides them on how to ensure their money has high impact.
Employees: 38
Volunteers: 3

New Start Trust

Alderman Downward House, 1st Floor, The Birtles, Civic Centre, Wythenshawe, Lancashire M22 5RF
T: 0161 498 0615
F: 0161 436 5570
E: info@newstarttrust.org
www.newstarttrust.org
Works to relieve poverty, sickness and distress for those people who are dependent on or affected by addiction to drugs.
Employees: 10
Volunteers: 2

Newcastle Action for Parent and Toddler Groups Initiative

Heaton Community Centre, Trewhitt Road, Heaton, Newcastle upon Tyne, Tyne and Wear NE6 5DY
T: 0191 265 6158 (also fax)
E: karen@napi.org.uk
www.napi.org.uk
Project Manager: Karen Williams
To promote the education and development of under school aged children in the City of Newcastle upon Tyne by the provision of advice, information and support services for parent and toddler groups and like groups.
Employees: 12
Income: ££220.00 (2014-15)

Newcastle Council for Voluntary Service

Higham House, Higham Place, Newcastle upon Tyne NE1 8AF
T: 0191 232 7445
F: 0191 230 5640
E: sally.young@cvsnewcastle.org.uk
www.cvsnewcastle.org.uk
Chief Executive: Sally.Young
Newcastle CVS works to support, develop, promote, connect and represent voluntary and community organisations in Newcastle. Our work helps to make Newcastle a better place by helping to develop a thriving voluntary and community sector. We do this through our three service areas: supporting and developing local organisations to thrive; networking and involving local organisations to engage; representing and influencing on behalf of the voluntary and community sector. Newcastle CVS also runs Ellison Services, a community accountancy organisation providing payroll
Employees: 32
Volunteers: 70
Regional offices: 1
Income: £998,000 (2012-13)

Newcastle Tenants and Residents Federation

Fawdon Community Centre, Fawdon Park Road, Fawdon, Newcastle upon Tyne, Tyne and Wear NE3 2PL
T: 0191 285 2724
E: enquiries@newcastletenantsfed.org.uk
www.newcastletenantsfed.org.uk
Newcastle Tenants and Residents Federation is a registered charity representing tenants and residents associations (TARAs) throughout Newcastle upon Tyne. We are also one of the oldest Federation's in the country, having been formed in 1977. Our focus is on working with tenants and residents to relieve deprivation and improve housing conditions and living environments across the city.
Employees: 4
Volunteers: 2

Newlife

Newlife Centre, Hemlock Way, Cannock, Staffordshire WS11 7GF
T: 01543 462777
E: enquiries@info.newlifecharity.co.uk
www.newlifecharity.co.uk
Medical research, awareness and service, relevant to all birth defects.

NHS Confederation

29 Bressenden Place, London SW1E 5DD
T: 020 7074 3282
F: 020 7959 7273
E: info@nhsconfed.org
www.nhsconfed.org
We help our members provide better health and healthcare by: influencing the development and implementation of policy and the wider public debate on the full range of health and health services issues, speaking out independently on behalf of our members; supporting health leaders through information sharing and networking; promoting excellence in employment to improve the working lives of staff and, through them, to provide better care for patients; providing tailored services and products to enable boards to develop their objectives.
Employees: 40

Niemann-Pick Disease Group UK

Suite 2, Vermont House, Concord, Washington, Tyne and Wear NE37 2SQ
T: 0191 415 0693
E: niemann-pick@zetnet.co.uk
www.niemannpick.org.uk
Executive Director: Toni Mathieson
The group aims to make a positive difference to the lives of those affected by Niemann-Pick diseases and their families, through the provision of effective support in the three main areas of care, information and research.
Employees: 4
Volunteers: 12

No Panic

Jubilee House, 74 High Street, Madeley, Telford, Shropshire TF5 4AH
T: 01952 680460
Helpline: 0844 967 4848
E: admin@nopanic.org.uk
www.nopanic.org.uk
Chairperson: Keith Stenning
Works for the relief and rehabilitation of people suffering from panic attacks, phobias and obsessive/compulsive disorders.
Employees: 2
Volunteers: 70

Noise Abatement Society

44 Grand Parade, Brighton BN2 9QA
T: 01273 682223
E: nas@noiseabatementsociety.fsnet.co.uk
www.noiseabatementsociety.com
The Noise Abatement Society is a registered charity. Its aims are to eliminate excessive noise in all its forms by campaigning to raise awareness, by lobbying parliament and through education to improve the quality of life for all. It is an active and effective problem-solving organisation with strong contacts in government. The society runs the only telephone noise helpline in the UK.

Nordoff-Robbins Music Therapy

2 Lissenden Gardens, London NW5 1PQ
T: 020 7267 4496
F: 020 7267 4369
E: admin@nordoff-robbins.org.uk
www.nordoff-robbins.org.uk
Provides music therapy treatment for people with special needs and training for music therapists.
Employees: 50
Volunteers: 50

Norfolk Community Law Service Ltd

E: ros@ncls.co.uk

Norm UK

PO Box 71, Stone, Staffordshire ST15 0SF
T: 01785 814044 (also fax)
E: info@norm-uk.org
www.15square.org.uk
Aims to advance the education of the public in all matters relating to circumcision and other forms of surgical alteration of the genitals, including alternative treatments and offering information and advice on such matters.
Employees: 1
Volunteers: 14

North Taunton Partnership

Priorswood Community Centre, 13-14 Priorswood Place, Eastwick Road, Taunton, Somerset TA2 7JW
T: 01823 353643
E: lesley.priorswoodcc@yahoo.co.uk
www.priorswoodcommunitycentre.co.uk
Manager: Lesley Thomas
The Charity's objects are to promote charitable purposes for the benefit of the community of North Taunton and in particular the advancement of education, the promotion of health and the relief of poverty, sickness and distress. These aims are achieved by offering advice surgeries, social groups, exercise classes and activities for young people during the school holidays through our Pride in Priorswood program.
Employees: 4
Volunteers: 32
Regional offices: 1
Income: £81,087 (2014-15)

Northallerton & District Voluntary Service Association

Community House, 10 South Parade, Northallerton, North Yorkshire DL7 8SE
T: 01609 780458
E: secretary@ndvsa.co.uk
www.ndvsa.co.uk
Manager: Hazel Kirby
NDVSA is a registered Charity providing advice, information, training and support to volunteers and voluntary and community groups in the local area. We also provide some services for local people.
Employees: 12
Volunteers: 100+

Northern Ireland Council for Voluntary Action

61 Duncairn Gardens, Belfast BT15 2GB
T: 028 9087 7777
F: 028 9087 7799
E: info@nicva.org
www.nicva.org
Chief Executive: Seamus McAleavey
NICVA is an umbrella organisation, seeking to represent the interests of voluntary and community organisations throughout Northern Ireland. In its role as a voluntary sector development agency, NICVA acts as a catalyst to promote innovation and new approaches to the challenge of social need.
Employees: 45

Norwich Door To Door

E: n-norwich@btconnect.com

Norwood

Broadway House, Stanmore, Middlesex HA7 4HB
T: 020 8954 4555
F: 020 8420 6800
E: suzanne.nehard@norwood.org.uk
www.norwood.org.uk
Chief Executive: Norma Brier
Norwood is Anglo-Jewry's largest children and family services organisation, supporting children and their families, and adults, in coping with learning disabilities and social disadvantage. Every year we help thousands of children and their families by providing vital, specialised care to the most vulnerable members of our community.
Employees: 1100
Volunteers: 700
Regional offices: 4

Notts Housing Advice

E: admin@nottshousingadvice.org.uk

Nova Wakefield District Limited

11 Upper York Street, Wakefield, Wakefield, West Yorkshire WF1 3FQ
T: 01924 367418
E: fiona.cooper@nova-wd.org.uk
www.nova-wd.org.uk
CEO: Alison Haskins
Nova Wakefield District is the support agency for the community and voluntary sector. We work with organisations big and small throughout the district, helping with development, volunteering, funding, contracts, governance and influencing issues pertinent to the sector.
Employees: 13
Volunteers: 13

NSPCC

Weston House, 42 Curtain Road, London EC2A 3NH
T: 020 7825 2500
Helpline: 0808 800 5000
F: 020 7825 2525
E: info@nspcc.org.uk
www.nspcc.org.uk
Chief Executive: Andrew Flanagan
Employees: 2600
Volunteers: 27500
Regional offices: 60

Nubian Life Resource Centre Ltd

50 Commonwealth Avenue, London W12 7QR
T: 020 8749 8017
E: info@nubian-life.org.uk
Provides for the relief of elderly African Caribbean people living in the UK.
Employees: 14

Nuffield Trust

59 New Cavendish Street, London W1G 7LP
T: 020 7631 8450
F: 020 7631 8451
E: info@nuffieldtrust.org.uk
www.nuffieldtrust.org.uk
Chief Operating Officer: Kim Beazor
The Trust's mission is to promote independent analysis and informed debate on UK healthcare policy, with a particular focus on long-term, strategic direction. The core objectives are: to improve the health of the people of the UK, to improve the quality of healthcare and to improve the quality of health policy; to communicate evidence and encourage an exchange around developed or developing knowledge in order to illuminate recognised and emerging issues.
Employees: 5

Number One Community Trust (TW) Ltd

1 Rowan Tree Road, Tunbridge Wells, Kent TN2 5PX
T: 01892 514544
E: onecommunity@btconnect.com
www.numberonecommunitytrust.org.uk
Chair of Trustees: Adrian Cory
Runs a community centre in a deprived area offering a wide range of services including pre-school, café and a variety of clubs/groups for people of all ages. Aims to: promote the physical, mental and spiritual health and wellbeing of local residents; improve the social and economic wellbeing of local residents; support the advancement of education and training; assist those who are seeking employment; and encourage environmental improvements in the neighbourhood.
Employees: 9
Volunteers: 47
Regional offices: 1
Income: £227,308 (2012-13)

Nurture Group Network

18a Victoria Park Square, Bethnal Green, London E2 9PF
T: 020 3475 8980
E: info@nurturegroups.org
www.nurturegroups.org
Chief Executive: Kevin Kibble
To promote nurture groups as an effective way of meeting the needs of vulnerable children and young people and to ensure their continuing quality through the delivery of accredited training, quality monitoring, publications, research and information exchange.
Employees: 11
Regional offices: 2
Income: £185,667 (2012-13)

NYAS (National Youth Advocacy Service)

Egerton House, 2 Tower Road, Birkenhead, Wirral, Merseyside CH41 1FN
T: 0151 649 8700
Helpline: 0300 330 3131
F: 0151 649 8701
E: main@nyas.net
www.nyas.net
Chief Executive: Christine Renouf
NYAS offers an unusual range of preventive interdisciplinary welfare and legal services, information, consultation, support and representation to children, young people and vulnerable adults in England and Wales. It has a team of in-house lawyers and a sessional workforce of more than 350 children's advocates and caseworkers, who include some of the most experienced welfare professionals in the country.
Employees: 130
Volunteers: 65
Regional offices: 8

Nystagmus Network

25 PenyLan Terrace, Cardiff, South Glamorgan CF23 9EU
T: 0845 634 2630
Helpline: 029 2045 4242
E: info@nystagmusnet.org
www.nystagmusnet.org
Chair: Richard Wilson
NN provides support and information to people with nystagmus. We raise awareness of the challenges presented by this incurable eye condition which affects at least 60,000 people in the UK. We also encourage and fund scientific, medical and social research into nystagmus.
Employees: 3
Volunteers: 12
Income: £120,000 (2014-15)

Oakleaf Enterprise

101 Walnut Tree Close, Guildford, Surrey GU1 4UQ
T: 01483 303649
F: 01483 537069
E: deeptiparmar@oakleaf-enterprise.org
www.oakleaf-enterprise.org
Oakleaf is the only mental health charity in Surrey working as a social enterprise to provide vocational training for those suffering from mental health issues. We offer training in horticulture, upholstery, IT and print finishing, enabling people to acquire new skills and ultimately return to work. Alongside these we offer a range of Social Inclusion Activities that cater towards building confidence, physical health and wellbeing. Through their placement at Oakleaf, clients are able to gain up-to-date qualifications, practical experience and increase their confidence levels.
Employees: 20
Volunteers: 40

Oasis Charitable Trust

Oasis Trust, 1 Kennington Road, London SE1 7QP
T: 020 7921 4200
E: enquiries@oasisuk.org
www.oasistrust.org
Group CEO: Joy Madeiros
Oasis is a community, housing, education and social-transformation charity committed to building communities where everyone can belong, overcome life's obstacles and reach their God-given potential. Working in 36 communities we pioneer integrated services such as Academies, food banks, youth work, housing provision and Community Churches. Inspired by the teachings of Jesus Christ, Oasis is a fully inclusive movement working to

make life in all its fullness a greater reality for every person and community.

OBJECT

PO Box 63639, London SW9 1BQ
E: ido@object.org.uk
www.object.org.uk

OCD Action

Suite 506-507, Davina House,
137-149 Goswell Road, London EC1V 7ET
T: 020 7253 5272
Helpline: 0845 390 6232
E: info@ocdaction.org.uk
www.ocdaction.org.uk
Director: Joel Rose
OCD Action is the largest national charity focusing on Obsessive Compulsive Disorder. The charity provides support and information to anybody affected by OCD, works to raise awareness of the disorder amongst the public and healthcare workers, and strives to secure a better deal for people with OCD. Formed by a group of leading professionals and volunteers in 1994, the charity is recognised as a strong voice for people with OCD and a vital source of help.
Employees: 7
Volunteers: 30
Regional offices: 2
Income: £270,000 (2012-13)

Ockenden International

Constitution Hill, Woking,
Surrey GU22 7UU
T: 01483 772012
E: oi@ockenden.org.uk
www.ockenden.org.uk
Ockenden works to promote independence and self-reliance amongst refugees, displaced people, returnees and their host communities throughout the world.

Odyssey Trust (UK)

Omnibus Business Centre,
39-41 North Road, London N7 9DP
T: 020 7700 6177
F: 020 7700 6232
E: info@theodyssey.co.uk
www.theodyssey.co.uk
The Trust provides high-quality treatment and support services that respond to the changing needs of people affected by substance misuse.

Off Centre Hackney

E: martin.williams@offcentre.org.uk

Officers' Association

1st Floor, Mountbarrow House,
London SW1W 9RB
T: 020 7808 4160
F: 020 7808 4161
E: info@officersassociation.org.uk
www.officersassociation.org.uk
The Officers' Association (OA), founded over 90 years ago, is the only charity dedicated exclusively to supporting officers and ex-officers and their dependants from all three services. It achieves this in two ways: providing employment services for service leavers and ex-serving officers; providing benevolence services in the form of financial and welfare support. The OA offers a resource based on a thorough understanding of the background and needs of commissioned officers and their families.
Employees: 24
Volunteers: 600

Olmec

London SE11 5JA
T: 0845 880 0110
E: bparker@olmec-ec.org.uk
www.olmec-ec.org.uk
We are a dynamic community investment foundation and work alongside disadvantaged communities to deliver programmes that lead to positive impact. We are driven by principles of self-help, empowerment and social justice and our work ranges from addressing issues of under-representation of minority communities, to breaking down the barriers to employment faced by refugees. We also engage in research and use it as a tool to influence policy and provision.
Employees: 8

One Plus One Marriage and Partnership Research

1 Benjamin Street, London EC1M 5QG
T: 020 7553 9530
E: kb@oneplusone.org.uk
www.oneplusone.org.uk
Director: Penny Mansfield
OnePlusOne puts research into practice, investigating what makes relationships work - or fall apart. We support individuals and couples to manage relationship issues earlier and more effectively, and champion the adoption and implementation of policies and services that value relationships, espouse early relationship support and encourage a culture of relationship support. We run self-help websites www.thecoupleconnection.net for individuals and couples and www.theparentconnection.org.uk for separated parents or those considering separation.
Employees: 23
Volunteers: 8
Income: £2,387,000 (2014-15)

One World Trust

3 Whitehall Court, London SW1A 2EL
T: 020 7766 3470
F: 020 7839 7718
E: gbergh@oneworldtrust.org
www.oneworldtrust.org
The One World Trust promotes education and research into the changes required within global organisations in order to achieve the eradication of poverty, injustice and war. It conducts research on practical ways to make global organisations more responsive to the people they affect, and on how the rule of law can be applied equally to all. It educates political leaders and opinion-formers about the findings of its research.
Employees: 8
Volunteers: 12

Online Centres Foundation

The Workstation, 15 Paternoster Row,
Sheffield, Unknown S1 2BX
T: 0114 227 0035
E: alison.broadley@ukonlinecentres.com
www.ukonlinecentres.com

Onside

E: martine.vantomme@onside-advocacy.org.uk

Open College Network YHR

OCNYHR, OCN House,
Lower Warrengate, Wakefield,
West Yorkshire WF1 1SA
T: 01924 434600
F: 01924 364213
E: enquiries@ocnyhr.org.uk
www.ocnyhr.org.uk
Chief Executive: John Lawton
OCNYHR is a national Awarding Organisation committed to providing a high quality and responsive accreditation service. Regulated by Ofqual, OCNYHR offers a wide range of qualifications within the Qualifications and Credit Framework (QCF). At OCNYHR, we also provide our Recognised Centres with bespoke accreditation through our Customised Accreditation Service. OCNYHR is also an Access Validating Agency, licensed by the Quality Assurance Agency (QAA), to

develop, approve and certificate Access to Higher Education Diplomas.
Employees: 30
Income: £1,500,000 (2012-13)

Open Doors International Language School

E: croberts@odils.com

Open Spaces Society

25a Bell Street, Henley-on-Thames, Oxfordshire RG9 2BA
T: 01491 573535
E: hq@oss.org.uk
www.oss.org.uk
General Secretary: Kate Ashbrook
We campaign to create and conserve common land, village greens, open spaces and rights of public access, in town and country, in England and Wales.
Employees: 5
Volunteers: 40

Operation Black Vote

18A Victoria Park Square, London E2 9PB
T: 020 8983 5474
F: 020 7684 3889
E: simon@charter88.org.uk
www.obv.org.uk
Operation Black Vote began in July 1996 as a collaboration between two organisations: Charter88 (which campaigns for democratic reform) and the 1990 Trust, the only national Black generic policy research and networking organisation, which uses information technology as a primary means of communication.
Employees: 8
Volunteers: 4

Operation Florian

6 Worcester Close, Bracebridge Heath, Lincoln, Lincolnshire LN4 2TY
T: 01522 569728 (also fax)
E: opflorian@aol.com
www.operationflorian.com
Operation Florian was established as a charity in 1995. It is a UK Fire Service Humanitarian Charity working to promote the protection of life amongst communities in need, world wide, by the provision of equipment and training to improve fire fighting and rescue capabilities.
Employees: 1

Opportunity Links

Trust Court, Vision Park, Histon, Cambridge CB24 9PW
T: 01223 566522
F: 01223 500281
E: info@openobjects.com
www.opportunity-links.org.uk
Managing Director: Paul Bogen
Opportunity Links works with the public sector to develop and manage quality information that supports families in making important life choices.
Employees: 62
Volunteers: 4
Regional offices: 2

Optua

Optua House, Hill View Business Park, Claydon, Ipswich, Suffolk IP6 0AJ
T: 01473 836777
F: 01473 836778
E: enquiries@optua.org.uk
www.optua.org.uk
Chief Executive: Colin Poole
We are a Suffolk-based disability charity providing a range of services and opportunities for disabled people including leisure and sport activities, community transport, advice and advocacy, community brain injury services and homecare.
Employees: 230
Volunteers: 300
Regional offices: 2

OPUS

26 Fernhurst Road, London SW6 7JW
T: 020 7736 3844
E: director@opus.org.uk
www.opus.org.uk
Chair: Steve Oram
OPUS is an organisation of people who believe that it is important that we and others develop a deeper understanding of organisational and societal processes and the way in which we relate to them; and that we use such understanding to act with authority and responsibility in our various roles. OPUS exists therefore to promote the development of the reflective citizen.
Volunteers: 350
Regional offices: 24
Income: £89,330 (2014-15)

Orbis Charitable Trust

4th Floor, Fergusson House, 124-128 City Road, London EC1V 2NJ
T: 020 7608 7260
F: 020 7278 5231
E: info@orbis.org.uk
www.orbis.org.uk
Orbis is a nonprofit humanitarian organisation dedicated to blindness prevention and treatment in developing countries.
Employees: 28
Volunteers: 1

Orione Care

13 Lower Teddington Road, Hampton Wick, Kingston upon Thames KT1 4EU
T: 020 8977 5130
E: info@orionecare.org
www.orionecare.org
Orione Care is a working name of The Sons of Divine Providence, a charity that provides housing and care services for older people and people with learning disabilities. The charity has a Roman Catholic ethos but people of all faiths and none are welcome to use its services.
Employees: 112
Income: £3,600,000 (2012-13)

Ormiston Families

Central Office, 333 Felixstowe Road, Ipswich, Suffolk IP3 9BU
T: 01473 705038
F: 01473 705025
E: income.generation@ormiston.org
www.ormiston.org
Chief Executive: Mark Heasman
Ormiston Families supports children, young people and their families to manage the challenges they face and improve their life chances. We run four core programmes across the East of England supporting young children, prisoners' families, school students and local communities. Our vision is that ' every child and young person is loved, nurtured and valued'.
Employees: 155
Volunteers: 300

Orphans In Need

22a Atlas Way, Sheffield S4 7QQ
T: 0800 999 0852
E: info@orphansinneed.org
www.orphansinneed.org
Orphans in Need helps some of the world's most vulnerable and needy people. It is committed to the alleviation of all forms of poverty and deprivation, in all parts of the globe. However, the organisation's primary focus is on orphans and widows; often the weakest members of any society, and the most affected by the scourge of poverty.
Employees: 4
Volunteers: 30
Regional offices: 2

Orphans Relief Fund and Charitable Trust

163-165 Dukes Road, Park Royal, London W3 0SL
T: 020 8205 8272
F: 020 8205 8922
E: orfact@hotmail.com
www.orfact.co.uk
Works for the relief of poverty and advancement of education for orphans, widows, refugees, the impoverished and the vulnerable around the world. This is carried out through education and support services, vocational training and development projects and emergency aid and relief.
Employees: 6
Volunteers: 6

Otherwise Club

1 Croxley Road, London W9 3HH
T: 020 8969 0893
E: info@otherwiseclub.org
www.theotherwiseclub.org.uk
Aims to advance the education of children whose families have opted for out-of-school education and who remain responsible for their children's education at all times, without distinction of race, sex, political, religious or other opinions, through the provision of facilities.

Outreach International

The Cambodia Trust, 4C Station Yard, Thame, Oxfordshire OX9 3UH
T: 01844 214844
E: www.outreachinternational.co.uk
www.cambodiatrust.com
Outreach International is committed to cross-cultural exchange and education. We combine the desire of young people to travel and work overseas with the needs of local communities. We give volunteers a deep understanding of traditional life in Ecuador, Cambodia and the Pacific coast of Mexico, whilst providing benefits to the host communities and children from humble backgrounds.

Outsiders

4S Leroy House, 436 Essex Road, London N1 3QP
T: 01997 421019
F: 020 7460 2247
E: trust@outsiders.org.uk
www.outsiders.org.uk/outsidersclub
Provides help for people with physical and social disabilities, especially those who live in emotional isolation.

Ovacome

B5 City Cloisters, 196 Old Street, London EC1V 9FR
T: 020 7299 6654
Helpline: 020 7299 6650
E: ovacome@ovacome.org.uk
www.ovacome.org.uk
Ovacome is a support organisation for all those affected by ovarian cancer. It links sufferers, provides information, runs a support line, and awareness-raising activities.
Employees: 6

Ovarian Cancer Action

London NW1 0JH
T: 0300 456 4700
F: 0300 456 4708
E: info@ovarian.org.uk
www.ovarian.org.uk
Chief Executive: Gilda Witte
Ovarian Cancer Action (OCA) is the UK's leading ovarian cancer charity, dedicated to improving survival rates for women with ovarian cancer. It funds innovative research into the disease at the Ovarian Cancer Action Research Centre (OCARC); raises awareness of the symptoms with national awareness campaigns aimed at women and healthcare workers; and gives a voice to those affected by it, acting as an advocate with policy makers, healthcare professionals and scientists.
Employees: 10
Volunteers: 50
Regional offices: 1

Overeaters Anonymous

PO Box 19, Stretford, Manchester M32 9EB
T: 07000 784985
E: oagbnsb@hotmail.com
www.oagb.org.uk
Welcomes those with the desire to stop eating compulsively, offering identification and acceptance; relieves our compulsion to overeat/undereat, or an obsession with food/dieting by living by spiritual principles based on the 12 steps of Alcoholics Anonymous.

Overseas Development Institute

203 Blackfriars Road, London SE1 8NJ
T: 020 7922 0300
F: 020 7922 0399
E: p.gee@odi.org.uk
www.odi.org.uk
Director: Alison Evans
Our mission is to inspire and inform policy and practice that lead to the reduction of poverty, the alleviation of suffering and the achievement of sustainable livelihoods in developing countries. We do this by locking together high-quality applied research, practical policy advice, and policy-focused dissemination and debate. We work with partners in the public and private sectors, in both developing and developed countries.
Employees: 184
Volunteers: 20

Oxfam GB

John Smith Drive, Cowley, Oxford, Oxfordshire OX4 2JY
T: 0300 200 1300
F: 01865 472600
E: givetime@oxfam.org.uk
www.oxfam.org.uk
CEO Oxfam GB: Mark Goldring
Oxfam is a development, relief, and campaigning organisation that works with others to achieve a just world without poverty.
Employees: 4951
Volunteers: 27000
Regional offices: 8

P3

E: andrew.regan@p3charity.org

PAC

5 Torriano Mews, London NW5 2RZ
T: 020 7284 0555
Helpline: 020 7284 5879
F: 020 7482 2367
E: advice@pac.org.uk
www.pac.org.uk
CEO: Peter Sandiford
PAC provides confidential advice, information and support for anyone affected by adoption or any other form of permanent care, including adoptive parents, adopted adults, birth parents and other birth family members, foster carers where permanence is the plan, special guardians and prospective adopters. Services include: advice line; individual counselling; individual, couple and family consultations; family therapeutic work; support with contact arrangements between adoptive and birth families; support for birth

relatives, including fortnightly birth mothers drop-in.
Employees: 25
Volunteers: 4

PACE

34 Hartham Road, London N7 9JL
T: 020 7715 0385
Helpline: 020 7700 1323
E: info@pacehealth.org.uk
www.pacehealth.org.uk
Chief Executive Officer: Margaret Unwin
PACE is London's leading charity promoting the mental health and emotional well-being of the lesbian, gay, bisexual and transgender community. PACE also provides online services that can be accessed nationally. We are committed to responding to the changing needs of LGBT people, and offering appropriate, sensitive, LGBT-delivered support services to help people move through their difficult times.
Employees: 23
Volunteers: 22

PACT (Parents and Children together)

7 Southern Court, South Street, Reading, Berkshire RG1 4QS
T: 0300 456 4800
E: info@pactcharity.org
www.pactcharity.org
Chief Executive: Jan Fishwick
PACT helps hundreds of families every year through adoption services and community projects. PACT is one of the UK's leading Voluntary Adoption Agencies (VAA) placing children with secure and loving families and supporting them with specialist therapeutic support.
Employees: 70
Volunteers: 50
Regional offices: 3
Income: £4,851,000 (2014-15)

Pain Relief Foundation

Clinical Sciences Centre, University Hospital Aintree, Lower Lane, Liverpool L9 7AL
T: 0151 529 5820
F: 0151 529 5821
E: secretary@painrelieffoundation.org.uk
www.painrelieffoundation.org.uk
Administrator: D Emsley
Aims to research human chronic pain to find the causes and mechanisms of why chronic pain persists. Also to find new and improved methods of treating all such conditions to ease the suffering of patients. Our ultimate aim is to find cures for all pain. Additionally, we provide ongoing education for health professionals at all levels and disciplines who are dealing with human chronic pain at the point of treatment.
Employees: 6
Regional offices: 1

Painswick Rococo Garden Trust

E: rococogarden@hotmail.co.uk

Paintings in Hospitals

Floor One, Menier Chocolate Factory, 51 Southwark Street, London SE1 1RU
T: 020 7407 3222
F: 020 7403 7721
E: mail@paintingsinhospitals.org.uk
www.paintingsinhospitals.org.uk
Director: Stuart Davie
Aims to relieve sick, infirm and convalescent persons by providing pictures and works of art on loan in order to improve the environment of hospitals and other healthcare establishments.
Employees: 5
Volunteers: 50
Regional offices: 7

Papworth Trust

Bernard Sunley Centre, Papworth Everard, Cambridge, Cambridgeshire CB23 3RG
T: 01480 357200
Helpline: 0800 952 5000
F: 01480 357201
E: info@papworth.org.uk
www.papworth.org.uk
Chief Executive: Adrian Bagg
Papworth Trust is a leading disability charity. We support over 20,000 people each year through a wide range of services, including accessible homes, personal care, leisure and learning opportunities, and support for people to find and keep jobs.
Employees: 500
Regional offices: 24

Parents for Inclusion

London
E: info@parentsforinclusion.org
www.parentsforinclusion.org
Parents for Inclusion is a network of parents of disabled children and children with special needs. In our families and as an organisation we have worked together with disabled people to build inclusive communities in ordinary life, where all people are truly welcome. We work closely with disabled adults, to bring their understanding and experience to parents, so that parents can become real allies to their disabled children.
Employees: 2
Volunteers: 5

Parents in Partnership

Cornerstone House, 14 Willis Road, Croydon, Surrey CR2 8DA
T: 020 8684 9082
E: office@pipcroydon.com
www.pipcroydon.com
Chairman: Jackie Sanders
Employees: 5
Volunteers: 4
Regional offices: 1

PARITY

Constables, Windsor Road, Ascot, Berkshire SL5 7LF
T: 01344 621167 (also fax)
E: postmaster@parity-uk.org
www.parity-uk.org
Chair: John Mays
Fosters and promotes equal treatment of the sexes under the law and by public authority, for example in state pensions, other social security provisions, bus concessions, etc.
Volunteers: 10
Regional offices: 1

Parkinson's Disease Society of the UK

215 Vauxhall Bridge Road, London SW1V 1EJ
T: 020 7931 8080
F: 020 7233 9908
E: enquiries@parkinsons.org.uk
www.parkinsons.org.uk
Helps and supports people with Parkinson's and their relatives; collects and shares information on Parkinson's; and encourages and provides funds for research into the disease.
Employees: 150
Volunteers: 3500
Regional offices: 14

Parliamentary Advisory Council for Transport Safety

3rd Floor, Clutha House, 10 Storey's Gate, London SW1P 3AY
T: 020 7222 7732
F: 020 7222 7106
E: admin@pacts.org.uk
www.pacts.org.uk
Executive Director: Robert Gifford
To protect human life through the promotion of transport safety for the public benefit; to

exercise scrutiny of legislative and policy proposals.
Employees: 3
Volunteers: 5

Partially Sighted Society

1 Bennetthorpe, Doncaster, South Yorkshire DN2 6AA
T: 0844 477 4966
F: 0844 477 4969
E: info@partsight.org.uk
www.partsight.org.uk
Executive Director: Anita Plant
Provides help, advice and training in enabling people with a visual impairment to make the best use of their remaining vision. Directly assists partially sighted people in their daily lives; promotes research and development in order to better understand the problems of being partially sighted. In-house design and print facility to produce heavily lined stationery.
Employees: 4
Regional offices: 1

Partners of Prisoners and Families Support Group

Valentine House, 1079 Rochdale Road, Blackley, Manchester M9 8AJ
T: 0161 702 1000
Helpline: 0808 808 2003
F: 0161 850 1988
E: mail@partnersofprisoners.co.uk
www.partnersofprisoners.co.uk
CEO: Diane Curry OBE
Provides information, advice and support to the partners, families and friends of those in prison.

Partnership at Work

301B The Argent Centre, 60 Frederick Street, Birmingham B1 3HS
T: 0121 244 3752
F: 0121 244 9752
E: info@partnershipatwork.org.uk
We aim to work collaboratively with voluntary youth, community and play organisations to improve the quality of working lives for their staff and volunteers. We do this by providing sector-specific information, advice and support on human resource management and employment legislation.
Employees: 4
Volunteers: 3
Regional offices: 1

Patients Association

PO Box 935, Harrow, Middlesex HA1 3YJ
T: 020 8423 9111
Helpline: 0845 608 4455
F: 020 8423 9119
E: mailbox@patients-association.com
www.patients-association.org.uk
The Patients Association is a healthcare charity that for more than 40 years has advocated for greater and equitable access to high-quality, accurate and independent information for patients, and for greater and equitable access to high-quality care and for involvement in decision-making as a right.
Employees: 5
Volunteers: 11

Patients Forum

Riverbank House, 1 Putney Bridge Approach, London SW6 3JD
T: 020 7736 7903
F: 020 7736 7932
E: support@datadial.net
www.thepatientsforum.org.uk
The Patients Forum is a network of national and regional organisations concerned with the healthcare interests of patients and their families and carers. Full membership is open to national and umbrella organisations representing the interests of users of health services, and their families and carers. Associate (non-voting) membership can be obtained for healthcare service providers, as well as all regulatory bodies.
Employees: 1
Regional offices: 1

Pax Christi

Christian Peace Education Centre, St Joseph's, Watford Way, London NW4 2LH
T: 020 8203 4884
F: 020 8203 5234
E: info@paxchristi.org.uk
www.paxchristi.org.uk
Founded in the Catholic Church, but open to all faiths, Pax Christi is a gospel-based lay-inspired peacemaking movement. It strives to help both the Church and the wider community proclaim peace through the witnesses and actions of its members. The three major objectives of Pax Christi are: reconciliation; the promotion of a culture of peace and non-violence; and providing the means to bring about peace (for example through training and education resources).
Employees: 1
Volunteers: 9

Pay and Employment Rights Service (Yorkshire) Ltd

E: fawzia@pers.org.uk

PayPal Giving Fund

Surrey TW9 1EH
T: 020 8439 2381
E: info@paypalgivingfund.org
www.paypalgivingfund.org.uk
CEO: Aldridge, Nick
PayPal Giving Fund UK is a registered charity (No. 1110538) and enables eBay and PayPal users to give to good causes quickly and easily. PayPal Giving Fund certifies charities to participate in the eBay for Charity programme, and collects donations from eBay and PayPal users. It also distributes those donations and Gift Aid to donors' chosen charities, which receive 100% of the funds raised.

PDSA for Pets in Need of Vets

Head Office, Whitechapel Way, Priorslee, Telford TF2 9PQ
T: 01952 290999
F: 01952 291035
E: rydstrom.marilyn@pdsa.org.uk
www.pdsa.org.uk
Director General: Marilyn Rydstrom
PDSA cares for the pets of people in need by providing free veterinary services to their sick and injured animals and promoting responsible pet ownership.
Employees: 1780
Volunteers: 4850
Regional offices: 6

Peace Brigades International UK Section (PBI UK)

1B Waterlow Road, London N19 5NJ
T: 020 7281 5370
E: admin@peacebrigades.org.uk
www.peacebrigades.org.uk
Director: Susi Bascon
Peace Brigades International provides protective accompaniment to human rights defenders (HRDs) at risk in Colombia, Guatemala, Honduras, Kenya, Mexico and Nepal. The presence of PBI volunteers represents the international community's concerns and deters against threats being carried out. This is backed up by international political and diplomatic support and dialogue with authorities at all levels. PBI UK also lobbies the UK government, EU and UN bodies for better mechanisms and policies to protect HRDs worldwide.
Employees: 3
Volunteers: 30
Regional offices: 1
Income: £270,000 (2011-12)

Peace Direct

Development House, London EC2A 4JX
T: 0845 456 9714
F: 020 7794 2489
E: robert@peacedirect.org
www.peacedirect.org
Peace Direct's focus is grassroots peace-building in areas of conflict across the world. This is achieved through funding projects, including collaborative projects and one-off grants; persuasion and promotion of the value of non-violent approaches; and learning through peace activities around the world.
Employees: 7

Peace Pledge Union

1 Peace Passage, London N7 0BT
T: 020 7424 9444
F: 020 7482 6390
E: mail@ppu.org.uk
www.ppu.org.uk
The oldest, secular pacifist organisation in the UK, the Union supports research, provides advice and information about the causes and effects of wars and violence, and ways of resolving conflicts peacefully.
Employees: 2
Volunteers: 4

Peacemakers

41 Bull St, Birmingham, West Midlands B4 6AF
T: 0121 236 4796
E: info@peacemakers.org.uk
www.peacemakers.org.uk
Director: Sara Hagel
Peacemakers exists to help create a more peaceful world, with more caring and resilient communities. We want a world where people are equipped to deal non-violently and creatively with the inevitable conflicts that arise. Our contribution to promoting a more harmonious society in the West Midlands is the development of peace-making behaviour of children and adults in schools.
Employees: 5
Volunteers: 1
Income: £133,000 (2013-14)

Peel Institute

Peel Centre, Percy Circus, London WC1X 9EY
T: 020 7837 6082
F: 020 7278 3855
E: admin@peelinstitute.org.uk
www.peelinstitute.org.uk
Chief Executive: Rob Hamilton
A community hub in the heart of King's Cross, providing a wide range of services for all ages and sections of the local community. Activities include crèche, child care, youth services, adult education, advice and advocacy to sports and older people's projects, all provided in a fully accessible purpose built community centre.
Employees: 33
Volunteers: 50
Income: £750,000 (2013-14)

Pelvic Pain Support Network

PO Box 6559, Poole, Dorset BH12 9DP
T: 01202 603447
E: info@pelvicpain.org.uk
www.pelvicpain.org.uk
The Network's volunteers are patients and carers who have been supporting those with pelvic pain, their carers and families since the year 2000. We attend local, national and international events and represent pelvic pain patients at many meetings, seminars and conferences.
Volunteers: 5

Pensions Advisory Service

11 Belgrave Road, London SW1V 1RB T: 020 7630 2272
F: 020 7592 7000
E: barry.wilkins@pensionsadvisoryservice.org.uk
www.pensionsadvisoryservice.org.uk
Chief Executive: Malcolm McLean
The Pensions Advisory Service, is an independent non-profit organisation that provides free information, advice and guidance on the whole spectrum of pensions covering state, company, personal and stakeholder schemes.
Employees: 35
Volunteers: 450

Penwith Community Development Trust

E: diana.higton@pcdt.org.uk

People & Planet

16-17 Turl Street, Oxford, Oxfordshire OX1 3DH
T: 01865 264180
E: people@peopleandplanet.org
www.peopleandplanet.org
People & Planet is the largest student network in Britain campaigning to end world poverty, defend human rights and protect the environment. We're a student-led movement that empowers young people with the skills, confidence and knowledge they need to make change happen, at home and globally.

People of God Trust

1 Carysfort House, 14 West Halkin Street, London SW1X 8JS
T: 020 7235 2841
E: pogtrust@gmail.com
www.ccc4vat2.org.uk
Honorary Secretary: Simon Bryden-Brook
A lay initiative, promoting the Catholic religion in accordance with the Second Vatican Council, largely by making grants to appropriate organisations.
Volunteers: 2
Regional offices: 1
Income: £5,500 (2014-15)

People's Trust for Endangered Species

15 Cloisters House, 8 Battersea Park Road, London SW8 4BG
T: 020 7498 4533
F: 020 7498 4459
E: jill@ptes.org
www.ptes.org
Chief Executive: Jill Nelson
PTES protects endangered species worldwide and advances public awareness of which species are endangered, rare or threatened. It gives grants and runs selected conservation programmes. The prime aims of PTES activities are to protect endangered species through conservation strategies that are informed by scientific research; to educate the public and promote open debate between the public, policy makers and conservation scientists about issues surrounding endangered species and their conservation.
Employees: 13
Volunteers: 1000

Permaculture Association (Britain)

BCM Permaculture Association, London WC1N 3XX
T: 0845 458 1805
E: office@permaculture.org.uk
www.permaculture.org.uk
CEO: Andy Goldring
The Permaculture Association is the national charity that supports and promotes permaculture design throughout the UK and worldwide through education, research and networking.
Employees: 10
Volunteers: 150

Perthes Association

PO Box 773, Guildford, Surrey GU1 1XN
T: 01483 306637
E: info@perthes.org.uk
www.perthes.org.uk
Perthes disease is a form of osteochondritis. A potentially crippling disease of the hip, Perthes disease is a childhood disorder, which affects the head of the femur. The association supports children with Perthes disease and associated conditions through the purchase of wheelchairs, buggies and more specialist equipment which are loaned free to members (parents and carers) allowing the children to play with their siblings and friends, and enjoy a better quality of life.
Employees: 4
Volunteers: 20

Pestalozzi International Village Trust

Ladybird Lane, Sedlescombe, Battle, East Sussex TN33 0UF
T: 01424 870444
F: 01424 870655
E: debbie.martin@pestalozzi.org.uk
www.pestalozzi.org.uk
Chief Executive: Paul Evans
Employees: 20
Volunteers: 6
Regional offices: 1

Pesticide Action Network UK

London EC2A 4LT
T: 020 7065 0905
F: 020 7065 0907
E: admin@pan-uk.org
www.pan-uk.org
Director: Linda Craig
(PAN UK) works to eliminate the dangers of toxic pesticides, our exposure to them, and their presence in the environment where we live and work. Nationally and globally, we promote safer alternatives, the production of healthy food, and sustainable farming.
Employees: 15
Volunteers: 3

Peter le Marchant Trust

Canalside Moorings Beeches Road, Loughborough, Leicestershire LE11 2NS
T: 01509 265590
E: lynnsmith@peterlemarchanttrust.co.uk
www.peterlemarchanttrust.co.uk
The Trust provides trips and holidays on special boats for adults and children with disabilities.

Peter Rigby Trust

The London Centre for Children with Cerebral Palsy, 54 Muswell Hill, London N10 3ST
T: 020 8444 7242
F: 020 8444 7241
E: kath@cplondon.org.uk
www.cplondon.org.uk
CEO: Marc Crank
We provide educational services for children with cerebral palsy. We have an independent approved school for children aged 3 to 11 years. We specialise in an approach known as Conductive Education. We also have an early intervention service and outreach support service within mainstream schools.
Employees: 26
Volunteers: 11
Regional offices: 1

PEYTU

2nd Floor, Scrapstore House, 21 Sevier Street, St Werburgh's, Bristol, Avon BS2 9LB
T: 0117 908 0601
F: 0117 908 0622
E: admin@peytu.co.uk
www.peytu.co.uk
Chief Executive Officer: Sandra Meadows
Independent, not-for-profit and approved by Local Authorities. As a registered charity, our aim is to improve outcomes for children and young people by providing training, information, consultancy and support for those working with and/or caring for them. Our work broadly encompasses workforce development and enhancing opportunities for employment, further education and the promotion of social welfare and recreation for all families.
Employees: 6
Regional offices: 1
Income: £369,670 (2012-13)

PFEG (Personal Finance Education Group)

Fifth Floor, 14 Bonhill Street, London EC2A 4BX
T: 020 7330 9470
Helpline: 0300 666 0127
F: 020 7374 6147
E: info@pfeg.org
www.pfeg.org
Chief Executive: Wendy van den Hende
PFEG is an educational charity and its mission is to make sure that all young people leaving school have the confidence, skills and knowledge in financial matters to take part fully in society. It offers a range of advice and resources and supports UK teachers working with children and young people aged 4 to 19 from all backgrounds.
Employees: 17
Volunteers: 100

PHAB

Summit House, Wandle Road, Croydon CR0 1DF
T: 020 8667 9443
F: 020 8681 1399
E: info@phabengland.org.uk
www.phabengland.org.uk
Via a network of clubs, projects, publications and activities, PHAB promotes and encourages people with and without physical disabilities to come together on equal terms, to achieve complete integration within the wider community.
Employees: 30
Volunteers: 15000
Regional offices: 4

Pharmacist Support

5th Floor, 196 Deansgate, Manchester, Greater Manchester M3 3WF
T: 0808 168 2233
F: 0161 441 0319
E: info@pharmacistsupport.org
www.pharmacistsupport.org
Charity Manager: Diane Leicester-Hallam
Pharmacist Support is an independent charity providing a range of free and confidential services to pharmacists and their families, former pharmacists, pre-registration trainees and pharmacy students. Support includes financial assistance, an information and enquiry service, a stress helpline, debt, benefits and employment advice and addiction support.
Employees: 9
Volunteers: 30
Income: £898,613 (2012-13)

Philadelphia Association

4 Marty's Yard, 17 Hampstead High Street, London NW3 1QW
T: 020 7794 2652 (also fax)
E: office@philadelphia-association.co.uk
www.philadelphia-association.org.uk
The Association helps to relieve mental illness of all descriptions; to maintain therapeutic community households; to offer a forum for research, study and training in community therapy and psychotherapy according to the Association's own philosophy; and to publish relevant texts.
Employees: 1

Phoenix Domestic Abuse & Support Services Ltd

E: kateormerod@phoenixsupport.org.uk

Phoenix Futures

3rd Floor, Asra House, 1 Long Lane, London SE1 4PG
T: 020 7234 9740
F: 020 7234 9770
E: info@phoenix-futures.org.uk
www.phoenix-futures.org.uk
Chief Executive: Karen Biggs
Employees: 550
Volunteers: 50
Regional offices: 4

Pilgrim Hearts Trust

24 Yorkshire Place, Warfield, 24 Yorkshire Place, Bracknell RG42 3XE
T: 01344 307030 (also fax)
E: pilgrim.hearts@gmail.com
www.pilgrimhearts.org.uk
Director: Elaine Chalmers-Brown
Pilgrim Hearts is there to assist those who are homeless and on the edge and those who for whatever reason are not able to benefit from all of life's opportunities. It is a Christian organisation devoted to helping marginalised people, and those with disabilities, from all walks of life and backgrounds. We provide assistance to other organisations and community groups both in the voluntary and public sector.
Employees: 5

Pilgrim Trust

Cowley House, 9 Little College Street, London SW1P 3HS
T: 020 7222 4723
E: georgina@thepilgrimtrust.org.uk
www.thepilgrimtrust.org.uk

Pilotlight

Holborn, London WC2A 3ED
T: 020 7396 7414
F: 020 7396 7467
E: info@pilotlight.org.uk
www.pilotlight.org.uk
Pilotlight helps small charities to build their capacity in order to plan for sustainability, growth and, where appropriate, replication. The membership of senior business people donate their time to supporting the charities through a combination of coaching and consultancy. The Pilotlight process is designed to enable members to make a difference to small charities in just a few hours a month, and educates this influential group about the charitable sector through practical experience.
Employees: 3

Pituitary Foundation

The Pituitary Foundation, 86 Colston Street, Bristol BS1 5BB
T: 0117 370 1333
Helpline: 0117 370 1320
E: helpline@pituitary.org.uk
www.pituitary.org.uk
The Pituitary Foundation is a national support and information organisation for pituitary patients, their families, friends and carers. The Pituitary Foundation's Objectives are: To promote the relief and treatment of persons suffering from pituitary disorders and related conditions and diseases, and their families, friends and carers, and to provide information and support; To promote and support research and to disseminate for the public benefit the results of any such research.
Employees: 7
Volunteers: 110
Regional offices: 31

Place2Be

326 City Road, London EC1V 2PT
T: 020 7923 5527
F: 020 7481 1894
E: enquiries@theplace2be.org.uk
www.theplace2be.org.uk
The Place2Be was established in 1994 in response to increasing concern about the extent and depth of emotional and behavioural difficulties displayed in classrooms and playgrounds.
Volunteers: 350

Plan UK

London NW1 7HS
T: 020 7482 9777
F: 020 7482 9778
E: mail@plan-international.org.uk
www.plan-uk.org
Plan is a child-centred development agency with no political or religious affiliations, enabling families and communities in the poorest countries to make lasting improvements to the lives of their children.
Employees: 64
Volunteers: 34

Plant Heritage

12 Home Farm, Loseley Park, Guildford, Surrey GU3 1HS
T: 01483 447540
F: 01483 458933
E: info@plantheritage.org.uk
www.plantheritage.com
Chief Executive Officer: Chief Executive Officer
Plant Heritage (or National Council for the Conservation of Plants and Gardens to give its full name) is the only charity working to conserve cultivated plants through the National Plant Collections scheme and the Threatened Plants Project.
Employees: 8
Volunteers: 500

Plunkett Foundation

Banbury Road, Woodstock, Oxfordshire OX20 1LH
T: 01993 810730
F: 01993 810849
E: info@plunkett.co.uk
www.plunkett.co.uk
The Plunkett Foundation is an educational charity, based near Oxford in the UK, which supports the development of rural group enterprise worldwide. The Foundation draws on 80 years' practical experience of working with partners from the private sector to promote and implement economic self-help solutions to rural problems.
Employees: 16

Police Foundation

Room 1.13, The Foundry, 17 Oval Way, Kennington, London SE11 5RR
T: 020 3752 5630
E: sue.roberts@police-foundation.org.uk
www.police-foundation.org.uk
Director: Dr Rick Muir
The Police Foundation is the country's only independent charity focused on responding to public concerns about policing, informing their understanding of policing issues and challenging the police service and the government to improve policing for the benefit of all citizens. It does so by promoting debate on policing and police reform, providing commentary, knowledge and insight on important issues and contemporary developments and turning new ideas into policy and practice.
Employees: 10
Volunteers: 1
Regional offices: 1
Income: £831,000 (2014-15)

Policy Studies Institute

50 Hanson Street, London W1W 6UP
T: 020 7911 7500
F: 020 7911 7501
E: psi-admin@psi.org.uk
www.psi.org.uk
One of Britain's leading independent research institutes, conducting research to promote economic wellbeing and improve quality of life. PSI undertakes and publishes research studies relevant to social, economic, industrial and environmental policy. In 1998 it merged to become an independent subsidiary of the University of Westminster. PSI takes a

politically neutral stance on issues of public policy and its income is derived from funds for individual research projects: funding sources include government, professional agencies, charitable trusts and private companies.
Volunteers: 46

Polycystic Kidney Disease Charity

91 Royal College Street, London NW1 0SE
T: 020 7387 0543
Helpline: 0300 111 1234
E: tess.harris@pkdcharity.org.uk
www.pkdcharity.org.uk
Chief Executive: Tess Harris
We provide information, advice and support to those affected by polycystic kidney disease (PKD). We aim to fund research into determining the causes of PKD, discovering treatments and a cure, and raise awareness of PKD, providing information about PKD to patients, the public, the medical community and the media.
Employees: 2
Volunteers: 50
Income: £90,000 (2011-12)

Pontifical Mission Societies

23 Eccleston Square, London SW1V 1NU
T: 020 7821 9755
E: director@missio.org.uk
www.missio.org.uk

Portchester Community Association

The Portchester Hub, 2, New Parade, 38, West Street, Portchester, Fareham, Hampshire PO16 9UY
T: 023 9221 0048
E: admin@portchesterca.org.uk
www.portchesterca.org.uk
Manager: Sarah Moss
Provide social, educational & leisure activities, facilities and services to local people (all ages) and groups through the Portchester Hub, outreach and partnerships. Also run Community learning, Pre-school/ancillary services; Sections (sports, arts, interest groups); community projects, specific activities for older people and volunteering.
Employees: 10
Volunteers: 80
Regional offices: 1
Income: £271,504 (2012-13)

Portman Group Trust

London W1G 9DQ
T: 020 7907 3700
F: 020 7907 3710
E: advice@portmangroup.org.uk
www.portmangroup.org.uk
Supported by the UK's leading drinks producers, the Trust is concerned solely with social responsibility issues surrounding alcohol. It endorses the preservation, protection and promotion of public health through the provision of education and research on alcohol-related matters.

Positive Body Image

PO Box 23266, London SE14 5FQ
E: info@positivebodyimage.co.uk
Positive Body Image aims to use a holistic approach to health and fitness to help individuals improve their physical, mental and spiritual wellbeing and, in so doing, help them to improve their self-image and achieve their potential. Positive Body Image was established to help address the health inequalities experienced by ethnic minority women, but its programmes and services are open to all women.

Positively UK

345 City Road, London EC1V 1LR
T: 020 7713 0444
E: info@positivelyuk.org
www.positivelyuk.org
Positively UK is the only national charity working to improve the quality of life of people affected by HIV; enabling them to make informed choices and challenging stigma and discrimination. All direct support is carried out by people who are themselves HIV positive and therefore have personal experience of the social and health implications of living with the virus.

Potential Plus UK

Suite 1.2, Challenge House, Sherwood Drive, Bletchley, Milton Keynes MK3 6DP
T: 01908 646433
E: amazingchildren@nagcbritain.org.uk
www.potentialplusuk.org
Chief Executive: Denise Yates
Supports gifted children, their parents, families and teachers and disseminates information concerning gifted children.
Employees: 9
Volunteers: 120

Powerhouse

St Luke's Community Centre, 85 Tarling Road, Canning Town, London E16 1HN
T: 020 7366 6336
F: 020 7366 6337
E: info@thepowerhouse.org.uk
www.thepowerhouse.org.uk
Powerhouse is an organisation of women with learning difficulties. It is committed to promoting women's rights through advocacy, campaigning, one-to-one support, training and awareness-raising.

Practical Action

The Schumacher Centre, Bourton on Dunsmore, Rugby, Warwickshire CV23 9QZ
T: 01926 634400
E: practicalaction@practicalaction.org.uk
www.practicalaction.org
We believe technology can transform lives and should be available to the many not the few. Through technology we enable poor communities build on their skills and knowledge to produce sustainable solutions, finding out what people are doing and helping them do it better. Founded in 1966 by E F Schumacher, for fifty years we've been delivering life-changing projects alongside local communities, building access to knowledge and influencing for change for poor men and women.

Prader-Willi Syndrome Association UK

125A London Road, Derby, Derbyshire DE1 2QQ
T: 01332 365676
F: 01332 360401
E: admin@pwsa.co.uk
www.pwsa.co.uk
Chief Executive Officer: Susan Passmore
Prader-Willi syndrome is a complex genetic disorder, present from birth. The Association exists to contact and support families concerned with the disorder; to inform health professionals, families and the public in general about the disorder; to raise funds and foster research into its causes and alleviation.
Employees: 9
Volunteers: 70
Regional offices: 1

Pre-school Learning Alliance

The Fitzpatrick Building, 188 York Way, London N7 9AD
T: 020 7697 2595
F: 020 3137 2493
E: info@pre-school.org.uk
www.pre-school.org.uk
Chief Executive: Neil Leitch
The Alliance is the largest and most representative early years membership organisation and voluntary sector provider of quality affordable childcare and education in England. We represent the interests of 14,000 member settings and give direct support to them, via information and advice, specialist publication, acclaimed training programmes and campaigns to influence early years policy and practice.
Employees: 2000
Volunteers: 763
Regional offices: 30
Income: £36,732,000 (2012-13)

Primary Ciliary Dyskinesia Family Support Group

15 Shuttleworth Grove, Wavendon Gate, Milton Keynes MK7 7RX
T: 01908 281635
Helpline: 0300 111 0122
E: chair@pcdsupport.org.uk
www.pcdsupport.org.uk
Chairman: Fiona Copeland
The Group provides support to patients with PCD (also known as Kartagener's syndrome and immotile cilia syndrome) and parents of children known to have the syndrome. It brings the disease to the attention of the medical profession and the public and raises funds for research.
Volunteers: 8
Income: £14,000 (2012-13)

Primary Sclerosing Cholangitis Trust

Hollibury House, 12 Limont Road, Southport, Merseyside PR8 3NJ
T: 01704 808740
E: info@psctrust.com
www.psctrust.com
The Primary Sclerosing Cholangitis (PSC) Trust is dedicated to discovering the cause and cure of PSC, a chronic progressive liver disease, and related conditions.
Volunteers: 12
Regional offices: 1

PRIMHE

c/o Tipton Care Org, Glebefields Health Centre, St Marks Road, Tipton, West Midlands DY4 0SN
T: 0121 530 8021 (also fax)
E: admin@primhe.org.uk
www.primhe.org.uk
Chair of Trustees: Dr Ian Walton
Helping primary healthcare professionals and staff achieve and deliver the best standards of mental healthcare. PRIMHE provides mental health support, services, resources, education and training.
Volunteers: 5
Regional offices: 1

Prince's Trust

Clarence House, London SW1A 1BA
T: 020 7543 1234
E: info@princes-trust.org.uk
www.princes-trust.org.uk
Employees: 800
Volunteers: 10000
Regional offices: 9

Prison Advice and Care Trust

Park Place, 12 Lawn Lane, London SW8 1UD
T: 020 7735 9535
E: info@prisonadvice.org.uk
www.prisonadvice.org.uk
Director: Andy Keen-Downs
The Trust's mission is to support prisoners and their families to make a fresh start and to minimise the harm that can be caused by imprisonment on offenders, families and communities.
Employees: 83
Volunteers: 300
Regional offices: 1

Prison Chat UK

PO Box 49449, Penge, London SE20 8YG
T: 020 8778 7741
E: prisonchatuk@aol.com
www.prisonchatuk.com
An online community giving support to those who have a loved one inside the British prison system. All members are connected to the prison system in some way and can offer advice and share their experiences, so creating a community for people to go and get support and answers when a loved one has been taken into custody.

Prison Fellowship England and Wales

PO Box 68226, London SW1P 9WR
T: 020 7799 2500
E: info@prisonfellowship.org.uk
www.prisonfellowship.org.uk
Chief Executive: Natalie Cronin
Prison Fellowship aims to show Christ's love to prisoners by coming alongside them, praying and supporting them to change. We offer our services to all who request them, regardless of their beliefs. We do this through our network of volunteer members and have over 1,500 volunteers throughout England and Wales.
Employees: 18
Volunteers: 1600

Prison Reform Trust

The Old Trading House, 15 Northburgh Street, London EC1V 0JR
T: 020 7251 5070
F: 020 7251 5076
E: geoff.dobson@prisonreformtrust.org.uk
www.prisonreformtrust.org.uk
Promotes public understanding of the need for improvements in our prison system; and encourages public interest in penal policy and practice.
Employees: 13
Volunteers: 3

Prisoners Abroad

89-93 Fonthill Road, London N4 3JH
T: 020 7561 6820
Helpline: 0808 172 0098
F: 020 7561 6821
E: info@prisonersabroad.org.uk
www.prisonersabroad.org.uk
Chief Executive: Pauline Crowe
Provides practical and emotional support to British citizens in prison overseas, their families and friends, and to ex-prisoners returning to the UK.
Employees: 25

Prisoners Advice Service

PO Box 46199, London EC1M 4XA
T: 020 7253 3323
Helpline: 0845 430 8923
F: 020 7253 8067
E: advice@prisonersadvice.org.uk
www.prisonersadvice.org.uk
PAS provides free, expert legal advice and information to prisoners in England and Wales regarding their rights and conditions of imprisonment; it takes up prisoners' complaints about their treatment inside prison by providing free advice and assistance on an individual and confidential basis. The service also produces a quarterly bulletin on new prison case law and policy, entitled Prisoners' Legal Rights Bulletin.
Employees: 6
Volunteers: 20

Prisoners Education Trust

Wandle House, Riverside Drive, Mitcham, Surrey CR4 4BU
T: 020 8648 7760
F: 020 8648 7762
E: info@prisonerseducation.org.uk
www.prisonerseducation.org.uk
Interim Director: Rachel Youngman
The Trust aims to offer prisoners a chance to change through education and promotes the importance of education in the successful resettlement of offenders. It makes grants to enable prisoners to study through distance learning and other courses that will enhance their chances of employment after release. It also runs projects developing support and advice for prisoner learners and enables prisoner learners to have a voice about education and learning.
Employees: 12
Volunteers: 12

Prisoners' Families and Friends Service

20 Trinity Street, London SE1 1DB
T: 020 7403 4091
F: 020 7403 9359
E: info@prisonersfamiliesandfriends.org.uk
www.prisonersfamiliesandfriends.org.uk
Employees: 4
Volunteers: 58

Professional Association for Childcare and Early Years (PACEY)

Royal Court, 81 Tweedy Road, Bromley, Kent BR1 1TG
T: 0300 003 0005
E: info@pacey.org.uk
www.pacey.org.uk
Chief Executive: Liz Bayram
PACEY is the Professional Association for Childcare and Early Years. A standard-setting organisation, we promote best practice and support childcare professionals to deliver high standards of care and learning. Since 1977 we have provided high quality support to our members and have worked with government, local authorities and others to raise standards. Together with our members - childminders, nannies and nursery workers - we are working to become the professional association for everyone in childcare and early years and ensure our members are recognised for the vital role they play in helping children get the best start in life.
Employees: 160
Regional offices: 7

Professionals Aid Council

10 St Christopher's Place, London W1U 1HZ
T: 020 7935 0641
E: admin@professionalsaid.org.uk
www.professionalsaid.org.uk
Chief Executive Officer: Finola McNicholl
PAC can give financial aid to university graduates and individuals from professional backgrounds. We also give small educational grants to help students whose funding has broken down after they have started their course. Limited grants may also be available to help families with the cost of children's education.
Employees: 4

Progress Educational Trust

140 Gray's Inn Road, London WC1X 8AX
T: 020 7278 7870
E: admin@progress.org.uk
www.progress.org.uk
Aims to enhance the public understanding of reproduction and genetics; to encourage discussion of their social, legal and ethical implication and to promote the need for further research in these areas of science and medicine.

Progress Employment Support

The Enterprise Centre, 291-305 Lytham Road, Blackpool, Lancashire FY4 1EW
T: 01253 477287
F: 01253 477276
E: deborah.parker@progressemployment.org
www.progressemployment.org
CEO: Deborah Parker
A values-driven supported employment agency achieving inclusive employment and business success, by supporting disabled people and their employers to benefit from working together.
Employees: 5
Regional offices: 1

Progressio

Units 912, The Stable Yard, Broomgrove Road, London SW9 9TL
T: 020 7733 1195
F: 020 7326 2059
E: enquiries@progressio.org.uk
www.progressio.org.uk
Executive Director: Mark Lister
Progressio is a UK-based charity working internationally to enable people in developing countries to change the situations that keep them poor. We work in 11 countries and have a history of working in fragile, post-conflict states, developing long-term partnerships with local organisations and community groups in Africa, Latin America, the Caribbean, the Middle East and Asia, providing practical support through around 100 development workers, mostly from the south, who share skills, know-how and training.
Employees: 80
Volunteers: 104

Promise Dreams

Promise House, Edwin House, Boundary Industrial Estate, Stafford Road, Wolverhampton, West Midlands WV10 7EL
T: 01902 212451
F: 01902 783625
E: info@promisedreams.co.uk
www.promisedreams.co.uk
Charity Manager: Beverley Bird
Promise Dreams is a national registered charity, dedicated to helping seriously ill and terminally ill children and their families turn a very special wish into reality.
Employees: 5
Regional offices: 1

Prospect Hospice

E: andrewthompson@prospect-hospice.net

Prospects for People with Learning Disabilities

69 Honey End Lane, Reading, Berkshire RG30 4EL
T: 0118 950 8781
E: paula@prospects.org.uk
www.prospects.org.uk
CEO: Paul Ashton
Prospects is a Christian organisation supporting people with learning disabilities so that they live their lives to the full through: residential homes and supported living; overseas partnerships; church-based ministry; involvement in Christian conferences.
Employees: 700
Volunteers: 1300
Regional offices: 7

Prostate Cancer UK

Fourth Floor, The Counting House, 53 Tooley Street, London SE1 2QN
T: 020 3310 7000
Helpline: 0800 074 8383
F: 020 3310 7107
E: info@prostatecanceruk.org
www.prostatecanceruk.org
Chief Executive: Owen Sharp
Prostate Cancer UK fight to help more men survive prostate cancer and enjoy a better quality of life. We support men through; our

helpline staffed by specialist nurses, our work in the community, and by providing vital information on all aspects of prostate disease. We find answers by funding research into causes, tests and treatments. And we lead change, raising the profile of the disease and improving care. We believe that men deserve better.
Employees: 185
Volunteers: 1263
Regional offices: 6
Income: £30,000,000 (2012-13)

Psoriasis and Psoriatic Arthritis Alliance

PO Box 111, St Albans AL2 3JQ
T: 0870 770 3212
F: 0870 770 3213
E: info@papaa.org
www.papaa.org
Aims to preserve, protect and relieve persons suffering from psoriatic arthropathy and associated conditions.

Psoriasis Association

Dick Coles House, 2 Queensbridge, Northampton, Northamptonshire NN4 7BF
T: 01604 251620
Helpline: 0845 676 0076
F: 01604 251621
E: mail@psoriasis-association.org.uk
www.psoriasis-association.org.uk
Chief Executive: Helen McAteer
The Association supports people with psoriasis, raises awareness of the condition and funds research into the causes, treatment and care.
Employees: 6
Volunteers: 2

Psychiatric Rehabilitation Association

Bayford Mews, Bayford Street, London E8 3SF
T: 020 8985 3570
E: ppra528898@aol.com
www.centreforbetterhealth.org.uk
Promotes the rehabilitation of the mentally sick on their return home, to employment and society by preparatory work and after-care in the community; and promotes practical measures in research for the prevention and combating of mental stress within the community.

Psychosynthesis and Education Trust

London SE1 2TH
T: 020 7403 2100
F: 020 7403 5562
E: enquiries@petrust.org.uk
www.psychosynthesis.edu
The Trust's main purpose is to gain recognition for the central role of soul and self in psychology, and to renew the soul in the everyday life of individuals, the family, groups, organisations and society. Other activities include promoting the practice of transpersonal counselling and psychotherapy by providing a training centre of excellence, and providing psychosynthesis educational techniques suitable for schools and adult education.
Employees: 29
Regional offices: 1

Public Concern at Work

Suite 301, 16 Baldwins Gardens, London EC1N 7RJ
T: 020 7404 6609
E: whistle@pcaw.co.uk
www.pcaw.org.uk
Acting as a leading, independent authority on public interest whistleblowing, PCaW aims to improve standards in the public, private and voluntary sectors and to assert the accountability of people in the workplace.

Public Fundraising Regulatory Association

Unit 11, Europoint Centre, 511 Lavington Street, London SE1 0NZ
T: 020 7401 8452
E: info@pfra.org.uk
www.pfra.org.uk
Chief Executive: Sally de la Bedoyere
The PFRA regulates the use of face-to-face fundraising by charities and professional fundraising organisations, principally on the street and doorstep. We work with local authorities to agree equitable access to fundraising sites and monitor their use to ensure fundraisers abide by the Institute of Fundraisings codes of practice.
Employees: 9
Regional offices: 1

Public Law Project

150 Caledonian Road, London N1 9RD
T: 020 7843 1260
F: 020 7837 7048
E: admin@publiclawproject.org.uk
www.publiclawproject.org.uk
Aims to improve access to public law remedies, such as judicial review, for people whose access is limited because of poverty, discrimination or other disadvantages.
Employees: 8
Volunteers: 3
Regional offices: 1

PublicMedia Projects CIC

82A, Highfield Road, Dartford, Kent DA1 2JJ
T: 01322 405540
E: vb@publicmedia.co.uk
www.publicmedia.co.uk
Enterprise Director: Vince Braithwaite
PublicMedia Projects is a social enterprise – community interest company which has been set-up to support the introduction of locally-based media services in the UK. Through new internet and radio services -etc., PublicMedia Projects aims to support the social and economic regeneration of local communities, and empower people to engage more effectively in civic society. These services will also create a space for the creative industries to produce content which is both entertaining and engaging.

QED – UK

Quest House, 243 Manningham Lane, Bradford BD8 7ER
T: 01274 483267
F: 01274 305689
E: info@qed-uk.org
www.qed-uk.org
Aims to improve the economic, social and education development of minority ethnic groups. Mainly focusing on disadvantaged South Asian communities.
Employees: 15
Volunteers: 20

Quaker Social Action

E: judithmoran@qsa.org.uk

Queen Alexandra College

Court Oak Road, Harborne, Birmingham B17 9TG
T: 0121 428 5050
F: 0121 428 5048
E: enquiries@qac.ac.uk
www.qac.ac.uk
Queen Alexandra College aims to challenge discrimination and exclusion by providing opportunities for people with visual impairment and other disabilities to learn, live and work independently.
Employees: 115
Volunteers: 10

Queen Elizabeth's Foundation for Disabled People

Leatherhead Court, Woodlands Road, Leatherhead, Surrey KT22 0BN
T: 01372 841100
F: 01372 844072
E: sue.moller@qef.org.uk
www.qef.org.uk
Chief Executive: Jonathan Powell
QEF works with people living with physical and learning disabilities or acquired brain injuries to gain new skills and increase independence. Whether it's learning everyday skills, rebuilding a life affected by brain injury, acquiring the skills to drive a specially adapted car or training for future employment, QEF supports disabled people to achieve goals for life.
Employees: 300
Volunteers: 300

Queen Victoria Seamen's Rest

121-131 East India Dock Road, Poplar, London E14 6DF
T: 020 7987 5466
E: enquiries@qvsr.org.uk
www.qvsr.org.uk
Provides secure and comfortable accommodation; fosters a spirit of community internally and externally; supports, empowers and enables individuals to enhance their quality of life; provides active rehabilitation opportunities; integrates our services into the lives of the local community.

QUIT

211 Old Street, London EC1V 9NR
T: 020 7251 1551
F: 020 7251 1661
E: reception@quit.org.uk
www.quit.org.uk
Helps smokers trying to stop smoking. QUIT provides practical, relevant and professional support to the 12 million smokers in Britain.
Employees: 60
Volunteers: 200

Race on the Agenda

c/o Resource for London, 356 Holloway Road, London N7 6PA
T: 020 7697 4093
E: rota@rota.org.uk
www.rota.org.uk
Chief Executive: Andy Gregg
To be a BAME-led social policy think-tank that focuses on race equality and issues affecting Britain's BAME communities, and creates an environment for the equalities third sector to flourish. To strengthen the voice of BAME communities through increased civic engagement and participation in society and provide representation of issues affecting BAME communities and the sector that was set up to serve them.
Employees: 7
Volunteers: 3
Regional offices: 1

Raglan Housing Association

Wright House, Poole, Dorset BH15 1BQ
T: 01202 678731
Helpline: 0845 070 7772
F: 01202 665091
E: info@raglan.org
www.raglan.org
Chief Executive: Alan Seabright
Raglan's purpose is to meet a variety of housing needs by providing quality, affordable homes, high-standard services and by promoting and encouraging sustainable communities. Our resident involvement policy offers a wide range of opportunities for volunteers to monitor performance and contribute to our drive for continuing improvement in the homes and services we deliver.
Employees: 400
Volunteers: 150
Regional offices: 6

Railway Children

1st Floor, 1 The Commons, Sandbach, Cheshire CW11 1EG
T: 01270 251571 (also fax)
E: enquiries@railwaychildren.org.uk
www.railwaychildren.org.uk
Railway Children exists to help street children. No child should have to live alone and at risk on the streets, and this belief is reflected in the charity's vision, which is to create a world of safety and opportunity for children who are at risk on the streets.
Employees: 6
Volunteers: 5

Rainbow Centre for Children affected by Life-Threatening Illnesses or Bereavement

27 Lilymead Avenue, Knowle, Bristol BS4 2BY
T: 0117 985 3343
E: contact@rainbowcentre.org.uk
www.rainbowcentre.org.uk
Centre Director: Angela Emms
The Rainbow Centre supports children and their families experiencing cancer and other life-threatening illnesses or bereavement, using counselling and complementary therapies.
Regional offices: 1

Rainbow Trust Children's Charity

6 Cleeve Court, Cleeve Road, Leatherhead, Surrey KT22 7UD
T: 01372 363438
F: 01372 363101
E: louise.whitby@rainbowtrust.org.uk
www.rainbowtrust.org.uk
Chief Executive: Heather Wood
Rainbow Trust provides emotional and practical support for families who have a child with a life-threatening or terminal illness. We offer the whole family individually tailored, high-quality support for as long as they need it.
Employees: 80
Volunteers: 50
Regional offices: 8

Rainforest Foundation UK

233A Kentish Town Road, London NW5 2JT
T: 020 7485 0193
F: 020 7485 0315
E: info@rainforestuk.org
www.rainforestfoundationuk.org
Executive Director: Simon Counsell
The Rainforest Foundation UK supports indigenous peoples of the world's rainforests in their efforts to protect the environment and fulfil their rights to life, land and livelihoods.
Employees: 20
Volunteers: 2

Rainy Day Trust

Federation House, 10 Vyse Street, Birmingham B18 6LT
T: 0121 237 1130
F: 0121 237 1133
E: diane@rainydaytrust.org.uk
www.rainydaytrust.org.uk
General Secretary: Diane Stevens
The Rainy Day Trust is a charity that exists solely to help people who have worked in the UK's home improvement and home enhancement industry including DIY/hardware stores, garden centres, pottery & glass, housewares and all the manufacturers, distributors and wholesalers who supply them. We can assist in variety of ways however all applicants should have worked for one/more of the above industries for at least three years.
Employees: 2
Volunteers: 5
Income: £165,385 (2013-14)

Raleigh International Trust

3rd Floor, Dean Bradley House, 52 Horseferry Road, London SW1P 2AF
T: 020 7183 1270
F: 020 7504 8094
E: s.adams@raleighinternational.org
www.raleighinternational.org
Chief Executive: Stacey Adams
Raleigh International supports people and communities to overcome the challenges they face, and help them to find the best solutions. By bringing together teams of young volunteers with communities in rural areas, and through a hands-on learning approach, we inspire and empower them to create lasting change. Our programmes focus on improving access to safe water and sanitation, building community resilience, and empowering communities to sustainably manage their natural resources. Alongside our local and international volunteers, project partners, local communities, funders, and 40,000 previous volunteers, we form a global community who are passionate about working together to build a sustainable future.
Employees: 102
Volunteers: 2,125
Regional offices: 5
Income: £6,867,000 (2013-14)

Ramblers' Association

2nd Floor, Camelford House, London SE1 7TW
T: 020 7339 8571
F: 020 7339 8501
E: ramblers@london.ramblers.org.uk
www.ramblers.org.uk
Promotes walking, protects rights of way, campaigns for access to open country and defends the beauty of the countryside.
Employees: 60
Volunteers: 5000
Regional offices: 3

Rape and Sexual Abuse Support Centre - Rape Crisis South London

PO Box 383, Croydon, Surrey CR9 2AW
T: 020 8683 3311
Helpline: 0808 802 9999
F: 020 8683 3366
E: info@rasasc.org.uk
www.rasasc.org.uk
Chief Executive Officer: Yvonne Traynor
A professional and passionate team working in a centre of excellence dedicated to the healing and empowerment of survivors of sexual violence by providing counselling, helpline support, advocacy through the criminal justice system, outreach to women involved in prostitution, training and information for other agencies. Services provided in Kingston, Southwark, Bexley and Crawley.
Employees: 38
Volunteers: 28
Regional offices: 4

Rapid Effective Assistance for Children with Potentially Terminal Illness

St Luke's House, 270 Sandycombe Road, Richmond Upon Thames, Surrey TW9 3NP
T: 020 8940 2575
F: 020 8940 2050
E: react@reactcharity.org
www.reactcharity.org
Identifies and responds to the needs of children and young people diagnosed as suffering from potentially terminal illnesses.
Employees: 4
Volunteers: 30
Regional offices: 1

Rare Breeds Survival Trust

Stoneleigh Park, Kenilworth, Warwickshire CV8 2LG
T: 024 7669 6551
F: 024 7669 6706
E: enquiries@rbst.org.uk
www.rbst.org.uk
CEO: Tom Beeston
The Rare Breeds Survival Trust is the leading national charity working to conserve and protect the UK's rare native breeds of farm animals from extinction. We believe in the value of the UK's rich and varied livestock heritage and that this needs to be conserved as a vital genetic resource for future generations and the benefit of agriculture.
Employees: 9
Volunteers: 250
Regional offices: 20

Rare Disease UK

Unit 4D, Leroy House, 436 Essex Road, London N1 3QP
T: 020 7704 3141
E: info@raredisease.org.uk
www.raredisease.org.uk
Chair: Alastair Kent
The national alliance for people with rare diseases and all who support them.

Rathbone

4th Floor, Churchgate House, 56 Oxford Street, Manchester M1 6EU
T: 0161 236 5358
F: 0161 238 6356
E: julie.lewis@rathboneuk.org
www.rathboneuk.org
Chief Executive: Richard Williams
Rathbone is a charity that provides education and training opportunities to over 14,000 young people annually. Rathbone is dedicated to working with young people who have not had their needs met by mainstream education. Many such young people require support to access opportunities that are tailored to their learning and social needs. Rathbone has four core areas: alternative school curriculum for young people aged 1416, apprenticeships, pre-vocational activities and youth engagement.
Employees: 750
Volunteers: 40
Regional offices: 89

Raw Material Music and Media Education

2 Robsart Street SW9 0DJ
T: 020 7737 6103
F: 020 7733 7533
E: tim@raw-material.org
www.raw-material.org
Promotes education and training in the creative and expressive arts and media.

Raynaud's & Scleroderma Association (RSA)

112 Crewe Road, Alsager, Cheshire ST7 2JA
T: 01270 872776
E: info@raynauds.org.uk
www.raynauds.org.uk
Chief Executive Officer: Elizabeth Bevins
Raynaud's is a common condition in which blood is prevented from reaching the

extremities of the body, mainly the fingers and toes, on exposure to the cold or any slight change in temperature. Scleroderma is an uncommon disease of the blood vessels, the immune system and the connective tissue. The Association's aims are to promote a better communication between doctors and patients, to disseminate information and to raise funds for research and welfare projects.
Employees: 6

RCJ Advice Bureau

Royal Courts of Justice, Strand,
London WC2A 2LL
T: 020 7947 7119
F: 020 7947 7167
E: james.banks@rcjadvice.org.uk
www.rcjadvice.org.uk
Chief Executive: James Banks
Works to provide access to justice to unrepresented litigants in the Royal Courts of Justice and the Principal Registry of the Family Division, through the provision of legal and other advice services.
Employees: 21
Volunteers: 35

Re-Solv

30A High Street, Stone,
Staffordshire ST15 8AW
T: 01785 817885
F: 01785 813205
E: information@re-solv.org
www.re-solv.org
Director: Stephen Ream
Re-Solv works to contribute to happier, healthier, safer social environments by preventing the death, suffering and crime, which may result as a consequence of solvent and volatile substance abuse (VSA).
Employees: 5
Volunteers: 14
Regional offices: 1

Re-Start

56 Davids Way, Hainault, Ilford,
Essex IG6 3BQ
T: 020 8501 1096
Helpline: 020 3087 5699
E: restartoffice@gmail.com
www.restartoffice.blogspot.com
CE: Moinul Khalique
Re-Start is a social-work-led voluntary organisation, working in partnership with Job Centre Plus We currently run a number of programmes, mainly of a solution-focused therapeutic nature, targeting specific groups, such as claimants of incapacity benefits in some of the most deprived parts of east and north east London. Many of the clients referred to us sometimes lack the motivation and determination to change their circumstances.
Employees: 1
Volunteers: -5

REACH

Camelford House,
87-89 Albert Embankment,
London SE1 7TP
T: 020 7582 6543
F: 020 7582 2423
E: mail@reachskills.org.uk
www.reachskills.org.uk
REACH's aims are to recruit and support people with managerial, professional, business and technical experience and match them with part-time voluntary roles throughout the UK, and to help voluntary organisations gain access to these potential volunteers and benefit fully from their expertise.
Employees: 7
Volunteers: 60
Regional offices: 1

Reach - Association for Children with Upper Limb Deficiency

Pearl Assurance House, Brook Street,
Tavistock, Devon PL19 0BN
T: 0845 130 6225
E: reach@reach.org.uk
www.reach.org.uk
National Coordinator: Jo Dixon
Reach was formed in 1978 by parents of children who were missing part of their arm or a hand, in order to lobby for the provision of a new artificial arm under the NHS. Since then Reach has grown to become a national organisation providing support and information for children with hand or arm deficiencies, and their parents.
Employees: 2
Volunteers: 25
Regional offices: 14

Reading Matters

Western House, Western Way,
Halifax Road, Bradford,
West Yorkshire BD6 2SZ
T: 01274 692219
E: rachel@readingmatters.org.uk
www.readingmatters.org.uk
Chief Executive: Rachel Kelly
Reading Matters improves reading skills. We specialise in one-to-one support to motivate children and young people to reach their potential by becoming confident and enthusiastic readers. As an effective literacy support charity, we support a network of trained volunteer Reading Mentors across West and South Yorkshire and train adults, young people and children across the UK to offer reading support.
Employees: 5
Volunteers: 90
Regional offices: 1
Income: £131,862 (2012-13)

Reading Mencap

21 Alexandra Road, Reading,
Berkshire RG1 5PE
T: 0118 966 2518
E: businessrelations@readingmencap.org.uk
www.readingmencap.org.uk/
CEO: Mandi Smith
We provide services from birth and throughout life for carers and children and adults with Learning Disability and Difficulties (LDD) and aim to reduce inequality in statutory services, combat isolation and discrimination, and to bring to local people an experience of having people with LDD as part of their community.
Employees: 22
Volunteers: 30
Income: £120,000 (2012-13)

Real Life Options

A1 Business Park, Knottingley Road,
Knottingley, West Yorkshire WF11 0BL
T: 01977 781800
F: 01977 795361
E: dave.rawnsley@reallifeoptions.org
www.reallifeoptions.org
Chief Executive: Brian Hutchinson
We all strive to enjoy our lives, experience excitement, make our own decisions and aim for the stars. Some of us may need support to help us achieve our goals and aspirations; this includes people with learning disabilities, autism or intellectual impairments. That's where Real Life Options excels. Across the UK we support people to make their own choices, to have the same experiences we take for granted and, above all, to enjoy their lives.
Employees: 2000
Volunteers: 2
Regional offices: 15
Income: £38,018,192 (2012-13)

Realife Trust

3 The Courtyard, Windhill, Bishop's Stortford, Hertfordshire CM23 2ND
T: 01279 504735
F: 01279 757658
E: info@realife.org.uk
www.realife.org.uk
Employees: 12
Volunteers: 20

Redbridge Council for Voluntary Service

3rd Floor, Forest House, 16-20 Clements Road, Ilford IG1 1BA
T: 020 8553 1004
F: 020 8911 9128
E: ross@redbridgecvs.net
www.redbridgecvs.net
Chief Officer: Ross Diamond

RedbridgeCVS is the umbrella body for the voluntary sector in the north east London Borough of Redbridge. We provide the functions of a CVS and a Volunteer Centre and provide a range of support services to local groups. We exist to support a strong, effective and independent voluntary and community sector in Redbridge.

Employees: 31
Volunteers: 20
Regional offices: 1
Income: £1,672,910 (2014-15)

RedR UK

250A Kennington Lane, London SE11 5RD
T: 020 7840 6000
F: 020 7582 8669
E: jo.barrett@redr.org.uk
www.redr.org.uk
CEO: Martin McCann

RedR is a leading international disaster relief charity that trains aid workers and provides skilled professionals to humanitarian programmes worldwide.

Employees: 120
Volunteers: 8
Regional offices: 6

Reedham Children's Trust

The Lodge, 23 Old Lodge Lane, Purley, Surrey CR8 4DJ
T: 020 8660 1461
F: 020 8763 1293
E: info@reedham-trust.org.uk
www.reedham-trust.org.uk
CEO: Sarah Smart

We help some of the most vulnerable children in our society who though death, illness, disability or substance abuse of a parent are left with a home environment that does not provide them with care and stability. We assist them to attend boarding schools thereby giving them space and security to thrive and receive a great education whilst also keeping the families together

Employees: 4

Refuge

4th Floor, International House, 1 St Katharine's Way, London E1W 1UN
T: 020 7395 7700
Helpline: 0808 200 0247
F: 020 7395 7721
E: info@refuge.org.uk
www.refuge.org.uk

Refuge is the national charity that provides a wide range of specialist domestic violence services to women and children experiencing domestic violence. On any given day our services support 3000 women and children.

Employees: 175
Volunteers: 12

Refugee Action

11 Belgrave Road, London SW1V 1RB
T: 020 7952 1511
E: lyna@refugee-action.org.uk
www.refugee-action.org
Chief Executive: Dave Garratt

Across England, Refugee Action works to: provide high-quality reception, advice and information to refugees and asylum seekers; promote the development of refugee communities; improve access to employment and mainstream services, and enhance opportunities for refugees and asylum-seekers; raise awareness, influence policy, and campaign for refugee rights; advise and assist asylum seekers and irregular migrants who are considering voluntary return.

Employees: 205
Volunteers: 200
Regional offices: 9

Refugee Council

London SW9 8BB
T: 020 7346 6700
F: 020 7582 9929
E: supporter@refugeecouncil.org.uk
www.refugeecouncil.org.uk
Employees: 350
Volunteers: 200
Regional offices: 8

Refugee Legal Centre

Nelson House, London E1 2DA
T: 020 7780 3320
E: rlc@refugee-legal-centre.org.uk
www.refugee-legal-centre.org.uk

Provides legal advice and representation (free of charge) to asylum seekers and refugees.

Refugee Therapy Centre

40 St John's Way, London N19 3RR
T: 020 7272 2565
E: aida@refugeetherapycentre.freeserve.co.uk
www.refugeetherapy.org.uk

Provides counselling, psychotherapy and associated treatment to children, adolescents and young refugees and asylum seekers and their families.

Regard

BM Regard, London WC1N 3XX
E: secretary@regard.org.uk
www.regard.org.uk

A national organisation of lesbians, gay men, bisexuals and transgender people (LGBT) who self-identify as disabled. We follow the Social Model of Disability. This is a way of thinking about disability that says it is society that needs to change by removing the barriers that deny us inclusion and equal rights. We offer information, support and campaign. Regard is run by its members for its members and has no paid staff.

Regional Studies Association

PO Box 2058, Seaford BN25 4QU
T: 01323 899698 (also fax)
E: support@rsc-london.ac.uk
www.regionalstudies.org

Provides, as an interdisciplinary group, a forum in which to discuss regional issues and to publish the results of related research.

Employees: 3
Volunteers: 12

Registry Trust Limited

E: mhurlston@hurlstons.com

Relate Brighton, Hove, Worthing and Districts

E: jo.carden@brightonrelate.org.uk

Relate Central Office

Herbert Gray College, Little Church Street, Rugby, Warwickshire CV21 3AP
T: 01788 563824
F: 01788 563825
E: enquiries@national.relate.org.uk
www.relate.org.uk

Aims to educate the public concerning the benefits of secure couple relationships, marriage and family life in order to improve the emotional, sexual and spiritual wellbeing of individuals that is derived from committed relationships.

Relate Lincolnshire

138 High Street, Lincoln,
Lincolnshire LN5 7PJ
T: 01522 524922
F: 01522 569238
E: ron.thorn@relate-lincs.org.uk
www.relate-lincs.org.uk
Centre Manager: Marilyn Merry
To enhance the health of adults and children by increasing public awareness of the benefit of committed relationships, marriage, and family life and working to prevent poverty, hardship and distress caused by the breakdown of such relationships Providing counselling, advice, education, guidance and relief to adults and/or children in relation to any aspect of contemporary life or work
Employees: 40
Volunteers: 20
Regional offices: 11
Income: £560,000 (2013-14)

Relatives and Residents Association

24 The Ivories, London N1 2HY
T: 020 7359 8148
Helpline: 020 7359 8136
F: 020 7226 6603
E: gillian.dalley@relres.org
www.relres.org
Chief Executive: Gillian Dalley
The Association exists for older people needing, or living in, residential care and the families and friends. As well as a listening ear, relatives need to know how to understand the complex regulations about paying for care, or to complain about the quality of care their loved ones are receiving. It offers support and information via its helpline; specific project work; influencing policy and practice; and working with local relatives and residents groups in care homes.
Employees: 5
Volunteers: 6
Regional offices: 20

Release

124-128 City Road, London EC1V 2NJ
T: 020 7324 2979
Helpline: 020 7324 2989
F: 020 7324 2977
E: ask@release.org.uk
www.release.org.uk
Executive Director: Niamh Eastwood
Release is the national centre of expertise on drugs, law and human rights. We provide legal advice to those affected by the UK drugs laws. We also provide a specialist drugs helpline. Advice can be sought via telephone or email.
Employees: 13
Volunteers: 50
Income: £600,000 (2014-15)

REMA

The Unity Centre,
St Leonards Road S65 1PD
T: 01709 720744
E: team@rema-online.org.uk
www.rema-online.org.uk
Chief Executive: Azizzum Akhtar
REMA is the infrastructure support organisation for the Black and Minority Ethnic Voluntary and Community Sector of Rotherham. Our Mission is to support the development of voluntary and community action that is effective, sustainable and brings about positive social change for the BME Voluntary, Community and Faith Sector (VCFS) and communities. We provide small group support, capacity building and recruitment advice. We also support voice and influence activity by hosting networks for the Bme communities
Employees: 5
Volunteers: 5
Income: £80,000 (2012-13)

Remap

D9 Chaucer Business Park, Watery Lane,
Kemsing, Kent TN15 6YU
T: 01732 760209
F: 01732 760204
E: data@remap.org.uk
www.remap.org.uk
Remap is an established national charity which provides one-off pieces of equipment for people with disabilities. Each year Remap helps about 4000 people in this way, helping them to lead more fulfilling and independent lives.
Employees: 5
Volunteers: 1500

Renaisi Limited

21 Garden Walk, London EC2A 3EQ
T: 020 7033 2600
F: 020 7033 2631
E: info@renaisi.com
www.renaisi.com
Chief Executive: Clive Tritton
Renaisi is an award-winning social enterprise that helps people and places to thrive. We do this by: developing strategies to maximise economic, social and cultural assets to create successful places; equipping and empowering individuals to find sustainable and secure employment; enabling resilient, confident, cohesive and flourishing communities.
Employees: 60
Income: £2,500,000 (2014-15)

Rescare

Steven Jackson House, 31 Buxton Road,
Heaviley, Stockport SK2 6LS
T: 0161 474 3723
Helpline: 0800 032 7330
E: office@rescare.org.uk
www.rescare.org.uk
Works for the relief and welfare of people with a learning disability in all types of residential accommodation. Gives help, support and advice to the families of such disabled people.

Rescue: the British Archaeological Trust

15A Bull Plain, Hertford SG14 1DX
T: 01992 553377
E: rescue@rescue-archaeology.freeserve.co.uk
www.rescue-archaeology.org.uk
Aims to preserve and record the archaeological and historic environment. Acts as a fundraising body and publications outlet, and works to increase public awareness of the destruction of our heritage.

Research Society of Process Oriented Psychology UK

c/o Interchange Studios,
Hampstead Town Hall Centre,
213 Haverstock Hill, London NW3 4QP
T: 0870 429 5296
E: contact@rspopuk.com
www.rspopuk.com
RS POP UK is the national forum and organising body for process work in the UK. It organises a full and exciting annual programme of workshops, classes, supervision, training and private therapy with teachers and therapists from the British and international process work community.

Resources for Autism

858 Finchley Road, Temple Fortune,
London NW11 6AB
T: 020 8458 3259
F: 020 8458 3222
E: liza.dresner@resourcesforautism.org.uk
www.resourcesforautism.org.uk
Director: Liza Dresner
Provides practical services including play and youth clubs, respite schemes, outreach home support, music and art therapy and advice

and information to individuals with an autistic spectrum condition and their families.
Employees: 220
Volunteers: 200
Regional offices: 1
Income: £1,500,000 (2014-15)

RESPECT

4th Floor, Development House,
56-64 Leonard Street, London EC2A 4LT
T: 020 7549 0578
Helpline: 0808 802 4040
E: info@respect.uk.net
www.respect.uk.net
Respect is the UK membership association for domestic violence perpetrator programmes and associated support services. Its key focus is on increasing the safety of those experiencing domestic violence through promoting effective interventions with perpetrators. An information and advice phone line is central to RESPECTs activities: this is used both by those carrying out abuse and those who have suffered it, as well as professionals who come into contact with domestic violence situations.
Employees: 12
Regional offices: 1

RESPOND

Respond, 3rd Floor, 24-32 Stephenson Way, London NW1 2HD
T: 020 7383 0700
E: admin@respond.org.uk
www.respond.org.uk
Chief Executive: Noelle Blackman
Respond exists to: lessen the effect of trauma and abuse on people with learning disabilities their families and supporters. We do this through providing psychotherapy for people with learning disabilities; advice and support for staff and families; training for professionals; education for people with learning disabilities; influencing generic services to make their services accessible; influencing learning disability services to consider the psychological impact of living with learning disabilities; undertaking research and disseminating our findings.
Regional offices: 1

Response International (HMD)

Office 11, Interlink House,
73a Maygrove Road, London NW6 2EG
T: 020 7372 6972
E: ri@responseinternational.org.uk
www.responseinternational.org.uk
Chief Executive: Philip Garvin
Emergency and rehabilitation services for victims of conflict: primary health, landmine action, rehabilitation of torture victims and amputees, reconstruction of health infrastructure, provision of prosthetics, training of health professionals.
Employees: 50
Volunteers: 15
Regional offices: 4

Restorative Justice Council

Beacon House, 113 Kingsway, Holborn, London WC2B 6PP
T: 020 7831 5700
E: enquiries@restorativejustice.org.uk
www.restorativejustice.org.uk
Chief executive officer: Jon Collins
The Restorative Justice Council (RJC) is the independent third sector membership body for the field of restorative practice. It provides quality assurance and a national voice advocating the widespread use of all forms of restorative practice, including restorative justice. The RJC's vision is of a restorative society where everyone has access to safe, high quality restorative practice wherever and whenever it is needed.
Employees: 19

Restricted Growth Association

PO Box 99, Lydney,
Gloucestershire GL15 9AW
T: 0300 111 1970
F: 0300 111 2454
E: office@restrictedgrowth.co.uk
www.restrictedgrowth.co.uk
The RGA is a self-help charity dealing with the medical and social consequences of restricted growth/dwarfism. It provides a telephone helpline, dedicated medical and benefits advisers and regular opportunities to meet others in a supportive social setting. The RGA also produces a variety of information publications about the different forms of dwarfism and provides members with a quarterly magazine.

Retirement Trust

Silton Cottage, Chantlers Hill,
Paddock Wood, Tonbridge, Kent TN12 6LX
T: 01892 838474
E: info@theretirementtrust.org.uk
www.theretirementtrust.org.uk
Chair: Roger Parkes
The Trust aims to bring pre-retirement advice, support and education to a wide range of employees.
Volunteers: 5

Rett UK

Langham House West, Mill Street,
Luton LU1 2NA
T: 01582 798910
Helpline: 01582 798911
E: info@rettuk.org
www.rettuk.org
Offers support, friendship and practical help to those families and carers who have a child or adult with Rett syndrome. Rett UK helps inform and train professionals in the fields of research, education, treatment, diagnosis, care and understanding of the condition.
Employees: 5
Volunteers: 120
Income: £207,598 (2014-15)

Returned Volunteer Action

5 Balls Pond Road, London N1 4AX
T: 020 7247 6406
E: retvolact@lineone.net
Returned Volunteer Action is a membership organisation open to both people who have been development volunteers or workers, and to those interested in the field. It provides information and training materials for those interested in becoming volunteers. A resource list is available on request.
Volunteers: 20
Income: £3,500 (2014-15)

Revolving Doors Agency

The Turnmill, 63 Clerkenwell Road,
London EC1M 5NP
T: 020 7253 4038
F: 020 7553 6079
E: admin@revolving-doors.org.uk
www.revolving-doors.co.uk
Revolving Doors agency is the UK's leading independent charity dedicated to working with people with mental health problems in touch with the criminal justice system.
Employees: 30
Volunteers: 1

RICA (Research Institute for Consumer Affairs)

Unit G03, The Wenlock,
50-52 Wharf Road, London N1 7EU
T: 020 7427 2460
E: mail@rica.org.uk
www.rica.org.uk
Co-Directors: Caroline Jacobs and Jasper Holmes
Rica is an independent consumer research charity with specialist expertise in product testing, user trials, focus groups and mystery shopping. Rica provides unbiased consumer information for older/disabled consumers e.g.. motoring guides including on car

adaptations, an online car search, and other relevant information. The aim of Rica is to increase awareness among manufacturers, service providers and policy makers to improve products and services to meet the needs of disabled and older consumers.
Employees: 6

Richmond Fellowship

80 Holloway Road, London N7 8JG
T: 020 7697 3300
F: 020 7697 3301
E: communications@richmondfellowship.org.uk
www.richmondfellowship.org.uk
Provides residential care, counselling and support, as well as rehabilitation and work skills, to men and women who are recovering from emotional disturbance, addiction and mental health problems. The Fellowship encourages greater public awareness and understanding of mental health problems.
Employees: 686
Regional offices: 4

Riding for the Disabled Association

Norfolk House, 1A Tournament Court, Edgehill Drive, Warwick, Warwickshire CV34 6LG
T: 0845 658 1082
F: 0845 658 1083
E: info@rda.org.uk
www.rda.org.uk
Chief Executive: Ed Bracher
RDA is a national charity dedicated to improving the lives of people with disabilities, through the provision of opportunities for riding and/or carriage driving. Through 500 member groups we enable people to improve their health and wellbeing, delivering a real and lasting therapy that not only benefits mobility and co-ordination, but also encourages confidence and self-worth whilst having fun. Currently 28,000 people with a wide range of disabilities and of all ages ride with RDA.
Employees: 17
Volunteers: 18000
Regional offices: 500

Right From the Start

84/86 Lewis Street, Aberbargoed, Bargoed, Caerphilly, Mid Glamorgan CF81 9EA
T: 01443 879426
F: 01443 879621
E: info@rfts.org.uk
www.rightfromthestart.co.uk
Project coordinator: Sian Williams
Supports families with Children within the Caerphilly Borough. Delivering Parenting Groups within the local communities and offering housing related support to families within their own home, covering a range of issues such as debt management, budgeting, managing accommodation, healthy living amongst other tenancy related support to ensure families are able to live independently within their own communities
Employees: 12
Volunteers: 5
Regional offices: 1

Rights of Women

52-54 Featherstone Street, London EC1Y 8RT
E: info@row.org.uk
www.rightsofwomen.org.uk
Director: Emma Scott
Rights of Women is a women's voluntary organisation committed to informing, educating and empowering women concerning their legal rights. We provide free legal advice on issues of family law including: divorce and relationship breakdown, children and contact issues, domestic violence, complaints about solicitors.
Income: £290,170 (2013-14)

RNIB National Library Service

Far Cromwell Road, Bredbury, Stockport SK6 2SG
Helpline: 0845 762 6843
F: 0161 355 2098
E: reader.advice@rnib.org.uk
www.rnib.org.uk/reading
Head of RNIB National Library Service: Helen Brazier
Provides books and information for blind and partially sighted children and adults in a range of accessible formats including audio (unabridged Daisy CDs), braille, Moon, large print (16pt type) and giant print (24pt type). We also provide free access to online reference information, braille sheet music, themed book lists and a quarterly reader magazine.
Employees: 35
Volunteers: 950
Regional offices: 2

RoadPeace

PO Box 2579, London NW10 3PW
T: 020 8838 5102
Helpline: 0845 450 0355
F: 020 8838 5103
E: rplist@roadpeace.org
www.roadpeace.org
Executive Director: Amy Aeron-Thomas
RoadPeace is Britain's national charity for road traffic victims, set up in 1992. RoadPeace provides support for people bereaved and injured in road crashes through a national helpline, and gives specialist advice and support. RoadPeace supports road danger reduction and the promotion of transport policies, which give greater consideration to vulnerable road users and the environment.
Employees: 4
Volunteers: 100

Roald Dahl's Marvellous Children's Charity

81a High Street, Great Missenden, Buckinghamshire HP16 0AL
T: 01494 890465
E: richardp@roalddahlcharity.org
www.roalddahlcharity.org
Chief Executive: Richard Piper
Making life better for children with severe, rare and under-supported health conditions. We create new Roald Dahl Nurse posts, give grants directly to families, and run a range of proactive programmes in partnership with others.
Employees: 11
Volunteers: 6
Income: £869,730 (2013-14)

Roots HR CIC

The Coach House, 30a Church Street, Kidderminster, Worcestershire DY10 2AX
T: 0845 543 8429
E: admin@rootshr.org.uk
www.rootshr.org.uk
Chief Executive : Jan Golding
Roots HR CIC is the UK's specialist consultancy for human resources and health and safety services for the social sector. We enable organisations to continually improve performance and sustainability through better people management, whilst ensuring an understanding of and compliance with employment legislation. Founded in 2009, we operate as a social enterprise, providing high quality and affordable services to social sector organisations.
Employees: 7
Regional offices: 1
Income: £300,000 (2014-15)

RoSA

P.O. Box 151, Rugby, Warwickshire CV21 3WR
T: 01788 551150
Helpline: 01788 551151
E: lindalewis.rosa@btconnect.com
www.rosasupport.org
Agency Director: Linda Lewis

We are an independent charity working with survivors of rape, sexual assault and childhood sexual abuse and their families. We offer a completely confidential service and support women, men, young people and children from the age of 5. All counsellors and support workers at RoSA have received comprehensive specialist training and work to BACP guidelines. We are the founder members of The Survivors Trust, a national umbrella agency.
Employees: 8
Volunteers: 50
Regional offices: 1
Income: ££125.00 (2013-14)

Rotary International in Great Britain and Ireland

Kinwarton Road, Alcester,
Warwickshire B49 6BP
T: 01789 765411
F: 01789 765570
E: secretary@ribi.org
www.ribi.org
There are some 58,000 Rotarians in Great Britain and Ireland in 1,845 clubs, helping those in need and working towards world understanding and peace.
Employees: 18
Volunteers: 60000

Rounders England

Unit 15, Venture 1 Business Park,
Long Acre Close, Holbrook Industrial Estate,
Sheffield, South Yorkshire S20 3FR
T: 0114 248 0357
E: oliver.wilson@roundersengland.co.uk
www.roundersengland.co.uk
Operations Director: Alison Steel
Rounders England is the sport's governing body in England. Based in Sheffield it provides a structure for the sport from the Board, county associations and clubs right the way through to individual members and volunteers.
Employees: 13
Volunteers: 1000+
Regional offices: 1
Income: £757,800 (2012-13)

Rowntree Society

Tanners Yard, Huntington Road,
Huntington, York,
North Yorkshire YO31 1ET
T: 01904 425499
E: burkeman@gn.apc.org
www.rowntreewalks.org
Volunteers: 12

Roy Castle Lung Cancer Foundation

200 London Road, Liverpool L3 9TA
T: 0871 220 5426
F: 0871 220 5427
E: roycastle@liv.ac.uk
www.roycastle.org
The Foundation secures the development of the Roy Castle International Centre for Lung Cancer research and health promotion; promotes and funds clinical laboratory and epidemiological research into the causes, prevention and treatment of lung cancer; provides amenities intended to improve the quality of life of the patients and relieve and alleviate the distress of relatives of the patients.
Employees: 60
Volunteers: 100
Regional offices: 2

Royal Academy of Dance

36 Battersea Square, London SW11 3RA
T: 020 7326 8000
F: 020 7924 3129
E: info@rad.org.uk
www.rad.org.uk
Chief Executive: Luke Rittner
The Royal Academy of Dance is a global organisation with over 13,000 members. With offices in 79 countries and headquarters in London, it is the largest ballet examination and teacher training institution in the world. Its mission is to promote knowledge, understanding and practice of dance internationally. It seeks to accomplish its mission through examining students of ballet, educating and training teachers of dance and promoting the study and performance of dance.
Employees: 180

Royal Agricultural Benevolent Institution

Shaw House, 27 West Way, Botley, Oxford,
Oxfordshire OX2 0QH
T: 01865 724931
Helpline: 01865 727888
F: 01865 202025
E: info@rabi.org.uk
www.rabi.org.uk
Chief Executive: Paul Burrows
The national farming charity for England and Wales. Helping those in need in the farming community during times of hardship.
Employees: 114

Royal Air Force Benevolent Fund

67 Portland Place, London W1B 1AR
T: 020 7580 8343
Helpline: 0800 169 2942
F: 020 7636 7005
E: enquiries@rafbf.org.uk
www.rafbf.org
Controller: Robert Wright
The Royal Air Force Benevolent Fund provides assistance to members and former members of the Royal Air Force, and their dependants, who need support as a consequence of poverty, sickness, disability, accident, infirmity or other adversity.
Employees: 120
Volunteers: 30
Regional offices: 2

Royal Air Force Music Charitable Trust

24 Bayford Drive, Newark,
Nottinghamshire NG24 2GS
T: 01636 707857
Helpline: 07748 945160
E: office@rafmusic.org.uk
www.rafmusic.org.uk
Administrator: Malcolm Goodman MBE
Promoting welfare funding through the performance of live music by Royal Air Force musicians.
Volunteers: 10
Regional offices: 1
Income: £15,000 (2013-14)

Royal Air Forces Association

117.5 Loughborough Road,
Leicester LE4 5ND
T: 0116 266 5224
Helpline: 0800 018 2361
F: 0116 266 5012
E: enquiries@rafa.org.uk
www.rafa.org.uk
Secretary General: Jane Easton
The RAF Association is a membership and charitable organisation offering support to all serving and former members of the RAF and their dependants during times of need. Its network of welfare officers provides advice, financial guidance, friendship and, where appropriate, can signpost to other agencies for assistance.
Employees: 179
Volunteers: 400
Regional offices: 9

Royal Alfred Seafarers Society

Head Office, Weston Acres, Woodmasterne Lane, Banstead, Surrey SM7 3HA
T: 01737 353763
F: 020 8401 2592
E: royalalfred@btopenworld.com
www.royalalfredseafarers.com
Provides long-term care for retired or disabled seafarers and their dependants.
Employees: 86
Volunteers: 2

Royal Association for Deaf people

18 Westside Centre, London Road, Stanway, Colchester, Essex CO3 8PH
T: 0845 688 2525
F: 0845 688 2526
E: info@royaldeaf.org.uk
www.royaldeaf.org.uk
RAD promote the welfare and interests of deaf people. We believe deaf people should receive the same access and opportunities as hearing people. We mainly support deaf people whose first or preferred language is British Sign Language (BSL) but also work with people with all forms of deafness including those who are hard of hearing, deafened or deafblind.
Employees: 100
Volunteers: 50
Regional offices: 3

Royal Blind Society for the UK

RBS House, 59/61 Sea Lane, Rustington, West Sussex BN16 2RQ
T: 01903 857023
F: 01903 859166
E: royalblindsoc@aol.com
www.royalblindsociety.org
Director: Graham Booth
Aims to assist blind and partially sighted people to cope with the additional costs of blindness, and to experience opportunities that they could not otherwise have.
Employees: 48
Volunteers: 25
Regional offices: 1

Royal British Legion

Haig House, 199 Borough High Street, London SE1 1AA
T: 020 7973 7200
F: 020 7973 7399
E: info@britishlegion.org.uk
www.britishlegion.org.uk
The Royal British Legion provides financial, social and emotional support to millions who have served and are currently serving in the Armed Forces, and their dependants. Currently, nearly 10.5 million people are eligible for our support and we receive thousands of calls for help every year.
Employees: 880
Volunteers: 600000
Regional offices: 65

Royal British Legion Industries Ltd

Hall Road, Aylesford, Kent ME20 7NL
T: 01622 795923
F: 01622 718744
E: phillip.defrain@rbli.co.uk
www.rbli.co.uk
RBLI provides employment, training and support for people, including those with disabilities, plus care and support for ex-servicemen, women and families.

Royal British Legion Women's Section

199 Borough High Stree, London SE1 1AA
T: 020 7973 7378
E: women@britishlegion.org.uk
www.rblws.org.uk
Promotes the welfare of ex-service women, the wives, widows, children and dependants of those who have served in any of HM Forces who find themselves in difficulties; to augment the activities of the Royal British Legion and to assist them in raising funds.

Royal College of General Practitioners

30 Euston Square, Stephenson Way, London NW1 2FB
T: 020 3188 7400
E: info@rcgp.org.uk
www.rcgp.org.uk
Encouraging, fostering and maintaining the highest possible standards in general medical practice.
Employees: 170
Regional offices: 31

Royal College of Midwives

15 Mansfield Street, London W1G 9NH
T: 020 7312 3535
F: 020 7313 3536
E: info@rcm.org.uk
www.rcm.org.uk
Aims to advance the art and science of midwifery and to maintain high professional standards.
Employees: 70
Volunteers: 2000
Regional offices: 4

Royal College of Obstetricians and Gynaecologists

27 Sussex Place, Regent's Park, London NW1 4RG
T: 020 7772 6200
E: iwylie@rcog.org.uk
www.rcog.org.uk
Chief Executive: Ian Wylie
The professional membership organisation for obstetricians and gynaecologists. We educate and examine doctors in the speciality both in the UK and throughout the world and we support their continuing development. We set standards for women's health and assist developing countries with maternal health education.
Employees: 140

Royal College of Paediatrics and Child Health

50 Hallam Street, London W1W 6DE
T: 020 7307 5616
E: enquiries@rcpch.ac.uk
www.rcpch.ac.uk
Promotes and publishes paediatric research; organises scientific meetings; advises government and other professional bodies on problems of child health; oversees the training of doctors specialising in paediatrics and child health; issues guidance on related issues.

Royal Commonwealth Society

Award House, 7-11, St Matthew Street, London SW1P 2JT
T: 020 3727 4300
E: info@thercs.org
www.thercs.org
Director: Michael Lake CBE
The Royal Commonwealth Society is a network of individuals and organisations committed to improving the lives and prospects of Commonwealth citizens worldwide. Promoting an understanding of the values and working of the Commonwealth, the Society engages with its educational, civil society, business and governmental networks to address issues that matter to the citizens of the Commonwealth and the world.
Employees: 9
Volunteers: 1

Royal Corps of Signals Benevolent Fund

Regimental Headquarters, Griffin House, Blandford Camp, Blandford Forum, Dorset DT11 8RH
T: 01258 482081
E: soinc-rhq-regtsec@mod.uk
Regimental Secretary: Colonel Terry Canham
Employees: 5

Royal Geographical Society

1 Kensington Gore, London SW7 2AR
T: 020 7591 3088
E: enquiries@rgs.org
www.rgs.org
A world-leading society for geographers and geographical learning dedicated to the promotion and development of knowledge together with its application to the challenges facing society and the environment.

Royal Humane Society

Brettenham House, Lancaster Place, London WC2E 7EP
T: 020 7836 8155
E: info@royalhumanesociety.org.uk
www.royalhumanesociety.org.uk
The Royal Humane Society is a charity that assesses acts of bravery in the saving of human life and makes awards. These range from certificates and testimonials to bronze, silver and gold medals.

Royal Institute of British Architects

66 Portland Place, London W1B 1AD
T: 020 7580 5533
E: info@inst.riba.org
www.architecture.com
RIBA is the UK body for architecture and the architectural profession. Providing support for 40,500 members worldwide in the form of training, technical services, publications and events, and set standards for the education of architects, both in the UK and overseas.

Royal Life Saving Society UK

River House, High Street, Broom, Warwickshire B50 4HN
T: 01789 773994
F: 01789 773995
E: lifesavers@rlss.org.uk
www.lifesavers.org.uk
Employees: 29
Volunteers: 13500
Regional offices: 50

Royal Literary Fund

3 Johnson's Court, Off Fleet Street, London EC4A 3EA
T: 020 7353 7159
F: 020 7353 1350
E: eileen.gunn@rlf.org.uk
www.rlf.org.uk
Chief Executive: Eileen Gunn
Provides assistance to established published authors of several books who are in financial difficulties due to personal or professional setbacks.
Employees: 4

Royal London Society

16 Manor Road, Bexhill-on-Sea, East Sussex TN40 1SP
T: 01424 218097
E: office@royallondonsociety.org.uk
www.royallondonsociety.org.uk

Royal London Society for the Blind

Dorton House, Wilderness Avenue, Seal, Sevenoaks, Kent TN15 0EB
T: 01732 592665
Helpline: 01732 592500
F: 01732 592668
E: enquiries@rlsb.org.uk
www.rlsb.org.uk
Chief Executive: Brian Cooney
The RLSB exists to provide education, training, transition and employment services that enable people who are blind or partially sighted to overcome the discrimination they face and the social exclusion and poverty that many experience.
Employees: 300
Volunteers: 25
Regional offices: 3

Royal Masonic Benevolent Institution

20 Great Queen Street, London WC2B 5BG
T: 020 7596 2400
E: enquiries@rmbi.org.uk
www.rmbi.org.uk
Provides support to freemasons and their dependants, by providing residential or nursing accommodation through our homes situated throughout the country.

Royal Medical Benevolent Fund

24 King's Road, Wimbledon, London SW19 8QN
T: 020 8540 9194
F: 020 8542 0494
E: cbogle@rmbf.org
www.rmbf.org
Chief Executive Officer: Steve Crone
The objectives of the charity are to prevent or relieve poverty and to relieve need arising from youth, age, ill health, disability and bereavement among people who are doctors or who have worked as doctors, and medical students and the dependants of such individuals.
Employees: 13
Volunteers: 300

Royal National Institute of the Blind

105 Judd Street, London WC1H 9NE
T: 020 7388 1266
F: 020 7388 2034
E: helpline@rnib.org.uk
www.rnib.org.uk
RNIB are the UK's leading charity offering information, support and advice to over two million people with sight problems. We fight for equal rights for people with sight problems. We fund pioneering research into preventing and treating eye disease and promote eye health by running public health awareness campaigns.
Employees: 2923
Volunteers: 5000
Regional offices: 5

Royal National Lifeboat Institution

West Quay Road, Poole, Dorset BH15 1HZ
T: 01202 663000
F: 01202 663167
E: info@rnli.org.uk
www.rnli.org.uk
Employees: 1000
Volunteers: 4600
Regional offices: 10

Royal National Mission to Deep Sea Fishermen

Mather House, 4400 Parkway, Solent Business Park, Hampshire PO15 7FJ
T: 020 7487 5101
E: enquiries@rnmdsf.org.uk
www.fishermensmission.org.uk
Supports fishermen and their families throughout the UK and in the Falkland Islands.

Royal Naval Benevolent Society for Officers

70 Porchester Terrace, Bayswater, London W2 3TP
T: 020 7402 5231
E: rnoc@arno.org.uk
www.arno.org.uk
CEO: Cdr Mike Goldthorpe
The Society, working title RNOC, provides financial assistance when in need to officers of the Royal Navy and Royal Marines, and their respective reserves, both active service

and retired, and to their widows, ex-wives and dependants.
Employees: 3

Royal Naval Benevolent Trust

Castaway House, 311 Twyford Avenue, Portsmouth PO2 8RN
T: 023 9269 0112
F: 023 9266 0852
E: rnbt@rnbt.org.uk
www.rnbt.org.uk
The RNBT exists to give help, in cases of need, to those who are serving or have served as ratings in the Royal Navy or as other ranks in the Royal Marines, and their dependants. The RNBT also manages its own care home in Gillingham, Kent, which offers first-class nursing and personal care in excellent accommodation for former sailors, Royal Marines, their wives and widows.
Employees: 100
Volunteers: 30

Royal Navy and Royal Marine Children's Fund

311 Twyford Avenue, Stamshaw, Portsmouth, Hampshire PO2 8RN
T: 023 9263 9534
F: 023 9267 7574
E: rnchildren@btconnect.com
www.rnrmchildrensfund.org.uk
RN & RM Children's Fund: Monique Bateman MBE
Assists children, under the age of 25, of serving and ex-serving members of RN and RM who are in need, hardship or distress. Assistance may be given in the form of grants to individuals or by paying for goods or services or facilities for those in need.
Employees: 4
Volunteers: 12
Regional offices: 1

Royal Society

6 Carlton House Terrace, London SW1Y 5AG
T: 020 7451 2500
E: info@royalsoc.ac.uk
www.royalsociety.org
Promotes the natural sciences, including mathematics and all applied sciences such as engineering and medicine. The Society encourages both national and international scientific activities (in a similar way to national academies overseas), adhering to many international, non-governmental scientific organisations and promoting co-operative research and exchanges through agreements with overseas academies.

Royal Society for Public Health

John Snow House, 59 Mansell Street, London E1 8AN
T: 020 7265 7300
E: info@rsph.org.uk
www.rsph.org.uk
Chief Executive: Shirley Cramer
RSPH is an independent, multi-disciplinary charity dedicated to the improvement of the public's health and wellbeing. Formed in October 2008 with the merger of the Royal Society of Health and the Royal Institute of Public Health, we help inform policy and practice, working to educate, empower and support communities and individuals to live healthily.
Employees: 45

Royal Society for the Prevention of Accidents

RoSPA House, 28 Calthorpe Road, Edgbaston, Birmingham, West Midlands B15 1RP
T: 0121 248 2000
F: 0121 248 2001
E: tmullarkey@rospa.com
www.rospa.com
Chief Executive: Tom Mullarkey
The Royal Society for the Prevention of Accidents (RoSPA) is a registered charity with a mission to save lives and reduce injuries. It promotes safety and the prevention of accidents in the home, on the road, at work, at leisure and in schools and colleges. RoSPA's various activities include collecting data, carrying out research, training and providing expert consultancy.
Employees: 130
Regional offices: 3

Royal Society for the Prevention of Cruelty to Animals

Wilberforce Way, Southwater, Horsham, West Sussex RH13 9RS
T: 0300 123 0100
Helpline: 0300 123 4555
F: 0303 123 0100
E: enq@rspca.org.uk
www.rspca.org.uk
Chief Executive: Mark Watts
The RSPCA will, by all lawful means, promote kindness to, prevent cruelty to, and alleviate suffering of animals.
Employees: 1668
Volunteers: 7000
Regional offices: 5

Royal Society for the Protection of Birds

The Lodge, Potton Road, Sandy, Bedfordshire SG19 2DL
T: 01767 680551
F: 01767 691178
E: alan.sharpe@rspb.org.uk
www.rspb.org.uk
Chief Executive: Mike Clarke
The RSPB speaks out for birds and wildlife, tackling the problems that threaten our environment. Our work helps all nature, every buzzing, crawling, slithering, fluttering part of it, and we look after wild places for you to enjoy too. We have a million members who are inspired by nature and give it a voice. Nature is amazing! Help us keep it that way.
Employees: 2151
Volunteers: 15765
Regional offices: 14

Royal Society of Health

38A St George's Drive, London SW1V 4BH
T: 020 7630 0121
F: 020 7976 6847
E: rsph@rsph.org
www.rsph.org
Chief Executive: Richard Parish
Our aim is to promote continuous improvement in human health worldwide, through education, communication and the encouragement of scientific research.
Employees: 25
Volunteers: 1

Royal Society of Medicine

1 Wimpole Street, London W1G 0AE
T: 020 7290 2900
F: 020 7290 2989
E: tansy.allen@rsm.ac.uk
www.rsm.ac.uk
Chief Executive: Ian Balmer
The RSM is an independent, apolitical organisation and one of the largest providers of continuing medical education in the UK. We provide accredited courses, which are vital in allowing healthcare professionals their continuing freedom to practice. Our aims are: to provide a broad range of educational activities for medical and healthcare professionals including students of these disciplines; to promote an exchange of

information and ideas on the science, practice and organisation of medicine.
Employees: 192
Volunteers: 500

Royal Television Society

3 Dorset Rise, London EC4Y 8EN
T: 020 7822 2810
F: 020 7822 2811
E: info@rts.org.uk
www.rts.org.uk
Chief Executive: Theresa Wise
The society's objective and principal activity is the advancement of public education in the science, practice, technology and art of television.
Employees: 12
Volunteers: 600

Royal Theatrical Fund

11 Garrick Street, Covent Garden, London WC2E 9AR
T: 020 7836 3322
F: 020 7379 8273
E: admin@trtf.com
www.trtf.com
Chair: Paul Gane
The Fund helps those in the entertainment media who cannot work through illness, adversity or infirmity.
Employees: 2

Royal UK Beneficent Association (Rukba)

18 Avonmore Road, London W14 8RR
T: 020 7605 4200
F: 020 7605 4201
E: charity@independentage.org
www.rukba.org.uk
Grants annuities and provides friendship for older people who are impoverished or infirm.
Employees: 218
Volunteers: 1100
Regional offices: 15

RP Fighting Blindness

PO Box 350, Buckingham MK18 1GZ
T: 01280 821334
Helpline: 0845 123 2354
E: info@rpfightingblindness.org.uk
www.rpfightingblindness.org.uk
Chief Executive: Tina Houlihan
RP Fighting Blindness aims to raise funds for scientific research to provide treatments for retinitis pigmentosa (RP). RP Fighting Blindness provides Information & Support services to people with RP and their families.
Employees: 14
Volunteers: 110

Rugby Football Foundation

Rugby House, 200 Whitton Road
T: 020 8831 7985
E: foundation@therfu.com
www.rfu.com/rff
RFF Administrator: Fran Thornber

Runnymede Trust

7 Plough Yard, Shoreditch, London EC2A 3LP
T: 020 7377 9222
F: 020 7377 6622
E: info@runnymedetrust.org
www.runnymedetrust.org
Director: Dr Robert Berkeley
The Runnymede Trust is an independent policy research organisation focusing on equality and justice through the promotion of a successful multi-ethnic society. Founded as a charitable educational trust, Runnymede has a long track record in policy research, working in close collaboration with eminent thinkers and policy makers in the public, private and voluntary sectors.
Employees: 12
Volunteers: 2

Rural Action Yorkshire

E: leah.swain@ruralyorkshire.org.uk

Rural Community Action Nottinghamshire

Newstead Centre, Tilford Road, Newstead, Nottinghamshire NG15 0BS
T: 01623 727600
E: rcrowder@rcan.org.uk
www.rcan.org.uk
Chief Executive: Robert Crowder
Rural Community Action Nottinghamshire (RCAN) is an independent voluntary organisation and registered charity, which exists to promote the social and economic well-being of rural communities. Examples of our work include tackling health issues, solving transport access problems, improving community facilities, and addressing social exclusion by developing initiatives which allows everyone to play a full part in the life of their community.
Employees: 17
Volunteers: 30
Income: £765,000 (2014-15)

Rural Housing Trust

Unit 8, Graphite Square, London SE11 5EE
T: 020 7793 8114
E: info@ruralhousing.org.uk
www.ruralhousing.org.uk
Provides affordable housing for local people in villages throughout England.

Rural Media Company

Sullivan House, Hereford, Herefordshire HR4 9HG
T: 01432 344039
F: 01432 270539
E: helenj@ruralmedia.co.uk
www.ruralmedia.co.uk
Chief Executive: Nic Millington
The Rural Media Company brings community and informal education, training and advocacy together with professional filmmaking and media industry skills. Working throughout the UK with local, regional and national partners in public, voluntary and independent organisations, to develop short and long term projects, as well as undertaking commissions for video/DVD.
Employees: 17
Volunteers: 10
Regional offices: 1

RYA Sailability

RYA House, Ensign Way, Hamble, Southampton, Hampshire SO31 4YA
T: 0845 345 0403
F: 023 8060 4286
E: info@ryasailability.org
www.rya.org.uk/sailability
The RYA programme for disability sailing. Committed to development of sailing clubs and organisations throughout the UK to promote, encourage and find people with disabilities to take up sailing in all its forms.
Employees: 3

SABRE Research UK

PO Box 18653, Hampstead, London NW3 4UJ
T: 020 7722 9394
E: office@sabre.org.uk
www.sabre.org.uk
Founder/Trustee: Susan Green
An independent charity that represents the interests of patients and research volunteers by raising awareness of the need to apply rigorous research methodology to the way animal research is conducted and evaluated. A more evidence-based approach is essential if the value of animal experiments is to be determined and the safety and efficacy of medical research to be improved. The charity has no links to political parties, animal lobby groups or the pharmaceutical industry.
Volunteers: 4

SAD Association

PO Box 989, Steyning BN44 3HG
E: info@sada.org.uk
www.sada.org.uk
Informs the public and health professions about SAD (seasonal affective disorder) and supports and advises sufferers of the illness.
Volunteers: 7

Safe Partnership Limited

3 East Street, Wareham, Dorset BH20 4NN
T: 01929 55100
F: 01929 553300
E: malcolm@safepartnership.org
www.safepartnership.org
Chief Executive: Malcolm Macleod
Safe Partnership is the national charity that provides home security and advice to vulnerable victims of crimes such as domestic violence, burglary, robbery, distraction burglary, identity theft and hate crime and to those in fear of such crimes. We also undertake proactive, preventative work with young people, to help them recognise the early signs of relationship abuse to prevent them becoming victims or perpetrators of violence and crime when they grow up.
Employees: 11
Volunteers: 5

SafeHands for Mothers

23 Fitzjohns Avenue, London NW3 5JY
T: 020 7433 0792
E: ndm@safehands.org
www.safehands.org
Founder Director: Nancy Durrell McKenna
Our vision is a world where no woman dies in pregnancy and childbirth. We work to achieve this through the production of films; documentaries that raise awareness of important issues such as FGM, Obstetric Fistula, Child Marriage, HIV/AIDS, Family Planning and films which educate and inspire frontline health workers, women and their communities.
Employees: 3
Volunteers: 2
Income: £353,735 (2012-13)

Safer Places

PO Box 2489, Essex CM18 6NS
T: 0845 074 3216
Helpline: 0330 102 5811
E: allison.gardner@saferplaces.co.uk
www.saferplaces.co.uk
Director of Business Services: Allison Gardner
Safer Places is an independent domestic abuse charity dedicated to supporting adults and children affected by domestic abuse. We provide a wide range of services to support clients and respond to their individual needs and circumstances, whether it is in our safe accommodation or in the community. Work in a holistic and empowering way to help enable clients to live independent lives free from domestic abuse. Services are available in East Hertfordshire, Essex and Southend.
Employees: 77
Volunteers: 28
Income: £3,400,000 (2014-15)

Saferworld

The Grayston Centre, 28 Charles Square, London N1 6HT
T: 020 7324 4646
F: 020 7324 4647
E: communications@saferworld.org.uk
www.saferworld.org.uk
Executive Director: Paul Murphy
Employees: 99
Regional offices: 8

SAGGA

5 Portway Drive, Tutbury, Burton-on-Trent, Staffordshire DE13 9HU
T: 01283 520685
E: treasurer@sagga.org.uk
www.sagga.org.uk
Provides a pool of professional people with experience of the Scout and Guide movement who are ready to assist with projects connected with the movement; takes an independent look at progress and developments within the movement; supports and encourages Scout and Guide clubs in institutions of higher education.

Sahara Communities Abroad (SACOMA)

108 Cranbrook Road, Ilford, Essex IG1 4LZ
T: 020 8554 9444 (also fax)
E: perez@sacoma.org.uk
www.sacomauk.com
Chief Executive: Perez Ochieng
Supports African migrant communities to develop skills for enterprise and work. We provide information, advice and guidance on matters such as housing, welfare, pensions, business start up, training and education. We provide accredited training and business support for SMEs.
Employees: 24
Volunteers: 40

Sailors' Children's Society

Francis Reckitt House, Cottingham Road, Hull HU6 7RJ
T: 01482 342331
E: info@sailors-families.org.uk
www.sailorschildren.org.uk
Chief Officer: Deanne Thomas
A maritime charity caring for the children of deceased and disabled seafarers and those in severe financial hardship. The aim of the Society is to provide not only the basic necessities of life such as clothing but to allow the children to partake in everyday activities. Financial support includes single parent families, and families where one of the parents is too ill, or disabled to work, and the other acts as carer.
Employees: 6

Sailors' Society

74 St Annes Road, Southampton, Hampshire SO19 9FF
T: 023 8051 5950
F: 023 8051 5951
E: admin@sailors-society.org
www.sailors-society.org
Chief Executive: Stuart Rivers
The objectives for which the Society is established are the advancement of the Christian religion, the advancement of education and the relief of poverty and distress among the world's seafarers and their families.
Employees: 76

Salmon Youth Centre

E: sam.adofo@salmonyouthcentre.org

Salvation Army

Territorial HQ, 101 Newington Causeway, London SE1 6BN
T: 020 7367 4864
F: 020 7367 4728
E: thq@salvationarmy.org.uk
www.salvationarmy.org.uk
Expresses practical Christianity through social action regardless of class, creed or sex. Programmes include homeless and drug rehabilitation centres, and nearly 16,000 church and community centres. Also supports the work of the emergency services by providing refreshments, shelter and counselling at major incidents.
Employees: 4000
Volunteers: 40000
Regional offices: 18

Samaritans

The Upper Mill, Kingston Road, Ewell, Surrey KT17 2AF
T: 020 8394 8300
Helpline: 0845 790 9090
F: 020 8394 8301
E: supportercare@samaritans.org
www.samaritans.org
Chief Executive: Dominic Rudd
Available 24 hours a day to provide confidential emotional support for people who are experiencing feelings of distress and despair, including those that may lead to suicide.
Employees: 75
Volunteers: 15400
Regional offices: 203

SANE

1st Floor, Cityside House, 40 Adler Street, London E1 1EE
T: 020 7375 1002
Helpline: 0845 767 8000
F: 020 7375 2162
E: info@sane.org.uk
www.sane.org.uk
Chief Executive: Marjorie Wallace
SANE is a national mental health charity that works to: raise awareness; combat stigma and increase understanding of mental illness; initiate research into causes, treatments and experiences of mental illness; provide emotional support and information to anyone affected by mental illness, including families, friends and carers. One-to-one support: helpline, Textcare and email. Peer support: Support Forum. For more information, visit the SANE website.
Employees: 30
Volunteers: 120
Regional offices: 1

Sangat Advice Centre

Sancroft Road, Harrow HA3 7NS
T: 020 8427 0659
F: 020 8863 2196
E: info@sangat.org.uk
www.sangat.org.uk
Manager: Kanti Nagda
Sangat Advice Centre provides legal advice on welfare benefits, housing, immigration, debt etc. We represent clients at the immigration and welfare benefits tribunals. We also provide IT learning facilities and assist BME carers.
Employees: 4
Volunteers: 6

Savana

Wood House, Etruria Road, Hanley, Stoke on Trent, Staffordshire ST1 5NQ
T: 01782 433205
Helpline: 01782 433204
E: info@savana.org.uk
www.savana.org.uk
Chief Operations Officer: Kay Glover
Savana is a company limited by guarantee with charitable status providing support services for those who have experienced or who are affected by (incl. relatives and supporters) any form of sexual violence or abuse including within domestic abuse, whether recently or in the past
Employees: 12
Volunteers: 30
Regional offices: 1

SAVE Britain's Heritage

70 Cowcross Street, London EC1M 6EJ
T: 020 7253 3500
E: save@btinternet.com
www.savebritainsheritage.org
Campaigns for the retention and rehabilitation of historic buildings and areas.

Save the Children UK

1 St John's Lane, London EC1M 4AR
T: 020 7012 6400
F: 020 7012 6963
E: supporter.care@savethechildren.org.uk
www.savethechildren.org.uk
Aims to relieve the distress and hardship, and to promote the welfare of children in any country or countries, place or places with particular emphasis on disaster relief, emergency response, campaigns and programmes.
Employees: 3673
Volunteers: 11000
Regional offices: 567

SBA The Solicitors' Charity

1 Jaggard Way, London SW12 8SG
T: 020 8675 6440
E: sec@sba.org.uk
www.sba.org.uk
Aims to financially assist solicitors and their dependants in need, who are or have been on the roll for England and Wales.

SCA Group

Amplevine House, Dukes Road, Southampton, Hampshire SO14 0ST
T: 023 8036 6663
F: 023 8036 6666
E: rosalind.lucas@scagroup.co.uk
www.scagroup.co.uk
CEO: Maria Mills
The Social Care in Action (SCA) Group is one of the leading social enterprises in the UK. Established over 20 years ago, SCA provides an outstanding range of health and social care services including care, NHS dentistry, transport, a health and wellbeing centre, an award-winning training centre and consultancy services. Everything SCA does is focussed on supporting its customers to lead better lives.
Employees: 596
Volunteers: 100
Regional offices: 4

School for Social Entrepreneurs

18 Victoria Park Square, London E2 9PF
T: 020 8981 0300
F: 020 8983 4655
E: office@sse.org.uk
www.sse.org.uk
The School for Social Entrepreneurs exists to provide training and opportunities to enable people to use their creative and entrepreneurial abilities more fully for social benefit. We also want to recruit more innovative and capable people into voluntary and other organisations.
Employees: 14

School Governors' One-Stop Shop

Unit 11, Shepperton House, London N1 3DF
T: 020 7354 9805
F: 020 7288 9549
E: info@sgoss.org.uk
www.sgoss.org.uk
Chief Executive: Steve Acklam

SGOSS is dedicated to recruiting volunteers to fill some of the 40,000 school governor vacancies that exist across England. Governors do not have to know about education or be a parent, they simply need to be over 18 and want to make a difference. All of SGOSS's services are free to volunteers, employers, schools and local authorities.
Employees: 17
Volunteers: 11500
Regional offices: 1

School Library Association

1 Pine Court, Kembrey Park, Swindon, Wiltshire SN2 8AD
T: 01793 530166
F: 01793 481182
E: info@sla.org.uk
www.sla.org.uk
Director: Tricia Adams
Promotes the development of school libraries as central to the curriculum at primary and secondary level and acts as a national voice for school libraries.
Employees: 6
Volunteers: 20
Income: £300,000 (2012-13)

School-Home Support (SHS)

Cityside House, 40 Adler Street, Whitechapel, London E1 1EE
T: 020 7426 5000
F: 020 7426 5001
E: enquiries@schoolhomesupport.org.uk
www.schoolhomesupport.org.uk
Chief Executive: Jan Tallis
Through the use of highly trained, independent practitioners based in schools, SHS works with disadvantaged children and their families to overcome the barriers that get in the way of learning. Currently working in 90 schools in London, as well as offering training in family support work in London, Yorkshire and the North East.
Employees: 100
Regional offices: 1

SciDevNet

London W1D 3TE
T: 020 7291 3690
F: 020 7843 4596
E: info@scidev.net
www.scidev.net
SciDev.Net aims to: promote for the public's benefit the advancement of education in science, technology and other matters connected with the development of society and in particular to disseminate useful research findings and provide for a critical discussion; undertake any other charitable purpose.
Employees: 5

Scoliosis Association (UK)

4 Ivebury Court, London W10 6RA
T: 020 8964 5343
Helpline: 020 8964 1166
E: info@sauk.org.uk
www.sauk.org.uk
Chair of Trustees: Dr Stephanie Clark
SAUK is the only national support organisation for people with scoliosis and their families. SAUK aims to: provide advice, support and information to people affected by scoliosis, and their families; raise awareness among health professionals and the general public.
Employees: 5
Volunteers: 4

Scope

PO Box 833, Milton Keynes MK12 5NY
Helpline: 0808 800 3333
F: 01908 321051
E: response@scope.org.uk
www.scope.org.uk
Chief Executive: Mark Atkinson
We're all about changing society for the better, so that disabled people and their families can have the same opportunities as everyone else. We work with disabled people and their families at every stage of their lives. We offer practical support from information services to education and everyday care. We challenge assumptions about disability, we influence decision-makers and we show what can be possible. Visit the Scope website.
Employees: 3375
Regional offices: 4

Scottish Council for Voluntary Organisations

Mansfield Traquair Centre, 15 Mansfield Place, Edinburgh EH3 6BB
T: 0131 474 8000
Helpline: 0800 169 0022
F: 0131 556 0279
E: enquiries@scvo.org.uk
www.scvo.org.uk
Chief Executive: Martin Sime
The Scottish Council for Voluntary Organisations (SCVO) is the membership organisation for Scotland's charities, voluntary organisations and social enterprises. SCVO works in partnership with the voluntary sector to advance our shared values and interests. We have over 1500 members who range from individuals and grassroots groups, to Scotland-wide organisations and intermediary bodies. Through lobbying and campaigning SCVO works to advance the interests of our members and the people and communities that they support.
Employees: 100
Volunteers: Varies
Regional offices: 3
Income: £14,513,735 (2012-13)

Scripture Union

Bletchley, Milton Keynes, Buckinghamshire MK2 2EB
T: 01908 856000
F: 01908 856111
E: info@scriptureunion.org.uk
www.scriptureunion.org.uk
National Director: Tim Hastie-Smith
Scripture Union is a Christian mission movement working with churches to make disciples of Jesus Christ among children, young people and families. Activities include running holidays, church-based events and school Christian groups, producing a wide range of publications and supporting those who use its resources through training programmes.
Employees: 76
Volunteers: 3900
Regional offices: 7

Sea Watch Foundation

Ewyn y Don, Bull Bay, Amlwch, Anglesey LL68 9SD
T: 01545 561227
F: 01407 832892
E: info@seawatchfoundation.org.uk
www.seawatchfoundation.org.uk
Scientific Director: Dr Peter Evans
The principal objective of the charity is the study, preservation and protection of cetaceans and promoting awareness for the benefit of the public.
Employees: 4
Volunteers: 15
Regional offices: 1
Income: £140,000 (2012-13)

Seafarers UK

(King George's Fund for Sailors), 8 Hatherley Street, London SW1P 2QT
T: 020 7932 0000
F: 020 7932 0095
E: seafarers@seafarers-uk.org
www.seafarers-uk.org
Director General: Commodore Barry Bryant
Employees: 22
Volunteers: 100+
Regional offices: 2

Seafarers' Advice & Information Line

30 King William Walk, Greenwich SE10 9HU
T: 020 8269 0565
Helpline: 0845 741 3318
F: 020 8269 0794
E: advice@sailine.org.uk
www.sailine.org.uk
Chief Executive: Emma Knight
Seafarer's Advice & Information Line (SAIL) is a Citizens Advice service dedicated to working and retired seafarers, and their families across the UK. All advice is free and confidential. See www.sailine.org.uk
Employees: 8
Volunteers: 2

SEAP

E: aoife.murphy@seap.org.uk

SeeAbility

Newplan House, 41 East Street, Epsom, Surrey KT17 1BL
T: 01372 755000
F: 01372 755001
E: d.scott-ralphs@seeability.org
www.seeability.org
Chief Executive: David Scott-Ralphs
SeeAbility works to enrich the lives of people with sight loss and multiple disabilities across the UK. We provide housing and personal support, day activities, specialist therapeutic support and a range of advisory services.
Employees: 500
Volunteers: 250
Regional offices: 2
Income: £15,122,538 (2013-14)

Selby Trust Ltd

The Selby Centre, Selby Road, White Hart Lane, Tottenham, London E17 8JL
T: 020 8885 5499
F: 020 8493 8517
E: selbytrust@aol.com
www.selbytrust.co.uk/
Chief Executive: Sona Mahtani
The Selby Trust promotes education and leisure activities to local residents, communities and young people facing multiple disadvantages through lack of education, poor health, living on low incomes or in unemployment or needing new skills. The vision of the Selby Trust to provide affordable workspace in an environmentally friendly manner with the strong participation of diverse local communities of all cultures is delivered through its motto of "Many Cultures One Community".
Employees: 20
Volunteers: 10
Income: £927,570 (2013-14)

Self Help Africa

Second Floor Suite, Westgate House, Dickens Court, Off Hills Lane, Shrewsbury, Shropshire SY1 1QU
T: 01743 277170
F: 01952 247158
E: infouk@selfhelpafrica.net
www.selfhelpafrica.org
Self Help Africa works with rural communities in eight African countries to help them improve their farms and their livelihoods. Self Help Africa helps people in rural Africa grow enough food to feed themselves, earn a living and access basic services. Self Help Africa equips people with the skills they need to move out of poverty by training farmers in new techniques and teaching basic business skills.
Employees: 14
Volunteers: 50
Regional offices: 11

Self injury Support

PO Box 3240, Bristol BS2 2EF
T: 0117 927 9600
Helpline: 0808 800 8088
E: info@selfinjurysupport.org.uk
www.selfinjurysupport.org.uk
Director: Hilary Lindsay
To provide support to women and girls affected by self-injury/self harm. To raise awareness of the issue by providing information (for professionals, individuals and family, friends and carers) and training for workers in contact with people who self-injure. Helpline 0808 800 8088. Text Support 0780 047 2908
Employees: 5
Volunteers: 45
Income: £105,000 (2013-14)

self management uk

32-36 Loman Street, Southwark, London SE1 0EH
T: 0333 344 5840
E: marketing@selfmanagementuk.org
www.selfmanagementuk.org
Chief Executive: Renata Drinkwater
self management uk is a leading charity which supports people with long-term health conditions. We have over 10 years' experience of delivering self-management training, support and education to well over 120,000 patients. Our aims are: To provide self-management support and training for people living with long-term conditions, increasing their wellbeing and confidence; To promote the value of self-management; To develop innovative and cost-effective ways to deliver self-management education.
Employees: 40
Volunteers: 100
Regional offices: 2

Sense

London N4 3SR
T: 020 7272 7774
F: 020 7272 6012
E: jacqui.penalver@sense.org.uk
www.sense.org.uk
Sense is a national voluntary organisation that works with and campaigns for the needs of children and adults who are deafblind, providing advice, support, information and services for them, their families, carers and the professionals who work with them.
Employees: 1600
Volunteers: 500
Regional offices: 13

Sequal Trust

3 Ploughmans Corner, Wharf Road, Ellesmere, Shropshire SY12 0EJ
T: 01691 624222 (also fax)
E: info@thesequaltrust.org.uk
www.thesequaltrust.org.uk
Chair: Dorcas Munday
The Sequal Trust is a national charity that fundraises to provide communication aids for disabled people with speech, movement and/or severe learning difficulties.
Employees: 4

Sesame Institute (UK)

27 Blackfriars Road, London SE1 8NY
T: 020 7633 9690
E: info@sesame-institute.org
www.sesame-institute.org
Makes possible a fuller life, through applied drama and movement, for those with mental health difficulties, people working with a physical challenge and others.

Shaftesbury Young People

The Chapel, Royal Victoria Patriotic Building, John Archer Way, London SW18 3SX
T: 020 8875 1555
F: 020 8875 1954
E: info@shaftesbury.org.uk
www.shaftesbury.org.uk
Cares for, educate and encourages looked after children and young people and children in need.

Shannon Trust

38 Ebury Street, London SW1W 0LU
T: 020 7730 4917
E: sue@shannontrust.org.uk
www.shannontrust.org.uk
CEO: David Ahern
Employees: 4
Volunteers: 160

Shape London

Deane House Studios, 27 Greenwood Place, London NW5 1LB
T: 0845 521 3457
F: 0845 521 3458
E: info@shapearts.org.uk
www.shapearts.org.uk
CEO: Tony Heaton

Our strategy reflects the artistic and political 'journey' of the disability and deaf communities and seeks to offer them a new platform to profile their work. Our strategy invests in disabled and deaf people as equals and seeks to ensure that they can play an active role in the cultural life of London and the UK. In order to achieve these aims, Shape will work in partnership with other arts organisations to build their capacity and their understanding of the creative potential of disabled and deaf people.

Employees: 18
Volunteers: 350
Regional offices: 4

Shaping Our Lives National User Network

BM Box 4845, London WC1N 3XX
T: 0845 241 0383
E: information@shapingourlives.org.uk
www.shapingourlives.org.uk
Chair: Peter Beresford

Shaping Our Lives is a national user controlled independent organisation started in 1996. We work with a wide variety of service users including people with physical and/or sensory impairments, older people, users/survivors of mental health services, young people with experience of being 'looked after', people with learning difficulties and others. Through networking, research and development we support the development of user involvement that aims to deliver better outcomes for service users.

Employees: 2

ShareAction

Ground Floor, 16 Crucifix Lane, London SE1 3JW
T: 020 7403 7800
E: info@shareaction.org
www.shareaction.org
Chief Executive: Catherine Howarth

ShareAction is a groundbreaking charity that promotes Responsible Investment by pension funds and fund managers. Bringing together leading charities, trade unions, faith groups and individual investors, our aim is to catalyse a shift at each level of the investment chain, so that Responsible Investment becomes the norm.

Employees: 15
Volunteers: 60
Income: £370,000 (2012-13)

Shared Care Network

63-66 Easton Business Centre, Felix Road, Easton, Bristol BS5 0HE
T: 0117 941 5361
F: 0117 941 5362
E: shared-care@bristol.ac.uk
www.shortbreaksnetwork.org.uk

We are the national organisation representing family-based short break schemes for disabled children.

Employees: 15
Regional offices: 9

Shared Lives Plus

G04 The Cotton Exchange, Old Hall Street, Liverpool, Merseyside L3 9JR
T: 0151 227 3499
F: 0151 236 3590
E: deborah@sharedlivesplus.org.uk
www.sharedlivesplus.org.uk
Chief Executive: Alex Fox

Shared Lives Plus is a UK charity established to represent the interests of all those involved in delivering very small, individualised, community-based services such as Shared Lives (formerly known as Adult Placement). Shared Lives Plus promotes Shared Lives, Homeshare and other small community micro services as an important resource to those seeking individualised services; promotes a legislative environment that ensures safety and quality but allows small community services to flourish.

Employees: 14
Volunteers: 50
Regional offices: 3

Shaw Trust Ltd

Fox Talbot House, Greenways Business Park, Bellinger Close, Malmesbury Road, Chippenham, Wiltshire SN15 1BN
T: 01225 716300
Helpline: 01225 779471
F: 01225 716301
E: sheila.tsiaparis@shaw-trust.org.uk
www.shaw-trust.org.uk
Director General: Tim Pape

Runs work programmes to help people with disabilities find employment and to remain in their jobs.

Employees: 1200
Volunteers: 200
Regional offices: 5

Shelter

88 Old Street, London EC1V 9HU
T: 020 7505 2000
F: 020 7505 2169
E: info@shelter.org.uk
www.shelter.org.uk
Employees: 800
Volunteers: 800

Shelterbox Trust

1A Water Ma Trout Industrial Estate, Helston, Cornwall TR13 0LW
T: 01326 569782
E: ageocur@aol.com
www.shelterbox.org
Chief Executive: Alison Wallace

ShelterBox is an international disaster relief charity that provides emergency shelter and life-saving supplies to families around the world who are affected by disasters. Each big, green ShelterBox is tailored to every disaster but typically contains a disaster relief tent for an extended family, blankets, water purification and storage equipment, cooking utensils, a stove, a basic tool kit, a children's activity pack and other vital items.

Employees: 60
Volunteers: 500
Regional offices: 2

SHINE

42 Park Road, Peterborough PE1 2UQ
T: 01733 555988
E: info@shinecharity.org.uk
www.shinecharity.org.uk

Provides services to people with spina bifida and/or hydrocephalus, and their carers, and promotes their interests in order to help them develop their abilities, receive the best possible services and make the most of life.

Shipwrecked Fishermen and Mariners' Royal Benevolent Society

Shipwrecked Mariners' Society, 1 North Pallant, Chichester, West Sussex PO19 1TL
T: 01243 789329
Helpline: 01243 787761
F: 01243 530853
E: general@shipwreckedmariners.org.uk
www.shipwreckedmariners.org.uk
Chief Executive: Malcolm Williams

The Shipwrecked Mariners' Society exists to provide financial help to merchant seafarers,

fishermen and their dependants who are in need. We pay an immediate grant to the widow of a serving seafarer who dies, whether at sea or ashore. Regular grants are paid to elderly seafarers and widows whose circumstances justify ongoing support. Special grants are made to meet particular needs in crisis situations.
Employees: 7
Volunteers: 200

Shpresa Programme (Albanian for Hope)

Mansfield House, 30 Avenons Road, Plaistow E13 3HT
T: 020 7511 1586
E: shpresaprogramme@yahoo.co.uk
www.shpresaprogramme.com
Project Director: Luljeta Nuzi
Aims to enable the Albanian-speaking community in UK to settle and fully participate in society and realise their full potential. We want to promote a positive identity and recognition of our community's cultural and linguistic heritage, both among Albanian speakers and wider society so that we can contribute to community cohesion in the UK.
Employees: 5
Volunteers: 31

Sightsavers International

Grosvenor Hall, Bolnore Road, Haywards Heath, West Sussex RH16 4BX
T: 01444 446600
F: 01444 446688
E: charper@sightsavers.org
www.sightsavers.org
Chief Executive: Caroline Harper
Sightsavers is an international charity that is dedicated to combating blindness in developing countries. We work with partners in over 33 countries, in poor and least-served communities, to support activities that prevent and cure blindness, restore sight and provide education and training for the blind and visually impaired.
Employees: 325
Regional offices: 6

Signalong Group

Stratford House, Waterside Court, Neptune Way, Rochester, Kent ME2 4NZ
T: 0845 450 8422
F: 0845 450 8428
E: mkennard@signalong.org.uk
www.signalong.org.uk
Operations Manager: Tracy Goode
Charity specialising in communication resources and training in learning disabilities and autism. Its aims are to improve communication skills, leading to greater independence, fulfilment of potential, reduction in disturbed and challenging behaviour, improved self-esteem and improved relationships.
Employees: 4
Volunteers: 24

Signature

Mersey House, Mandale Business Park, Belmont, Durham DH1 1TH
T: 0191 383 1155
F: 0191 383 7914
E: joanne.lavender@signature.org.uk
www.signature.org.uk
Works towards the improvement of communication with deaf, deafened, hard of hearing and deafblind people in particular by the education, training and examination of students and tutors in the different modes of communication used by such persons.
Employees: 33
Regional offices: 2

SignHealth

5 Baring Road, Beaconsfield, Buckinghamshire HP9 2NB
T: 01494 687600
E: info@signhealth.org.uk
www.signhealth.org.uk
Chief Executive: Steve Powell
SignHealth is a charity that aims for a world where the risk of deaf people developing preventable health problems is removed, and where equality, respect and fulfilment are enjoyed by deaf people experiencing mental health problems. SignHealth is committed to bringing better healthcare and equality of service provision to deaf people in the UK.
Employees: 120
Volunteers: 20
Regional offices: 6
Income: £4,417,208 (2012-13)

Single Parent Action Network

Millpond, Baptist Street, Bristol BS5 0YW
T: 0117 951 4231
F: 0117 935 5208
E: info@spanuk.org.uk
www.singleparents.org.uk
Director: Sue Cohen
SPAN is a uniquely diverse organisation supporting single parents to empower themselves throughout the UK. SPAN aims to give a voice to one-parent families living in poverty and isolation, and support the setting up and development of self-help groups. SPAN develops partnerships with organisations and agencies to improve policies for one-parent families.
Employees: 17
Volunteers: 5

Sir Halley Stewart Trust

22 Earith Road, Willingham, Cambridge, Cambridgeshire CB24 5LS
T: 01954 260707 (also fax)
E: email@sirhalleystewart.org.uk
www.sirhalleystewart.org.uk
Trust Administrator: Sue West
The trust aims to promote and assist innovative research activities or pioneering developments in medical, social and religious fields. It emphasises prevention rather than alleviation of human suffering. Certain priorities apply, please refer to Trust website for current details.
Employees: 1
Income: £106,300 (2013-14)

SITRA (Services)

3rd Floor, 55 Bondway, London SW8 1SJ
T: 020 7793 4710
F: 020 7793 4715
E: berihum@sitra.org
www.sitra.org
Chief Executive: Vic Rayner
Provides policy, information, training, events and consultancy services to the housing with care and support sector. Sitra has some 600 member organisations including supported housing providers, housing associations and local authorities. We publish a popular monthly bulletin.
Employees: 30
Regional offices: 4

Skill Force

Edwinstowe House, High Street, Edwinstowe, Mansfield, Nottinghamshire NG21 9PR
T: 01623 827619
E: enquiries@skillforce.org
www.skillforce.org
The mission of Skill Force is to develop young people in order to raise standards in wider key skills, self-esteem and employability.
Employees: 250

Skills for Care Ltd

Albion Court, 5 Albion Place, Leeds, West Yorkshire LS1 6JL
T: 0113 245 1716
F: 0113 243 6417
E: sharon.allen@skillsforcare.org.uk
www.skillsforcare.org.uk
Chief Executive: Andrea Rowe

Skills for Care is the not-for-profit organisation that aims to improve adult social care services across the whole of England by supporting employers' workforce development activity. Our vision is to put employers in the driving seat on social care workforce issues; to create a trained and qualified workforce providing high-quality care; and to provide an expert voice on the social care workforce.
Employees: 200
Volunteers: 24
Regional offices: 9

Skills for Communities

265 Anlaby Road, Hull,
Humberside HU3 2SE
T: 0870 803 2768
F: 0870 803 2769
E: info@skills4communities.co.uk
www.skills4communities.co.uk
Skills for Communities has the following aims: develop and provide a range of multidisciplinary support and education services within a broad therapeutic framework for young people and their families; promote social inclusion, particularly through the provision of training and employment opportunities; provision of advice and counselling to the youth of the community on pregnancy and teenage problems, and help to asylum seekers and refugees through training, advice, information and guidance the unemployed and local service providers.
Employees: 4
Volunteers: 2
Regional offices: 2

Skillset Sector Skills Council

Focus Point, 21 Caledonian Road N1 9GB
T: 020 7713 9800
E: michellec@skillset.org
www.skillset.org
HR and Office Manager: Michelle Care

Skillshare International

Imperial House, St Nicholas Circle,
Imperial House, Leicester,
Leicestershire LE1 4LF
T: 0116 254 1862
E: info@skillshare.org
www.skillshare.org
CEO: Dr Cliff Allum
Skillshare International works for sustainable development in partnership with people and communities in Africa and Asia. We do this by sharing and developing skills through projects and volunteer placements. Our programmes focus on sustainable livelihoods, sport for development, HIV and AIDS, gender justice and conflict management.
Employees: 38
Volunteers: 260
Regional offices: 7
Income: £1,400,000 (2014-15)

Small Charities Coalition

Unit 9/10, 83 Crampton Street,
London SE17 3BQ
T: 020 7358 6490
E: info@smallcharities.org.uk
www.smallcharities.org.uk
Acting CEO: John Barrett
Small Charities Coalition is a national umbrella and capacity-building organisation with over 7,000 members UK-wide. We exist to help trustees, staff and volunteers of small charities access the skills, tools, and information they need to get going and do what they do best. We do this through a free skills matching service, free online resources and information, low cost training, free online and phone helpline and championing the voice of small charities.
Employees: 3
Volunteers: 10
Regional offices: 1

Smile International

PO Box 3, Orpington, Kent BR5 1WZ
T: 01689 870932
E: ruth.doubleday@smileinternational.org
www.smileinternational.org
CEO: Clive Doubleday
Smile International is passionate about helping to relieve suffering and poverty around the world through our Feeding, Educating, Empowering and Developing programmes in Africa, Asia and Europe.
Employees: 4
Volunteers: 203
Income: £1,282,733 (2013-14)

Smile Support & Care

Eastleigh Community Enterprise Centre,
Unit 3, Barton Park, Eastleigh,
Hampshire SO50 6RR
T: 023 8061 6215
E: stuart.baldwin@smilesupport.org.uk
www.smilesupport.org.uk
Chief Executive: Stuart Baldwin
Smile Support & Care supports children and young adults with disabilities both in their own home, in the community and at our respite centre in Waterlooville, Hampshire. Working in southern England, we ensure the people we support can exercise choice over the way they take short breaks or engage in any other activity. We are Care Quality Commission registered, Investors in People and ISO 9001 quality assured. For more information, see our website.
Employees: 110
Volunteers: 30
Regional offices: 2
Income: £1,500,000 (2014-15)

Social Care Institute for Excellence

1st Floor, Goldings House, Hayes Lane,
London SE1 2HB
T: 020 7089 6871
F: 020 7089 6841
E: stephen.goulder@scie.org.uk
www.scie.org.uk
Chief Executive: Julie Jones
The Social Care Institute for Excellence (SCIE) was established by government in 2001 to improve social care services for adults and children in the UK. We achieve this by identifying good practice and helping to embed it in everyday social care provision.
Employees: 65

Social Emotional and Behavioural Difficulties Association

C/O Goldwyn School, Godinton Lane,
Great Chart, Ashford, Great Chart,
Kent TN23 3BT
T: 01233 662958
E: admin@sebda.org
www.sebda.org
Chair: Nicki Jennings
SEBDA is a long-established charity that provides accredited specialist training, information and support to professionals working with children with social, emotional and behavioural difficulties. Members receive free copies of the Association's research journal, discounts on courses and conferences and detailed updates on policy and practice in its popular newsletter.
Employees: 1
Volunteers: 50

Social Enterprise Coalition

South Bank House, Black Prince Road,
London SE1 7SJ
T: 020 7793 2323
F: 020 7968 4922
E: info@socialenterprise.org.uk
www.socialenterprise.org.uk
The Social Enterprise Coalition (SEC) is the UK trade body that brings together all types of social enterprise to promote the sector and share knowledge.
Employees: 7

Social Market Foundation

11 Tufton Street, London SW1P 3QB
T: 020 7227 4400
E: enquiries@smf.co.uk
www.smf.co.uk
The Social Market Foundation is a leading UK think-tank, developing innovative ideas across a broad range of economic and social policy. It champions policy ideas that marry markets with social justice and takes a pro-market rather than free-market approach. Its work is characterised by the belief that governments have an important role to play in correcting market failures and setting the framework within which markets can operate in a way that benefits individuals and society.
Employees: 12

Social Partnership

44 Castle Street, Liverpool L2 7LA
T: 0151 258 1331
F: 0151 709 7779
E: generalenquiries@tsp.org.uk
The Social Partnership (TSP) aims to reintegrate socially excluded people into the community both socially and economically through the provision of education, training and employment opportunities.
Employees: 45
Volunteers: 3

Social Perspectives Network

c/o SCIE, Goldings House, 2 Hay's Lane, London SE1 2HB
T: 020 7089 6840
F: 020 7089 6841
E: media@scie.org.uk
www.spn.org.uk
We are a broad-based coalition of service users/survivors, carers, policy makers, academics, students, practitioners working to ensure that social perspectives are put at the heart of the evolving mental health policy, practice, research and legislative agendas. Social perspectives are holistic and look at the social issues that affect people's mental health such as experiences of stigma and discrimination, relationships, employment, access to housing and quality health and social care services.
Employees: 1
Volunteers: 25

Social Research Association

London NW1 6QB
T: 020 7388 2391
E: admin@the-sra.org.uk
www.the-sra.org.uk
Chair of the Board of Trustees: Patten Smith
We are the professional membership body for social researchers. Promoting high-quality standards of social research, we seek to represent, support, connect and inform our members and the wider social research community.
Employees: 2
Volunteers: 10
Regional offices: 3

Social Venture Network UK

Chandos House, 128 Cotham Brow, Bristol, Avon BS6 6AE
E: info@svnuk.org
www.svneurope.com
A network of socially and environmentally engaged entrepreneurs dedicated to changing the way the world does business. The network creates opportunities for learning, partnerships, and launching new ventures and is associated with SVN United States and SVN Asia.
Volunteers: 3
Regional offices: 1

Society for Co-operative Studies

c/o Patricia Juby, Co-operative UK, Holyoake House, Hanover Street, Manchester M60 0AS
T: 01452 308406
E: pajuby@gmail.com
www.co-opstudies.org
The Society welcomes into membership, co-operative members, employees, managers, specialist practitioners, academics and others who share an interest in the UK and world Co-operative Movement. It seeks to advance the education of members and the public on all aspects of the Co-operative Movement, co-operative forms of structure and, in particular, to commission, identify, and publish research on the Co-operative Movement and the exchange of information and experience on co-operative study and research.

Society for Endocrinology

22 Apex Court, Woodlands, Bradley Stoke, Bristol, Avon BS32 4JT
T: 01454 642200
F: 01454 642205
E: sally.spencer@endocrinology.org
www.endocrinology.org
Chief Executive: Ian Russell
The Society for Endocrinology is the major British society representing scientists, clinicians and nurses who work with hormones. It advances education and research in endocrinology, as well as acting as the discipline's voice with an aim of raising its profile.
Employees: 80

Society For General Microbiology

Marlborough House, Basingstoke Road, Spencers Wood, Reading, Berkshire RG7 1AG
T: 0118 988 1800
E: info@sgm.ac.uk
www.sgm.ac.uk
CEO: Dr Simon Festing
Society for General Microbiology (SGM) is a membership organisation for scientists who work in all areas of microbiology. SGM publishes key academic journals in microbiology and virology, organises international scientific conferences and provides an international forum for communication among microbiologists and supports their professional development. SGM promotes the understanding of microbiology to a diverse range of stakeholders, including policy makers, students, teachers, journalists and the wider public through a framework of communication activities and resources.
Employees: 36
Volunteers: 80

Society for Mucopolysaccharide Diseases

MPS House, Repton Place, White Lion Road, Amersham, Buckinghamshire HP7 9LP
T: 0345 389 9901
F: 0845 389 9902
E: mps@mpssociety.org.uk
www.mpssociety.org.uk
Group Chief Executive: Christine Lavery
Provides support and individual advocacy to those affected by Mucopolysaccharide, Fabry and other lysosomal diseases throughout the UK. Publishes a wide range of information booklets and a quarterly newsletter. Organises conferences, training and funds research into MPS diseases.
Employees: 16
Volunteers: 200
Regional offices: 1

Society for Promoting Christian Knowledge

36 Causton Street, London SW1P 4ST
T: 020 7592 3900
F: 020 7592 3939
E: pphillips@spck.org.uk
www.spck.org.uk
Chief Executive: Sam Richardson
Promotes Christian knowledge by: communicating the faith in its rich diversity; helping people to understand it and to

develop their personal faith; equipping Christians for mission and ministry.
Employees: 30

Society for the Assistance of Ladies in Reduced Circumstances

Lancaster House, 25 Hornyold Road, Malvern, Worcestershire WR14 1QQ
T: 0300 365 1886
E: john.sands@salrc.org.uk
www.salrc.org.uk
General Secretary: John Sands
The Society makes grants to working-age women resident in the UK who are living alone in their own home (either owned or rented) and in genuine financial need, irrespective of social status.
Employees: 4
Income: £886,012 (2013-14)

Society for the Protection of Ancient Buildings

37 Spital Square, London E1 6DY
T: 020 7377 1644
Helpline: 020 7456 0916
F: 020 7247 5296
E: info@spab.org.uk
www.spab.org.uk
Secretary: Philip Venning
Aims to educate public opinion in the conservative repair of historic buildings and to prevent ill-considered and conjectural restoration. Offers advice and courses for homeowners and building professionals. SPAB is a membership organisation. Its respected magazine, Cornerstone, is sent to all members on a quarterly basis. We advise, we educate, we campaign.

Society for the Protection of Animals Abroad

14 John Street, London WC1N 2EB
T: 020 7831 3999
F: 020 7831 5999
E: john@spana.org
www.spana.org
Chief Executive: Jeremy Hulme
With 19 veterinary centres and 21 mobile clinics, SPANA treated over 300,000 animals last year throughout North and West Africa and the Middle East. Our efforts are concentrated on those areas where the need is greatest: wherever animals are mistreated, neglected or struggling to survive without proper care.
Employees: 17
Volunteers: 20

Society for the Protection of Unborn Children

London SW1P 2JT
T: 020 7222 5845
F: 020 7222 0630
E: information@spuc.org.uk
www.spuc.org.uk
Affirms, defends and promotes the existence and value of human life from the moment of conception; reasserts the principle laid down in UN Declaration of the Rights of the Child that the child needs special safeguards and care, including appropriate legal protection, before as well as after birth; defends and promotes welfare of mothers during pregnancy and of their children; examines existing or proposed laws, legislation or regulations relating to abortion, supporting or opposing as appropriate.
Employees: 34
Volunteers: 100
Regional offices: 6

Society of Analytical Psychology

1 Daleham Gardens, Hampstead, London NW3 5BY
T: 020 7435 7696
F: 020 7431 1495
E: chair@thesap.org.uk
www.thesap.org.uk
Chair: Penny Pickles
The Society's main functions are the development of analytical psychology; training of adult analysts and psychotherapists; provision of Jungian analysis to members of the public through the society's Clinic, plus a consultation and referral service; education through public events and the Journal of Analytical Psychology; professional association for Jungian analysts and psychotherapists
Employees: 17
Volunteers: 100
Income: £316,559 (2012-13)

Society of Antiquaries of London

Burlington House, Piccadilly, London W1J 0BE
T: 020 7479 7080
F: 020 7287 6967
E: admin@sal.org.uk
www.sal.org.uk
General Secretary: John Lewis
The Society of Antiquaries of London's goals are the encouragement, advancement and furtherance of the study and knowledge of the antiquities and history of this and other countries.
Employees: 20
Regional offices: 1

Society of Authors

84 Drayton Gardens, London SW10 9SB
T: 020 7373 6642
F: 020 7373 5768
E: info@societyofauthors.org
www.societyofauthors.org
General Secretary: Mark Le Fanu
The Society is a trade union with 8,500 members. It lobbies for the profession and gives individual advice and help to members on business issues (e.g.. contracts, copyright, publishers, agents, etc.). Members receive a quarterly journal, The Author.
Employees: 14

Society of Biology

Charles Darwin House, 12 Roger Street, London WC1N 2JU
T: 020 7685 2550
E: info@societyofbiology.org
www.societyofbiology.org
Chief Executive: Dr Mark Downs
Aims to advance the science and practice of biology and education in biology and to coordinate and encourage the study of biology and its application.
Employees: 30
Volunteers: 200
Income: £2,600,000 (2012-13)

Society of Homeopaths

11 Brookfield, Duncan Close, Moulton Park, Northampton, Northamptonshire NN1 6WL
T: 01604 621400
F: 01604 622622
E: julie_rowland@homeopathy-soh.org
www.homeopathy-soh.org
Established in 1978, it is the largest organisation representing professional homeopaths in Europe, with over 1,500 members on its register. Members practice in accordance with the society's Code of Ethics and Practice and carry full public liability and indemnity insurance.
Employees: 20
Volunteers: 20
Regional offices: 1

Soil Association

Bristol House, Bristol BS1 6BY
T: 0117 914 2454
F: 0117 925 2504
E: development@soilassociation.org
www.soilassociation.org
Aims to educate the general public about organic agriculture, gardening and food, and their benefits for both human health and the environment; promotes the production and consumption of organically grown food; lobbies the authorities for an agricultural

policy that is based on ecological and sustainable principles.
Employees: 150
Volunteers: 10
Regional offices: 2

Solihull Carers Centre

E: sueshahmiri@solihullcarers.org

SOLVE IT

Satra Innovation Park, Rockingham Road, Kettering, Northamptonshire NN16 9JH
T: 01536 414690
E: manager.solveit@gmail.com
www.solveitonline.co.uk
Business Manager: Deborah Clarke
SOLVE IT provides a free service to young people, parents, carers and those adults affected by volatile substance abuse (VSA), promoting a general awareness to the dangers of these substances, working towards the prevention of related deaths, illness, accidents and social exclusion. It provides education, early intervention, a confidential support and counselling service for those affected by such abuse, including families, training and support for professionals.
Employees: 5
Volunteers: 8
Regional offices: 1

SOS Children's Villages UK

St Andrew's House, 59 St Andrew's Street, Cambridge, Cambridgeshire CB2 3BZ
T: 01223 365589
F: 01223 322613
E: info@sos-uk.org.uk
www.soschildrensvillages.org.uk
Provides loving care and a secure future for homeless, orphaned and abandoned children throughout the world.
Employees: 9
Volunteers: 2

Sound and Music

3rd Floor, Somerset House, London WC2R 1LA
T: 020 7759 1800
E: info@soundandmusic.org
www.soundandmusic.org
Chief Executive: Susanna Eastburn
Sound and Music's vision is to create a world where new music and sound prospers, transforming lives, challenging expectations and celebrating the work of its creators.
Employees: 10
Regional offices: 1

Sound Seekers

c/o UCL Ear Institute, 332-336 Gray's Inn Road, London WC1X 8EE
T: 020 7833 0035
E: help@sound-seekers.org.uk
www.sound-seekers.org.uk
Chief Executive: Lucy Carter
Sound Seekers is dedicated to helping deaf people, particularly children, in the poorest communities of the developing world. We work in partnership with local organisations to deliver sustainable and cost-effective projects that advance understanding of deaf people's needs and improve their access to health services, education, and social support, together with initiatives that enable people to avoid, or overcome, the effects of deafness.
Employees: 4
Volunteers: 30
Regional offices: 1
Income: £417,118 (2013-14)

South Lancashire Learning Disability Training Consortium

E: ceo@slldtc.co.uk

Southampton and Winchester Visitors Group

SWVG, PO Box 1615, Southampton, Hampshire SO17 3WF
T: 07503 176350
E: info@swvg-refugees.org.uk
www.swvg-refugees.org.uk
Chair: Anne Leeming
SWVG is a group of volunteers who befriend and support asylum seekers and refugees in the Southampton area. We offer financial assistance to those who are homeless and destitute. Through our legal justice project we have access to advice from a leading immigration solicitor. We try to give asylum seekers a voice by reaching out to churches, schools and community groups and we campaign for a fairer asylum system.
Employees: 2
Volunteers: 60
Income: £82,098 (2014-15)

Southbank Mosaics CIC

St John's Crypt, 73 Waterloo Road, London, 73 Waterloo Road, London SE1 8UD
T: 020 7620 6070
F: 020 7928 6724
E: david@southbankmosaics.com
www.southbankmosaics.com
Director: David Tootill
To make the neighbourhood more attractive through the highest quality public realm installations: sculptures, fountains, seating, murals etc. We train students in artisan craft and will open a small independent university to teach mosaic. We work with special needs children and take referrals from health and social services. We aim to provide an alternative to custody for local youth in trouble with the police. We support ex-offenders coming out of prison.
Employees: 8
Volunteers: 300
Income: £150,000 (2014-15)

Southend Association of Voluntary Services

E: asemmence@savs-southend.co.uk

Sova

Head Office, Unit 201, Lincoln House, 1-3 Brixton road, London SW9 6DE
T: 020 7793 0404
F: 020 7793 5858
E: mail@sova.org.uk
www.sova.org.uk
Chief Operating Officer: Sophie Wilson
Sova works in England and Wales with the National Offender Management Service, the Prison Service, probation areas, JobCentre Plus, Social Services and other organisations to strengthen communities by involving local volunteers in promoting social inclusion and reducing crime. Paid staff and volunteers utilise skills to encourage the positive development of a wide client group including offenders, prisoners, young people on youth offending orders, those at risk of offending and asylum seekers.
Employees: 150
Volunteers: 1000

Spadework Ltd

Teston Road, Offham, West Malling, Kent ME19 5NA
T: 01732 870002
F: 01732 842827
E: spadework1@btconnect.com
www.spadework.net
Provides training opportunities for adults with learning and/or physical disabilities to prepare them for an independent life within the community.
Employees: 13
Volunteers: 20
Regional offices: 2

Spare Tyre Theatre Company

E: lucy@sparetyre.org

Speakability (Action for Dysphasic Adults)

240 City Road, London EC1V 2PR
T: 020 7261 9572
Helpline: 0808 808 9572
E: melanie@speakability.org.uk
www.speakability.org.uk
Chief Executive: Melanie Derbyshire
Speakability is a national charity supporting and empowering people with Aphasia (whatever the cause) and their carers, by offering a free helpline and information service, training resources for carers and a UK-wide network of Aphasia Self-Help Groups. As the voice of people with Aphasia, Speakabilty also campaigns for greater understanding of this communication disability and better service provision.
Employees: 5
Volunteers: 100+

Special Kids In the UK

PO Box 617, Addlestone KT15 9AP
T: 01932 356416
E: information@specialkidsintheuk.org
www.specialkidsintheuk.org
Special Kids in the UK is a charity for families who have a child of any age with additional needs. The charity aims to bring families together, offering friendship and support.

Spinal Injuries Association

SIA House, 2 Trueman Place, Oldbrook, Milton Keynes MK6 2HH
T: 01908 604191
Helpline: 0800 980 0501
E: sia@spinal.co.uk
www.spinal.co.uk
Chief Executive Officer: Sue Browning
SIA is a national, user-led organisation for people with spinal cord injuries and their families. Our purpose is to promote the integration and full participation in society of our members, by encouraging them to become fulfilled and in control of their lives.
Employees: 50
Volunteers: 100

Spinal Muscular Atrophy Support UK

40 Cygnet Court, Timothy's Bridge Road, Stratford upon Avon, Warwickshire CV37 9NW
T: 01789 267520
F: 01789 268371
E: office@smasupportuk.org.uk
www.smasupportuk.org.uk
Managing Director: Doug Henderson
We inform, support and empower families and individuals affected by all forms of SMA and raise awareness of the condition. We also fund and support the research community addressing the causes, treatment and management of SMA.
Employees: 13
Volunteers: 170

Spitalfields City Farm

Buxton street, London E1 5AR
T: 020 7247 8762
F: 020 7247 5452
E: mhairi@spitalfieldscityfarm.org
www.spitalfieldscityfarm.org
Director: Mhairi Weir
Spitalfields City Farm is a community space that inspires and that everyone can enjoy. We challenge people to respect themselves, each other, their environment and animals. We strive to be sustainable and lead by example. We aim to give people the opportunity to become active members of their community and encourage their participation in the development of the Farm, and to explore and promote the benefits of healthy and sustainable lifestyles
Employees: 16
Volunteers: 350
Income: £350,000 (2012-13)

Sport and Recreation Alliance

4th Floor, Burwood House, London SW1H 0QT
T: 020 7976 3900
F: 020 7976 3901
E: info@sportandrecreation.org.uk
www.sportandrecreation.org.uk
Chief Executive: Tim Lamb
Employees: 20

Sports Leaders UK

Clyde House, 10 Milburn Avenue, Oldbrook, Milton Keynes MK6 2WA
T: 01908 689194
F: 01908 393744
E: info@sportsleaders.org
www.sportsleaders.org
The new name for the British Sports Trust, Sports Leaders UK believes in inspiring people and communities through leadership qualifications in sport. Sports Leaders UK believes that everyone has the potential to make a meaningful contribution to their local community, but not everyone has the opportunity or the motivation. Our Sports Leader Awards help people learn essential skills such as working with and organising others, as well as motivational, communication and teamwork skills.
Employees: 32
Volunteers: 1

Spurgeon's Child Care

74 Wellingborough Road, Rushden, Northamptonshire NN10 9TY
T: 01933 417405
E: info@spurgeons.org
www.spurgeons.org

ssafa

Queen Elizabeth House, 4 St Dunstans Hill, London EC3R 8AD
T: 020 7403 8783
F: 020 7403 8815
E: terry.c@ssafa.org.uk
www.ssafa.org.uk
We provide support for the serving men and women in todays Armed Forces and for those who have served even if it was only for a single day. We also care for the needs of their families and dependants. Last year alone, our professional staff and trained volunteers gave assistance to more than 50,000 people. We helped to make a real difference to many lives.
Employees: 680
Volunteers: 7000
Regional offices: 100

St Albans Mencap

E: macpheemartyn@aol.com

St Andrew's Healthcare

St Andrew's Hospital, Billing Road, Northampton, Northamptonshire NN1 5DG
T: 01604 616000
E: treading@standrew.co.uk
www.stah.org
Chief Executive and Medical Director: Philip Sugarman
St Andrew's Healthcare, a not-for-profit charity, aims to be the UK's leading independent provider of specialist mental healthcare, complementing and working in partnership with the NHS.
Employees: 2500
Volunteers: 110

St Francis Leprosy Guild

73 St Charles Square, London W10 6EJ
T: 020 8969 1345
E: enquiries@stfrancisleprosy.org
www.stfrancisleprosy.org
President: Mr Michael Forbes Smith
St Francis Leprosy Guild supports those caring for leprosy patients in Asia, Africa and South America. Although leprosy can now be cured by multi-drug therapy, many new cases are still being discovered and thousands of

cured patients have disabilities and need care and support. Each year the Guild sends grants to eighty hospitals, clinics and centres in 25 countries. Its 'elective' programme helps medical students in the UK to work with leprosy patients abroad.
Employees: 1
Volunteers: 10
Income: £201,500 (2013-14)

St John Ambulance

27 St John's Lane, London EC1M 4BU
T: 020 7324 4000
F: 020 7324 4001
E: chief-executive@nhq.sja.org.uk
www.sja.org.uk
Everyone who needs it should receive first aid from those around them. No one should suffer for the lack of trained first aiders. Our mission is: to provide an effective and efficient charitable first aid service to local communities; to provide training and products to satisfy first aid and related health and safety needs for all of society; and to encourage personal development for people of all ages, through training and by membership of our organisation.
Volunteers: 44000
Regional offices: 45

St John of God Care Services

Saint Bede's House, Morton Park Way, Darlington, County Durham DL1 4XZ
T: 01325 373701
F: 01325 373707
E: enquiries@sjog.org.uk
Employees: 700
Volunteers: 40
Regional offices: 6

St Joseph's Hospice Association

Jospice, Ince Road, Thornton, Liverpool L23 4UE
T: 0151 924 3812
E: enquiries@jospice.org.uk
www.jospice.org.uk
Maintains hospices to care for the incurably sick and destitute, both in Britain and the third world (Central and South America, India and Pakistan).

St Loye's Foundation

Beaufort House, 51,New North Road, Exeter EX4 4EP
T: 01392 255428
F: 01392 420889
E: info@stloyes.ac.uk
www.stloyes.org.uk
CEO: Eilis Rainsford
St Loye's Foundation is a national charity and service provider, based in Exeter, Devon for over 75 years. We also have satellite offices in Warrington, Cardiff and North Devon. We specialise in helping people with health, disability and social issues by providing a range of services, including Employment Training, Care and Support and Learning and Skills. Across all these services individuals are given the support and practical knowledge they need to access employment.
Employees: 120
Volunteers: 6
Regional offices: 6

St Peters House Project

1-3 The Pavement, Grovehill Road, Redhill, Surrey RH1 6TW
T: 01737 773917
Helpline: 01737 763000
E: stephanie@stpetershouse.org.uk
www.stpetershouse.org.uk
Project Director: Stephanie Phillips
Employees: 7
Volunteers: 3
Income: £124,000 (2012-13)

St Vincent de Paul Society (England and Wales)

5th Floor, London SE1 1JG
T: 020 7407 4644
F: 020 7407 4634
E: info@svp.org.uk
www.svp.org.uk
Chief Executive: Elizabeth Palmer
The St Vincent de Paul Society is an international Christian voluntary organisation dedicated to tackling poverty and disadvantage by providing direct practical assistance to anyone in need. Active in England and Wales since 1844, today it continues to address social and material need in all its many forms.
Employees: 130
Volunteers: 10000
Regional offices: 1100

Staffordshire Council of Voluntary Youth Services

42a, Eastgate Street, Stafford, Staffordshire ST16 2LY
T: 01785 240378
E: phil@staffscvys.org.uk
www.staffscvys.org.uk
Staffordshire Council of Voluntary Youth: Phil Pusey
Staffordshire Council of Voluntary Youth Services will ensure that Staffordshire County will be internally and externally recognised as having a dynamic voluntary youth sector made up of strong, sustainable, local organisations run by capable people committed to meaningful engagement and effective partnership working providing safe environments for thousands of children and young people to maximise their personal potential through personal & social development.
Employees: 8
Volunteers: 6000
Income: £350,000 (2012-13)

STAGETEXT

1st Floor, 54 Commercial Street, London E1 6LT
T: 020 7377 0540
F: 020 7247 5622
E: enquiries@stagetext.org
www.stagetext.org
Chief Executive: Tabitha Allum
STAGETEXT provides and promotes the use of captioning and live speech-to-text transcription (subtitling) in cultural and entertainment venues to enable deaf, deafened and hard of hearing people to access the arts.
Employees: 7
Income: £543,000 (2012-13)

STAR (Student Action for Refugees)

356 Holloway Road N7 6PA
T: 020 7697 4130
E: staradmin@star-network.org.uk
www.star-network.org.uk
Chief Executive: Emma Williams
STAR is the national charity of students welcoming refugees to the UK. Our 12,000 student activists run groups at over 30 universities. They volunteer at local refugee projects, educate fellow students about asylum in the UK, campaign for refugee protection and fundraise for STAR
Employees: 7
Volunteers: 45

STARS - Syncope Trust And Reflex anoxic Seizures

PO Box 175, Stratford upon Avon, Warwickshire CV37 8YD
T: 01789 450564
F: 01789 450682
E: info@stars.org.uk
www.stars.org.uk
STARS aims to ensure that anyone presenting with unexplained loss of consciousness receives the correct diagnosis, the appropriate treatment, informed support and sign posting to the appropriate medical professional. STARS offers information and advice to help manage symptoms and regain quality of life. This is achieved through our 24 hour helpline, DoH approved resources and

patients day offering advice and support to patients, carers and medical professionals.
Employees: 1
Volunteers: 3
Regional offices: 1

Staying First

Mulliner House, Flanders Road W4 1NN
T: 020 8996 8893
E: lorna.revell@sbhg.co.uk
Director: Graham Raine
To provide advice, practical assistance and help to people living in West London to enable them to live in comfort and security in their own homes. Housing advice (private tenants and owner occupiers only), small repairs and home improvement agency for residents in Kensington and Chelsea. Small repairs for residents in Westminster. Furniture recycling and reuse in West London. Debt and welfare benefits advice provided to a number of registered social housing providers.
Employees: 42
Volunteers: 15
Regional offices: 1

Stephen Lawrence Charitable Trust

2nd Floor, Downstream Building, 1 London Bridge, London SE1 9BG
T: 020 8100 2800
E: information@stephenlawrence.org.uk
www.stephenlawrence.org.uk
As an educational charity, our mission is to promote diversity in architecture and associated professions, improve the educational achievements of black and ethnic-minority students, and help young people find pathways out of poverty into sustainable, rewarding careers in architecture, building construction and other fields associated with urban design and regeneration.
Employees: 4
Volunteers: 20

Steps Charity Worldwide

Wright House, Crouchley Lane, Lymm, Cheshire WA13 0AS
T: 01925 750271
F: 01925 750270
E: info@steps-charity.org.uk
www.steps-charity.org.uk
Acting Chief Executive Officer: Loredana Guteg Wyatt
We provide quality support, information and a voice for families and people with lower limb conditions (hip dysplasia/clubfoot/lower limb deficiency). In order to do this we are committed to furthering research, innovation, services and best practice through a partnership approach.
Employees: 4
Volunteers: 3

Stickler Syndrome Support Group

PO Box 3351, Littlehampton BN16 9GB
T: 01903 785771
E: info@stickler.org.uk
www.stickler.org.uk
Founder and Honorary President: Wendy Hughes
The Stickler Syndrome Support Group provides support for sufferers and their families, plus medical and other professionals with an interest in the syndrome. This support is provided through publications, telephone, website, conferences and family days.
Volunteers: 8

Stillbirth and Neonatal Death Society

28 Portland Place, London W1B 1LY
T: 020 7436 7940
F: 020 7436 3715
E: support@uk-sands.org
www.uk-sands.org
Director: Neal Long
Employees: 19
Regional offices: 95 groups

Stonewall

The Tower Building, 11 York Road, London SE1 7NX
T: 020 7593 1850
Helpline: 0800 050 2020
F: 020 7593 1877
E: info@stonewall.org.uk
www.stonewall.org.uk
Chief Executive Officer: Ben Summerskill
Campaigns to achieve legal and social justice for: lesbians, gay men and bisexuals; challenges discrimination and prejudice; promotes new research and has an information service offering information about LGB rights.
Employees: 70
Volunteers: 200
Regional offices: 3

Stonewall Housing

Unit 2A, Leroy House, 436 Essex Road, London N1 3QP
T: 020 7359 6242
Helpline: 020 7359 5767
F: 020 7359 9419
E: bob@stonewallhousing.org
www.stonewallhousing.org
Chief Executive: Bob Green
Stonewall Housing provides housing, advice, care and support to lesbian, gay, bisexual and transgender people so they feel safe and secure and are able to achieve their full potential.
Employees: 16
Volunteers: 2

Stonham

Malt House, 281 Field End Road, Eastcote, Middlesex HA4 9XQ
T: 020 8868 9000
F: 020 8868 9292
E: robert.weatherall@homegroup.org.uk
www.stonham.org.uk
Executive Director: Paul Rydquist
Stonham is England's largest provider of housing and support for socially excluded and vulnerable adults. We run 545 projects across the country and work with over 15,000 people each year, in a mix of residential services and in floating support services (where we support people living in their own homes).
Employees: 2500
Regional offices: 3

Stop Abuse for Everyone

1 Queens Road, Exeter EX2 9ER
T: 01392 269545
E: chris.collier@btinternet.com
www.safe-services.org.uk
Manager: Janet Collier
Stop Abuse For Everyone (SAFE) works with all those affected by and experiencing all forms of domestic violence and abuse (DVA) in Exeter, East and Mid Devon. It provides: A Refuge for women, children and young people; Independent Domestic Violence Advisors who offer support through MARAC, court and other processes; Support in the community for children, young people and young men; Awareness-raising work in schools and colleges; Pattern Changing courses for women wishing to move on in their lives and learn how to do so in a specialist and supportive environment.
Employees: 7
Volunteers: 9
Regional offices: 1
Income: £566,263 (2013-14)

Strategic Planning Society

Buxton House, 7 Highbury Hill,
London N5 1SU
T: 0845 056 3663
E: membership@sps.org.uk
www.sps.org.uk
Campaigns to develop an understanding of the need for long-range planning in both the private and public sectors of the economy. Aims to enhance the skills of long-range planners and to exchange and extend the information available to long-range planners.

Street Child Africa

Brabant House, Portsmouth Road,
Thames Ditton, Surrey KT7 0EY
T: 020 8972 9820
F: 020 8972 9821
E: info@streetchildafrica.org.uk
www.streetchildafrica.org.uk
Director: Anthony Morton-King
Street Child Africa's mission is to champion the rights of African street children and other children at risk. We work in Senegal, Ghana, Uganda, the DRC, Zambia and Mozambique, directly with African partners. Through our partners we support children with education, skills training and a chance to return to their families and communities.
Employees: 10
Volunteers: 7
Regional offices: 1
Income: £640,000 (2012-13)

Streetscene

StreetScene Addiction Recovery,
(Registered office), 55 Cobham Road,
Ferndown, Dorset Bh21 7RB
T: 01202 540337
Helpline: 01202 551254
F: 01202 765946
E: tessa@streetscene.org.uk
www.streetscene.org.uk
CEO: Tessa Corner
Provider of care for people with problems of addiction to drugs / alcohol including; residential treatment, supported after care, day care, re-integration, simple detox. 54 beds of rehab in 3 different locations, 54 beds of support in 6 different locations. Based in Dorset and Hampshire. Abstinence based philosophy.
Employees: 52
Volunteers: 15

Stroke Association

Stroke Association House, 240 City Road,
London EC1V 2PR
T: 020 7566 0300
Helpline: 0303 303 3100
F: 020 7490 2686
E: jbarrick@stroke.org.uk
www.stroke.org.uk
Chief Executive: Jon Barrick
The Stroke Association is a charity. We believe in life after stroke and together we can conquer stroke. We work directly with stroke survivors and their families and carers, with health and social care professionals and with scientists and researchers. We campaign to improve stroke care and support people to make the best recovery they can. We fund research to develop new treatments and ways of preventing stroke.
Employees: 783
Volunteers: 4000
Regional offices: 16
Income: £37,500,000 (2014-15)

Student Christian Movement

Unit 504F, The Big Peg, 120 Vyse Street,
The Jewellery Quarter,
Birmingham B18 6NE
T: 0121 200 3355
E: scm@movement.org.uk
www.movement.org.uk
National Coordinator: Hilary Topp
We're a student-led movement inspired by Jesus to act for justice and show God's love in the world. As a community we come together to pray, worship and explore faith in an open and non-judgemental environment. The movement is made up of a network of groups and individual members across Britain, as well as link churches and affiliated chaplaincies.
Employees: 5
Volunteers: 10
Regional offices: 1
Income: £177,913 (2014-15)

Sturge Weber Foundation (UK)

348 Pinhoe Road, Exeter EX4 8AF
T: 01392 464675
E: support@sturgeweber.org.uk
www.sturgeweber.org.uk
Chair: Jenny Denham
Sturge Weber syndrome is a rare neurological disorder, the symptoms of which usually occur in the child's first year of life. The Foundation aims to help and support parents; to raise public and professional awareness and to raise funds in order to do so.
Volunteers: 6

Sue Ryder

First Floor, 16 Upper Woburn Place,
London WC1H 0AF
T: 0845 050 1953
F: 020 7400 0441
E: info@sueryder.org
www.sueryder.org
Sue Ryder Care's mission is care that liberates lives. We inspire, support and care for people with long-term neurological conditions and palliative care needs in our care centres, hospices, their own homes and in the community.
Employees: 2500

Support After Murder and Manslaughter

L&D Tally Ho!, Pershore Road, Edgbaston,
Birmingham B5 7RN
T: 0121 471 1200
Helpline: 0845 872 3440
F: 0121 471 1201
E: samm.national@gmail.com
www.samm.org.uk
National Coordinator: Heather Meyer
Offers understanding and support to families and friends bereaved through murder and manslaughter; raises public awareness about the effects of murder and manslaughter; takes up issues of concern arising from the affects of murder and manslaughter; and promotes and supports research into the effects of murder and manslaughter on society. All volunteers, trustees etc. have themselves been bereaved by murder.
Employees: 4
Volunteers: 55
Income: £140,000 (2012-13)

Support After Murder and Manslaughter Abroad

SISEC Ltd, 21 Holborn Viaduct,
London EC1A 2DY
T: 0845 123 2384
E: lianne@sammabroad.org
www.sammabroad.org
Director/Trustee: Eve Henderson
Support After Murder and Manslaughter Abroad started in 2001. We provide peer support, emotional support, information and practical support. We also work to improve the support families receive in the UK after a murder abroad. We seek to provide feedback to the many government agencies involved after a murder abroad, so that they may improve the services they offer and reduce the distress they cause to bereaved families.
Volunteers: 7

Supporters Direct

3rd Floor, Victoria House, Bloomsbury Square, London WC1B 4SE
T: 020 7273 1596
F: 020 7273 1605
E: info@supporters-direct.coop
www.supporters-direct.org
Chief Executive: David Lampitt
Supporters Direct helps form and support supporters' trusts, which are not-for-profit, volunteer-run groups of supporters of particular sports clubs who wish to take a stake in the ownership and management of their clubs and reorientate those clubs towards their communities using social enterprise business models.
Employees: 11
Volunteers: 11
Regional offices: 2

SupportLine

PO Box 2860, Romford, Essex RM7 1JA
T: 01708 765222
Helpline: 01708 765200
E: info@supportline.org.uk
www.supportline.org.uk
Chair: Peter Barrell
Provides emotional support and information by telephone helpline, email and post. Service for children young people and adults primarily aimed at those who are vulnerable, at risk, isolated and victims of any form of abuse. We help people develop healthy positive coping strategies, increase their confidence and self-esteem and develop an inner feeling of strength. The service specialises in providing support for adult survivors of childhood abuse.
Employees: 1
Volunteers: 6
Income: £45,057 (2014-15)

Surf Life Saving Great Britain

19 Southernhay West, Exeter, Devon EX1 1PJ
T: 01392 218007
F: 01392 217808
E: mail@slsgb.org.uk
www.surflifesaving.org.uk
CEO: Esther Pearson
Aims to provide a safe and enjoyable environment on British beaches, promoting and controlling the work of lifesaving, resuscitation and first aid.
Employees: 8
Volunteers: 100
Regional offices: 1

Surrey Nurturing Links

E: jharris@surreynurturinglinks.org.uk

Survival International

6 Charterhouse Buildings, Goswell Road, London EC1M 7ET
T: 020 7687 8700
E: info@survivalinternational.org
www.survivalinternational.org
Survival International is the global movement for tribal peoples' rights. They help tribal peoples to defend their lands, protect their lives and determine their own futures.

Survivors of Bereavement by Suicide

The Flamsteed Centre, Albert Street, Ilkeston, Derbyshire DE7 5GU
T: 0115 944 1117
Helpline: 0300 111 5065
E: sobs.admin@care4free.net
www.uk-sobs.org.uk
Chair of the Trustees: Ann Culley
We exist to meet the needs and break the isolation of those bereaved by the suicide of a close relative or friend. Many of those helping have, themselves, been bereaved by suicide. Our aim is to provide a safe, confidential, environment, in which bereaved people can share their experiences and feelings, thus giving and gaining support from each other.
Employees: 3
Volunteers: 180
Regional offices: 55

Survivors Trust

Unit 2, Eastlands Court Business Centre, St Peters Road, Rugby, Warwickshire CV21 3RP
T: 01788 550554
F: 01788 551150
E: info@thesurvivorstrust.org
www.thesurvivorstrust.org
The Survivors Trust is a national umbrella agency for 126 specialist voluntary sector agencies providing a range of counselling, therapeutic and support services working with women, men and children who are victims/survivors of rape, sexual violence and childhood sexual abuse.
Employees: 2

Sustain: the Alliance for Better Food and Farming

94 White Lion Street, London N1 9PF
T: 020 7837 1228
E: sustain@sustainweb.org
www.sustainweb.org
Advocates food and agriculture policies and practices that enhance the health and welfare of people and animals, improves the working and living environment, and promotes equity and enriches society and culture.

Sustrans

Head Office, Sustrans, 2 Cathedral Square, College Green, Bristol BS1 5DD
T: 0117 926 8893
F: 0117 929 4173
E: info@sustrans.org.uk
www.sustrans.org.uk
MD: Malcolm Shepherd
Sustrans works with communities, policy-makers and partner organisations so that people can choose healthier, cleaner and cheaper journeys and enjoy better, safer spaces where they live. All over the UK, we make a positive difference to people's lives.
Employees: 300
Volunteers: 1200
Regional offices: 10

Sutton Trust

9th Floor, Millbank Tower, London SW1P 4QP
T: 020 7802 1660
F: 020 7802 1661
E: info@suttontrust.com
www.suttontrust.com
The main objective of the trust is to support innovative projects that provide educational opportunities for young people from non-privileged backgrounds. Projects range from early years (0-3 year olds), through primary and secondary schooling, to further and higher education, including research projects, with an emphasis on innovative start-up projects that have the scope to benefit large numbers in the future. The trust does not fund individuals or capital projects.
Employees: 6

Suzy Lamplugh Trust

218 Strand, London WC2R 1AT
T: 020 7091 0014
F: 020 7091 0015
E: info@suzylamplugh.org
www.suzylamplugh.org
Employees: 18
Volunteers: 3

Swan Advice Network

Leigh House, 1 Wells Hill, Radstock, Bath BA3 3RN
Helpline: 01761 432445
E: swan.management@btconnect.com
www.swan.btck.co.uk
Manager: Sarah Williams
Swan exists to relieve need and hardship amongst people in Bath and North East Somerset and surrounding areas by providing a range of advice, information and access services. Current services include transport provision for the elderly or disabled on low incomes, a housing advice service, benefits advice services including help with universal

credit, and administration of the Bath and District Deposit Bond Service for those seeking accommodation in the private rented sector.
Employees: 7
Volunteers: 24
Regional offices: 1
Income: £127,647 (2014-15)

SWAN UK (Syndromes Without A Name)

Genetic Alliance UK, Unit 4D Leroy House, 436 Essex Rd, London N1 3QP
T: 020 7704 3141
E: info@undiagnosed.org.uk
www.undiagnosed.org.uk
Director of Genetic Alliance UK: Alastair Kent
SWAN UK supports families of children with undiagnosed genetic conditions. SWAN UK is an initiative of Genetic alliance UK offering information and support to families of children with undiagnosed genetic conditions.

TAEN - The Age and Employment Network

Headland House, 308-312 Gray's Inn Road, London WC1X 8DP
T: 020 7837 4762
E: info@taen.org.uk
www.taen.org.uk
Chief Executive: Chris Ball
TAEN - The Age and Employment Network works to remove age barriers to employment opportunities and for an effective job market that works better for people in mid and later life, employers and the economy. TAEN is not an employment agency but can direct individuals looking for work, who want to change direction, develop their careers or undertake training, to relevant organisations and a number of useful resources.

Take a Break Warwickshire

Canterbury House, Exhall Grange Campus, Easter Way, Ash Green, Coventry, Warwickshire CV7 9HP
T: 024 7664 4909 F: 024 7664 4959
E: kim@tabw.org.uk
www.tabw.org.uk
Director: Kim Fathers
Take-a-Break Warwickshire provides community based short breaks for children and young people who have a disability or life threatening illness and adults with a learning disability.
Employees: 220
Volunteers: 15
Regional offices: 1
Income: £1,813,230 (2014-15)

Talking Newspaper Association of the UK

10 Browning Road, Heathfield, East Sussex TN21 8DB
T: 01435 866102
E: info@tnauk.org.uk
www.tnauk.org.uk
Chief Executive: John Kerby
National Talking Newspapers and Magazines provides magazines and newspapers in audio and full (electronic) text for people unable to read normal print, mainly due to visual impairment, with the aim of giving them the same choice of magazines and newspapers as sighted people. Part of RNIB Group.
Employees: 30
Volunteers: 200

Tall Ships Youth Trust

2A The Hard, Portsmouth PO1 3PT
T: 023 9283 2055
F: 023 9281 5769
E: info@tallships.org
www.tallships.org
Employees: 10
Volunteers: 1500
Regional offices: 50

Target Tuberculosis

82 Queens Road, Brighton, East Sussex BN1 3XE
T: 01273 827070
F: 01273 821059
E: info@targettb.org.uk
www.targettuberculosis.org.uk
Tackles tuberculosis as a disease as well as the social and economic issues around it. Forms partnerships with local organisations mainly in the Indian subcontinent and sub-Saharan Africa. Aims to bring TB treatment close to the patient and improve the quality of life for patients and families.
Employees: 3
Volunteers: 6

TASHA Foundation

Alexandra House, 241 High Street, Brentford, Middlesex TW8 0NE
T: 020 8560 4583 (also fax)
E: enquiries@tasha-foundation.org.uk
www.tasha-foundation.org.uk
Provides one-to-one counselling for those experiencing problems with drug use, suffering from anxiety and stress. Supports individuals experiencing mental health problems.
Employees: 14
Volunteers: 15
Regional offices: 4

TaxAid UK

Room 304, Linton House, Southwark, London SE1 0LH
T: 020 7803 4950
Helpline: 0345 120 3779
F: 020 7803 4955
E: admin@taxaid.org.uk
www.taxaid.org.uk
Director: Rosina Pullman
TaxAid runs a free, confidential helpline, helping people on low incomes with their tax affairs. It offers face-to-face appointments in London, Birmingham, Manchester, Newcastle, Plymouth and Shropshire. It also runs training programmes for voluntary sector.
Employees: 11
Volunteers: 40

TBPI Group

1 Malvern Rise, Hadfield, Glossop, Derbyshire SK13 1QW
E: kwf1961@talktalk.net
www.tbpi-group.org
Supplies information and support to adults coping with a trauma brachial plexus injury and helps them achieve a better understanding of the impact these injuries may have on the individual, and their family.

Teacher Support Network

40A Drayton Park, London N5 1EW
T: 020 7697 2750
Helpline: 0800 056 2561
F: 020 7554 5239
E: enquiries@teachersupport.info
www.teachersupport.info
Chief Executive: Julian Stanley
We believe that all teachers should have access to the practical and emotional support they need to improve their personal wellbeing and effectiveness. If, as a society, we are to achieve the best possible education for our young people, then supporting teachers is a must. Teacher Support Network is the largest provider of support services to UK

schoolteachers. We provide counselling, coaching and advice free of charge.
Employees: 25
Volunteers: 327
Regional offices: 3

Tearfund

100 Church Road, Teddington, Middlesex TW11 8QE
T: 0845 355 8355
F: 020 8943 3594
E: enquiries@tearfund.org
www.tearfund.org
Aims to relieve poverty, suffering and distress, prevent disease and ill health among the people of the world and to promote Christian education and evangelism.
Employees: 300
Volunteers: 3300
Regional offices: 13

Teenage Cancer Trust

3rd Floor, 93 Newman Street, London W1T 3EZ
T: 020 7612 0370
F: 020 7612 0371
E: hello@teenagecancertrust.org
www.teenagecancertrust.org
Chief Executive: Siobhan Dunn
Teenage Cancer Trust is the only UK charity dedicated to improving the quality of life and chances of survival for young people with cancer aged 13 to 24. The charity funds and builds specialist units in NHS hospitals and provides dedicated staff, bringing young people together so they can be treated by teenage cancer experts in the best place for them. Teenage Cancer Trust relies on donations to fund its work.
Employees: 105

Telephones for the Blind Fund

7 Huntersfield Close, Reigate, Surrey RH2 0DX
T: 01737 248032
E: info@tftb.org.uk
www.tftb.org.uk
Provides financial support for installation and rental for a BT line for the benefit of the blind. Applicants must be registered blind or partially sighted, living alone and on low income. Applications must be made through registered support workers. Free mobile phones may also be given on application and with the same criteria.
Volunteers: 5

Television Trust for the Environment

46 Bloomsbury Street, London WC1B 3QJ
T: 020 7147 7420
E: tve@tve.org.uk
www.tve.org
Promotes global public awareness of sustainable development through television and the other audio-visual media. TVE aims to provide videos on the environment and development of NGOs in low and middle income countries free of charge, and to raise funding for film-makers in the developing world to make these programmes.

Template Foundation

The Centre, 1 Bath Place, Barnet, Hertfordshire EN5 5XE
T: 020 8441 2567
E: info@thecentrelondon.org
The Foundation's objectives are to advance the education of the public through the promotion and further study of human behavioural sciences, philosophy, history, the art of human expression and living derived from the Template and Emin archives, including arts such as theatre, dance and music.
Employees: 5
Volunteers: 200

Terrence Higgins Trust

London WC1X 8DP
T: 020 7812 1600
Helpline: 0845 122 1200
F: 020 7812 1696
E: info@tht.org.uk
www.tht.org.uk
Chief Executive: Sir Nick Partridge
HIV and sexual health charity.
Employees: 350
Volunteers: 1000
Regional offices: 17

Textile Institute International

1st Floor, St James's Buildings, Oxford Street, Manchester M1 6FQ
T: 0161 237 1188
E: tiihq@textileint.org.uk
www.textileinstitute.org
Promotes professionalism in all areas associated with the textile industries worldwide.

Thames Reach

E: ashley.nur@thamesreach.org.uk

The Adolescent and Children's Trust (TACT)

303 Hither Green Lane, Hither Green, London SE13 6TJ
T: 020 8695 8142
F: 020 8695 8141
E: enquiries@tactcare.org.uk
www.tactcare.org.uk
Chief Executive: Kevin Williams
TACT is the UK's largest charity provider of fostering and adoption services. Our core work involves providing high-quality and well-supported fostering or adoptive families for children and young people in the care of local authorities. We are dedicated to providing creative, effective and outcome-focused services. We also campaign and fundraise on behalf of children and young people in care, carers and adoptive families.
Employees: 152
Volunteers: 2
Regional offices: 9

The Arthrogryposis Group (TAG)

45 Milton Road, Hanwell, London W7 1LQ
Helpline: 0800 028 4447
E: admin@taguk.org.uk
www.taguk.org.uk
The Arthrogryposis Group (TAG) is the only organisation in the UK providing contact, information and support to people with Arthrogryposis and their families. TAG provides members with information about Arthrogryposis and can put them in touch with other families. TAG also provides an information service for professionals involved in the management of the condition. TAG encourages public awareness of Arthrogryposis and also supports research.
Volunteers: 30

The BB Group

Rochester House, 4 Belvedere Road, London SE19 2AT
T: 020 8771 3377
F: 020 8771 8550
E: sadie.westwood@thebbgroup.org
www.thebbgroup.org
CEO: Emma-Jane Cross
The BB Group is an international charity based in the UK. We build communities through socially mediated support connecting people in need with those who can help. Our 2 lead services are Mindful, a national charity that helps young people to improve and sustain positive mental health, emotional resilience and wellbeing; and BeatBullying, an international bullying prevention charity working and campaigning to make bullying unacceptable.
Employees: 50
Volunteers: 15000
Income: £2,500,000 (2011-12)

The Brendoncare Foundation

The Old Malthouse, Victoria Road, Winchester, Hampshire SO23 7DU
T: 01962 852133
E: jlamont@brendoncare.org.uk
www.brendoncare.org.uk
Chief Executive: Carole Sawyers

The Brendoncare Foundation is a registered charity, dedicated to improving the quality of life for older people through our care homes, close care facilities and social clubs across the South of England. We have 10 care homes, each with its own distinctive character, some with specialist dementia units. Brendoncare Clubs are friendship and wellbeing clubs dedicated to providing opportunities for social interaction and to meet new friends in a welcoming and supportive environment.
Employees: 750
Volunteers: 600
Regional offices: 1

The Brooke

5th Floor Friars Bridge Court,
41-45 Blackfriars Road SE1 8NZ
T: 020 3012 3456
F: 020 3012 0156
E: info@thebrooke.org
www.thebrooke.org
The Brooke is an international animal welfare organisation dedicated to improving the lives of working horses, donkeys and mules in the poorest parts of the world. We provide veterinary treatment and community programmes across Africa, Asia and Latin America. The Brooke's goal is to increase the number of working animals we help to two million a year by 2016.
Employees: 100
Volunteers: 30

The Cambridge Centre

E: paula.myers@cambridgecentre.org

The Churches Conservation Trust

Society Building, 8 All Saints Street,
London N1 9RL
T: 0845 303 2760
F: 020 7841 0434
E: central@thecct.org.uk
www.visitchurches.org.uk
Chief Executive: Crispin Truman
CCT is the national charity protecting historic churches at risk. We've saved over 340 beautiful buildings which attract almost two million visitors a year. We aim to: Inspire people to enjoy, understand and support England's historic churches; Protect history through the conservation, regeneration and presentation of our unique collection; Create value, ensuring that its social, environmental and economic value is realised.
Employees: 68
Volunteers: 1700
Regional offices: 3
Income: £12,900,000 (2014-15)

The Clinic for Boundaries Studies

49-51 East Road, London N1 6AH
T: 020 3468 4194
E: jcoe@professionalboundaries.org.uk
www.professionalboundaries.org.uk
Managing Director: Jonathan Coe
The clinic provides specialist support services for the public alongside training and professional development services for practitioners. It is also involved in research and development around professional boundaries and conduct.
Employees: 12

The Compassionate Friends

SE8 3HS
Helpline: 0345 123 2304
E: helpline@tcf.org.uk
www.tcf.org.uk
We are an organisation of bereaved parents offering support and befriending to others after the loss of a child, of any age, from any cause. We have a National Helpline (helpline@tcf.org.uk), with calls taken only by bereaved parents, which is available for support and information 365 days a year. We also have a website which includes a Members Forum which enables those who join up to speak electronically to others similarly bereaved.

The Cry-sis Helpline

BM Cry-sis, London WC1N 3XX
Helpline: 0845 122 8669
E: info@cry-sis.org.uk
www.cry-sis.org.uk
From its modest beginnings, Cry-sis has developed to become a well-respected and national charity. It offers support to families with excessively crying, sleepless and demanding babies. To achieve this, Cry-sis runs a national telephone helpline that is available to callers every day of the year between 9.00am and 10.00pm. Call cost a maximum of 2 pence per minute plus your telephone providers access charge.
Employees: 1
Volunteers: 30

The Dante Leigh Foundation

84 St Gothard Road, West Norwood,
London SE27 9QP
T: 07904 694089
E: mail@dlf-disabilitysupport.org.uk
www.dlf-disabilitysupport.org.uk
Co-Founder: Jean Leigh
Our main aims are to research into the needs and requirements of disabled people, especially young adults with learning difficulties and to work with other organisations to have these 'needs' met whilst raising disability awareness as an everyday issue.
Volunteers: 10
Income: ££602.00 (2013-14)

The Drinkaware Trust

Samuel House, 6 St Albans Street,
London SW1Y 4SQ
T: 020 7766 9900
F: 020 7504 8217
E: llam@drinkaware.co.uk
www.drinkaware.co.uk
Chief Executive: Elaine Hindal
Drinkaware aims to change the UK's drinking habits for the better. We promote responsible drinking and find innovative ways to challenge the national drinking culture to help reduce alcohol misuse and minimise alcohol-related harm.
Regional offices: 1

The Duke of Edinburgh's Award

Gulliver House, Madeira Walk, Windsor,
Berkshire SL4 1EU
T: 01753 727400
F: 01753 810666
E: info@dofe.org
www.dofe.org
Chief Executive: Peter Westgarth
Employees: 112
Volunteers: 50000
Regional offices: 11

The Ear Foundation

Marjorie Sherman House, 83 Sherwin Road,
Lenton, Nottingham,
Nottinghamshire NG7 2FB
T: 0115 942 1985
F: 0115 924 9054
E: info@earfoundation.org.uk
www.earfoundation.org.uk
Chief Executive: Sue Archbold
Employees: 16
Volunteers: 80
Regional offices: 1

The Eikon Charity

on Fullbrook School site, Selsdon Road,
New Haw, Addlestone, Surrey KT15 3HP
T: 01932 347434
E: info@eikon.org.uk
www.eikon.org.uk
CEO: Chris Hickford
The Eikon Charity aims to help socially and economically disadvantaged young people achieve their full potential, and has been working in local Surrey communities for almost two decades, delivering a variety of support programmes for vulnerable young

people who are at risk of falling in to crisis: developing an addiction, becoming homeless, being excluded from school etc. We strongly believe in early intervention - helping young people overcome issues before they become significant problems.
Employees: 14
Volunteers: 50
Income: £410,838 (2012-13)

The Electrical Safety Council

Unit 331-3 Great Guildford Business Square, 30 Great Guildford Street, London SE1 0HS
T: 020 3463 5100
E: enquiries@esc.org.uk
www.esc.org.uk
Director General: Philip Buckle
The Electrical Safety Council (ESC) is a UK charity committed to reducing deaths and injuries caused by electrical accidents in the home. We work closely with industry, government, media and consumer organisations to raise awareness of the dangers of electricity.
Employees: 20
Regional offices: 1

The Encephalitis Society

32 Castlegate, Malton, North Yorkshire YO17 7DT
T: 01653 692583
Helpline: 01653 699599
E: mail@encephalitis.info
www.encephalitis.info
Chief Executive Officer: Ava Easton
Aims to improve the quality of life of all people affected, directly and indirectly, by Encephalitis. We support people affected, provide information on the condition and its consequences in different formats, raise awareness of the condition, and conduct research. The Society is the only resource of our kind in the world.
Employees: 9
Volunteers: 30
Income: £501,441 (2014-15)

The Fairlight Trust

Fairlight, The Avenue, North Ascot, Berkshire SL5 7LY
T: 01344 874681
E: lindsay@fairlightolc.co.uk
Chair: Josephine Collier
The charity's main aims are to support vulnerable women, especially those in prostitution and with related issues, and their children; to provide aftercare for women and children who have previously accessed its services.
Employees: 20
Volunteers: 21
Income: £1,368,272 (2012-13)

The Farming Community Network

Manor Farm, Guilsborough Road, West Haddon, Northampton, Northamptonshire NN6 7AQ
T: 01788 510866
Helpline: 0300 011 1999
E: mail@fcn.org.uk
www.fcn.org.uk
Chief Executive Officer: Charles W Smith
The Farming Community Network is a UK network of volunteers from the farming community and rural churches, providing a national helpline and visiting service to farming people and families facing difficulties. The network provides pastoral and practical support for as long as it is needed, helping people to find a positive way forward through their problems.
Employees: 12
Volunteers: 389

The Federation

505 Barking Road, Plaistow, London E13 8PS
T: 020 8692 2525
F: 020 8469 4103
E: info@thefederation.org.uk
www.thefederation.org.uk
The Federation is a national membership organisation and registered charity, representing the needs of diverse communities and professionals from the drug, alcohol, criminal justice, mental health and related sectors. We offer a particular expertise in issues pertaining to black and minority Ethnic (BME) communities and professionals.
Employees: 4

The Forum for Health and Wellbeing

Office 2/3, St Mark's Community Centre, 218 Tollgate Road, Beckton, London E6 5YA
T: 020 7474 3176
E: enquiries@bemccf.org.uk
www.fhwb.co.uk
Director: Sahdia Warraich
The Forum aims to develop and improve services that effectively meet the health and social care needs of black and ethnic minority communities. It develops a strong, collective and informed voice for black and ethnic minority groups, service users and carers. The Forum aims to build the infrastructure of the black and ethnic minority voluntary, community and faith sector to deliver their own health and social care services through providing tailored capacity building and development support, and access to funding.
Employees: 11

The Giving Machine

E: joanne@me2club.org.uk

The Grace Eyre Foundation

36 Montefiore Road, Hove, East Sussex BN3 6EP
T: 01273 201900
E: mburgess@grace-eyre.org
www.grace-eyre.org
CEO: Eva Jarvis
We support people with learning disabilities and/or mental health needs across Sussex to develop their independence, obtain housing, find employment and learn new skills.
Employees: 240
Volunteers: 88
Income: £5,210 (2014-15)

The Grandparents' Association

Moot House, The Stow, Harlow, Essex CM20 3AG
T: 01279 428040 (also fax)
Helpline: 0845 434 9585
E: info@grandparents-association.org.uk
www.grandparents-association.org.uk
Chief Executive: Lynn Chesterman
The Grandparents' Association is the only national membership organisation dealing with all grandparent issues, such as bringing up your grandchildren full-time (kinship care), denied contact and childcare, in public and private law. We provide information and support by way of our helpline, welfare benefits advice service, support groups and various publications and leaflets.
Employees: 11
Volunteers: 80
Regional offices: 2
Income: £303,051 (2014-15)

The Grange

E: karen.pinchbeck@grangecentre.org.uk

The Greensand Trust

E: alexe.rose@greensandtrust.org

The Harland Trust

66 High Street, Weston Favell, Northampton, Northamptonshire NN3 3JX
T: 07752 647208
E: alan.harland@ntlworld.com

This trust supports individuals in need and charitable causes know to the Trustees at home and overseas. It applies charitable resources at the point of need in an accountable manner. This trust aims to grow in the future. Anyone wishing to donate to The Harland Trust or leave a legacy should contact the trust directly using the contact details provided here.

The Haven

Effie Road, London SW6 1TB
T: 020 7384 0000
F: 020 7384 0001
E: info@thehaven.org.uk
www.thehaven.org.uk
Chief Executive: Pamela Healy OBE
Being diagnosed with breast cancer and undergoing treatment affects people physically and emotionally. The Haven offers a free programme of care to support patients and their families during this time. Staffed by a specialist team, Havens are welcoming places providing support, information and complementary therapies before, during and after medical treatment. Working alongside healthcare professionals, Havens promote integrated breast cancer care where conventional and complementary medicine work together.
Employees: 45
Volunteers: 75
Regional offices: 4
Income: £3,000,000 (2013-14)

The Haven

E: hcss@havenrefuge.org.uk

The Heritage Alliance

Clutha House, 10 Storeys Gate, Westminster, London SW1P 3AY
T: 020 7233 0500
E: kate.pugh@theheritagealliance.org.uk
www.theheritagealliance.org.uk
Chief Executive: Kate Pugh
The Heritage Alliance is the largest coalition of heritage interests in England. Established in 2002 by key voluntary sector bodies, it brings together nearly 90 major national and regional non-government organisations concerned with heritage. Between them, Alliance members represent nearly five million people across Britain. The Alliance provides a forum for members to formulate and promote policy on core issues, make their voices heard collectively and share information and networks.
Volunteers: 6

The IARS International Institute

14 Dock Offices, Surrey Quays Road, London SE16 7PQ
T: 020 7064 4380
E: t.gavrielides@iars.org.uk
www.iars.org.uk
Director: Dr Theo Gavrielides
The IARS International Institute is user-led and user-focused charity with a mission to give everyone a chance to forge a safer, fairer and more inclusive society. Over the last 10 years, the Institute has been providing world-class and cutting-edge educational, research, policy and networking services of local, national and international significance. We are focused on empowering the most marginalised communities through direct service delivery, while enabling organisations to achieve, measure and improve their social impact.
Employees: 10
Volunteers: 15
Regional offices: 1
Income: £450,000 (2014-15)

The Leprosy Mission

Goldhay Way, Orton Goldhay, Peterborough, Cambridgeshire PE2 5GZ
T: 01733 370505
F: 01733 404880
E: post@tlmew.org.uk
www.leprosymission.org.uk
National Director: Peter Walker
Our vision is a world without leprosy. Our goal is to eradicate the causes and consequences of the disease. This means more than just detecting and curing the leprosy bacillus. It means addressing the underlying cause as well as working to prevent disability and restore dignity and wholeness to people's lives.
Employees: 40

The Lesbian and Gay Foundation

Number 5, Richmond Street, Manchester M1 3HF
T: 0845 330 3030
F: 0161 235 8036
E: info@lgf.org.uk
www.lgf.org.uk
Chief Executive: Paul Martin
The Lesbian and Gay Foundation is a community-based charity, working to end homophobia and empower people across the north west of England and beyond. In 2013/14 we provided advice, information, support and services to over 40,000 people. The Lesbian and Gay Foundation provides direct services and resources for more LGB people than any other charity of its kind in the UK.
Employees: 49
Volunteers: 200
Regional offices: 1

The Lindsay Leg Club Foundation

PO Box 689, Ipswich IP1 9BN
T: 01473 749565
E: lynn.bullock@legclubfoundation.com
www.legclub.org
President: Ellie Lindsay
The aims of the Lindsay Leg Cub Foundation are twofold: To support the network of Leg Clubs operating around the UK, Europe, Australia and Tasmania, and to communicate the benefits of the Leg Club model to stakeholders. The model features the treatment of patients suffering from or at risk of leg ulceration within a social model of care. Stakeholders include patients, healthcare providers, clinicians, healthcare media
Income: £100,000 (2011-12)

The Lodge Trust

The Lodge, Main Street, Market Overton, Oakham, Rutland LE15 7PL
T: 01572 767234
F: 01572 767503
E: admin@lodgetrust.org.uk
www.lodgetrust.org.uk
CEO: David Whitmarsh
Provides individual support for adults with learning disabilities in Christian homes and working environments.
Employees: 75
Volunteers: 25
Regional offices: 1

The Log Cabin

259 Northfield Avenue, Ealing, London W5 4UA
T: 020 8840 3400
F: 020 8840 6780
E: vivien.dymock@logcabin.org.uk
www.logcabin.org.uk
Director: Sharon Flynn
The Log Cabin makes a positive difference to the lives of 250 children and young people with additional needs and disabilities or who are in need by providing exciting and stimulating play opportunities in a safe, caring, inclusive and fun environment. Founded in 1978, we are open 6 days a week. Services include an after school club, all-day holiday playschemes, Saturday sessions, sessions for

young families and projects for older young people.
Employees: 17
Volunteers: 10
Income: £604,370 (2014-15)

The Makaton Charity

Westmead House, Farnborough, Hampshire GU14 7LP
T: 01276 606760
Helpline: 01276 606777
F: 01276 36725
E: info@makaton.org
www.makaton.org
Chief Executive Officer: Lysa Schwartz
Makaton uses signs, symbols and speech to help people communicate. Today over 100,000 children and adults, use Makaton symbols and signs, either as their main method of communication or as a way to support speech. The Makaton Charity is responsible for developing and sharing Makaton so that everyone who needs to use Makaton can. We support families and professionals, provide training, resources, information and work with others to influence change for people with communication difficulties.
Employees: 14
Income: £1,096,057 (2013-14)

The Mare and Foal Sanctuary

Honeysuckle Farm, Haccombe with Coombe, Newton Abbot, Devon TQ12 4SA
T: 01626 355969
E: office@mareandfoal.org
www.mareandfoal.org
Rescues, provides care for and prevents cruelty and suffering among horses and ponies that are in need of attention because of sickness, maltreatment, ill usage or other causes and provides temporary or permanent homes for such horses and ponies.
Employees: 31
Volunteers: 25

The Marine Society and Sea Cadets

202 Lambeth Road, London SE1 7JW
T: 020 7654 7000
F: 020 7928 8914
E: info@ms-sc.org
www.ms-sc.org
Chief Executive: Martin Coles
To be the leading maritime charity for youth development and lifelong learning. Our vision for Sea Cadets is to give young people the best possible head start in life through nautical adventure and fun and for the Marine Society to be the first in learning and personal development for seafarers.
Employees: 180
Volunteers: 9000
Regional offices: 6

The Matthew Project

Nedeham House, 22 St Stephens Road, Norwich, Norfolk NR1 3QU
T: 01603 626123
F: 01603 630411
E: rachael.graham@matthewproject.org
www.matthewproject.org
Chief Executive Officer: Paul Martin
The Matthew Project works across Norfolk and Suffolk with young people and adults: Supporting people with drug and alcohol related issues; Providing innovative education about the risks of drugs and alcohol; Empowering people to make more informed choices.
Employees: 132
Volunteers: 29
Regional offices: 1
Income: £3,434,000 (2013-14)

The MedicAlert Foundation

MedicAlert House, 327-329 Witan Court, Upper Fourth Street, Milton Keynes MK9 1EH
Helpline: 01908 951045
F: 01908 951071
E: info@medicalert.org.uk
www.medicalert.org.uk
CEO: Mark Rawden
MedicAlert provides vital details in an emergency, because every moment matters. We support members with a wide range of medical conditions and allergies, which we help to describe on custom made medical ID jewellery. MedicAlert keeps secure, detailed medical records for our members. This information can be accessed in an emergency, 24/7 from anywhere in the world, using our emergency telephone number and we are able to converse in over 100 languages.
Employees: 42
Volunteers: 460

The Migraine Trust

London WC1B 4HP
T: 020 7631 6970
Helpline: 020 7631 6975
F: 020 7436 2886
E: info@migrainetrust.org
www.migrainetrust.org
Chief Executive: Wendy Thomas
The Migraine Trust is the health and medical research charity for migraine in the UK. We seek to educate health professionals, raise awareness of migraine as a serious public health issue and empower, inform and support those affected by migraine by providing them with evidence based information. The Migraine Trust funds and promotes research into migraine in order to better understand it, improve diagnosis and treatment and ultimately to find a cure.

The National Autistic Society

393 City Road, London EC1V 1NG
T: 020 7833 2299
Helpline: 0808 800 4104
F: 020 7833 9666
E: nas@nas.org.uk
www.autism.org.uk
Chief Executive: Mark Lever
The National Autistic Society (NAS) is the UK's leading charity for people affected by autism. The NAS provides information, advice, training and support for individuals and their families; information and training for health, education and other professionals working with people with autism and their families; residential, supported living, outreach and day services for adults; specialist schools and education, outreach services for children and young people; employment training and support and social programmes for adults with autism.
Employees: 2782
Volunteers: 1000
Regional offices: 12

The Nationwide Foundation

Nationwide House, Pipers Way, Swindon, Wiltshire SN38 2SN
Helpline: 01793 655113
E: enquiries@nationwidefoundation.org.uk
www.nationwidefoundation.org.uk
interim Chief Executive: Leigh Pearce
The Nationwide Foundation makes grants and social investments to charitable causes in the UK. It aims to create decent affordable homes for people in need. The three areas the Nationwide Foundation focuses on are: bringing empty properties into use as homes for people in need; improving the living conditions of vulnerable private rented sector tenants; and supporting alternative scalable housing models.
Employees: 3

The Neuro Foundation

Quayside House, 38 High Street, Kingston upon Thames, Surrey KT1 1HL
T: 020 8439 1234
F: 020 8439 1200
E: info@nfauk.org
www.nfauk.org
Charity Manager: Mike Mills
The Neuro Foundation works to raise awareness of neurofibromatosis; provide help, support and advice to those affected, their families and the professionals working with them; provide relevant, up-to-date information and facilitate research.
Employees: 6
Regional offices: 1

The NFSH Charitable Trust Ltd

21 York Road, Northampton, Northamptonshire NN1 5QG
T: 01604 603247
F: 01604 603534
E: office@thehealingtrust.org.uk
www.thehealingtrust.org.uk
Chair: Alan Knott
Employees: 5
Volunteers: 4000
Regional offices: 65

The Not Forgotten Association

4th Floor, 2 Grosvenor Gardens, London SW1W 0DH
T: 020 7730 2400
F: 020 7730 0020
E: admin@nfassociation.org
www.nfassociation.org
Chief Executive: Piers Storie-Pugh
A tri-service charity which provides entertainment and recreation for the serving wounded, injured or sick and for ex-service men and women with disabilities. This is achieved through a unique programme of concerts, outings, holidays, events and the provision of televisions and/or TV Licences. Our aim is to provide comradeship, challenge, hope and something to which ex-service men and women can look forward.
Employees: 7
Volunteers: 25
Income: £1,082,000 (2014-15)

The Orpheus Centre

E: jessicabolton@orpheus.org.uk

The Printing Charity

First Floor, Underwood House, 235 Three Bridges Road, Crawley, West Sussex RH10 1LS
T: 01293 542820
F: 01293 542826
E: info@theprintingcharity.org.uk
www.theprintingcharity.org.uk
Chief Executive : Stephen Gilbert
The Printing Charity helps individuals and their families, helps people of all ages, wants to help more people. Whatever a person's job is or was for three years in an organisation that produces a printed output – printing, publishing, operating presses, driving, cleaning, advertising, photography, graphic arts, making ink, recycling paper – the charity is there to help through regular financial assistance, one-off grants and its two sheltered homes for retired printers.

The Queen's Nursing Institute

1A Henrietta Place, London W1G 0LZ
T: 020 7549 1400
E: matthew.bradby@qni.org.uk
www.qni.org.uk
Chief Executive: Dr Crystal Oldman
The Queen's Nursing Institute is the charity dedicated to patient care in the home and in the community. We work with nurses and decision-makers to make sure that high-quality nursing is available for everyone, where and when they need it.
Employees: 14
Income: £750,000 (2013-14)

The Radio Amateurs' Emergency Network

Far Cockcroft, Rishworth, Sowerby Bridge, West Yorkshire HX6 4SB
T: 0303 040 1080
E: cosec@raynet-uk.net
www.raynet-uk.net
Chairman: C Clark
The Radio Amateurs' Emergency Network, known as RAYNET, provides communications to government, emergency and voluntary organisations in times of emergency or community support.
Volunteers: 1600
Regional offices: 14

The Respite Association

4 Lowgate Lane, Bicker, Boston, Lincolnshire PE20 3DG
T: 01775 820176
E: help@respiteassociation.org
www.respiteassociation.org
CEO: Preston Keeling
Aims to relieve the stress on unpaid carers by offering assistance with funding alternative care enabling a short respite break. As of 2013 we have also added a smaller service to the above now offering some Carers free holiday accommodation in Skegness or Blackpool for a break WITHOUT the person they normally care for to enable a proper break. Details of both schemes on our website as are application forms.
Employees: 2
Volunteers: 12
Regional offices: 1
Income: £107,000 (2013-14)

The Rivers Trust

Rain-Charm House, Kyl Cober Parc, Stoke Climsland, Callington, Cornwall PL17 8PH
T: 01579 372142
E: alan@theriverstrust.org
www.theriverstrust.org
Chief Executive: Arlin Rickard
The Rivers Trust is an umbrella environmental charity representing the rivers trust movement in England, Wales and Northern Ireland. It works by promoting practical and sustainable solutions at a river catchment scale to environmental issues across the UK and Europe.
Employees: 10
Income: £1,070,549 (2013-14)

The Royal National College for the Blind

Venns Lane, Hereford, Herefordshire HR1 1DT
T: 01432 265725
F: 01432 842979
E: peter.okeefe@rnc.ac.uk
www.rnc.ac.uk
CEO: Mrs Sheila Tallon
Vision: To enable people who are blind or partially sighted, together with those who may have additional disabilities, achieve their full potential and integration in society.
Employees: 174
Volunteers: 21

The Royal Star and Garter Homes

15 Castle Mews, Hampton, Middlesex TW12 2NP
T: 020 8481 7676
F: 020 8481 7677
E: general.enquiries@starandgarter.org
www.starandgarter.org
Chief Executive: Mike Barter

The Royal Star & Garter Homes is a charity founded in 1916 to care for the severely injured young men returning from the battlegrounds of the First World War. Today we provide specialist care to the whole military family in our friendly, modern and comfortable Homes in Solihull and Surbiton.

Regional offices: 1

The Scout Association

Gilwell Park, Chingford, London E4 7QW
T: 020 8433 7100
F: 020 8433 7108
E: info.centre@scout.org.uk
www.scouts.org.uk
Chief Executive: Matt Hyde

Scouting exists to actively engage and support young people in their personal development, empowering them to make a positive contribution to society.

Employees: 240
Volunteers: 89013

The Seeing Dogs Alliance

116 Potters Lane, Send, Woking, Surrey GU23 7AL
T: 01483 765556
F: 01483 750846
E: info@seeingdogs.org.uk
www.seeingdogs.org.uk

Furthers the mobility of blind persons through the use of trained training guide dogs, known as Seeing Dogs.

Employees: 1
Volunteers: 20

The Sick Children's Trust

80 Ashfield Street, London E1 2BJ
T: 020 7791 2266
F: 020 7709 8358
E: claudette@sickchildrenstrust.org
www.sickchildrenstrust.org
Chief Executive: Claudette Watson

Provides high-quality 'home from home' accommodation for families whose children are receiving hospital treatment for serious illnesses. We exist to support and promote the child's recovery and further to support the fabric and wellbeing of the family as a whole.

Employees: 26
Volunteers: 10
Regional offices: 7

The Sickle Cell Society

54 Station Road, London NW10 4UA
T: 020 8961 7795
F: 020 8961 8346
E: info@sicklecellsociety.org
www.sicklecellsociety.org

Our aim is to enable and assist individuals with a sickle cell disorder to realise their full economic and social potential. Objectives are to provide relief for persons with sickle cell disorders, the relief of poverty, provision of recreational activities and improvement of public information, assisting in research into the causes, treatment of the condition and dissemination of such information.

Employees: 6
Volunteers: 20
Regional offices: 2

The SMA Trust

1C Atherstone Barns, Atherstone on Stour, Stratford upon Avon, Warwickshire CV37 8NE
T: 01789 801155
E: mandy@smatrust.org
www.smatrust.org
Chief Executive: Joanna Mitchell

We are the only Uk charity solely dedicated to funding medical research into Spinal Muscular atrophy (SMA). Our objective is to be active and progressive in the search for a cure and treatments for SMA.

Employees: 4
Volunteers: 6-10
Regional offices: 1
Income: £350,000 (2013-14)

The Somerville Foundation

Saracens House, 25 St Margarets Green, Ipswich, Suffolk IP4 2BN
T: 01473 252007
Helpline: 0800 854759
F: 01473 281823
E: admin@thesf.org.uk
www.thesf.org.uk
National Director: John Richardson

Supports young people and adults born with a heart condition in the UK. Offers support, information and advice to help them stay in control, empowering patients to enable them to take control of their lives and manage their own heart condition. We listen to the patients and respond to their needs, providing them with the support they need and want.

Employees: 5
Volunteers: 10
Regional offices: 1
Income: £107,700 (2013-14)

The Tavistock Centre for Couple Relationships

The Tavistock Centre, 70 Warren Street, London W1T 5PB
T: 020 7380 1975
F: 020 7388 6162
E: tccr@tccr.org.uk
www.tccr.org.uk
CEO: Susanna Abse

TCCR is the leading provider of highly specialised and affordable couple counselling and psychotherapy. We offer a range of relationship, psychosexual and parenting support services throughout London. Our services include: relationship counselling; couple psychotherapy; wellbeing service brief counselling; parenting together; psychosexual therapy; divorce and separation unit.

Employees: 42

The Therapy Database

23 Holybourne Avenue, London SW15 4JJ
T: 020 8788 5370
E: admin@therapydatbase.info
www.therapydatabase.info
Trustee Director: Gerard Bonham-Carter

We enable doctors to fulfil their duty to gain their patients' fully informed consent to treatment. We enable patients to fully understand their treatment options. Patients benefit from the powerful placebo effect when they undergo treatments that they believe in. We achieve both goals by enabling patients to access comprehensive and balanced information on Western mainstream treatments and on the alternatives. This fulfils a DOH requirement for valid consent.

Employees: 1
Volunteers: 9

The Vince Hines Foundation

The Acton Centre, Acton Old Town Hall, High Street, London W3 6NE
Helpline: 0303 040 2690
F: 0870 974 8524
E: cmass@ubol.com
www.ubol.com

The Charity was formed in 1975, and operated continuously since. Its focus is on self-help and grassroots support. It provides general support to members of the community on matters dealing with community, education and training. This includes information, advice and guidance, with a focus on the harder to reach and those not in education, training and employment. Support to volunteers and the formation of new groups, including those involved in the performing arts.

The Wildlife Trusts

The Kiln, Waterside, Mather Road, Newark, Nottinghamshire NG24 1WT
T: 01636 677711
F: 01636 670001
E: enquiry@wildlifetrusts.org
www.wildlifetrusts.org
CEO: Stephanie Hilborne
Aims to protect wildlife for the future, and to educate the public in the understanding and appreciation of nature and the need for its conservation.
Employees: 2000
Volunteers: 43000
Regional offices: 47

Theatres Trust

22 Charing Cross Road, London WC2H 0QL
T: 020 7836 8591
E: info@theatrestrust.org.uk
www.theatrestrust.org.uk
Director: Mhora Samuel
The Theatres Trust is the national advisory public body for theatres, protecting theatres for everyone. We operate nationally in England, Wales, Scotland and Northern Ireland providing an authoritative and knowledgeable source of expert advice and information on theatres, promoting the value of theatre buildings and championing their future.
Employees: 9
Volunteers: 2

Thera Trust

The West House, Alpha Court, Swingbridge Road, Grantham, Lincolnshire NG31 7XT
T: 01476 562777
F: 01476 565677
E: sarah.frost@thera.co.uk
www.thera.co.uk
Thera Trust offers those with a learning disability support and is thereby helping them to get the most out of life.
Employees: 650

Think Global

CAN Mezzanine, 32-36 Loman Street, London SE1 0EH
T: 020 7922 7930
F: 020 7922 7929
E: info@think-global.org.uk
www.think-global.org.uk
Chief Executive: Tom Franklin
Think Global promotes education for a just and sustainable world. We have a network of 200 member organisations that share this commitment and we work with them to change UK education for the better. Our mission is to promote education that puts learning in a global context, fostering critical and creative thinking; self-awareness and open-mindedness towards difference; understanding of global issues and power relationships; and optimism and action for a better world.
Employees: 10

Third Age Trust (National Office U3A)

The Old Municipal Buildings, 19 East Street, Bromley, Kent BR1 1QE
T: 020 8466 6139
E: national.office@u3a.org.uk
www.u3a.org.uk
Chairman: Barbara Lewis
The Third Age Trust is the national representative body for the Universities of the Third Age in the UK. U3As are democratic self-funded self-managed later life learning organisations providing daytime education activities for people no longer in full-time employment.
Employees: 10

This Way Up Youth Project

The Bethany Centre, 155a Kineton Green Road, Olton, Solihull B92 7EG
Helpline: 0121 439 9181
E: ann@twup.org.uk
www.twup.org.uk
CEO: Pete English
Our team works in local Solihull schools supporting young people affected by loss through family breakdown or bereavement. We offer help to those trying to come to terms with this difficult life changing event through our Lost & Found Course. We also train Christian youth and community workers across the country to deliver our course so that more young people can be helped to turn their lives the right way up.
Employees: 6
Volunteers: 5
Regional offices: 1

Thomas Pocklington Trust

5 Castle Row, Horticultural Place, London W4 4JQ
T: 020 8995 0880
F: 020 8987 9965
E: info@pocklington-trust.org.uk
www.pocklington-trust.org.uk
Provides quality housing care and support services for adult people with sight loss. Sponsors social and public health research in the field of visual impairment.
Employees: 19
Volunteers: 116
Regional offices: 10

Thrive

The Geoffrey Udall Centre, Beech Hill Road, Beech Hill, Reading, Berkshire RG7 2AT
T: 0118 988 5688
F: 0118 988 5677
E: info@thrive.org.uk
www.thrive.org.uk / www.carryongardening.org.uk
Chief Executive: Kathryn Rossiter
Thrive is a national charity whose mission is to research, educate and promote the use and advantages of gardening for people with a disability. It is the only national charity of its kind working to bring change to disabled people through gardening. This is done by offering advice and information, supporting health and education professionals, carrying out research, and running local gardening projects in Battersea, Reading, Birmingham and Gateshead.
Employees: 50
Volunteers: 110
Regional offices: 4

Through the Roof

PO Box 353, Epsom, Surrey KT18 5WS
T: 01372 749955
E: info@throughtheroof.org
www.throughtheroof.org
CEO: Tim Wood
Mission: transforming lives through disabled people. Our work: providing life-changing opportunities and equipping churches, communities and individuals. Our vision: a world where people live interdependently, mutually giving and receiving as God intended.

Tibet Relief Fund

2 Baltic Place, 287 Kingsland Road, London N1 5AQ
T: 020 3119 0041
E: info@tibetrelieffund.co.uk
www.tibetrelieffund.co.uk
Chief Executive: Philippa Carrick
Tibet Relief Fund was set up to respond to the needs of Tibetan refugees, following the Chinese invasion of Tibet in 1950. Today, we provide vital support to Tibetans in exile in India and Nepal and inside Tibet, including emergency aid to newly arrived refugees and education, healthcare and income-

generating projects for the long-term. Tibet Relief Fund also runs a sponsorship programme to support children, university students, elderly people, monks and nuns.
Employees: 6
Volunteers: 3

Time Banking UK

The Exchange, Brick Row, Stroud, Gloucestershire GL5 1DF
T: 01453 750952
E: info@timebanks.co.uk
www.timebanking.org
Chief Executive: Sarah Bird
We provide information, practical support, inspiration and training to anyone wanting to use time banking as a tool to build community and encourage active citizenship.
Employees: 4
Regional offices: 1
Income: £116,636 (2013-14)

Time For God

Community House, 46-50 East Parade, Harrogate, North Yorkshire HG1 5RR
T: 01423 536248
F: 05602 053964
E: office@timeforgod.org
www.timeforgod.org
Director: Paul Webster
TfG is a faith based organisation which matches volunteers with long term volunteering placements. It is supported by all the major Christian denominations in the UK. With over 40 years experience, our projects are based in areas of social need. The majority of our work involves placing international volunteers in placements in the UK, however we also have opportunities for UK volunteers to travel abroad.
Employees: 6
Volunteers: 100
Regional offices: 1

TimeBank

One KX, 120 Cromer Street, London WC1H 8BS
T: 020 3111 0700
E: helpdesk@timebank.org.uk
www.timebank.org.uk
Chief Executive: Helen Walker
TimeBank is a national volunteering charity. We recruit and train volunteers to deliver mentoring projects to tackle complex social problems. We also work with businesses to engage their staff in volunteering. We believe that great volunteering can transform the lives of both volunteers and beneficiaries by building stronger, happier and more inclusive communities.

Tiny Tickers

76 Chiswick Lane, London, 4 Fennel Court, Methley W4 2LA
T: 07773 3034533
Helpline: 07793 093181
E: jon@tinytickers.org
www.tinytickers.org
Chief Executive: Jon Arnold
Around 1,000 newborn babies will leave UK hospitals this year with no one realising they are suffering from a major heart condition. Tiny Tickers is the only national charity with the sole aim of improving the early detection, diagnosis and care for babies with serious heart problems and their families.
Employees: 4
Volunteers: 4
Income: £107,000 (2014-15)

TOC H

PO Box 15824, Birmingham, West Midlands B13 3JU
T: 0121 443 3552
E: info@toch.org.uk
www.toch.org.uk
Chair of Trustees: Terry Drummond
Striving to eliminate social exclusion, Toc H is a charity committed to building a fairer society. Toc H provides alternative education, self-development and mentoring programmes for young people, in partnership with schools, local authorities and youth agencies. The charity also offers community centres. Toc H has a 20 Bed Outdoor pursuits center in Langdale in the Lake District.
Volunteers: 300
Income: £121,000 (2014-15)

Together for Short Lives

4th Floor, Bridge House, Bristol, Avon BS1 1QB
T: 0117 989 7820
Helpline: 0845 108 2201
E: info@togetherforshortlives.org.uk
www.togetherforshortlives.org.uk
Chief Executive: Barbara Gelb
We estimate that there are 23,500 children and young people across the UK unlikely to reach adulthood. Together for Short Lives is the only charity working across the UK representing all these children and their families as well as the organisations and people that support them. We want to help ensure that all of these children and their families get the best possible care and support whenever and wherever they need it.
Employees: 30
Volunteers: 2

Together Trust

Together Trust Centre, Schools Hill, Cheadle, Cheshire SK8 1JE
T: 0161 283 4848
F: 0161 283 4747
E: enquiries@togethertrust.org.uk
www.togethertrust.org.uk
Chief Executive: Mark Lee
We provide a range of social care, special education, community support and consultancy services in the North West of England and surrounding areas. In addition to local authority funded places, Together Trust services can be purchased by families, carers, and service users over the age of 18 or their brokers via a direct payment, individual budget, individual service fund or personal/private funds.
Employees: 770
Volunteers: 50
Income: £22,980,000 (2014-15)

Together Working for Wellbeing

12 Old Street, London EC1V 9BE
T: 020 7780 7300
F: 020 7780 7301
E: contactus@together-uk.org
www.together-uk.org
MACA is a leading national charity providing high-quality services in the community and hospitals and prisons for people with mental-health needs and their carers.
Employees: 800
Regional offices: 3

Tommy's

Nicholas House, 3 Laurence Pountney Hill, London EC4R 0BB
T: 020 7398 3400
Helpline: 0800 014 7800
F: 020 7398 3479
E: mailbox@tommys.org
www.tommys.org
Chief Executive: Jane Brewin
Tommy's is dedicated to funding research into the cause and prevention of miscarriage, stillbirth and premature birth, as well as promoting pregnancy health through a national information programme.
Employees: 22
Volunteers: 1

Tomorrow's People Trust

1st Floor, Minster House, York Road, Eastbourne, East Sussex BN21 4ST
T: 01323 418143
E: alevitt@tomorrows-people.co.uk
www.tomorrows-people.org.uk
Chief Executive: Debbie Scott

Tomorrow's People is a national employment charity helping long-term unemployed people out of welfare dependency and into jobs and self-sufficiency. Advisers work with individuals directly in their communities helping them to overcome their barriers to work, and develop the confidence, motivation and skills they need to move forward in their lives. Since 1984 we have helped more than 440,000 people on their journey back to work.
Employees: 135
Regional offices: 15

Tools for Self Reliance

Netley Marsh Workshops, Ringwood Road, Netley Marsh, Southampton, Hampshire SO40 7GY
T: 023 8086 9697
E: felicity@tfsr.org
www.tfsr.org
Chief Executive: Sarah Ingleby
Tools for Self Reliance works with partners in Ghana, Malawi, Sierra Leone, Tanzania, Uganda and Zambia. Our mission is to reduce poverty in Africa by helping people build sustainable livelihoods through the provision of tools and training. We aim to empower men and women to gain meaningful employment through our vocational, business and life skills training and the provision of tool kits for their trade.
Employees: 10
Volunteers: 800
Income: £749,402 (2012-13)

Torch Trust for the Blind

Torch House, Torch Way, Northampton Road, Market Harborough, Leicestershire LE16 9HL
T: 01858 438260
F: 01858 438275
E: volunteers@torchtrust.org
www.torchtrust.org
Chief Executive: Gordon Temple
The principal aim of the Torch Trust is to meet the spiritual needs of blind and partially sighted people through producing Christian literature in accessible media and promoting Christian fellowship across the UK and around the world.
Employees: 40
Volunteers: 81

Torridge Community Transport Association

E: john.conniss@torridge-cta.org.uk

Tourette's Action (Tourette Syndrome (UK) Association)

The Meads Business Centre, 19 Kingsmead, Farnborough, Hampshire GU14 7SR
T: 01252 362638
Helpline: 0300 777 8427
E: help@tourettes-action.org.uk
www.tourettes-action.org.uk
Chief Executive: Suzanne Dobson
Tourette's Action is the Uk's leading support and research charity for people with Tourette Syndrome (TS) and their families. We want people with TS to receive the practical support and social acceptance they need to help them live their lives to the full. We deal with all forms of TS including the most challenging.
Employees: 8
Volunteers: 8

Tourism for All UK

7A Pixel Mill, 44 Appleby Road, Kendal, Cumbria LA9 6ES
T: 0845 124 9971
E: info@tourismforall.org.uk
www.tourismforall.org.uk
Chief Executive: Ray Veal
Tourism for All UK is an independent charity supporting leisure and tourism opportunities for all, operating an information service to older and disabled people, and working with the industry and government to raise the standards of welcome to all guests.
Employees: 1
Volunteers: 2
Regional offices: 1

Tower Hamlets CVS

E: khadiru.mahdi@thcvs.org.uk

Town and Country Planning Association

17 Carlton House Terrace, London SW1Y 5AS
T: 020 7930 8903
F: 020 7930 3280
E: tcpa@tcpa.org.uk
www.tcpa.org.uk
Provides an informed and independent voice on national, regional and environmental planning policies and legislation, and to campaign for more local initiatives and decentralisation of decision-making.
Employees: 7
Volunteers: 40

Townswomen's Guilds

Tomlinson House, 329 Tyburn Road, Birmingham B24 8HJ
T: 0121 326 0400
F: 0121 326 1976
E: tghq@townswomen.org.uk
www.the-tg.com
National Chair: Pauline Meyers
Aims to advance the social awareness of all women, irrespective of race, creed or political affiliation.

Toynbee Hall

28 Commercial Street, London E1 6LS
T: 020 7247 6943
F: 020 7377 5964
E: alexandra.wilkinson@toynbeehall.org.uk
www.toynbeehall.org.uk/
Chief Executive: Graham Fisher
Toynbee Hall is a community organisation that pioneers ways to reduce poverty and disadvantage. Based in East London, we provide free legal, debt and general support service advice; as well as elderly and youth programmes. We have been a catalyst for social reform in the UK for 130 years, and continue to bring together communities, organisations and policy makers to create new ways to help those who find themselves in poverty today.
Employees: 75
Volunteers: 100+
Income: £6,000,000 (2013-14)

TPAS England

Suite 4B, Trafford Plaza, 73 Seymour Grove, Manchester, Greater Manchester M16 0LD
T: 0161 868 3500
F: 0161 877 6256
E: info@tpas.org.uk
www.tpas.org.uk
Acting Chief Executive: Jenny Osbourne
TPAS exists to promote resident and community empowerment. We are a membership organisation of housing associations, local authorities and tenants groups. We provide training, conferences, advice and consultancy services.
Employees: 15
Volunteers: 50

Tracheo-Oesophageal Fistula Support Group

St George's Centre, 91 Victoria Road, Netherfield, Nottingham NG4 2NN
T: 0115 961 3092
F: 0115 961 3097
E: info@tofs.org.uk
www.tofs.org.uk

Supports the families and carers of children born unable to swallow because of oesophageal atresia, tracheo-oesophageal atresia, tracheo-oesophageal fistula and associated conditions.
Employees: 3
Volunteers: 45

Trafford Carers Centre

E: kelly.hunter@traffordcarerscentre.org.uk

Training Opportunities

Hanover House, Wolverhampton, West Midlands WV2 3BY
T: 01902 877920
E: topps@totalise.co.uk
www.topps.org.uk
Provides information, support and training to women returning to the workplace and young people and women who wish to set up a small business or social enterprise.

Transaid

137 Euston Road, London NW1 2AA
T: 020 7387 8136
F: 020 7387 2669
E: info@transaid.org
www.transaid.org
Chief Executive: Gary Forster
Transaid is an international NGO working through the application of best practice in transport and logistics to alleviate poverty, facilitating access to basic services such as healthcare, and encouraging economic growth and development.
Employees: 6
Volunteers: 10
Regional offices: 3

Transform Africa

GQ Leroy House, 436 Essex Road, London N1 3QP
T: 020 7354 5455
F: 020 7354 5499
E: charles@transformafrica.org
www.transformafrica.org
Chief Executive Officer: Charles Kazibwe
Transform Africa aims to strengthen and empower African organisations and their communities to more effectively tackle poverty and its causes. We offer training services and work in partnership with local organisations to support local communities.
Employees: 3

Transparency International (UK)

London SE1 0EH
T: 020 7922 7906
F: 020 7785 6355
E: info@transparency.org.uk
www.transparency.org.uk
We are the UK national chapter of the global anti-corruption non-governmental organisation, Transparency International (TI). TI, which is co-ordinated by an international secretariat in Berlin, is a coalition of more than 90 autonomous national chapters who are committed to fighting corruption using transparency as a major tool. TI is dedicated to combating corruption at the national and international levels through constructive partnerships with governments, the private sector, civil society and international organisations.
Volunteers: 20
Regional offices: 1

Transplant Sport UK

Basepoint Business Centre, Winnall Valley Road, Winchester, Hampshire SO23 0LD
T: 0115 837 0878
E: office@transplantsport.org.uk
www.transplantsport.org.uk
CEO: Kevin Kibble
We are a registered charity whose main aim is to raise awareness of the need for organ donation in the UK and worldwide. Through organising sports and social events for transplant recipients Transplant Sport UK shows the benefits of organ donation and prove that you can lead a normal and active life again after transplantation.
Employees: 3
Volunteers: 100
Regional offices: 1

Transport Trust

202 Lambeth Road, London SE1 7JY
T: 020 7928 6464
E: hq@thetransporttrust.org.uk
www.transporttrust.com
Promotes and encourages the permanent preservation, for the benefit of the nation, of transport items of historical or technical interest and books, drawings, films, photographs and recordings of all forms of transport by rail, air and water.

Travelling Light Theatre Company

Barton Hill Settlement, 43 Ducie Road, Barton Hill, Bristol, Avon BS5 0AX
T: 0117 377 3166
E: info@travellinglighttheatre.org.uk
www.travellinglighttheatre.org.uk
General Manager: Dienka Hines
Travelling Light Theatre Company creates exciting and inspiring theatre for and with young people from its base in Barton Hill, Bristol. We are world-renowned for our innovative devised productions which tour locally and nationally to venues and schools. Our participation programme works with young people from babies to 25's, including projects for children with additional needs. We work closely with our local community showcasing our work with free performances, storytelling sessions, and schools theatre workshops.
Employees: 7
Volunteers: 7
Regional offices: 1

Tree Council

71 Newcomen Street, London SE1 1YT
T: 020 7407 9992
F: 020 7407 9908
E: info@treecouncil.org.uk
www.treecouncil.org.uk
Director General: Pauline Buchanan Black
Promotes for the public benefit, the improvement and development of the environment through the planting, care, nurture and cultivation of trees in town and country.
Employees: 5
Volunteers: 8000

Trees for Cities

Prince Consort Lodge, Kennington Park, Kennington Park Place, London SE11 4AS
T: 020 7587 1320
F: 020 7793 9042
E: david@treesforcities.org
www.treesforcities.org
Chief Executive: David Eliott
Planting trees and greening cities worldwide
Employees: 24
Volunteers: 50
Income: £1,140,000 (2014-15)

Treloar Trust

Holybourne, Alton, Hampshire GU34 4GL
T: 01420 547400
E: info@treloar.org.uk
www.treloar.org.uk
CEO: Tony Reid
The Treloar Trust exists to provide education, independence training and care for physically disabled young people from all over the UK. It aims to provide support and opportunities and to develop individual students' confidence and abilities in all aspects of their lives.

Trigeminal Neuralgia Association

PO Box 234, Oxted, Surrey RH8 8BE
Helpline: 01883 370214
E: admin@tna.org.uk
www.tna.org.uk
Chairman: Jillie Abbott
We exist to reach those affected by trigeminal neuralgia (TN) (sufferers, carers, healthcare professionals and the wider public); to provide evidence-based information, support and encouragement: with opportunities for people to express their feelings and concerns with those who understand their situation, and encouragement to actively self-manage their TN and to add to the body of knowledge about TN by increasing the level of knowledge about TN and TNA UK amongst healthcare professionals, policy-makers and others.
Employees: 1
Volunteers: 20
Regional offices: 1
Income: £69,929 (2013-14)

Tropical Health and Education Trust

5th Floor, 1 Wimpole Street, London W1G 0AE
T: 020 7290 3892
F: 020 7290 3890
E: sharon@thet.org
www.thet.org
Chief Executive: Andrew Purkis
THET is committed to improving access to and the quality of health services in developing countries. We believe that the most effective way of doing this is to work in partnership with those delivering and running healthcare, helping to strengthen and extend existing services.
Employees: 12
Volunteers: 4

Trust

E: fundraising@trust-london.com

Trust for the Study of Adolescence Ltd

23 New Road, Brighton, East Sussex BN1 1WZ
T: 01273 693311
F: 01273 679907
E: info@youngpeopleinfocus.org.uk
www.tsa.uk.com
Employees: 29

Trust for Urban Ecology

T: 020 8293 1904
E: information@tcv.org.uk
www.urbanecology.org.uk
Supports the conservation of the natural elements of the urban landscape; promotes the use of urban nature areas for the health, enjoyment and education of all sections of the community; and provides information, advice and expertise on the design, creation and management of urban greenspaces.

Tuberous Sclerosis Association

PO Box 8001, Derby DE1 0YA
T: 01332 290734 (also fax)
E: development-support@tuberous-sclerosis.org
www.tuberous-sclerosis.org
Chief Executive: Jayne Spink
Offers support to people with tuberous sclerosis complex and their families or carers. Promoting education, publicity and information to increase awareness and understanding. There are specialist advisers to advise on any problems relating to TSC.
Employees: 11 P/T

Turning Point

Standon House, 21 Mansell Street, London E1 8AA
T: 020 7481 7600
F: 020 7480 6288
E: info@turning-point.co.uk
www.turning-point.co.uk
Turning Point is the UK's leading social care organisation. We provide services for people with complex needs, including those affected by drug and alcohol misuse, mental health problems and those with a learning disability. We provide services in 200 locations and worked with around 130,000 people last year.
Employees: 1800
Regional offices: 200

Tutu Foundation UK

18 Victoria Park Square, London E2 9PF
T: 020 8980 9737
E: info@tutufoundationuk.org
www.tutufoundationul.org
The Tutu Foundation UK builds peace in fractured communities in the UK using Ubuntu, a model inspired by Archbishop Desmond Tutu's peace and reconciliation work all over the world. To successfully tackle the anti-social behaviour and violence in our communities, underlying attitudes and behaviours must first be addressed in order to build a lasting peace.
Employees: 2
Volunteers: 70
Regional offices: 1

Twin Ltd

3rd Floor, 1 Curtain Road, London EC2A 3LT
T: 020 7375 1221
E: info@twin.org.uk
www.twin.org.uk
Uses trade positively to redress the imbalance between north and south, to build better livelihoods for the poorest and weakest in the trading chain and to provoke development and longer term shifts in the political and economic environment.

Twins and Multiple Births Association

MANOR HOUSE, CHURCH HILL, ALDERSHOT, Hampshire GU12 4JU
T: 01252 332344
Helpline: 0800 138 0509
E: enquiries@tamba.org.uk
www.tamba.org.uk
CEO: Keith Reed
Tamba exists to enable the families of twins, triplets and more to meet the challenge of their unique experience.
Employees: 12
Volunteers: 100
Regional offices: 2

UCCF

5 Blue Boar Street, Oxford OX1 4EE
T: 01865 253678
F: 0116 255 5672
E: helpdesk@uccf.org.uk
www.uccf.org.uk
IT Manager: David Holland
Employees: 106
Volunteers: 50

UK Acquired Brain Injury Forum

c/o Royal Hospital for Neuro Disability, West Hill, Putney, London SW15 3SW
T: 020 8780 4500
E: info@rhn.org.uk
www.ukabif.org.uk
The UK Acquired Brain Injury Forum (UKABIF) is a not-for-profit coalition of organisations and individuals that seeks to

promote understanding of all aspects of acquired brain injury and to provide information and expert input to policy makers, service providers and the general public to promote the interests of brain injured people and their families.
Employees: 1

UK Community Foundations

12 Angel Gate, 320-326 City Road, London EC1V 2PT
T: 020 7713 9326
F: 020 7713 9327
E: lkarban@ukcommunityfoundations.org
www.ukcommunityfoundations.org
Chief Executive: Stephen Hammersley
UKCF is the UK wide organisation supporting and promoting UK community foundations. Community foundations are charities dedicated to strengthening local communities. They manage funds donated by individuals and organisations, building endowment and acting as the vital link between donors and local needs.
Employees: 10
Income: £11,400,000 (2013-14)

UK Council for International Student Affairs

London N1 0NX
T: 020 7288 4330
Helpline: 020 7107 9922
F: 020 7288 4360
E: membership@ukcisa.org.uk
www.ukcisa.org.uk
Chief Executive: Dominic Scott
The UK Council for International Student Affairs (UKCISA) is the UK's national advisory body serving the interests of international students and those who work with them. It aims to encourage best practice, professional development and the highest quality of institutional support for international students throughout the education sector, increase support for international education and raise awareness of its values and benefits, and promote opportunities for greater student mobility.
Employees: 17

UK Council for Psychotherapy

2nd Floor, Edward House, 2 Wakley Street EC1V 7LT
T: 020 7014 9955
F: 020 7014 9977
E: info@ukcp.org.uk
www.psychotherapy.org.uk
Employees: 20

UK Council on Deafness

Westwood Park, London Road, Little Horkesley, Colchester C06 4BS
T: 01206 274075
F: 01206 274077
E: c.long@deafcouncil.org.uk
www.deafcouncil.org.uk
The national infrastructure organisation for voluntary sector organisations working with deaf people. Our mission is to create an environment in which voluntary sector organisations working with deaf people can flourish. We aim to support members in their work with deaf people and to encourage cooperation between members in promoting and representing the diverse interests of deaf people.
Employees: 3

UK Health Forum

Fleetbank House, 2-6 Salisbury Square, London EC4Y 8JX
T: 020 7832 6920
F: 020 7832 6921
E: dan.french@ukhealthforum.org.uk
www.ukhealthforum.org.uk
Chief Executive: Paul Lincoln
Aims to preserve and protect the health of the public and to advance public education about all matters concerning avoidable chronic disease and its prevention.
Employees: 20

UK Neighbourhood Watch Trust

1st Floor, 52 London Road, Oadby, Leicester LE2 5DH
T: 0116 271 0052
E: uknwt@neighbourhoodwatch.net
www.neighbourhoodwatch.net
Chair: Roy Rudham
The UKNWT supports and promotes the Neighbourhood Watch movement by providing an effective and informative two-way communications channel through its website. The Trust promotes best practice throughout the Neighbourhood Watch movement; encourages the exchange of views and ideas through a range of online forums; broadens the appeal of Neighbourhood Watch through an editorial approach on the website that reflects the concerns and interests of all sections of society, ethnic groupings and age ranges.

UK Overseas Territories Conservation Forum

Icknield Court, Back Street, Wendover, Buckinghamshire HP22 6EB
T: 01733 569325
F: 020 8020 7217
E: cwensink@ukotcf.org
www.ukotcf.org
Honorary Executive Director : Dr Mike Pienkowski
UKOTCF exists to protect and promote the diverse and increasingly threatened plant and animal species and natural habitats of UK's Overseas Territories (UKOTs) and Crown Dependencies. It aims to do this by providing assistance in the form of expertise, information and liaison between non-governmental organisations and governments, both in the UK and in the Territories themselves. UKOTCF has over 25 years experience working with partners in the UKOTs on various projects.
Volunteers: 14
Income: £264,803 (2012-13)

UK Public Health Association

2nd Floor, 28 Portland Place, London W1B 1DE
T: 0870 010 1932
F: 020 7061 3393
E: info@ukpha.org.uk
www.ukpha.org.uk
Promotes and defends public health in the UK; brings together local and national statutory and non-governmental organisations, professional associations, trade unions, voluntary and community groups and individuals; promotes the development of healthy public policy at all levels of government, including the European Union, in order to ensure that the health needs of the UK become a permanent feature of national policy and spending decisions.
Employees: 7
Volunteers: 20

UK Thalassaemia Society

19 The Broadway, Southgate Circus, London N14 6PH
T: 020 8882 0011
F: 020 8882 8618
E: office@ukts.org
www.ukts.org
Campaigns on behalf of people suffering from thalassaemia; promotes and coordinates research; educates people on the problems of thalassaemia; offers counselling to sufferers and carriers.
Employees: 2

UK Youth

Avon Tyrrell, Bransgore,
Hampshire BH23 8EE
T: 01425 672347
F: 01425 673883
E: info@ukyouth.org
www.ukyouth.org
Employees: 59
Volunteers: 40000

Unique - Rare Chromosome Disorder Support Group

G1, The Stables, Station Rd West, Oxted,
Surrey RH8 9EE
T: 01883 723306
Helpline: 01883 723356
E: craig@rarechromo.org
www.rarechromo.org
Chief Executive Officer: Beverly Searle

Unique provides specialist information and support to anyone born, often sick & disabled, with a rare chromosome disorder and their families. Our aim is to alleviate feelings of isolation by linking families whose children have similar clinical and/or practical problems caused by rare chromosome disorders. Unique provides family support services to more than 4,000 UK families.

Employees: 8
Volunteers: 200
Income: £300,000 (2014-15)

United Kingdom Homecare Association

Group House, 2nd Floor,
52 Sutton Court Road, Sutton,
Surrey SM1 4SL
T: 020 8288 1551
F: 020 8288 1550
E: enquiries@ukhca.co.uk
www.ukhca.co.uk

The professional association of home care providers from the independent, voluntary, not-for-profit and statutory sectors. UKHCA helps organisations that provide social care, which may include nursing services, to people in their own homes, promoting high standards of care and providing representation with national and regional policy makers and regulators. The association represents over 1,500 members across the UK.

Employees: 10
Volunteers: 14

United Kingdom Sports Association for People with Learning Disability

2E Leroy House, 436 Essex Road,
London N1 3QP
T: 020 7490 3057
F: 020 7251 8861
E: info@uksportsassociation.org
www.uksportsassociation.org
Chief Executive: Tracey McCillen

The UK Sports Association (UKSA) promotes, facilitates and supports talented sports people with learning disability in the UK to train, compete and excel in national and international sport. UKSA leads eligibility and classification, is recognised by UK Sport, is a member of the British Paralympic Association and is the official GB member of the International Sports Federation for Para Athletes with Intellectual Disability (INAS), a member of the International Paralympic Committee.

Employees: 3
Volunteers: 30

United Kingdom's Disabled People's Council

Litchurch Plaza, Litchurch Lane,
Derby DE24 8AA
T: 01332 295551
F: 01332 295580
E: info@ukdpc.net
www.bcodp.org.uk

Aims to relieve the disability of people with physical, mental or sensory impairments and to further their independence and full participation in the community.

Employees: 10
Volunteers: 50
Regional offices: 1

United Nations Association

3 Whitehall Court, London SW1A 2EL
T: 020 7930 2931
F: 020 7930 5893
E: richardson@una.org.uk
www.una-uk.org

Campaigns for fuller implementation of the UN Charter in British policy decisions. It aims to educate government and as wide a cross-section of the British public as possible in understanding the principles and purposes of the UN. Particular interests include: UN and conflict; international security and disarmament; human rights; refugee issues; economic and social, sustainable development; environmental protection, culture of peace.

Employees: 20
Regional offices: 130

United Response

Vantage House, 1 Weir Road,
Wimbledon Park, London SW19 8UX
T: 020 8246 5200
F: 020 8780 9538
E: su.sayer@unitedresponse.org.uk
www.unitedresponse.org.uk
Chief Executive: Su Sayer

United Response is a national charity that works with people with learning disabilities, mental health needs and physical disabilities in over 200 localities across England and Wales. Our mission is to enable people to take control of their lives and our vision is of a society where people with disabilities or mental health needs are equal participants and have access to the same rights and opportunities as everyone else.

Employees: 2900
Volunteers: 300
Regional offices: 4

United Trusts

PO Box 14, 8 Nelson Road, Edge Hill,
Liverpool L69 7AA
T: 0151 709 8252
F: 0151 708 5621
E: information@unitedtrusts.org.uk
www.unitedtrusts.org.uk

Fundraising to support the relief of poverty, the advancement of education and such other purposes beneficial to the community. United Trust endorses the Workplace Charity Fund.

Employees: 4
Volunteers: 20

Universities Federation for Animal Welfare

The Old School, Brewhouse Hill,
Wheathampstead, Hertfordshire AL4 8AN
T: 01582 831818
F: 01582 831414
E: ufaw@ufaw.org.uk
www.ufaw.org.uk

Promotes humane behaviour towards animals by enlisting the energies of members of the universities and professional people. Obtains and disseminates accurate information relating to the welfare of animals.

Employees: 8

Universities UK

Woburn House, 20 Tavistock Square,
London WC1H 9HQ
T: 020 7419 4111
Helpline: 020 7419 5523
F: 020 7388 8649
E: info@universitiesuk.ac.uk
www.universitiesuk.ac.uk
Chief Executive: Nicola Dandridge

Universities UK is the major representative body and membership organisation for the higher education sector. Its members are the executive heads of UK universities. Within it are the England and Northern Ireland Council, Universities Scotland and Higher Education Wales. Our mission is to be the essential voice and best support for a vibrant, successful and diverse university sector, to influence and create policy for HE, and to provide an environment where the sector can flourish.
Employees: 81
Regional offices: 2

University Association for Contemporary European Studies

School of Public Policy, University College London, London WC1H 9QU
T: 020 7679 4975
F: 020 7679 4973
E: admin@uaces.org
www.uaces.org
The academic association for contemporary European Studies.
Employees: 3

UNLOCK - for people with convictions

Maidstone Community Support Centre, 39-48 Marsham Street, Maidstone, Kent ME14 1HH
T: 01622 230705
Helpline: 01634 247350
E: admin@unlock.org.uk
www.unlock.org.uk
Director (Operations): Julie Harmsworth
Unlock is an independent award-winning charity which provides information, advice and advocacy for people with convictions. Our staff and volunteers combine professional training with personal experience to help others overcome the long-term problems that having a conviction can bring. Our knowledge and insight helps us to work with government, employers and others, to change policies and practices to create a fairer and more inclusive society so that people with convictions can move on in their lives.
Employees: 4
Volunteers: 6

UnLtd - the Foundation for Social Entrepreneurs

123 Whitecross Street, Islington, London EC1Y 8JJ
T: 020 7566 1100
E: pa@unltd.org.uk
www.unltd.org.uk
Chief Executive: Cliff Prior
UnLtd is a charity that supports social entrepreneurs - people with vision, drive, commitment and passion who want to change the world for the better. We do this by providing a complete package of funding and support, to help these individuals make their ideas a reality.
Employees: 76
Volunteers: 3
Regional offices: 3
Income: £12,854,579 (2014-15)

Upkeep

2 The Courtyard, 48 New North Road, Exeter BX4 4EP
T: 020 7256 7646
E: info@upkeep.org.uk
www.upkeep.org.uk
Director: Sarah Bentley
Upkeep promotes good practice in building care. We deliver short courses on building repair, maintenance and improvement. We believe that good maintenance of existing buildings is key to a sustainable future. Upkeep also runs the Charities Facilities Management Group, the network for people who look after buildings and facilities issues in the voluntary sector. The CFM Group was set up in 2000 and has 250 member-charities nationwide.
Employees: 1
Volunteers: 2
Regional offices: 1

Urban Forum

33 Corsham Street, London N1 6DR
T: 020 7253 4816
F: 020 7253 4817
E: info@urbanforum.org.uk
www.urbanforum.org.uk
Urban Forum is an umbrella body for community and voluntary groups with interests in urban and regional policy, especially regeneration.
Employees: 5
Volunteers: 15

Urostomy Association

4 Demontfort Way, Uttoxeter, Staffordshire ST14 8XY
T: 01889 563191
E: secretary.ua@classmail.co.uk
www.urostomyassociation.org.uk
National Secretary: Hazel Pixley
Charity set up in 1971 to provide support for people having a urinary diversion (e.g. urostomy, mitrofanoff, neo-bladder, bladder reconstruction). 16 local branches; magazine published three times a year; leaflets and other publications available.
Employees: 2
Volunteers: 100
Income: £125,000 (2013-14)

Us in a Bus

Queens House, Philanthropic Road, Redhill RH1 4DZ
T: 01737 764774
E: info@usinabus.org.uk
www.usinabus.org.uk
Chief Executive: Janet Gurney
Us in a Bus delivers services to people with profound learning disabilities and/or complex needs, in their own home and in the community, across Surrey and the surrounding areas. We also provide training in Intensive Interaction for families, carers, support staff and other professionals nationwide. Us in a Bus enables people with profound learning disabilities and/or complex needs to connect with others through interaction, play and self expression.
Employees: 14
Volunteers: 2
Regional offices: 1

Variety

E: stuart.rogers@variety.org.uk

Vegetarian Society UK Ltd

Parkdale, Dunham Road, Altrincham,
Cheshire WA14 4QG
T: 0161 925 2000
F: 0161 926 9182
E: info@vegsoc.org
www.vegsoc.org
Chief Executive: Lynne Elliot
The Vegetarian Society influences, inspires and supports people to embrace and maintain a vegetarian lifestyle. We organise National Vegetarian Week each year and we run the Cordon Vert Vegetarian Cookery School in Altrincham, Cheshire.
Employees: 28
Volunteers: 150
Regional offices: 1
Income: £1,306,000 (2013-14)

Victa Children Ltd

Silverstone House, 46 Newport Road,
Woolstone, Milton Keynes,
Buckinghamshire MK15 0AA
T: 01908 240831
F: 01908 668868
E: admin@victa.org.uk
www.victa.org.uk
Chief Executive: Tracie Tappenden
VICTA supports blind and partially sighted children, young people and their families by providing: Grants; Annual family weekend; Family days; International Youth trips for 18+; Youth weekends for 18+; Youth weekends for 14 – 17; Multi European camps for 16+; Family Support. For more information please visit our website www.victa.org.uk
Employees: 6
Volunteers: 40
Regional offices: 1

Victim Support

Hallam House, 56-60 Hallam Street,
London W1W 6JL
T: 020 7268 0200
E: contact@victimsupport.org.uk
www.victimsupport.org.uk
Chief Executive: Mark Castle
Victim Support is the independent national charity for people affected by crime. Staff and volunteers offer free and confidential information and support for victims of any crime, whether or not it has been reported and regardless of when it happened. The organisation operates via a network of affiliated local charities, the Witness Service and the Victim Supportline.
Employees: 1000
Volunteers: 3000
Regional offices: 5

Viewpoint

E: leslie@hertsviewpoint.co.uk

Village Aid

Suite 1, Fearnehough House,
Riverside Business Park, Buxton Road,
Bakewell, Derbyshire DE45 1GJ
T: 01629 814434
F: 01629 812272
E: keith@villageaid.org
www.villageaid.org
We work with the most marginalised rural communities in West Africa, establishing partnerships with African communities and local organisations to enhance sustainable development and find solutions using African resources and experience. In the UK we aim to raise awareness of development issues and present positive images of African people and their abilities.
Employees: 3
Volunteers: 3

Vine Day Centre, The

PO BOX 442, 33 Station Road, Aldershot,
Aldershot, Hampshire GU11 9FQ
T: 01252 400196
E: mags.mercer@thevinealdershot.org.uk
www.vinedaycentre.org.uk
Chief Executive Officer: Mags Mercer
The Vine Day Centre has been established in the community of Aldershot, North East Hampshire since 1987, supporting vulnerable and homeless adults since inception and registered as a charity in February 2003. Our primary aim is to reduce social isolation, to facilitate and enable change, and to improve the quality of life for homeless and vulnerable men and women aged 25 years and over.
Employees: 7
Volunteers: 25
Regional offices: 1
Income: £157,000 (2014-15)

VISION 2020 UK

PO Box 70172, London WC1A 9HH
T: 07837 692026
E: m.broom@vision2020uk.org.uk
www.vision2020uk.org.uk
CEO: Mercy Jeyasingham
VISION 2020 UK (Charity No.1146746) is the umbrella organisation which facilitates greater collaboration and co-operation between organisations within the UK, which focus on vision impairment and operate on a national, regional or international basis.
Employees: 4
Income: £110,000 (2013-14)

Vision Aid Overseas

12 The Bell Centre, Newton Road,
Manor Royal, Crawley,
West Sussex RH10 2FZ
T: 01293 535016
F: 01293 535026
E: info@visionaidoverseas.org
www.vao.org.uk
Director: Dr Natalie Briggs
Vision Aid Overseas is a charity dedicated to people in the developing world whose lives are blighted by poor eyesight.
Employees: 7
Volunteers: 1200

Vision Homes Association

Trigate, 210-222 Hagley Road West,
Oldbury B68 0NP
T: 0121 434 4644
F: 0121 434 5655
E: caroline@visionhomes.org
www.visionhomes.org.uk
Chief Executive: Ewa Stefanowska
Pursues ways of improving facilities and services for adults who have vision impairments and/or additional disabilities. Promotes the provisions of residential accommodation and home support throughout the UK.
Employees: 110
Volunteers: 2
Regional offices: 1

Visionary - linking local sight loss charities

5/14 Western Harbour View, Leith,
Edinburgh, Leith, Edinburgh EH6 6PF
T: 020 8417 0942
E: visionary@visionary.org.uk
www.visionary.org.uk
Chief Executive: Angela Tinker
Visionary supports local independent charities that support blind and partially sighted people across the UK. Our core aims:
To Connect: bringing the network of local societies together and learning from best practices
To Influence: consulting members on issues that affect them, representing them on the national stage
To Develop: offering direct support to members, providing advice, learning opportunities, guidance and funding to facilitate the development of new local societies and services from existing local societies
Employees: 2
Volunteers: 12

Vista

Viata House, 1a Salisbury Road, Leicester, Leicestershire LE1 7QR
T: 0116 249 0909
Helpline: 0116 249 8839
E: info@vistablind.org.uk
www.vistablind.org.uk
Chief Executive: Paul Bott
Vista is the leading provider of services to blind and partially sighted people in Leicester, Leicestershire and Rutland. Vista run 4 residential care homes, providing care to older people and to adults with learning disability and sight loss. They also run community services including social groups, rehabilitation and deaf/blind services
Employees: 250
Volunteers: 100
Regional offices: 2
Income: £5,700,000 (2012-13)

Vita Nova

11 Roumelia Lane, Boscombe, Dorset BH5 1EU
T: 01202 309999
E: office@vitanova.co.uk
www.vitanova.co.uk
Chief Executive: Simon Bull
Vita Nova is an arts organisation that supports those who have been through drugs/alcohol addiction and those with mental health issues. Vita Nova also provides awareness education to primary and secondary schools, colleges and universities.
Employees: 4
Volunteers: 10
Income: £100,000 (2013-14)

Vitalise

12 City Forum, 250 City Road, London EC1V 8AF
T: 0845 345 1972
F: 0845 345 1978
E: info@vitalise.org.uk
www.vitalise.org.uk
Aims to enable visually impaired and disabled people to exercise choice, and to provide vital breaks for carers and inspirational opportunities for volunteers.
Employees: 290
Volunteers: 6000

Vitiligo Society

24 Greencoat Place, London SW1P 1RD
T: 020 7840 0855
Helpline: 0800 018 2631
E: general@vitiligosociety.org.uk
www.vitiligosociety.org.uk
Promotes a positive approach to living with vitiligo. Offers support and understanding to people with vitiligo and their families and advice on how to cope with the condition. Funds research to establish the causes of vitiligo and finding safe and effective treatments.
Employees: 1
Volunteers: 4

Voice Care Network UK

25 The Square, Kenilworth, Warwickshire CV8 1EF
T: 01926 864000 (also fax)
E: info@voicecare.org.uk
www.voicecare.org.uk
Chair: Jeremy Stoke
VCN provides information and practical help for people to keep their voices healthy, to avoid voice loss, to communicate skillfully and with confidence through its professional members who are: teachers and coaches of speaking voice; speech and language therapists experienced in clinical treatment for voice disorders.
Employees: 1
Volunteers: 230

Voluntary Action Calderdale

Resource Centre, Hall Street, Halifax, West Yorkshire HX1 5AY
T: 01422 348777
E: info@cvac.org.uk
www.cvac.org.uk
Chief Officer: Soo Nevison
We are established as a local infrastructure organisation supporting the VCS in Calderdale. We also run small projects that support the local communities in our Borough with an aim to improve life chances for anyone living in Calderdale.
Employees: 12
Volunteers: 45
Income: £750,000 (2012-13)

Voluntary Action History Society

WC1H 0AL
E: georginabrewis@yahoo.co.uk
www.vahs.org.uk
Chair: Dr Peter Grant
The Voluntary Action History Society (VAHS) aims to advance the historical understanding and analysis of voluntary action. VAHS is a network of postgraduate students, academics and voluntary sector practitioners. Activities include a seminar series at the Institute of Historical Research; conferences and workshops; New Researchers group for postgraduates and early-career scholars; and an edited blog.
Volunteers: 15

Voluntary Action Islington

200a Pentonville Road, London N1 9JP
T: 020 7832 5800
F: 020 7832 5835
E: mike.sherriff@vai.org.uk
www.vai.org.uk
Chief Executive: Mike Sherriff
Voluntary Action Islington provides services to community groups in Islington, including the accredited Volunteer Centre for the borough. We have a resource centre with training and meeting rooms available for hire
Employees: 6
Volunteers: 15
Income: £539,000 (2013-14)

Voluntary Action South West Surrey

39 Castle Street, Guildford GU1 3UQ
T: 01483 504626
E: c.dunnett@vasws.org.uk
www.voluntaryactionsws.org.uk
Chief Officer: Carol Dunnett
We provide information, advice and support for voluntary and community organisations in the Boroughs of Guildford and Waverley. We run a volunteer brokerage service both online and through our Volunteer Centres. We have a supported volunteer programme and a project that supports older people to volunteer.
Employees: 10
Volunteers: 20
Regional offices: 1
Income: £150,000 (2012-13)

Voluntary Arts Network

Network Office, 121 Cathedral Road, Cardiff CF11 9PH
T: 029 2039 5395
E: info@voluntaryarts.org
www.voluntaryarts.org
Chief Executive: Robin Simpson
Voluntary Arts Network promotes participation in the arts and crafts across the UK and Republic of Ireland. We recognise that they are a key part of our culture and are vital to our health, and to our social and economic development. Over half the UK adult population already takes part in arts and crafts activity for self-improvement, social networking and leisure. Activities include folk, dance, drama, literature, music, visual arts, crafts, applied arts and festivals.
Employees: 18
Regional offices: 5

Voluntary Norfolk

St Clements House, 2-16 Colegate, Norwich, Norfolk NR3 1BQ
T: 01603 614474
F: 01603 764109
E: admin@voluntarynorfolk.org.uk
www.voluntarynorfolk.org.uk/
CEO: Alan Hopley
Voluntary Norfolk supports volunteers and voluntary organisations, recruiting, training and deploying many hundreds of volunteers each year. We deliver projects including a volunteering website, befriending, employability services and neighbourhood development programmes. Via our social enterprise, Charity BackRoom, we offer a wide range of individually-tailored back-office services including HR and employment law, DBS checks and payroll. We provide support for charities to raise funds through grant applications and appeals via our subsidiary, Blue Tree Fundraising.
Employees: 50
Volunteers: 500
Regional offices: 3
Income: £1,500,000 (2013-14)

Voluntary Sector Training

45 Stortford Road, Great Dunmow, Essex CM6 1DQ
T: 01371 876747
E: maddy@voluntarysectortraining.org.uk
www.voluntarysectortraining.org.uk
Director: Linda Riley
We are an independent charity providing affordable, relevant and accessible training for charities and community groups in Essex & beyond. We want to support the development of a strong, effective and diverse voluntary and community sector. We run a programme of regular one day courses all over Essex for staff, volunteers, trustees and committee members. Or we can come up with a course tailored to your charity's needs and deliver it in house.
Employees: 5
Volunteers: 3
Regional offices: 1
Income: £172,000 (2014-15)

Voluntary Services Lewisham

300 Stanstead Road, London SE23 1DE
T: 020 8291 1747
E: evelyn@vslonline.org.uk
www.vslonline.org.uk
CEO: Evelyn Brady
To provide direct voluntary services to Lewisham Residents including: befriending, gardening transport projects plus drop-ins and wellbeing workshops for people experiencing mental health difficulties. To recruit, train, place and support volunteers in roles that develop skills and build confidence and enhance the lives of our service users. To liaise with other groups and agencies with the aim to build partnerships that enable the delivery of quality effective services.
Employees: 9
Volunteers: 200
Income: £275,000 (2014-15)

Volunteer Centre Greenwich

E: annie@volunteersgreenwich.co.uk

Volunteers for Rural India

12 Eastleigh Avenue, Harrow, Middlesex HA2 0UF
T: 020 8864 4740
Helpline: 07786 570377
E: enquiries@vri-online.org.uk
www.vri-online.org.uk
Chair: Shobhana Snow
VRI aims to relieve poverty in India, by undertaking voluntary work, raising funds to assist village development schemes and educating the public in the UK about Indian culture and traditions and other aspects of Indian life.
Volunteers: 16
Regional offices: 1
Income: £10,000 (2013-14)

Voscur

Royal Oak House, Royal Oak Avenue, Bristol BS1 4GB
T: 0117 909 9949
E: info@voscur.org
www.voscur.org
Chief Executive: Wendy Stephenson
Voscur supports, develops and represents Bristol's voluntary and community sector. It strengthens and advocates for local organisations so they can improve the quality of life of individuals and communities. As the city's volunteering hub, it also supports individuals to create positive social change, particularly those often excluded from such opportunities. It facilitates partnerships within and between the public, private and voluntary sectors to create social impact, add value to public spending and increase social inclusion.
Volunteers: 46
Income: £738,988 (2013-14)

VSO

317 Putney Bridge Road, London SW15 2PN
T: 020 8780 7200
F: 020 8780 7300
E: david.son@vso.org.uk
www.vso.org.uk
VSO is an international development agency working through international volunteering. VSO's purpose is to build reciprocal local and global partnerships that bring people together to share skills, creativity and learning to build a fairer world.
Employees: 700
Volunteers: 1450
Regional offices: 5

Wainwright Trust

Plowmans, Crazies Hill, Reading, Berkshire RG10 8LU
T: 0118 940 2632
E: secretary@wainwrighttrust.org.uk
www.wainwrighttrust.org.uk
Chair: Susanne Lawrence
The Trust seeks to promote diversity and improve equality of opportunity and fairness of treatment in the workplace, and to combat all forms of discrimination in the workplace, whether arising from gender, race, colour, nationality, ethnic or national origins, religion or belief, sexual orientation, disability of family or other status. It does this by spreading knowledge of good practice.

Wales Council for Voluntary Action

Baltic House, Mount Stuart Square, Cardiff Bay, Cardiff CF10 5FH
T: 0800 288 8329
F: 029 2043 1701
E: help@wcva.org.uk
www.wcva.org.uk
Chief Executive: Ruth Marks
Supports working relationships between the voluntary sector, and government and public bodies; supports and promotes the work of voluntary and community groups at national and local level; supports and promotes volunteering and the interest of volunteers; promotes community cohesion and inclusion and build social capital; develops and supports new initiatives; enhances resources available

to the voluntary sector; and improves its performance and effectiveness.
Employees: 99
Regional offices: 3
Income: £20,855,366 (2013-14)

Walsall Society for the Blind

Hawley House, 11 Hatherton Road, Walsall, West Midlands WS1 1XS
T: 01922 627683
E: areed@wsftb.co.uk
www.walsallblind.org
C.E.O: Amanda Reed
Our mission is to provide information, support and friendship to those affected by sight loss within the Borough of Walsall. Our Services include: A Community officer; A Community Engagement Officer; Talking Newspaper and Magazine Service; A Social Activity Centre; An Eye Clinic Liaison Officer; Transcription Service.
Employees: 13
Volunteers: 40
Regional offices: 1
Income: £182,953 (2014-15)

Walsingham Support

Walsingham House, 1331-1337 High Road, Whetstone, London N20 9HR
T: 020 8343 5600
F: 020 8446 9156
E: enquiries@walsingham.com
www.walsingham.com
Chief Executive: Paul Snell
Walsingham Support is a leading national charity providing highly personalised services for over 420 people with learning disabilities, autism, brain injuries and complex needs.
Employees: 900

War on Want

London N1 7JP
T: 020 7324 5040
F: 020 7324 5041
E: drudkin@waronwant.org
www.waronwant.org
Executive Director: John Hilary
War on Want fights poverty in developing countries in partnership and solidarity with people affected by globalisation. We campaign for human rights and against the root causes of global poverty, inequality and injustice.
Employees: 19
Volunteers: 5

War Widows Association of Great Britain and Northern Ireland

C/O 199 Borough High Street, London SE1 1AA
T: 0845 241 2189
E: info@warwidows.org.uk
www.warwidows.org.uk/
The association seeks to improve the conditions of war widows in Great Britain. This is done by regular meetings with Ministers and pension authorities. We hold regular national and local events, publish a regular newsletter and ensure that widows are represented at significant national events of remembrance.

Waste Watch

London EC2A 4LT
T: 020 7089 2100
F: 020 7403 4802
E: info@wastewatch.org.uk
www.wastewatch.org.uk
Aims to be the leading cross-sectoral national organisation that educates, informs and raises awareness on waste reduction, re-use and recycling.
Employees: 28
Volunteers: 2
Regional offices: 1

Water for Africa

12 The Midway, Newcastle-under-Lyme, Staffordshire ST5 1QG
T: 01782 593289
E: info@waterforafrica.org.uk
www.waterforafrica.org.uk
We believe that water, sanitation and health are basic human rights and the key to emerging long-term from poverty. We have set up and successfully run a UK-led organisation over the last four years managed by local professionals. Its service has provided a fast, professional, targeted service directly to benefit the people of Africa who need it most at the fraction of the cost of the cost of traditional methods.
Volunteers: 3

WaterAid

Second floor, London SE11 5JD
T: 0845 600 0433
F: 020 7793 4545
E: wateraid@wateraid.org
www.wateraid.org
Chief Executive: Barbara Frost
WaterAid is a leading independent organisation that enables the world's poorest people to gain access to safe water, sanitation and hygiene education. We work in Africa, Asia and the Pacific region and campaign globally with our partners to realise our vision of a world where everyone has access to these basic human rights.
Employees: 518
Volunteers: 600
Regional offices: 20

WAY Widowed and Young

Suite 17, The College Business Centre, Uttoxeter New Road, Derby, Derbyshire DE22 3WZ
E: enquiries@widowedandyoung.org.uk
www.widowedandyoung.org.uk
Chairperson: Georgia Elms
WAY Widowed and Young helps men and women widowed when aged 50 or under to rebuild their lives, whether or not they have children. We offer support and friendship through a national network of groups, message board and chatroom, newsletter, book loan service and weekend trips for members.
Employees: 2
Volunteers: 50

WDC, Whale and Dolphin Conservation

Brookfield House, 38 St Paul Street, Chippenham, Wiltshire SN15 1LY
T: 01249 449500
E: info@whales.org
www.whales.org
Raises public awareness of all the threats facing whales, dolphins and porpoises. The society funds, throughout the world, research and conservation methods concerning whales, dolphins and porpoises and their habitats, and campaigns for their protection from all threats.

Weight Concern

1-19 Torrington Place, London WC1E 7HB
T: 020 7679 1853
F: 020 7679 8354
E: enquiries@weightconcern.org.uk
www.weightconcern.org.uk
Executive Director: Dr Laura McGowan
Weight Concern exists to tackle the issue of obesity in the UK. Our vision is to support and empower people to live a healthy lifestyle, and our mission is to increase the understanding of both health professionals and the public about the causes, consequences and treatments of overweight and obesity. We aim to provide clear, evidence-based information on obesity and weight-management to provide a 'voice' for those who have first-hand experience of being overweight.
Employees: 4
Volunteers: 3

Wellbeing of Women

27 Sussex Place, London NW1 4SP
T: 020 7772 6400
F: 020 7724 7725
E: hello@wellbeingofwomen.org.uk
www.wellbeingofwomen.org.uk
Director: Liz Campbell
Wellbeing of Women is a charity dedicated to improving the health of women and babies, to make a difference to everybody's lives today and tomorrow. We provide information, to raise awareness of health issues to keep women and babies well today. We fund medical research and training grants, which have and will continue to develop better treatments and outcomes for tomorrow.
Employees: 10

WellChild

16 Royal Crescent, Cheltenham, Gloucestershire GL50 3DA
T: 01242 530007
E: info@wellchild.org.uk
www.wellchild.org.uk
Chief Executive: Colin Dyer
WellChild is the national charity for sick children. We provide essential practical and emotional support for seriously ill children, young people and those who care for them across the UK to ensure they receive the best possible quality of care.
Employees: 26
Volunteers: 250
Regional offices: 1

Wellcome Trust

Gibbs Building, 215 Euston Road, London NW1 2BE
T: 020 7611 7210
F: 020 7611 8800
E: s.wallcraft@wellcome.ac.uk
www.wellcome.ac.uk
Aims to protect, preserve and advance all or any aspects of the health and welfare of humankind and to advance and promote knowledge and education by engaging in, encouraging and supporting research into any of the biosciences.
Employees: 500

Wells for India

The Winchester Centre, 68 St George's Street, Winchester, Hampshire SO23 8AH
T: 01962 848043
F: 01962 848029
E: office@wellsforindia.org
www.wellsforindia.org
Employees: 2
Volunteers: 27

Welwitschia Welfare Centre

Imperial House, 64 Willoughby Lane, Tottenham, London N17 0SP
T: 020 8808 1255
F: 020 8885 3471
E: info@wwcuk.org
www.wwcuk.org
Chief Executive: Pedro Lunguela
The WWC is a voluntary community charity organisation. It was set up to help Angolan community and other Portuguese-speaking migrants, refugees access the mainstream services, not to suffer in silence through lack of knowledge of their rights and entitlements in their host country. It also combats poverty and helps the community integrate into British society. WWC services are now also offered to other minority ethnic groups.
Employees: 2
Volunteers: 8
Income: £13,100 (2014-15)

WESC Foundation

E: kgaulton@wescfoundation.ac.uk

West Harton Churches Action Station Ltd

Boldon Lane, South Shields, Tyne & Wear NE34 0AS
T: 0191 455 8122
E: ceo@actionstation.org.uk
www.actionstation.org.uk
Manager: Dave Kippax
To reduce social isolation, increase job readiness of the community, increase the overall health of the community and promote individuals working together for the benefit of the local community. To provide a one stop shop.
Employees: 6
Volunteers: 43
Income: £200,000 (2012-13)

West Indian Standing Conference

5 Westminster Bridge Road, London SE1 7XW
T: 020 7928 7861
F: 020 7928 0343
E: wiscorg@tiscali.co.uk
www.wisc.btck.co.uk
Aims to be a representative body for West Indians in Britain and to research into, report upon, and make representations as appropriate concerning the conditions of that community. It establishes and co-ordinates projects to monitor, assist and inform statutory and voluntary agencies of the needs of the West Indian community.
Employees: 6
Volunteers: 3

Western Lodge

85 Trinity Road, Tooting, London SW17 7SQ
T: 020 8696 1564
F: 020 8672 6232
E: info@westernlodge.org.uk
www.westernlodge.org.uk
Chair of the Board of Trustee's: Mr R Plummer
Western Lodge is a 10 bed medium support hostel for male clients over the age of 30years. All clients need to have support needs in addition to being homeless and priority is given to Wandsworth clients. The project is staffed 24/7 and full support is given to all clients.
Employees: 5
Regional offices: 1

Westminster Drug Project

7th Floor, Kingsway House, 103 Kingsway, Holborn, London WC2B 6QX
T: 020 7421 3100
F: 020 7421 3199
E: communications@wdp-drugs.org.uk
www.wdp-drugs.org.uk
Chief Executive Officer: Stuart Campbell
WDP is a vibrant and innovative charity committed to helping all those who are affected by drug and alcohol use. We believe that with the right support, people can make long-lasting change in their lives to improve health, wellbeing and social integration. We provide drug and alcohol services across London and the south east of England. We work with individuals, families and communities to help people recover from drug dependency and to reduce crime.
Employees: 360
Volunteers: 100
Regional offices: 24

Weston Park Hospital Development Fund Ltd

23 Northumberland Road, Sheffield, South Yorkshire S10 2TX
T: 0114 226 5391
Helpline: 0114 226 5666
E: karen.holmes@cancersupportcentre.co.uk
www.cancersupportcentre.co.uk
Centre Manager: Karen Holmes
Providing Information, support and advice for cancer patients and their families and friends,

via a drop-in centre. Health care professionals available to take enquiries.
Employees: 10
Volunteers: 14
Regional offices: 1
Income: £413,200 (2014-15)

WheelPower

Stoke Mandeville Stadium, Guttmann Road, Stoke Mandeville, Buckinghamshire, Buckinghamshire HP21 9PP
T: 01296 395995
F: 01296 424171
E: nigel.roberts@wheelpower.org.uk
www.wheelpower.org.uk
Chief Executive: Martin McElhatton
WheelPower British Wheelchair Sport provides, promotes and develops opportunities for men, women and children with disabilities to participate in recreational and competitive wheelchair sport from grass roots to international level throughout the UK.
Employees: 10
Volunteers: 250
Regional offices: 1
Income: £1,600,000 (2012-13)

Whitehall and Industry Group

80 Petty France, London SW1H 9EX
T: 020 7222 1166
F: 020 7222 1167
E: charitynext@wig.co.uk
www.wig.co.uk
Chief Executive: Mark Gibson
The Whitehall and Industry Group is an independent, not-for-profit and non-lobbying membership organisation. Established in 1984, we have a charitable purpose to build understanding and cooperation between the public, private and voluntary sectors for the greater public good a nation better governed, business better managed and society better served.
Employees: 23

Whizz-Kidz

Bressenden Place, Victoria, London SW1E 5BH
T: 020 7233 6600
E: info@whizz-kidz.org.uk
www.whizz-kidz.org.uk
Whizz-Kidz improves the quality of life of young disabled people under 18 in the UK through the provision of customised mobility equipment such as powered and manual wheelchairs and tricycles. The charity provides help and advice to children and their families and raises awareness of mobility-related issues through national campaigning.

Who Cares' Trust

Kemp House, 152-160 City Road, London EC1V 2NP
T: 020 7251 3117
F: 020 7251 3123
E: mailbox@thewhocarestrust.org.uk
www.thewhocarestrust.org.uk
Aims to improve the delivery of public care and the day-to-day life experience of children and young people in public care through promoting and acting on their views.
Employees: 27
Volunteers: 1

Wigan and Leigh CVS

E: sue.barrett@gmcvo.org.uk

Wildfowl and Wetlands Trust

Slimbridge, Gloucestershire GL2 7BT
T: 01453 891900
F: 01453 890827
E: kath.brice@wwt.org.uk
www.wwt.org.uk
Chief Executive: Martin Spray
The Wildfowl and Wetlands Trust (WWT) is the largest international wetland conservation charity in the UK. Its mission is to promote, protect and develop wetlands and their wildlife. WWT operates nine visitor centres in the UK aimed at bringing people closer to wetland wildlife.
Employees: 420
Volunteers: 520
Regional offices: 9

Wildlife Aid

Randalls Farm House, Randalls Road, Leatherhead, Surrey KT22 0AL
T: 01372 377332
Helpline: 0906 180 0132
F: 01372 375183
E: becky@wildlifeaid.org.uk
www.wildlifeaid.com
Managing Trustee: Simon Cowell
Wildlife Aid is a registered charity dedicated to the rescue, care and rehabilitation of sick, injured and orphaned British wildlife. Based in Leatherhead, Surrey, since its opening over 25 years ago the centre has grown to be one of the largest wildlife rehabilitation hospitals in the country, dealing with more than 20,000 incidents each year.
Employees: 3
Volunteers: 300
Regional offices: 1

Wildlife and Countryside Link

89 Albert Embankment, London SE1 7TP
T: 020 7820 8600
F: 020 7820 8620
E: enquiry@wcl.org.uk
www.wcl.org.uk
Wildlife and Countryside Link brings together environmental voluntary organisations in the UK united by their common interest in the conservation and enjoyment of the natural and historic environment. Our aim is to maximise the efficiency and effectiveness of the voluntary sector through collaboration. Through Link, groups of people from different organisations get together to exchange information, develop and promote policies, and work to effect change.
Employees: 5
Volunteers: 2

William Sutton Trust

William Sutton Housing Association, Sutton Court, Tring, Hertfordshire HP23 5BB
T: 01442 891100
E: customerservice@affinitysutton.com
www.affinitysutton.com
A registered charity and a housing association registered with The Housing Corporation, which provides affordable housing and associated community support for people in housing need in 44 local authority areas throughout England, including London.

Williams Syndrome Foundation Ltd

161 High Street, Tonbridge, Kent TN9 1BX
T: 01732 365152
E: enquiries@williams-syndrome.org.uk
www.williams-syndrome.org.uk
CEO: Elizabeth Hurst
Provides support and expert research backed information to those with WS and those who care for and educate them. Fundraises and supports research and exchanges information on William's syndrome, a rare disorder caused by an abnormality in chromosomes. Puts parents in touch through a national contact network. Stimulates interest, particularly among the medical profession, in the condition. Runs social and information events. Subsidises respite breaks and supported holidays.

Wincanton Community Venture

E: sueplace@balsamcentre.org.uk

Windle Trust International

37A Oxford Road, Cowley, Oxford OX4 2EN
T: 01865 712900
E: cathryn@windle.org.uk
www.windle.org.uk

Windsor Leadership Trust

Adair House, Madeira Walk, Windsor, Berkshire SL4 1EU
T: 01753 830202
F: 01753 842775
E: office@windsorleadershiptrust.org.uk
www.windsorleadershiptrust.org.uk
Chief Executive: Dr James McCalman
For 15 years, the Windsor Leadership Trust has been bringing together top leaders from every sector to reflect on how they can use their influence, decisions and actions to benefit their organisations, and wider society. Through our programmes we enable leaders to explore for themselves the responsibilities of leadership. The different programme levels reflect the increasingly complex challenges leaders face as their roles become more strategic and their leadership responsibilities grow.
Employees: 10

Winston's Wish

3rd Floor, Cheltenham House, Clarence Street, Cheltenham, Gloucestershire GL50 3JR
T: 01242 515157
Helpline: 0845 203 0405
E: info@winstonswish.org.uk
www.winstonswish.org.uk
Chief Executive: Fergus Crow
Winston's Wish helps children rebuild their lives after the death of a parent or sibling, enabling them to face the future with confidence and hope. We offer practical support and guidance to families, professionals and anyone concerned about a grieving child. We want children to avoid the problems that can occur in later life if they are unable to express their grief.

Wish - a voice for women's mental health

15 Old Ford Road, London E2 9PL
T: 020 8980 3618
F: 020 8980 1596
E: info@womenatwish.org.uk
www.womenatwish.org.uk
Director: Joyce Kallevik
Wish is the only national, user-led charity working with women with mental health needs in prison, hospital and the community. It provides independent advocacy, emotional support and practical guidance at all stages of a woman's journey through the Mental Health and Criminal Justice Systems. Wish acts to increase women's participation in the services they receive, and campaigns to get their voice heard at a policy level.
Employees: 15
Volunteers: 25
Regional offices: 2

Wishing Well

4 Laurel Avenue, Fleetwood, Lancashire FY7 7PT
T: 01253 773546
E: wishingwellappeal@yahoo.co.uk
www.wishingwellcharity.org
Lead Trustee: Jason O'Flaherty
Wishing Well is a small international development charity. We work with children and families, promote volunteering and support community development initiatives. Wishing Well is currently working in Romania and in the UK. Our projects include: providing educational support to young Roma children; advocacy; work with children with HIV and special needs; delivering a schools NGO community development training programme and promoting volunteering, including coordinating National Volunteering Week.
Employees: 2
Volunteers: 20
Regional offices: 1

Woking Association of Voluntary Service

E: sylvie@wavs.org.uk

Wolverhampton Domestic Violence Forum

P O Box 4984, Wolverhampton, West Midlands WV1 9GE
T: 01902 555643
E: wdvf@wolverhampton.gov.uk
Strategy Co-ordinator: Kathy Cole-Evans
WDVF aims to work in partnership to stop domestic violence and abuse, to ensure the safety and empowerment of victims and their children, and to bring perpetrators to justice. Integrated partnership working is key to achieving our aims. We work closely with a number of local partnerships, and collectively develop and implement multi-agency strategies and action plans towards meeting these aims.
Employees: 8

WOMANKIND Worldwide

2nd Floor, Development House, London EC2A 4LT
T: 020 7549 0360
F: 020 7549 0361
E: info@womankind.org.uk
www.womankind.org.uk
Chief Executive: Jackie Ballard
Employees: 24
Volunteers: 12

Women and Girls' Network

PO Box 13095, London W14 0FE
T: 020 7610 4678
E: info@wgn.org.uk
www.wgn.org.uk
Offers counselling to women and girls who have experienced any form of violence, whether physical, sexual or emotional.

Women and Manual Trades

Tindlemanor, 52-54 Featherstone Street, London EC1Y 8RT
T: 020 7251 9192
F: 020 7251 9193
E: info@wamt.org
www.wamt.org
Info & support for women training and working in the manual building trades. Campaigns to make women "on the tools" the norm rather than the exception.
Employees: 6

Women's Aid Federation of England

PO Box 3245, Bristol BS2 2EH
Helpline: 0808 200 0247
E: info@womensaid.org.uk
www.womensaid.org.uk
Chief Executive: Polly Neate
Women's Aid is that national charity working to end domestic abuse against women and children. Our three key aims: To improve the protection available to abused women and children by ensuring that their needs and experiences inform developments in law, policy and practice; To work towards the prevention of gender based violence through public awareness and education; To ensure the provision of high quality services for abused women and children.
Employees: 63
Volunteers: 1
Regional offices: 2
Income: £2,572,485 (2014-15)

Women's Engineering Society (WES)

Michael Faraday House, Six Hills Way, Stevenage, Herts. SG1 2AY
T: 01438 765506
E: info@wes.org.uk
www.wes.org.uk
The Women's Engineering Society aims to: support members of WES and women in general to achieve their potential as engineers, scientists and technologists; encourage the study and application of engineering; help engineering companies to promote gender diversity and equality in the workplace; lobby Government, organisations and policy makers to strive for equality, both in the workplace and in the promotion of engineering as a career.
Employees: 1
Volunteers: 100+
Regional offices: 1
Income: £50,000 (2012-13)

Women's Environmental Network

PO Box 30626, London E2 7EY
T: 020 7481 9004
F: 020 7481 9144
E: info@wen.org.uk
www.wen.org.uk
Campaigns on environmental and health issues from a woman's perspective, and informs and empowers women and men who care about the environment.
Employees: 11
Volunteers: 2
Regional offices: 100

Women's Farm and Garden Association

175 Gloucester Street, Cirencester, Gloucestershire GL7 2DP
T: 01285 658339
E: admin@wfga.org.uk
www.wfga.org.uk
Creates interest in and promotes the study and practice of agriculture and horticulture among women throughout the UK. Trains returners through the Women Returners to Amenity Gardening Scheme (WRAGS). Offers a programme of specialist workshops, tours and visits to its membership. Offers grants to the membership through the Christine Ladley Fund for education and work-related funding.
Employees: 15

Women's Health Advice Centre

1 Council Road, Ashington, Ashington, Northumberland NE63 8RZ
T: 01670 853977
E: cathhale@whac.uk.com
www.whac-online.co.uk
Manager: Cath Hale
Incorporated charity aiming to provide people (14+) in Northumberland with quality counselling, personal development, education and information on issues contributing to their general health and well being. Specialising in Domestic and sexual abuse, bereavement, mental health, relationship problems, self esteem and suicide.
Employees: 6
Volunteers: 25
Regional offices: 1
Income: £150,000 (2012-13)

Women's Resource Centre

Ground Floor East, London EC1V 0BB
T: 020 7324 3030
F: 020 7324 3050
E: info@wrc.org.uk
www.wrc.org.uk
Chief Executive: Vivienne Hayes
The Women's Resource Centre is a charity that supports women's organisations to be more effective and sustainable. We provide training, information, resources and one-to-one support on a range of organisational development issues. We also lobby decision-makers on behalf of the women's not-for-profit sector for improved representation and funding. Our members work in a wide range of fields delivering services to and campaigning on behalf of some of the most marginalised communities of women.
Employees: 18

Women's Royal Naval Service Benevolent Trust

311 Twyford Avenue, Stamshaw, Portsmouth, Hampshire PO2 8RN
T: 023 9265 5301
F: 023 9267 9040
E: generalsecretary@wrnsbt.org.uk
www.wrnsbt.org.uk
General Secretary: Sarah Ayton
The primary aim of the Trust is to provide relief in cases of necessity or distress amongst its members and their dependants. The Trust is also empowered, in suitable cases, to make grants for the education of dependants.
Employees: 2
Volunteers: 20
Regional offices: 1
Income: £509,000 (2012-13)

Women's Technology and Education Centre

Blackburne House Centre For Women, Blackburne Place, Liverpool L8 7PE
T: 0151 709 4356
E: bh.wtec@blackburnehouse.co.uk
www.blackburnehouse.co.uk
Promotes education and training for women; establishes and promotes equal opportunities in education and training. Encourages women into non-traditional jobs.

Women's Therapy Centre

10 Manor Gardens, London N7 6JS
T: 020 7263 7860
Helpline: 020 7263 6200
F: 020 7272 4222
E: enquiries@womenstherapycentre.co.uk
www.womenstherapycentre.co.uk
Chief Executive: Monika Schwartz
We offer both group and individual psychoanalytic psychotherapy for women. Therapy is offered on a sliding scale according to financial means. Please see website for up-to-date information on making an appointment.
Employees: 10
Volunteers: 10
Regional offices: 1

Woodcraft Folk

13 Ritherdon Road, London SW17 8QE
T: 020 7703 4173
F: 020 8767 2457
E: info@woodcraft.org.uk
www.woodcraft.org.uk
Unites children, young people and all who are young in spirit. Directs the energy and enthusiasm of youth towards the transformation of society, educating members in the principles of universal tolerance, equality and friendship.
Volunteers: 3500
Regional offices: 500

Wooden Spoon Society

Fleet, Hampshire GU51 3PD
T: 01252 773720
F: 01276 502134
E: idoorbar@woodenspoon.com
www.woodenspoon.com
Enhances the quality and prospect of life for children and young persons in the UK and Ireland who are disadvantaged, either physically, mentally or socially.
Employees: 23
Volunteers: 400
Regional offices: 1

Woodgreen The Animal Charity

King's Bush Farm, London Road, Godmanchester, Cambridgeshire PE29 2NH
T: 0844 248 8181
F: 01480 832815
E: paula.loveday-smith@woodgreen.org.uk
www.woodgreen.org.uk
Chief Executive : Paula Loveday-Smith
Animal welfare and rehoming charity
Employees: 270
Regional offices: 3

Woodland Trust

Kempton Way, Grantham, Lincolnshire NG31 6LL
T: 01476 581111
F: 01476 590808
E: hilaryallison@woodlandtrust.org.uk
www.woodlandtrust.org.uk
The Trust is the UK's leading charity dedicated to protecting, restoring and expanding our native woods. Our long-term aims are to enable the creation of more new native woods, to protect native woods, trees and their wildlife for the future, and to restore our native woodland heritage.
Employees: 320
Volunteers: 1000+
Regional offices: 4

Worcester Volunteer Centre

33, The Tything, Worcester, Worcestershire WR1 1JL
T: 01905 24741
F: 01907 23688
E: sally@wvc.org.uk
www.worcestervolunteercentre.org.uk
Chief Officer: Sally Ellison
Local Infrastructure organisation and Volunteer recruitment centre. Aim to promote volunteering, community action & deliver community services through volunteers
Employees: 15
Volunteers: 110
Income: £300,000 (2012-13)

Work Foundation

21 Palmer Street, London SW1Y 0AD
T: 020 7976 3500
E: partnership@theworkfoundation.com
www.theworkfoundation.com
The Work Foundation aims to improve productivity and performance of all British organisations by enriching the quality and integrity of working life. Our unique understanding of the importance and developing human capital enables us to work with our clients to bring about in-depth sustainable change, through our distinctive brand of research, consultancy, advocacy, leadership and coaching programmes.

Workaid

The Old Boot Factory, 71 Townsend Road, Chesham, Bucks., Buckinghamshire HP5 2AA
T: 01494 775220
E: publicity@workaid.org
www.workaid.org
General Manager: John Fox
Supplying refurbished donated tools, sewing/knitting machines and horticultural equipment to vocational training projects in East Africa and the UK.
Employees: 4
Volunteers: 280
Income: £220,000 (2014-15)

Workers' Educational Association

4 Loop Sreet, London EC2A 4XW
T: 020 7426 3450
F: 020 7426 3451
E: london@wea.org.uk
www.wea.org.uk
General Secretary: Ruth Spellman
The WEA creates and delivers around 14,000 courses for adults each year in response to local need across England and Scotland, often in partnership with community groups and local charities. We believe that education is lifelong and should continue beyond school, college and university in order to help people develop their full human potential in society.
Employees: 3500
Volunteers: 4000
Regional offices: 10

Working Families

London EC1V 0AA
T: 020 7253 7243
Helpline: 0300 012 0312
F: 020 7253 6253
E: office@workingfamilies.org.uk
www.workingfamilies.org.uk
Employees: 12
Volunteers: 10

Working with Words

Carlton Centre, Carlton Road, Sidcup, Kent DA14 6AH
T: 020 8302 4619
E: words@mcch.org.uk
www.mcch.org.uk/workingwithwords/index.aspx
Design and Contracts Manager: Colin Thomas
There are 1.2 million people with learning disabilities and 1.7 million adults with low literacy in the UK. Working with Words can help you reach this audience. We produce accessible information and easy read documents, making it easy to understand for people with learning disabilities and low literacy. All of our documents are created using Government and European guidelines and are proof read by our target audience.

World Association of Girl Guides and Girl Scouts

World Bureau, Olave Centre, 12C Lyndhurst Road, London NW3 5PQ
T: 020 7794 1181
F: 020 7431 3764
E: waggs@wagggsworld.org
www.wagggs.org/en/
Provides a dynamic, flexible, values-based educational programme that is relevant to girls' needs. Strives for excellence by providing opportunities to enable girls to make informed decisions. The largest voluntary organisation for girls and young women in the world, WAGGGS bases its work on spiritual values and has a commitment to peace and world citizenship.
Employees: 51
Volunteers: 1000000
Regional offices: 1

World Development Movement

66 Offley Road, London SW9 0LS
T: 020 7820 4900
F: 020 7820 4949
E: wdm@wdm.org.uk
www.wdm.org.uk
Director: Nick Dearden
World Development Movement (WDM) tackles the underlying causes of poverty. We lobby decision-makers to change the policies that keep people poor. We research and promote positive alternatives. We work alongside people in the developing world who are standing up to injustice.
Employees: 30
Volunteers: 5
Regional offices: 1

World Emergency Relief

20 York Buildings, London WC2N 6JU
T: 0870 429 2129
F: 020 7839 8202
E: hannah@wer-uk.org
www.worldemergencyrelief.org
Delivers practical, emotional, spiritual and economic aid to children and disaster victims in developing countries.
Employees: 7
Volunteers: 3

World Society for the Protection of Animals

5th Floor, 222 Gray's Inn Road,
London WC1X 8HB
T: 020 7587 5000
F: 020 7587 5057
E: wspa@wspa.org.uk
www.wspa.org.uk
For 25 years, WSPA has aimed to promote the concept of animal welfare in regions of the world where there are few, if any, measures to protect animals. Politically, we have campaigned to convince governments and key decision-makers to change practices and introduce new laws to protect or improve the welfare of animals.
Employees: 50
Volunteers: 4
Regional offices: 10

World Vision UK

World Vision House, Opal Drive, Fox Milne,
Milton Keynes MK15 0ZR
T: 01908 841000
F: 01908 841001
E: info@worldvision.org.uk
www.worldvision.org.uk
Chief Executive Officer: Justin Byworth
World Vision is a Christian relief, development and advocacy organisation dedicated to working with children, families and communities to overcome poverty and injustice.

Worshipful Company of Information Technologists

39A Bartholomew Close,
London EC1A 7JN
T: 020 7600 1992
F: 020 7600 1991
E: caroline@wcit.org.uk
www.wcit.org.uk
Getting the maximum benefit from IT is now a prerequisite, not just for commercial organisations but also for the charity sector. We work with a wide range of not-for-profit organisations with the aim of helping them to gain the maximum benefit from their IT. Our members give their time and expertise to provide pro bono IT advice (usually at a strategic level).
Employees: 4
Volunteers: 200

Worster-Drought Syndrome Support Group

10 St Vincent Chase, Braintree,
Essex CM7 9UJ
Helpline: 01376 348948
E: j.leech@btopenworld.com
www.wdssg.org.uk
Chair: Jacqueline Leech
Helps support those with WDS, a rare form of cerebral palsy, and their families.
Volunteers: 6

Worthing Women's Aid Trading as Safe in Sussex

Safe in Sussex, PO Box 4127, Worthing,
West Sussex BN11 1AF
T: 01903 219994
Helpline: 01903 231939
E: louise@safeinsussex.org.uk
www.safeinsussex.org
Services Manager: Sharon Howard
Providing domestic abuse awareness through Freedom and Education. The provision of a refuge service for women and their children. Facilitation of the Freedom Programme for women and educational programmes for young people.
Employees: 15
Volunteers: 18
Regional offices: 1

WPF Therapy

23 Magdalen Street, London SE1 2EN
T: 020 7378 2000
F: 020 7378 2010
E: counselling@wpf.org.uk
www.wpf.org.uk
Chief Executive: Joan Baxter
WPF Therapy works to broaden access to good psychological therapies. It provides therapy to a high standard tailored for each individual as well as training for counsellors and psychotherapists with a wide range of accredited training programmes. The organisation's clinical services and training cover ongoing psychodynamic counselling, psychodynamic psychotherapy, time-limited psychodynamic counselling, group analytic psychotherapy and CBT (cognitive behavioural therapy).
Employees: 150
Volunteers: 100
Regional offices: 27

WRVS

Garden House, Milton Hill, Steventon,
Abingdon, Oxfordshire OX13 6AD
T: 01235 442900
Helpline: 0845 600 5885
F: 01235 861166
E: enquiries@royalvoluntaryservice.org.uk
www.wrvs.org.uk
Chief Executive: Lynne Berry
Works independently and in partnership with government departments, local authorities and the private sector in carrying out welfare and emergency work through a nationwide network based on local authority areas in England, Scotland and Wales. WRVS is the largest active voluntary organisation in the UK.
Employees: 1600
Volunteers: 65000

WWV

5 Russell Town Lane, Bristol BS5 9LT
T: 0117 955 9042
E: wwv@wwv.org.uk
www.wwv.org.uk
Director: Mike Silvey
WWV believes in the power of voluntary work as a catalyst for change. We are specialists in the use of volunteering to enable young people and people at risk of being marginalised to take control of their lives and expand their horizons, enhancing well-being, employability and life satisfaction. We work one-to-one with ex-offenders, disadvantaged young people and wounded and injured servicemen, veterans and their families.
Employees: 22
Volunteers: 9

Wycombe Women's Aid Ltd

P.O. Box 1477, High Wycombe,
Buckinghamshire HP11 9HP
T: 01494 461367
F: 01494 452622
E: wwal@btconnect.com
www.wycombewomensaid.org.uk
Director: Lisbeth Harvey
Wycombe Women's Aid provides support to women and children experiencing the effects of domestic violence by offering safe, temporary and emergency accommodation as well as practical and emotional support within the refuge and through outreach in the Wycombe, South Bucks and Chiltern Districts of Bucks. This is achieved using an equal opportunities approach incorporated in a women-centred philosophy.
Employees: 17
Volunteers: 1
Income: £546,648 (2013-14)

Y Care International

Kemp House, London EC1V 2NP
T: 020 7549 3150
F: 020 7549 3151
E: enq@ycareinternational.org
www.ycareinternational.org
YCI works with vulnerable and disadvantaged young people in developing countries, focusing on street and working children, girls and young women, young refugees and displaced and young people with disabilities.
Employees: 15
Volunteers: 2

YHA (England and Wales) Ltd

Trevelyan House, Dimple Road, Matlock, Derbyshire DE4 3YH
T: 01629 592654
F: 01629 592702
E: customerservices@yha.org.uk
www.ywcagb.org.uk
YHA operates a network of more than 200 youth hostels across England and Wales. Our accommodation is open to all and everyone can experience a warm welcome, comfortable accommodation, good food and affordable prices. We also have more than 230,000 members, who receive many additional benefits, most notably an exemption from paying a non-member supplement each time they stay with YHA.
Employees: 1150
Volunteers: 5250
Regional offices: 80

YMCA England

London EC1M 3JF
T: 0845 873 6633
E: enquiries@england.ymca.org.uk
www.ymca.org.uk
The YMCA is a leading Christian charity committed to supporting all young people, particularly in times of need. YMCA England supports and represents the work of over 140 YMCAs providing professional and relevant services that make a difference to the lives of young people in over 250 communities.
Employees: 884
Volunteers: 250
Regional offices: 7

YMCA Indian Student Hostel

41 Fitzroy Square, London W1T 6AQ
T: 020 7387 0411
F: 020 7383 4735
E: gs@indianymca.org
www.indianymca.org
General Secretary/CEO: Thomas Abraham
YMCA stands for worldwide fellowship based on the equal value of all persons, respect and freedom for all, tolerance and understanding between people of different opinions and concern of the needs. YMCA Indian Student Hostel is a project of the National Council of YMCAs of India (NCYI), for the mental, spiritual and physical wellbeing of the youth in accordance with the YMCA worldwide. It provides a home for the youth and helps new arrivals.
Employees: 30
Volunteers: 9

Yorkshire Cat Rescue

The Farm, Lower Pierce Close, Cross Roads, Keighley, West Yorkshire BD22 9AQ
T: 01535 647184
E: mail@yorkshirecatrescue.org
www.yorkshirecatrescue.org
Founder and Chief Executive Officer: Sara Atkinson
A half way home for unwanted and stray cats and kittens in Yorkshire. All cats are neutered, microchipped, vaccinated, treated for worms and fleas. Volunteers needed for cat care, fundraising, admin and to help out in our charity shops in Keighley and Halifax.
Employees: 8
Volunteers: 75
Regional offices: 1
Income: £250,000 (2013-14)

Yorkshire Coast Enterprise Ltd

E: jennifer.crowther@yce.org.uk

Young Christian Workers

St. Antony's House, Eleventh Street, Trafford Park, Manchester M17 1JF
T: 0161 872 6017
E: info@ycwimpact.com
www.ycwimpact.com
National President: Phil Callaghan
The Young Christian Workers (YCW) is an organisation for 16-30 year olds (YCW) and Impact 13-17 years; it is for young people and run by young people. Our purpose is to help all young people live life to the full and realise their potential. The mission of the YCW is lived out among young people in the working world, paid or unpaid work, or those studying. YCW encourage them to grow in confidence and responsibility.
Employees: 2
Volunteers: 50
Income: £44,492 (2014-15)

Young Enterprise

Peterley House, Peterley Road, Cowley, Oxford OX4 2TZ
T: 01865 776845
E: info@young-enterprise.org.uk
www.young-enterprise.org.uk
With direct practical experience, the organisation introduces young people to the world of commerce and industry. It gives school and college students the opportunity to acquire a basic understanding of the world of work and wealth creation.

Young Epilepsy

St Piers Lane, Lingfield, Surrey RH7 6PW
T: 01342 832243
Helpline: 01342 831342
F: 01342 834639
E: info@youngepilepsy.org.uk
www.youngepilepsy.org.uk
Chief Executive: Carol Long
Young Epilepsy is the national charity working exclusively on behalf of children and young people with epilepsy. With over 100 years of experience we are a leading provider of specialist health and education services. The charity offers support, information, training for health, social care and education professionals and campaigns to improve access to, and quality of, health and education services.
Employees: 750
Volunteers: 50
Regional offices: 1

Young Explorers Trust

Stretton Cottage, Wellow Road, Ollerton, Newark, Nottinghamshire NG22 9AX
T: 01623 861027
E: ted@theyet.org
www.theyet.org
Chairman of Trustees: Graham Derrick
YET is a registered charity promoting safe and responsible expeditions. It aims to give young people the opportunity to take part in exploration, discovery and challenging adventure to help foster the qualities of service, self-sufficiency and leadership. By giving advice to youth expeditions it aims to help schools, youth organisations and peer groups to run their own expeditions in a safe

and responsible manner. It can also give grant aid to individuals and expeditions.
Volunteers: 20

Young Lancashire

Preston's College, Fulwood Campus, St Vincent's Road, PRESTON, Lancashire PR2 8UR
T: 01772 556127
F: 01772 251334
E: grahamw@younglancashire.org.uk
www.younglancashire.org.uk
CEO: Graham Whalley
Young Lancashire is a local infrastructure organisation which offers support to all front line voluntary children, young people and family based organisations to achieve the highest standards of practice and effectiveness in their work by building their capacity to deliver quality services. Our mission is to support children, young people and family based organisations to achieve the highest standards of practice and effectiveness in their work by building their capacity to deliver quality services.
Employees: 5
Volunteers: 14
Income: £252,645 (2013-14)

Young People Matter

E: m.dawes@youngpeoplematter.org

Young People's Support Foundation

E: k.roberts@ypsf.co.uk

Young People's Trust for the Environment and Nature Conservation

43 South Street, South Petherton, Somerset TA13 5AE
T: 01935 385962
E: peter.littlewood@ypte.org.uk
www.yptenc.org.uk
Encourages young people's understanding of the environment and the need for sustainability.

YoungMinds

Suite 11, Baden Place, Crosby Row, London SE1 1YW
T: 020 7089 5050
Helpline: 0808 802 5544
E: ymenquiries@youngminds.org.uk
www.youngminds.org.uk
Chief Executive: Sarah Brennan
YoungMinds is the UK's leading charity committed to improving the emotional wellbeing and mental health of children and young people. Driven by their experiences we campaign, research and influence policy and practice.
Employees: 35
Volunteers: 15

Youth Access

67 Alderbrook Road, London SW12 8AD
T: 020 8772 9900
E: admin@youthaccess.org.uk
www.youthaccess.org.uk
Director: Barbara Rayment
Youth Access is the national membership organisation for young people's information, advice, counselling and support services (YIACS). It promotes and encourages the growth of young people's counselling and advisory services; promotes good practice in these services; provides a forum for individuals and agencies; and promotes public recognition of the importance of these services.
Employees: 5

Youth at Risk

The Old Warehouse, 31 Upper King Street, Royston, Hertfordshire SG8 9AZ
T: 01763 241120
F: 01763 244735
E: sue@youthatrisk.org.uk
www.youthatrisk.org.uk
Chief Executive Officer: Sue Handly
Our mission is to enable society's most disadvantaged, difficult and damaged young people to transform their lives and build a future beyond their present expectations; the main activity is to advance the social education of young people at risk either from physical, mental or sexual abuse, drug or other substance abuse, criminal activity, poverty, homelessness, unemployment or illiteracy.
Employees: 11
Volunteers: 800

Youth Sport Trust

SportPark, Loughborough University, 3 Oakwood Drive, Loughborough, Leicestershire LE11 3QF
T: 01509 226600
E: info@youthsporttrust.org
www.youthsporttrust.org
Our charity is passionate about helping all young people to achieve their potential by delivering high-quality physical education and sport.
Regional offices: 1

YouthNet

1st Floor, 50 Featherstone Street, London EC1Y 8RT
T: 020 7250 5700
F: 020 7250 3695
E: media@youthnet.org
www.youthnet.org
Chief Executive: Emma Thomas
YouthNet helps young people make choices today for a brighter tomorrow, by providing impartial information and support about anything and everything for 16 to 25 year olds, whenever and wherever they need it; inspiring them to get involved. YouthNet do this primarily through their three websites: TheSite.org, do-it.org and Lifetracks.com
Employees: 50
Regional offices: 1

Youthscape

3A Upper George Street, Luton, Bedfordshire LU1 2QX
T: 01582 877220
E: chris.curtis@youthscape.co.uk
CEO: Chris Curtis

YWCA England and Wales

New Barkley House, 234 Botley Road, Oxford OX2 0HP
T: 01865 304209
F: 01865 204805
E: info@platform51.org
www.ywca-gb.org.uk
YWCA is the leading charity working with the most disadvantaged young women in England and Wales. Young women face unique problems in today's society. They are largely unheard and lack influence. We want a future where they can overcome prejudice and take charge of their own lives. We run services to support them and campaign with them to combat the discrimination they face.
Employees: 250
Regional offices: 19

Zoological Society of London

Regent's Park, London NW1 4RY
T: 020 7449 6253
F: 020 7586 5743
E: ian.meyrick@zsl.org
www.zsl.org
Director General: Ralph Armond

By conducting scientific research, we promote zoology and the conservation of biological diversity, the welfare of animals and care and breeding of endangered species. We foster public interest and participation in conservation worldwide.

Employees: 725
Volunteers: 300
Regional offices: 1

Zurich Community Trust (UK) Limited

PO Box 1288, Swindon, Wiltshire SN1 1FL
T: 01793 511227
F: 01793 506982
E: kate.hodges@zct.org.uk
www.zct.org.uk
Head of Zurich Community Trust: Pam Webb

The umbrella for all Zurich's community involvement in the UK and supports the most disadvantaged people. A registered charity in its own right, Zurich Community Trust gives time, money and skills donated by Zurich and its employees in the UK. The Zurich Community Trust has a long history of pioneering grant-making to support less popular issues and works in genuine partnership with charities and supports around 600 local, national and overseas charities each year.

Employees: 18
Volunteers: 2600
Income: £2,833,000 (2012-13)

INDEX
THE VOLUNTARY
AGENCIES DIRECTORY

ABUSE & VIOLENCE – VICTIMS' & SURVIVORS' SUPPORT SERVICES

ACCOMMODATION & HOUSING

See also HOMELESSNESS SUPPORT; HOSPICES; RESIDENTIAL & CARE HOMES

EX-OFFENDERS

EX-SERVICEMEN & WOMEN

HOLIDAY & HOSTEL ACCOMMODATION

HOSPITAL / NEAR HOSPITAL ACCOMMODATION

FOR OLDER PEOPLE

VULNERABLE ADULTS

WOMEN

YOUNG PEOPLE & CHILDREN

ADDICTION SUPPORT SERVICES

See also ALCOHOL AWARENESS & SUPPORTGROUPS; DRUG AWARENESS & SUPPORT GROUPS; GAMBLING SUPPORTGROUPS; SMOKING 'STOP SMOKING' SUPPORT GROUPS; ARTS AND CULTURE

ADMINISTRATION

See GOVERNANCE & ADMINISTRATION

ADOPTION & FOSTERING SERVICES

ADULT EDUCATION & TRAINING

See also LITERACY & NUMERACY

BENEVOLENT SOCIETIES

BENGALI COMMUNITY GROUPS

BEREAVEMENT SUPPORT GROUPS

BIPOLAR DISORDERS

BIRD PROTECTION

BISEXUAL SUPPORT GROUPS

See GAY/LESBIAN/BISEXUAL/ TRANSGENDER SUPPORT GROUPS

BLINDNESS & SIGHT IMPAIRMENT

OVERSEAS AID

RESOURCES FOR

BLOOD DISORDERS

BUDDHIST FAITH

BUILDINGS & OPEN SPACE PROVISION

See also ACCOMMODATION & HOUSING

BUSINESS & ENTERPRISE DEVELOPMENT

BUSINESS & INDUSTRY TRAINING

CANCER RESEARCH & SUPPORT GROUPS

CARDIAC CONDITIONS & RESEARCH

CAREERS GUIDANCE & ADVICE

CARERS

CAT WELFARE

CEREBAL PALSY

CHILD PROTECTION

CHILDBIRTH SUPPORT SERVICES

See also POST-NATAL SUPPORT GROUPS; PREGNANCY; STILLBIRTH & NEONATAL DEATH

MULTIPLE BIRTHS

CHILDCARE PROVISION

CHILDREN & YOUNG PEOPLE

See also BEHAVIOURAL DIFFICULTIES-SUPPORT FOR PARENTS & CARERS; CHILD PROTECTION; CHILDCARE PROVISION, CHILDREN'S ACTIVITY SCHEMES & CLUBS; COUNSELLING & PSYCHOTHERAPY SERVICES; EXCHANGE AND OVERSEAS PROGRAMMES; FURTHER & HIGHER EDUCATION; HELPLINES; INFANT & CHILDREN HEALTH SUPPORT GROUPS; INFANT, PRIMARY & SECONDARY SCHOOL EDUCATION; INFANT DEATH; OUTDOOR EDUCATION & RESIDENTIAL COURSES; PRE-SCHOOL EDUCATION

CHILDREN'S ACTIVITY SCHEMES & CLUBS

CHILDREN'S HEALTH

See INFANT & CHILDREN'S HEALTH SUPPORT GROUPS

CHINESE COMMUNITY GROUPS

CHRISTIAN FAITH GROUPS

CHILDREN & YOUNG PEOPLE

OVERSEAS AID

CHROMOSOMAL DISORDERS

CHRONIC FATIGUE SYNDROME

See ME

CIRCULATORY DISORDERS

CIRCUMCISION

CITIZENSHIP

COMMUNICATIONS & MEDIA HANDLING

COMMUNITY DEVELOPMENT & RESOURCES

See also UMBRELLA & RESOURCE BODIES; VOLUNTARY ACTION AND VOLUNTEER CENTRES; HOMELESSNESS

COMPLEMENTARY MEDICINE

COMPUTERS & THE INTERNET

CONGENITAL DISORDERS

CONGOLESE COMMUNITY GROUPS

CONSERVATION GROUPS

CONTINENCE (INCONTINENCE) ADVICE & SUPPORT

COUNSELLING & PSYCHOTHERAPY SERVICES

CRIME & JUSTICE

DANCE

DEAFNESS & HEARING IMPAIRMENTS

DEMENTIA SUPPORT GROUPS

DENTAL HEALTH

DERMATOLOGY & SKIN DISORDERS

DIABETES RESEARCH & SUPPORT

DISABILITIES

ACCESS TO ENVIRONMENTS

ACCOMMODATION

ADVICE & INFORMATION

CHILDREN

DEAFBLINDNESS

EDUCATION & VOCATIONAL TRAINING SUPPORT

EMPLOYMENT & PROGRESSION SERVICES

OVERSEAS AID RECREATION

REHABILITATION SERVICES

RESOURCES FOR

RESPITE CARE & SHORT BREAKS

SPORT

ENVIRONMENTAL HEALTH & POLLUTION

ENZYME DEFICIENCY DISORDERS

EPILEPSY

EQUAL OPPORTUNITIES & DIVERSITY

See also AFRICAN & AFRO-CARIBBEAN SUPPORT GROUPS; OLDER PEOPLE; WOMEN

ETHIOPIAN COMMUNITY GROUPS

EX-SERVICEMEN & WOMEN SUPPORT SERVICES

EXCHANGE & OVERSEAS PROGRAMMES

FACIAL DISFIGUREMENT

FAMILY SUPPORT

See also GRANDPARENTS; PARENTING; BEHAVIOURAL DIFFICULTIES – SUPPORT FOR PARENTS & CARERS

(DEALING WITH) ADDICTIONS

(DEALING WITH) BEHAVIOURAL PROBLEMS

HEALTH

METABOLIC DEFICIENCY DISORDERS

MULTIPLE SCLEROSIS

MUSCULAR DISORDERS

MUSEUMS

MUSIC

MUSLIM FAITH

MYALGIC ENCEPHALOMYELITIS (CHRONIC FATIGUE SYNDROME)

NEONATAL DEATH

NEURODEVELOPMENTAL DISORDERS

NEUROLOGICAL DISORDERS

OBESITY

OLDER PEOPLE ADVISORY & SUPPORT GROUPS

EDUCATION & TRAINING

GRANTS & LOANS

HOUSING & CARE PROVISION

HEALTH CARE

RECREATION

RETIREMENT

ORGAN DONATION & REGISTERS

OUTDOOR EDUCATION & RESIDENTIAL COURSES

OVERSEAS AID & DEVELOPMENT

CHILDREN & YOUNG PEOPLE

EDUCATION & TRAINING

EQUIPMENT

HEALTH

HOMELESSNESS

VOLUNTEERS

WATER AID

PAIN MANAGEMENT

PALLIATIVE CARE

PARENTING

PATIENT CARE & ENVIRONMENT

PEACE CAMPAIGNS

See also POLITICAL ENGAGEMENT

PHOBIAS & PANIC ATTACKS

POLITICAL ENGAGEMENT

See also PEACE CAMPAIGNS

POST-NATAL SUPPORT GROUPS

See also CHILDBIRTH; PREGNANCY; STILLBIRTH & NEONATAL DEATH

POVERTY RELIEF

PRE-SCHOOL EDUCATION

PREGNANCY

PRISON & PROBATION SERVICES

PROFESSIONAL BODIES' INFORMATION SERVICES

PSYCHOLOGY

RECYCLING & WASTE MANAGEMENT

REFUGEE & ASYLUM SEEKERS SUPPORT GROUPS

REHABILITATION

ADDICTIONS

PHYSICAL

REPRODUCTIVE & SEXUAL HEALTH CARE

RESEARCH SUPPORT & POLICY DEVELOPMENT

CITZENSHIP

COMMUNITY DEVELOPMENT

EDUCATION

ENVIRONMENT

HERITAGE

SOCIAL POLICY & CHANGE

RESIDENTIAL & CARE HOMES

EX-SERVICEMEN/WOMEN

FOR PEOPLE WITH DISABILITIES, LEARNING DISABILITIES & MENTAL HEALTH PROBLEMS

RESPITE CARE

RHEUMATISM

RURAL & FARMING COMMUNITIES

SEAFARERS & MARITIME WORKERS

SEXUAL ABUSE

See ABUSE & VIOLENCE - VICTIMS' & SURVIVORS' SUPPORT SERVICES

SIGHT IMPAIRMENT

See BLINDNESS & SIGHT IMPAIRMENT

SMOKING 'STOP SMOKING' SUPPORT GROUPS

SOCIAL CARE & WELFARE

TECHNOLOGY

THEATRES

THERAPY SERVICES AND CENTRES

EDUCATIONAL & SPECIAL NEEDS

MEDICAL & HEALTH BENEFITS

WOMEN

TOWN PLANNING

TRAINING

TRANSGENDER SUPPORT GROUPS

TRANSPORT

TRAVELLER GROUPS

TREE PRESERVATION

UMBRELLA & RESOURCE BODIES

ADVICE & INFORMATION

ACCOMMODATION

EDUCATION

HEALTH